SIGNLL Conference on Computational Natural Language Learning 2017

Proceedings of the CoNLL 2017 Shared Task: Multilingual Parsing from Raw Text to Universal Dependencies

Vancouver, Canada
3 – 4 August 2017

ISBN: 978-1-5108-4565-7

CoNLL 2017

**The SIGNLL Conference on
Computational Natural Language Learning**

**Proceedings of the CoNLL 2017 Shared Task: Multilingual
Parsing from Raw Text to Universal Dependencies**

August 3-4, 2017
Vancouver, Canada

Sponsors:

Google, Inc.

DFKI Berlin

CRACKER project

text & form

ÚFAL

Charles University

LINDAT/CLARIN

Introduction

This volume contains papers describing systems submitted to the *CoNLL 2017 Shared Task: Multilingual Parsing from Raw Text to Universal Dependencies* and an overview paper summarizing the task, its features, evaluation methodology for the main and additional metrics, and some interesting observations about the submitted systems and the task as a whole.

This Shared Task (`http://universaldependencies.org/conll17/`) can be seen as an extension of the CoNLL 2007 Shared Task on parsing, but there are many important differences that make this year's task unique with several "firsts". Most importantly, the data for this task come from the Universal Dependencies project (`http://universaldependencies.org`), which provides annotated treebanks for a large number of languages using the same annotation scheme for all of them. In the shared task setting, this allows for more meaningful comparison between systems as well as languages, since differences are much more likely due to true parser differences rather than differences caused by annotation schemes. In addition, the number of languages for which training data were available is unprecedented for a single shared task: a total of 64 treebanks in 45 languages have been provided for training the systems. Additional data have been provided too, as were some baseline systems for those who wanted to try only some particular aspect of parsing. Overall, the task can be described as "closed", since only pre-approved data could be used.

For evaluation, there were 81 datasets (standard datasets for the treebank languages provided for training, plus more test sets in known languages, but based on a specially created and annotated parallel corpus, and four surprise language test sets). Participants had to process all the test sets. The TIRA platform has been used for evaluation, as was the case already for the CoNLL 2015 and 2016 Shared Tasks, meaning that participants had to provide their code on a designated virtual machine to be run by the organizers to produce official results. However, test data have been published after the official evaluation period, and participants could run their systems at home to produce additional results they were allowed to include in the system description papers. There was one main evaluation metric – Labeled Attachment Score – for the main ranking table evaluating dependency parsing performance, plus additional metrics for tokenization, word and sentence segmentation, POS tagging, lemmatization and disambiguation of morphological features, and separate metrics computed for interesting subsets of the evaluation data.

A total of 32 systems ran successfully and have been ranked (`http://universaldependencies.org/conll17/results.html`). While there are clear overall winners, we would like to thank all participants for working hard on their submissions and adapting their systems not only to the datasets available, but also to the evaluation platform. We would like to thank all of them for their effort, since it is the participants who are the core of any shared task's success.

We would like to thank the CoNLL organizers for their support and the reviewers for helping to improve the submitted system papers. Special thanks go to Martin Potthast of the TIRA platform for handling such a large number of systems, running often for several hours each, and for being very responsive and helpful to us and all system participants, round the clock during the evaluation week and beyond. We also thank to the 200+ people working on the Universal Dependencies project during the past three years, without whom there would be no data.

Jan Hajič, Daniel Zeman, Joakim Nivre, Filip Ginter, Slav Petrov, Milan Straka, Martin Popel, Eduard Bejček

Organizers of the CoNLL 2017 Shared Task: Multilingual Parsing from Raw Text to Universal Dependencies

Prague, June 2017

Chair:

Jan Hajič, Charles University

Management group:

Daniel Zeman, Charles University
Joakim Nivre, Uppsala University
Filip Ginter, University of Turku
Slav Petrov, Google

Milan Straka, Charles University
Martin Popel, Charles University
Eduard Bejček, Charles University (Shared Task Proceedings Publication Chair)

TIRA support:

Martin Potthast, University of Weimar

Support group:

Christopher Manning, Stanford University
Marie-Catherine de Marneffe, Ohio State University
Yoav Goldberg, Bar Ilan University
Reut Tsarfaty, Open University of Israel
Sampo Pyysalo, University of Cambridge

Francis Tyers, UiT Norgga árktalaš universitehta
Jenna Kanerva, University of Turku
Çağrı Çöltekin, University of Tübingen
Juhani Luotolahti, University of Turku

Program Committee:

Lauriane Aufrant, LIMSI-CNRS, DGA
Miguel Ballesteros, IBM Research
Tiberiu Boroș, Romanian Academy
Agnieszka Falenska, University of Stuttgart
Marcos Garcia, Universidade da Coruña
Filip Ginter, University of Turku
Giuseppe Celano, Leipzig University
Johannes Heinecke, Orange Labs
James Henderson, Xerox Research Centre Europe
Jenna Kanerva, University of Turku
Ömer Kırnap, Koç University
Adam Lopez, University of Edinburgh
Christopher Manning, Stanford University
Paola Merlo, University of Geneva
Dat Quoc Nguyen, Macquarie University
Joakim Nivre, Uppsala University

Hiroshi Noji, Nara Institute of Science and Technology
Jungyeul Park, University of Arizona
Martin Popel, Charles University
Sudeshna Sarkar, IIT Kharagpur
Sebastian Schuster, Stanford University
Djamé Seddah, Université Paris Sorbonne
Tianze Shi, Cornell University
Pavel Sofroniev, University of Tübingen
Francis Tyers, UiT Norgga árktalaš universitehta
David Vilares, Universidade da Coruña
Hao Wang, Shanghai JiaoTong University
Katsumasa Yoshikawa, IBM Research
Deniz Yuret, Koç University
Zdeněk Žabokrtský, Charles University
Lilja Øvrelid, University of Oslo

Table of Contents

Conference Program

Overview

Systems

Systems (continued)

CoNLL 2017 Shared Task: Multilingual Parsing from Raw Text to Universal Dependencies

Daniel Zeman[1], Martin Popel[1], Milan Straka[1], Jan Hajič[1], Joakim Nivre[2],
Filip Ginter[3], Juhani Luotolahti[3], Sampo Pyysalo[4], Slav Petrov[5], Martin Potthast[6],
Francis Tyers[7], Elena Badmaeva[8], Memduh Gökırmak[9], Anna Nedoluzhko[1], Silvie
Cinková[1], Jan Hajič jr.[1], Jaroslava Hlaváčová[1], Václava Kettnerová[1], Zdeňka Urešová[1],
Jenna Kanerva[3], Stina Ojala[3], Anna Missilä[3], Christopher Manning[10], Sebastian
Schuster[10], Siva Reddy[10], Dima Taji[11], Nizar Habash[11], Herman Leung[12],
Marie-Catherine de Marneffe[13], Manuela Sanguinetti[14], Maria Simi[15], Hiroshi
Kanayama[16], Valeria de Paiva[17], Kira Droganova[1], Héctor Martínez Alonso[18], Çağrı
Çöltekin[19], Umut Sulubacak[9], Hans Uszkoreit[20], Vivien Macketanz[20], Aljoscha
Burchardt[20], Kim Harris[21], Katrin Marheinecke[21], Georg Rehm[20], Tolga Kayadelen[5],
Mohammed Attia[5], Ali Elkahky[5], Zhuoran Yu[5], Emily Pitler[5], Saran Lertpradit[5],
Michael Mandl[5], Jesse Kirchner[5], Hector Fernandez Alcalde[5], Jana Strnadová[5], Esha
Banerjee[5], Ruli Manurung[5], Antonio Stella[5], Atsuko Shimada[5], Sookyoung Kwak[5],
Gustavo Mendonça[5], Tatiana Lando[5], Rattima Nitisaroj[5], and Josie Li[5]

[1]Charles University, Faculty of Mathematics and Physics
[2]Uppsala University, [3]University of Turku, [4]University of Cambridge
[5]Google, [6]Bauhaus-Universität Weimar, [7]UiT The Arctic University of Norway
[8]University of the Basque Country, [9]Istanbul Technical University
[10]Stanford University, [11]New York University Abu Dhabi, [12]City University of Hong Kong
[13]Ohio State University, [14]University of Turin, [15]University of Pisa, [16]IBM Research, [17]Nuance
Communications, [18]INRIA – Paris 7, [19]University of Tübingen, [20]DFKI, [21]text & form

```
{zeman|popel|straka|hajic}@ufal.mff.cuni.cz
joakim.nivre@lingfil.uu.se, {figint|mjluot}@utu.fi
slav@google.com, martin.potthast@uni-weimar.de
```


Abstract

The Conference on Computational Natural Language Learning (CoNLL) features a shared task, in which participants train and test their learning systems on the same data sets. In 2017, one of two tasks was devoted to learning dependency parsers for a large number of languages, in a real-world setting without any gold-standard annotation on input. All test sets followed a unified annotation scheme, namely that of Universal Dependencies. In this paper, we define the task and evaluation methodology, describe data preparation, report and analyze the main results, and provide a brief categorization of the different approaches of the participating systems.

1 Introduction

Ten years ago, two CoNLL shared tasks were a major milestone for parsing research in general and dependency parsing in particular. For the first time dependency treebanks in more than ten languages were available for learning parsers. Many of them were used in follow-up work, evaluating parsers on multiple languages became standard, and multiple state-of-the-art, open-source parsers became available, facilitating production of dependency structures to be used in downstream applications. While the two tasks (Buchholz and Marsi, 2006; Nivre et al., 2007) were extremely important in setting the scene for the following years, there were also limitations that complicated application of their results: (1) gold-standard to-

1

Proceedings of the CoNLL 2017 Shared Task: Multilingual Parsing from Raw Text to Universal Dependencies, pages 1–19,
Vancouver, Canada, August 3-4, 2017. © 2017 Association for Computational Linguistics

kenization and part-of-speech tags in the test data moved the tasks away from real-world scenarios, and (2) incompatible annotation schemes made cross-linguistic comparison impossible. CoNLL 2017 has picked up the threads of those pioneering tasks and addressed these two issues.[1]

The focus of the 2017 task was learning syntactic dependency parsers that can work in a real-world setting, starting from raw text, and that can work over many typologically different languages, even surprise languages for which there is little or no training data, by exploiting a common syntactic annotation standard. This task has been made possible by the Universal Dependencies initiative (UD) (Nivre et al., 2016), which has developed treebanks for 50+ languages with cross-linguistically consistent annotation and recoverability of the original raw texts.

Participating systems had to find labeled syntactic dependencies between words, i.e., a syntactic head for each word, and a label classifying the type of the dependency relation. No gold-standard annotation (tokenization, sentence segmentation, lemmas, morphology) was available in the input text. However, teams wishing to concentrate just on parsing were able to use segmentation and morphology predicted by the baseline UDPipe system (Straka et al., 2016).

2 Data

In general, we wanted the participating systems to be able to use any data that is available free of charge for research and educational purposes (so that follow-up research is not obstructed). We deliberately did not place upper bounds on data sizes (in contrast to e.g. Nivre et al. (2007)), despite the fact that processing large amounts of data may be difficult for some teams. Our primary objective was to determine the capability of current parsers with the data that is currently available.

In practice, the task was formally closed, i.e., we listed the approved data resources so that all participants were aware of their options. However, the selection was rather broad, ranging from Wikipedia dumps over the OPUS parallel corpora (Tiedemann, 2012) to morphological transducers. Some of the resources were proposed by the participating teams.

We provided dependency-annotated training and test data, and also large quantities of crawled raw texts. Other language resources are available from third-party servers and we only referred to the respective download sites.

2.1 Training Data: UD 2.0

Training and development data come from the Universal Dependencies (UD) 2.0 collection (Nivre et al., 2017b). Unlike previous UD releases, the test data was not included in UD 2.0. It was kept hidden until the evaluation phase of the shared task terminated. In some cases, the underlying texts had been known from previous UD releases but the annotation had not (UD 2.0 follows new annotation guidelines that are not backward-compatible).

64 UD treebanks in 45 languages were available for training. 15 languages had two or more training treebanks from different sources, often also from different domains.

56 treebanks contained designated development data. Participants were asked not to use it for training proper but only for evaluation, development, tuning hyperparameters, doing error analysis etc. The 8 remaining treebanks were small and had only training data (and even these were extremely small in some cases, especially for Kazakh and Uyghur). For those treebanks cross-validation had to be used during development, but the entire dataset could be used for training once hyperparameters were determined.

Participants received the training and development data with gold-standard tokenization, sentence segmentation, POS tags and dependency relations; and for some languages also lemmas and/or morphological features.

Cross-domain and cross-language training was allowed and encouraged. Participants were free to train models on any combination of the training treebanks and apply it to any test set. They were even allowed to use the training portions of the 6 UD 2.0 treebanks that were excluded from evaluation (see Section 2.3).

2.2 Supporting Data

To enable the induction of custom embeddings and the use of semi-supervised methods in general, the participants were provided with supporting resources primarily consisting of large text corpora for (nearly) all of the languages in the task, as well as embeddings pre-trained on these corpora.

Raw texts The supporting raw data was gathered from CommonCrawl, which is a publicly available web crawl created and maintained by the non-profit CommonCrawl foundation.[2] The data is publicly available in the Amazon cloud both as raw HTML and as plain text. It is collected from a number of independent crawls from 2008 to 2017, and totals petabytes in size.

We used cld2[3] as the language detection engine because of its speed, available Python bindings and large coverage of languages. Language detection was carried out on the first 1024 bytes of each plaintext document. Deduplication was carried out using hashed document URLs, a simple strategy found in our tests to be effective for coarse duplicate removal. The data for each language was capped at 100,000 tokens per a single input file.

Automatic tokenization, morphology and parsing The raw texts were further processed in order to generate automatic tokenization, segmentation, morphological annotations and dependency trees.

At first, basic cleaning was performed – paragraphs with erroneous encoding or less than 16 characters were dropped, remaining paragraphs converted to Normalization Form KC (NFKC)[4] and again deduplicated. Then the texts were segmented and tokenized, multi-word tokens split into words, and sentences with less than 5 words dropped. Because we wanted to publish the resulting corpus, we shuffled the sentences and also dropped sentences with more than 80 words at this point for licensing reasons. The segmentation and tokenization was obtained using the baseline UDPipe models described in Section 5. These models were also used to further generate automatic morphological annotations (lemmas, UPOS, XPOS and FEATS) and dependency trees.

The resulting corpus contains 5.9 M sentences and 90 G words in 45 languages and is available in CoNLL-U format (Ginter et al., 2017). The per-language sizes of the corpus are listed in Table 1

Precomputed word embeddings We also precomputed word embeddings using the segmented and tokenized plain texts. Because UD words can contain spaces, these in-word spaces were con-

Language	Words
English (en)	9,441 M
German (de)	6,003 M
Portuguese (pt)	5,900 M
Spanish (es)	5,721 M
French (fr)	5,242 M
Polish (pl)	5,208 M
Indonesian (id)	5,205 M
Japanese (ja)	5,179 M
Italian (it)	5,136 M
Vietnamese (vi)	4,066 M
Turkish (tr)	3,477 M
Russian (ru)	3,201 M
Swedish (sv)	2,932 M
Dutch (nl)	2,914 M
Romanian (ro)	2,776 M
Czech (cs)	2,005 M
Hungarian (hu)	1,624 M
Danish (da)	1,564 M
Chinese (zh)	1,530 M
Norwegian-Bokmål (no)	1,305 M
Persian (fa)	1,120 M
Finnish (fi)	1,008 M
Arabic (ar)	963 M
Catalan (ca)	860 M
Slovak (sk)	811 M
Greek (el)	731 M
Hebrew (he)	615 M
Croatian (hr)	583 M
Ukrainian (uk)	538 M
Korean (ko)	527 M
Slovenian (sl)	522 M
Bulgarian (bg)	370 M
Estonian (et)	328 M
Latvian (lv)	276 M
Galician (gl)	262 M
Latin (la)	244 M
Basque (eu)	155 M
Hindi (hi)	91 M
Norwegian-Nynorsk (no)	76 M
Kazakh (kk)	54 M
Urdu (ur)	46 M
Irish (ga)	24 M
Ancient Greek (grc)	7 M
Uyghur (ug)	3 M
Kurdish (kmr)	3 M
Upper Sorbian (hsb)	2 M
Buryat (bxr)	413 K
North Sámi (sme)	331 K
Old Church Slavonic (cu)	28 K
Total	90,669 M

Table 1: The supporting data overview: the number of words (M = million; K = thousand) for each language.

[2] http://commoncrawl.org/ Except for Ancient Greek, which was gathered from the Perseus Digital Library.
[3] http://github.com/CLD2Owners/cld2
[4] http://unicode.org/reports/tr15/

verted to Unicode character *NO-BREAK SPACE* (U+00A0).[5]

The dimensionality of the word embeddings was chosen to be 100 after thorough discussion – more dimensions may yield better results and are commonly used, but even with just 100, the uncompressed word embeddings for the 45 languages take 135 GiB. Also note that Andor et al. (2016) achieved state-of-the-art results with 64 dimensions.

The word embeddings were precomputed using `word2vec` (Mikolov et al., 2013) with the following options:

```
word2vec -min-count 10 -size 100
    -window 10 -negative 5 -iter 2
    -threads 16 -cbow 0 -binary 0.
```

The precomputed word embeddings are available on-line (Ginter et al., 2017).

2.3 Test Data: UD 2.0

The main part of test data comprises test sets corresponding to 63 of the 64 training treebanks.[6] Test sets from two different treebanks of one language were evaluated separately as if they were different languages. Every test set contained at least 10,000 words or punctuation marks. UD 2.0 treebanks that were smaller than 10,000 words were excluded from the evaluation. Among the treebanks that were able to provide the required amount of test data, there are 8 treebanks so small that the remaining data could not be split to training and development portions; for two of them, the data left for training is only a tiny sample (529 words in Kazakh, 1662 in Uyghur). There was no upper limit on the test data; the largest treebank had a test set comprising 170K words.

Although the 63 test sets correspond to UD 2.0 treebanks, they were not released with UD 2.0. They were kept hidden and only published after the evaluation phase of the shared task (Nivre et al., 2017a).

2.4 New Parallel Test Sets

In addition, there were test sets for which no corresponding training data sets exist: 4 "surprise" languages (described in Section 2.5) and 14 test sets of a new Parallel UD (PUD) treebank (described in this section). These test sets were created for this shared task, i.e., not included in any previous UD release.

The PUD treebank consists of 1000 sentences currently in 18 languages (15 K to 27 K words, depending on the language), which were randomly picked from on-line newswire and Wikipedia;[7] usually only a few sentences per source document. 750 sentences were originally English, the remaining 250 sentences come from German, French, Italian and Spanish texts. They were translated by professional translators to 14 languages (i.e., 15 languages with the original: Arabic, Chinese, English, French, German, Hindi, Indonesian, Italian, Japanese, Korean, Portuguese, Russian, Spanish, Thai and Turkish; but four languages— Chinese, Indonesian, Korean and Thai—were excluded from the shared task due to consistency issues). Translators were instructed to prefer translations closer to original grammatical structure, provided it is still a fluent sentence in the target language. In some cases, picking a correct translation was difficult because the translators did not see the context of the original document. The translations were organized at DFKI and text & form, Germany; they were then tokenized, morphologically and syntactically annotated at Google following guidelines based on McDonald et al. (2013), and finally converted to proper UD v2 annotation style by volunteers from the UD community using the Udapi framework (Popel et al., 2017).[8] Three additional translations (Czech, Finnish and Swedish) were contributed and annotated natively in UD v2 by teams from Charles University, University of Turku and Uppsala University, respectively.

The Google dependency representation predates Universal Dependencies, deriving from the scheme used by McDonald et al. (2013), i.e., Stanford Dependencies 2.0 with the option to make copula verbs heads (de Marneffe and Manning, 2008, section 4.7) and Google Universal POS tags (Petrov et al., 2011). Various tree transformations were needed to convert it to UD.[9] For example, prepositions and copula verbs are phrasal heads in Google annotation but must be dependent function words in UD. Similarly, some POS tags differ in the two schemes; particularly hard were conjunc-

---

[5]Using `udpipe --output=horizontal`.

[6]We had to withdraw the test set from the Italian ParTUT treebank because it turned out to significantly overlap with the training data of the larger Italian treebank in UD 2.0.

[7]The two domains are encoded in sentence ids but this information is not visible to the systems participating in the shared task.

[8]`http://udapi.github.io/`

[9]using ud.Google2ud from the Udapi framework

tions, where the Google tag set does not distinguish coordinators (CCONJ in UD) from subordinators (SCONJ). Some bugs, for example where verbs had multiple subjects or objects, or where function words were not leaves, were detected automatically[10] and fixed manually.

Finally, the most prominent consistency issues lay in tokenization and word segmentation, especially in languages where it interacts with morphology or where the writing system does not clearly mark word boundaries. The tokenizers used before manual annotation were not necessarily compatible with existing UD treebanks, yet in the shared task it was essential to make the segmentation consistent with the training data. We were able to fix some problems, such as unmarked multi-word tokens in European languages,[11] and we were even able to re-segment Japanese (note that this often involved new dependency relations); on the other hand, we had to exclude Korean for not being able to fix it in time.

Many transformations were specific to individual languages. For example, in the original tokenization of Arabic, the definite article *al-* was separated from the modified word, which is comparable to the D3 tokenization scheme (Habash, 2010). This scheme was inconsistent with the tokenization of the Arabic training data, hence it had to be changed. Text-level normalization further involved removal of the *shadda* diacritical mark (marking consonant gemination), which is optional in Arabic orthography and does not occur in the training data. On the POS level, the active and passive participles and verbal nouns (masdars) were annotated as verbs. For Arabic, however, these should be mapped to NOUN. Once we changed the tags, we also had to modify the surrounding relations to those used with nominals.

Like some UD treebanks, the parallel data contains information on document boundaries. They are projected as empty lines to the raw text presented to parsers, and they can be exploited to improve sentence segmentation. Note that due to the way the sentences were collected, the paragraphs are rather short.[12]

The fact that the data is parallel was not exploited in this task. Participating systems were told the language code so they could select an appropriate model. All parallel test sets were in languages that have at least one training treebank in UD 2.0 (although the domain may differ).

After the evaluation phase these parallel test sets were published together with the main test data; in the future they will become part of regular UD releases.

2.5 Surprise Languages

The second type of additional test sets were surprise languages, which had not been previously released in UD. Names of surprise languages (Buryat, Kurmanji Kurdish, North Sámi and Upper Sorbian) and small samples of gold-standard data (about 20 sentences) were published one week before the beginning of the evaluation phase. Crawled raw texts were provided too, though in much smaller quantity than for the other languages. The point of having surprise languages was to encourage participants to pursue truly multilingual approaches to parsing, utilizing data from other languages.

As with all other test sets, the systems were able to use segmentation and part-of-speech tags predicted by the baseline UDPipe system (in this case UDPipe was trained and applied in a 10-fold cross-validation manner directly on the test data; hence this is the only annotation that the participants were given but could not produce with their own models).

Note that the smallest non-surprise languages (Kazakh, Uyghur) were asking for multilingual approaches as well, given that the amount of their own training data was close to zero. The difference was that participants at least knew in advance what these languages were and had more time to determine the most suitable training model. On the other hand, the segmentation and tagging models for these languages were only trained on the tiny training data, i.e., they were much worse than the models for the surprise languages. In this sense parsing of Kazakh and Uyghur was even harder than parsing the surprise languages.

When compared to the training data available in UD 2.0, the genetically closest language to Kazakh and Uyghur is Turkish; but it uses a dif-

---

[10] using ud.MarkBugs from the Udapi framework

[11] using Udapi's ud.de.AddMwt for German, and similarly for Spanish (es), French (fr) and Portuguese (pt). For all languages, we applied ud.ComplyWithText to make sure the concatenation of tokens matches exactly the original raw text.

[12] A special case is Arabic where we artificially marked every sentence as a separate paragraph, to make it more consistent with somewhat unusual segmentation of the existing UD Arabic treebank. This gave an advantage to systems that were able to take paragraph boundaries into account, including those that re-used the baseline segmentation.

ferent writing system, and the Turkish dataset itself is not particularly large. For Kurmanji Kurdish, the closest relative is Persian, again with different script and other reservations. Buryat is a Mongolic language written in Cyrillic script and does not have any close relative in UD. North Sámi is an Finno-Ugric language; Finnish and Estonian UD data could be expected to be somewhat similar. Finally, Upper Sorbian is a West Slavic language spoken in Germany; among the many Slavic languages in UD, Czech and Polish are its closest relatives.

In summary, the test data consisted of 81 files in 49 languages (55 test sets from "big" UD 2.0 treebanks, 8 "small" treebanks, 14 parallel test sets and 4 surprise-language test sets).

3   Evaluation Metrics

The standard evaluation metric of dependency parsing is the *labeled attachment score (LAS)*, i.e., the percentage of nodes with correctly assigned reference to parent node, including the label (type) of the relation. When parsers are applied to raw text, the metric must be adjusted to the possibility that the number of nodes in gold-standard annotation and in the system output vary. Therefore, the evaluation starts with aligning system nodes and gold nodes. A dependency relation cannot be counted as correct if one of the nodes could not be aligned to a gold node. LAS is then re-defined as the harmonic mean (F_1) of precision P and recall R, where

$$P = \frac{\#correctRelations}{\#systemNodes} \quad (1)$$

$$R = \frac{\#correctRelations}{\#goldNodes} \quad (2)$$

$$LAS = \frac{2PR}{P + R} \quad (3)$$

Note that attachment of all nodes including punctuation is evaluated. LAS is computed separately for each of the 81 test files and a macro-average of all these scores serves as the main metric for system ranking in the task.

3.1   Token Alignment

UD defines two levels of token/word segmentation. The lower level corresponds to what is usually understood as tokenization. However, unlike some popular tokenization schemes, it does not include any normalization of the non-whitespace characters. We can safely assume that any two tokenizations of a text differ only in whitespace while the remaining characters are identical. There is thus a 1-1 mapping between gold and system non-whitespace characters, and two tokens are aligned if all their characters match.

3.2   Syntactic Word Alignment

The higher segmentation level is based on the notion of *syntactic word*. Some languages contain *multi-word tokens* (MWT) that are regarded as contractions of multiple syntactic words. For example, the German token *zum* is a contraction of the preposition *zu* "to" and the article *dem* "the".

Syntactic words constitute independent nodes in dependency trees. As shown by the example, it is not required that the MWT is a pure concatenation of the participating words; the simple token alignment thus does not work when MWTs are involved. Fortunately, the CoNLL-U file format used in UD clearly marks all MWTs so we can detect them both in system output and in gold data. Whenever one or more MWTs have overlapping spans of surface character offsets, the longest common subsequence algorithm is used to align syntactic words within these spans.

3.3   Sentence Segmentation

Words are aligned and dependencies are evaluated in the entire file without considering sentence segmentation. Still, the accuracy of sentence boundaries has an indirect impact on LAS: any missing or extra sentence boundary necessarily makes one or more dependency relations incorrect.

3.4   Invalid Output

If a system fails to produce one of the 81 files or if the file is not valid CoNLL-U format, the score of that file (counting towards the system's macro-average) is zero.

Formal validity is defined more leniently than for UD-released treebanks. For example, a non-existent dependency type does not render the whole file invalid, it only costs the system one incorrect relation. However, cycles and multi-root sentences are disallowed. A file is also invalid if there are character mismatches that could make the token alignment algorithm fail.

3.5 CLAS

Content-word Labeled Attachment Score (CLAS) has been proposed as an alternative parsing metric that is tailored to the UD annotation style and more suitable for cross-language comparison (Nivre and Fang, 2017). It differs from LAS in that it only considers relations between content words. Attachment of function words is disregarded because it corresponds to morphological features in other languages (and morphology is not evaluated in this shared task). Furthermore, languages with many function words (e.g., English) have longer sentences than morphologically rich languages (e.g., Finnish), hence a single error in Finnish costs the parser significantly more than an error in English. CLAS also disregards attachment of punctuation.

As CLAS is still experimental, we have designated full LAS as our main evaluation metric; nevertheless, a large evaluation campaign like this is a great opportunity to study the behavior of the new metric, and we present both scores in Section 6.

4 Evaluation Methodology

Key goals of any empirical evaluation are to ensure a blind evaluation, its replicability, and its reproducibility. To facilitate these goals, we employed the cloud-based evaluation platform TIRA (Potthast et al., 2014),[13] which implements the evaluation as a service paradigm (Hanbury et al., 2015). In doing so, we depart from the traditional submission of system output to shared tasks, which lacks in these regards, toward the submission of working software. Naturally, software submissions bring about additional overhead for both organizers and participants, whereas the goal of an evaluation platform like TIRA is to reduce this overhead to a bearable level. Still being an early prototype, though, TIRA fulfills this goal only with some reservations. Nevertheless, the scale of the CoNLL 2017 UD Shared Task also served as a test of scalability of the evaluation as a service paradigm in general as well as that of TIRA in particular.

4.1 Blind Evaluation

Traditionally, evaluations in shared tasks are half-blind (the test data are shared with participants while the ground truth is withheld), whereas outside shared tasks, say, during paper-writing, evaluations are typically pseudo-blind (the test data and

---

[13] http://www.tira.io/

ground truth are accessible, yet, ignored until the to-be-evaluated software is ready). In both cases, remaining blind to the test data is one of the cornerstones of evaluation, and has a significant impact on the validity of evaluation results. While outside shared tasks, one can only trust that paper authors do not spoil their evaluation by implicitly or explicitly exploiting their knowledge of the test data, within shared tasks, another factor comes into play, namely the fact that shared tasks are also competitions.

Dependent on its prestige, winning a shared task comes along with a lot of visibility, so that supplying participants with the test data up front bears risks of mistakes that spoil the ground truth, and of cheating. Here, TIRA implements a proper solution which ensures blind evaluation, an airlock for data. On demand, software deployed at TIRA is locked in the datalock together with the test data, where it can process the data and have its output recorded. Otherwise, all communication channels to the outside are closed or tightly moderated to prevent data leakage. However, closing down all communication channels also has its downsides, since participants cannot check up on their running software anymore, or have to ask organizers to do so, which increases the turnaround time to fix bugs. Participants were only able to learn whether they achieved a non-zero score on each of the 81 test files; a zero score signaled a bug, in which case the task moderator would make the diagnostic output visible to the participants. Such interaction was only possible when the system run completed; before that, even the task moderator would not see whether the system was really producing output and not just sitting in an endless loop. Especially given the scale of operations this year, this turned out to be a major obstacle for some participants; TIRA needs to be improved by offering more fine-grained process monitoring tools, both for organizers and participants.

4.2 Replicability and Reproducibility

The replicability of an evaluation depends on whether the same results can be obtained from re-running an experiment using the same setup, whereas reproducibility refers to achieving results that are commensurate with a reference evaluation, for instance, when exchanging the test data with alternative test data. Both are important aspects of an evaluation, the former pertaining to its reliability, and the latter to its validity. Ensuring both requires that a to-be-evaluated software is preserved in working condition for as long as possible. Traditionally, shared tasks do not take charge of participant software preservation, mostly because the software remains with participants, and since open sourcing the software underlying a paper is still the exception rather than the rule. To ensure both, TIRA supplies participants with a virtual machine, offering a range of commonly used operating systems in order not to limit the choice of technology stacks and development environments. Once deployed and tested, the virtual machines are archived to preserve the software within.

Many participants agreed to share their code so that we decided to collect the respective projects in a kind of open source proceedings at GitHub.[14]

4.3 Resource Allocation

The allocation of an appropriate amount of computing resources (especially CPUs and RAM, whereas disk space is cheap enough) to each participant proved to be difficult, since minimal requirements were unknown. When asked, participants typically request liberal amounts of resources, just to be on the safe side, whereas assigning too much up front would not be economical nor scale well. We hence applied a least commitment strategy with an initial assignment of 1 CPU and 4 GB RAM. More resources were granted on request, the limit being the size of the underlying hardware. When it comes to exploiting available resources, a lot depends on programming prowess, whereas more resources do not necessarily translate into better performance. This is best exemplified by the fact that with 4 CPUs and 16 GB RAM, the winning team Stanford used only a quarter the amount of resources of the second and third winners, respectively. The team on fourth (sixth) place was even more frugal, getting by with 1 CPU and 8 GB RAM (4 GB RAM). All of the aforementioned teams' approaches exceed the LAS level of 70%.

5 Baseline System

5.1 UDPipe

We prepared a set of baseline models using UD-Pipe (Straka et al., 2016) version 1.1. A slightly improved version—UDPipe 1.2—was submitted

by Straka and Straková (2017) as one of the competing systems. Straka and Straková (2017) describe both these versions in more detail.

The baseline models were released together with the UD 2.0 training data, one model for each treebank. Because only training and development data were available during baseline model training, we put aside a part of the training data for hyperparameter tuning, and evaluated the baseline model performance on development data. We called this data split *baseline model split*. The baseline models, the baseline model split, and also UD 2.0 training data with morphology predicted by 10-fold jack-knifing (cross-validation), are available on-line (Straka, 2017).

UDPipe baseline models are able to reconstruct nearly all annotation from CoNLL-U files – they can generate segmentation, tokenization, multiword token splitting, morphological annotation (lemmas, UPOS, XPOS and FEATS) and dependency trees. Participants were free to use any part of the model in their systems – for all test sets, we provided UDPipe processed variants in addition to raw text inputs. We provided the UDPipe processed variant even for surprise languages – however, only segmentation, tokenization and morphology, generated by 10-fold jack-knifing, as described in Section 2.5.

Baseline UDPipe Shared Task System We further used the baseline models as a baseline system in the shared task. We used the corresponding models for the UD 2.0 test data.

For the new parallel treebanks, we used UD 2.0 baseline models of the corresponding languages. If there were several treebanks for one language, we arbitrarily chose the one named after the language only (e.g., we chose `ru` and not `ru_syntagrus`). Unfortunately, we did not explicitly mention this choice to the participants and this arbitrary choice had a large impact on results – some contestant systems fell below UDPipe baseline just because of choosing different treebanks to train on for the parallel treebanks. (On the other hand, there was no guarantee that the models selected in the baseline system would be optimal.)

For each surprise language, we also chose one baseline model to apply. Even if most words are unknown to the baseline model, universal POS tags can be used to drive the parsing, making the baseline model act similar to a delexicalized parser. We chose a baseline model to maximize

---

Team	LAS
1. Stanford (Dozat et al.)	76.30
2. C2L2 (Shi et al.)	75.00
3. IMS (Björkelund et al.)	74.42
4. HIT-SCIR (Che et al.)	72.11
5. LATTICE (Lim and Poibeau)	70.93
6. NAIST SATO (Sato et al.)	70.14
7. Koç University (Kırnap et al.)	69.76
8. ÚFAL (Straka and Straková)	69.52
9. UParse (Vania et al.)	68.87
10. Orange (Heinecke and Asadullah)	68.61
11. TurkuNLP (Kanerva et al.)	68.59
12. darc (Yu et al.)	68.41
13. BASELINE UDPipe 1.1	68.35
14. MQuni (Nguyen et al.)	68.05
15. fbaml (Qian and Liu)	67.87
16. LyS (Vilares and Gómez-Rodríguez)	67.81
17. LIMSI (Aufrant and Wisniewski)	67.72
18. RACAI (Dumitrescu et al.)	67.71
19. IIT Kharagpur (Das et al.)	67.61
20. naistCL (no paper)	67.59
21. Wanghao-ftd-SJTU (Wang et al.)	66.53
22. UALING (Hornby et al.)	65.24
23. Uppsala (de Lhoneux et al.)	65.11
24. METU (Akkuş et al.)	61.98
25. CLCL (Moor et al.)	61.82
26. Mengest (Ji et al.)	61.33
27. ParisNLP (De La Clergerie et al.)	60.02
28. OpenU (More and Tsarfaty)	56.56
29. TRL (Kanayama et al.)	43.07
30. MetaRomance (Garcia and Gamallo)	34.05
31. UT (no paper)	21.10
32. ECNU (no paper)	3.18
33. Wenba-NLU (no paper)	0.58

Table 2: Ranking of the participating systems by the main evaluation metric, the labeled attachment F_1-score, macro-averaged over 81 test sets. Pairs of systems with significantly ($p < 0.05$) different LAS are separated by a line. Names of several teams are abbreviated in the table: LyS-FASTPARSE, OpenU NLP Lab, Orange – Deskiñ and ÚFAL – UDPipe 1.2. Citations refer to the corresponding system-description papers in this volume.

the accuracy on the released sample for each surprise language, resulting in Finnish FTB, Polish, Finnish FTB and Slovak models for the surprise

Team	CLAS F_1
1. Stanford (Stanford)	72.57
2. C2L2 (Ithaca)	70.91
3. IMS (Stuttgart)	70.18
4. HIT-SCIR (Harbin)	67.63
5. LATTICE (Paris)	66.16
6. NAIST SATO (Nara)	65.15
7. Koç University (İstanbul)	64.61
8. ÚFAL – UDPipe 1.2 (Praha)	64.36
9. Orange – Deskiñ (Lannion)	64.15
10. TurkuNLP (Turku)	63.61
11. UParse (Edinburgh)	63.55
12. darc (Tübingen)	63.24
13. BASELINE UDPipe 1.1	63.02

Table 3: Average CLAS F_1 score.

languages Buryat, Kurmanji, North Sámi and Upper Sorbian, respectively.

5.2 SyntaxNet

Another set of baseline models was prepared by Alberti et al. (2017) based on improved version of the SyntaxNet system (Andor et al., 2016). Pretrained models were provided for UD 2.0 data.

However, no SyntaxNet models were prepared for the surprise languages, therefore, the SyntaxNet baseline is not part of the official results.

6 Results

6.1 Official Parsing Results

Table 2 gives the main ranking of participating systems by the LAS F_1 score macro-averaged over all 81 test files. The table also shows the performance of the baseline UDPipe system; the baseline is relatively strong and only 12 of the 32 systems managed to outperform it.

We used bootstrap resampling to compute 95% confidence intervals: they are in the range ± 0.11 to ± 0.15 (% LAS) for all systems except the three lowest-scoring ones. We used paired bootstrap resampling to compute whether the difference in LAS is significant ($p < 0.05$) for each pair of systems.[15]

6.2 Secondary Metrics

In addition to the main LAS ranking, we evaluated the systems along multiple other axes, which may

---

[15] using Udapi's eval.Conll17, marked by the presence or absence of vertical lines in Table 2.

Team	Toks	Wrds	Sents
1. IMS	98.92	98.81	89.10
2. LIMSI	**98.95**	98.68	88.49
3. ÚFAL – UDPipe 1.2	98.89	98.63	**88.68**
4. HIT-SCIR	**98.95**	98.62	**88.91**
5. ParisNLP	98.85	98.58	88.61
6. Wanghao-ftd-SJTU	98.81	98.55	88.40
darc	98.81	98.55	**88.66**
8. BASELINE UDPipe	98.77	98.50	88.49
C2L2	98.77	98.50	88.49
CLCL	98.77	98.50	88.49
IIT Kharagpur	98.77	98.50	88.49
Koç University	98.77	98.50	88.49
LATTICE	98.77	98.50	88.49
LyS-FASTPARSE	98.77	98.50	88.49
METU	98.77	98.50	88.49
MQuni	98.77	98.50	88.49
NAIST SATO	98.77	98.50	88.49
Orange – Deskiñ	98.77	98.50	88.49
Stanford	98.77	98.50	88.49
TurkuNLP	98.77	98.50	88.49
UALING	98.77	98.50	88.49
UParse	98.77	98.50	88.49
naistCL	98.77	98.50	88.49
24. RACAI	98.58	98.39	87.52
25. OpenU NLP Lab	**98.77**	98.38	**88.49**
26. Uppsala	97.64	98.20	**89.03**

Table 4: Tokenization, word segmentation and sentence segmentation (ordered by word F_1 scores; out-of-order scores in the other two columns are bold).

Team	UPOS	Feats	Lemm
1. Stanford	93.09	38.81	82.46
2. IMS	91.98	82.99	62.83
3. ParisNLP	91.91	38.89	75.32
4. ÚFAL – UDPipe 1.2	91.22	82.50	71.17
5. HIT-SCIR	91.13	81.90	83.74
6. TurkuNLP	91.10	82.58	82.64
7. LIMSI	91.05	82.49	82.64
8. darc	91.00	82.48	82.60
9. CLCL	90.88	82.31	82.46
10. BASELINE UDPipe	90.88	82.31	82.45
C2L2	90.88	82.31	82.46
IIT Kharagpur	90.88	82.31	82.46
Koç University	90.88	82.31	82.46
LATTICE	90.88	82.31	82.46
LyS-FASTPARSE	90.88	82.31	79.14
NAIST SATO	90.88	82.31	82.46
Orange – Deskiñ	90.88	38.81	15.38
UALING	90.88	82.31	82.46
UParse	90.88	82.31	82.46
naistCL	90.88	82.31	82.46

Table 5: Universal POS tags, features and lemmas (ordered by UPOS F_1 scores).

shed more light on their strengths and weaknesses. This section provides an overview of selected secondary metrics for systems matching or surpassing the baseline; a large number of additional results is available at the shared task website.[16]

The website also features a LAS ranking of unofficial system runs, i.e. those that were not marked by their teams as primary runs, or were even run after the official evaluation phase closed and test data were unblinded. At least two differences from the official results are remarkable; both seem to be partially inflicted by the blind evaluation on TIRA and the inability of the participants to see the diagnostic messages from their software. In the first case, the Dynet library seems to pro-

duce suboptimal results when deployed on a machine different from the one where it was trained. Several teams used the library and may have been affected; for the Uppsala team (de Lhoneux et al., 2017) the issue led to official LAS = 65.11 (23rd place) instead of 69.66 (9th place). In the second case, the ParisNLP system (De La Clergerie et al., 2017) used a wrong method of recognizing the input language, which was not supported in the test data (but unfortunately it was possible to get along with it in development and trial data). Simply crashing could mean that the task moderator would show the team their diagnostic output and they would fix the bug; however, the parser was robust enough to switch to a language-agnostic mode and produced results that were not great, but also not so bad to alert the moderator and make him investigate. Thus the official LAS of the system is 60.02 (27th place) while without the bug it could have been 70.35 (6th place).

Table 3 ranks the systems by CLAS instead of LAS (see Section 3.5). The scores are lower than LAS but differences in system ranking are minimal, possibly indicating that optimization towards

[16] http://universaldependencies.org/
conll17/results.html

one of the metrics does not make the parser bad with respect to the other.

Table 4 evaluates detection of tokens, syntactic words and sentences. Half of the systems simply trusted the segmentation offered by the baseline system. 7 systems were able to improve baseline segmentation. For most languages and in aggregate, the ability to improve parsing scores through better segmentation was probably negligible, but for a few languages, such as Chinese and Vietnamese, the UDPipe baseline segmentation was not so strong and several teams, notably IMS, appear to have improved their LAS by several percent through use of improved segmentation.

The systems were not required to generate any morphological annotation (part-of-speech tags, features or lemmas). Some parsers do not even need morphology and learn to predict syntactic dependencies directly from text. Nevertheless, systems that did output POS tags, and had them at least as good as the baseline system, are evaluated in Table 5. Note that as with segmentation, morphology predicted by the baseline system was available and some systems simply copied it to the output.

6.3 Partial Results

Table 6 gives the LAS F_1 score averaged over the 55 "big" treebanks (training data larger than test data, development data available). Higher scores reflect the fact that models for these test sets are easier to learn: enough data is available, no cross-lingual or cross-domain learning is necessary (the parallel test sets are not included here). When compared to Table 2, four new teams now surpass the baseline, LyS-FASTPARSE being the best among them. The likely explanation is that the systems can learn good models but are not so good at picking the right model for unknown domains and languages.

Table 7 gives the LAS F_1 score on the four surprise languages only. The globally best system, Stanford, now falls back to the fourth rank while C2L2 (Cornell University) apparently employs the most successful strategy for underresourced languages. Another immediate observation is that our surprise languages are very hard to parse; accuracy under 50% is hardly useful for any downstream processing. However, there are significant language-by-language differences, the best score on Upper Sorbian surpassing 60%. This proba-

Team	LAS F_1
1. Stanford (Stanford)	81.77
2. C2L2 (Ithaca)	79.85
3. IMS (Stuttgart)	79.60
4. HIT-SCIR (Harbin)	77.45
5. LATTICE (Paris)	75.79
6. NAIST SATO (Nara)	75.64
7. LyS-FASTPARSE (A Coruña)	74.55
8. Koç University (İstanbul)	74.39
9. ÚFAL – UDPipe 1.2 (Praha)	74.38
10. TurkuNLP (Turku)	74.19
11. Orange – Deskiñ (Lannion)	74.13
12. MQuni (Sydney)	74.03
13. LIMSI (Paris)	73.64
14. UParse (Edinburgh)	73.56
15. darc (Tübingen)	73.31
16. fbaml (Palo Alto)	73.11
17. BASELINE UDPipe 1.1	73.04

Table 6: Average attachment score on the 55 "big" treebanks.

bly owes to the presence of many Slavic treebanks in training data, including some of the largest datasets in UD.

In contrast, the results on the 8 small non-surprise treebanks (Table 8) are higher on average, but again the variance is huge. Uyghur (best score 43.51) is worse than three surprise languages, and Kazakh (best score 29.22) is the least parsable test set of all (see Table 10). These two treebanks are outliers in the size of training data (529 words Kazakh and 1662 words Uyghur, while the other "small" treebanks have between 10K and 20K words). However, the only "training data" of the surprise languages are samples of 147 to 460 words, yet they seem to be easier for some systems. It would be interesting to know whether the more successful systems took a similar approach to Kazakh and Uyghur as to the surprise languages.

Table 9 gives the average LAS on the 14 new parallel test sets (PUD). Three of them (Turkish, Arabic and Hindi) proved difficult to parse for any model trained on the UD 2.0 training data; it seems likely that besides domain differences, inconsistent application of the UD annotation guidelines played a role, too.

See Table 10 for a ranking of all test sets by the best LAS achieved on them by any parser. Note that this cannot be directly interpreted as a

Team	LAS F_1
1. C2L2 (Ithaca)	47.54
2. IMS (Stuttgart)	45.32
3. HIT-SCIR (Harbin)	42.64
4. Stanford (Stanford)	40.57
5. ParisNLP (Paris)	39.22
6. UParse (Edinburgh)	39.17
7. Koç University (İstanbul)	38.81
8. Orange – Deskiñ (Lannion)	38.72
9. LIMSI (Paris)	37.57
10. IIT Kharagpur (Kharagpur)	37.17
11. BASELINE UDPipe 1.1	37.07

Table 7: Average attachment score on the 4 surprise languages: Buryat (bxr), Kurmanji (kmr), North Sámi (sme) and Upper Sorbian (hsb).

Team	LAS F_1
1. C2L2 (Ithaca)	61.49
2. Stanford (Stanford)	61.02
3. IMS (Stuttgart)	58.76
4. LATTICE (Paris)	54.78
5. HIT-SCIR (Harbin)	54.77
6. fbaml (Palo Alto)	54.64
7. RACAI (Bucureşti)	54.26
8. TurkuNLP (Turku)	54.19
9. ÚFAL – UDPipe 1.2 (Praha)	53.76
10. NAIST SATO (Nara)	53.52
11. Koç University (İstanbul)	53.36
12. darc (Tübingen)	52.46
13. UALING (Tucson)	52.27
14. Wanghao-ftd-SJTU (Shanghai)	52.13
15. BASELINE UDPipe 1.1	51.80

Table 8: Average attachment score on the 8 small treebanks: French ParTUT, Galician Tree-Gal, Irish, Kazakh, Latin, Slovenian SST, Uyghur and Ukrainian.

ranking of languages by their parsing difficulty: many treebanks have high ranks simply because the corresponding training data is large. The table also gives a secondary ranking by CLAS and indicates the system that achieved the best LAS / CLAS (mostly the same system won by both metrics). Finally, the best score of word and sentence segmentation is given (without indicating the best-scoring system). Vietnamese proved to be the hardest language in terms of word segmentation; it is not surprising given that its writ-

Team	LAS F_1
1. Stanford (Stanford)	73.73
2. C2L2 (Ithaca)	71.49
3. IMS (Stuttgart)	71.31
4. LATTICE (Paris)	70.77
5. NAIST SATO (Nara)	69.83
6. Koç University (İstanbul)	69.76
7. HIT-SCIR (Harbin)	69.51
8. MQuni (Sydney)	69.28
9. ÚFAL – UDPipe 1.2 (Praha)	69.00
10. UParse (Edinburgh)	68.91
11. Orange – Deskiñ (Lannion)	68.64
12. TurkuNLP (Turku)	68.56
13. BASELINE UDPipe 1.1	68.33

Table 9: Average attachment score on the 14 parallel test sets (PUD).

ing system allows spaces inside words. Second hardest was Hebrew, probably due to a large number of multi-word tokens. In both cases the poor segmentation correlates with poor parsing accuracy. Sentence segmentation was particularly difficult for treebanks without punctuation, i.e., most of the classical languages and spoken data (the best score achieved on the Spoken Slovenian Treebank is only 21.41%). On the other hand, the paragraph boundaries available in some treebanks made sentence detection significantly easier (the extreme being Arabic PUD with one sentence per paragraph; some systems were able to exploit this anomaly and get 100% correct segmentation).

7   Analysis of Submitted Systems

Table 11 gives an overview of 29 of the systems evaluated in the shared task. The overview is based on a post-evaluation questionnaire to which 29 of 32 teams responded. The abbreviations used in Table 11 are explained in Table 12.

As we can see from Table 11, the typical system uses the baseline models for segmentation and morphological analysis (including part-of-speech tagging), employs a single parsing model with pre-trained word embeddings provided by the organizers, and does not make use of any additional data. For readability, all the cells corresponding to use of baseline models (and lack of additional data) have been shaded gray.

Only 7 teams have developed their own word and sentence segmenters, while an additional 5

Treebank	LAS F$_1$	CLAS F$_1$	Best system	Word	Sent
1. ru_syntagrus	92.60	1. 90.11	Stanford	99.69	98.64
2. hi	91.59	6. 87.92	Stanford	100.00	99.29
3. sl	91.51	**2. 88.98**	Stanford	99.96	99.24
4. pt_br	91.36	8. 87.48	Stanford	99.86	96.84
5. ja	91.13	26. 83.18	TRL	98.59	95.11
6. ca	90.70	**10. 86.70**	Stanford	99.97	99.43
7. it	90.68	13. 86.18	Stanford	99.85	99.07
8. cs_cac	90.43	**4. 88.31**	Stanford	99.99	100.00
9. pl	90.32	5. 87.94	Stanford	99.90	99.59
10. cs	90.17	**3. 88.44**	Stanford	99.99	95.10
11. es_ancora	89.99	14. 86.15	Stanford	99.95	98.67
12. no_bokmaal	89.88	**7. 87.67**	Stanford	99.88	96.44
13. bg	89.81	11. 86.53	Stanford	99.92	93.36
14. no_nynorsk	88.81	12. 86.41	Stanford	99.93	94.56
15. fi_pud	88.47	**9. 86.82**	Stanford	99.63	93.67
16. it_pud	88.14	17. 84.49	Stanford	99.27	97.81
17. fr_partut	88.13	24. 83.58	C2L2	99.56	99.13
18. nl_lassysmall	87.71	**15. 85.22**	Stanford	99.99	85.33
19. pt	87.65	25. 83.27	Stanford	99.54	91.67
20. el	87.38	**23. 83.59**	Stanford	99.94	92.68
21. fr_sequoia	87.31	**20. 84.09**	C2L2	99.49	84.60
22. es	87.29	32. 82.08	Stanford	99.81	95.37
23. la_ittb	87.02	**16. 84.94**	Stanford	99.99	94.34
24. fi_ftb	86.81	19. 84.12	Stanford	99.99	86.98
25. fa	86.31	28. 82.93	Stanford	99.65	99.25
26. sk	86.04	**21. 83.86**	Stanford	100.00	85.32
27. ro	85.92	33. 81.87	Stanford	99.77	96.57
28. sv	85.87	**22. 83.71**	Stanford	99.87	97.26
29. cs_cltt	85.82	27. 83.05	C2L2	99.82	95.69
30. fi	85.64	**18. 84.25**	Stanford	99.69	90.88
31. en_pud	85.51	29. 82.63	Stanford	99.74	98.06
32. fr	85.51	31. 82.14	Stanford	99.50	94.58
33. hr	85.25	**30. 82.36**	Stanford	99.93	97.75
34. en_partut	84.46	39. 79.80	C2L2	99.61	98.40
35. cs_pud	84.42	**35. 81.60**	Stanford	99.29	96.43
36. ja_pud	83.75	50. 75.63	HIT-SCIR	94.93	97.52
37. ru	83.65	**34. 81.80**	Stanford	99.94	97.16
38. gl	83.23	43. 78.05	Stanford	99.98	96.36
39. da	82.97	**37. 80.03**	Stanford	100.00	82.59
40. sv_lines	82.89	38. 79.92	Stanford	99.98	87.89
41. ko	82.49	**36. 80.85**	Stanford	99.73	93.05
42. ur	82.28	49. 75.88	Stanford	100.00	98.60
43. en	82.23	**41. 78.99**	Stanford	99.03	78.01
44. en_lines	82.09	42. 78.71	Stanford	99.96	87.55
45. eu	81.44	**40. 79.71**	Stanford	99.99	99.83
46. es_pud	81.05	53. 74.60	Stanford	99.48	98.19
47. de	80.71	**46. 76.97**	Stanford	99.67	80.47
48. nl	80.48	52. 75.19	Stanford	99.88	77.14
49. id	79.19	**45. 77.15**	Stanford	100.00	92.66
50. fr_pud	78.81	**44. 77.37**	Stanford	98.87	96.55
51. sv_pud	78.49	47. 76.48	Stanford	98.56	95.52
52. pt_pud	78.48	56. 72.80	C2L2	99.45	97.32
53. hu	77.56	**48. 76.08**	Stanford	99.85	96.56
54. cu	76.84	51. 75.59	IMS	100.00	50.44
55. ru_pud	75.71	55. 73.13	Stanford	98.29	98.95
56. uk	75.33	57. 71.72	Stanford	99.92	95.75
57. grc_proiel	75.28	60. 69.73	IMS	100.00	51.38
58. de_pud	74.86	**54. 73.96**	Stanford	98.00	91.40
59. gl_treegal	74.34	65. 67.59	C2L2	98.76	86.74
60. lv	74.01	**58. 70.22**	Stanford	99.45	98.80
61. grc	73.19	64. 67.59	Stanford	100.00	98.96
62. ar	72.90	**61. 69.15**	IMS	95.53	85.69
63. et	71.65	**59. 69.85**	Stanford	99.89	93.66
64. la_proiel	71.55	63. 68.93	IMS	100.00	40.63
65. got	71.36	**62. 69.02**	IMS	100.00	41.65
66. ga	70.06	67. 61.38	Stanford	99.73	96.92
67. zh	68.56	**66. 64.23**	IMS	94.57	98.80
68. he	68.16	68. 61.10	IMS	91.37	100.00
69. la	63.37	70. 58.96	Stanford	100.00	99.20
70. tr	62.79	**69. 60.01**	Stanford	97.95	97.04
71. hsb	61.70	71. 56.32	C2L2 / Stanford	99.84	91.65
72. sl_sst	59.07	72. 54.30	C2L2	100.00	21.41
73. hi_pud	54.49	73. 48.87	Stanford	99.65	94.85
74. ar_pud	49.94	75. 46.32	IMS	96.05	100.00
75. sme	48.96	**74. 48.42**	C2L2	99.88	99.13
76. kmr	47.53	76. 44.54	C2L2	98.85	98.64
77. vi	47.51	77. 44.12	IMS	87.30	92.95
78. ug	43.51	78. 34.07	IMS	99.94	70.47
79. tr_pud	38.22	79. 32.32	IMS	96.93	93.91
80. bxr	32.24	80. 26.32	IMS / ParisNLP	99.35	93.69
81. kk	29.22	81. 25.14	RACAI	96.56	89.35

Table 10: Treebank ranking by best parser LAS. Bold CLAS is higher than the preceding one. Best F$_1$ of word and sentence segmentation is also shown. ISO 639 language codes are optionally followed by a treebank code.

teams have retrained or improved the baseline models, or combined them with other techniques. When it comes to part-of-speech tags and morphology, 7 teams use their own systems and 4 use modified versions of the baseline, while 2 teams predict tags jointly with parsing and 3 teams do not predict morphology at all.

For parsing, most teams use a single parsing model – transition-based, graph-based or even rule-based – but 4 teams build ensemble systems in one way or the other. It is worth noting that, whereas the C2L2 and IMS systems are ensembles, the winning Stanford system is not, which makes its performance even more impressive.

The majority of parsers incorporate pre-trained word embeddings. Only 3 parsers use word embeddings without pre-training, and only 4 parsers do not incorporate word embeddings at all. Except for training word embeddings, the additional data provided (or permitted) appears to have been used very sparingly.

When it comes to the surprise languages (and some of the other low-resource languages), the dominant approach is to use a cross-lingual parser, single- or multi-source, and often delexicalized. Finally, for the parallel test sets, most teams have picked a model trained on a single treebank from the same language, but at least 4 teams have trained models on multiple treebanks.

8 Conclusion

The CoNLL 2017 Shared Task on UD parsing was novel in several respects. Besides using cross-linguistically consistent linguistic representations and emphasizing end-to-end processing of text, as discussed in the introduction, it was unusual also in featuring a very large number of languages, in integrating cross-lingual learning for resource-poor languages, and in using a multiply parallel test set.

It was the first large-scale evaluation on data annotated in the Universal Dependencies style. For most UD languages the results represent a new state of the art for dependency parsing. The numbers are not directly comparable to some older work for various reasons (different annotation schemes, gold-standard POS tags, tokenization etc.) but the way the task was organized should ensure their reproducibility and comparability in the future. Furthermore, parsing results are now more comparable across languages than ever before.

System	R	Segment	Morph/POS	Parsing	Embed	AddData	Surp	Para
C2L2	2	Base	Aux	Ensemble-GT	Random	None	Cross-MD	Single
CLCL	25	Base	Base	Single	Random	None	Cross-M	?
darc	12	UDP	Own	Single-T	Base	None	Cross	Single
fbaml	15	Own	Own	Single	Base	None	Mono	?
HIT-SCIR	4	Own	None	Single/Ensemble	Base	OPUS	Cross	Single
IIT Kharagpur	19	Base	Base	Single-T	Base	None	Cross-MD	All/Single
IMS	3	B/O	Own	Ensemble-GT	Base	None	Cross	All
Koç University	7	Base	Base	Single	Crawl	None	Cross	?
LATTICE	5	Base	Base	Single	B/O/FB	Wiki/OPUS	Cross	All
LIMSI	17	B/UDP	Base	B/Single-T	Base	OPUS	Cross	Single
LyS-FASTPARSE	16	Base	Base	Single-T	Base	None	Cross	Single
Mengest	26	Base	Base	Single-T	Crawl	None	Canon	Single
MetaRomance	30	Base	Base	Single-R	None	None	Canon	?
METU	24	Base	Base	Single-T	Base	PTB/CCG	Cross	Single
MQuni	14	Base	Joint	Single-G	Random	None	Mono	Single
NAIST SATO	6	Base	Base	Single	Base	None	Canon	Single
OpenU NLP Lab	28	B/UDP	B/O	Single-T	None	None	Cross	Single
Orange-Deskiñ	10	Base	None	Single	Crawl	None	Cross	Single
ParisNLP	27	B/UDP/O	B/UDP/O/AG	Single	B/C	None	Cross	Single
RACAI	18	Own	Own	Single-G	Crawl	None	Cross	?
Stanford	1	Base	Own	Single-G	B/FB	None	Cross-MD	Single
TRL	29	Own	Own	Single-R	None	None	Cross-SD	Single
TurkuNLP	11	Base	Base/UDP	Single-T	Crawl	None	Cross-S	Single
UALING	22	Base	Base	Base	Base	None	Cross	?
ÚFAL – UDPipe 1.2	8	Own	UDP	Single-T	Treebank	None	Cross	All/Single
UParse	9	Base	Base	B/Single-G	O/FB	OPUS	Cross	Single
Uppsala	23	Own	None	Single-T	Treebank	None	Cross-M	Single
UT	31	Base	Own/AG	Ensemble	FB	None	Cross-S	?
Wanghao-ftd-SJTU	21	Own	Base	Single	None	None	Cross-D	?

Table 11: Classification of participating systems. The second column repeats the main system ranking.

Two new language resources were produced whose usefulness reaches far beyond the task itself: A UD-style parallel treebank in 18 languages, and a large, web-crawled parsebank in 48 languages, over 90 billion words in total.

The analysis of the shared task results has so far only scratched the surface, and we refer to the system description papers for more in-depth analysis of individual systems and their performance. For many previous CoNLL shared tasks, the task itself has only been the starting point of a long and fruitful research strand, enabled by the resources created for the task. We hope and believe that the 2017 UD parsing task will join this tradition.

Acknowledgments

We are grateful to all the contributors to Universal Dependencies; without their effort a task like this simply wouldn't be possible.

The work described herein, including data preparation for the *CoNLL 2017 UD Shared Task*, has been supported by the following grants and projects: "CRACKER," H2020 Project No. 645357 of the European Commission; "MANYLA," Grant No. GA15-10472S of the Grant Agency of the Czech Republic; FIN-CLARIN.

The data for the *CoNLL 2017 UD Shared Task* are available via the LINDAT/CLARIN repository, which is part of a research infrastructure project funded by the Ministry of Education, Youth and Sports of the Czech Republic, Project. No. LM2015071.

The parallel evaluation set was made possible by contributions from DFKI (sentence selection and translation), Google (initial treebanking) and UD volunteers (translation to additional languages, annotation and conversion to UD v2).

References

Burak Kerim Akkuş, Heval Azizoğlu, and Ruket Çakıcı. 2017. Initial explorations of CCG supertagging for Universal Dependency parsing. In *Proceedings of the CoNLL 2017 Shared Task: Multilingual Parsing from Raw Text to Universal Dependencies*. Association for Computational Linguistics.

Chris Alberti, Daniel Andor, Ivan Bogatyy, Michael Collins, Dan Gillick, Lingpeng Kong, Terry Koo, Ji Ma, Mark Omernick, Slav Petrov, Chayut Thanapirom, Zora Tung, and David Weiss. 2017. Syntaxnet models for the conll

Abbreviation	Explanation
Segment	**Word and sentence segmentation**
B(ase)	Baseline UDPipe
UDP	Adapted/retrained UDPipe
O(wn)	Own system for word and sentence segmentation
Morph	**Morphological analysis (including part-of-speech tags)**
None	No prediction of tags or morphological features
B(ase)	Baseline UDPipe
UDP	Adapted/retrained UDPipe
Own	Own system for predicting tags and/or morphological features
AG	Apertium/Giellatekno morphological analyzers
Aux	Tags predicted as an auxiliary task during parser training
Joint	Tags predicted jointly with parsing
Parsing	**Parsing technique**
B(ase)	Baseline UDPipe
Single	Single parser
Ensemble	Ensemble of several parsers
Suffixes	G = Graph-based
	T = Transition-based
	R = Rule-based (with statistics or unsupervised learning)
Embed	**Word embeddings**
B(ase)	Pre-trained word embeddings provided by organizers
C(rawl)	Word embeddings trained on the crawled data provided by organizers
Treebank	Word embeddings trained (only) on the UD treebanks
O	Word embeddings trained on data from OPUS
FB	Pre-trained embeddings released by Facebook
Random	Randomly initialized (trained only with parser)
AddData	**Additional data used (over and above treebanks + raw text)**
None	No additional data
OPUS	Parallel data from OPUS
Wiki	Wikipedia dumps
PTB	Penn Treebank (sic)
CCG	CCGBank (sic)
Surp	**Approach to surprise languages**
Mono	Monolingual parser trained on dev data
Canon	Single canonical model for all surprise languages
Cross	Cross-lingual parsing
Suffixes	S = Single-source
	M = Multi-source
	D = Delexicalized
Para	**Approach to parallel test sets**
Single	Model trained on a single treebank from each language
All	Model trained on all treebanks from each language

Table 12: Abbreviations used in Table 11.

2017 shared task. *CoRR* abs/1703.04929. http://arxiv.org/abs/1703.04929.

Daniel Andor, Chris Alberti, David Weiss, Aliaksei Severyn, Alessandro Presta, Kuzman Ganchev, Slav Petrov, and Michael Collins. 2016. Globally normalized transition-based neural networks. In *Proceedings of the 54th Annual Meeting of the Association for Computational Linguistics, ACL 2016, August 7-12, 2016, Berlin, Germany, Volume 1: Long Papers*. http://aclweb.org/anthology/P/P16/P16-1231.pdf.

Lauriane Aufrant and Guillaume Wisniewski. 2017. LIMSI@CoNLL'17: UD shared task. In *Proceedings of the CoNLL 2017 Shared Task: Multilingual Parsing from Raw Text to Universal Dependencies*. Association for Computational Linguistics.

Anders Björkelund, Agnieszka Faleńska, Xiang Yu, and Jonas Kuhn. 2017. IMS at the CoNLL 2017 UD shared task: CRFs and perceptrons meet neural networks. In *Proceedings of the CoNLL 2017 Shared Task: Multilingual Parsing from Raw Text to Universal Dependencies*. Association for Computational Linguistics.

Sabine Buchholz and Erwin Marsi. 2006. CoNLL-X shared task on multilingual dependency parsing. In *Proceedings of the 10th Conference on Computational Natural Language Learning (CoNLL-X)*. Association for Computational Linguistics, pages 149–164. http://anthology.aclweb.org/W/W06/W06-29.pdf#page=165.

Wanxiang Che, Jiang Guo, Yuxuan Wang, Bo Zheng, Huaipeng Zhao, Yang Liu, and Ting Liu. 2017. The HIT-SCIR system for end-to-end parsing of Universal Dependencies. In *Proceedings of the CoNLL 2017 Shared Task: Multilingual Parsing from Raw Text to Universal Dependencies*. Association for Computational Linguistics.

Ayan Das, Zaffar Affan, and Sudeshna Sarkar. 2017. Delexicalized transfer parsing for low-resource languages using transformed and combined treebanks. In *Proceedings of the CoNLL 2017 Shared Task: Multilingual Parsing from Raw Text to Universal Dependencies*. Association for Computational Linguistics.

Eric De La Clergerie, Benoît Sagot, and Djamé Seddah. 2017. The ParisNLP entry at the CoNLL UD shared task 2017: A tale of a #parsingtragedy. In *Proceedings of the CoNLL 2017 Shared Task: Multilingual Parsing from Raw Text to Universal Dependencies*. Association for Computational Linguistics.

Miryam de Lhoneux, Yan Shao, Ali Basirat, Eliyahu Kiperwasser, Sara Stymne, Yoav Goldberg, and Joakim Nivre. 2017. From raw text to Universal Dependencies - look, no tags! In *Proceedings of the CoNLL 2017 Shared Task: Multilingual Parsing from Raw Text to Universal Dependencies*. Association for Computational Linguistics.

Marie-Catherine de Marneffe and Christopher D. Manning. 2008. Stanford typed dependencies manual. Technical report, Stanford University. http://nlp.stanford.edu/software/dependencies_manual.pdf.

Timothy Dozat, Peng Qi, and Christopher D. Manning. 2017. Stanford's graph-based neural dependency parser at the CoNLL 2017 shared task. In *Proceedings of the CoNLL 2017 Shared Task: Multilingual Parsing from Raw Text to Universal Dependencies*. Association for Computational Linguistics.

Stefan Daniel Dumitrescu, Tiberiu Boroş, and Dan Tufiş. 2017. RACAI's natural language processing pipeline for Universal Dependencies. In *Proceedings of the CoNLL 2017 Shared Task: Multilingual Parsing from Raw Text to Universal Dependencies*. Association for Computational Linguistics.

Marcos Garcia and Pablo Gamallo. 2017. A rule-based system for cross-lingual parsing of Romance languages with universal dependencies. In *Proceedings of the CoNLL 2017 Shared Task: Multilingual Parsing from Raw Text to Universal Dependencies*. Association for Computational Linguistics.

Filip Ginter, Jan Hajič, Juhani Luotolahti, Milan Straka, and Daniel Zeman. 2017. CoNLL 2017 shared task - automatically annotated raw texts and word embeddings. LINDAT/CLARIN digital library at the Institute of Formal and Applied Linguistics, Charles University. http://hdl.handle.net/11234/1-1989.

Nizar Y Habash. 2010. *Introduction to Arabic natural language processing*, volume 3. Morgan & Claypool Publishers.

Allan Hanbury, Henning Müller, Krisztian Balog, Torben Brodt, Gordon V. Cormack, Ivan Eggel, Tim Gollub, Frank Hopfgartner, Jayashree Kalpathy-Cramer, Noriko Kando, Anastasia Krithara, Jimmy Lin, Simon Mercer, and Martin Potthast. 2015. Evaluation-as-a-Service: Overview and Outlook. *ArXiv e-prints* http://arxiv.org/abs/1512.07454.

Johannes Heinecke and Munshi Asadullah. 2017. Multi-model and crosslingual dependency analysis. In *Proceedings of the CoNLL 2017 Shared Task: Multilingual Parsing from Raw Text to Universal Dependencies*. Association for Computational Linguistics.

Ryan Hornby, Clark Taylor, and Jungyeul Park. 2017. Corpus selection approaches for multilingual parsing from raw text to Universal Dependencies. In *Proceedings of the CoNLL 2017 Shared Task: Multilingual Parsing from Raw Text to Universal Dependencies*. Association for Computational Linguistics.

Tao Ji, Yuanbin Wu, and Man Lan. 2017. A fast and lightweight system for multilingual dependency parsing. In *Proceedings of the CoNLL 2017 Shared Task: Multilingual Parsing from Raw Text to Universal Dependencies*. Association for Computational Linguistics.

Hiroshi Kanayama, Masayasu Muraoka, and Katsumasa Yoshikawa. 2017. A semi-universal pipelined approach to the CoNLL 2017 UD shared task. In *Proceedings of the CoNLL 2017 Shared Task: Multilingual Parsing from Raw Text to Universal Dependencies*. Association for Computational Linguistics.

Jenna Kanerva, Juhani Luotolahti, and Filip Ginter. 2017. TurkuNLP: Delexicalized pre-training of word embeddings for dependency parsing. In *Proceedings of the CoNLL 2017 Shared Task: Multilingual Parsing from Raw Text to Universal Dependencies*. Association for Computational Linguistics.

Ömer Kırnap, Berkay Furkan Önder, and Deniz Yuret. 2017. Parsing with context embeddings. In *Proceedings of the CoNLL 2017 Shared Task: Multilingual Parsing from Raw Text to Universal Dependencies*. Association for Computational Linguistics.

Kyungtae Lim and Thierry Poibeau. 2017. A system for multilingual dependency parsing based on bidirectional LSTM feature representations. In *Proceedings of the CoNLL 2017 Shared Task: Multilingual Parsing from Raw Text to Universal Dependencies*. Association for Computational Linguistics.

Ryan McDonald, Joakim Nivre, Yvonne Quirmbach-Brundage, Yoav Goldberg, Dipanjan Das, Kuzman Ganchev, Keith Hall, Slav Petrov, Hao Zhang, Oscar Täckström, Claudia Bedini, Núria Bertomeu Castelló, and Jungmee Lee. 2013. Universal dependency annotation for multilingual parsing. In *Proceedings of the 51st Annual Meeting of the Association for Computational Linguistics*. Sofia, Bulgaria.

Tomas Mikolov, Ilya Sutskever, Kai Chen, Gregory S. Corrado, and Jeffrey Dean. 2013. Distributed representations of words and phrases and their compositionality. In *Advances in Neural Information Processing Systems 26: 27th Annual Conference on Neural Information Processing Systems*. pages

3111–3119. http://papers.nips.cc/paper/5021-distributed-representations-of-words-and-phrases-and-their-compositionality.

Christophe Moor, Paola Merlo, James Henderson, and Haozhou Wang. 2017. Geneva DINN parser: a neural network dependency parser ten years later. In *Proceedings of the CoNLL 2017 Shared Task: Multilingual Parsing from Raw Text to Universal Dependencies*. Association for Computational Linguistics.

Amir More and Reut Tsarfaty. 2017. Universal joint morph-syntactic processing: The Open University of Israel's submission to the CoNLL 2017. In *Proceedings of the CoNLL 2017 Shared Task: Multilingual Parsing from Raw Text to Universal Dependencies*. Association for Computational Linguistics.

Dat Quoc Nguyen, Mark Dras, and Mark Johnson. 2017. A novel neural network model for joint POS tagging and graph-based dependency parsing. In *Proceedings of the CoNLL 2017 Shared Task: Multilingual Parsing from Raw Text to Universal Dependencies*. Association for Computational Linguistics.

Joakim Nivre, Željko Agić, Lars Ahrenberg, Lene Antonsen, Maria Jesus Aranzabe, Masayuki Asahara, Luma Ateyah, Mohammed Attia, Aitziber Atutxa, Elena Badmaeva, Miguel Ballesteros, Esha Banerjee, Sebastian Bank, John Bauer, Kepa Bengoetxea, Riyaz Ahmad Bhat, Eckhard Bick, Cristina Bosco, Gosse Bouma, Sam Bowman, Aljoscha Burchardt, Marie Candito, Gauthier Caron, Gülşen Cebiroğlu Eryiğit, Giuseppe G. A. Celano, Savas Cetin, Fabricio Chalub, Jinho Choi, Yongseok Cho, Silvie Cinková, Çağrı Çöltekin, Miriam Connor, Marie-Catherine de Marneffe, Valeria de Paiva, Arantza Diaz de Ilarraza, Kaja Dobrovoljc, Timothy Dozat, Kira Droganova, Marhaba Eli, Ali Elkahky, Tomaž Erjavec, Richárd Farkas, Hector Fernandez Alcalde, Jennifer Foster, Cláudia Freitas, Katarína Gajdošová, Daniel Galbraith, Marcos Garcia, Filip Ginter, Iakes Goenaga, Koldo Gojenola, Memduh Gökırmak, Yoav Goldberg, Xavier Gómez Guinovart, Berta Gonzáles Saavedra, Matias Grioni, Normunds Grūzītis, Bruno Guillaume, Nizar Habash, Jan Hajič, Jan Hajič jr., Linh Hà Mỹ, Kim Harris, Dag Haug, Barbora Hladká, Jaroslava Hlaváčová, Petter Hohle, Radu Ion, Elena Irimia, Anders Johannsen, Fredrik Jørgensen, Hüner Kaşıkara, Hiroshi Kanayama, Jenna Kanerva, Tolga Kayadelen, Václava Kettnerová, Jesse Kirchner, Natalia Kotsyba, Simon Krek, Sookyoung Kwak, Veronika Laippala, Lorenzo Lambertino, Tatiana Lando, Phương Lê Hồng, Alessandro Lenci, Saran Lertpradit, Herman Leung, Cheuk Ying Li, Josie Li, Nikola Ljubešić, Olga Loginova, Olga Lyashevskaya, Teresa Lynn, Vivien Macketanz, Aibek Makazhanov, Michael Mandl, Christopher Manning, Ruli Manurung, Cătălina Mărănduc, David Mareček, Katrin Marheinecke, Héctor Martínez Alonso, André Martins, Jan Mašek, Yuji Matsumoto, Ryan McDonald, Gustavo Mendonça, Anna Missilä, Verginica Mititelu, Yusuke Miyao, Simonetta Montemagni, Amir More, Laura Moreno Romero, Shunsuke Mori, Bohdan Moskalevskyi, Kadri Muischnek, Nina Mustafina, Kaili Müürisep, Pinkey Nainwani, Anna Nedoluzhko, Lương Nguyễn Thị, Huyền Nguyễn Thị Minh, Vitaly Nikolaev, Rattima Nitisaroj, Hanna Nurmi, Stina Ojala, Petya Osenova, Lilja Øvrelid, Elena Pascual, Marco Passarotti, Cenel-Augusto Perez, Guy Perrier, Slav Petrov, Jussi Piitulainen, Emily Pitler, Barbara Plank, Martin Popel, Lauma Pretkalniņa, Prokopis Prokopidis, Tiina Puolakainen, Sampo Pyysalo, Alexandre Rademaker, Livy Real, Siva Reddy, Georg Rehm, Larissa Rinaldi, Laura Rituma, Rudolf Rosa, Davide Rovati, Shadi Saleh, Manuela Sanguinetti, Baiba Saulīte, Yanin Sawanakunanon, Sebastian Schuster, Djamé Seddah, Wolfgang Seeker, Mojgan Seraji, Lena Shakurova, Mo Shen, Atsuko Shimada, Muh Shohibussirri, Natalia Silveira, Maria Simi, Radu Simionescu, Katalin Simkó, Mária Šimková, Kiril Simov, Aaron Smith, Antonio Stella, Jana Strnadová, Alane Suhr, Umut Sulubacak, Zsolt Szántó, Dima Taji, Takaaki Tanaka, Trond Trosterud, Anna Trukhina, Reut Tsarfaty, Francis Tyers, Sumire Uematsu, Zdeňka Urešová, Larraitz Uria, Hans Uszkoreit, Gertjan van Noord, Viktor Varga, Veronika Vincze, Jonathan North Washington, Zhuoran Yu, Zdeněk Žabokrtský, Daniel Zeman, and Hanzhi Zhu. 2017a. Universal dependencies 2.0 – CoNLL 2017 shared task development and test data. LINDAT/CLARIN digital library at the Institute of Formal and Applied Linguistics, Charles University. http://hdl.handle.net/11234/1-2184.

Joakim Nivre, Željko Agić, Lars Ahrenberg, Maria Jesus Aranzabe, Masayuki Asahara, Aitziber Atutxa, Miguel Ballesteros, John Bauer, Kepa Bengoetxea, Riyaz Ahmad Bhat, Eckhard Bick, Cristina Bosco, Gosse Bouma, Sam Bowman, Marie Candito, Gülşen Cebiroğlu Eryiğit, Giuseppe G. A. Celano, Fabricio Chalub, Jinho Choi, Çağrı Çöltekin, Miriam Connor, Elizabeth Davidson, Marie-Catherine de Marneffe, Valeria de Paiva, Arantza Diaz de Ilarraza, Kaja Dobrovoljc, Timothy Dozat, Kira Droganova, Puneet Dwivedi, Marhaba Eli, Tomaž Erjavec, Richárd Farkas, Jennifer Foster, Cláudia Freitas, Katarína Gajdošová, Daniel Galbraith, Marcos Garcia, Filip Ginter, Iakes Goenaga, Koldo Gojenola, Memduh Gökırmak, Yoav Goldberg, Xavier Gómez Guinovart, Berta Gonzáles Saavedra, Matias Grioni, Normunds Grūzītis, Bruno Guillaume, Nizar Habash, Jan Hajič, Linh Hà Mỹ, Dag Haug, Barbora Hladká, Petter Hohle, Radu Ion, Elena Irimia, Anders Johannsen, Fredrik Jørgensen, Hüner Kaşıkara, Hiroshi Kanayama, Jenna Kanerva, Natalia Kotsyba, Simon Krek, Veronika Laippala, Phương Lê Hồng, Alessandro Lenci, Nikola Ljubešić, Olga Lyashevskaya, Teresa Lynn, Aibek Makazhanov, Christopher Manning, Cătălina Mărănduc, David Mareček, Héctor Martínez Alonso, André Martins, Jan Mašek, Yuji Matsumoto, Ryan McDonald, Anna Missilä, Verginica Mititelu, Yusuke Miyao, Simonetta Montemagni, Amir More, Shunsuke Mori, Bohdan Moskalevskyi, Kadri Muischnek, Nina

Mustafina, Kaili Müürisep, Lương Nguyễn Thị, Huyền Nguyễn Thị Minh, Vitaly Nikolaev, Hanna Nurmi, Stina Ojala, Petya Osenova, Lilja Øvrelid, Elena Pascual, Marco Passarotti, Cenel-Augusto Perez, Guy Perrier, Slav Petrov, Jussi Piitulainen, Barbara Plank, Martin Popel, Lauma Pretkalniņa, Prokopis Prokopidis, Tiina Puolakainen, Sampo Pyysalo, Alexandre Rademaker, Loganathan Ramasamy, Livy Real, Laura Rituma, Rudolf Rosa, Shadi Saleh, Manuela Sanguinetti, Baiba Saulīte, Sebastian Schuster, Djamé Seddah, Wolfgang Seeker, Mojgan Seraji, Lena Shakurova, Mo Shen, Dmitry Sichinava, Natalia Silveira, Maria Simi, Radu Simionescu, Katalin Simkó, Mária Šimková, Kiril Simov, Aaron Smith, Alane Suhr, Umut Sulubacak, Zsolt Szántó, Dima Taji, Takaaki Tanaka, Reut Tsarfaty, Francis Tyers, Sumire Uematsu, Larraitz Uria, Gertjan van Noord, Viktor Varga, Veronika Vincze, Jonathan North Washington, Zdeněk Žabokrtský, Amir Zeldes, Daniel Zeman, and Hanzhi Zhu. 2017b. Universal Dependencies 2.0. LINDAT/CLARIN digital library at the Institute of Formal and Applied Linguistics, Charles University, Prague. http://hdl.handle.net/11234/1-1983.

Joakim Nivre, Marie-Catherine de Marneffe, Filip Ginter, Yoav Goldberg, Jan Hajič, Christopher Manning, Ryan McDonald, Slav Petrov, Sampo Pyysalo, Natalia Silveira, Reut Tsarfaty, and Daniel Zeman. 2016. Universal Dependencies v1: A multilingual treebank collection. In *Proceedings of the 10th International Conference on Language Resources and Evaluation (LREC 2016)*. European Language Resources Association, Portorož, Slovenia, pages 1659–1666.

Joakim Nivre and Chiao-Ting Fang. 2017. Universal dependency evaluation. In *Proceedings of the NoDaLiDa 2017 Workshop on Universal Dependencies (UDW 2017)*. pages 86–95.

Joakim Nivre, Johan Hall, Sandra Kübler, Ryan McDonald, Jens Nilsson, Sebastian Riedel, and Deniz Yuret. 2007. The CoNLL 2007 shared task on dependency parsing. In *Proceedings of the CoNLL Shared Task Session of EMNLP-CoNLL 2007*. Association for Computational Linguistics, pages 915–932. http://www.aclweb.org/anthology/D/D07/D07-1.pdf#page=949.

Slav Petrov, Dipanjan Das, and Ryan T. McDonald. 2011. A universal part-of-speech tagset. *CoRR* abs/1104.2086. http://arxiv.org/abs/1104.2086.

Slav Petrov and Ryan McDonald. 2012. Overview of the 2012 shared task on parsing the web. In *Proceedings of the First Workshop on Syntactic Analysis of Non-Canonical Language (SANCL)*. Montréal, Canada. http://www.petrovi.de/data/sancl12.pdf.

Martin Popel, Zdeněk Žabokrtský, and Martin Vojtek. 2017. Udapi: Universal API for universal dependencies. In *NoDaLiDa 2017 Workshop on Universal Dependencies*. Göteborgs universitet, Göteborg, Sweden, pages 96–101. http://aclweb.org/anthology/W/W17/W17-0412.pdf.

Martin Potthast, Tim Gollub, Francisco Rangel, Paolo Rosso, Efstathios Stamatatos, and Benno Stein. 2014. Improving the reproducibility of PAN's shared tasks: Plagiarism detection, author identification, and author profiling. In Evangelos Kanoulas, Mihai Lupu, Paul Clough, Mark Sanderson, Mark Hall, Allan Hanbury, and Elaine Toms, editors, *Information Access Evaluation meets Multilinguality, Multimodality, and Visualization. 5th International Conference of the CLEF Initiative (CLEF 14)*. Springer, Berlin Heidelberg New York, pages 268–299. https://doi.org/10.1007/978-3-319-11382-1_22.

Xian Qian and Yang Liu. 2017. A non-DNN feature engineering approach to dependency parsing – FBAML at CoNLL 2017 shared task. In *Proceedings of the CoNLL 2017 Shared Task: Multilingual Parsing from Raw Text to Universal Dependencies*. Association for Computational Linguistics.

Motoki Sato, Hitoshi Manabe, Hiroshi Noji, and Yuji Matsumoto. 2017. Adversarial training for cross-domain universal dependency parsing. In *Proceedings of the CoNLL 2017 Shared Task: Multilingual Parsing from Raw Text to Universal Dependencies*. Association for Computational Linguistics.

Djamé Seddah, Sandra Kübler, and Reut Tsarfaty. 2014. Introducing the SPMRL 2014 shared task on parsing morphologically-rich languages. In *First Joint Workshop on Statistical Parsing of Morphologically Rich Languages and Syntactic Analysis of Non-Canonical Languages*. Dublin, Ireland, pages 103–109. http://www.aclweb.org/anthology/W14-6111.

Djamé Seddah, Reut Tsarfaty, Sandra Kübler, Marie Candito, Jinho D. Choi, Richárd Farkas, Jennifer Foster, Iakes Goenaga, Koldo Gojenola, Yoav Goldberg, Spence Green, Nizar Habash, Marco Kuhlmann, Wolfgang Maier, Joakim Nivre, Adam Przepiórkowski, Ryan Roth, Wolfgang Seeker, Yannick Versley, Veronika Vincze, Marcin Woliński, Alina Wróblewska, and Eric Villemonte de la Clérgerie. 2013. Overview of the SPMRL 2013 shared task: Cross-framework evaluation of parsing morphologically rich languages. In *Proceedings of the Fourth Workshop on Statistical Parsing of Morphologically Rich Languages*. Association for Computational Linguistics, Seattle, Washington, USA, pages 146–182. http://www.aclweb.org/anthology/W13-4917.

Tianze Shi, Felix G. Wu, Xilun Chen, and Yao Cheng. 2017. Combining global models for parsing Universal Dependencies. In *Proceedings of the CoNLL 2017 Shared Task: Multilingual Parsing from Raw Text to Universal Dependencies*. Association for Computational Linguistics.

Milan Straka. 2017. CoNLL 2017 shared task - UD-Pipe baseline models and supplementary materials. LINDAT/CLARIN digital library at the Institute of Formal and Applied Linguistics, Charles University. http://hdl.handle.net/11234/1-1990.

Milan Straka, Jan Hajič, and Jana Straková. 2016. UD-Pipe: trainable pipeline for processing CoNLL-U files performing tokenization, morphological analysis, POS tagging and parsing. In *Proceedings of the 10th International Conference on Language Resources and Evaluation (LREC 2016)*. European Language Resources Association, Portorož, Slovenia.

Milan Straka and Jana Straková. 2017. Tokenizing, POS tagging, lemmatizing and parsing UD 2.0 with UDPipe. In *Proceedings of the CoNLL 2017 Shared Task: Multilingual Parsing from Raw Text to Universal Dependencies*. Association for Computational Linguistics.

Jörg Tiedemann. 2012. Parallel data, tools and interfaces in OPUS. In Nicoletta Calzolari (Conference Chair), Khalid Choukri, Thierry Declerck, Mehmet Ugur Dogan, Bente Maegaard, Joseph Mariani, Jan Odijk, and Stelios Piperidis, editors, *Proceedings of the Eight International Conference on Language Resources and Evaluation (LREC'12)*. European Language Resources Association (ELRA), Istanbul, Turkey.

Clara Vania, Xingxing Zhang, and Adam Lopez. 2017. UParse: the Edinburgh system for the CoNLL 2017 UD shared task. In *Proceedings of the CoNLL 2017 Shared Task: Multilingual Parsing from Raw Text to Universal Dependencies*. Association for Computational Linguistics.

David Vilares and Carlos Gómez-Rodríguez. 2017. A non-projective greedy dependency parser with bidirectional LSTMs. In *Proceedings of the CoNLL 2017 Shared Task: Multilingual Parsing from Raw Text to Universal Dependencies*. Association for Computational Linguistics.

Hao Wang, Hai Zhao, and Zhisong Zhang. 2017. A transition-based system for universal dependency parsing. In *Proceedings of the CoNLL 2017 Shared Task: Multilingual Parsing from Raw Text to Universal Dependencies*. Association for Computational Linguistics.

Kuan Yu, Pavel Sofroniev, and Erik Schill. 2017. The parse is darc and full of errors: Universal dependency parsing with transition-based and graph-based algorithms. In *Proceedings of the CoNLL 2017 Shared Task: Multilingual Parsing from Raw Text to Universal Dependencies*. Association for Computational Linguistics.

Stanford's Graph-based Neural Dependency Parser at the CoNLL 2017 Shared Task

Timothy Dozat
Stanford University
tdozat@stanford.edu

Peng Qi
Stanford University
pengqi@stanford.edu

Christopher D. Manning
Stanford University
manning@stanford.edu

Abstract

This paper describes the neural dependency parser submitted by Stanford to the CoNLL 2017 Shared Task on parsing Universal Dependencies. Our system uses relatively simple LSTM networks to produce part of speech tags and labeled dependency parses from segmented and tokenized sequences of words. In order to address the rare word problem that abounds in languages with complex morphology, we include a character-based word representation that uses an LSTM to produce embeddings from sequences of characters. Our system was ranked first according to all five relevant metrics for the system: UPOS tagging (93.09%), XPOS tagging (82.27%), unlabeled attachment score (81.30%), labeled attachment score (76.30%), and content word labeled attachment score (72.57%).

1 Introduction

In this paper, we describe Stanford's approach to tackling the CoNLL 2017 shared task on Universal Dependency parsing (Nivre et al., 2016; Zeman et al., 2017; Nivre et al., 2017b,a). Our system builds on the deep biaffine neural dependency parser presented by Dozat and Manning (2017), which uses a well-tuned LSTM network to produce vector representations for each word, then uses those vector representations in novel biaffine classifiers to predict the head token of each dependent and the class of the resulting edge. In order to adapt it to the wide variety of different treebanks in Universal Dependencies, we make two noteworthy extensions to the system: first, we incorporate a word representation built up from character sequences using an LSTM, theorizing that

this should improve the model's ability to adapt to rare or unknown words in languages with rich morphology; second, we train our own taggers for the treebanks using nearly identical architecture to the one used for parsing, in order to capitalize on potential improvements in part of speech tag quality over baseline or off-the-shelf taggers. This approach gets state-of-the-art results on the macro average of the shared task datasets according to all five POS tagging and attachment accuracy metrics.

One noteworthy feature of our approach is its relative simplicity. It uses a single tagger/parser pair per language, trained on only words and tags; thus we refrain from taking advantage of ensembling, lemmas, or morphological features, any one of which could potentially push accuracy even higher.

2 Architecture

2.1 Deep biaffine parser

The basic architecture of our approach follows that of Dozat and Manning (2017), which is closely related to Kiperwasser and Goldberg (2016), the first neural graph-based (McDonald et al., 2005) parser.[1] In Dozat and Manning's 2017 parser, the input to the model is a sequence of tokens and their part of speech tags, which is then put through a multilayer bidirectional LSTM network. The output state of the final LSTM layer (which excludes the cell state) is then fed through four separate ReLU layers, producing four specialized vector representations: one for the word as a dependent seeking its head; one for the word as a head seeking all its dependents; another for the word as a dependent deciding on its label; and a fourth for the word as head deciding on the labels of its depen-

---

[1] For other neural graph-based parsers, cf. Cheng et al. (2016); Hashimoto et al. (2016); Zhang et al. (2016)

20

Proceedings of the CoNLL 2017 Shared Task: Multilingual Parsing from Raw Text to Universal Dependencies, pages 20–30,
Vancouver, Canada, August 3-4, 2017. © 2017 Association for Computational Linguistics

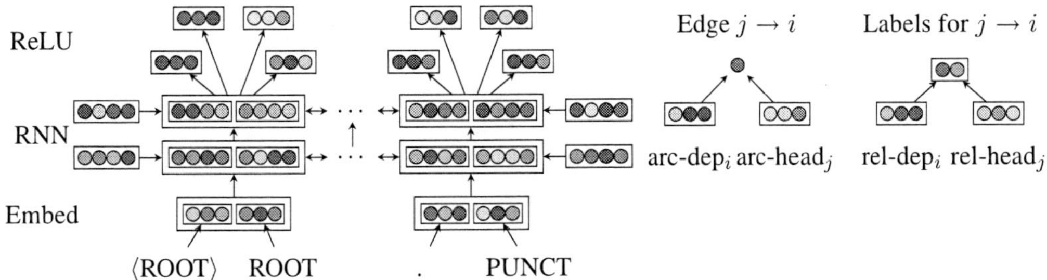

Figure 1: The architecture of our parser. Arrows indicate structural dependence, but not necessarily trainable parameters.

dents.[2] These vectors are then used in two biaffine classifiers: the first computes a score for each pair of tokens, with the highest score for a given token indicating that token's most probable head; the second computes a score for each label for a given token/head pair, with the highest score representing the most probable label for the arc from the head to the dependent. This is shown graphically in Figure 1.

Put formally, given a sequence of n word embeddings (to be described in more detail in Section 2.2) $(\mathbf{v}_1^{(word)}, \ldots, \mathbf{v}_n^{(word)})$ and n tag embeddings $(\mathbf{v}_1^{(tag)}, \ldots, \mathbf{v}_n^{(tag)})$, we concatenate each pair together and feed the result into a BiLSTM with initial state $\mathbf{r}_0$:[3]

$$\mathbf{x}_i = \mathbf{v}_i^{(word)} \oplus \mathbf{v}_i^{(tag)} \tag{1}$$

$$\mathbf{r}_i = \text{BiLSTM}\big(\mathbf{r}_0, (\mathbf{x}_1, \ldots, \mathbf{x}_n)\big)_i \tag{2}$$

$$\mathbf{h}_i, \mathbf{c}_i = \text{split}(\mathbf{r}_i) \tag{3}$$

We then produce four distinct vectors from each recurrent hidden state $\mathbf{h}_i$ (without the recurrent cell state $\mathbf{c}_i$) using ReLU perceptron layers:

$$\mathbf{h}_i^{(arc\text{-}dep)} = \text{MLP}^{(arc\text{-}dep)}(\mathbf{h}_i) \tag{4}$$

$$\mathbf{h}_i^{(arc\text{-}head)} = \text{MLP}^{(arc\text{-}head)}(\mathbf{h}_i) \tag{5}$$

$$\mathbf{h}_i^{(rel\text{-}dep)} = \text{MLP}^{(rel\text{-}dep)}(\mathbf{h}_i) \tag{6}$$

$$\mathbf{h}_i^{(rel\text{-}head)} = \text{MLP}^{(rel\text{-}head)}(\mathbf{h}_i) \tag{7}$$

In order to produce a prediction $y_i'^{(arc)}$ for token i, we use a biaffine classifier involving the (arc)

---

[2]Interestingly, other researchers have found similar approaches to be beneficial for other tasks; cf. Reed and de Freitas (2016); Miller et al. (2016); Daniluk et al. (2017)

[3]We adopt the convention of using lowercase italics for scalars, lowercase bold for vectors, uppercase italics for matrices, and uppercase bold for tensors. We maintain this convention when indexing and stacking; so $\mathbf{a}_i$ is the ith vector of matrix A, and matrix A is the stack of all vectors $\mathbf{a}_i$.

hidden vectors:

$$\mathbf{s}_i^{(arc)} = H^{(arc\text{-}head)} W^{(arc)} \mathbf{h}_i^{(arc\text{-}dep)} \tag{8}$$
$$+ H^{(arc\text{-}head)} \mathbf{b}^{\top(arc)}$$

$$y_i'^{(arc)} = \arg\max_j s_{ij}^{(arc)} \tag{9}$$

Note first the similarity between line 8 and a traditional affine classifier of the form $W\mathbf{h} + \mathbf{b}$, with each of W and $\mathbf{b}$ first being transformed by $H^{(arc\text{-}head)}$. Note also that both terms of the biaffine layer have intuitive interpretations: the first relates to the probability of word j being the head of word i given the information in both $\mathbf{h}^{(arc)}$ vectors (for example, the probability of word i depending on word j given that word i is *the* and word j is *cat*); the second relates to the probability of word j being the head of word i given only the information in the head's vector (for example, the probability of word i depending on word j given that word j is *the*, which should be very small no matter what word i is).

After deciding on a head y_i' for word i, we use another biaffine transformation—this time involving the (rel) hidden vectors—to produce a predicted label:

$$\mathbf{s}_i^{(rel)} = \mathbf{h}_{y_i'^{(arc)}}^{\top(rel\text{-}head)} U^{(rel)} \mathbf{h}_i^{(rel\text{-}dep)} \tag{10}$$
$$+ W^{(rel)}\big(\mathbf{h}_i^{(rel\text{-}dep)} \oplus \mathbf{h}_{y_i'^{(arc)}}^{(rel\text{-}head)}\big)$$
$$+ \mathbf{b}^{(rel)}$$

$$y_i'^{(rel)} = \arg\max_j s_{ij}^{(rel)} \tag{11}$$

Again, each term in line 10 has an intuitive interpretation: the first term relates to the probability of observing a label given the information in both $\mathbf{h}^{(rel)}$ vectors (e.g. the probability of the label *det* given word i is *the* with head *cat*); the second relates to the probability of observing a label given

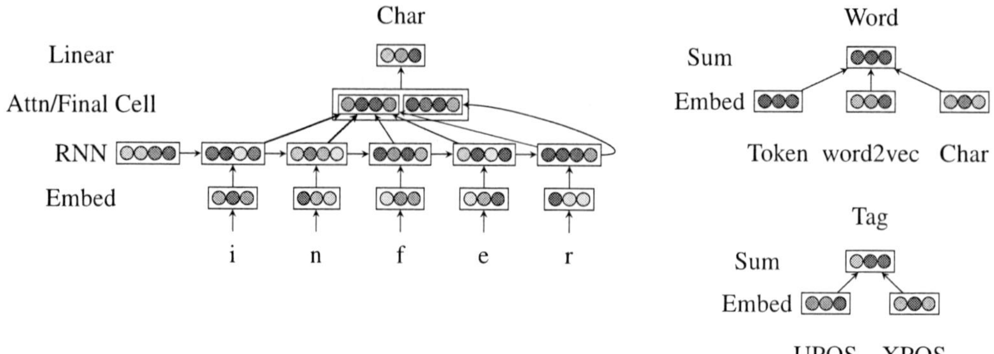

Figure 2: The architecture of our embedding model. Arrows indicate structural dependence, but not necessarily trainable parameters.

either $\mathbf{h}^{(rel)}$ vector (e.g. the probability of the label *det* given that word i is *the* or that word j is *cat*); the last relates to the prior probability of observing a label.

We jointly train these two biaffine classifiers by optimizing the sum of their softmax cross-entropy losses. At test time, we ensure the tree is well-formed by iteratively identifying and fixing cycles for each proposed root and selecting the one with the highest score, which is both simple and sufficient for our purposes. [4]

2.2 Character-level model

Dozat and Manning (2017) represented words as the sum of a pretrained vector[5] and a holistic word embedding for frequent words. However, that approach seems insufficient for languages with rich morphology; so we add a third representation built up from sequences of characters. Each character is given a trainable vector embedding, and each sequence of character embeddings is fed into a unidirectional LSTM. However, the LSTM produces a *sequence* of recurrent states $(\mathbf{r}_1, \ldots, \mathbf{r}_n)$, which we need to convert into a single vector. The simplest approach is to take the last one—which would represent a summary of all the information aggregated one character at a time—and linearly transform it to the desired dimensionality. Another approach, suggested by Cao and Rei (2016), is to use attention over the hidden states, and then

trasform the resulting context vector to the desired size; in theory, this should both allow the model to learn morpheme information more easily by attending more closely to the LSTM output at morpheme boundaries. We choose to combine both approaches, using the hidden states for attention and the cell state for summarizing, shown in Figure 2.

That is, given a sequence of n character embeddings and an initial state $\mathbf{r}_0$ for the LSTM, we each embedding into an LSTM as before, extracting hidden and cell states:

$$\mathbf{r}_i = \mathrm{LSTM}\big(\mathbf{r}_0, (\mathbf{v}_1^{(char)}, \ldots, \mathbf{v}_n^{(char)})\big)_i \tag{12}$$

$$\mathbf{h}_i, \mathbf{c}_i = \mathrm{split}(\mathbf{r}_i) \tag{13}$$

We then compute linear attention over the stack of hidden vectors H and concatenate it to the final cell state:

$$\mathbf{a} = \mathrm{softmax}\big(H\mathbf{w}^{(attn)}\big) \tag{14}$$

$$\tilde{\mathbf{h}} = H^\top \mathbf{a} \tag{15}$$

$$\hat{\mathbf{v}} = W\big(\tilde{\mathbf{h}} \oplus \mathbf{c}_n\big) \tag{16}$$

In this way we use the hidden states for attention and the cell state as a final summary vector.

After computing the character-level word embedding, we add together elementwise the pretrained embedding, the holistic frequent token embedding, and the newly generated character-level embedding. We also add together embeddings for the language's UPOS and XPOS tags. The resulting two vectors are used as input to the BiLSTM parser in Section 2.1.

---

[4]Although in the future we intend to implement than the Chu-Liu/Edmonds algorithm for nonprojective MST parsing (Chu and Liu, 1965; Edmonds, 1967)

[5]We use the provided CoNLL vectors trained on word2vec (Mikolov et al., 2013); for Gothic, which had no provided vector embeddings, we used Facebook's FastText vectors (Bojanowski et al., 2016)

2.3 POS tagger

The final piece of our system is a separately-trained part of speech tagger. The architecture for the tagger is almost identical to that of the parser (and shares fundamental properties with other neural taggers; cf. Ling et al. (2015); Plank et al. (2016))—it uses a BiLSTM over word vectors (using the tripartite representation from Section 2.2), then uses ReLU layers to produce one vector representation for each type of tag.

Thus we use a BiLSTM, as with the parser architecture:

$$\mathbf{r}_i = \text{BiLSTM}\big(\mathbf{r}_0, (\mathbf{v}_1^{(word)}, \ldots, \mathbf{v}_n^{(word)})\big)_i \tag{17}$$

$$\mathbf{h}_i, \mathbf{c}_i = \text{split}(\mathbf{r}_i) \tag{18}$$

And we use affine classifiers for each type of tag, which we add together for the parser:

$$\mathbf{h}_i^{(pos)} = \text{MLP}^{(pos)}(\mathbf{h}_i) \tag{19}$$

$$\mathbf{s}_i^{(pos)} = W\mathbf{h}_i^{(pos)} + \mathbf{b}^{(pos)} \tag{20}$$

$$y_i'^{(pos)} = \arg\max_j s_{ij}^{(pos)} \tag{21}$$

The tag classifiers are trained jointly using cross-entropy losses that are summed together during optimization, but the tagger is trained independently from the parser.

3 Training details

Our model largely adopts the same hyperparameter configuration laid out by Dozat and Manning (2017), with a few exceptions. The parser uses three BiLSTM layers with 100-dimensional word and tag embeddings and 200-dimensional recurrent states (in each direction); the arc classifier uses 400-dimensional head/dependent vector states and the label classifier uses 100-dimensional ones; we drop word and tag embeddings independently with 33% probability;[6] we use same-mask dropout (Gal and Ghahramani, 2015) in the LSTM, ReLU layers, and classifiers, dropping input and recurrent connections with 33% probability; and we optimize with Adam (Kingma and Ba, 2014), setting the learning rate to $2e^{-3}$ and $\beta_1 = \beta_2 = .9$. We train models for up to 30,000 training steps (where one step/iteration is a single minibatch with approximately 5,000 tokens), at

---

[6]When only one is dropped, we scale the other by a factor of two

first saving the model every 100 steps if fewer than 1,000 iterations have passed, and afterwards only saving if validation accuracy increases (or training accuracy for languages with no validation data). When 5,000 training steps pass without improving accuracy, we terminate training.

For the character model, we use 100-dimensional uncased character embeddings with 400-dimensional recurrent states. We don't drop characters but do include 33% dropout in the LSTM and attention connections.

In the tagger we use nearly identical settings, with a few exceptions: the BiLSTM is only two layers deep, we increase the dropout between recurrent connections to 50%, and we use cased character embeddings.

Our approach for dealing with the surprise languages was to train delexicalized "language family" parsers with the same architecture detailed in Section 2.1 on UDPipe v1.1 (Straka et al., 2016)'s UPOS tags with no word-level information. For Buryat (Altaic), we used as input the training datasets for Turkish, Uyghur, Kazakh, Korean, and Japanese; for Kurmanji (Indo-Iranian), we used Persian, Urdu, and Hindi; for North Sámi (Uralic), we used Finnish, Finnish-FTB, Estonian, and Hungarian; and for Upper Sorbian (Slavic), we used Bulgarian, Czech, Old Church Slavonic, Polish, Russian, Russian-SynTagRus, Slovak, Slovenian, Slovenian-SST, and Ukrainian.

There's substantial variability in training and testing speed across treebanks, but on an NVidia Titan X GPU the models train at 100 to 1000 sentences/sec and test at 1000 to 5000 sentences/sec. Even without GPU acceleration a tagger or parser can be run on an entire test treebank in ten to twenty seconds. By far the greatest runtime overhead comes not from the model itself, but from reading in the large matrices of pretrained embeddings, which can take several minutes. A full run over the 81 test sets on the TIRA virtual machine (Potthast et al., 2014) takes about 16 hours, but when parallelized on faster machines it can be done in under an hour.

4 Results

Our model uses a provided tokenization and segmentation and produces UPOS tags, XPOS tags, arcs, and labels. Thus the relevant metrics for the system are UPOS accuracy, XPOS accuracy, unlabeled attachment score, labeled attachment score,

	UPOS	XPOS	UAS	LAS	CLAS		UPOS	XPOS	UAS	LAS	CLAS
ar	89.36	**87.66**	76.59	71.97	68.17	*hsb*	90.30	99.84	67.83	60.01	**56.32**
ar_pud	71.17	0.00	58.87	49.50	46.06	*hu*	**95.34**	99.82	**82.35**	**77.56**	**76.08**
bg	**98.75**	**96.71**	**92.89**	**89.81**	**86.53**	*id*	**94.09**	99.99	85.17	**79.19**	**77.15**
bxr	84.12	99.35	**51.19**	30.00	25.37	*it*	**98.04**	**97.93**	**92.51**	**90.68**	**86.18**
ca	**98.59**	**98.58**	**92.88**	**90.70**	**86.70**	*it_pud*	93.74	2.48	**91.08**	**88.14**	**84.49**
cs	**98.83**	**95.86**	**92.62**	**90.17**	**88.44**	*ja*	88.14	89.68	75.42	74.72	65.90
cs_cac	**99.05**	**95.16**	**93.14**	**90.43**	**88.31**	*ja_pud*	89.41	7.50	78.64	77.92	68.95
cs_cltt	**97.91**	**89.98**	86.02	82.56	79.62	*kk*	57.36	55.72	43.51	25.13	19.32
cs_pud	96.42	**92.60**	**89.11**	**84.42**	**81.60**	*kmr*	90.04	89.84	47.71	35.05	28.72
cu	**95.90**	**96.20**	77.10	71.84	70.49	*ko*	**96.14**	**93.02**	**85.90**	**82.49**	**80.85**
da	**97.40**	99.69	**85.33**	**82.97**	**80.03**	*la*	90.67	76.69	72.56	63.37	58.96
de	**94.41**	**97.29**	**84.10**	**80.71**	**76.97**	*la_ittb*	**98.36**	**94.79**	**89.44**	**87.02**	**84.94**
de_pud	85.71	20.89	80.88	74.86	**73.96**	*la_proiel*	**96.72**	**96.93**	73.71	69.35	66.56
el	**97.74**	**97.76**	**89.73**	**87.38**	**83.59**	*lv*	**93.59**	80.05	**79.26**	**74.01**	**70.22**
en	**95.11**	**94.82**	84.74	82.23	**78.99**	*nl*	93.24	90.61	85.17	80.48	75.19
en_lines	**96.64**	**95.41**	85.16	82.09	78.71	*nl_lassysmall*	**98.39**	99.93	**89.56**	**87.71**	**85.22**
en_partut	**95.22**	**95.08**	86.10	82.54	77.40	*no_bokmaal*	**98.35**	99.75	**91.60**	**89.88**	**87.67**
en_pud	**95.40**	**94.29**	88.22	85.51	82.63	*no_nynorsk*	**98.11**	99.85	**90.75**	**88.81**	**86.41**
es	**96.59**	99.69	**90.01**	**87.29**	**82.08**	*pl*	**98.15**	**91.97**	**93.98**	**90.32**	**87.94**
es_ancora	**98.72**	**98.73**	**92.11**	**89.99**	**86.15**	*pt*	**97.24**	83.04	**89.90**	**87.65**	**83.27**
es_pud	88.39	1.76	88.14	81.05	74.60	*pt_br*	**98.22**	**98.22**	**92.76**	**91.36**	**87.48**
et	**93.01**	**95.05**	78.08	71.65	69.85	*pt_pud*	88.99	0.00	83.27	77.14	71.68
eu	95.89	**99.96**	85.28	81.44	79.71	*ro*	**97.59**	**96.98**	**90.43**	**85.92**	**81.87**
fa	**97.15**	**97.12**	**89.64**	**86.31**	**82.93**	*ru*	**96.99**	**96.73**	87.15	83.65	**81.80**
fi	**96.62**	**97.37**	**87.97**	**85.64**	**84.25**	*ru_pud*	86.85	80.17	82.31	75.71	73.13
fi_ftb	**96.30**	**95.31**	**89.24**	**86.81**	**84.12**	*ru_syntagrus*	**98.59**	**99.57**	**94.00**	**92.60**	**90.11**
fi_pud	**97.54**	0.00	**90.60**	**88.47**	**86.82**	*sk*	**96.87**	85.00	**89.58**	**86.04**	**83.86**
fr	96.20	98.87	**88.57**	**85.51**	**82.14**	*sl*	**98.63**	94.74	**93.34**	**91.51**	**88.98**
fr_partut	**96.16**	**95.88**	88.64	85.05	79.49	*sl_sst*	**94.04**	**86.87**	61.71	56.02	51.04
fr_pud	89.32	2.40	83.45	78.81	**77.37**	*sme*	86.81	88.98	51.13	37.21	39.22
fr_sequoia	**97.41**	99.06	88.48	86.53	83.37	*sv*	**97.70**	**96.40**	**88.50**	**85.87**	**83.71**
ga	**92.43**	**91.31**	78.50	70.06	**61.38**	*sv_lines*	**96.74**	**94.84**	**86.51**	**82.89**	**79.92**
gl	**97.72**	**97.50**	85.87	83.23	78.05	*sv_pud*	**94.33**	**92.33**	**81.90**	**78.49**	**76.48**
gl_treegal	**94.51**	**91.65**	78.28	73.39	66.02	*tr*	**93.86**	**93.11**	**69.62**	**62.79**	**60.01**
got	**95.74**	**96.49**	73.10	66.82	63.87	*tr_pud*	72.73	0.00	58.72	37.72	31.71
grc	**92.64**	**84.47**	**78.42**	**73.19**	67.59	*ug*	76.65	78.69	56.86	39.79	30.11
grc_proiel	**97.06**	**97.51**	78.30	74.25	68.83	*uk*	**94.31**	79.42	**81.44**	**75.33**	**71.72**
he	82.42	82.45	67.70	63.94	56.78	*ur*	**93.95**	**92.30**	**87.98**	**82.28**	**75.88**
hi	**97.50**	**97.01**	**94.70**	**91.59**	**87.92**	*vi*	75.28	73.56	46.14	42.13	38.59
hi_pud	85.48	34.82	**67.24**	**54.49**	**48.87**	*zh*	85.26	85.07	68.95	65.88	62.03
hr	**97.68**	99.93	**90.11**	**85.25**	**82.36**						

	UPOS	XPOS	UAS	LAS	CLAS
All treebanks	93.09	82.27	81.30	76.30	72.57
Large treebanks	95.58	94.56	85.16	81.77	78.40
Parallell treebanks	88.25	30.66	80.17	73.73	69.88
Small treebanks	87.02	82.03	70.19	61.02	54.76
Surprise treebanks	–	–	54.47	40.57	37.41

Table 1: Results on each treebank in the shared task plus the macro average over all of them. State of the art performance by the system is in bold.

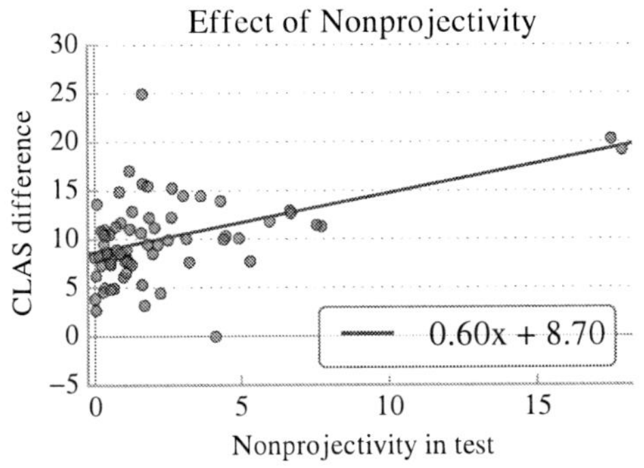

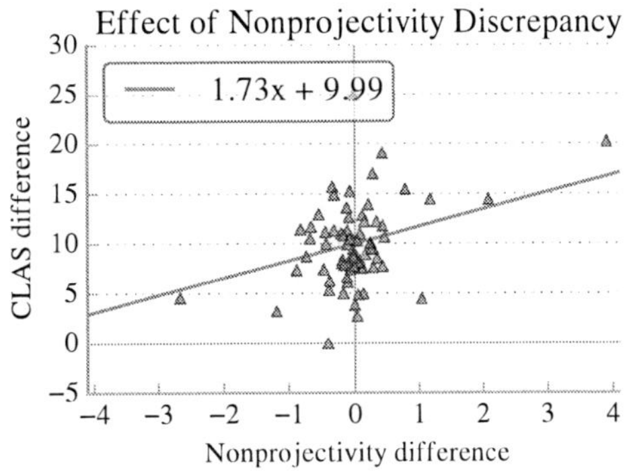

(a) Difference in CLAS between our parser and UDPipe v1.1 as a function of the nonprojectivity of the test set

(b) Difference in CLAS between our parser and UDPipe v1.1 as a function of the difference between the nonprojectivity of the test and training sets

Figure 3: How the percent of nonprojective arcs in the training and test set influence accuracy of our graph-based and a transition-based parser

and content labeled attachment score. Our system achieves the highest aggregated score on all five of these metrics in the shared task. Below we explore where our model does particularly well, and where it can be improved. We choose to evaluate on CLAS performance because we feel it more accurately reflects model performance, being a principled extension of the common practice of removing punctuation from evaluation. We also exclude surprise languages from the following analyses.

One small point to that end is that our system assumes tokenization and segmentation has already been done; we therefore trained on gold segmentation and evaluated using the segmentation provided by UDPipe. For most treebanks this was easily sufficient, but for Vietnamese, Chinese, Japanese, and Arabic, UDPipe's lower performance at segmenting or tokenizing was correlated with a relatively large gap between CLAS and gold-aligned CLAS. Because our model reports comparable numbers for nearly all other treebanks, we take this to mean that alignment errors propagated through the system into parsing errors.

4.1 Nonprojectivity

In Universal Dependencies, unlike many other popular benchmarks, several treebanks have a large fraction of crossing dependencies, so any competitive system will need to be able to produce nonprojective arcs. One of the most frequently used approaches for producing fully nonprojective parsers in transition-based systems is to add the `swap` action (Nivre, 2009). This makes any arbitrary nonprojective arc possible, but increases the number of transition steps required to produce that arc. One valid concern is that this might bias the model toward producing projective arcs; in our graph-based system, by contrast, there's little reason to think nonprojective arcs should be harder to predict than projective ones. Here we aim to explore how the fraction of nonprojective arcs in a treebank affects the performance of the two types of systems.

To test the relative performance of a graph-based and a transition-based model, we compute the difference in per-treebank CLAS performance between our parser and the UDPipe v1.1 baseline (Straka et al., 2016), which uses a transition-based parser with the `swap` operation (Straka et al., 2015). We then plot this against the frequency of nonprojective arcs in the test set. To determine whether there is a significant relationship between the difference in performance, we fit the data to a generalized linear mixed effects regression model (Fisher, 1930), using Markov chain Monte Carlo sampling (Hadfield, 2010). We include log data size, morphological complexity (see Section 5.2), and training set projectivity as random effects. We plot the data with the learned regression lines in Figure 3a. What we find is that the margin between the performance of the graph-based and transition-based parsers increases with the nonprojectivity of the test set significantly ($p < 0.001$).

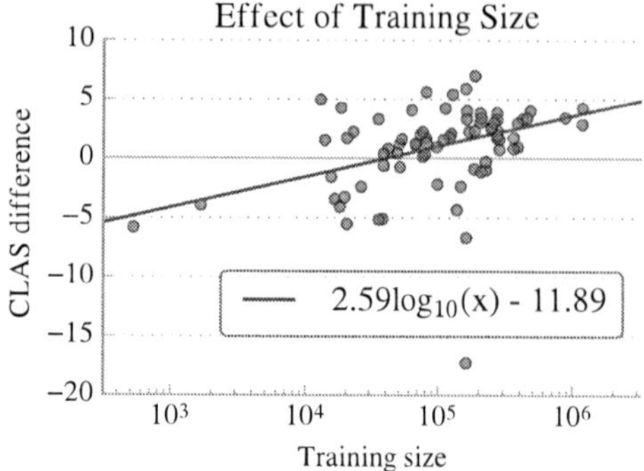

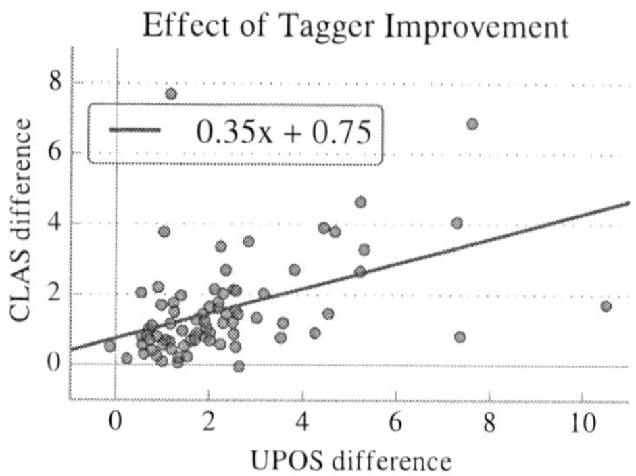

Figure 4: Performance difference between our model and the highest-performing model other than ours as a function of log training data size

Figure 5: Performance difference between a version of our model trained on our own predicted tags and a version trained on UDPipe v1.1 tags as a function of the performance difference between our taggers and the UDPipe taggers

This remains significant even when outliers[7] are excluded ($p < 0.05$). To the extent that UDPipe represents a typical nonprojective transition-based parser, our results suggest that a graph-based approach is better suited to parsing UD treebanks that have significant syntactic freedom or complexity than a transition-based one.

Predicting crossing arcs requires more operations (and therefore more long-term planning on behalf of the parser) when using the `swap` feature in a transition-based system, but in our graph-based system they can be predicted as easily as projective arcs. One might hypothesize that because of this, a transition-based `swapping` system would need to see more examples of crossing dependencies than a graph-based system in order to generalize well. The data shown in Figure 3b support this hypothesis: we computed the difference between the projectivity of each test and training set, and used this as the fixed effect in another mixed effects model with data size, morphological complexity, and train/test nonprojectivity as random effects. We find that when the training set has drastically fewer crossing dependencies than the test set, the graph-based model achieves relatively higher accuracy; but when the transition-based parser can train on many crossing arcs, the models are closer in performance ($p < 0.001$), even when excluding the same outliers ($p < 0.05$). This suggests that the graph-based approach learns and generalizes crossing dependencies more efficiently than the transition-

based approach, although this again comes with the assumption that UDPipe's parser is representative of most transition-based `swapping` parsers when it comes to producing nonprojective parses.

4.2 Data size

We use the same hyperparameter configuration for all datasets, regardless of how much training data there is for that treebank, which means we may have overfit to small training datasets or underfit to large ones. To test this, we computed the per-treebank difference between the test CLAS performance of our model and that of the highest-performing model other than ours, and plotted that ratio against the log training data size in Figure 4. We fit the differences to another mixed effects regression model with train/test projectivity and morphological complexity set as random effects, finding that our system on average tends to do relatively better on larger datasets compared to other approaches and worse on smaller ones ($p < 0.001$). When the outliers are excluded,[8] this tendency is still significant ($p < 0.001$). This suggests that our model is overfitting to smaller datasets, and that increasing regularization or decreasing model capacity may improve accuracy for lower-resource languages.

---

[7]Korean (top); Ancient Greek, Latin (right)

[8]Kazakh, Uyghur (left); Japanese (bottom); Czech-CAC, Russian-SynTagRus, Czech (right)

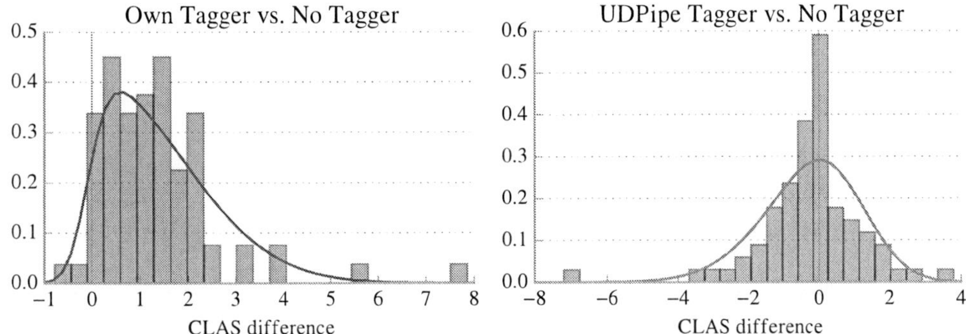

Figure 6: Performance difference between parsers using our taggers and parsers without tags (left) and between parsers using UDPipe v1.1's tags and parsers without tags (right), with both histograms fit to skew normal distributions

5 Ablation Studies

5.1 POS Tagger

We chose to train our parsers on our own predicted tags instead of using provided taggers; here we aim to justify that strategy empirically with an ablation study. We trained another set of parsers with otherwise identical hyperparameter settings using the baseline tags provided by UDPipe v1.1, and computed the difference in CLAS between our reported models and the new ones. We also computed the difference in UPOS accuracy between UDPipe v1.1's taggers and our own. In Figure 5, we plot how the difference in tagger quality affects the CLAS of the parser, making two noteworthy observations. The first is that the performance difference between the set of models trained on our own tags is statistically significantly better than the performance of the models trained on UDPipe tags according to a Wilcoxon test ($p < 0.001$). The second is that this can be explained by the improvement of our tagger over UDPipe v1.1, again accounting for dataset size, nonprojectivity, and morphology in a mixed effects model ($p < 0.001$). This suggests that improving upstream tagger performance is an effective way of improving downstream parser accuracy. We also examined the effect of training size on the difference in parser performance, finding no significant correlation ($p > 0.05$).

The approach laid out in this paper uses one neural network to tag the sequences of tokens, and a second neural network to produce a parse from the tokens and tags. One might ask to what extent the tagger network is actually necessary, for a number of reasons: presumably whatever predictive patterns it learns from the token sequences would also be learnable by the parser network; errors by the tagger are likely to be propagated by the parser; and Ballesteros et al. (2015) found that POS tags are drastically less important for character-based parsers. In order to examine how useful the POS tag information is to our character-based system, we trained an additional set of parsers without UPOS or XPOS input, comparing them to the other two, with the differences graphed in Figure 6. We find that the variant with no POS tag input is likewise significantly worse than our reported model according to a Wilcoxon test ($p < 0.001$), but not statistically different from the one trained with UDPipe tags ($p > 0.05$). This suggests that predicted POS tags are still useful for achieving maximal parsing accuracy in our system, provided the tagger's performance is sufficiently high.

5.2 Character model

One of the ways in which we build on Dozat and Manning's 2017 work is by adding a character-level word representation similar to that of Ballesteros et al. (2015), hypothesizing that it should allow the model to more effectively learn the relationships between words in languages with rich morphology and loose word order. We test this using another ablation study; we trained a second set of taggers and parsers on the dataset with only whole token and pretrained vectors, leaving out the vector composed from character sequences

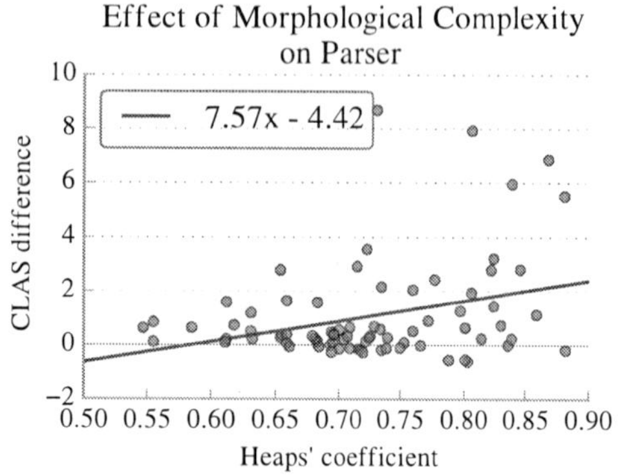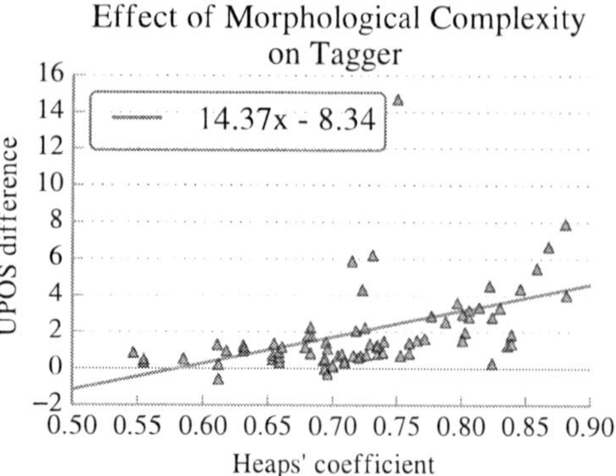

Figure 7: Performance difference between our character-based approach and a pure token-based approach for parsing (left) and tagging (right) as a function of approximated morphological complexity

(for maximal comparability, we use the original character-based taggers for the token-based parsers). As morphological complexity increases, the difference between the models should increase as well.

The basis of our approach to quantifying morphological complexity will be the assumption that in a morphologically complex language, the ratio between the size of the vocabulary $|V^{(X)}|$ of a corpus to the size of the corpus $|X|$ will be relatively high, because the same lemma may occur with many different forms; but in a morphologically simplex language, that ratio will be smaller, because a given lemma will normally appear with only a few forms. Assuming both languages have the same number of lemmas, the vocabulary size of the complex language will then be larger. The most principled way of modeling this intuition is through Heaps' law (Herdan, 1960; Heaps, 1978) in Equation 22, which says that the log vocabulary size increases linearly in the log corpus size.

$$\log(|V^{(X)}|) = w \log(|X|) + b \qquad (22)$$

We can take advantage of Heaps' law directly in approximating morphological complexity. Morphologically richer languages should increase the size of their vocabulary at a faster rate as the corpus size grows, because a new token being added to the corpus has a higher probability of having a previously observed lemma with a previously unobserved morphological form, thereby increasing the vocabulary size; in a morphologically simplex language, previously observed lemmas are unlikely to have many morphological forms that could increase $|V|$. Therefore, we would expect

the parameter w of Equation 22 to be higher for languages with rich morphology. We computed this value for each treebank, and the results generally align with our intuition (although not without some variation, attributable to domain and dataset size): Hindi and Urdu—which have significant allomorphy—are among the lowest, having $w = .555$ and $.585$ respectively; English and Vietnamese have .631 and .661; Spanish and Portuguese have .7 and .704; and Finnish, Estonian, and Hungarian have some of the highest, at .806, .822, and .846.

Thus we use the coefficient w in Equation 22 as our metric for morphological richness, and plot the difference between models trained with character-level word embeddings and token-level word embeddings against this value in Figure 7. First we perform a Wilcoxon signed rank test, finding that the difference between the two approaches is statistically significant for the taggers ($p < 0.001$) and parsers ($p < 0.001$). Then we fit a mixed effects model to the data with treebank size and training/test projectivity as random effects, finding that the character-level approach tends to significantly improve performance more as complexity grows both for parsing ($p < 0.005$) and tagging ($p < 0.001$).[9] This indicates that incorporating subword information into UD parsing models is a promising way to improve performance on languages with significant morphology.

____

[9]The assumption of linearity is clearly wrong, but the negative y-values preclude using a log-linear model on which we run significance tests

6 Conclusion

In this paper we describe our relatively simple neural system for parsing that achieved state-of-the-art performance on the 2017 CoNLL Shared Task on UD parsing without utilizing lemmas, morphological features, or ensembling. The system uses BiLSTM networks for tagging and parsing, and includes character-level word representations in addition to token-level ones. We also examined what can be learned more generally from our model's performance. We explore the relative performance of nonprojective graph-based and transition-based architectures on this task, finding evidence that modern graph-based parsers might be better at producing nonprojective arcs (with some caveats). Additionally, our network performs better when there's an abundance of data, suggesting that more regularization could improve accuracy on lower-resource languages.

We also sought to quantitatively justify the additional complexity of our system. We considered how important the POS tagger is to the system, comparing the downstream performance of parsers using our tagger, the baseline tagger, and no tagger at all. We find that our tagger beats both baselines significantly, whereas the two baselines don't statistically differ from each other, indicating that POS tags can help our system but must be sufficiently accurate. The character-based approach was found to significantly boost performance on languages that scored high on our metric for morphological complexity—both for parsing and tagging—suggesting that constructing token representation from subtoken information is effective for capturing the influence of morphology on syntax, and the naïve approach of using only holistic word embeddings is insufficient. Our success at the shared task demonstrates that a well-tuned, straightforward neural approach to parsing and tagging can get state-of-the-art performance for datasets with a wide variety of syntactic properties.

References

Miguel Ballesteros, Chris Dyer, and Noah A Smith. 2015. Improved transition-based parsing by modeling characters instead of words with lstms. *EMNLP* .

Piotr Bojanowski, Edouard Grave, Armand Joulin, and Tomas Mikolov. 2016. Enriching word vectors with subword information. *EMNLP* .

Kris Cao and Marek Rei. 2016. A joint model for word embedding and word morphology. *ACL 2016* page 18.

Hao Cheng, Hao Fang, Xiaodong He, Jianfeng Gao, and Li Deng. 2016. Bi-directional attention with agreement for dependency parsing. *EMNLP 2016* .

Yoeng-Jin Chu and Tseng-Hong Liu. 1965. On shortest arborescence of a directed graph. *Scientia Sinica* 14(10):1396.

Michal Daniluk, Tim Rocktäschel, Johannes Welbl, and Sebastian Riedel. 2017. Frustratingly short attention spans in neural language modeling. *ICLR 2017* .

Timothy Dozat and Christopher D. Manning. 2017. Deep biaffine attention for neural dependency parsing. *ICLR 2017* .

Jack Edmonds. 1967. Optimum branchings. *Journal of Research of the national Bureau of Standards B* 71(4):233–240.

Ronald Aylmer Fisher. 1930. *The genetical theory of natural selection: a complete variorum edition*. Oxford University Press.

Yarin Gal and Zoubin Ghahramani. 2015. Dropout as a bayesian approximation: Representing model uncertainty in deep learning. *International Conference on Machine Learning* .

Jarrod D Hadfield. 2010. Mcmc methods for multiresponse generalized linear mixed models: The MCMCglmm R package. *Journal of Statistical Software* 33(2):1–22. http://www.jstatsoft.org/v33/i02/.

Kazuma Hashimoto, Caiming Xiong, Yoshimasa Tsuruoka, and Richard Socher. 2016. A joint many-task model: Growing a neural network for multiple nlp tasks. *arXiv preprint arXiv:1611.01587* .

Harold Stanley Heaps. 1978. *Information retrieval: Computational and theoretical aspects*. Academic Press, Inc.

Gustav Herdan. 1960. *Type-token mathematics*, volume 4. Mouton.

Diederik Kingma and Jimmy Ba. 2014. Adam: A method for stochastic optimization. *International Conference on Learning Representations* .

Eliyahu Kiperwasser and Yoav Goldberg. 2016. Simple and accurate dependency parsing using bidirectional LSTM feature representations. *Transactions of the Association for Computational Linguistics* 4:313–327.

Wang Ling, Tiago Luís, Luís Marujo, Ramón Fernandez Astudillo, Silvio Amir, Chris Dyer, Alan W Black, and Isabel Trancoso. 2015. Finding function in form: Compositional character models for open vocabulary word representation. *NAACL* .

Ryan McDonald, Fernando Pereira, Kiril Ribarov, and Jan Hajič. 2005. Non-projective dependency parsing using spanning tree algorithms. In *Proceedings of the conference on Human Language Technology and Empirical Methods in Natural Language Processing*. Association for Computational Linguistics, pages 523–530.

Tomas Mikolov, Kai Chen, Greg Corrado, and Jeffrey Dean. 2013. Efficient estimation of word representations in vector space. *International Conference on Learning Representations* .

Alexander H. Miller, Adam Fisch, Jesse Dodge, Amir-Hossein Karimi, Antoine Bordes, and Jason Weston. 2016. Key-value memory networks for directly reading documents. In *ACL 2016*. pages 1400–1409.

Joakim Nivre. 2009. Non-projective dependency parsing in expected linear time. In *Proceedings of the Joint Conference of the 47th Annual Meeting of the ACL and the 4th International Joint Conference on Natural Language Processing of the AFNLP: Volume 1-Volume 1*. Association for Computational Linguistics, pages 351–359.

Joakim Nivre, Željko Agić, Lars Ahrenberg, et al. 2017a. Universal dependencies 2.0 CoNLL 2017 shared task development and test data. LIN-DAT/CLARIN digital library at the Institute of Formal and Applied Linguistics, Charles University. http://hdl.handle.net/11234/1-2184.

Joakim Nivre, Marie-Catherine de Marneffe, Filip Ginter, Yoav Goldberg, Jan Hajič, Christopher Manning, Ryan McDonald, Slav Petrov, Sampo Pyysalo, Natalia Silveira, Reut Tsarfaty, and Daniel Zeman. 2016. Universal Dependencies v1: A multilingual treebank collection. In *Proceedings of the 10th International Conference on Language Resources and Evaluation (LREC 2016)*. European Language Resources Association, Portoro, Slovenia, pages 1659–1666.

Joakim Nivre et al. 2017b. Universal Dependencies 2.0. LINDAT/CLARIN digital library at the Institute of Formal and Applied Linguistics, Charles University, Prague, http://hdl.handle.net/11234/1-1983. http://hdl.handle.net/11234/1-1983.

Barbara Plank, Anders Søgaard, and Yoav Goldberg. 2016. Multilingual part-of-speech tagging with bidirectional long short-term memory models and auxiliary loss. *ACL* .

Martin Potthast, Tim Gollub, Francisco Rangel, Paolo Rosso, Efstathios Stamatatos, and Benno Stein. 2014. Improving the reproducibility of PAN's shared tasks: Plagiarism detection, author identification, and author profiling. In Evangelos Kanoulas, Mihai Lupu, Paul Clough, Mark Sanderson, Mark Hall, Allan Hanbury, and Elaine Toms, editors, *Information Access Evaluation meets Multilinguality, Multimodality, and Visualization. 5th International Conference of the CLEF Initiative (CLEF 14)*. Springer, Berlin Heidelberg New York, pages 268–299. https://doi.org/10.1007/978-3-319-11382-1_22.

Scott E. Reed and Nando de Freitas. 2016. Neural programmer-interpreters. *ICLR 2016* .

Milan Straka, Jan Hajic, Jana Straková, and Jan Hajic jr. 2015. Parsing universal dependency treebanks using neural networks and search-based oracle. In *International Workshop on Treebanks and Linguistic Theories (TLT14)*. page 208.

Milan Straka, Jan Hajič, and Jana Straková. 2016. UD-Pipe: trainable pipeline for processing CoNLL-U files performing tokenization, morphological analysis, POS tagging and parsing. In *Proceedings of the 10th International Conference on Language Resources and Evaluation (LREC 2016)*. European Language Resources Association, Portoro, Slovenia.

Daniel Zeman, Martin Popel, Milan Straka, Jan Hajič, Joakim Nivre, Filip Ginter, Juhani Luotolahti, Sampo Pyysalo, Slav Petrov, Martin Potthast, Francis Tyers, Elena Badmaeva, Memduh Gökırmak, Anna Nedoluzhko, Silvie Cinková, Jan Hajič jr., Jaroslava Hlaváčová, Václava Kettnerová, Zdeňka Urešová, Jenna Kanerva, Stina Ojala, Anna Missilä, Christopher Manning, Sebastian Schuster, Siva Reddy, Dima Taji, Nizar Habash, Herman Leung, Marie-Catherine de Marneffe, Manuela Sanguinetti, Maria Simi, Hiroshi Kanayama, Valeria de Paiva, Kira Droganova, Héctor Martínez Alonso, Hans Uszkoreit, Vivien Macketanz, Aljoscha Burchardt, Kim Harris, Katrin Marheinecke, Georg Rehm, Tolga Kayadelen, Mohammed Attia, Ali Elkahky, Zhuoran Yu, Emily Pitler, Saran Lertpradit, Michael Mandl, Jesse Kirchner, Hector Fernandez Alcalde, Jana Strnadova, Esha Banerjee, Ruli Manurung, Antonio Stella, Atsuko Shimada, Sookyoung Kwak, Gustavo Mendonça, Tatiana Lando, Rattima Nitisaroj, and Josie Li. 2017. CoNLL 2017 Shared Task: Multilingual Parsing from Raw Text to Universal Dependencies. In *Proceedings of the CoNLL 2017 Shared Task: Multilingual Parsing from Raw Text to Universal Dependencies*. Association for Computational Linguistics.

Xingxing Zhang, Jianpeng Cheng, and Mirella Lapata. 2016. Dependency parsing as head selection. *EACL 2017* .

Combining Global Models for Parsing Universal Dependencies

Tianze Shi   **Felix G. Wu**   **Xilun Chen**   **Yao Cheng**
Cornell University
{tianze,felixgwu,xlchen,yc2258}@cs.cornell.edu

Abstract

We describe our entry, C2L2, to the CoNLL 2017 shared task on parsing Universal Dependencies from raw text. Our system features an ensemble of three global parsing paradigms, one graph-based and two transition-based. Each model leverages character-level bi-directional LSTMs as lexical feature extractors to encode morphological information. Though relying on baseline tokenizers and focusing only on parsing, our system ranked second in the official end-to-end evaluation with a macro-average of 75.00 LAS F1 score over 81 test treebanks. In addition, we had the top average performance on the four surprise languages and on the small treebank subset.

1 Introduction

General Parsing Approach Our submitted system to the CoNLL 2017 shared task (Zeman et al., 2017) focuses only on the task of dependency parsing, assuming that tokenization, sentence boundary detection, part-of-speech (POS) tagging and morphological features are already handled by a baseline model. In this paper, we highlight our neural-network-based feature extractors and ensemble of global parsing models, including two novel global transition-based models.

Bi-directional long-short term memory networks (Graves and Schmidhuber, 2005, bi-LSTMs) have recently achieved state-of-the-art performance on syntactic parsing (Kiperwasser and Goldberg, 2016; Cross and Huang, 2016; Dozat and Manning, 2017). Our system leverages the representational power of bi-LSTMs to generate compact features for both graph-based and transition-based parsing frameworks. The latter further enables the application of dynamic programming techniques (Huang and Sagae, 2010; Kuhlmann et al., 2011) for global training and exact decoding. With just two bi-LSTM vectors as features, all three global parsing paradigms in our system have efficient $O(n^3)$ implementations. The full system consists of 3-5 each of these unlabeled parsing models (9-15 in total, depending on the treebank), and another ensemble of arc labelers.

Adaptation of General Approach to the Shared Task The CoNLL 2017 shared task presents two unique challenges: 1. A large fraction of the datasets are morphologically-rich languages. Some languages have an exceedingly-high out-of-vocabulary ratio of over 30%. 2. For many languages, very little training data is provided. Furthermore, there are four surprise language, for which we only have tens of sample sentences.

We address the first challenge with character-level bi-LSTMs, which have previously been shown to be effective in multi-lingual POS tagging (Plank et al., 2016) and dependency parsing (Ballesteros et al., 2015; Alberti et al., 2017). Character-level representation gives better coverage, and it directly learns sub-word information through end-to-end training.

The second challenge is approached by transferring delexicalized information. For each of those languages with little training data, we select the most similar language according to linguistic typology. We then train delexicalized models taking only part-of-speech and morphology tags as input features, which are made available through baseline prediction during test time.

Our full system scored a macro-average LAS F1 score of 75.00, which ranked second among all participating systems. Additionally, in the categories of small treebanks and surprise languages, we obtained the best average performance.

Proceedings of the CoNLL 2017 Shared Task: Multilingual Parsing from Raw Text to Universal Dependencies, pages 31–39,
Vancouver, Canada, August 3-4, 2017. © 2017 Association for Computational Linguistics

2 System Overview

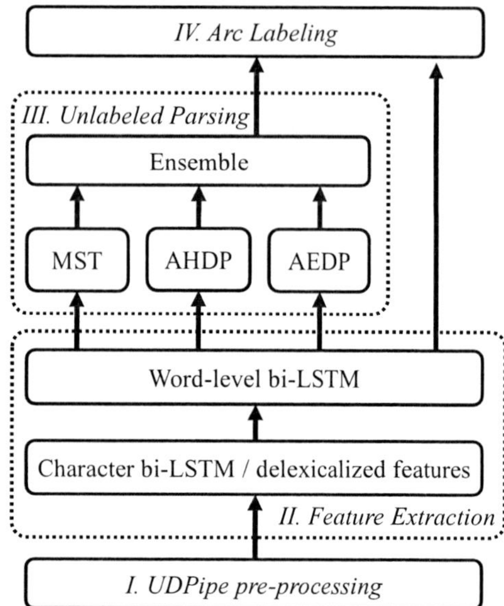

Figure 1: Overview of our system.

Figure 1 illustrates our pipelined system. It processes raw texts in four stages starting from baseline UDPipe (Straka et al., 2016) tokenization and sentence delimitation. For this stage we use predictions provided by the organizers instead of training our own UDPipe models.

For each sentence, Stage II (§3) extracts a dense feature vector for each word in the sentence. For most languages, we employ character-level bi-LSTMs to capture morphological information. On top of the character-level representations, there is another layer of bi-LSTMs processing at the word level, the output of which gives context-sensitive features associated with every word in the sentence. For the four surprise languages and a selected set of languages with small training treebanks, we substitute the character-level encodings of each word in Stage II with concatenation of part-of-speech (POS) tag embeddings and morphological feature embeddings, but keep the word-level bi-LSTMs. We call these *delexicalized* features as opposed to the *lexicalized* features in the general case. All later stages are kept the same. The POS tags and morphological features are provided by baseline UDPipe predictions.

Stage III (§4.1) focuses on unlabeled parsing with an ensemble of three global models, one first-order graph-based maximal spanning tree algorithm (MST), and two transition-based, namely

arc-hybrid and arc-eager dynamic programming (AHDP and AEDP). They share the same underlying feature extractors. We combine outputs from the unlabeled parsing models with a uniform weight reparsing model (Sagae and Lavie, 2006).

The final stage (§4.2) of our system is arc labeling. Based on the extracted LSTM features and predicted unlabeled parse trees, this stage assigns the highest scoring label to each arc. Similar to Stage III, we train multiple models with different random initializations, and the ensemble prediction is obtained via majority vote.

Our system was implemented with DyNet (Neubig et al., 2017). Each single model is of small size and runs efficiently. The submitted full system completed the test phase in 4.64 hours with 2 threads. We provide implementation details for all the modules and training process in §6. The code is available at `https://github.com/CoNLL-UD-2017/C2L2`.

3 Feature Extractors

In Stage II of our system, we first extract features for each word in isolation, then consider one sentence at a time for context-sensitive representations. These two feature extractors both leverage the representational power of bi-LSTMs.

3.1 Character LSTMs

Among the most straightforward ways for representing a word are through binary features or word embeddings. Though popular in many existing parsers, they are not ideal for languages with high out-of-vocabulary (OOV) ratios. In Universal Dependencies, the 56 development sets have an average OOV ratio of 14.4%, with four languages (et, hu, ko and sk) higher than 30%, posing a severe challenge for lexical representation. On the other hand, the average out-of-charset (OOC) ratio is 0.03%, with the highest (zh) not exceeding 0.1%, suggesting the promise of character-level representations in terms of coverage.

Our system adopts character-level bi-LSTMs similar to Plank et al. (2016) and Ballesteros et al. (2015). They show that the obtained sub-word information is especially useful for rare and OOV words in morphologically-rich languages.

Formally, for a word w with its character sequence [BOW, $c_1, ..., c_m$, EOW], with two special begin-of-word (BOW, or c_0) and end-of-word (EOW, or c_{m+1}) symbols, we run a forward and a backward LSTM at layer l:

$$[\overrightarrow{c_i^l}] = \text{LSTM}_{\text{forward}}([\overrightarrow{c_i^{l-1}}])$$

$$[\overleftarrow{c_i^l}] = \text{LSTM}_{\text{backward}}([\overleftarrow{c_i^{l-1}}])$$

$$\overleftrightarrow{c_i^l} = \overrightarrow{c_i^l} \circ \overleftarrow{c_i^l}$$

each c_i^l denotes the vector representation at layer l for c_i, $\circ$ denotes concatenation of vectors, and $[\cdot]$ is a shorthand for a list of vectors. The inputs to the first layer c_i^0 are character embeddings that are jointly trained with the model. We take the concatenation of $\overrightarrow{c_{m+1}}$ and $\overleftarrow{c_0}$ at the final layer of the LSTMs as the output vectors. We use two-layer bi-LSTMs in our system.

Efficiency Improvement Considering the Zipfian distribution for word frequencies, most of the time is spent on getting char bi-LSTM representations for frequent words. On the other hand, for those words, it is considerably easier to train decent representations even without char bi-LSTMs. We thus directly learn the dense word vectors for frequent words, as a proxy for character-level bi-LSTMs and they can be considered as fast look-up tables without actually running the LSTMs[1] .

3.2 Delexicalized Features

For languages with small treebanks, the provided data is not adequate to learn character bi-LSTMs. We choose to use the available delexicalized information predicted by UDPipe. Namely, we use information from two fields: universal POS tags (UPOS) and morphological tags.

To get dense vectors for each word w in the same form as the output of char bi-LSTMs, we use the concatenation of UPOS embeddings $\overrightarrow{p_w}$ and the bag-of-morphology (BOM) embeddings $\text{pool}(\{\overrightarrow{m_w}\})$. The BOM embeddings require a pooling function $\text{pool}(\cdot)$ because each word may receive multiple morphological tags. In our system, we use element-wise max operator as the pooling function.

3.3 Word-level LSTMs

The character bi-LSTM vector for each word is computed in isolation from other words in the sentence. In this module, we again leverage bi-LSTMs for integration of contextual information.

---

[1] In retrospect, we could have used pre-trained word vectors as extra features.

Similar to §3.1, we pad a sentence with two special begin-of-sentence (BOS, or w_0), and end-of-sentence (EOS, or w_{n+1}) symbols into $[\text{BOS}, w_1, ..., w_n, \text{EOS}]$. Inputs to the first layer are character bi-LSTM encodings, or concatenation of POS-tag and BOM embeddings in the case of delexicalized models. We take the bi-directional vectors $\overleftrightarrow{w_i}$ at the final layer as the context-sensitive representation associated with w_i. All parsing components to be described in the following section will build from these vectors.

4 Parsing Components

Our system parses a sentence in two steps, first predicting the unlabeled parse tree, and next predicting the label for each arc in the unlabeled tree.

4.1 Global Models for Unlabeled Parsing

Our system includes one graph-based and two transition-based, a total of three different global parsing paradigms. All of these models only handle projective cases. For this reason, before training, we projectivize all gold-standard trees in the training sets.

First-order Graph-based Parsing Our graph-based model is based on the popular edge-factored Eisner's algorithm (Eisner, 1996; Eisner and Satta, 1999). Each potential arc (h, m) in the graph ($O(n^2)$ in total with sentence length n) is first scored with a function $\text{score}^{\text{MST}}(h, m)$. Then Eisner's algorithm is used to find the maximum spanning tree among all possible projective trees:

$$\underset{\text{valid parses } y}{\arg\max} \sum_{(h,m)\in y} \text{score}^{\text{MST}}(h, m)$$

Following Dozat and Manning (2017), we use a deep bi-affine scoring function:

$$\text{score}^{\text{MST}}(h, m) = v_h^{\mathsf{T}} U v_m + b_h \cdot v_h + b_m \cdot v_m + b$$

where

$$v_h = \text{MLP}^{\text{MST-head}}(\overleftrightarrow{h})$$

$$v_m = \text{MLP}^{\text{MST-mod}}(\overleftrightarrow{m})$$

are representations transformed by two multi-layer perceptrons (MLPs) from their bi-LSTM vectors. We train separate MLPs for head and modifier transformation. The weight matrix U, bias vectors b_h, b_m and term b are parameters of the function.

Global Transition-based Parsing We include global training and exact decoders for two transition systems, arc-hybrid and arc-eager. They are based on dynamic programming approaches (Huang and Sagae, 2010; Kuhlmann et al., 2011), thus we call the two models AHDP and AEDP.

The dynamic programming shares computation for parser configurations with the same extracted features. In our system, we only use two bi-LSTM vectors, one from the top of the stack ($\vec{s_0}$), and one from the top of the buffer ($\vec{b_0}$). This compact set of features enables dynamic programming to compress the exponentially-large search space down to $O(n^3)$ for the two transition systems.

Below we illustrate the AHDP decoder, with AEDP being similar. The bare deduction system, adapted from Kuhlmann et al. (2011) is:

$$\text{sh}\ \frac{[i,j]}{[j,j+1]} \quad \text{re}_{\curvearrowleft}\ \frac{[k,i]\ \ [i,j]}{[k,j]}k \curvearrowright i$$

$$\text{re}_{\curvearrowright}\ \frac{[k,i]\ \ [i,j]}{[k,j]}i \curvearrowleft j$$

each deduction item $[i,j]$ corresponds to a push computation detailed in Kuhlmann et al. (2011). For the purpose of our decoder, the deduction item can also be understood as a parser configuration with w_i being s_0 and w_j being b_0. The deduction system has an axiom $[0,1]$ and goal $[0,n+1]$ corresponding to initial and terminal configurations.

Next, we incorporate scoring functions:

$$\frac{[i,j]:v}{[j,j+1]:0}(\text{sh}) \quad \frac{[k,i]:v_1\ \ [i,j]:v_2}{[k,j]:v_1+v_2+\Delta}(\text{re}_{\curvearrowleft})$$

where $\Delta = \text{score}_{\text{sh}}(\vec{w_k},\vec{w_i}) + \text{score}_{\text{re}_{\curvearrowleft}}(\vec{w_i},\vec{w_j})$. The scoring functions are bi-affine and take the same form as $\text{score}^{\text{MST}}(\cdot)$. The highest-scoring proof for the goal item $[0,n+1]$ constitutes the predicted transition sequence.

Training We employ discriminative training strategies for all three global parsing models. Cost-augmented decoding (Taskar et al., 2005; Smith, 2011) is applied during training. A correct parse tree is instructed to get higher scores than an incorrect parse tree by a margin set to be the number of incorrectly-attached nodes (Hamming distance). This technique has previously been applied in training a neural MST parser (Kiperwasser and Goldberg, 2016).

	UAS F1	LAS F1	Official Ranking
Big Treebanks	85.16	79.85	2
Small Treebanks	70.59	61.49	1
PUD Treebanks	80.17	71.49	2
Surprise Languages	58.40	47.54	1
Overall	80.35	75.00	2

Table 1: Official UAS and LAS scores on the test sets. Rankings are based on the macro-average LAS F1 scores over all treebanks in the set.

Target	Source	UAS F1	LAS F1	Official Ranking
bxr	hi	50.79	31.98	2
hsb	cs	69.45	61.70	1
kmr	fa	54.51	47.53	1
sme	fi	58.85	48.96	1
Average		58.40	47.54	1

Table 2: Evaluation results of our system on the surprise languages. We show the source treebanks from which we trained the delexicalized parsers.

4.2 Arc Labeling

We separate out the stage of arc labeling and adopt a simple labeler proposed by Kiperwasser and Goldberg (2016). For a predicted arc with h as the head and m being the modifier, their associated vectors are concatenated to be the input to a MLP. Each dimension of the output from the MLP corresponds to the score for a potential label, And we select the label with the highest score:

$$\text{label}(h,m) = \underset{l}{\arg\max}\ \text{MLP}_l^{\text{label}}(\vec{h}\circ\vec{m})$$

The arc-labeling models are trained with gold-standard (h,m) tuples. And we use a discriminative hinge loss, with margin of 1.

5 Results

The main official evaluation results are given in Table 1. Our system achieved second place in overall ranking. When considering average performance on small treebanks (8 treebanks) and surprise languages (4 treebanks, detailed in Table 2), we scored the first among all teams.

We show per-treebank LAS F1 results in Figure 2. Our system lacks customized modules

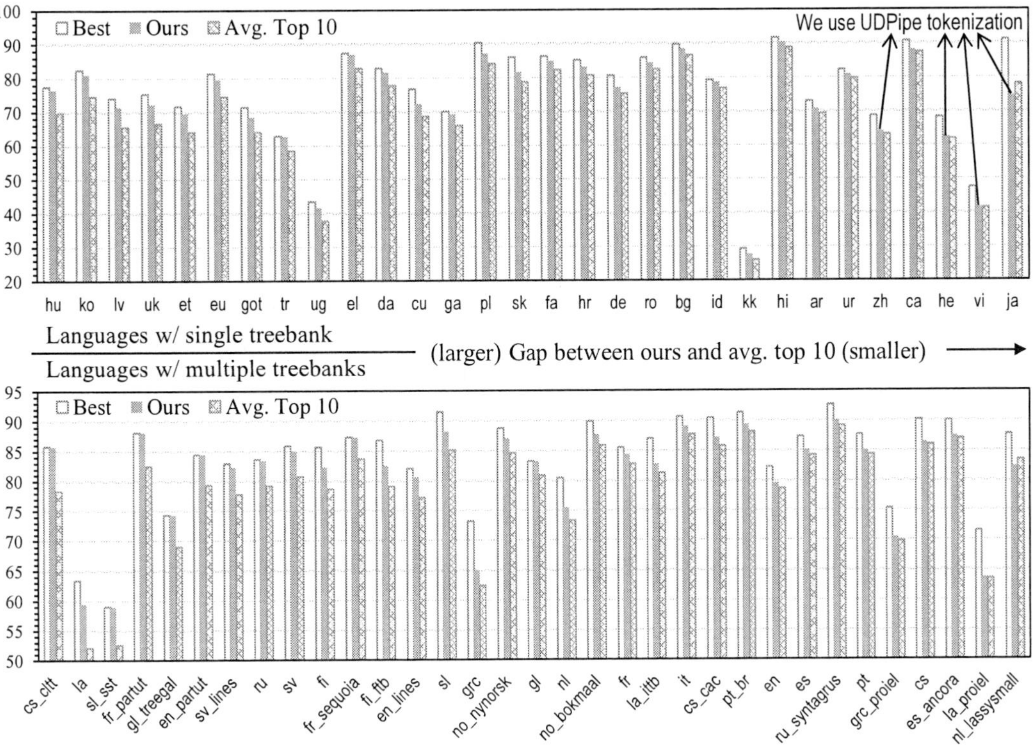

Figure 2: LAS F1 score per treebank. The top/bottom row results are on languages with single/multiple treebank(s). For comparison, we include the best official result and the average of the top ten results on each treebank. Each row is sorted by the gap between our system and the average of the top ten.

for tokenization and sentence boundary detection, which is reflected by the gap between our system and the best-performing systems on ja, vi, he and zh. The other large source of gaps comes from languages with large non-projective ratios, such as grc, la and nl. The global transition-based AHDP and AEDP models are not compatible with non-projective parsing, and we did not implement or test with non-projective graph-based parsers due to time and resource constraints.

Our system performs relatively well on languages with high OOV ratios, such as hu, ko, lv and et, with the help of character bi-LSTMs. In addition, the strategies of concatenating multiple training treebanks for the same language (see §6) brought success on small treebanks.

Table 3 gives the performance of our system on the 14 additional parallel treebanks. The results are largely consistent with in-domain evaluation results, and we ranked within top third for most treebanks except ja_pud, en_pud and ru_pud. We did not implement our own tokenizer for Japanese, explaining the gap. For the other two

languages, our selected models were not domain-robust. We perform a post-evaluation analysis and parse the PUD treebanks (Nivre et al., 2017a) with models trained on the canonical treebanks. The two languages observe an improvement on LAS scores of 7.53 and 14.73 respectively.

Ablation Analaysis To examine the effect of individual components in our ensemble system, we evaluate several variations, where we use single or an incomplete set of models for unlabeled parsing and arc-labeling. Results are shown in Table 4. AEDP gives higher unlabeled parsing performance, and an ensemble of three instances of AEDPs achieves comparable performance to our full system. The arc-labeling ensemble gives another gain in LAS result of 0.31.

6   Implementation Details

Our system was trained on the UD 2.0 dataset (Nivre et al., 2016, 2017b), with the provided training and development splits when available. For languages without development sets, we split

Target Treebank	Selected Model	LAS F1	Rank
pt_pud	pt	78.48	1
de_pud	de	73.92	2
sv_pud	sv	77.97	2
fr_pud	fr	78.25	2
es_pud	es	80.50	2
fi_pud	fi	85.42	2
it_pud	it	86.74	2
tr_pud	tr	37.65	3
ar_pud	ar	49.03	3
hi_pud	hi	54.12	3
cs_pud	cs_cac	82.23	3
cs_pud	cs*	83.38*	2*
ja_pud	ja	78.22	6
ru_pud	ru_syntagrus	61.82	22
ru_pud	ru*	76.55*	1*
en_pud	en_lines	76.56	23
en_pud	en*	84.09*	2*
Average		71.49	2

Table 3: Evaluation results of our system on PUD treebanks. We give post-evaluation (non-official) results* where we tested with models trained on treebanks with canonical language codes. The table is sorted by our rankings.

Unlabeled Parser	Arc Labeler	LAS F1
Full	Full	75.00
3×AEDP	Full	74.79
Full	Single	74.69
1×AEDP	Full	74.32
1×AHDP	Full	74.00
1×MST	Full	73.75

Table 4: Ablation of our ensemble system.

the training sets into train/dev sets with ratio 0.9/0.1. We did not use any additional data. All neural network computation was implemented with DyNet (Neubig et al., 2017).

Stage I of our system is the baseline system UDPipe 1.1, and we directly used the outputs provided by the organizers. We implemented modules for all later stages. They were trained with gold-standard features and tokenizations. For all languages and all treebanks, we trained models with 2-layer-deep and 192-unit-wide (96 units for each direction) word-level bi-LSTMs as feature extractors. Lexicalized character bi-LSTMs are 2 layers deep and 128 units wide, with 64-dimensional input character embeddings. For languages without lexicalized feature extractors, we used concatenation of 64-dimensional UPOS embeddings, and max pooling of 64-dimensional morphological embeddings as input to word-level bi-LSTMs.

The word-level bi-LSTM feature vectors were passed through MLPs with 1 hidden layer and 192 hidden units, before the bi-affine scoring functions for MST, AHDP and AEDP unlabeled parsing. In arc-labelers, we concatenated the word-level feature vectors and passed it through a 1-layer MLP with 192 hidden units to get scores for the arc labels. Output layer size depends on the number of labels appearing in the training set for the concerned treebank. We projected language-specific arc tags into universal ones before training.

All the aforementioned hidden layers used tanh as activation functions. And the parameters were uniformly initialized (Glorot and Bengio, 2010), except for the weight matrices in the bi-affine scoring functions, which were initialized to be orthogonal (Saxe et al., 2013). We did not use any pretrained word embeddings.

We applied dropout at every stage. MLPs had dropout rates of 0.3 (Srivastava et al., 2014). Bi-LSTMs, both character-level and word-level, also had dropout rates of 0.3 for input and recurrent connections (Gal and Ghahramani, 2016). Further, we zeroed out input vectors to word-level LSTMs for 15% of the time, to encourage the models gain more information from context.

When we trained each model, we randomly shuffled the training set before starting each epoch, and grouped sentences into mini-batches of approximately 100 words. The discriminative loss functions were optimized via Adam optimizer (Kingma and Ba, 2015), with default hyperparameters except initial learning rate set to be 0.002. We evaluated the models with development data after every 500 mini-batches. We halved the learning rate if the performance plateaued in 5 consecutive evaluations, The process was repeated 3 times before we terminated the training process.

We employed the technique of stack-propagation (Zhang and Weiss, 2016), where the auxiliary task of UPOS prediction was used as a regularizer. It received 0.1 the weight of other components in computing the loss.

For the languages with multiple treebanks, we first concatenated the training treebanks and trained a general model. We then fine-tuned the models on the respective individual treebanks.

To speed up training,we simultaneously trained MST, AHDP, AEDP and arc labeling models with shared LSTM feature extractors. Their losses were linearly combined with weights 0.6, 0.3, 0.3, 1.5 respectively. After a joint model had been trained, we fine-tuned each of the four tasks separately.

Our final system included ensembles both for unlabeled parsing and arc labeling. They were obtained with different random initializations of the neural network, but trained in the same fashion. For languages with multiple treebanks, we trained 3 sets of models (3 for each parsing paradigm, 9 unlabeled parsing models in total, plus 3 for arc labeling). For languages with single treebanks, we trained 5 sets of models.

For surprise languages, we first trained delexicalized models using the training data in a most similar language according to the WALS features (Dryer and Haspelmath, 2013). We selected `fi`, `fa`, `hi`, `cs` for `sme`, `kmr`, `bxr`, `hsb` respectively. We then fine-tuned the models on the sample data for these languages. We treated `kk` and `ug` similarly as they have quite small training sets. Both of them used `tr` as the source language.

The entire training process of all models in the ensemble for all treebanks was done using 8 CPU cores (2 $\times$ Intel i7-4790 @ 3.60GHz) in approximately one week. Each model required at most 2GB RAM plus the amount needed for holding the training sets. On the online evaluation platform TIRA (Potthast et al., 2014), the test phase for our full model finished in 4.64 hours with 2 threads. Each model required at most 500MB RAM plus the amount needed for holding the test sets.

Acknowledgments

The first author was supported by a Google focused research grant. The second author was supported by Kilian Q. Weinberger with IIS-1550179, IIS-1525919, IIS-1618134 grants from National Science Foundation. The fourth author was supported by DARPA DEFT Grant FA8750-13-2-0015. We thank Lillian Lee for her helpful input and support throughout the shared task. And we thank the two anonymous reviewers for their valuable comments.

References

Chris Alberti, Daniel Andor, Ivan Bogatyy, Michael Collins, Dan Gillick, Lingpeng Kong, Terry Koo, Ji Ma, Mark Omernick, Slav Petrov, Chayut Thanapirom, Zora Tung, and David Weiss. 2017. SyntaxNet models for the CoNLL 2017 shared task. *arXiv:1703.04929.* http://arxiv.org/abs/1703.04929.

Miguel Ballesteros, Chris Dyer, and Noah A. Smith. 2015. Improved transition-based parsing by modeling characters instead of words with LSTMs. In *Proceedings of the 2015 Conference on Empirical Methods in Natural Language Processing*. Association for Computational Linguistics, pages 349–359. https://doi.org/10.18653/v1/D15-1041.

James Cross and Liang Huang. 2016. Incremental parsing with minimal features using bidirectional LSTM. In *Proceedings of the 54th Annual Meeting of the Association for Computational Linguistics (Volume 2: Short Papers)*. Association for Computational Linguistics, pages 32–37. https://doi.org/10.18653/v1/P16-2006.

Timothy Dozat and Christopher D. Manning. 2017. Deep biaffine attention for neural dependency parsing. In *Proceedings of the 5th International Conference on Learning Representations*.

Matthew S. Dryer and Martin Haspelmath, editors. 2013. *WALS Online.* Max Planck Institute for Evolutionary Anthropology, Leipzig. http://wals.info/.

Jason Eisner. 1996. Three new probabilistic models for dependency parsing: An exploration. In *Proceedings of the 16th International Conference on Computational Linguistics*. http://aclweb.org/anthology/C96-1058.

Jason Eisner and Giorgio Satta. 1999. Efficient parsing for bilexical context-free grammars and head automaton grammars. In *Proceedings of the 37th Annual Meeting of the Association for Computational Linguistics*. pages 457–464. http://aclweb.org/anthology/P99-1059.

Yarin Gal and Zoubin Ghahramani. 2016. A theoretically grounded application of dropout in recurrent neural networks. In *Advances in Neural Information Processing Systems*. pages 1019–1027.

Xavier Glorot and Yoshua Bengio. 2010. Understanding the difficulty of training deep feedforward neural networks. In *Proceedings of the 13th International Conference on Artificial Intelligence and Statistics*. volume 9, pages 249–256.

Alex Graves and Jürgen Schmidhuber. 2005. Framewise phoneme classification with bidirectional LSTM and other neural network architectures. *Neural Networks* 18(56):602–610. https://doi.org/10.1016/j.neunet.2005.06.042.

Liang Huang and Kenji Sagae. 2010. Dynamic programming for linear-time incremental parsing. In

Proceedings of the 48th Annual Meeting of the Association for Computational Linguistics. Association for Computational Linguistics, pages 1077–1086. http://aclweb.org/anthology/P10-1110.

Diederik Kingma and Jimmy Ba. 2015. Adam: A method for stochastic optimization. In *Proceedings of the 4th International Conference on Learning Representations.*

Eliyahu Kiperwasser and Yoav Goldberg. 2016. Simple and accurate dependency parsing using bidirectional LSTM feature representations. *Transactions of the Association for Computational Linguistics* 4:313–327. http://aclweb.org/anthology/Q16-1023.

Marco Kuhlmann, Carlos Gómez-Rodrìguez, and Giorgio Satta. 2011. Dynamic programming algorithms for transition-based dependency parsers. In *Proceedings of the 49th Annual Meeting of the Association for Computational Linguistics: Human Language Technologies.* Association for Computational Linguistics, pages 673–682. http://aclweb.org/anthology/P11-1068.

Graham Neubig, Chris Dyer, Yoav Goldberg, Austin Matthews, Waleed Ammar, Antonios Anastasopoulos, Miguel Ballesteros, David Chiang, Daniel Clothiaux, Trevor Cohn, Kevin Duh, Manaal Faruqui, Cynthia Gan, Dan Garrette, Yangfeng Ji, Lingpeng Kong, Adhiguna Kuncoro, Gaurav Kumar, Chaitanya Malaviya, Paul Michel, Yusuke Oda, Matthew Richardson, Naomi Saphra, Swabha Swayamdipta, and Pengcheng Yin. 2017. DyNet: The dynamic neural network toolkit. *arXiv:1701.03980.* http://arxiv.org/abs/1701.03980.

Joakim Nivre, Željko Agić, Lars Ahrenberg, et al. 2017a. Universal dependencies 2.0 CoNLL 2017 shared task development and test data. LINDAT/CLARIN digital library at the Institute of Formal and Applied Linguistics, Charles University. http://hdl.handle.net/11234/1-2184.

Joakim Nivre, Marie-Catherine de Marneffe, Filip Ginter, Yoav Goldberg, Jan Hajič, Christopher Manning, Ryan McDonald, Slav Petrov, Sampo Pyysalo, Natalia Silveira, Reut Tsarfaty, and Daniel Zeman. 2016. Universal Dependencies v1: A multilingual treebank collection. In *Proceedings of the 10th International Conference on Language Resources and Evaluation.* European Language Resources Association, Portoro, Slovenia, pages 1659–1666.

Joakim Nivre et al. 2017b. Universal Dependencies 2.0. LINDAT/CLARIN digital library at the Institute of Formal and Applied Linguistics, Charles University, Prague. http://hdl.handle.net/11234/1-1983.

Barbara Plank, Anders Søgaard, and Yoav Goldberg. 2016. Multilingual part-of-speech tagging with bidirectional long short-term memory models and auxiliary loss. In *Proceedings of the 54th Annual Meeting of the Association for Computational Linguistics (Volume 2: Short Papers).* Association for Computational Linguistics, pages 412–418. https://doi.org/10.18653/v1/P16-2067.

Martin Potthast, Tim Gollub, Francisco Rangel, Paolo Rosso, Efstathios Stamatatos, and Benno Stein. 2014. Improving the reproducibility of PAN's shared tasks: Plagiarism detection, author identification, and author profiling. In Evangelos Kanoulas, Mihai Lupu, Paul Clough, Mark Sanderson, Mark Hall, Allan Hanbury, and Elaine Toms, editors, *Information Access Evaluation meets Multilinguality, Multimodality, and Visualization. 5th International Conference of the CLEF Initiative.* Springer, Berlin Heidelberg New York, pages 268–299. https://doi.org/10.1007/978-3-319-11382-1_22.

Kenji Sagae and Alon Lavie. 2006. Parser combination by reparsing. In *Proceedings of the Human Language Technology Conference of the North American Chapter of the ACL, Companion Volume: Short Papers.* pages 129–132. http://aclweb.org/anthology/N06-2033.

Andrew M. Saxe, James L. McClelland, and Surya Ganguli. 2013. Exact solutions to the nonlinear dynamics of learning in deep linear neural networks. In *Proceedings of the International Conference on Learning Representations.*

Noah A. Smith. 2011. *Linguistic Structure Prediction,* volume 4 of *Synthesis Lectures on Human Language Technologies.* Morgan & Claypool Publishers.

Nitish Srivastava, Geoffrey E. Hinton, Alex Krizhevsky, Ilya Sutskever, and Ruslan Salakhutdinov. 2014. Dropout: A simple way to prevent neural networks from overfitting. *Journal of Machine Learning Research* 15(1):1929–1958.

Milan Straka, Jan Hajič, and Jana Straková. 2016. UDPipe: trainable pipeline for processing CoNLL-U files performing tokenization, morphological analysis, POS tagging and parsing. In *Proceedings of the 10th International Conference on Language Resources and Evaluation.* European Language Resources Association, Portoro, Slovenia.

Ben Taskar, Vassil Chatalbashev, Daphne Koller, and Carlos Guestrin. 2005. Learning structured prediction models: A large margin approach. In *Proceedings of the 22nd International Conference on Machine Learning.* pages 896–903.

Daniel Zeman, Martin Popel, Milan Straka, Jan Hajič, Joakim Nivre, Filip Ginter, Juhani Luotolahti, Sampo Pyysalo, Slav Petrov, Martin Potthast, Francis Tyers, Elena Badmaeva, Memduh Gökırmak, Anna Nedoluzhko, Silvie Cinková, Jan Hajič jr., Jaroslava Hlaváčová, Václava Kettnerová, Zdeňka Urešová, Jenna Kanerva, Stina Ojala, Anna Missilä, Christopher Manning, Sebastian Schuster, Siva Reddy, Dima Taji, Nizar Habash, Herman Leung, Marie-Catherine de Marneffe, Manuela Sanguinetti, Maria Simi, Hiroshi Kanayama, Valeria de Paiva,

Kira Droganova, Hĕctor Martínez Alonso, Hans Uszkoreit, Vivien Macketanz, Aljoscha Burchardt, Kim Harris, Katrin Marheinecke, Georg Rehm, Tolga Kayadelen, Mohammed Attia, Ali Elkahky, Zhuoran Yu, Emily Pitler, Saran Lertpradit, Michael Mandl, Jesse Kirchner, Hector Fernandez Alcalde, Jana Strnadova, Esha Banerjee, Ruli Manurung, Antonio Stella, Atsuko Shimada, Sookyoung Kwak, Gustavo Mendonça, Tatiana Lando, Rattima Nitisaroj, and Josie Li. 2017. CoNLL 2017 Shared Task: Multilingual Parsing from Raw Text to Universal Dependencies. In *Proceedings of the CoNLL 2017 Shared Task: Multilingual Parsing from Raw Text to Universal Dependencies*. Association for Computational Linguistics.

Yuan Zhang and David Weiss. 2016. Stack-propagation: Improved representation learning for syntax. In *Proceedings of the 54th Annual Meeting of the Association for Computational Linguistics (Volume 1: Long Papers)*. Association for Computational Linguistics, pages 1557–1566. https://doi.org/10.18653/v1/P16-1147.

IMS at the CoNLL 2017 UD Shared Task:
CRFs and Perceptrons Meet Neural Networks

Anders Björkelund[*] and **Agnieszka Falenska**[*] and **Xiang Yu**[*] and **Jonas Kuhn**
Institute for Natural Language Processing
University of Stuttgart
`{anders,falenska,xiangyu,jonas}@ims.uni-stuttgart.de`

Abstract

This paper presents the IMS contribution to the CoNLL 2017 Shared Task. In the preprocessing step we employed a CRF POS/morphological tagger and a neural tagger predicting supertags. On some languages, we also applied word segmentation with the CRF tagger and sentence segmentation with a perceptron-based parser. For parsing we took an ensemble approach by blending multiple instances of three parsers with very different architectures. Our system achieved the third place overall and the second place for the surprise languages.

1 Introduction

This paper presents the IMS contribution to the CoNLL 2017 UD Shared Task (Zeman et al., 2017). Our submission to the Shared Task (ST) ranked third. Our overall approach relies on established techniques for improving accuracies of dependency parsers, including strong preprocessing, supertagging and parser combination.

The task was to predict dependency trees from raw text. To make the ST more accessible to participants, the organizers provided baseline predictions for all preprocessing steps (including word and sentence segmentation and POS/morphological feature predictions) using the baseline UDPipe system (Straka et al., 2016). We scrutinized the baseline and considered where we could improve over it. It turns out that, although the UDPipe baseline is a strong one, considerable parsing accuracy improvements can be gained by improving the preprocessing steps. In particular, we applied our own POS/morphology tagging using a CRF tagger and supertagging (Ouchi et al.,

---

2014) with a neural tagger. Additionally, we performed our own word and/or sentence segmentation on a subset of the test sets.

For the parsing step we applied an ensemble approach using three different parsers, sometimes using multiple instances of the same parser: one graph-based parser trained with the perceptron; one transition-based beam search parser also trained with the perceptron; and one greedy transition-based parser trained with neural networks. The parser outputs were combined through blending (also known as reparsing; Sagae and Lavie, 2006) using the Chu-Liu-Edmonds algorithm (Chu and Liu, 1965; Edmonds, 1967).

The final test runs were carried out on the TIRA platform (Potthast et al., 2014) where participants were assigned a virtual machine. To ensure that our final test run would finish on time on the VM, we established a time budget for each treebank and set a goal that a full test run should finish within 24 hours. Thus we applied a combination search under a time constraint to limit the maximal number of instances of the individual parsers.

An interesting aspect of the ST was the introduction of four surprise languages. These languages were only announced one week before the test phase at which point the participants were provided with roughly 20 gold standard sentences for each language. Unfortunately, among the allowed external resources the amount of parallel data for the surprise languages was rather limited. This prevented us from using cross-lingual techniques or multilingual word vectors. We therefore resorted to blending models trained on the small samples as well as delexicalized models trained on other source languages.

Another challenge of the ST were 14 parallel new test domains for the known languages. Since the UD annotation scheme is applied on all of the treebanks, this suggests that the training data of

---

[*]All three authors contributed equally.

Proceedings of the CoNLL 2017 Shared Task: Multilingual Parsing from Raw Text to Universal Dependencies, pages 40–51,
Vancouver, Canada, August 3-4, 2017. © 2017 Association for Computational Linguistics

the same language from different domains could be combined. We made several experiments in this direction and trained models on merged treebanks for most of the parallel test sets (Section 7).

The remainder of this paper is organized as follows. Section 2 discusses our preprocessing steps, including word and sentence segmentation, POS and morphological tagging, and supertagging. In Section 3 we describe the three baseline parsers, while blending is reviewed in Section 4. In Section 5 we go through our pipeline and show results on the development data. Sections 6 and 7 describe our approaches to the surprise languages and parallel test sets, respectively. Our official test set results are shown in Section 8 and Section 9 concludes.

2   Preprocessing

For most data sets word and sentence segmentation plays a minimal role, as it is delivered almost for free by means of whitespaces, sentence-final punctuation and capital letters. Therefore our overall architecture applies word/sentence segmentation pipeline only on treebanks for which this task is non-trivial (see Figure 1). These test sets can roughly be grouped into two categories: Languages where tokenization is challenging, e.g., Chinese and Japanese, but also languages such as Arabic and Hebrew, where many orthographic tokens are segmented into smaller syntactic words with transformations. The second category comprises the treebanks where the detection of sentence boundaries is difficult, mostly classical texts.

2.1   Word Segmentation

We applied our own word segmentation on six languages: Arabic, French, Hebrew, Japanese, Vietnamese, and Chinese. We selected them by analyzing the UDPipe baseline and picking out cases where we potentially could surpass it.

For Arabic, French and Hebrew, the difficulty lies in splitting *orthographic* words (i.e., multiword tokens) into several *syntactic* words (e.g., clitics). Additionally the orthographic words are often not the simple concatenation of their components. For example in French, the multiword token *des* would be split into two syntactic words *de* and *les*. We cast this problem as classification by predicting the Levenshtein edit script to transform a multiword token into its components.

Concretely with the French example, we take the multiword token *des* as input, and predict *de&les*, where & is an artificial delimiter to split the token. To reduce the tag set, we used the Levenshtein edit script "=2+&le=1" instead of *de&les* as the target class, which means keeping the first 2 characters, adding "&le", then keeping 1 character, so that *des* can be transformed into *de&les* (thus split into *de* and *les*). Using edit scripts reduced the tag set size from about 12,000 to 1,000 for Arabic and from 14,000 to 600 for Hebrew.

For Japanese, Vietnamese and Chinese, we simply applied a standard chunking method: for each character (or phoneme in Vietnamese), we predicted the chunk boundary, jointly with the POS tag of the word.

In both cases, we used the state-of-the-art morphological CRF tagger[1] MarMoT (Müller et al., 2013) to predict the tags (edit scripts or chunk boundaries). We used second order models for Arabic, French and Hebrew, and third order models for Japanese, Vietnamese and Chinese.

2.2   Sentence boundary detection

We applied our own sentence segmentation on nine languages (see Figure 1). For some of them, like Gothic or Latin PROIEL, typical orthographic features (e.g., punctuation or capitalization) that indicate sentence boundaries are not present and UDPipe was achieving extremely low scores (23.51 and 19.76 F1 respectively). The others were selected empirically by tests on the development data.

We employed a beam-search transition-based parser extended to predict sentence boundaries (Björkelund et al., 2016). This parser (referred to as **TPSeg**) is an extension of our transition-based parser (see Section 3.2) using the perceptron and is trained using DLASO updates (Björkelund and Kuhn, 2014; Björkelund et al., 2016). It marks sentence boundaries with an additional transition. For this parser the input is not just a pre-tokenized sentence, but a pre-tokenized document. As documents during test-time we used paragraphs from the raw input text, assuming that no sentence would span across a paragraph break.

A training instance for the parser is a document (rather than a sentence). Some treebanks have the entire training set represented as a single paragraph (document). Initial experiments showed that

---

[1] `http://cistern.cis.lmu.de/marmot/`

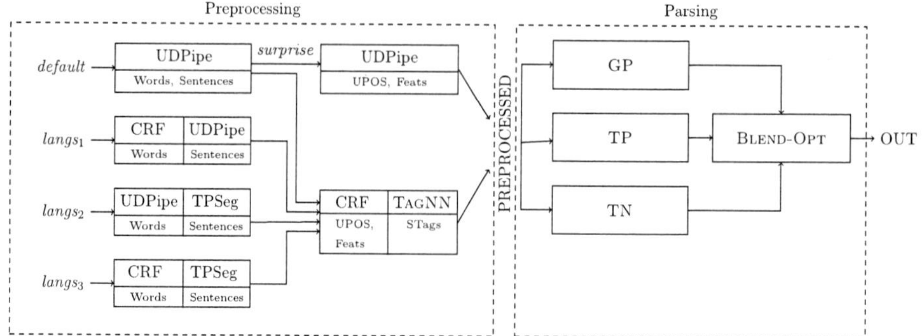

Figure 1: System architecture, where *langs₁*: he, ja, fr, fr_sequoia, fr_partut, fr_pud, vi, zh; *langs₂*: cu, en, et, got, grc_proiel, la, la_ittb, la_proiel, nl_lassysmall, sl_sst; *langs₃*: ar, ar_pud.

training the parser on a single document took considerable time and also did not perform very well. Instead, we created artificial documents for training by taking chunks of 10 sentences from the training set and treating them as documents (irrespective of whether they went across paragraphs).

We trained the parser using gold word segmentation and POS/morphology information. At test time we relied on UDPipe predictions in most cases. However, for Arabic, the only language where we did both word and sentence segmentation, we applied our own POS/morphology tagger since the word segmentation had changed. Additionally, we applied our tagger on Old Church Slavonic, Estonian, Gothic, Ancient Greek PROIEL and Dutch LassySmall since we found that this lead to better sentence segmentation results on the development sets.

2.3 Part-of-Speech and Morphological Tagging

We used MarMoT to jointly predict POS tags and morphological features. We annotated the training sets via 5-fold jackknifing. All parsers for all languages except the surprise ones were trained on jackknifed features. We did not use XPOS tags and lemmas. We used MarMoT with default hyperparameters.

2.4 Supertags

Supertags (Joshi and Bangalore, 1994) are labels for tokens which encode syntactic information, e.g., the head direction or the subcategorization frame. Supertagging has recently been proposed to provide syntactic information to the feature model of statistical dependency parsers (Ambati et al. (2013; 2014), Ouchi et al. (2014)).

We follow the definition of supertagging from Ouchi et al. (2014) and extract supertag tag sets from the treebanks. We use their Model 1 to design our supertags. That is, we encode the dependency relation (*label*), the relative head direction (*hdir*) and the presence of left and right dependents (*hasLdep*, *hasRdep*) and follow the template *label/hdir+hasLdep_hasRdep*.

We used an in-house neural-based tagger (**TagNN**) to predict the supertags (Yu et al., 2017). It takes the context of a word within a window size of 15. The input word representations are concatenations of three components: output of a character-based Convolutional Neural Network (CNN), pretrained word embeddings provided by the ST organizers, and a binary code indicating the target word. The word representations of the whole context-window are then fed into another CNN to predict the supertag of the target word. We used TagNN instead of CRF for supertagging, since it performed considerably better in the preliminary experiments.

3 Baseline parsers

Surdeanu and Manning (2010) show that combining a set of parsers with a simple voting scheme can improve parsing performance. Martins et al. (2013) demonstrate that self-application, i.e., stacking a parser on its own output, only leads to minuscule improvements.[2] Therefore to profit from combining components one of the most significant factor is their diversity. Thus we experimented with three parsers with quite different ar-

______
[2]In fact, even supertagging can be regarded as a form of stacking. Also in this case, the key ingredient is that the suppertagger is architecturally sufficiently different from the parser (Faleńska et al., 2015).

chitectures and additionally varied their settings.

3.1 Graph-based perceptron parser

As the graph-based parser we used *mate*[3] (Bohnet, 2010), henceforth referred to as **GP**. This is a state-of-the-art graph- and perceptron-based parser. The parser uses the Carreras (2007) extension of the Eisner (1997) decoding algorithm to build a projective parse tree. It then applies the non-projective approximation algorithm of McDonald and Pereira (2006) to recover non-projective dependencies. We train the parser using the default number of training epochs (10).

We modified the publicly available sources of this parser in two ways. First, we extended the feature set with features based on the supertags following Faleńska et al. (2015). Second, we changed the perceptron implementation to shuffle the training instances between epochs.[4] Shuffling enables us to obtain different instances of the parser trained with different random seeds, which are used in the blending step.

Since the time complexity of the Carreras (2007) decoder is quite high ($O(n^4)$) this parser required a considerable amount of time to parse long sentences. Therefore, while applying this parser in the blending scenario, we skipped all sentences longer than 50 tokens.[5] We additionally made sure that for each treebank we had at least one parser that was not GP, so that all sentences would be parsed.

3.2 Transition-based beam-perceptron parser

We apply an in-house transition-based beam search parser trained with the perceptron (Björkelund and Nivre, 2015), henceforth referred to as **TP**.[6] We have previously extended this parser to accommodate features from supertags (Faleńska et al., 2015). It uses the ArcStandard system extended with a Swap transition (Nivre, 2009) and is trained using the improved oracle by Nivre et al. (2009).

The parser is trained with a globally optimized structured perceptron (Zhang and Clark, 2008) using max-violation updates (Huang et al., 2012).

We use the default settings for beam size (20) and number of training epochs (also 20). Similarly to GP, we employ different seeds for the random number generator used during shuffling of the training instances in order to obtain multiple different models.

3.3 Transition-based greedy neural parser

We use an in-house transition-based greedy parser with neural networks (Yu and Vu, 2017), henceforth referred to as **TN**.[7]

The parser uses a CNN to compose word representations from characters, it also takes the embeddings of word forms, universal POS tags and supertags and concatenates all of them as input features. The input is then fed into two hidden layers with ReLU non-linearity, and finally predicts the transition with a softmax layer. The parser uses the same Swap transition system and oracle as TP. We use the default hyperparameters during training and testing.

During training the parser additionally predicts the supertag of the top token in the stack and includes the tagging cross-entropy into the cost function. This approach is similar to stack-propagation (Zhang and Weiss, 2016), where the tagging task is only used as a regularizer.

4 Blending

To enhance the performance of the baseline single parsers we combined them using blending (Sagae and Lavie, 2006). We trained multiple instances of each baseline parser using different random seeds. We parsed every sentence and assigned scores to arcs depending on how frequent they were in the predicted trees. We used the Chu-Liu-Edmonds algorithm to decode the maximum spanning tree from the resultant graph. This way we obtained the majority decision of the parser instances under the tree constraint.

As a baseline for blending (**BLEND-BL**), we took four instances from each of the baseline parsers: The four GP instances were trained with different random seeds. The four TP instances further split into two groups: two parse from left to right (TP-l2r) and two parse from right to left (TP-r2l). The four TN instances differ not only in the parsing direction, but also in the word embeddings, two use pretrained embeddings

---

[3] http://code.google.com/p/mate-tools

[4] The publicly available version does not shuffle.

[5] For the baseline results on the development sets (Tables 3 and 4), the parser was applied to all sentences.

[6] This parser as well as the variant that we applied for sentence segmentation (TPSeg) is available on the first author's website.

[7] This parser as well as the neural tagger used for supertagging (TAGNN) is available on the third author's website.

from the organizers (TN-l2r-vec, TN-r2l-vec) and two use randomly initialized embeddings (TN-l2r-rand, TN-r2l-rand).

The 4+4+4 combination was rather arbitrary and simply based on the intuition that different parsers should be equally represented and as diverse as possible. However, this might not be the optimal combination since different parsers are better at different treebanks. Also, given the relatively limited computing resources on the VM, we needed to optimize the number of blended instances in terms of speed.

We thus applied a combination search under a time constraint. First we measured time needed by each parser to parse every development treebank on the VM as an estimation of time usage for the test run. We then defined a time budget of 1,000 seconds for each treebank, and checked all combinations of the parsers on the development set under the time budget. We took the combinations from a pool of 24 individual instances, divided into seven groups: $8\times$GP; $4\times$TP-l2r; $4\times$TP-r2l; $2\times$TN-l2r-rand; $2\times$TN-l2r-vec; $2\times$TN-r2l-rand; $2\times$TN-r2l-vec.

Note that enumerating all combinations of individual instances is not feasible (2^{24} combinations). Thus we applied a two-step heuristic search. First we searched for the optimal number of instances from the 7 groups, by drawing samples from the pool of instances with only different random seed (at most $9 \times 5 \times 5 \times 3 \times 3 \times 3 \times 3 = 18,225$ possibilities). Once the optimal numbers of instances were found, we then searched exhaustively for the optimal instances (**BLEND-OPT**).

5   Evaluation

In this section we evaluate the aforementioned methods on the 55 treebanks for which development data was available.

5.1   Word and sentence segmentation

As discussed in Section 2, we applied our own word and/or sentence segmentation to a subset of languages. The corresponding results on the development sets are shown in Tables 1 and 2.

For word tokenization both our methods (predicting edit script and tagging with chunk boundaries) outperform the UDPipe baseline by 2.64 F1-score points on average. The biggest gains are achieved for Hebrew (4.57 points) and Vietnamese (4.67 points).

Using the TPSeg parser to predict sentence boundaries results in an average improvement of 9.32 points on sentence segmentation F1-score over the UDPipe baseline. Especially the difficult data sets that do not use orthographic features to indicate sentence boundaries improve by a big margin, for example Latin PROIEL by 18.76 and Gothic by 15.73.

Most importantly, the improvements in word and sentence segmentation F1-score roughly translate into LAS improvements with a 1:1 and a 5:1 ratio, respectively.

	UDPipe	CRF	Δ LAS
ar	93.86	95.53	2.04
fr	99.18	99.66	0.60
fr_sequoia	98.65	99.35	0.90
he	88.15	92.72	4.82
ja	89.53	92.10	5.08
vi	83.99	88.66	5.57
zh	88.95	92.76	5.47
average	91.76	94.40	3.50

Table 1: F1 scores for word segmentation and gains in LAS for TP.

	UDPipe	TPSeg	Δ LAS
ar	77.99	94.01	0.83
cu	37.09	48.03	3.16
en	76.35	78.69	0.66
et	84.91	86.40	0.54
got	23.51	39.24	4.01
grc_proiel	41.95	54.38	1.91
la_ittb	77.38	80.55	0.47
la_proiel	19.76	38.52	4.00
nl_lassysmall	79.31	82.35	0.82
average	57.58	66.91	1.82

Table 2: F1 score for sentence segmentation and gains in LAS for TP.

5.2   Preprocessing and Supertags

To see the improvements stemming from our preprocessing steps we run the baseline parsers in four incremental settings: (1) using only the UDPipe baseline predictions, (2) replacing POS and morphological features with CRF predictions, (3) adding supertags, and (4) applying our own word and sentence segmentation. Table 3 shows the average LAS for each parser across the 55 development sets for the consecutive experiments. For each set of experiments the parsers were trained on corresponding jackknifed annotations for POS, morphology, and supertags. Gold word and sentence segmentation was used while training parsers in all settings.

The table shows that replacing the POS and morphological tagging with the CRF instead of baseline UDPipe predictions improves the parsers by 0.66 on average.[8] The introduction of supertags brings an additional 0.88 points which demonstrates that supertags are a useful source of syntactic features for dependency parsers, irrespective of architecture. Replacing the word and sentence segmentation from UDPipe with our own improves on average by 0.74 points. It is worth noting that this improvement stems only from the 15 treebanks where we applied our own segmentation, although the averages in Table 3 are computed across all 55 treebanks.

	UDPipe	CRF	+STags	+segm.
GP	75.46	76.01	+1.12	+0.74
TP (l2r)	74.69	75.49	+0.97	+0.78
TN (l2r-vec)	74.95	75.58	+0.54	+0.71
average	75.03	75.69	+0.88	+0.74

Table 3: Average (across 55 treebanks) gains in parsing accuracies (LAS) for incremental changes to UDPipe preprocessing baseline.

5.3 Development Results

Our overall results on the development sets are shown in Table 4. The table shows the performance of the preprocessing steps, the individual baseline parsers, and the results of the two blends. The 15 treebanks where we applied our own word and/or sentence segmentation are marked explicitly in the table, for the other cases we used the UDPipe baseline.

The three single baseline parsers achieved similar average performances. Each one of them performed the highest on some of the treebanks, but not on all. It is worth noting that the strongest baseline parser, GP, is perceptron-based rather than a neural model. That is not to say that perceptrons generally are stronger than neural models (our neural TN parser is a greedy parser, and other participants in the Shared Task present considerably stronger neural models), however it indicates that perceptrons are not miles behind the more recent neural-based parsers.

Blending parsers yield a strong boost over the

baselines. BLEND-BL improves roughly 2-3 points depending on the choice of baseline. By searching for optimal combinations under the time budget, this can be further improved by 0.49 on average (BLEND-OPT). The search reduced the number of models from 660 to 438. In particular, there were 221 instances of GP, 79 of TP, and 138 of TN.

6 Surprise languages

The implementation of the surprise languages in the Shared Task was done in a rather peculiar way with respect to preprocessing. The test sets were annotated by the organizers through cross-validation. That is, the test sets were provided with predicted (by UDPipe) POS and morphological tags. Participants were provided with a small sample (about 20 sentences) for each surprise language, however only with gold standard preprocessing. This meant that it was difficult to use the samples for tuning/development since we would either have to use gold standard preprocessing, or apply cross-validation on the samples ourselves which most likely would have resulted in considerably worse preprocessing than that which was delivered for the test sets. We chose to consistently use gold preprocessing for all development experiments on the surprise languages.

A straightforward approach to the surprise languages is to use delexicalized parser transfer (Zeman and Resnik, 2008). The idea is to train a parser on a source treebank using only nonlexical features (in our case universal POS tags and morphological features) and apply it on sentences from the target language. We followed Rosa and Zabokrtský (2015) and performed multi-source delexicalized transfer by blending together models trained on several languages. Contrary to them, we treat the source languages equally and blend them with the same weight.

We trained delexicalized TP and GP parsers for 40 source languages (we took the 40 biggest treebanks, excluding the domain specific ones). We refrained from training TN since the main motivation of this parser is that it operates on characters. Therefore, using it in the delexicalized setting does not make sense.

To narrow down the number of possible source language parsers, we used TP to select the best six source languages for each surprise language using the sample data. We then searched for the optimal

---

[8]The actual improvements on the POS and morphological tagging tasks amount to 0.68 and 1.17, respectively.

	Preprocessing (F1)				Baseline parsers (LAS)			Blending (LAS)	
	Words	Sentences	UPOS	Feats	GP	TP	TN	Blend-BL	Blend-Opt
ar$^{\otimes\odot}$	95.53	94.01	90.73	86.40	70.88	70.54	71.35	72.59	72.99
bg	99.84	92.41	97.88	96.22	84.81	84.65	83.35	85.93	86.09
ca	99.96	98.77	98.16	97.50	87.04	86.75	85.11	87.59	87.90
cs	99.96	92.41	98.68	93.65	87.36	86.75	83.74	87.42	87.45
cs_cac	100.00	99.09	99.07	91.01	87.37	86.52	85.41	87.56	88.17
cs_cltt	98.65	74.11	90.30	79.69	73.01	72.83	73.94	76.84	77.30
cu$^{\odot}$	100.00	48.03	94.92	89.26	73.35	72.45	73.02	75.27	75.86
da	99.68	84.36	95.22	94.59	78.01	76.98	74.59	79.63	80.01
de	99.91	92.25	92.95	84.72	78.72	77.83	75.10	80.02	80.54
el	99.87	88.67	95.77	91.03	81.53	80.78	80.06	83.45	84.16
en$^{\odot}$	98.69	78.69	93.09	94.03	78.37	77.27	76.93	79.11	79.41
en_lines	99.93	87.36	94.92	99.93	76.51	76.23	76.41	78.59	79.35
en_partut	99.46	97.62	94.23	93.35	76.58	76.15	77.35	79.41	80.12
es	99.80	98.07	96.12	96.97	84.91	84.25	83.00	85.08	85.25
es_ancora	99.94	96.33	98.10	97.57	86.66	86.18	85.16	87.07	87.30
et$^{\odot}$	99.79	86.40	89.20	84.13	63.56	62.15	63.87	66.49	67.76
eu	99.99	99.00	94.14	89.83	74.99	73.73	74.47	76.96	77.59
fa	99.69	97.14	96.16	96.24	82.86	82.43	81.97	84.21	84.42
fi	99.69	86.47	95.49	93.01	80.08	78.99	78.34	81.71	82.13
fi_ftb	99.93	82.52	92.85	93.15	79.97	79.03	80.35	81.17	82.02
fr$^{\otimes}$	99.66	97.09	96.90	96.78	87.24	86.93	86.25	87.76	87.92
fr_sequoia$^{\otimes}$	99.35	90.20	96.58	95.68	84.30	83.42	83.01	85.54	86.17
gl	99.93	98.04	96.80	99.80	80.33	79.31	78.89	81.74	81.87
got$^{\odot}$	100.00	39.24	94.75	87.90	68.29	67.59	67.35	70.65	71.01
grc	99.98	99.17	88.34	89.58	65.77	64.06	64.28	68.14	69.09
grc_proiel$^{\odot}$	100.00	54.38	96.64	90.57	75.07	74.29	73.98	77.30	77.80
he$^{\otimes}$	92.72	98.57	89.24	87.21	68.89	68.75	68.31	70.94	71.02
hi	100.00	98.46	96.12	90.89	88.92	88.83	89.73	90.09	90.45
hr	99.98	97.23	96.70	87.57	80.54	79.91	79.15	82.41	82.99
hu	99.91	94.55	93.84	72.72	72.06	72.00	70.84	76.13	76.50
id	99.99	90.83	93.33	99.56	75.26	74.80	73.68	77.38	77.43
it	99.70	93.20	97.14	97.31	85.70	84.80	84.48	86.35	86.77
ja$^{\otimes}$	92.10	99.71	89.82	92.08	78.52	78.66	79.58	79.71	80.04
ko	99.45	91.10	93.10	99.17	70.47	71.13	74.37	74.03	76.41
la_ittb$^{\odot}$	99.88	80.55	96.79	92.41	76.10	75.40	75.67	78.21	79.16
la_proiel$^{\odot}$	99.99	38.52	95.83	89.46	68.99	67.05	67.82	71.45	71.99
lv	98.91	96.48	91.29	85.40	67.08	65.03	65.31	69.19	70.25
nl	99.87	92.11	94.38	92.92	79.04	78.29	76.36	80.18	80.72
nl_lassysmall$^{\odot}$	99.90	82.35	96.01	95.74	79.03	77.85	76.27	80.41	80.98
no_bokmaal	99.89	96.91	97.55	96.36	86.17	85.90	84.89	86.79	87.01
no_nynorsk	99.92	93.05	97.05	96.01	84.56	84.19	83.55	85.36	85.50
pl	99.87	99.56	96.12	85.71	84.67	83.78	83.66	85.89	86.89
pt	99.74	89.27	96.86	95.05	86.04	85.71	84.53	87.20	87.56
pt_br	99.83	96.65	97.39	99.71	86.99	86.49	86.33	87.88	87.87
ro	99.55	95.16	96.68	96.13	82.05	81.61	80.12	83.19	83.37
ru	99.92	96.18	95.44	87.50	80.22	79.60	78.89	81.89	82.37
ru_syntagrus	99.68	97.67	98.15	94.40	89.10	88.45	86.79	89.37	89.19
sk	100.00	77.85	95.04	80.13	78.49	77.92	76.71	80.10	80.70
sl	99.94	99.59	97.13	90.54	85.92	84.33	82.42	87.05	87.40
sv	99.77	95.59	95.52	94.80	77.11	76.34	75.28	79.18	79.96
sv_lines	99.97	87.28	94.50	99.97	76.10	75.65	75.93	78.00	78.80
tr	97.88	96.98	91.35	86.17	58.05	58.07	57.04	61.42	62.16
ur	99.99	98.37	93.46	80.24	79.02	78.45	79.78	80.70	80.96
vi$^{\otimes}$	88.66	96.28	80.64	88.56	47.01	47.62	47.76	49.66	49.77
zh$^{\otimes}$	92.76	97.60	86.23	91.57	62.93	63.28	63.37	66.17	66.80
average	99.07	89.45	94.56	91.78	77.87	77.24	76.83	79.52	80.01

Table 4: Development results. The treebanks for which we did our own word and/or sentence segmentation are marked with $^{\otimes}$ and $^{\odot}$ respectively. The TP and TN models correspond to TP-l2r TN-l2r-vec, respectively.

combination (across both parsers) where, instead of a time budget, we arbitrarily set the maximum number of parsers to eight.

sme_{lex}	51.02	hsb_{lex}	65.00
fi_{delex}	51.02	cs_{delex}	78.04
$\text{no\_bokmaal}_{delex}$	47.62	sl_{delex}	76.74
et_{delex}	47.62	sk_{delex}	75.43
BLEND-OPT	60.54	BLEND-OPT	78.70

(a) Target language: sme (c) Target language: hsb

kmr_{lex}	48.76	bxr_{lex}	41.83
fa_{delex}	42.15	eu_{delex}	37.25
el_{delex}	33.88	ur_{delex}	35.95
uk_{delex}	29.75	hi_{delex}	35.29
BLEND-OPT	44.63	BLEND-OPT	44.44

(b) Target language: kmr (d) Target language: bxr

Table 5: Parsing accuracy (LAS) for surprise languages: the three best delexicalized TP-l2r parsers and lexicalized parser obtained by leave-one-out jackknifing.

In addition to the delexicalized models, we also trained lexicalized TP and GP models[9] on the sample data and applied leave-one-out jackknifing.[10] A comparison between the three best delexicalized TP models and the lexicalized TP parser is shown in Table 5. Only for Upper Sorbian were transferred models able to surpass the model trained on the very small training data. Interestingly, the blended models were much better than any of the models for all languages except Kurmanji. Therefore we decided not to use any of the delexicalized models for this language. For the other three surprise languages we used ultimately blended eight delexicalized (selected as described above) and eight lexicalized models, the intuition being that this would give equal weight to lexicalized and delexicalized models.

7 Parallel datasets

For the 14 additional parallel datasets (PUD) we used parsers trained on their corresponding languages. For several languages there were more than one treebank in the training data for the corresponding PUD test set. This begs the question as to whether the models used for the PUD test sets should be trained only on the primary treebank, or on the combination of all training sets corresponding to that language. For the main treebanks, initial experiments indicated that this was a bad idea and parsers performed better when training sets were not combined. However, for the PUD test sets we had no information on the annotation scheme nor the domain, which made it difficult to decide whether to use only the primary training set or all available.

For each language with multiple training sets, we trained one parser on each training set as well as on their concatenation. We applied these models on the development sets and created a confusion matrix. Without prior knowledge about the PUD treebanks, we estimated the expected LAS as the average LAS of the development sets and chose the model that maximizes the estimation.

Table 6 shows such a confusion matrix for Swedish using the TN parser. The expected LAS for PUD (right-most column) is highest when trained on the concatenation of the two treebanks. This observation held for all the languages with multiple treebanks that we tested and we therefore used models trained on the concatenation of all training data with two exceptions: For Czech time prevented us from training models and creating a confusion matrix and we only used models trained on the primary treebank. For Finish FTB the README distributed with the treebank states that this treebank is a conversion that tries to approximate the primary Finish treebank. This suggests that it does not entirely conform to the Finish UD standard. We assumed that the Finish PUD test set would be closer to the primary treebank and therefore chose to use only the model trained on the primary treebank.

	sv	sv_lines	exp. sv_pud
sv	75.28	63.54	69.41
sv_lines	67.78	75.93	71.86
sv_concat	75.31	75.23	75.27

Table 6: Confusion matrix for Swedish with expected LAS on Swedish PUD.

8 Test Set results

Our final results on the test sets are shown in Table 7. Overall we ranked third in the Shared Task with a macro-average LAS of 74.42 behind two teams: Stanford and Cornell. Both of them used

---

[9]We did not train lexicalized TN models since it had problems with exploding gradients and convergence due to the small size of the sample data.

[10]That is, for a sample set of 20 sentences this boils down to 20-fold cross-validation.

state-of-the-art neural-based parsers (Zeman et al., 2017).

Our efforts to improve the preprocessing scores paid off. On most of the languages where we applied our word and/or sentence segmentation we achieved the best parsing results. On the secondary evaluation metrics we ranked first for word segmentation and sentence segmentation, second for POS tagging, and first for morphological tagging. Additionally we were second on parsing the surprise languages.

As it turns out, all PUD treebanks were presumably annotated following the guidelines of the primary treebanks. This most likely lowered our results a little bit for some of the PUD treebanks. However, for Russian PUD our results are abnormally low compared to many other participants. We scored about 13 points behind the top result, in comparison to an average distance of less than 2 points. This is most likely an artifact of how the non-primary (SynTagRus) Russian treebank is considerably larger than the primary Russian treebank, which means that a parser trained on the concatenation is mostly dominated by the SynTagRus annotation style and domains.

9 Conclusion

We have presented the IMS contribution to the CoNLL 2017 UD Shared Task. We have shown that tuning the preprocessing methods is a way to achieve competitive parsing performance. We made use of a CRF tagger for POS and morphological features and very strong word and sentence segmentation tools.

None of our baseline parsers alone would rank third. We therefore used blending to combine them. In general, we can confirm the observation of Surdeanu and Manning (2010) that the diversity of parsers is important. Additionally, we observed that both the diversity of parser architectures and number of instances of the same parser can improve performance. Furthermore, our automatized combination search method could be seen as a case of a "sparsely" weighted voting scheme.

We confirmed two of our previous findings on a larger scale. (1) Syntactic information can help sentence segmentation (Björkelund et al., 2016). (2) Supertags improve parsing performance across all languages (Faleńska et al., 2015).

For the surprise languages we blended delexicalized models from other languages with lexical-ized models trained on the small in-language sample data. This approach seems to have been robust and rendered us second rank for surprise languages. However, further analysis would be required in order to understand whether the lexicalized or delexicalized models in general fare better in this setting.

As for the PUD treebanks we found that, although the UD annotation scheme should be consistent across treebanks, combining training sets for one language is not useful for parsing the PUD test sets. Whether this depends on annotation idiosyncrasies or domain differences is an open question and deserves further attention.

Acknowledgments

This work was supported by the Deutsche Forschungsgemeinschaft (DFG) via the SFB 732, project D8. We express our gratitude to the organizers of the Shared Task (Zeman et al., 2017), the treebank providers (Nivre et al., 2017) and baseline system authors (Straka et al., 2016). We also thank our colleagues Özlem Çetinoğlu and Kyle Richardson for the contribution of ideas.

References

Bharat Ram Ambati, Tejaswini Deoskar, and Mark Steedman. 2013. Using CCG categories to improve Hindi dependency parsing. In *Proceedings of the 51st Annual Meeting of the Association for Computational Linguistics (Volume 2: Short Papers)*. Association for Computational Linguistics, Sofia, Bulgaria, pages 604–609. http://www.aclweb.org/anthology/P13-2107.

Bharat Ram Ambati, Tejaswini Deoskar, and Mark Steedman. 2014. Improving Dependency Parsers using Combinatory Categorial Grammar. In *Proceedings of the 14th Conference of the European Chapter of the Association for Computational Linguistics, volume 2: Short Papers*. Association for Computational Linguistics, Gothenburg, Sweden, pages 159–163. http://www.aclweb.org/anthology/E14-4031.

Anders Björkelund, Agnieszka Faleńska, Wolfgang Seeker, and Jonas Kuhn. 2016. How to train dependency parsers with inexact search for joint sentence boundary detection and parsing of entire documents. In *Proceedings of the 54th Annual Meeting of the Association for Computational Linguistics (Volume 1: Long Papers)*. Association for Computational Linguistics, Berlin, Germany, pages 1924–1934. http://www.aclweb.org/anthology/P16-1181.

Anders Björkelund and Jonas Kuhn. 2014. Learning structured perceptrons for coreference resolu-

	Words	Sent.	UPOS	Feats	LAS	Rank
ar[⊗][⊙]	95.53	77.71	90.62	87.15	72.90	1
bg	99.91	92.83	97.95	96.47	87.65	3
ca	99.97	98.95	97.97	97.16	87.74	4
cs	99.90	92.03	98.44	93.14	86.39	5
cs_cac	99.99	100.0	98.76	90.72	86.99	3
cs_cltt	99.35	95.06	96.79	87.88	80.67	4
cu[⊙]	99.96	50.44	94.94	88.90	76.84	1
da	99.69	79.36	95.27	94.83	79.52	3
de	99.65	79.11	92.24	83.11	75.47	3
el	99.88	90.79	96.53	91.37	84.96	3
en[⊙]	98.67	74.72	93.29	94.40	78.71	5
en_lines	99.94	85.84	95.08	99.94	78.25	4
en_partut	99.49	97.51	93.32	92.69	79.37	5
es	99.69	94.15	95.53	96.34	83.15	9
es_ancora	99.95	97.05	98.19	97.72	87.12	5
et[⊙]	99.77	85.21	89.50	84.62	67.60	3
eu	99.96	99.58	94.01	89.57	77.97	3
fa	99.64	98.00	96.21	96.34	83.34	3
fi	99.63	84.56	95.15	92.43	81.21	3
fi_ftb	99.88	83.83	92.80	93.43	81.33	3
fr[⊗]	99.46	93.59	96.22	96.12	83.82	3
fr_sequoia[⊗]	99.49	83.75	96.61	96.10	85.40	4
gl	99.92	96.15	96.87	99.75	81.60	3
got[⊙]	100.0	41.65	95.03	88.36	71.36	1
grc	99.95	98.43	87.59	88.00	68.23	2
grc_proiel[⊙]	100.0	51.38	96.48	90.24	75.28	1
he[⊗]	91.37	99.39	87.34	85.06	68.16	1
hi	100.0	99.20	96.28	91.03	90.41	2
hr	99.93	96.92	96.48	85.82	82.51	3
hu	99.82	93.85	92.63	72.61	73.55	3
id	99.99	91.15	93.42	99.45	77.70	3
it	99.73	97.10	97.43	97.37	87.85	3
ja[⊗]	91.68	94.92	89.07	91.66	78.21	5
ko	99.73	93.05	93.74	99.34	79.51	3
la_ittb[⊙]	99.99	93.37	97.41	94.27	84.09	2
la_proiel[⊙]	100.0	40.63	95.63	89.22	71.55	1
lv	98.91	98.59	89.72	84.14	68.03	3
nl	99.88	77.14	91.38	90.04	75.07	3
nl_lassysmall[⊙]	99.93	84.59	97.61	97.55	86.86	2
no_bokmaal	99.75	95.76	97.12	95.56	85.98	5
no_nynorsk	99.85	91.23	96.80	95.25	85.05	4
pl	99.88	98.91	96.35	86.53	86.75	3
pt	99.52	89.79	96.58	94.62	85.11	2
pt_br	99.84	96.84	97.36	99.73	87.10	7
ro	99.64	93.42	96.86	96.24	83.50	3
ru	99.91	96.42	95.45	87.27	81.49	3
ru_syntagrus	99.57	97.81	98.18	94.55	89.80	3
sk	100.0	83.53	94.60	81.23	80.53	3
sl	99.96	99.24	96.90	90.08	85.86	4
sv	99.84	96.37	96.10	95.15	82.28	3
sv_lines	99.98	86.44	94.40	99.98	78.88	3
tr	97.89	96.63	91.54	86.82	62.39	3
ur	100.0	98.32	92.98	81.03	80.93	3
vi[⊗]	86.67	92.59	77.88	86.33	47.51	1
zh[⊗]	92.81	98.19	86.33	91.71	68.56	1
average	99.01	88.96	94.45	91.75	79.60	3

(a) Big treebanks.

	Words	Sent.	UPOS	Feats	LAS	Rank
bxr	99.35	91.81	84.12	81.65	32.24	1
hsb	99.84	90.69	90.30	74.20	61.67	2
kmr	98.85	97.02	90.04	81.61	46.70	2
sme	99.88	98.79	86.81	81.93	40.67	2
average	99.48	94.58	87.82	79.85	45.32	2

(b) Surprise treebanks. All preprocessing by UDPipe.

	Words	Sent.	UPOS	Feats	LAS	Rank
ar_pud[⊗][⊙]	93.32	96.79	73.89	24.66	49.94	1
cs_pud	99.29	96.43	95.76	89.89	81.00	5
de_pud	98.00	86.49	84.53	31.67	71.88	3
en_pud	99.66	97.13	93.95	89.27	81.55	4
es_pud	99.47	93.42	88.48	40.47	78.63	9
fi_pud	99.61	93.67	96.77	95.35	85.21	3
fr_pud[⊗]	98.87	92.32	58.62	36.83	77.60	3
hi_pud	97.81	90.83	83.68	16.84	53.57	4
it_pud	99.17	96.58	93.22	57.34	86.16	4
ja_pud	93.44	94.89	91.07	54.44	81.98	3
pt_pud	99.42	95.65	88.36	43.51	75.53	5
ru_pud	97.18	98.95	87.19	33.35	62.72	21
sv_pud	98.26	90.20	90.32	53.47	74.41	3
tr_pud	96.62	93.91	71.39	23.62	38.23	1
average	97.87	94.09	87.69	50.89	71.31	3

(c) PUD treebanks.

	Words	Sent.	UPOS	Feats	LAS	Rank
fr_partut[⊗]	99.56	98.00	95.92	93.50	83.82	4
ga	99.29	95.81	89.99	80.05	69.22	3
gl_treegal	98.62	81.63	92.32	91.31	71.30	3
kk	94.91	81.38	58.48	45.49	25.29	5
la[⊙]	99.99	93.75	84.41	75.56	51.82	5
sl_sst[⊙]	99.82	21.41	90.91	84.82	55.88	3
ug	98.52	63.55	74.96	98.52	43.51	1
uk	99.81	92.59	89.68	74.88	69.27	3
average	98.81	78.52	84.58	80.52	58.76	3

(d) Small treebanks.

Table 7: Test results. The treebanks for which we did our own word and/or sentence segmentation are marked with ⊗ and ⊙ respectively.

tion with latent antecedents and non-local features. In *Proceedings of the 52nd Annual Meeting of the Association for Computational Linguistics (Volume 1: Long Papers)*. Association for Computational Linguistics, Baltimore, Maryland, pages 47–57. http://www.aclweb.org/anthology/P14-1005.

Anders Björkelund and Joakim Nivre. 2015. Non-deterministic oracles for unrestricted non-projective transition-based dependency parsing. In *Proceedings of the 14th International Conference on Parsing Technologies*. Association for Computational Linguistics, Bilbao, Spain, pages 76–86. http://www.aclweb.org/anthology/W15-2210.

Bernd Bohnet. 2010. Top accuracy and fast dependency parsing is not a contradiction. In *Proceedings of the 23rd International Conference on Computational Linguistics (Coling 2010)*. Coling 2010 Organizing Committee, Beijing, China, pages 89–97. http://www.aclweb.org/anthology/C10-1011.

Xavier Carreras. 2007. Experiments with a higher-order projective dependency parser. In *Proceedings of the CoNLL Shared Task Session of EMNLP-CoNLL 2007*. Association for Computational Linguistics, Prague, Czech Republic, pages 957–961. http://www.aclweb.org/anthology/D/D07/D07-1101.

Yoeng-jin Chu and Tseng-hong Liu. 1965. On the shortest aborescence of a directed graph. *Science Sinica* 14:1396–1400.

Jack Edmonds. 1967. Optimum branchings. *Journal of Research of the National Bureau of Standards* 71(B):233–240.

Jason Eisner. 1997. Bilexical grammars and a cubic-time probabilistic parser. In *Proceedings of the 5th International Workshop on Parsing Technologies (IWPT)*. MIT, Cambridge, MA, pages 54–65. http://cs.jhu.edu/ jason/papers/#eisner-1997-iwpt.

Agnieszka Faleńska, Anders Björkelund, Özlem Çetinoğlu, and Wolfgang Seeker. 2015. Stacking or supertagging for dependency parsing – what's the difference? In *Proceedings of the 14th International Conference on Parsing Technologies*. Association for Computational Linguistics, Bilbao, Spain, pages 118–129. http://www.aclweb.org/anthology/W15-2215.

Liang Huang, Suphan Fayong, and Yang Guo. 2012. Structured perceptron with inexact search. In *Proceedings of the 2012 Conference of the North American Chapter of the Association for Computational Linguistics: Human Language Technologies*. Association for Computational Linguistics, Montréal, Canada, pages 142–151. http://www.aclweb.org/anthology/N12-1015.

Aravind K. Joshi and Srinivas Bangalore. 1994. Disambiguation of Super Parts of Speech (or Supertags): Almost Parsing. In *Proceedings of the 15th Conference on Computational Linguistics - Volume 1*. Association for Computational Linguistics, Stroudsburg, PA, USA, COLING '94, pages 154–160. https://doi.org/10.3115/991886.991912.

A. Martins, M. Almeida, and N. A. Smith. 2013. "turning on the turbo: Fast third-order non-projective turbo parsers". In *Annual Meeting of the Association for Computational Linguistics - ACL*. volume -, pages 617–622.

Ryan McDonald and Fernando Pereira. 2006. Online learning of approximate dependency parsing algorithms. In *Proceedings of the 11th Conference of the European Chapter of the ACL (EACL 2006)*. Association for Computational Linguistics, Trento, Italy, pages 81–88. http://www.aclweb.org/anthology-new/E/E06/E06-1011.pdf.

Thomas Müller, Helmut Schmid, and Hinrich Schütze. 2013. Efficient Higher-Order CRFs for Morphological Tagging. In *In Proceedings of EMNLP*.

Joakim Nivre. 2009. Non-projective dependency parsing in expected linear time. In *Proceedings of the Joint Conference of the 47th Annual Meeting of the ACL and the 4th International Joint Conference on Natural Language Processing of the AFNLP*. Association for Computational Linguistics, Suntec, Singapore, pages 351–359. http://www.aclweb.org/anthology/P/P09/P09-1040.

Joakim Nivre, Željko Agić, Lars Ahrenberg, et al. 2017. Universal dependencies 2.0 CoNLL 2017 shared task development and test data. LINDAT/CLARIN digital library at the Institute of Formal and Applied Linguistics, Charles University. http://hdl.handle.net/11234/1-2184.

Joakim Nivre, Marco Kuhlmann, and Johan Hall. 2009. An improved oracle for dependency parsing with online reordering. In *Proceedings of the 11th International Conference on Parsing Technologies (IWPT'09)*. Association for Computational Linguistics, Paris, France, pages 73–76. http://www.aclweb.org/anthology/W09-3811.

Hiroki Ouchi, Kevin Duh, and Yuji Matsumoto. 2014. Improving Dependency Parsers with Supertags. In *Proceedings of the 14th Conference of the European Chapter of the Association for Computational Linguistics, volume 2: Short Papers*. Association for Computational Linguistics, Gothenburg, Sweden, pages 154–158. http://www.aclweb.org/anthology/E14-4030.

Martin Potthast, Tim Gollub, Francisco Rangel, Paolo Rosso, Efstathios Stamatatos, and Benno Stein. 2014. Improving the reproducibility of PAN's shared tasks: Plagiarism detection, author identification, and author profiling. In Evangelos Kanoulas, Mihai Lupu, Paul Clough, Mark Sanderson, Mark Hall, Allan Hanbury, and Elaine Toms, editors, *Information Access Evaluation meets Multilinguality, Multimodality, and Visualization. 5th*

International Conference of the CLEF Initiative (CLEF 14). Springer, Berlin Heidelberg New York, pages 268–299. https://doi.org/10.1007/978-3-319-11382-1_22.

Rudolf Rosa and Zdenek Zabokrtský. 2015. Kl-cpos3 - a language similarity measure for delexicalized parser transfer. In *Proceedings of the 53rd Annual Meeting of the Association for Computational Linguistics and the 7th International Joint Conference on Natural Language Processing of the Asian Federation of Natural Language Processing, ACL 2015, July 26-31, 2015, Beijing, China, Volume 2: Short Papers*. pages 243–249. http://aclweb.org/anthology/P/P15/P15-2040.pdf.

Kenji Sagae and Alon Lavie. 2006. Parser combination by reparsing. In *Proceedings of the Human Language Technology Conference of the NAACL, Companion Volume: Short Papers*. Association for Computational Linguistics, New York City, USA, pages 129–132. http://www.aclweb.org/anthology/N/N06/N06-2033.

Milan Straka, Jan Hajič, and Jana Straková. 2016. UDPipe: trainable pipeline for processing CoNLL-U files performing tokenization, morphological analysis, pos tagging and parsing. In *Proceedings of the Tenth International Conference on Language Resources and Evaluation (LREC'16)*. European Language Resources Association (ELRA), Paris, France. http://www.lrec-conf.org/proceedings/lrec2016/pdf/873_Paper.pdf.

Mihai Surdeanu and Christopher D Manning. 2010. Ensemble models for dependency parsing: cheap and good? In *Human Language Technologies: The 2010 Annual Conference of the North American Chapter of the Association for Computational Linguistics*. Association for Computational Linguistics, pages 649–652.

Xiang Yu, Agnieszka Falenska, and Ngoc Thang Vu. 2017. A general-purpose tagger with convolutional neural networks. In *arXiv preprint arXiv:1706.01723*.

Xiang Yu and Ngoc Thang Vu. 2017. Character composition model with convolutional neural networks for dependency parsing on morphologically rich languages. In *Proceedings of the 52nd Annual Meeting of the Association for Computational Linguistics*. Association for Computational Linguistics, Vancouver, Canada.

Daniel Zeman, Martin Popel, Milan Straka, Jan Hajič, Joakim Nivre, Filip Ginter, Juhani Luotolahti, Sampo Pyysalo, Slav Petrov, Martin Potthast, Francis Tyers, Elena Badmaeva, Memduh Gökırmak, Anna Nedoluzhko, Silvie Cinková, Jan Hajič jr., Jaroslava Hlaváčová, Václava Kettnerová, Zdeňka Urešová, Jenna Kanerva, Stina Ojala, Anna Missilä, Christopher Manning, Sebastian Schuster, Siva Reddy, Dima Taji, Nizar Habash, Herman Leung,

Marie-Catherine de Marneffe, Manuela Sanguinetti, Maria Simi, Hiroshi Kanayama, Valeria de Paiva, Kira Droganova, Hěctor Martínez Alonso, Hans Uszkoreit, Vivien Macketanz, Aljoscha Burchardt, Kim Harris, Katrin Marheinecke, Georg Rehm, Tolga Kayadelen, Mohammed Attia, Ali Elkahky, Zhuoran Yu, Emily Pitler, Saran Lertpradit, Michael Mandl, Jesse Kirchner, Hector Fernandez Alcalde, Jana Strnadova, Esha Banerjee, Ruli Manurung, Antonio Stella, Atsuko Shimada, Sookyoung Kwak, Gustavo Mendonça, Tatiana Lando, Rattima Nitisaroj, and Josie Li. 2017. CoNLL 2017 Shared Task: Multilingual Parsing from Raw Text to Universal Dependencies. In *Proceedings of the CoNLL 2017 Shared Task: Multilingual Parsing from Raw Text to Universal Dependencies*. Association for Computational Linguistics.

Daniel Zeman and Philip Resnik. 2008. Cross-language parser adaptation between related languages. In *Third International Joint Conference on Natural Language Processing, IJCNLP 2008, Hyderabad, India, January 7-12, 2008*. pages 35–42. http://aclweb.org/anthology/I/I08/I08-3008.pdf.

Yuan Zhang and David Weiss. 2016. Stack-propagation: Improved representation learning for syntax. In *Proceedings of the 54th Annual Meeting of the Association for Computational Linguistics (Volume 1: Long Papers)*. Association for Computational Linguistics, pages 1557–1566. https://doi.org/10.18653/v1/P16-1147.

Yue Zhang and Stephen Clark. 2008. A tale of two parsers: Investigating and combining graph-based and transition-based dependency parsing. In *Proceedings of the 2008 Conference on Empirical Methods in Natural Language Processing*. Association for Computational Linguistics, Honolulu, Hawaii, pages 562–571. http://www.aclweb.org/anthology/D08-1059.

The HIT-SCIR System for End-to-End Parsing of Universal Dependencies

Wanxiang Che, Jiang Guo, Yuxuan Wang, Bo Zheng
Huaipeng Zhao, Yang Liu, Dechuan Teng and **Ting Liu**
Center for Social Computing and Information Retrieval
Harbin Institute of Technology, Harbin, China 150001
{wxche,jguo,yxwang,bzheng,hpzhao,yliu,dcteng,tliu}@ir.hit.edu.cn

Abstract

This paper describes our system (HIT-SCIR) for the CoNLL 2017 shared task: Multilingual Parsing from Raw Text to Universal Dependencies. Our system includes three pipelined components: *tokenization*, *Part-of-Speech* (POS) *tagging* and *dependency parsing*. We use character-based bidirectional long short-term memory (LSTM) networks for both tokenization and POS tagging. Afterwards, we employ a list-based transition-based algorithm for general non-projective parsing and present an improved Stack-LSTM-based architecture for representing each transition state and making predictions.

Furthermore, to parse low/zero-resource languages and cross-domain data, we use a model transfer approach to make effective use of existing resources. We demonstrate substantial gains against the UDPipe baseline, with an average improvement of 3.76% in LAS of all languages. And finally, we rank the 4th place on the official test sets.

1 Introduction

Our system for the CoNLL 2017 shared task (Zeman et al., 2017) is a pipeline which includes three cascaded modules, *tokenization*, *Part-of-Speech* (POS) *tagging* and *dependency parsing*.

- Tokenization. This module includes two components, the *sentence segmenter* and the *word segmenter* which recognize the sentence and word boundaries respectively (Section 2.1).

- POS tagging. We focus mainly on universal POS tags, and don't use language-specific POS as well as other morphological features (Section 2.2).

- Dependency parsing. To handle the non-projective dependencies in most of the languages (or treebanks) provided in the task, we employ the list-based transition parsing algorithm (Choi and McCallum, 2013), equipped with an improved Stack-LSTM-based model for representing the transition states, i.e., configurations (Section 2.3).

We mainly concentrate on parsing in this task, and make use of UDPipe (v1.1) (Straka et al., 2016a) for most of the pre-processing steps. However, our preliminary experiments showed that the UDPipe tokenizer and POS tagger perform rather poorly in some languages and specific domains. Therefore, we develop our own tokenizer and POS tagger for a subset of languages.

To deal with the *parallel test sets* (cross-domain) and low/zero-resource languages, we adopt the neural transfer approaches proposed in our previous studies (Guo et al., 2015, 2016) to encourage knowledge transfer across different but related languages or treebanks.

Experiments on 81 test sets demonstrate that our system (HIT-SCIR: software4) obtains an average improvement of 3.76% in LAS as compared with the UDPipe baseline, and ranks the 4th place in this task.

2 System Architecture

2.1 Tokenization

2.1.1 Sentence Segmentation

We develop our own sentence segmentation models for the languages which have white spaces as token separators and on which UDPipe doesn't

Proceedings of the CoNLL 2017 Shared Task: Multilingual Parsing from Raw Text to Universal Dependencies, pages 52–62,
Vancouver, Canada, August 3-4, 2017. © 2017 Association for Computational Linguistics

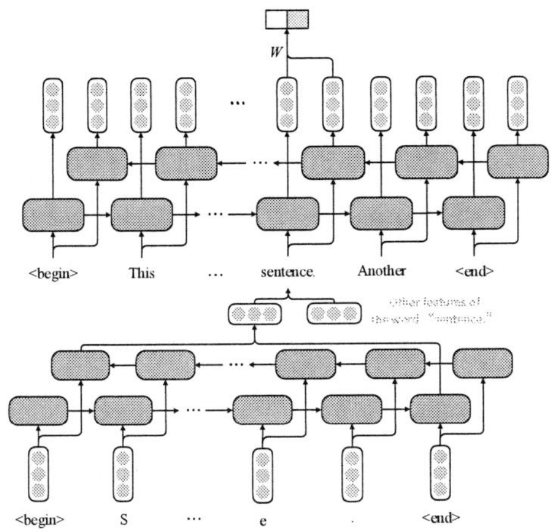

Figure 1: The hierarchical Bi-LSTM model for sentence segmentation.

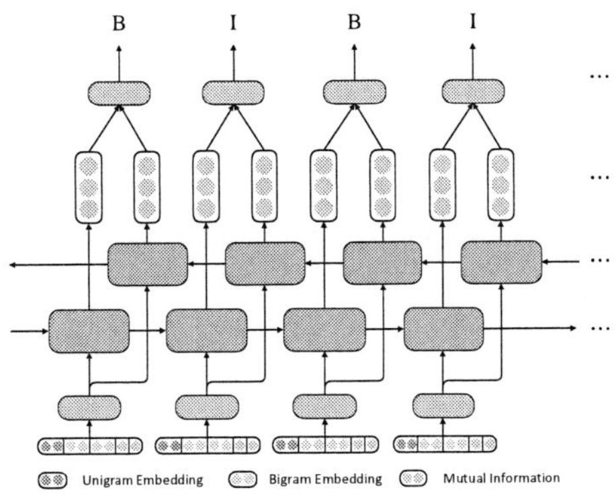

Figure 2: The word segmentation model. 'B' denotes the beginning position and 'I' denotes the middle or ending positions of a word.

perform well. We formalize the sentence segmentation process as a binary classification problem, that is to classify each token as either the end of a sentence or not. We notice that character-level information is critical for sentence segmentation, since texts are not tokenized yet in the current phase. Therefore, we develop a hierarchical LSTM-based model, as illustrated in Figure 1, in which characters in each token are composed using a character-based bidirectional LSTM (Bi-LSTM) network and then concatenated with additional token-level features (e.g., token embedding, the first character of this token, etc.) and passed through a token-level Bi-LSTM. The hidden states of the token-level Bi-LSTM are finally used for classification through a softmax layer.

We follow the strategy of the UDPipe tokenizer (Straka et al., 2016a) and employ a sliding window to incrementally segment a document into sentences.

In addition, we notice that for certain treebanks (e.g., la_ittb and cs_cltt), some punctuation-related rules derived from the training data can be highly effective. To be more specific, some punctuations that appear as the end of a sentence with high probability will be used directly for determining sentence boundaries. Therefore, we develop additional rule-based systems for these data instead of using the neural models as describe above.

2.1.2 Word Segmentation

We develop our own word segmentation models particularly for languages which do not have ex-plicit word boundary markers, i.e., white spaces, including *Chinese, Japanese* and *Vietnamese*.[1]

Our word segmentation model is also built on Bi-LSTM networks, and incorporates rich statistics-based features gathered from large-scale unlabeled data. Specifically, we utilize features like character-unigram embeddings, character-bigram embeddings and the pointwise mutual information (Liang, 2005) (PMI) of adjacent characters. Formally, the input of our model at each time step t can be computed as:

$$z_t = [U_t; B_{t-1}; B_t; \text{PMI}(c_{t-1}, c_t); \text{PMI}(c_t, c_{t+1})] \tag{1}$$

$$x_t = max\{0, Wz_t + b\} \tag{2}$$

where U_t and B_t denote the unigram embedding and bigram embedding respectively at position t and PMI denotes the pointwise mutual information between two characters.

The PMI values are computed through:

$$\text{PMI}(c_1, c_2) = \log \frac{p(c_1 c_2)}{p(c_1) p(c_2)} \tag{3}$$

where c_1 and c_2 are two characters, $p(c_1)$, $p(c_2)$ and $p(c_1 c_2)$ are counted on the raw data provided by the shared task. $p(s)$ denotes the probability string s appears in the raw data. We scale PMI

---

[1] *Vietnamese* requires word segmentation because white spaces occur both inter- and intra-words. When segmenting *Vietnamese*, white space-separated tokens are used as inputs, rather than characters as in *Chinese* and *Japanese*. In addition, we don't consider *Korean* here since the *Korean* input texts have already been segmented in the corpus provided by the task.

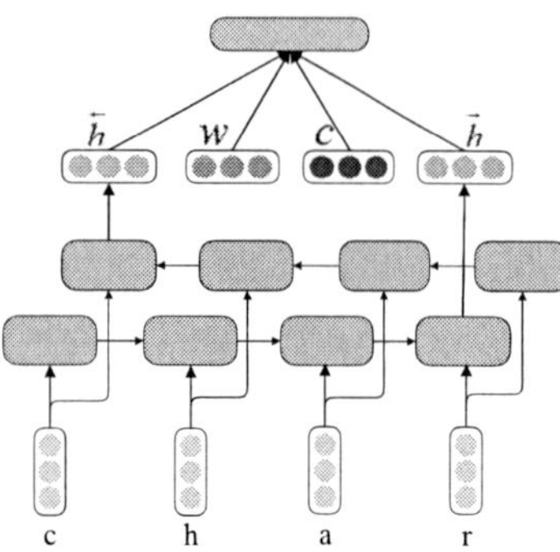

Figure 3: Structure of the character-based composition model for learning word representations. 'w' denotes the pre-trained word embedding, 'c' denotes the Brown cluster embedding.

with their Z-scores, the Z-score of a PMI value x is $\frac{x-\mu}{\sigma}$, where μ and σ are the mean and standard deviation of the PMI distribution, respectively.

Figure 2 shows the architecture of our word segmentation model.

The character-unigram embeddings and character-bigram embeddings are obtained using word2vec (Mikolov et al., 2013) on the raw data.

2.2 Part-of-Speech Tagging

The UDPipe POS tagger is trained using averaged perceptron with feature engineering. In our system, we use a model similar to the one for sentence segmentation (Section 2.1.1), i.e., a hierarchical Bi-LSTM model which outperforms UDPipe on most of datasets with much fewer features. Concretely, each word is modeled using a character-based Bi-LSTM, so that word prefix and suffix features can be effectively incorporated, which is particularly important for morphologically rich languages. In addition, modeling from characters alleviates the problem of Out-of-Vocabulary (OOV) words.

The character-based compositional embedding of each word is then concatenated with a pre-trained word embedding and a Brown cluster embedding, resulting in the final word representation which is fed as input of a word-level Bi-LSTM for POS tagging. Formally,

$$x = \max\{0, W[\overrightarrow{h}; \overleftarrow{h}; w; c] + q\} \quad (4)$$

Figure 3 illustrates the structure of the character-based composition model.

2.3 Dependency Parsing

The transition-based dependency parsing algorithm with a list-based arc-eager transition system proposed by Choi and McCallum (2013) is used in our parser. We base our parser mainly on the Stack-LSTM model proposed by Dyer et al. (2015), where three Stack-LSTMs are utilized to incrementally obtain the representations of the buffer β, the stack σ and the transition action sequence A. In addition, a dependency-based Recursive Neural Network (RecNN) is used to compute the partially constructed tree representation. However, compared with the arc-standard algorithm (Nivre, 2004) used by Dyer et al. (2015), the list-based arc-eager transition system has an extra component in each configuration, i.e., the deque δ. So we use an additional Stack-LSTM to learn the representation of δ. More importantly, we introduce two LSTM-based techniques, namely *Bi-LSTM Subtraction* and *Incremental Tree-LSTM* (explained below) for modeling the buffer and sub-tree representations in our model.

The pre-trained word embedding (100-dimensional), Brown cluster embedding (100-dimensional), along with a 100-dimensional randomly initialized word embedding updated while training,[2] and a 50-dimensional embedding for UPOS are concatenated and passed through a non-linear layer to obtain the representation of each word.

Representations of the four components in our transition system are concatenated and passed through a hidden layer to obtain the representation of the parsing state at time t:

$$e_t = \max\{0, W[s_t; b_t; p_t; a_t] + d\} \quad (5)$$

where s_t, b_t, p_t and a_t are the representation of σ, β, δ and A respectively. d is the bias. e_t is finally used to compute the probability distribution of possible transition actions at time t through a softmax layer. Figure 4 shows the architecture.

2.3.1 Bi-LSTM Subtraction

We regard the buffer as a *segment* and use the subtraction between LSTM hidden vectors of the segment head and tail as its representation. To include the information of words out of the buffer, we apply subtraction on bidirectional LSTM representations over the whole sentence (Wang et al.,

---

[2]Unfortunately we did not have access to enough raw text of *Gothic*, thus no pre-trained word embedding nor Brown cluster is utilized for it.

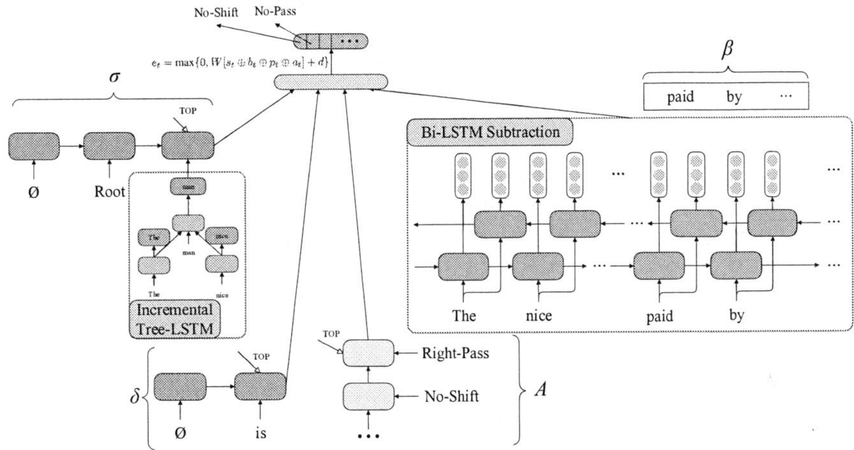

Figure 4: Example transition state representation based on LSTMs. The buffer β is represented by Bi-LSTM Subtraction, the sub-trees are computed by Incremental Tree-LSTM.

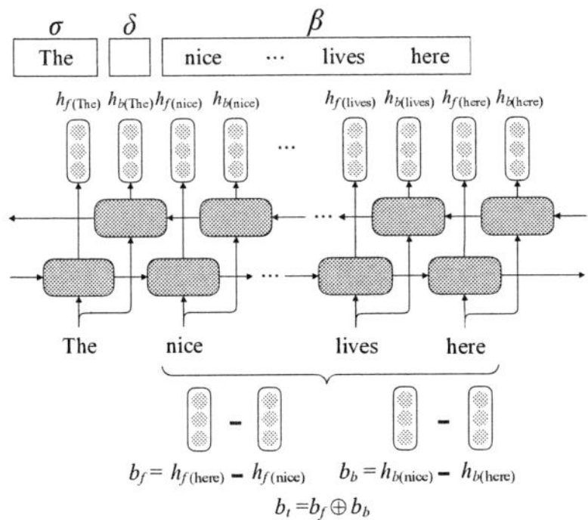

Figure 5: Illustration of Bi-LSTM Subtraction for buffer representation learning. $h_f(*)$ and $h_b(*)$ indicate the hidden vectors of forward and backward LSTM respectively. b_t is the resulting buffer representation.

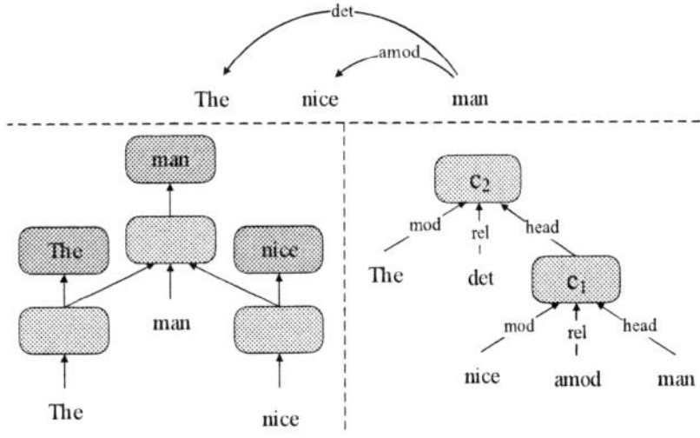

Figure 6: Representations of a dependency sub-tree (above) computed by Tree-LSTM (left) and dependency-based RecNN (right).

2016; Kiperwasser and Goldberg, 2016; Cross and Huang, 2016), thus called **Bi-LSTM Subtraction**.

The forward and backward subtractions are calculated independently, i.e., $b_f = h_f(l) - h_f(f)$ and $b_b = b_b(f) - b_b(l)$, where $h_f(f)$ and $h_f(l)$ are the hidden vectors of the first and the last words in the forward LSTM, $h_b(f)$ and $h_b(l)$ are the hidden vectors of the first and the last words in the backward LSTM. Then b_f and b_b are concatenated as the buffer representation. As illustrated in Figure 5, the forward and backward subtractions for the buffer are $b_f = h_f(here) - h_f(nice)$ and $b_b = h_b(nice) - h_b(here)$ respectively.

2.3.2 Incremental Tree-LSTM

We use a Tree-LSTM (Tai et al., 2015; Zhu et al., 2015) in our parser to model the sub-trees during parsing. The example in Figure 6 shows the differences between RecNN (Dyer et al., 2015) and Tree-LSTM. In RecNN, the representation of a sub-tree is computed by recursively combining head-modifier pairs. Whereas in Tree-LSTM, a head is combined with all of its modifiers simultaneously in each LSTM unit.

However, our implementation of Tree-LSTM is different from the conventional one. Unlike traditional bottom-up Tree-LSTMs in which each head and all of its modifiers are combined simultaneously, the modifiers are found incrementally during our parsing procedure. Therefore, we propose **Incremental Tree-LSTM**, which obtains sub-tree representations incrementally. To be more specific, each time a dependency arc is generated,

55

we collect representations of all the found modifiers of the head and combine them along with the embedding of the head as the representation of the sub-tree. The original embedding rather than the current representation of the head is utilized to avoid the reuse of modifier information, since the current representation of the head contains information of its modifiers found previously.

2.3.3 Parser Ensembling

For a majority of languages, we found that the parsing performance can be improved by simply integrating two separately trained models. More specifically, for each language two models with different random seeds are trained separately. While predicting, in each state, both models are used to calculate the scores for valid transitions under this configuration as described above. Then the score distributions computed by two models are summed to get the final scores for the valid transitions, among which the one with the highest score will be taken as the next transition.

3 Transfer Parsing across Domains and Languages

3.1 Cross-Domain Transfer

For 15 out of 45 languages presented in the task, multiple treebanks from different domains are provided. To exploit the benefits from these cross-domain data, we use a simple inductive transfer approach which has two stages:

1. Multiple treebanks of each language are combined to train an unified parser.

2. The unified parser is then fine-tuned on the training treebank of each domain, to obtain target domain-specific parsers.

In practice, for each language considered here, we treat the largest treebank as our source-domain data, and the rest as target-domain data. Only target-domain models are fine-tuned from the unified parser, while the source-domain parser is trained separately using the source treebank alone.

For the new *parallel test sets* in test phase, we simply use the model trained on source-domain data, without any assumption on the target domain.

3.2 Cross-Lingual Transfer

We consider the languages which have less than 900 sentences in the training treebank as *low-*

Target	hu	uk	qa	ug	kk
Source	fi_ftb	ru_syntagrus	en	tr	tr

Table 1: Cross-lingual transfer settings for low-resource target languages.

resource, and employ the cross-lingual model transfer approach described in Guo et al. (2015, 2016) to benefit from existing resource-rich languages.

The low-resource languages here include *Ukrainian* (uk), *Irish* (ga), *Uyghur* (ug) and *Kazakh* (kk). We determine their source language (treebank) according to the language families they belong to and their linguistic typological similarity. Specifically, the transfer setting is shown in Table 1.

The transfer approach is similar to cross-domain transfer as described above, with one important difference. Here, we use cross-lingual word embeddings and Brown clusters derived by the *robust projection* approach (Guo et al., 2015) when training the unified parser, to encourage knowledge transfer across languages at lexical level. Specifically, for each source and target language pair $\langle src, tgt \rangle$, we derive an alignment matrix $A_{tgt|src}$ from a collected bilingual parallel corpus, where each element $A_{tgt|src}(i,j)$ is the normalized count of alignments between corresponding words in their vocabularies:

$$A_{tgt|src}(i,j) = \frac{\#(V_{tgt}^{(i)} \leftrightarrow V_{src}^{(j)})}{\sum_k \#(V_{tgt}^{(i)} \leftrightarrow V_{src}^{(k)})} \quad (6)$$

Given a pre-trained source language word embedding matrix E_{src}, the resulting word embedding matrix for the target language can be simply computed as:

$$E_{tgt} = A_{tgt|src} \cdot E_{src} \quad (7)$$

Therefore, the embedding of each word in the target language is the weighted average of the embeddings of its translation words in our bilingual parallel corpus.

The cross-lingual Brown clusters are obtained using the PROJECTED clustering approach described in (Täckström et al., 2012), which assigns a target word to the cluster with which it is most often aligned:

$$c(w_i^{tgt}) = \arg\max_k \sum_j A_{tgt|src}(i,j) \cdot \mathbb{1}[c(w_j^{src}) = k] \quad (8)$$

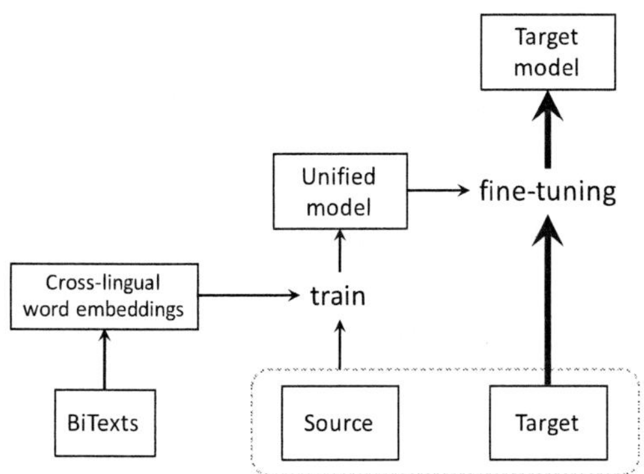

Figure 7: The cross-lingual transfer approach.

Target	bxr	kmr	sme	hsb
Source	tr & ug & kk	fa	fi_ftb & fi	cs

Table 2: Cross-lingual delexicalized transfer settings for surprise languages.

After that, target language-specific parsers are obtained through fine-tuning on their own treebanks. Figure 7 illustrates the flow of our transfer approach.

For the *surprise languages* in the final test phase, we use the transfer settings in Table 2. We use multi-source **delexicalized transfer** for surprise language parsing, considering that bilingual parallel data which is required for obtaining cross-lingual word embeddings is not available for these languages.

4 Experiments

We first describe our experiment setups and strategies for processing different languages (treebanks) in each module. Then we present the results and analysis.

4.1 Experimental Settings

4.1.1 Model Selection Strategies

For *sentence segmentation*, we apply our own models for a subset of languages on which UDPipe yields poor performance, and use UDPipe for the rest languages.[3] Specifically, we use the rule-based model for la_ittb and cs_cltt,[4] and use the Bi-LSTM-based model (Figure 1) for sk, en, en_lines, fi_ftb, got, nl_lassysmall, grc_proiel, la_ittb, cu,

la_proiel, da and sl_sst. For *word segmentation*, we use our Bi-LSTM-based model for zh, ja, ja_pud and vi, which don't have explicit word boundary markers, i.e., white spaces.

We use our own POS taggers for all of the languages, except for the surprise languages, which we rely on UDPipe for all pre-processing steps.

Our strategies for parsing are shown in Table 3. We determine the optimal parser (single, ensemble or transfer) for each treebank according to the performance on the development data.

4.1.2 Data and Tools

We use the provided 100-dimensional multilingual word embeddings[5] in our tokenization, POS tagging and parsing models, and use the Wikipedia and CommonCrawl data for training Brown clusters. The number of clusters is set to 256.

For cross-lingual transfer parsing of low-resource languages, we use parallel data from OPUS to derive cross-lingual word embeddings.[6] The *fast_align* toolkit (Dyer et al., 2013) is used for word alignment.[7]

We use the Dynet toolkit for the implementation of all our neural models.[8]

4.2 Effects of Different Parts in Dependency Parsing

We conduct experiments on the development sets of 4 treebanks to investigate the contributions of the two architectures we proposed (i.e., the Incremental Tree-LSTM and the Bi-LSTM Subtraction) and the Brown cluster. The LAS of different experiment settings are presented in Table 4. Results show that Brown clusters and both architectures help to improve the parsing performance in most situations. And the ensemble method we eventually choosed which incorporated the two architectures as well as Brown clusters and utilized two models for predicting yield the best performance.

4.3 Effect of Transfer Parsing

To investigate the effect of transfer parsing on cross-domain and cross-lingual data, we compare our transferred system with the supervised system on a subset of treebanks. Evaluation is conducted

---

[3] We use the same hyper-parameter settings as provided by the organizers to train the UDPipe models.

[4] However, the rule-based model does not yield good performance on the two test sets. We suggest that the rules we use are overfitting the development sets to some degree.

[5] lindat.mff.cuni.cz/repository/xmlui/handle/11234/1-1989
[6] opus.lingfil.uu.se
[7] https://github.com/clab/fast_align
[8] github.com/clab/dynet

Strategy	ltcode
Single	cs_cac, bg, ja, he
Ensemble (2)	cs, ru_syntagrus, la_ittb, fi_ftb, grc_proiel, es_ancora, es, de, hi, ca, en, fi, sk, ro, hr, pl, ar, eu, fa, id, ko, da, sv, cu, ur, zh, tr, got, sv_lines, lv, gl, et, el, vi, hu
Cross-domain Transfer	no_bokmaal, no_nynorsk, la, la_proiel, grc, pt, pt_br, sl, sl_sst, nl, nl_lassysmall, en_lines, en_partut, fr, fr_sequoia, fr_partut, it, it_partut[†], gl_treegal, cs_cltt, ru
Cross-lingual Transfer	uk, ga, ug, kk
Delexicalized Transfer	bxr, kmr, sme, hsb

Table 3: Model selection strategies for all treebanks. [†] it_partut is excluded from the final test sets. But it's used in our transfer parsing as a source treebank.

Settings	cs	de	en	ko
Baseline	86.79	80.08	81.87	67.21
B	87.51	80.01	82.48	68.19
T	87.43	80.01	82.24	68.29
B + T	87.67	80.24	82.73	68.34
B + T + C	87.62	81.45	83.37	70.24
Ensemble (2)	**88.52**	**81.92**	**83.99**	**71.38**

Table 4: Experiment results (LAS) on development sets with different settings. B: Bi-LSTM Subtraction, T: Incremental Tree-LSTM, C: Brown cluster. Ensemble is produced with models we eventually submitted.

on the development data or through 5-fold cross-validation when development data is not available. Results are shown in Table 5 and 6 respectively. We can see that both cross-domain and cross-lingual transfer parsing improve over the supervised systems significantly.

4.4 Results

The overall results of our end-to-end universal parsing system on 81 test treebanks are shown in Table 7, with comparison to the UDPipe baseline models. We obtain substantial gains over UDPipe on 76 out of 81 treebanks, with 3.76% improvements in average LAS. It spent about 9 hours to evaluate all of 81 test sets end-to-end and needed up to 4GB memory on the TIRA virtual machine.

4.5 Post-Evaluation

We realized a small problem in our implementation of the word segmentation models after official evaluation. After revision, we re-evaluated our models on the four test treebanks: zh, vi, ja

ltcode	Supervised		Transfer	
	UAS	LAS	UAS	LAS
cs_cltt	81.23	77.80	85.38	83.08
en_lines	82.30	78.44	83.65	79.75
en_partut	82.66	78.72	85.97	82.08
fr_sequoia	88.68	86.67	89.46	87.79
la_proiel	78.77	73.18	79.67	74.46
no_bokmaal	89.76	87.50	90.49	88.37
no_nynorsk	88.39	85.84	89.41	87.08
nl_lassysmall	86.11	82.65	87.39	84.02
pt_br	91.59	89.65	91.93	90.16
Average	*85.50*	*82.27*	***87.04***	***84.09***

Table 5: Effects of cross-domain transfer parsing on a subset of development sets.

and ja_pud. The post-evaluation results are shown in Table 8. On zh, vi and ja_pud, we outperform the rank-1 system significantly. We can see that the performance of word segmentation is crucial for the pipeline system.

5 Conclusion and Future Work

Our CoNLL-2017 system on end-to-end universal parsing includes three cascaded modules, *tokenization*, *POS tagging* and dependency parsing. We develop effective neural models for each task, with particular utilization of bidirectional LSTM networks. Furthermore, we use transfer parsing approaches for cross-domain and cross-lingual adaption, that can effectively exploit resources from multiple treebanks. We obtain significant improvements against the UDPipe baseline systems on most of the test sets, and obtain the 4th place in the final evaluation.

ltcode	Supervised		Transfer	
	UAS	LAS	UAS	LAS
uk	78.75	72.47	86.27	80.92
ga	76.66	67.08	80.83	73.44
ug	58.53	38.32	67.19	52.23
Average	*71.31*	*59.29*	***78.10***	***68.86***

Table 6: Effects of cross-lingual transfer parsing on ug uk and ga. 5-fold cross-validation is used for evaluation.

6 Credits

There are a few references we would like to give proper credit, especially to data providers: the core Universal Dependencies paper from LREC 2016 (Nivre et al., 2016), the UD version 2.0 datasets (Nivre et al., 2017b,a), the baseline UDPipe models (Straka et al., 2016b), the baseline SyntaxNet models (Weiss et al., 2015) and the evaluation platform TIRA (Potthast et al., 2014).

Acknowledgments

This work was supported by the National Key Basic Research Program of China via grant 2014CB340503 and the National Natural Science Foundation of China (NSFC) via grant 61300113 and 61632011.

References

Jinho D. Choi and Andrew McCallum. 2013. Transition-based dependency parsing with selectional branching. In *Proc. of ACL*. pages 1052–1062.

James Cross and Liang Huang. 2016. Incremental parsing with minimal features using bi-directional lstm. In *Proc. of ACL*. pages 32–37.

Chris Dyer, Miguel Ballesteros, Wang Ling, Austin Matthews, and Noah A. Smith. 2015. Transition-based dependency parsing with stack long short-term memory. In *Proc. of ACL and IJCNLP*. pages 334–343.

Chris Dyer, Victor Chahuneau, and Noah A. Smith. 2013. A simple, fast, and effective reparameterization of ibm model 2. In *NAACL*. Association for Computational Linguistics, Atlanta, Georgia, pages 644–648.

Jiang Guo, Wanxiang Che, David Yarowsky, Haifeng Wang, and Ting Liu. 2015. Cross-lingual dependency parsing based on distributed representations. In *Proceedings of the 53rd Annual Meeting of the Association for Computational Linguistics and the 7th International Joint Conference on Natural Language Processing (Volume 1: Long Papers)*. pages 1234–1244.

Jiang Guo, Wanxiang Che, David Yarowsky, Haifeng Wang, and Ting Liu. 2016. A representation learning framework for multi-source transfer parsing. In *AAAI*. pages 2734–2740.

Eliyahu Kiperwasser and Yoav Goldberg. 2016. Simple and accurate dependency parsing using bidirectional lstm feature representations. *TACL* 4:313–327.

Percy Liang. 2005. *Semi-supervised learning for natural language*. Master thesis, Massachusetts Institute of Technology.

Tomas Mikolov, Kai Chen, Greg Corrado, and Jeffrey Dean. 2013. Efficient estimation of word representations in vector space. *International Conference on Learning Representations (ICLR) Workshop* .

Joakim Nivre. 2004. Incrementality in deterministic dependency parsing. In *Proc. of the Workshop on Incremental Parsing: Bringing Engineering and Cognition Together*. pages 50–57.

Joakim Nivre, Željko Agić, Lars Ahrenberg, Lene Antonsen, Maria Jesus Aranzabe, Masayuki Asahara, Luma Ateyah, Mohammed Attia, Aitziber Atutxa, Elena Badmaeva, Miguel Ballesteros, Esha Banerjee, Sebastian Bank, John Bauer, Kepa Bengoetxea, Riyaz Ahmad Bhat, Eckhard Bick, Cristina Bosco, Gosse Bouma, Sam Bowman, Aljoscha Burchardt, Marie Candito, Gauthier Caron, Gülşen Cebirolu Eryiit, Giuseppe G. A. Celano, Savas Cetin, Fabricio Chalub, Jinho Choi, Yongseok Cho, Silvie Cinková, Çar Çöltekin, Miriam Connor, Marie-Catherine de Marneffe, Valeria de Paiva, Arantza Diaz de Ilarraza, Kaja Dobrovoljc, Timothy Dozat, Kira Droganova, Marhaba Eli, Ali Elkahky, Tomaž Erjavec, Richárd Farkas, Hector Fernandez Alcalde, Jennifer Foster, Cláudia Freitas, Katarína Gajdošová, Daniel Galbraith, Marcos Garcia, Filip Ginter, Iakes Goenaga, Koldo Gojenola, Memduh Gökrmak, Yoav Goldberg, Xavier Gómez Guinovart, Berta Gonzáles Saavedra, Matias Grioni, Normunds Grūzītis, Bruno Guillaume, Nizar Habash, Jan Hajič, Jan Hajič jr., Linh Hà M, Kim Harris, Dag Haug, Barbora Hladká, Jaroslava Hlaváčová, Petter Hohle, Radu Ion, Elena Irimia, Anders Johannsen, Fredrik Jørgensen, Hüner Kaşkara, Hiroshi Kanayama, Jenna Kanerva, Tolga Kayadelen, Václava Kettnerová, Jesse Kirchner, Natalia Kotsyba, Simon Krek, Sookyoung Kwak, Veronika Laippala, Lorenzo Lambertino, Tatiana Lando, Phng Lê Hng, Alessandro Lenci, Saran Lertpradit, Herman Leung, Cheuk Ying Li, Josie Li, Nikola Ljubešić, Olga Loginova, Olga Lyashevskaya, Teresa Lynn, Vivien Macketanz, Aibek Makazhanov, Michael Mandl, Christopher Manning, Ruli Manurung, Cătălina Mărănduc, David Mareček, Katrin Marheinecke, Héctor Martínez Alonso, André Martins,

ltcode	UDPipe 1.1		Ours		ltcode	UDPipe 1.1		Ours	
	UAS	LAS	UAS	LAS		UAS	LAS	UAS	LAS
ar	71.19	65.30	74.13	69.12	hsb	61.70	53.83	66.64	59.27
ar_pud	53.55	43.14	57.18	48.01	hu	71.46	64.30	74.68	66.29
bg	87.79	83.64	90.30	86.73	id	80.91	74.61	83.06	76.66
bxr‡	46.97	31.50	46.04	27.66	it	88.03	85.28	90.05	87.77
ca	88.62	85.39	90.79	88.27	it_pud	87.04	83.70	88.59	85.51
cs	86.46	82.87	89.57	86.52	ja	73.52	72.21	81.94	80.85
cs_cac	86.49	82.46	87.66	83.87	ja_pud	77.13	76.28	84.38	83.75
cs_cltt	76.26	71.64	84.96	81.89	kk	41.92	24.51	42.11	24.76
cs_pud	84.42	79.80	85.79	80.75	kmr	46.20	32.35	52.55	44.70
cu	69.68	62.76	72.19	65.80	ko	66.40	59.09	76.95	71.82
da	76.94	73.38	81.14	78.03	la	54.35	43.77	59.15	48.75
de	74.27	69.11	79.03	74.79	la_ittb	80.78	76.98	84.07	81.03
de_pud	73.64	66.53	77.90	71.11	la_proiel	63.50	57.54	68.94	63.48
el	83.00	79.26	85.72	82.82	lv	67.14	59.95	71.91	64.97
en	78.87	75.84	82.88	79.94	nl	74.94	68.90	78.90	73.43
en_lines	77.39	72.94	82.70	78.73	nl_lassysmall	81.37	78.15	89.06	86.85
en_partut	77.83	73.64	85.57	81.98	no_bokmaal	86.14	83.27	89.09	86.90
en_pud	82.74	78.95	84.97	81.86	no_nynorsk	84.88	81.56	87.95	85.43
es	84.84	81.47	87.20	84.22	pl	85.08	78.78	88.18	83.75
es_ancora	86.97	83.78	89.94	87.39	pt	85.77	82.11	87.75	84.90
es_pud‡	84.71	77.65	82.34	72.67	pt_br	87.75	85.36	90.51	88.71
et	67.71	58.79	73.09	65.10	pt_pud	80.10	73.96	81.18	72.33
eu	74.39	69.15	79.29	73.85	ro	85.50	79.88	87.30	82.21
fa	83.36	79.24	86.24	82.08	ru	79.28	74.03	84.32	80.58
fi	77.90	73.75	81.98	77.73	ru_pud‡	75.67	68.31	72.33	61.60
fi_ftb	78.77	74.03	82.79	78.08	ru_syntagrus	89.30	86.76	91.71	89.77
fi_pud	82.24	78.65	82.76	78.99	sk	78.14	72.75	84.38	79.82
fr	84.13	80.75	86.07	82.67	sl	84.68	81.15	89.54	87.08
fr_partut	81.69	77.38	88.39	84.86	sl_sst	53.79	46.45	60.36	54.06
fr_pud	78.62	73.63	82.55	77.51	sme	46.06	30.6	52.51	38.91
fr_sequoia	82.62	79.98	87.11	85.09	sv	80.78	76.73	83.93	80.58
ga	72.08	61.52	73.48	61.62	sv_lines	79.18	74.29	81.77	77.30
gl	80.66	77.31	83.31	80.23	sv_pud	75.09	70.62	75.15	70.70
gl_treegal	71.17	65.82	72.65	66.51	tr	60.48	53.19	64.14	56.43
got	67.13	59.81	67.61	60.52	tr_pud‡	55.01	34.53	54.17	34.15
grc	62.74	56.04	66.86	59.84	ug‡	53.58	34.18	51.57	34.52
grc_proiel	70.42	65.22	74.19	69.39	uk	69.78	60.76	71.22	63.08
he	61.54	57.23	64.30	60.07	ur	83.67	76.69	86.41	79.72
hi	90.97	86.77	93.31	89.48	vi	42.12	37.47	47.53	42.52
hi_pud	63.43	50.85	67.24	54.14	zh	61.5	57.40	68.95	65.10
hr	83.20	77.18	86.58	81.30	*Average*	**74.41**	**68.35**	**77.81**	**72.11**

Table 7: End-to-end parsing results on all test treebanks. ‡ indicates the test sets on which UDPipe performs better. Among the 5 sets, es_pud, ru_pud and tr_pud are parallel test sets on which we simply use the model trained from the source treebank. We suggest better strategies should be explored.

ltcode	Ours (b/r)		Ours (a/r)		Rank-1	
	WSeg	LAS	WSeg	LAS	WSeg	LAS
ja	92.95	80.85	94.70	84.37	**98.59**	**91.13**
ja_pud	94.02	83.75	**95.54**	**85.33**	94.93	83.75
vi	84.70	42.52	**91.40**	**48.98**	87.30	47.51
zh	91.19	65.10	**95.21**	**70.49**	94.57	68.56

Table 8: Post-evaluation results on zh, vi, ja and ja_pud. b/r: before revision. a/r: after revision.

Jan Mašek, Yuji Matsumoto, Ryan McDonald, Gustavo Mendonça, Anna Missilä, Verginica Mititelu, Yusuke Miyao, Simonetta Montemagni, Amir More, Laura Moreno Romero, Shunsuke Mori, Bohdan Moskalevskyi, Kadri Muischnek, Nina Mustafina, Kaili Müürisep, Pinkey Nainwani, Anna Nedoluzhko, Lng Nguyn Th, Huyn Nguyn Th Minh, Vitaly Nikolaev, Rattima Nitisaroj, Hanna Nurmi, Stina Ojala, Petya Osenova, Lilja Øvrelid, Elena Pascual, Marco Passarotti, Cenel-Augusto Perez, Guy Perrier, Slav Petrov, Jussi Piitulainen, Emily Pitler, Barbara Plank, Martin Popel, Lauma Pretkalnia, Prokopis Prokopidis, Tiina Puolakainen, Sampo Pyysalo, Alexandre Rademaker, Livy Real, Siva Reddy, Georg Rehm, Larissa Rinaldi, Laura Rituma, Rudolf Rosa, Davide Rovati, Shadi Saleh, Manuela Sanguinetti, Baiba Saulīte, Yanin Sawanakunanon, Sebastian Schuster, Djamé Seddah, Wolfgang Seeker, Mojgan Seraji, Lena Shakurova, Mo Shen, Atsuko Shimada, Muh Shohibussirri, Natalia Silveira, Maria Simi, Radu Simionescu, Katalin Simkó, Mária Šimková, Kiril Simov, Aaron Smith, Antonio Stella, Jana Strnadová, Alane Suhr, Umut Sulubacak, Zsolt Szántó, Dima Taji, Takaaki Tanaka, Trond Trosterud, Anna Trukhina, Reut Tsarfaty, Francis Tyers, Sumire Uematsu, Zdeňka Urešová, Larraitz Uria, Hans Uszkoreit, Gertjan van Noord, Viktor Varga, Veronika Vincze, Jonathan North Washington, Zhuoran Yu, Zdeněk Žabokrtský, Daniel Zeman, and Hanzhi Zhu. 2017a. Universal dependencies 2.0 CoNLL 2017 shared task development and test data. LINDAT/CLARIN digital library at the Institute of Formal and Applied Linguistics, Charles University. http://hdl.handle.net/11234/1-2184.

Joakim Nivre, Željko Agić, Lars Ahrenberg, Maria Jesus Aranzabe, Masayuki Asahara, Aitziber Atutxa, Miguel Ballesteros, John Bauer, Kepa Bengoetxea, Riyaz Ahmad Bhat, Eckhard Bick, Cristina Bosco, Gosse Bouma, Sam Bowman, Marie Candito, Gülşen Cebirolu Eryiit, Giuseppe G. A. Celano, Fabricio Chalub, Jinho Choi, Çar Çöltekin, Miriam Connor, Elizabeth Davidson, Marie-Catherine de Marneffe, Valeria de Paiva, Arantza Diaz de Ilarraza, Kaja Dobrovoljc, Timothy Dozat, Kira Droganova, Puneet Dwivedi, Marhaba Eli, Tomaž Erjavec, Richárd Farkas, Jennifer Foster, Cláudia Freitas, Katarína Gajdošová, Daniel Galbraith, Marcos Garcia, Filip Ginter, Iakes Goenaga, Koldo Gojenola, Memduh Gökrmak, Yoav Goldberg, Xavier Gómez Guinovart, Berta Gonzáles Saavedra, Matias Grioni, Normunds Grūzītis, Bruno Guillaume, Nizar Habash, Jan Hajič, Linh Hà M, Dag Haug, Barbora Hladká, Petter Hohle, Radu Ion, Elena Irimia, Anders Johannsen, Fredrik Jørgensen, Hüner Kaşkara, Hiroshi Kanayama, Jenna Kanerva, Natalia Kotsyba, Simon Krek, Veronika Laippala, Phng Lê Hng, Alessandro Lenci, Nikola Ljubešić, Olga Lyashevskaya, Teresa Lynn, Aibek Makazhanov, Christopher Manning, Cătălina Mărănduc, David Mareček, Héctor Martínez Alonso, André Martins, Jan Mašek, Yuji Matsumoto, Ryan McDonald, Anna Missilä, Verginica Mititelu, Yusuke Miyao, Simonetta Montemagni, Amir More, Shunsuke Mori, Bohdan Moskalevskyi, Kadri Muischnek, Nina Mustafina, Kaili Müürisep, Lng Nguyn Th, Huyn Nguyn Th Minh, Vitaly Nikolaev, Hanna Nurmi, Stina Ojala, Petya Osenova, Lilja Øvrelid, Elena Pascual, Marco Passarotti, Cenel-Augusto Perez, Guy Perrier, Slav Petrov, Jussi Piitulainen, Barbara Plank, Martin Popel, Lauma Pretkalnia, Prokopis Prokopidis, Tiina Puolakainen, Sampo Pyysalo, Alexandre Rademaker, Loganathan Ramasamy, Livy Real, Laura Rituma, Rudolf Rosa, Shadi Saleh, Manuela Sanguinetti, Baiba Saulite, Sebastian Schuster, Djamé Seddah, Wolfgang Seeker, Mojgan Seraji, Lena Shakurova, Mo Shen, Dmitry Sichinava, Natalia Silveira, Maria Simi, Radu Simionescu, Katalin Simkó, Mária Šimková, Kiril Simov, Aaron Smith, Alane Suhr, Umut Sulubacak, Zsolt Szántó, Dima Taji, Takaaki Tanaka, Reut Tsarfaty, Francis Tyers, Sumire Uematsu, Larraitz Uria, Gertjan van Noord, Viktor Varga, Veronika Vincze, Jonathan North Washington, Zdeněk Žabokrtský,

Amir Zeldes, Daniel Zeman, and Hanzhi Zhu. 2017b. Universal Dependencies 2.0. LINDAT/CLARIN digital library at the Institute of Formal and Applied Linguistics, Charles University, Prague, http://hdl.handle.net/11234/1-1983. http://hdl.handle.net/11234/1-1983.

Joakim Nivre, Marie-Catherine de Marneffe, Filip Ginter, Yoav Goldberg, Jan Hajič, Christopher Manning, Ryan McDonald, Slav Petrov, Sampo Pyysalo, Natalia Silveira, Reut Tsarfaty, and Daniel Zeman. 2016. Universal Dependencies v1: A multilingual treebank collection. In *Proceedings of the 10th International Conference on Language Resources and Evaluation (LREC 2016)*. European Language Resources Association, Portoro, Slovenia, pages 1659–1666.

Martin Potthast, Tim Gollub, Francisco Rangel, Paolo Rosso, Efstathios Stamatatos, and Benno Stein. 2014. Improving the reproducibility of PAN's shared tasks: Plagiarism detection, author identification, and author profiling. In Evangelos Kanoulas, Mihai Lupu, Paul Clough, Mark Sanderson, Mark Hall, Allan Hanbury, and Elaine Toms, editors, *Information Access Evaluation meets Multilinguality, Multimodality, and Visualization. 5th International Conference of the CLEF Initiative (CLEF 14)*. Springer, Berlin Heidelberg New York, pages 268–299. https://doi.org/10.1007/978-3-319-11382-1_22.

Milan Straka, Jan Hajic, and Jana Straková. 2016a. Ud-pipe: Trainable pipeline for processing conll-u files performing tokenization, morphological analysis, pos tagging and parsing. In *Proceedings of the Tenth International Conference on Language Resources and Evaluation (LREC 2016)*.

Milan Straka, Jan Hajič, and Jana Straková. 2016b. UDPipe: trainable pipeline for processing CoNLL-U files performing tokenization, morphological analysis, POS tagging and parsing. In *Proceedings of the 10th International Conference on Language Resources and Evaluation (LREC 2016)*. European Language Resources Association, Portoro, Slovenia.

Oscar Täckström, Ryan McDonald, and Jakob Uszkoreit. 2012. Cross-lingual word clusters for direct transfer of linguistic structure. In *NAACL*. Association for Computational Linguistics, Montréal, Canada, pages 477–487.

Kai Sheng Tai, Richard Socher, and Christopher D. Manning. 2015. Improved semantic representations from tree-structured long short-term memory networks. In *Proc. of ACL and IJCNLP*. pages 1556–1566.

Peilu Wang, Yao Qian, Frank K. Soong, Lei He, and Hai Zhao. 2016. Learning distributed word representations for bidirectional lstm recurrent neural network. In *Proc. of HLT-NAACL*.

David Weiss, Chris Alberti, Michael Collins, and Slav Petrov. 2015. Structured training for neural network transition-based parsing. *CoRR* abs/1506.06158. http://arxiv.org/abs/1506.06158.

Daniel Zeman, Martin Popel, Milan Straka, Jan Hajič, Joakim Nivre, Filip Ginter, Juhani Luotolahti, Sampo Pyysalo, Slav Petrov, Martin Potthast, Francis Tyers, Elena Badmaeva, Memduh Gökırmak, Anna Nedoluzhko, Silvie Cinková, Jan Hajič jr., Jaroslava Hlaváčová, Václava Kettnerová, Zdeňka Urešová, Jenna Kanerva, Stina Ojala, Anna Missilä, Christopher Manning, Sebastian Schuster, Siva Reddy, Dima Taji, Nizar Habash, Herman Leung, Marie-Catherine de Marneffe, Manuela Sanguinetti, Maria Simi, Hiroshi Kanayama, Valeria de Paiva, Kira Droganova, Hĕctor Martínez Alonso, Hans Uszkoreit, Vivien Macketanz, Aljoscha Burchardt, Kim Harris, Katrin Marheinecke, Georg Rehm, Tolga Kayadelen, Mohammed Attia, Ali Elkahky, Zhuoran Yu, Emily Pitler, Saran Lertpradit, Michael Mandl, Jesse Kirchner, Hector Fernandez Alcalde, Jana Strnadova, Esha Banerjee, Ruli Manurung, Antonio Stella, Atsuko Shimada, Sookyoung Kwak, Gustavo Mendonça, Tatiana Lando, Rattima Nitisaroj, and Josie Li. 2017. CoNLL 2017 Shared Task: Multilingual Parsing from Raw Text to Universal Dependencies. In *Proceedings of the CoNLL 2017 Shared Task: Multilingual Parsing from Raw Text to Universal Dependencies*. Association for Computational Linguistics.

Xiaodan Zhu, Parinaz Sobihani, and Hongyu Guo. 2015. Long short-term memory over recursive structures. In *Proc. of ICML*. pages 1604–1612.

A System for Multilingual Dependency Parsing based on Bidirectional LSTM Feature Representations

KyungTae Lim
LATTICE Laboratory
École Normale Supérieure & PSL Univ.
Univ. Sorbonne nouvelle & USPC
Paris, France
KISTI / DaeJeon, Korea
ktlim@ens.fr

Thierry Poibeau
LATTICE Laboratory
École Normale Supérieure & PSL Univ.
Univ. Sorbonne nouvelle & USPC
Paris, France
thierry.poibeau@ens.fr

Abstract

In this paper, we present our multilingual dependency parser developed for the *CoNLL 2017 UD Shared Task* dealing with "Multilingual Parsing from Raw Text to Universal Dependencies"[1]. Our parser extends the monolingual BIST-parser as a multi-source multilingual trainable parser. Thanks to multilingual word embeddings and one hot encodings for languages, our system can use both monolingual and multi-source training. We trained 69 monolingual language models and 13 multilingual models for the shared task. Our multilingual approach making use of different resources yield better results than the monolingual approach for 11 languages. Our system ranked 5th and achieved 70.93 overall LAS score over the 81 test corpora (macro-averaged LAS F1 score).

1 Introduction

Many existing parsers are trainable on monolingual data. Normally such systems take a monolingual corpus in input, along with monolingual word embeddings and possibly monolingual dictionaries as well as other knowledge sources. However for resource-poor languages such as Kurmanji and Buryat[2], there are generally not enough resources to train an efficient parser. One reasonable approach is then to infer knowledge from similar languages (Tiedemann, 2015). Developing tools to process several languages including resource-poor languages has been conducted in many different ways in the past (Heid and Raab, 1989). Thanks

to Universal Dependency (Nivre et al., 2016), it is now possible to train a system for several languages from the same set of POS tags. It has also been demonstrated that, with current machine learning approaches, parsing accuracy improves when using multilingual word embeddings (i.e. word embeddings inferred from corpora in different languages) even for resource-rich languages (Ammar et al., 2016a; Guo et al., 2015).

In this paper, we describe the development of a system using either a monolingual or multilingual strategy (depending on the kind of resources available for each language considered) for the CoNLL 2017 shared task (Zeman et al., 2017). For the multilingual model, we assume that learning over words and POS sequences is a first step from which better parsers can then be derived. For this reason, we re-used most of the training algorithms implemented for the BIST-parser since these have proven to be effective when dealing with sequential information even for long sentences, thanks to bidirectional LSTM feature representations (Kiperwasser and Goldberg, 2016).

In addition, our parser can also have recourse to multilingual word embeddings that merge different word vectors in a single vector space in order to get multi-source models. As for multilingual word embeddings, we extend the bilingual word mapping approach (Artetxe et al., 2016) to be able to deal with multilingual data. We have only used this approach based on multilingual word embeddings for two different language groups in this experiment: (*i*) for resource-poor languages for which less than 30 sentences were provided for training such as *surprise languages* and Kazakh, and (*ii*) for another group of 7 resource-rich languages that are all Indo-European languages. This is to show that even the analysis of resource-rich languages can be improved thanks to a multilingual approach.

---

[1] http://universaldependencies.org/conll17/

[2] http://universaldependencies.org/conll17/surprise.html

Proceedings of the CoNLL 2017 Shared Task: Multilingual Parsing from Raw Text to Universal Dependencies, pages 63–70,
Vancouver, Canada, August 3-4, 2017. © 2017 Association for Computational Linguistics

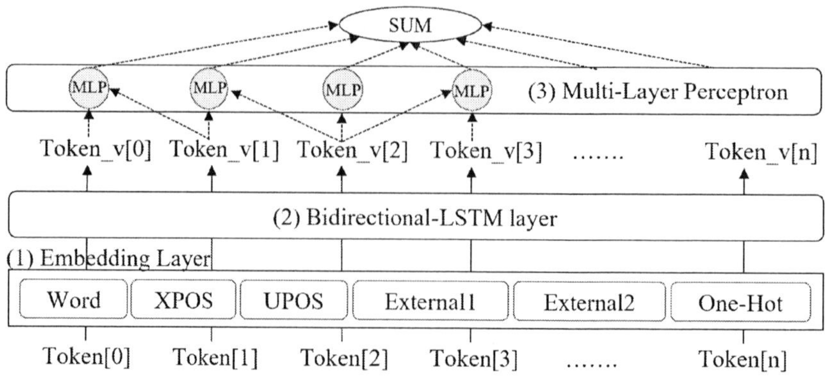

Figure 1: Overall system structure for training language models. **(1) Embedding Layer**: vectorized features that are feeding into Bidirectional LSTM. **(2) Bidirectional-LSTM**: train representation of each token as vector values based on bidirectional LSTM neural network. **(3) Multi-Layer Perceptron**: build candidate of parse trees based on trained(changed) features by bidirectional LSTM layer, and then calculate probabilistic scores for each of candidates. Finally, if it has multiple roots, revise it (section 3) or select the best parse tree.

Although we could theoretically train a single model for all the languages considered in the evaluation based on our multilingual approach, relevant results can only be obtained if one takes into account language similarities and typological information. Moreover, given the limited time and the specific resource environment designed for the shared task, it was hard to get better results using a multilingual approach than using a monolingual approach for resource-rich languages since training new word embeddings requires time. Thus, we processed 69 corpora with monolingual models, and only 13 corpora with our multilingual approach.

In what follows we describe the architecture of our system (section 2), our monolingual (section 3) as well as our multilingual approach (section 4). Finally, we compare the results with the baseline provided by UDPipe1.1 and with the results of other teams (section 5).

2 System Overview

Our system extends the Graph-based parser (Taskar et al., 2005) especially in BIST-parser that works by default with monolingual data. Basically the Graph-based BIST-parser uses bidirectional Long Short Term Memory (LSTM) feature representations thanks to two neural network layers (Kiperwasser and Goldberg, 2016). In order to select the best relation and head for each tokens in a sentence, Kiperwasser and Goldberg

link the output of the bidirectional LSTM with the Multi-Layer Perceptron (MLP) thanks to one neural layer. Here we adopt the same feature representation and MLP but different training features and decision models.

In order to adapt the parser to a multilingual approach, we add new parameters and new features to the training algorithm, notably the possibility to use multilingual word embeddings and one hot encoding to encode languages. Finally, the parser can be trained on monolingual and multilingual data depending on the parameters chosen for training. An overview of the overall architecture is given in Figure 1. Details on word embeddings along with the number of dimensions considered are given below.

- *Word*: randomly generated word embedding (100)

- **XPOS:** language-specific POS (25)

- **UPOS:** universal POS (25)

- **External embedding1:** pretrained word embedding (100)

- **External embedding2:** pretrained word embedding that is replaced with *Word* (100)

- **one-hot encoding:** one-hot encoding of the language ID (65)

Corpus	Embedding model	Bilingual Dic	Training corpora
Buryat	Buryat-Russian	wiki dump	brx(20), ru
Kurmanji	Kurmanji-English	wiki dump	kmr(20), en
North Sámi	North Sámi-Finnish	wiki dump	sme(20), fi, fi-fbt
Upper Sorbian	Upper Sorbian-Polish	OPUS	hsb(20), pl
Kazakh	Kazakh-Turkish	OPUS	kk(20), tr
Portuguese	7 languages*	Europarl7,WMT11	en, it, fr, es, pt, de, sv
Italian	7 languages*	Europarl7,WMT11	en, it, fr, es, pt, de, sv
Italian_ParTUT	7 languages*	Europarl7,WMT11	en, en_partut, fr_partut, it, it_partut
English_ParTUT	7 languages*	Europarl7,WMT11	en, en_partut, fr_partut, it_partut
French_ParTUT	7 languages*	Europarl7,WMT11	en_partut, fr(2), fr_partut, it_partut
Czech-CLTT	Czech	-	cs, cs_cac, cs_cltt
Galician-TreeGal	Galician	-	ga, ga_treegal
Slovenian-SST	Slovenian	-	sl, sl_sst

Table 1: Languages trained by a multilingual model. **Embedding model:** applied languages that were used for making multilingual word embeddings. **Bilingual Dic:** resources to generate bilingual dictionaries **Training corpora:** Training corpora that were used. **7 languages:** English, Italian, French, Spanish, Portuguese, German, Swedish. **(number):** the number of multiplication to expand the total amount of corpus.

Word refers to words taken from the training corpora and used as lexical features with vectorized embeddings in our parser. Both *XPOS* and *UPOS*[3] are used as delexicalized features. The content of *Word* and *POS* is set randomly when the training phase starts. In addition, two external word embeddings are added to the representations of words, one is concatenated with the *Word* vector additionally, and the other is used to replace the *Word* vector. For example, let *Word* be generated randomly with 100 dimensional vector values and *External1* and let *External2* be pretrained word embeddings made from different resources with 100 dimensional vector values. If we just add *External1* to an additional word embedding, then final word embedding could be *Word+External1* (200 dimensions) based on concatenation. However, if we add just *External2* as an additional word embedding, *Word* is deleted because it is replaced with *External2* so that final word embedding could be *External2* (100 dimensions). If both are used, final word embedding could be *External1 + External2* (*Word* is deleted because of *External2*). Since we have found if we can use two external word embeddings, replacing one word embedding as the *Word* made better results than concatenating two word embeddings based on experiments.

Since our goal is to develop a multilingual pars-

ing model, we took the idea of one-hot encodings from (Ammar et al., 2016a). The idea is to add language one-hot encoding as an additional feature while training multilingual models. It allows the model to directly focus on language specificities. There are 65 hot-encoding dimensions because there are 64 languages in UD 2.0 (Nivre et al., 2017) plus *unknown* languages.

3 Monolingual Model

There were 81 different corpora to be parsed within the CoNLL 2017 shared task. We used a monolingual approach for 69 corpora, and our results are detailed in section 5. As mentioned above, training a monolingual model in our system is very similar to training a BIST-parser model. However, we made two modifications to the original approach.

Multiple roots: The BIST-parser can generate multiple roots for a given sentence. This is not a problem in general but for the shared task we need to provide only one single root per sentence. Not detecting the right root for a sentence leads to major errors so the problem had to be addressed carefully. We chose to develop a simple algorithm: when the parser returns multiple roots, our system revises the overall sentence analysis so as to select one single primary root and change other previous roots as links pointing to the new head node. Choosing the primary root is the result of an

---

[3] http://universaldependencies.org/format.html

empirical process depending on the language considered (i.e. taking into account language-specific word order). For example, the primary root is the first head node in the case of an English sentence and the last one in the case of a Korean sentence. This very simple trick improved the LAS scores by 0.43 overall F1-measure on the development set.

Customizing for UD: Basically, the BIST-parser is not adapted to the Universal Dependency format. Thus several changes had to be made. First, we added both *XPOS* and *UPOS* categories to the parser. Second, if a word in a training sentence did not exist in external word embeddings, we replaced the word as a lemma of the word. Third, we used the external word embeddings provided by the shared task organizers[4] and concatenated them with the original *Word* embedding.

4 Multilingual Model

We processed 13 test corpora with our multilingual model. The F1-measure of our system for these corpora are better than with our monolingual system for resource-poor languages and even for most of the resource-rich languages.

4.1 Surprise Languages and Kazakh

There were four surprise languages provided for evaluation within the CONLL 2017 shared task: Buryat, Kurmanji, North Sámi and Upper Sorbian (all in the Universal Dependency format). Less than 30 sentences were provided for training, and Kazakh also had 30 sentences for training. We divided the training corpus in half: half od the data were set apart for development and never used for training.

Word embeddings. The first step for training multilingual model is finding topologically similar languages. Thus, we selected three languages for each surprise language in order to be able to derive multilingual word embeddings. The choice of languages was based on the *Word Atlas of Language Structures*[5] and on advices from linguists.

Bilingual Dictionary. There has been many attempts to build multilingual embeddings (Ammar et al., 2016b; Smith et al., 2017). One simple but powerful method is finding a linear transformation matrix from two monolingual embed-

dings. (Artetxe et al., 2016) propose to do this with pretrained word embeddings and bilingual dictionaries. We tried to follow their approach using monolingual embeddings provided by Facebook research[6] and building bilingual dictionaries. Unfortunately there were not many resources (even with a limited coverage) for building a bilingual dictionary in the case of surprise languages.

For some languages we were able to find bilingual dictionaries from OPUS[7]. When no corpus was available, we used Swadesh lists from Wikipedia dumps. Swadesh lists are composed of 207 bilingual words that are supposed to be *"basic concepts for the purposes of historical-comparative linguistics"*[8]. Finally, we transformed both embeddings in a single vector space.

Table1 shows details about the selected pairs of languages and the different sources used for our dictionaries. From these resources, we trained a multilingual model and after testing with the development set set apart for each pair of candidate languages, we picked up the best candidate for the different surprise languages and for Kazakh.

4.2 Italian and Portuguese

There have been several attempts aiming at training multilingual models for resource-rich languages (Guo et al., 2016; Ammar et al., 2016a). We have tested our multilingual system in a similar way as explained in the previous section for resource-rich languages, except that we of course changed the resources used. We used the multilingual word embeddings for 7 languages presented in Ammar et al.'s paper (average and brown cluster model), and then trained a multilingual model with the training set provided for the 7 languages considered. Although the size of word vectors for multilingual embeddings is almost 10 times smaller than with the monolingual embeddings made by Facebook research, the result (F1-measure) is slightly better than with the monolingual model for Italian and Portuguese, with 0.39 and 0.41 within development sets.

4.3 ParTUT corpora

We assumed that all ParTUT corpora are related with each other. Thus, we used a similar multilingual approach to parse the ParTUT corpora but we used different compositions of corpora for

---

[4]https://lindat.mff.cuni.cz/repository/xmlui/handle/11234/1-1989

[5]The Word Atlas of Language Structures provides information about different languages in the world (family, latitude and longitude, see http://wals.info).

[6]https://github.com/facebookresearch/fastText/
[7]http://opus.lingfil.uu.se/
[8]https://en.wikipedia.org/wiki/Swadesh_list

Corpus	LAS	UAS	Rank(LAS)	Rank(UAS)	Baseline(LAS)
Overall (81)	70.93	76.75	5	5	68.35
Big treebanks only (55)	75.79	80.55	5	5	73.04
PUD treebanks only (14)	70.77	77.64	4	4	68.33
Small treebanks only (8)	54.78	64.99	4	5	51.80
Surprise language only (4)	36.93	48.66	12	15	37.07
English_PUD	82.38	85.77	2	2	78.95
Russian_PUD	72.03	79.31	2	2	68.31
Spanish	85.22	88.40	2	3	81.47

Table 2: Official experiment results with rank. (number): number of corpora

Corpus	LATTICE	Baseline	Corpus	LATTICE	Baseline
Arabic_PUD	47.13	43.14	Croatian	80.96	77.18
Arabic	68.54	65.3	Hungarian	68.49	64.3
Bulgarian	85.6	83.64	Indonesian	76.6	74.61
Catalan	86.83	85.39	Italian_PUD	86.49	83.7
Czech-CAC	84.77	82.46	Japanese_PUD	77.41	76.28
Czech_PUD	80.86	79.8	Japanese	73.98	72.21
Czech	83.68	82.87	Korean	72.35	59.09
Old_Church_Slavonic	60.81	62.76	Latin-ITTB	74.33	76.98
Danish	76.47	73.38	Latin-PROIEL	55.04	57.54
Danish_PUD	71.45	66.53	Latin	51.95	43.77
German	75.09	69.11	Latvian	64.49	59.95
Greek	81.13	79.26	Dutch-LassySmall	75.67	78.15
English-LinES	76.17	72.94	Dutch	70.6	68.9
English_PUD	82.38	78.95	Norwegian-Bokmaal	85.55	83.27
English	78.91	75.84	Norwegian-Nynorsk	84.57	81.56
Spanish-AnCora	86.87	83.78	Polish	85.94	78.78
Spanish_PUD	79.87	77.65	Portuguese-BR	88.56	85.36
Spanish	85.22	81.47	Portuguese_PUD	76.56	73.96
Estonian	62.93	58.79	Romanian	81.93	79.88
Basque	72.13	69.15	Russian_PUD	72.03	68.31
Persian	82.63	79.24	Russian-SynTagRus	87.9	86.76
Finnish-FTB	79.44	74.03	Russian	78.42	74.03
Finnish_PUD	80.82	78.65	Slovak	79.23	72.75
Finnish	77.11	73.75	Slovenian	84.52	81.15
French_PUD	76.55	73.63	Swedish-LinES	78.15	74.29
French-Sequoia	83.7	79.98	Swedish_PUD	73.4	70.62
French	82.83	80.75	Swedish	81.07	76.73
Irish	64.39	61.52	Turkish_PUD	34.82	34.53
Galician	80.68	77.31	Turkish	58.89	53.19
Gothic	60.55	59.81	Uyghur	34.94	34.18
Ancient_Greek-PROIEL	60.58	65.22	Ukrainian	63.63	60.76
Ancient_Greek	51.5	56.04	Urdu	79.26	76.69
Hebrew	61.24	57.23	Vietnamese	39.87	37.47
Hindi_PUD	50.94	50.85	Chinese	61.94	57.4
Hindi	86.99	86.77	**Average**	**73.13**	**70.45**

Table 3: Official experiment results processed by monolingual models.

Corpus	LATTICE-Multi	LATTICE-Mono	Baseline
Buryat	27.08	19.7	31.5
Kurmanji	41.71	37.59	32.35
North Sámi	28.39	25.89	30.6
Upper Sorbian	50.54	41.23	53.83
Kazakh	22.11	19.98	24.51
Italian	87.75	87.98	85.28
Portuguese	84.08	84.08	82.11
English-ParTUT	80.45	77.62	73.64
French-ParTUT	83.26	80.66	77.38
Italian-ParTUT	84.09	80.36	-
Czech-CLTT	75.45	74.85	71.64
Galician-TreeGal	68.01	67.75	65.82
Slovenian-SST	49.94	48.06	46.45

Table 4: Official experiment results processed by multilingual models.

training, such as French_ParTUT with en_partut, fr_partut, it_partut and doubled-fr corpus. Finally, the best training compositions are listed in Table 1.

4.4 Czech-CLTT, Galician-TreeGal, Slovenian-SST

These three corpora have a small number of training sentences. We thus chose to train them together but with different language hot-encoding values.

5 Experimental Results

Because we wanted to focus on the dependency parsing task, we used automatically annotated corpora for testing and also trained all models with the annotated corpora provided by UDPipe (Straka et al., 2016).

As described in section 4, we used different word embeddings and training corpora for multilingual models. As for monolingual models, we simply trained the system with monolingual embeddings (see details in section 3).

Overall results. Table 2, 3 and 4 show the official results (except for it_ParTUT), using the F1-measure computed by the TIRA platform (Potthast et al., 2014) for the CoNLL 2017 Shared task[9]. Our system achieved 70.93 F1 (LAS) on the overall 81 test sets and ranked 5th out of 33 teams. The average gap between the baseline obtained with UDPipe1.1 (Straka et al., 2016) and our system is 2.58 LAS in our favor. Our system shows better results in avoiding over-fitting issues. Performance gaps are narrowed when considering only

PUD test sets (for example, our system ranked second best for processing English_PUD and Russian_PUD), which is encouraging for practical applications.

Multilingual model. Table 4 shows the results obtained when using the multilingual models on the small treebank dataset (fr_partut, ga, gl_treegal, kk, la, sl_sst, ug, uk). We ranked 4th, with 54.78 LAS score on this group of languages. However, in terms of extremely resource-poor languages (surprise languages), we have ranked only 12th, with 36.93 LAS score. This is slightly lower than the UDPipe1.1 baseline model: we assume this is the result of using half of the corpus for training surprise languages (section 4). If we compare monolingual models of surprise languages with multilingual ones, we see an improvement between 2.5 and 9.31 percent. The same kind of improvement can be observed for the ParTUT group. In this case, the multilingual approach improves performance by almost 3 points.

6 Conclusion

In this paper, we have described our system for multilingual dependency parsing that has been tested over the 81 Universal Dependency corpora provided for the CoNLL 2017 shared task. Our parser mainly extends the monolingual BIST-parser as a multi-source trainable parser. We proposed three main contributions: (*1*) the integration of multilingual word embeddings and one hot encodings for the different languages, which means our system can work using monolingual models as well as on multilingual ones. (*2*) a simple but

---

[9]http://universaldependencies.org/conll17/results.html

effective way to solve the multiple roots problem of the original BIST parser and (*3*) an original approach for the elaboration of multilingual dictionaries for resource-poor languages and the projection of monolingual word embeddings in a single vector space. Our system ranked 5th and achieved 70.93 overall F1-measure over the 81 test corpora provided for evaluation. We are confident there is room for improvement since this system is only preliminary and lots of components could be optimized. A better account of language typology could also help the process and show the benefit of linguistic knowledge in this kind of environment.

7 Acknowledgements

Kyung Tae Lim is supported by the ANR ERA-NET ATLANTIS project. This work is also supported by the LAKME project through a grant from Paris Sciences et Lettres within the framework of the IDEX (Initiatives d'Excellence) PSL reference ANR-10-IDEX-0001-02.

References

Waleed Ammar, George Mulcaire, Miguel Ballesteros, Chris Dyer, and Noah A. Smith. 2016a. One parser, many languages. *CoRR* abs/1602.01595. http://arxiv.org/abs/1602.01595.

Waleed Ammar, George Mulcaire, Yulia Tsvetkov, Guillaume Lample, Chris Dyer, and Noah A Smith. 2016b. Massively multilingual word embeddings. *arXiv preprint arXiv:1602.01925* .

Mikel Artetxe, Gorka Labaka, and Eneko Agirre. 2016. Learning principled bilingual mappings of word embeddings while preserving monolingual invariance. In *Proceedings of the 2016 Conference on Empirical Methods in Natural Language Processing*.

Jiang Guo, Wanxiang Che, David Yarowsky, Haifeng Wang, and Ting Liu. 2015. Cross-lingual dependency parsing based on distributed representations. In *Proceedings of ACL*.

Jiang Guo, Wanxiang Che, David Yarowsky, Haifeng Wang, and Ting Liu. 2016. A representation learning framework for multi-source transfer parsing. In *AAAI*. pages 2734–2740.

Ulrich Heid and Sybille Raab. 1989. Collocations in multilingual generation. In *Proceedings of the fourth conference on European chapter of the Association for Computational Linguistics*. Association for Computational Linguistics, pages 130–136.

Eliyahu Kiperwasser and Yoav Goldberg. 2016. Simple and accurate dependency parsing using bidirectional LSTM feature representations. *TACL* 4:313–327. https://transacl.org/ojs/index.php/tacl/article/view/885.

Joakim Nivre, Marie-Catherine de Marneffe, Filip Ginter, Yoav Goldberg, Jan Hajič, Christopher Manning, Ryan McDonald, Slav Petrov, Sampo Pyysalo, Natalia Silveira, Reut Tsarfaty, and Daniel Zeman. 2016. Universal Dependencies v1: A multilingual treebank collection. In *Proceedings of the 10th International Conference on Language Resources and Evaluation (LREC 2016)*. European Language Resources Association, Portorož, Slovenia, pages 1659–1666.

Joakim Nivre et al. 2017. Universal Dependencies 2.0. LINDAT/CLARIN digital library at the Institute of Formal and Applied Linguistics, Charles University, Prague, http://hdl.handle.net/11234/1-1983. http://hdl.handle.net/11234/1-1983.

Martin Potthast, Tim Gollub, Francisco Rangel, Paolo Rosso, Efstathios Stamatatos, and Benno Stein. 2014. Improving the reproducibility of PAN's shared tasks: Plagiarism detection, author identification, and author profiling. In Evangelos Kanoulas, Mihai Lupu, Paul Clough, Mark Sanderson, Mark Hall, Allan Hanbury, and Elaine Toms, editors, *Information Access Evaluation meets Multilinguality, Multimodality, and Visualization. 5th International Conference of the CLEF Initiative (CLEF 14)*. Springer, Berlin Heidelberg New York, pages 268–299. https://doi.org/10.1007/978-3-319-11382-1_22.

Samuel L. Smith, David H. P. Turban, Steven Hamblin, and Nils Y. Hammerla. 2017. Offline bilingual word vectors, orthogonal transformations and the inverted softmax. *CoRR* abs/1702.03859. http://arxiv.org/abs/1702.03859.

Milan Straka, Jan Hajič, and Jana Straková. 2016. UDPipe: trainable pipeline for processing CoNLL-U files performing tokenization, morphological analysis, POS tagging and parsing. In *Proceedings of the 10th International Conference on Language Resources and Evaluation (LREC 2016)*. European Language Resources Association, Portorož, Slovenia.

Ben Taskar, Vassil Chatalbashev, Daphne Koller, and Carlos Guestrin. 2005. Learning structured prediction models: A large margin approach. In *Proceedings of the 22nd international conference on Machine learning*. ACM, pages 896–903.

Jörg Tiedemann. 2015. Cross-lingual dependency parsing with universal dependencies and predicted pos labels. *Depling 2015* page 340.

Daniel Zeman, Martin Popel, Milan Straka, Jan Hajič, Joakim Nivre, Filip Ginter, Juhani Luotolahti, Sampo Pyysalo, Slav Petrov, Martin Potthast, Francis Tyers, Elena Badmaeva, Memduh Gökırmak,

Anna Nedoluzhko, Silvie Cinková, Jan Hajič jr., Jaroslava Hlaváčová, Václava Kettnerová, Zdeňka Urešová, Jenna Kanerva, Stina Ojala, Anna Missilä, Christopher Manning, Sebastian Schuster, Siva Reddy, Dima Taji, Nizar Habash, Herman Leung, Marie-Catherine de Marneffe, Manuela Sanguinetti, Maria Simi, Hiroshi Kanayama, Valeria de Paiva, Kira Droganova, Hĕctor Martínez Alonso, Hans Uszkoreit, Vivien Macketanz, Aljoscha Burchardt, Kim Harris, Katrin Marheinecke, Georg Rehm, Tolga Kayadelen, Mohammed Attia, Ali Elkahky, Zhuoran Yu, Emily Pitler, Saran Lertpradit, Michael Mandl, Jesse Kirchner, Hector Fernandez Alcalde, Jana Strnadova, Esha Banerjee, Ruli Manurung, Antonio Stella, Atsuko Shimada, Sookyoung Kwak, Gustavo Mendonça, Tatiana Lando, Rattima Nitisaroj, and Josie Li. 2017. CoNLL 2017 Shared Task: Multilingual Parsing from Raw Text to Universal Dependencies. In *Proceedings of the CoNLL 2017 Shared Task: Multilingual Parsing from Raw Text to Universal Dependencies*. Association for Computational Linguistics.

Adversarial Training for Cross-Domain Universal Dependency Parsing

Motoki Sato[1]   **Hitoshi Manabe**[1]   **Hiroshi Noji**[1]   **Yuji Matsumoto**[1,2]
[1] Nara Institute of Science and Technology
[2] RIKEN Center for Advanced Intelligence Project (AIP)
{ sato.motoki.sa7, manabe.hitoshi.me0, noji, matsu }@is.naist.jp

Abstract

We describe our submission to the CoNLL 2017 shared task, which exploits the shared common knowledge of a language across different domains via a domain adaptation technique. Our approach is an extension to the recently proposed adversarial training technique for domain adaptation, which we apply on top of a graph-based neural dependency parsing model on bidirectional LSTMs. In our experiments, we find our baseline graph-based parser already outperforms the official baseline model (UDPipe) by a large margin. Further, by applying our technique to the treebanks of the same language with different domains, we observe an additional gain in the performance, in particular for the domains with less training data.

1   Introduction

In the CoNLL 2017 shared task (Zeman et al., 2017), some language data is available in more than one treebanks typically from different annotation projects. While the treebanks differ in many respects such as the genre and the source of the text (i.e., original or translated text), the most notable difference is that the size of the treebanks often varies significantly. For example, there are three variants of English treebanks: *en*, *en_lines*, and *en_parunt*, in which the largest dataset *en* contains 12,543 training sentences while *en_lines* and *en_parunt* contain only 2,738 and 1,090 sentences, respectively.

In this paper, we describe our approach to improve the parser performance for the tree-banks with lesser training data (e.g., *en_lines* and *en_parunt*), by jointly learning with the dominant

treebank of the same language (e.g, *en*). We formulate our approach as a kind of domain adaptation, in which we treat the dominant treebank as the source domain while the others as the target domains.

Our approach to domain adaptation, which we call *SharedGateAdvNet*, is an extension to the recently proposed neural architecture for domain adaptation (Ganin and Lempitsky, 2015) with adversarial training (Goodfellow et al., 2014), which learns domain-invariant feature representations through an adversarial domain classifier. We extend this architecture with an additional neural layer for each domain, which captures domain-specific feature representations. To our knowledge this is the first study to apply the adversarial training-based domain adaptation to parsing.

We utilize this architecture to obtain the representation of each token of a sentence, and feed it into a graph-based dependency parsing model where each dependency arc score is calculated using bilinear attention (Dozat and Manning, 2017). Specifically, we obtain the domain-specific and domain-invariant feature representations for each token via separate bidirectional LSTMs (Bi-LSTMs), and then combine them via a gated mechanism.

Our baseline method is our reimplementation of the graph-based dependency parser with LSTMs (Dozat and Manning, 2017) trained with a single treebank. First, we observe that this model is already much stronger than the official baseline model of UDPipe (Straka et al., 2016) in most treebanks. We then apply our domain adaptation technique to the set of treebanks of the same language, and in most cases we observe a clear improvement of the scores, especially for the treebanks with lesser training data. We also try our architecture across multiple languages, i.e., a high-resource language with a large treebank, such as English,

Proceedings of the CoNLL 2017 Shared Task: Multilingual Parsing from Raw Text to Universal Dependencies, pages 71–79,
Vancouver, Canada, August 3-4, 2017. © 2017 Association for Computational Linguistics

and a low-resource language with a small data set. Interestingly, even though the mixed languages are completely different, we observe some score improvements in low-resource languages with this approach. Finally we rank the 6th place on the main result of the shared task.

2 System overview

The CoNLL 2017 shared task aims at parsing Universal Dependencies 2.0 (Nivre et al., 2017). While its concern is parsing in the wild, i.e., from the raw input text, in this work we focus only on the dependency parsing layer that receives the tokenized and POS tagged input text. For all preprocessing from sentence splitting to POS tagging, we use the provided UDPipe pipeline. For obtaining the training treebanks, we keep the gold word segmentation while assign the predicted POS tags with the UDPipe.[1]

We did a simple model selection with the development data for choosing the final submitted models. First, we trained our baseline graph-based LSTM parsing model (Section 3) independently for each treebank. Then for some languages with more than one treebank, or low-resource languages with a small treebank alone, we applied our proposed domain adaptation technique (Section 4) and obtained additional models. For treebanks for which we trained several models, we selected the best performing model on the development set in terms of LAS. For the other treebanks, we submitted our baseline graph-based parser.

For the parallel test sets (e.g., *en_pub*) with no training data, we use the model trained on the largest treebank of a target language. We did not pay much attention to the surprise languages. For Buryat (*bxr*), we just ran the model of Russian (*ru*). For the other three languages, we ran the model of English (*en*).

3 Biaffine Attention model

Our baseline model is the *biaffine* attention model (Dozat and Manning, 2017), which is an extension to the recently proposed dependency parsing method calculating the score of each arc independently from the representations of two tokens obtained by Bi-LSTMs (Kiperwasser and Goldberg, 2016). For labeled dependency parsing, this model

first predicts the best *unlabeled* dependency structure, and then assigns a label to each predicted arc with another classifier. For the first step, receiving the word and POS tag sequences as an input, the model calculates the score of every possible dependency arc. To obtain a well-formed dependency tree, these scores are given to the maximum spanning tree (MST) algorithm (Pemmaraju and Skiena, 2003), which finds the tree with the highest total score of all arcs. The overview of the biaffine model is shown in Figure 1.

Let w_t be the t-th token in the sentence. As an input the model receives the word embedding $\mathbf{w}_t \in \mathbb{R}^{d_{word}}$ and POS embedding $\mathbf{p}_t \in \mathbb{R}^{d_{pos}}$ for each w_t, which are concatenated to a vector $\mathbf{x}_t$. This input is mapped by Bi-LSTMs to a hidden vector $\mathbf{r}_t$, which is then fed into an extension of bilinear transformation called a *biaffine* function to obtain the score for an arc from w_i (head) to w_j (dependent):

$$
\begin{aligned}
\mathbf{r}_t &= \text{Bi-LSTM}(\mathbf{x}_t), & (1)\\
\mathbf{h}_i^{(arc-head)} &= \text{MLP}^{(arc-head)}(\mathbf{r}_i),\\
\mathbf{h}_j^{(arc-dep)} &= \text{MLP}^{(arc-dep)}(\mathbf{r}_j),\\
s_{i,j}^{(arc)} &= \mathbf{h}_i^{\text{T}(arc-head)} U^{(arc)} \mathbf{h}_j^{(arc-dep)}\\
&\quad + \mathbf{h}_i^{\text{T}(arc-head)} \mathbf{u}^{(arc)},
\end{aligned}
$$

where MLP is a multi layer perceptron. A weight matrix $U^{(arc)}$ determines the strength of a link from w_i to w_j while $\mathbf{u}^{(arc)}$ is used in the bias term, which controls the prior headedness of w_i.

After obtaining the best unlabeled tree from these scores, we assign the best label for every arc according to $\mathbf{s}_{i,j}^{(label)}$, in which the k-th element corresponds to the score of k-th label:

$$
\begin{aligned}
\mathbf{h}_i^{(label-head)} &= \text{MLP}^{(label-head)}(\mathbf{r}_i),\\
\mathbf{h}_j^{(label-dep)} &= \text{MLP}^{(label-dep)}(\mathbf{r}_j),\\
\mathbf{h}_{i,j}^{(label)} &= \mathbf{h}_i^{(label-head)} \oplus \mathbf{h}_j^{(label-dep)},\\
\mathbf{s}_{i,j}^{(label)} &= \mathbf{h}_i^{\text{T}(label-head)} \mathbf{U}^{(label)} \mathbf{h}_j^{(label-dep)}\\
&\quad + \mathbf{h}_{i,j}^{\text{T}(label)} W^{(label)} + \mathbf{u}^{(label)},
\end{aligned}
$$

where $\mathbf{U}^{(label)}$ is a third-order tensor, $W^{(label)}$ is a weight matrix, and $\mathbf{u}^{(label)}$ is a bias vector.

4 Domain Adaptation Techniques with Adversarial Training

Here we describe our network architectures for domain adaptation. We present two different net-

---

[1] We were not aware of the jack-knifed training data provided by the organizer at submission time.

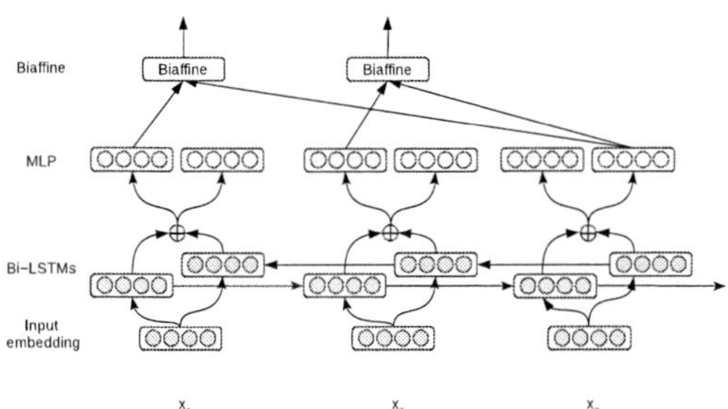

Figure 1: Overview of the biaffine model.

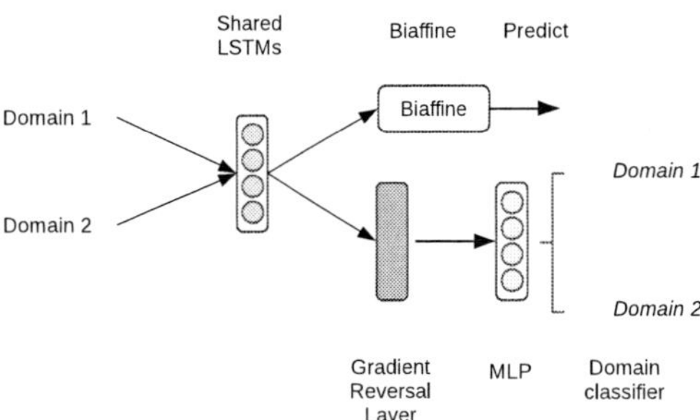

Figure 2: An application of the adversarial training for the biaffine model. In this basic architecture all domains are modeled with a common single Bi-LSTM network (Shared Bi-LSTMs).

works both using adversarial training; the main difference between them is whether we use a domain-specific feature representation for each domain. The basic architecture with adversarial training (Section 4.1) is an application of the existing domain adaptation technique (Ganin and Lempitsky, 2015) that does not employ domain-specific representations. We then extend this architecture to add a domain-specific component with a gated mechanism (Section 4.2).

In Section 5 we compare the empirical performances of these two approaches as well as several ablated settings.

4.1 Adversarial Training

Figure 2 describes the application of adversarial training (Ganin and Lempitsky, 2015) for the biaffine model. In this architecture all models for different domains are parameterized by the same LSTMs (Shared Bi-LSTMs), which output r_t (Eqn. 1) that are fed into the biaffine model. The key of this approach is a domain classifier, which also receives r_t and tries to classify the domain of the input. During training the classifier is trained to correctly classify the input domain. At the same time, we train the shared BiLSTM layers so that the domain classification task becomes harder. By this *adversarial* mechanism the model is encouraged to find the shared parameters that are not specific to a particular domain as much as possible. As a result, we expect the target domain model (with lesser training data) is trained to utilize the knowledge of the source domain effectively. Note that the domain classifier in Figure 2 is applied for every token in the input sentence.

This domain adaptation technique can be implemented by introducing the **gradient reversal layer** (GRL). The GRL has no parameters associated with it (apart from the hyper-parameter λ,

which is not updated with backpropagation). During the forward propagation GRL acts as an identity transform, while during the backpropagation GRL takes the gradient from the subsequent layer, multiplies it by λ and passes it to the preceding layer.

The parameter λ controls the trade-off between the two objectives (the domain classifier and the biaffine model) that shape the feature representation during training. The GRL layer $R_\lambda(\mathbf{x})$ for the forward and backward propagation is defined as follows:

$$R_\lambda(\mathbf{x}) = \mathbf{x}; \quad \frac{dR_\lambda}{d\mathbf{x}} = -\lambda \mathbf{I}.$$

4.2 Shared Gated Adversarial Networks

Now we present our extension to adversarial training described above, which we call the shared gated adversarial networks (*SharedGateAdvNet*).

Figure 3 shows the overall architecture. The largest difference from Figure 2 is the existence of the domain-specific Bi-LSTMs (Not-shared Bi-LSTMs) that we expect to capture the representations not fitted into the shared LSTMs and specialized to a particular domain. The model comprises of the following three components.

Shared Bi-LSTMs As in the basic model with adversarial training (Figure 2), the shared Bi-LSTMs in this model try to learn the domain invariant feature representation via a domain classifier, which facilitates effective domain adaptation.

Domain-specific Bi-LSTMs This domain-specific component captures the information that does not fit into the domain-invariant shared

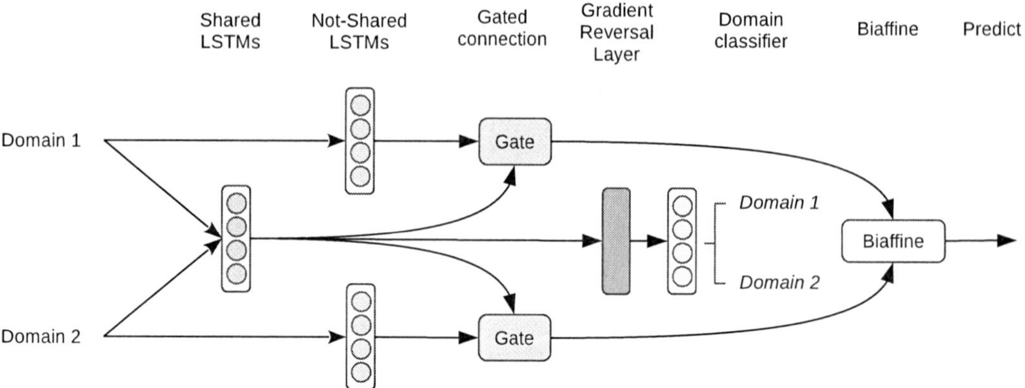

Figure 3: The architecture of SharedGateAdvNet. Each token in the input sentence is passed to the biaffine model through this network.

Bi-LSTMs. The domain-specific LSTMs exist on each domain. Figure 3 shows the case when two treebanks (domains) are trained at the same time. When training with three treebanks, there exist three Bi-LSTMs, one for each domain.

Gated connection The gated connection selects which information to use between the domain-invariant and domain-specific feature representations (the shared Bi-LSTMs and the domain-specific Bi-LSTMs). We get the combined representation $\mathbf{r}_t^{gate}$ from these two vectors as follows:

$$\mathbf{g}_t = \sigma(U^{(gate)}(\mathbf{r}_t^{dom} \oplus \mathbf{r}_t^{share}) + \mathbf{u}^{(gate)}),$$
$$\mathbf{r}_t^{gate} = \mathbf{g}_t \cdot \mathbf{r}_t^{share} + (1 - \mathbf{g}_t) \cdot \mathbf{r}_t^{dom},$$

where σ is the sigmoid function. $\mathbf{r}^{share}$ is the output of the shared Bi-LSTMs while $\mathbf{r}^{dom}$ is the output of the domain-specific Bi-LSTMs.

5 Experiments

5.1 Settings

For the settings of the biaffine models, we follow the same network settings as Dozat and Manning (2017): 3-layer, 400-dimentional LSTMs for each direction, 500-dimensional MLP for arc prediction, and 100-dimentional MLP for label prediction. We use the 100-dimensional pre-trained word embeddings trained by word2vec (Mikolov et al., 2013) [2] and the 100-dimensional randomly initialized POS tag embeddings. For the model

with adversarial training, we fix λ to 0.5.[3] We apply dropout (Srivastava et al., 2014) with a 0.33 rate at the input and output layers. For optimization, we use Adam (Kingma and Ba, 2014) with the batch size of 128 and gradient clipping of 5. We use early stopping (Caruana et al., 2001) based on the performance on the development set.

5.2 Preliminary Experiment

Before selecting the final submitted model for each treebank (Section 5.3) here we perform a small experiment on selected languages (English and French) to see the effectiveness of our domain adaptation techniques.

English experiment First, for English, we compare the performances of several domain adaptation techniques as well as the baselines without adaptation, to see which technique performs better. We compare the following six systems:

- **UDPipe**: The official baseline parser (Straka et al., 2016). This is a transition-based parser selecting each action using neural networks.

- **Biaffine**: Our reimplementation of the graph-based parser of Dozat and Manning (2017). We use Chainer (Tokui et al., 2015) for our implementation. We train this model independently on each treebank.

- **Biaffine-MIX**: A simple baseline of domain adaptation, which just trains a single biaffine model across different domains. We obtain

---

[2] The pre-trained word embeddings are provided by the CoNLL 2017 Shared Task organizers. These are trained with CommonCrawl and Wikipedia.

[3] We did not obtain any performance gains by scheduling λ in our preliminary experiments.

Method	en		en_lines		en_partut	
	UAS	LAS	UAS	LAS	UAS	LAS
UDPipe	83.83	80.13	79.00	74.68	78.26	74.23
Biaffine	86.19	82.45	81.94	77.64	80.01	75.52
Biaffine-MIX	86.19	82.28	82.23	76.95	83.34	78.02
Biaffine-MIX + Adv	86.05	82.36	82.47	77.45	83.38	78.37
SharedGateNet	86.17	82.42	82.67	**78.28**	84.06	80.09
SharedGateAdvNet	**86.27**	**82.47**	**82.69**	78.27	**84.32**	**80.35**

Table 1: The result of our preliminary English experiment across multiple domains. UDPipe and Biaffine are trained separately for each language, while the other models are trained across all domains jointly.

Method	en		en_lines		en_partut		fr		fr_partut		fr_sequoia	
	UAS	LAS	UAS	LAS	UAS	LAS	UAS	LAS	UAS	LAS	UAS	LAS
Biaffine	86.19	82.45	81.94	77.64	80.01	75.52	**90.39**	**88.11**	86.79	83.70	87.20	84.90
Ours (domain)	**86.27**	**82.47**	**82.69**	**78.27**	**84.32**	**80.35**	90.26	88.06	88.71	86.18	87.64	85.27
Ours (domain, lang)	85.47	81.75	82.03	77.58	83.60	79.51	90.07	87.71	**89.49**	**87.08**	**87.90**	**85.34**

Table 2: The result of our preliminary experiment across different languages (English and French). Ours (domain) is trained for each language across multiple domains by SharedGateAdvNet. Ours (domain, lang) is trained with all six treebanks of two languages jointly. Joint training of two languages brings a small improvement on the smaller French treebanks (fr_partut and fr_sequoia).

this by removing the domain classification component in Figure 2.

- **Biaffine-MIX + Adv**: The model in Figure 2, which shares the same parameters across multiple domains but adversarial training facilitates learning domain-invariant representations.

- **SharedGateNet**: A simpler version of our proposed architecture (Figure 3), which does not have the adversarial component but has the gated unit controlling the strength of the two, domain-invariant and domain-specific Bi-LSTMs.

- **SharedGateAdvNet**: Our full architecture (Figure 3) with both adversarial training and the gated unit.

The result is shown in Table 1. First, we find that our baseline biaffine parser already outperforms the official baseline parser (UDPipe) by a large margin (e.g., for English, 82.45 vs. 80.13 LAS), which suggests the strength of graph-based parsing with Bi-LSTMs that enable the model to capture the entire sentence as a context. By just mixing the training treebanks (Biaffine-MIX), we observe a score improvement for the domains with less data, *en_lines* and *en_parunt*, which only contain 2,738 and 1,090 sentences,

respectively. We also observe an additional small gain with adversarial training (Biaffine-MIX Adv). Comparing with this, our proposed architectures (SharedGateNet and SharedGateAdvNet) perform better. This shows the importance of having the domain-specific network layers. Our final architecture SharedGateAdvNet slightly outperforms SharedGateNet, indicating that the adversarial technique also has its own advantage.

Since SharedGateAdvNet consitently outperforms the others in English, we only try this method in the following experiments.

English and French experiment To see the effects of our approach when combining completely different data, i.e., different language treebanks, we perform a small experiment using two languages: English and French. French treebanks are also divided into three domains and also are imbalanced: *fr* (14,553 sentences), *fr_partut* (620 sentences), and *fr_sequoria* (2,231 sentences). We compare the models trained within each language (3 domains for each), and the model trained with all six treebanks of English and French. The result is shown in Figure 2. Interestingly, especially for *fr_partut* and *fr_sequoria*, we observe a small score improvement by jointly learning two languages. The best model for *fr* is the biaffine model without joint training. Note also that for *en*, the effect of the adaptation technique is very small, or

Language	UAS			LAS		
	UDPipe	Biaffine	SharedGateAdv	UDPipe	Biaffine	SharedGateAdv
ar	80.13	**82.97**	-	73.04	**76.35**	-
bg	88.02	**90.60**	-	83.22	**86.23**	-
ca	88.37	**90.57**	-	85.28	**87.42**	-
cs	88.14	**91.36**	91.23	84.68	**88.31**	88.29 (i)
cs_cac	86.81	89.03	**89.77**	83.50	85.65	**86.73** (i)
cs_cltt	72.65	75.88	**78.87**	69.01	71.43	**75.23** (i)
cu	80.41	**82.83**	-	73.19	**75.30**	-
da	78.40	**82.04**	-	74.74	**78.42**	-
de	79.40	**84.40**	-	74.11	**80.17**	-
el	82.37	**84.99**	-	78.69	**80.88**	-
en	83.83	86.19	**86.27**	80.13	82.45	**82.47** (i)
en_lines	79.00	81.94	**82.69**	74.68	77.64	**78.27** (i)
en_partut	78.26	80.01	**84.32**	74.23	75.52	**80.35** (i)
es	87.50	89.37	**89.49**	84.29	86.25	**86.33** (i)
es_ancora	87.53	**90.34**	90.26	84.54	**87.76**	87.61 (i)
et	69.26	**70.57**	-	**60.16**	59.01	-
eu	74.59	**77.58**	-	69.23	**70.06**	-
fa	83.89	**87.02**	-	79.81	**83.15**	-
fi	79.97	80.57	**81.74**	75.37	74.62	**75.98** (i)
fi_ftb	80.72	81.60	**82.21**	76.10	75.38	**76.20** (i)
fr	88.72	**90.39**	90.07	86.36	**88.11**	87.71 (ii)
fr_partut	77.82	86.79	**89.49**	73.67	83.70	**87.08** (ii)
fr_sequoia	84.35	87.20	**87.89**	81.93	84.90	**85.33** (ii)
ga	74.57	**80.28**	-	63.47	**72.70**	-
gl	80.66	83.73	**83.81**	77.17	80.08	**80.11** (i)
gl_treegal	72.32	78.48	**83.69**	66.43	73.62	**78.08** (i)
got	76.42	**78.21**	-	68.92	**70.32**	-
grc	62.12	66.13	**69.16**	55.23	58.77	**61.23** (i)
grc_proiel	77.35	80.74	**81.83**	72.03	75.43	**76.22** (i)
he	83.93	**86.12**	-	78.03	**80.13**	-
hi	91.29	**93.03**	-	86.90	**88.97**	-
hr	81.99	**85.66**	-	76.40	**79.79**	-
hu	71.52	**74.09**	-	**65.04**	63.31	-
id	80.76	**83.34**	-	74.08	**76.67**	-
it	87.77	90.09	**90.82**	85.04	87.62	**88.15** (i)
it_partut	82.02	82.66	**90.66**	78.47	78.72	**87.34** (i)
ja	94.31	**95.48**	-	92.94	**94.15**	-
kk	37.08	**64.51**	-	23.60	**37.09**	-
ko	63.71	**67.01**	-	56.41	**59.04**	-
la	56.93	67.41	**73.06**	47.13	58.65	**64.53** (i)
la_ittb	75.95	82.82	**83.29**	71.07	78.24	**78.69** (i)
la_proiel	75.31	79.30	**80.34**	69.11	72.83	**73.74** (i)
lv	56.93	**71.98**	-	47.13	**63.45**	-
nl	79.57	**85.44**	85.38	74.55	80.21	**80.28** (i)
nl_lassysmall	79.59	85.01	**86.59**	75.46	81.17	**82.53** (i)
no_bokmaal	87.52	**90.17**	-	84.38	**87.40**	-
no_nynorsk	85.79	**88.51**	-	82.49	**85.54**	-
pl	85.18	**86.84**	-	79.01	**81.15**	-
pt	88.37	90.75	**91.02**	85.20	87.84	87.79 (i)
pt_br	88.37	90.53	**90.93**	86.26	88.36	**88.75** (i)
ro	85.22	**88.04**	-	79.66	**82.35**	-
ru	80.13	82.79	**84.01**	75.07	77.14	**78.98** (i)
ru_syntagrus	89.69	**92.07**	91.86	86.84	**89.48**	89.23 (i)
sk	81.81	**84.09**	-	75.55	**77.41**	-
sl	81.81	87.12	**87.17**	80.72	**83.80**	83.73 (i)
sl_sst	63.71	77.56	**80.17**	55.39	69.67	**72.28** (i)
sv	77.94	80.32	**82.27**	73.64	75.28	**77.91** (i)
sv_lines	79.72	79.81	**82.71**	74.72	74.23	**77.87** (i)
tr	63.41	**64.77**	-	**55.70**	53.88	-
ug	62.50	74.80	**75.57**	38.46	52.67	**52.68** (iii)
uk	62.66	78.05	**79.59**	54.17	71.39	**72.93** (iii)
ur	83.05	**85.69**	-	76.15	**78.87**	-
vi	63.99	**65.98**	-	56.34	**57.91**	-
zh	74.03	**77.09**	-	68.75	**71.38**	-

Table 3: The result of our experiment for model selection on the development data. (i), (ii), and (iii) correspond to the differnt domain adaptation strategies found in the body.

negative, and these suggest our approach may be ineffective for a treebank that already contains sufficient amount of data.

Due to time constraints, we were unable to try many language pairs for joint training, but this result suggests the parser may benefit from training across different languages. For the final experiment for model selection below, we try some other pairs for some languages, and select those models when they perform better.

5.3 Model Selection

As we summarize in Section 2 we perform a simple model selection for each language with the development data in order to select the final submitted models. Besides a biaffine model with a single treebank, for some treebanks we additionally train other models with our SharedGateAdvNet. Our approach is divided into the following three strategies according to the languages:

(i) Training multiple domains within a single language. We try this for many languages, such as English (*en*), Czech (*cs*), Spanish (*es*), etc.

(ii) Training multiple domains *across* different languages. Based on the positive result of our preliminary experiment, we try this only for obtaining French models (training jointly with English treebanks).

(iii) Training two treebanks in different languages. We only try this for two very small treebanks: Ukrainian (*uk*), which we train with *en*, and Uyghur (*ug*), which we train with Russian (*ru*) that we find performs better than training with *en*.

See Table 3 for the results. Again, our baseline biaffine parser outperforms UDPipe in most treebanks. Training multiple domains in one language often brings performance gains, in particular for smaller treebanks, as in the case for English. For example, for Galician, LAS in *gl_treegal* largely improves from 73.63 to 78.08 with our joint training. The largest gain is obtained in Italian (*it_partut*), from 78.72 to 87.34, about 10 points improvement in LAS.

From these results, for example, we select our SharedGateAdvNet model for *cs_cac* while select the biaffine model for *cs*, which does not benefit from joint training.

Language	UAS			LAS		
	UDPipe	Ours	Stanford	UDPipe	Ours	Stanford
ar	71.19	**73.34**	76.59	65.30	**67.78**	71.96
ar_pub	53.55	**55.66**	58.87	43.14	**45.56**	49.50
bg	87.79	**89.95**	92.89	83.64	**85.97**	89.81
bxr	**46.97**	44.07	51.19	**31.50**	27.20	30.00
ca	88.62	**90.59**	92.88	85.39	**87.47**	90.70
cs	86.46	**89.74**	92.62	82.87	**86.50**	90.17
cs_cac	86.49	**90.09**	93.14	82.46	**86.41**	90.43
cs_cltt	76.26	**81.10**	86.02	71.64	**77.14**	82.56
cs_pub	84.42	**87.22**	89.11	79.80	**82.30**	84.42
cu	69.68	**72.19**	77.10	62.76	**65.13**	71.84
da	76.94	**80.90**	85.33	73.38	**77.08**	82.97
de	74.27	**78.43**	84.10	69.11	**74.04**	80.71
de_pub	73.64	**77.20**	80.88	66.53	**70.74**	74.86
el	83.00	**85.48**	89.73	79.26	**81.79**	87.38
en	78.87	**80.96**	84.74	75.84	**77.93**	82.23
en_lines	77.39	**81.87**	85.16	72.94	**77.53**	82.09
en_partut	77.83	**83.17**	86.10	73.64	**79.10**	82.54
en_pub	82.74	**84.75**	88.22	78.95	**81.18**	85.51
es	84.84	**87.80**	90.01	81.47	**84.25**	87.29
es_ancora	86.97	**89.93**	92.11	83.78	**87.27**	89.99
es_pub	84.71	**86.91**	88.14	77.65	**79.66**	81.05
et	67.71	**69.00**	78.08	**58.79**	57.72	71.65
eu	74.39	**77.94**	85.28	69.15	**70.71**	81.44
fa	83.36	**86.06**	89.64	79.24	**82.01**	86.31
fi	77.90	**80.17**	87.97	73.75	**74.71**	85.64
fi_ftb	78.77	**80.43**	89.24	74.03	**74.42**	86.81
fi_pub	82.24	**82.40**	90.60	**78.65**	77.11	88.47
fr	84.13	**85.88**	88.57	80.75	**82.43**	85.51
fr_partut	81.69	**84.79**	88.64	77.38	**80.31**	85.05
fr_pub	78.62	**80.32**	83.45	73.63	**75.20**	78.81
fr_sequoia	82.62	**85.85**	88.48	79.98	**83.10**	86.53
ga	72.08	**73.29**	78.50	61.52	**62.25**	70.06
gl	80.66	**83.51**	85.87	77.31	**80.13**	83.23
gl_treegal	71.17	**73.60**	78.28	65.82	**66.84**	73.39
got	67.13	**67.84**	73.10	59.81	**60.20**	66.82
grc	62.74	**68.85**	78.42	56.04	**61.28**	73.19
grc_proiel	70.42	**74.33**	78.30	65.22	**69.23**	74.25
he	61.54	**64.16**	67.70	57.23	**59.56**	63.94
hi	90.97	**92.64**	94.70	86.77	**88.70**	91.59
hi_pub	63.43	**65.29**	67.24	50.85	**52.81**	54.49
hr	83.20	**85.47**	90.11	77.18	**79.32**	85.25
hsb	**61.70**	49.38	67.83	**53.83**	41.32	60.01
hu	71.46	**71.87**	82.35	**64.30**	60.30	77.56
id	80.91	**83.11**	85.17	74.61	**76.50**	79.19
it	88.03	**89.93**	92.51	85.28	**87.39**	90.68
it_pub	87.04	**88.61**	91.08	83.70	**85.30**	88.14
ja	73.52	**74.46**	75.42	72.21	**73.27**	74.72
ja_pub	77.13	**77.65**	78.64	76.28	**76.78**	77.92
kk	**41.92**	40.12	43.51	**24.51**	22.49	25.13
kmr	**46.20**	31.68	47.71	**32.35**	23.18	35.05
ko	66.40	**71.48**	85.90	59.09	**64.46**	82.49
la	54.35	**63.60**	72.56	43.77	**52.19**	63.37
la_ittb	80.78	**85.53**	89.44	76.98	**82.20**	87.02
la_proiel	63.50	**67.68**	73.71	57.54	**61.34**	69.35
lv	67.14	**68.83**	79.26	59.95	**60.20**	74.01
nl	74.94	**79.16**	85.17	68.90	**73.22**	80.48
nl_lassysmall	81.37	**87.74**	89.56	78.15	**85.03**	87.71
no_bokmaal	86.14	**88.55**	91.60	83.27	**86.05**	89.88
no_nynorsk	84.88	**87.22**	90.75	81.56	**84.39**	88.81
pl	85.08	**86.89**	93.98	78.78	**80.68**	90.32
pt	85.77	**87.70**	89.90	82.11	**84.35**	87.65
pt_br	87.75	**90.06**	92.76	85.36	**87.73**	91.36
pt_pub	80.10	**82.58**	83.27	73.96	**76.35**	77.14
ro	85.50	**87.28**	90.43	79.88	**81.66**	85.92
ru	79.28	**82.75**	87.15	74.03	**77.63**	83.65
ru_syntagrus	89.30	**91.68**	82.31	86.76	**89.31**	75.71
ru_pub	75.67	**77.93**	94.00	68.31	**70.51**	92.60
sk	78.14	**81.11**	89.58	72.75	**75.28**	86.04
sl	84.68	**87.35**	93.34	81.15	**84.06**	91.51
sl_sst	53.79	**57.47**	61.71	46.45	**50.16**	56.02
sme	**46.06**	37.74	51.13	**30.60**	23.54	37.21
sv	80.78	**83.71**	88.50	76.73	**79.68**	85.87
sv_lines	79.18	**81.49**	86.51	74.29	**76.63**	82.89
sv_pub	75.09	**77.47**	81.90	70.62	**72.89**	78.49
tr	60.48	**62.48**	69.62	**53.19**	51.44	62.79
tr_pub	**55.01**	52.95	58.72	**34.53**	31.17	37.72
ug	**53.58**	51.45	56.86	**34.18**	33.19	39.79
uk	69.78	**70.22**	81.44	**60.76**	60.73	75.33
ur	83.67	**86.40**	87.98	76.69	**79.38**	82.28
vi	42.12	**44.01**	46.14	37.47	**38.99**	42.13
zh	61.50	**63.87**	68.95	57.40	**59.99**	65.88
AVG.	74.40	**76.35**	81.30	68.35	**70.13**	76.29

Table 4: The main result on the test data.

5.4 Evaluation on Test data

The main result of CoNLL 2017 shared task on
the test data is shown in Table 4. In addition to
the official baseline (UDPipe) and our system, we
also report the scores of the winning system by
the Stanford team. See Zeman et al. (2017) for the
overview of the other participating systems.

Our system outperforms UDPipe in many test
treebanks, 69 out of 81 treebanks. We find many
cases that UDPipe performs better are when the
training teebank is very small, e.g., Kazakh (*kk*),
Ukrainian (uk), and Uyghur (ug), or not available
at all, i.e., surprise languages: Buryat (*bxr*), Kurmanji (*kmr*), Upper Sorbian (*hsb*), and North Sàmi
(*sme*), for which our approach is somewhat naive
(Section 2) and UDPipe performs always better.
We can also see that for some treebanks (e.g., *et*,
fi_pub and *hu*), our system performs better in UAS
while worse in LAS. This may be due to the design
of the baseline biaffine model, which determines
the best unlabeled tree before assigning the labels
(Section 3), i.e., does not perform labeled parsing
as a single task.

Our system (NAIST-SATO) achieves the overall average LAS of 70.13, which is the 6th rank
among 33 participants in the shared task. UDPipe
(68.35) is the 13th rank.

6 Related Work

A related approach to us in parsing is Ammar et al.
(2016), where a single multilingual dependency
parser parses sentences in several languages. Differently from our final architecture their model
shares all parameters across different languages.
In this study, we found the importance of modeling language-specific syntactic features explicitly
with the separate Bi-LSTMs.

Our network architecture for domain adaptation
is an extension of Ganin and Lempitsky (2015),
which applies adversarial training (Goodfellow
et al., 2014) for the domain adaptation purpose.
There is little prior work applying this adversarial
domain adaptation technique to NLP tasks; Chen
et al. (2016) use it for cross-lingual sentiment classification, in which the adversarial component has
a classifier that tries to classify the language of an
input sentence. To our knowledge, this is the first
study applying adversarial training for parsing. In
addition to the simple application, we also proposed an extended architecture with the domain
specific LSTMs and demonstrated the importance

of them.

7 Conclusion

We have proposed a domain adaptation technique
with adversarial training for parsing. By applying it on the recent state-of-the-art graph-based dependency parsing model with Bi-LSTMs, we obtained a consistent score improvement, especially
for the treebanks having less training data. For
the architecture design, we found the importance
of preparing the network layer capturing the domain specific representation. We also performed a
small experiment for training across multiple languages and had an encouraging result. In this
work, we have not investigated incorporating information on language families, so a natural future
direction would be to investigate whether typological knowledge helps to select good combinations
of languages for training multilingual models.

Acknowledgments

We thank two anonymous reviewers for helpful
comments. This work was in part supported by
JSPS KAKENHI Grant Number 16H06981.

References

Waleed Ammar, George Mulcaire, Miguel Ballesteros,
Chris Dyer, and Noah A Smith. 2016. Many languages, one parser. *Transactions of the Association
for Computational Linguistics (TACL)* 5:431–444.

Rich Caruana, Steve Lawrence, and C. Lee Giles. 2001.
Overfitting in neural nets: Backpropagation, conju-
gate gradient, and early stopping. In T. K. Leen,
T. G. Dietterich, and V. Tresp, editors, *Advances
in Neural Information Processing Systems 13*, MIT
Press, pages 402–408.

Xilun Chen, Yu Sun, Ben Athiwaratkun, Claire Cardie,
and Kilian Weinberger. 2016. Adversarial deep averaging networks for cross-lingual sentiment classification. *arXiv preprint arXiv:1606.01614* .

Timothy Dozat and Christopher D Manning. 2017.
Deep biaffine attention for neural dependency pars-
ing. *Proc. International Conference on Learning
Representations (ICLR)* .

Yaroslav Ganin and Victor Lempitsky. 2015. Unsupervised domain adaptation by backpropagation. *arXiv
preprint arXiv:1409.7495* .

Ian Goodfellow, Jean Pouget-Abadie, Mehdi Mirza,
Bing Xu, David Warde-Farley, Sherjil Ozair, Aaron
Courville, and Yoshua Bengio. 2014. Generative adversarial nets. In *Advances in neural information
processing systems*. pages 2672–2680.

Diederik Kingma and Jimmy Ba. 2014. Adam: A method for stochastic optimization. *arXiv preprint arXiv:1412.6980* .

Eliyahu Kiperwasser and Yoav Goldberg. 2016. Simple and Accurate Dependency Parsing Using Bidirectional LSTM Feature Representations. *Transactions of the Association for Computational Linguistics* 4:313–327.

Tomas Mikolov, Ilya Sutskever, Kai Chen, Greg S Corrado, and Jeff Dean. 2013. Distributed representations of words and phrases and their compositionality. In *Advances in neural information processing systems*. pages 3111–3119.

Joakim Nivre, Željko Agić, Lars Ahrenberg, et al. 2017. Universal Dependencies 2.0. LINDAT/CLARIN digital library at the Institute of Formal and Applied Linguistics, Charles University, Prague. http://hdl.handle.net/11234/1-1983.

Sriram Pemmaraju and Steven S Skiena. 2003. *Computational Discrete Mathematics: Combinatorics and Graph Theory with Mathematica®*. Cambridge university press.

Nitish Srivastava, Geoffrey Hinton, Alex Krizhevsky, Ilya Sutskever, and Ruslan Salakhutdinov. 2014. Dropout: A simple way to prevent neural networks from overfitting. *Journal of Machine Learning Research* 15:1929–1958.

Milan Straka, Jan Hajič, and Jana Straková. 2016. UD-Pipe: trainable pipeline for processing CoNLL-U files performing tokenization, morphological analysis, pos tagging and parsing. In *Proceedings of the Tenth International Conference on Language Resources and Evaluation (LREC'16)*. European Language Resources Association (ELRA), Paris, France.

Seiya Tokui, Kenta Oono, Shohei Hido, and Justin Clayton. 2015. Chainer: a next-generation open source framework for deep learning. In *Proceedings of Workshop on Machine Learning Systems (LearningSys) in The Twenty-ninth Annual Conference on Neural Information Processing Systems (NIPS)*.

Daniel Zeman, Martin Popel, Milan Straka, Jan Hajič, Joakim Nivre, Filip Ginter, Juhani Luotolahti, Sampo Pyysalo, Slav Petrov, Martin Potthast, Francis Tyers, Elena Badmaeva, Memduh Gökırmak, Anna Nedoluzhko, Silvie Cinková, Jan Hajič jr., Jaroslava Hlaváčová, Václava Kettnerová, Zdeňka Urešová, Jenna Kanerva, Stina Ojala, Anna Missilä, Christopher Manning, Sebastian Schuster, Siva Reddy, Dima Taji, Nizar Habash, Herman Leung, Marie-Catherine de Marneffe, Manuela Sanguinetti, Maria Simi, Hiroshi Kanayama, Valeria de Paiva, Kira Droganova, Hěctor Martínez Alonso, Hans Uszkoreit, Vivien Macketanz, Aljoscha Burchardt, Kim Harris, Katrin Marheinecke, Georg Rehm, Tolga Kayadelen, Mohammed Attia, Ali Elkahky, Zhuoran Yu, Emily Pitler, Saran Lertpradit, Michael Mandl, Jesse Kirchner, Hector Fernandez Alcalde, Jana Strnadova, Esha Banerjee, Ruli Manurung, Antonio Stella, Atsuko Shimada, Sookyoung Kwak, Gustavo Mendonça, Tatiana Lando, Rattima Nitisaroj, and Josie Li. 2017. CoNLL 2017 Shared Task: Multilingual Parsing from Raw Text to Universal Dependencies. In *Proceedings of the CoNLL 2017 Shared Task: Multilingual Parsing from Raw Text to Universal Dependencies*. Association for Computational Linguistics.

Parsing with Context Embeddings

Ömer Kırnap   **Berkay Furkan Önder**   **Deniz Yuret**

Koç University
Artificial Intelligence Laboratory
İstanbul, Turkey
`okirnap,bonder17,dyuret@ku.edu.tr`

Abstract

We introduce *context embeddings*, dense vectors derived from a language model that represent the left/right context of a word instance, and demonstrate that context embeddings significantly improve the accuracy of our transition based parser. Our model consists of a bidirectional LSTM (BiLSTM) based language model that is pre-trained to predict words in plain text, and a multi-layer perceptron (MLP) decision model that uses features from the language model to predict the correct actions for an ArcHybrid transition based parser. We participated in the CoNLL 2017 UD Shared Task as the "Koç University" team and our system was ranked 7th out of 33 systems that parsed 81 treebanks in 49 languages.

1 Introduction

Recent studies in parsing natural language has seen a shift from shallow models that use high dimensional, sparse, hand engineered features, e.g. (Zhang and Nivre, 2011), to deeper models with dense feature vectors, e.g. (Chen and Manning, 2014). Shallow linear models cannot represent feature conjunctions that may be useful for parsing decisions, therefore designers of such models have to add specific combinations to the feature list by hand: for example Zhang and Nivre (2011) define 72 hand designed conjunctive combinations of 39 primitive features. Deep models can represent and automatically learn feature combinations that are useful for a given task, so the designer only has to come up with a list of primitive features. Two questions about feature representation still remain critical: what parts of the parser state to represent,

and how to represent these (typically discrete) features with continuous embedding vectors.

In this work we derive features for the parser from a bidirectional LSTM language model trained with pre-tokenized text to predict words in a sentence using both the left and the right context. In particular we derive *word embeddings* and *context embeddings* from the language model. Word embeddings represent the general features of a word type averaged over all its occurrences. Taking advantage of word embeddings derived from language models in other applications is common practice, however, using the same embedding for every occurrence of an ambiguous word ignores polysemy and meaning shifts. To mitigate this problem, we also construct and use *context embeddings* that represent the immediate context of a word *instance*. Context embeddings were previously shown to improve tasks such as part-of-speech induction (Yatbaz et al., 2012) and word sense induction (Başkaya et al., 2013). In this study, we derive context embeddings from the hidden states of the forward and backward LSTMs of the language model that are generated while predicting a word. These hidden states summarize the information from the left context and the right context of a word that was useful in predicting it. Our main contribution is to demonstrate that using context embeddings as features leads to a significant improvement in parsing performance.

The rest of the paper is organized as follows: Section 2 introduces basic components of a transition based neural network parser and describes related work based on their design choices. Section 3 describes the details of our model and training method. Section 4 discusses our results and Section 5 summarizes our contributions.

Proceedings of the CoNLL 2017 Shared Task: Multilingual Parsing from Raw Text to Universal Dependencies, pages 80–87,
Vancouver, Canada, August 3-4, 2017. © 2017 Association for Computational Linguistics

2 Related work

In this section, we describe related work in transition based neural network parsers in terms of their design decisions regarding common components.

2.1 Embedding words and features

In neural network parsers, words, part of speech tags, and other discrete features are represented with numeric vectors. These vectors can be initialized and optimized in a number of ways. The first choice is between binary (one-hot) vectors vs dense continuous vectors. If dense vectors are to be used, they can be initialized randomly or transferred from a model for a related task such as language modeling. Finally, once initialized, these vectors can be fixed or fine-tuned during the training of the dependency parser.

Chen and Manning (2014) initialize with pre-trained word vectors from (Collobert et al., 2011) in English and (Mikolov et al., 2013) in Chinese, and dense, randomly initialized vectors for POS tags. Similarly, Dyer et al. (2015) get pre-trained word embeddings from Bansal et al. (2014) and use POS tag vectors that are randomly initialized. Both studies fine-tune the vectors during parser training.

Kiperwasser and Goldberg (2016) start with random POS embeddings and fine-tuned word embeddings from (Dyer et al., 2015) and further optimize all embeddings during parser training. They also report that initialization with random word vectors give inferior performance.

In (Alberti et al., 2017), a character-level LSTM reads each word character by character and the last hidden state creates a *word representation*. The word representation is used as input to a word-level LSTM whose hidden states constitute the *lookahead representation* of each word. Finally, the lookahead representation is used by a *tagger* LSTM trained to predict POS tags. Concatenation of the *lookahead* and *tagger* representations of a word, together with additional features are used to represent the word in the parser model.

2.2 Feature extraction

A neural network parser uses a feature extractor that represents the state of the parser using continuous embeddings of its various elements. Chen and Manning (2014); Kiperwasser and Goldberg (2016); Andor et al. (2016) use POS tag and word embedding features of the stack's first and second words, their right and leftmost children, and the buffer's first word. They have done experiments with different subsets of those features, but they report their best performance using all of them. Alberti et al. (2017) extract the *tagger* features that are explained in 2.1 for the first and second words of the stack and the first word of the buffer plus the *lookahead* feature of buffer's first word. They also use the last two transitions executed by the parser (including shift and reduce operations) as binary encoded features in their parser model.

2.3 Decision module

A transition based parser composes the parse of a sentence by taking a number of parser actions. We name the component that picks a parser action using the extracted features the *decision module*. Chen and Manning (2014) use an MLP decision module with a hidden size of 200 whose input is a concatenation of word, POS tag, and dependency embeddings. Kuncoro et al. (2016) use an LSTM as the decision module instead, carrying internal state between actions. Dyer et al. (2015) introduce stack-LSTMs, which have the ability to recover earlier hidden states. They construct the parser state using three stack-LSTMs, representing the buffer, the stack, and the action history. Kiperwasser and Goldberg (2016) train a BiLSTM whose input is word and POS embeddings and whose hidden states are fed to an MLP that decides parsing actions.

2.4 Training

Parsing is a structured prediction problem and a number of training objectives and optimization methods have been proposed beyond simple likelihood maximization of correct parser actions.

Kiperwasser and Goldberg (2016) use dynamic oracle training proposed in (Goldberg and Nivre, 2012). In dynamic oracle training, the parser takes predicted actions rather than gold actions which lets it explore states otherwise not visited. Andor et al. (2016), use beam training based on (Collins and Roark, 2004). The objective in beam training is to maximize the probability of the whole sequence rather than a single action. Andor et al. (2016) use global normalization with beam search (Collins and Roark, 2004) which normalizes the total score of the action sequence instead of turning the score of each action into a probability. This allows the model to represent a richer set of probability distributions. They report that their MLP

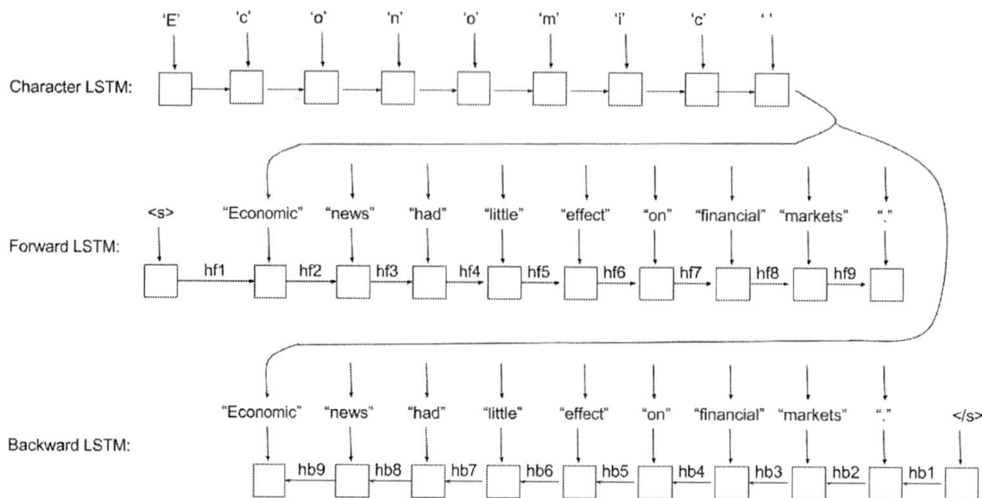

Figure 1: Processing of the sentence "Economic news had little effect on financial markets" by the bidirectional LSTM language model. Word embeddings are generated by the character LSTM. Each word is predicted (e.g. "news") by feeding the adjacent hidden states (e.g. "hf2" and "hb8") to a softmax layer.

based globally normalized parser performs better than locally normalized recurrent models.

3 Model

Our parser uses a bidirectional language model to generate word and context embeddings, an ArcHybrid transition system (Kuhlmann et al., 2011) to construct a parse tree, and a simple MLP decision module to pick the right parser actions. These components are detailed below. The model was implemented and trained using the Knet deep learning package in Julia (Yuret, 2016) and the source code is publicly available at `https://github.com/CoNLL-UD-2017`.

3.1 Language Model

We trained bidirectional language models to extract *word* and *context embeddings* using the Wikipedia data sets provided by task organizers (Ginter et al., 2017) and tokenized with UDPipe (Straka et al., 2016). Our language models consist of two parts: a character based unidirectional LSTM to produce word embeddings, and a word based bidirectional LSTM to predict words and produce context embeddings. First, each word of a sentence is padded in the beginning and the end by

a start character and an end character respectively. Next, the character based LSTM reads each word left to right and the final hidden layer is used as the *word embedding*. This step is repeated until all the words of an input sentence is mapped to dense embedding vectors. Next, those word embeddings become inputs to the BiLSTM, which tries to predict each word based on its left and right contexts. A *context embedding* for a word is created by concatenating the hidden vectors of the forward and backward LSTMs used in predicting that word.

Figure 1 depicts the language model processing an example sentence. The unidirectional character LSTM produces the word embeddings (shown for the word "Economic" in the Figure) which are fed as input to the bidirectional word LSTM. The bidirectional LSTM predicts a given word using the adjacent forward and backward hidden states at that position (e.g. the word "news" is predicted using "hf2" and "hb8").

The parser uses both word embeddings produced by the character LSTM (350 dimensions) and the context embeddings produced by the word LSTM (300+300 dimensions) as features. We did not fine-tune the LM weights during parser training.

The character and word LSTMs were trained end-to-end using backpropagation through time (Werbos, 1990) using Adam (Kingma and Ba, 2014) with default parameters and with gradients clipped at 5.0. Sentences that are longer than 28 words were skipped during LM training. In addition, if a word is longer than 65 characters, only the first 65 characters were used and the rest was ignored. The output vocabulary was restricted to the most frequent 20K words of each language. The training was stopped if there was no significant improvement in out-of-sample perplexity during the last 1M words. Table 3 includes the perplexity of each bidirectional language model we used.

3.2 The ArcHybrid transition system

We used the ArcHybrid transition system (Kuhlmann et al., 2011) in our model where the state of the parser $c = (\sigma, \beta, A)$, consists of a stack of tree fragments σ, a buffer of unused words β and a set A of dependency arcs. The initial state has an empty stack and dependency set and all words start in the buffer. The system has 3 types of transitions:

- $\text{shift}(\sigma, b|\beta, A) = (\sigma|b, \beta, A)$

- $\text{left}_d(\sigma|s, b|\beta, A) = (\sigma, b|\beta, A \cup \{(b, d, s)\})$

- $\text{right}_d(\sigma|s|t, \beta, A) = (\sigma|s, \beta, A \cup \{(s, d, t)\})$

where | denotes concatenation and (b, d, s) is a dependency arc between b (head) and s (modifier) with label d. The parser stops when the buffer is empty and there is a single word in the stack, which is assumed to be the root.

3.3 Features

Abbrev	Feature
c	context embedding
v	word embedding
p	universal POS tag
d	distance to the next word
a	number of left children
b	number of right children
A	set of left dependency labels
B	set of right dependency labels
L	dependency label of current word

Table 1: Possible features for each word

Table 1 lists the potential features our model is able to extract for each word. Context and word embeddings come from the language model. The 17 universal POS tags are mapped to 128 dimensional embedding vectors and the 37 universal dependency labels are mapped to 32 dimensional embedding vectors. These are initialized randomly and trained with the parser. To represent sets of dependency labels we simply add the embeddings of each element in the set. Each distinct left/right child count and distance is represented using a randomly initialized 16 dimensional embedding vector trained with the parser. Counts and distances larger than 10 were truncated to 10.

This leaves the question of which words to use and which of their features to extract. The transition system informs feature selection: ArcHybrid transitions directly effect the top word in the buffer and the top two words in the stack. Figure 2 lists the features that are actually extracted by our model to represent each parser state. $s0, s1, \ldots$ are stack words, $n0, n1, \ldots$ are buffer words, $s1r$ and $s0r$ are the rightmost children of the top two stack words, $n0l$ is the leftmost child of the top buffer word. The letters below each word are the features extracted for that word (using the notation in Table 1). Nonexistent features (e.g. the dependency label of $n0l$ when $n0$ does not have any left children) are represented with vectors of zeros.

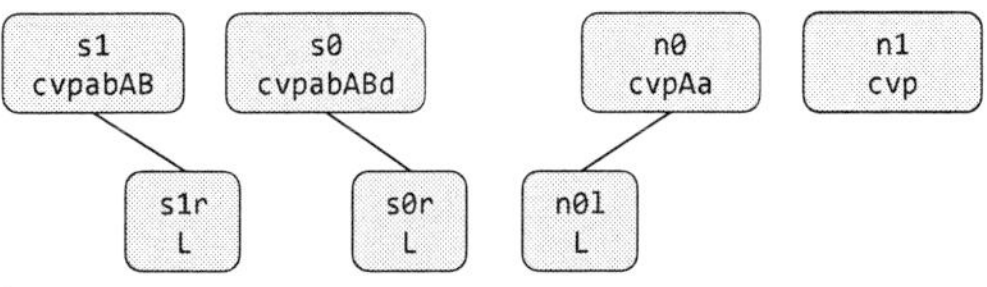

Figure 2: Features used by our model. See the text and Table 1 for an explanation of the notations.

3.4 Decision module

We use a simple MLP with a single hidden layer of 2048 units to choose parser actions. The embeddings of each feature are concatenated to provide the input to the decision module, which results in a 4664 dimensional input vector. Note that word and context embeddings come from the language model and are fixed, whereas the other embeddings are randomly initialized and trained with the MLP.

The output of the MLP is a 73 dimensional softmax layer. These represent the shift, 36 left and 36 right (labeled) actions of the parser: there are no actions for the "root" label.

To train the MLP we used Adam with a dropout rate of 0.5. We train 5 to 30 epochs, quitting with the best model when the dev score does not improve for 5 epochs.

3.5 Training

We followed different procedures for training languages that had training and development data, languages that did not have development data, and surprise languages that only had a small amount of sample data. We detail our methodology below.

3.5.1 Languages with training and development data

For most languages, a substantial amount of training data with gold parses along with development data were supplied. In this case we first trained our language models using the additional raw data (Ginter et al., 2017) provided by *CoNLL 2017 UD Shared Task Organizers* as described in 3.1. Next, the decision module (MLP part) is trained as described in 3.5 using the *context* and *word embeddings* from the language model as fixed inputs. The development data was used to determine when to stop training.

3.5.2 Languages without development data

For languages with no development data, we used 5 fold cross validation on the training data to determine the number of epochs for training. The MLP model is trained on each fold for up to 30 epochs during the 5 fold cross validation. If the LAS score on the test split does not improve for 5 epochs, training is stopped and the number of epochs to reach the best score is recorded. In the final step, the MLP model is trained using the whole training data for a number of epochs determined by the average of the 5 splits.

3.5.3 Surprise languages

The surprise languages did not come with raw data to train a language model, so we decided to use unlexicalized parsers for them. An unlexicalized model in our case is simply one that does not use the "c" and "v" features in Figure 2, i.e. no word and context embeddings. The surprise languages also did not have enough training data to train a parser. We decided that an unlexicalized parser trained on a related language may perform better than one trained on the small amount of sample data we had for each surprise language. We trained unlexicalized parsers for most of the languages

Language	Parent Language	LAS
North Sami	Estonian	60.48
Buryat	Turkish	47.68
Kurmanji	Bulgarian	46.87
Upper Sorbian	Croatian	65.98

Table 2: Parent models used for parsing surprise languages and LAS scores obtained after pre-train and finetuning.

provided in the task and tried them as "parent" languages for each surprise language. An unlexicalized model trained on the parent language was finetuned for the surprise language with its small amount of sample data. Table 2 lists the parent language used for each surprise language and the LAS score achieved on the sample data provided using 5-fold cross validation.[1]

4 Results and Discussion

We submitted our system to *CoNLL 2017 UD Shared Task* as the "Koç University" team and our scoring can be found under official *CoNLL 2017 UD Shared Task* website[2] replicated here in Table 3. All our experiments are done with UD version 2.0 datasets (Nivre et al., 2017). In this section we discuss our best/worst results relative to other task participants, and analyze the benefit of using context vectors.

4.1 Best and worst results

Looking at our best/worst results may give insights into the strengths and weaknesses of our approach. Relative to other participants, Finnish, Hungarian, and Turkish are among our best languages: all agglutinative languages with complex morphology. This may be due to our character based language model which can capture morphological features when constructing word vectors. Our worst results are in ancient languages: Ancient Greek, Gothic, Old Church Slavonic. We believe this is due to lack of raw text to construct high quality language models. Finally, our results for languages with large treebanks (Syntagrus and Czech) are also relatively worse than languages with smaller treebanks. A large treebank may offset the advantage

---

[1] Note that for two ancient languages, Gothic and Old Church Slavonic, our LM training was not successful, and we used unlexicalized models for them like the surprise languages.

[2] http://universaldependencies.org/conll17/results.html

Language	LM Perp.	Rank	LAS	Language	LM Perp.	Rank	LAS
ar	99.21	13	66.14	hsb	Not used	17	50.25
ar_pud	99.21	12	44.97	hu	27.83	4	69.55
bg	25.60	9	84.95	id	52.64	9	75.54
bxr	Not used	14	24.96	it	27.97	10	86.45
ca	18.49	10	86.09	it_pud	27.97	10	84.52
cs	37.65	20	81.55	ja	29.14	18	72.67
cs_cac	44.87	15	82.91	ja_pud	29.14	15	76.27
cs_cltt	52.64	10	73.88	kk	715.23	17	22.34
cs_pud	37.65	20	78.57	kmr	Not used	4	42.11
cu	Not used	26	58.63	ko	34.60	8	71.70
da	30.28	7	76.39	la	111.51	10	47.08
de	33.98	11	72.44	la_ittb	59.28	16	76.15
de_pud	33.98	6	70.96	la_proiel	130.01	13	59.36
el	20.14	7	81.35	lv	37.81	6	63.63
en	44.50	15	75.96	nl	32.43	11	70.24
en_lines	40.79	10	74.39	nl_lassysmall	35.62	8	80.85
en_ParTUT	51.57	11	75.71	no_bokmaal	34.38	12	83.73
en_pud	44.50	11	79.51	no_nynorsk	31.03	9	82.72
es	26.33	7	83.34	pl	27.97	9	80.84
es_ancora	26.33	9	85.63	pt	24.11	9	82.92
es_pud	26.33	8	78.74	pt_br	33.6	10	86.7
et	45.77	6	62.04	pt_pud	24.11	6	75.02
eu	39.92	8	71.47	ro	21.02	7	81.48
fa	63.29	12	79.56	ru	26.99	7	77.11
fi	29.36	5	77.72	ru_pud	26.99	3	71.2
fi_ftb	41.03	11	75.37	ru_syntagrus	29.36	20	85.24
fi_pud	29.36	4	82.37	sk	21.99	7	76.46
fr	18.76	9	81.30	sl_sst	194.75	8	49.56
fr_ParTUT	14.60	7	80.22	sme	Not used	4	37.93
fr_pud	18.76	6	76.04	sv	40.42	9	78.31
fr_sequoia	16.75	7	81.97	sv_lines	34.21	7	75.71
ga	56.32	8	63.22	sv_pud	40.42	6	72.36
gl	28.70	5	80.27	tr	57.31	6	56.8
gl_treegal	32.32	4	69.13	tr_pud	57.31	6	34.65
got	Not used	24	56.81	ug	866.74	21	31.59
grc	116.72	23	49.31	uk	36.16	6	63.76
grc_proiel	227.78	22	61.70	ur	105.38	11	77.64
he	78.75	10	58.98	vi	91.67	13	38.3
hi	37.36	10	87.23	zh	92.01	19	57.15
hi_pud	37.36	9	51.49	hr	33.29	7	79.22

Table 3: Our official results in *CoNLL 2017 UD Shared Task*

of extra information we capture from a language model trained on raw text. Our simple MLP model trained with a static oracle is probably not competitive on large datasets. Whether our pre-trained language model and context embeddings would boost the scores of more sophisticated approaches (e.g. stack-LSTMs or global normalization) is an open question.

4.2 Impact of context vectors

Feats	Hungarian	En-ParTUT	Latvian
p	63.6	76.6	55.9
v	73.5	75.9	63
c	72.2	76	63.5
v-c	76	79	67.6
p-c	78	82.5	70.6
p-v	76.6	80.8	67.7
p-fb	74.7	79.7	66.3
p-v-c	79.3	83.2	74.2

Table 4: Feature comparison results on three languages. p=postag, v=word-vector, c=context-vector, fb=Facebook-vector.

To analyze the impact of context vectors and other embeddings on parsing performance, we performed experiments on three corpora (Hungarian, English-ParTUT, Latvian) with different feature combinations. These corpora were chosen for their relatively small sizes to allow quick experimentation. We tried eight different feature combinations on each language. In each setting, we used a different subset of context, word, and postag embeddings. The "p-fb" setting uses postag embeddings and Facebook's pre-trained word embeddings (Bojanowski et al., 2016) instead of the ones from our language model. We can make some observations consistent across all three languages based on the results in Table 4:

- Word vectors from our BiLSTM language model perform slightly better than Facebook vectors (p-v vs p-fb).

- Both part-of-speech tags and context vectors have significant contributions (comparing v with p-v or v-c).

- Context vectors seem to provide independent information on top of part-of-speech tags that significantly boosts parser accuracy (p-v vs p-v-c).

5 Contributions

We introduced a transition based neural network parser that uses word and context embeddings derived from a bidirectional language model as features. Our experiments suggest that context embeddings can have a significant positive impact on parsing accuracy. Our source code is publicly available at `https://github.com/CoNLL-UD-2017`.

Acknowledgments

This work was supported by the Scientific and Technological Research Council of Turkey (TÜBİTAK) grants 114E628 and 215E201.

References

Chris Alberti, Daniel Andor, Ivan Bogatyy, Michael Collins, Dan Gillick, Lingpeng Kong, Terry Koo, Ji Ma, Mark Omernick, Slav Petrov, Chayut Thanapirom, Zora Tung, and David Weiss. 2017. Syntaxnet models for the conll 2017 shared task. *CoRR* abs/1703.04929. http://arxiv.org/abs/1703.04929.

Daniel Andor, Chris Alberti, David Weiss, Aliaksei Severyn, Alessandro Presta, Kuzman Ganchev, Slav Petrov, and Michael Collins. 2016. Globally normalized transition-based neural networks. *CoRR* abs/1603.06042. http://arxiv.org/abs/1603.06042.

Mohit Bansal, Kevin Gimpel, and Karen Livescu. 2014. Tailoring continuous word representations for dependency parsing. In *ACL (2)*. pages 809–815.

Osman Başkaya, Enis Sert, Volkan Cirik, and Deniz Yuret. 2013. Ai-ku: Using substitute vectors and co-occurrence modeling for word sense induction and disambiguation. In *Second Joint Conference on Lexical and Computational Semantics (*SEM), Volume 2: Proceedings of the Seventh International Workshop on Semantic Evaluation (SemEval 2013)*. Association for Computational Linguistics, Atlanta, Georgia, USA, pages 300–306. http://www.aclweb.org/anthology/S13-2050.

Piotr Bojanowski, Edouard Grave, Armand Joulin, and Tomas Mikolov. 2016. Enriching word vectors with subword information. *arXiv preprint arXiv:1607.04606* .

Danqi Chen and Christopher D Manning. 2014. A fast and accurate dependency parser using neural networks. In *EMNLP*. pages 740–750.

Michael Collins and Brian Roark. 2004. Incremental parsing with the perceptron algorithm. In *Proceedings of the 42nd Annual Meeting on Association for Computational Linguistics*. Association for Computational Linguistics, page 111.

Ronan Collobert, Jason Weston, Léon Bottou, Michael Karlen, Koray Kavukcuoglu, and Pavel Kuksa. 2011. Natural language processing (almost) from scratch. *Journal of Machine Learning Research* 12(Aug):2493–2537.

Chris Dyer, Miguel Ballesteros, Wang Ling, Austin Matthews, and Noah A. Smith. 2015. Transition-based dependency parsing with stack long short-term memory. *CoRR* abs/1505.08075. http://arxiv.org/abs/1505.08075.

Filip Ginter, Jan Hajič, Juhani Luotolahti, Milan Straka, and Daniel Zeman. 2017. CoNLL 2017 shared task - automatically annotated raw texts and word embeddings. LINDAT/CLARIN digital library at the Institute of Formal and Applied Linguistics, Charles University. http://hdl.handle.net/11234/1-1989.

Yoav Goldberg and Joakim Nivre. 2012. A dynamic oracle for arc-eager dependency parsing. In *COLING*. pages 959–976.

Diederik Kingma and Jimmy Ba. 2014. Adam: A method for stochastic optimization. *arXiv preprint arXiv:1412.6980* .

Eliyahu Kiperwasser and Yoav Goldberg. 2016. Simple and accurate dependency parsing using bidirectional LSTM feature representations. *CoRR* abs/1603.04351. http://arxiv.org/abs/1603.04351.

Marco Kuhlmann, Carlos Gómez-Rodríguez, and Giorgio Satta. 2011. Dynamic programming algorithms for transition-based dependency parsers. In *Proceedings of the 49th Annual Meeting of the Association for Computational Linguistics: Human Language Technologies-Volume 1*. Association for Computational Linguistics, pages 673–682.

Adhiguna Kuncoro, Yuichiro Sawai, Kevin Duh, and Yuji Matsumoto. 2016. Dependency parsing with lstms: An empirical evaluation. *CoRR* abs/1604.06529. http://arxiv.org/abs/1604.06529.

Tomas Mikolov, Ilya Sutskever, Kai Chen, Greg S Corrado, and Jeff Dean. 2013. Distributed representations of words and phrases and their compositionality. In *Advances in neural information processing systems*. pages 3111–3119.

Joakim Nivre et al. 2017. Universal Dependencies 2.0. LINDAT/CLARIN digital library at the Institute of Formal and Applied Linguistics, Charles University, Prague, http://hdl.handle.net/11234/1-1983. http://hdl.handle.net/11234/1-1983.

Milan Straka, Jan Hajič, and Jana Straková. 2016. UD-Pipe: trainable pipeline for processing CoNLL-U files performing tokenization, morphological analysis, POS tagging and parsing. In *Proceedings of the 10th International Conference on Language Resources and Evaluation (LREC 2016)*. European Language Resources Association, Portoro, Slovenia.

Paul J Werbos. 1990. Backpropagation through time: what it does and how to do it. *Proceedings of the IEEE* 78(10):1550–1560.

Mehmet Ali Yatbaz, Enis Sert, and Deniz Yuret. 2012. Learning syntactic categories using paradigmatic representations of word context. In *Proceedings of the 2012 Conference on Empirical Methods in Natural Language Processing (EMNLP-CONLL 2012)*. Association for Computational Linguistics, Jeju, Korea. http://denizyuret.blogspot.com/2012/05/learning-syntactic-categories-using.html.

Deniz Yuret. 2016. Knet: beginning deep learning with 100 lines of julia. In *Machine Learning Systems Workshop at NIPS 2016*.

Yue Zhang and Joakim Nivre. 2011. Transition-based dependency parsing with rich non-local features. In *Proceedings of the 49th Annual Meeting of the Association for Computational Linguistics: Human Language Technologies: short papers-Volume 2*. Association for Computational Linguistics, pages 188–193.

Tokenizing, POS Tagging, Lemmatizing and Parsing UD 2.0 with UDPipe

Milan Straka and **Jana Straková**
Charles University
Faculty of Mathematics and Physics
Institute of Formal and Applied Linguistics
{straka,strakova}@ufal.mff.cuni.cz

Abstract

We present an update to UDPipe 1.0 (Straka et al., 2016), a trainable pipeline which performs sentence segmentation, tokenization, POS tagging, lemmatization and dependency parsing. We provide models for all 50 languages of UD 2.0, and furthermore, the pipeline can be trained easily using data in CoNLL-U format.

For the purpose of the *CoNLL 2017 Shared Task: Multilingual Parsing from Raw Text to Universal Dependencies*, the updated UDPipe 1.1 was used as one of the baseline systems, finishing as the 13th system of 33 participants. A further improved UDPipe 1.2 participated in the shared task, placing as the 8th best system, while achieving low running times and moderately sized models.

The tool is available under open-source Mozilla Public Licence (MPL) and provides bindings for C++, Python (through `ufal.udpipe` PyPI package), Perl (through `UFAL::UDPipe` CPAN package), Java and C#.

1 Introduction

The Universal Dependencies project (Nivre et al., 2016) seeks to develop cross-linguistically consistent treebank annotation of morphology and syntax for many languages. The latest version of UD (Nivre et al., 2017a) consists of 70 dependency treebanks in 50 languages. As such, the UD project represents an excellent data source for developing multi-lingual NLP tools which perform sentence segmentation, tokenization, POS tagging, lemmatization and dependency tree parsing.

The goal of the *CoNLL 2017 Shared Task: Multilingual Parsing from Raw Text to Universal Dependencies* (*CoNLL 2017 UD Shared Task*) is to stimulate research in multi-lingual dependency parsers which process raw text only. The overview of the task and the results are presented in Zeman et al. (2017).

This paper describes UDPipe (Straka et al., 2016)[1] – an open-source tool which automatically generates sentence segmentation, tokenization, POS tagging, lemmatization and dependency trees, using UD version 2 treebanks as training data.

The contributions of this paper are:

- Description of *UDPipe 1.1 Baseline System*, which was used to provide baseline models for *CoNLL 2017 UD Shared Task* and pre-processed test sets for the *CoNLL 2017 UD Shared Task* participants. UDPipe 1.1 provided a strong baseline for the task, placing as the 13th (out of 33) best system in the official ranking. The *UDPipe 1.1 Baseline System* is described in Section 3.

- Description of *UDPipe 1.2 Participant System*, an improved variant of UDPipe 1.1, which was used as a contestant system in the *CoNLL 2017 UD Shared Task*, finishing 8th in the official ranking, while keeping very low software requirements. The *UDPipe 1.2 Participant System* is described in Section 4.

- Evaluation of search-based oracle and several transition-based system on UD 2.0 dependency trees (Section 5).

2 Related Work

There is a number of NLP pipelines available, e.g., Natural Language Processing Toolkit[2] (Bird et al.,

---

[1] http://ufal.mff.cuni.cz/udpipe
[2] NLTK, http://nltk.org

Proceedings of the CoNLL 2017 Shared Task: Multilingual Parsing from Raw Text to Universal Dependencies, pages 88–99,
Vancouver, Canada, August 3-4, 2017. © 2017 Association for Computational Linguistics

2009) or OpenNLP[3] to name a few. We designed yet another one, UDPipe, with the aim to provide extremely simple tool which can be trained easily using only a CoNLL-U file without additional resources or feature engineering.

Deep neural networks have recently achieved remarkable results in many areas of machine learning. In NLP, end-to-end approaches were initially explored by Collobert et al. (2011). With a practical method for precomputing word embeddings (Mikolov et al., 2013) and routine utilization of recurrent neural networks (Hochreiter and Schmidhuber, 1997; Cho et al., 2014), deep neural networks achieved state-of-the-art results in many NLP areas like POS tagging (Ling et al., 2015), named entity recognition (Yang et al., 2016) or machine translation (Vaswani et al., 2017). The wave of neural network parsers was started recently by Chen and Manning (2014) who presented fast and accurate transition-based parser. Many other parser models followed, employing various techniques like stack LSTM (Dyer et al., 2015), global normalization (Andor et al., 2016), biaffine attention (Dozat and Manning, 2016) or recurrent neural network grammars (Kuncoro et al., 2016), improving LAS score in English and Chinese dependency parsing by more than 2 points in 2016.

3 UDPipe 1.1 Baseline System

UDPipe 1.0 (Straka et al., 2016)[4] is a trainable pipeline performing sentence segmentation, tokenization, POS tagging, lemmatization and dependency parsing. It is fully trainable using CoNLL-U version 1 files and the pretrained models for UD 1.2 treebanks are provided.

For the purpose of the *CoNLL 2017 UD Shared Task*, we implemented a new version UDPipe 1.1 which processes CoNLL-U version 2 files. UDPipe 1.1 was used as one of the baseline systems in the shared task. *UDPipe 1.1 Baseline System* was trained and tuned in the training phase of *CoNLL 2017 UD Shared Task* on the UD 2.0 training data and the trained models and outputs were available to the participants.

In this Section, we describe the *UDPipe 1.1 Baseline System*, focusing on the differences to the previous version described in (Straka et al., 2016): the tokenizer (Section 3.1), the tagger (Sec-

tion 3.2), the parser (Section 3.3), the hyperparameter search support (Section 3.4), the training details (Section 3.5) and evaluation (Section 3.6).

3.1 Tokenizer

In UD and in CoNLL-U files, the text is structured on several levels – a *document* consists of *paragraphs* composed of (possibly partial) *sentences*, which are sequences of *tokens*. A token is also usually a *word* (unit used in further morphological and syntactic processing), but a single token may be composed of several syntactic words (for example, token *zum* consists of words *zu* and *dem* in German). The original text can be therefore reconstructed as a concatenation of tokens with adequate spaces, but not as a concatenation of words.

Sentence Segmentation and Tokenization

Sentence segmentation and tokenization is performed jointly (as it was in UDPipe 1.0) using a single-layer bidirectional GRU network which predicts for each character whether it is the last one in a sentence, the last one in a token, or not the last one in a token. Spaces are usually not allowed in tokens and therefore the network does not need to predict end-of-token before a space (it only learns to separate adjacent tokens, like for example *Hi!* or *cannot*).

Multi-Word Token Splitting

In UDPipe 1.0, a case insensitive dictionary was used to split tokens into words. This approach is beneficial if there is a fixed number of multi-word tokens in the language (which is the case for example in German).

In *UDPipe 1.1 Baseline System* we also employ automatically generated suffix rules – a token with a specific suffix is split, using the non-matching part of the token as prefix of the first words, and a fixed sequence of first word suffix and other words (e.g, in Polish we create a rule $\star lem \rightarrow \star l + em$). The rules are generated automatically by keeping all such rules present in the training data, which do not trigger incorrectly too often. The contribution of suffix rules is evaluated in Section 5.

Documents and Paragraphs

We use an improved sentence segmenter in *UDPipe 1.1 Baseline System*. The segmenter learns sentence boundaries in the text in a standard way as in *UDPipe 1.1 Baseline System*, but it omits the sentence breaks at the end of a paragraph or a document. The reason for excluding these boundaries

---

[3]https://opennlp.apache.org
[4]http://ufal.mff.cuni.cz/udpipe

from the training data is that the ends of paragraphs and documents are frequently recognized by layout (e.g. newspaper headlines) and if the recognizer is trained to recognize these sentence breaks, it tends to erroneously split regular sentences.

Additionally, we now also mark paragraph boundaries (recognized by empty lines) and document boundaries (corresponding to files being processed, storing file names as document ids) when running the segmenter.

Spaces in Tokens

Additional feature allowed in CoNLL-U version 2 files is presence of spaces in tokens. If spaces in tokens are allowed, the GRU tokenizer network must be modified to predict token breaks in front of spaces. On the other side, many UD 2.0 languages do not allow spaces in tokens (and in such languages a space in a token might confuse the following systems in the pipeline), therefore, it is configurable whether spaces in tokens are allowed, with the default being to allow spaces in tokens if there is any token with spaces in the training data.

Precise Reconstruction of Spaces

Unfortunately, neither CoNLL-U version 1 nor version 2 provide a standardized way of storing inter-token spaces which would allow reconstructing the original plain text. Therefore, *UDPipe 1.1 Baseline System* supports several UDPipe-specific MISC fields that are used for this purpose.

CoNLL-U defines `SpaceAfter=No` MISC feature which denotes that a given token is not followed by a space. We extend this scheme in a compatible way by introducing `SpacesAfter=spaces` and `SpacesBefore=spaces` fields. These fields store the spaces following and preceding this token, with `SpacesBefore` by default empty and `SpacesAfter` being by default empty or one space depending on `SpaceAfter=No` presence. Therefore, these fields are not needed if tokens are separated by no space or a single space. The spaces are encoded by a means of a C-like escaping mechanism, with escape sequences `\s`, `\t`, `\r`, `\n`, `\p`, `\\` for space, tab, CR, LF, | and \ characters, respectively.

If spaces in tokens are allowed, these spaces cannot be represented faithfully in the FORM field which disallows tabs and new line characters. Therefore, UDPipe utilizes an additional MISC field `SpacesInToken=token_with_spaces` representing the token with original spaces. Once again, with the default value being the value of the FORM field, the field is needed only if the token spaces cannot be represented in the FORM field.

All described MISC fields are generated automatically by *UDPipe 1.1 Baseline System* tokenizer, with `SpacesBefore` used only at the beginning of a sentence.

Furthermore, we also provide an optional way of storing the document-level character offsets of all tokens, using `TokenOffset` MISC field. The values of this field employ Python-like `start:end` format.

Detokenization

To train the tokenizer, the original plain texts of the CoNLL-U files are required. These plain texts can be reconstructed using the `SpaceAfter=No` feature. However, very little UD version 1 corpora contains this information. Therefore, UDPipe 1.0 offers a way of generating these features using a different raw text in the concerned language (Straka et al., 2016).

Fortunately, most UD 2.0 treebanks do include the `SpaceAfter=No` feature. We perform detokenization only for Dannish, Finnish-FTB and Slovenian-SST.

Inference

When employing the segmenter and tokenizer GRU network during inference, it is important to normalize spaces in the given text. The reason is that during training, tokens were either adjacent or separated by a single space, so we need to modify the network input during inference accordingly.

During inference, we precompute as much network operations on character embeddings as possible[5] (to be specific, we cache 6 matrix products for every character embedding in each GRU). Consequently, the inference is almost twice as fast.

3.2 Tagger

The tagger utilized by *UDPipe 1.1 Baseline System* is nearly identical to the previous version in UDPipe 1.0. A guesser generates several (UPOS, XPOS, FEATS) triplets for each word according to its last four characters, and an averaged perceptron tagger with a fixed set of features disambiguates the generated tags (Straka et al., 2016; Straková et al., 2014).

---

[5] Similarly to Devlin et al. (2014).

The lemmatizer is analogous. A guesser produces (lemma rule, UPOS) pairs, where the lemma rule generates a lemma from a word by stripping some prefix and suffix and prepending and appending new prefix and suffix. To generate correct lemma rules, the guesser generates the results not only according to the last four characters of a word, but also using word prefix. Again, the disambiguation is performed by an averaged perceptron tagger.

We prefer to perform lemmatization and POS tagging separately (not as a joint task), because we found out that utilization of two different guessers and two different feature sets improves the performance of our system (Straka et al., 2016).

The only change in *UDPipe 1.1 Baseline System* is a possibility to store lemmas not only as lemma rules, i.e., relatively, but also as "absolute" lemmas. This change was required by the fact that some languages such as Persian contain a lot of empty lemmas which are difficult to encode using relative lemma rules, and because Latin-PROIEL treebank uses `greek.expression` lemma for all Greek forms.

3.3 Dependency Parsing

UDPipe 1.0 utilizes fast transition-based neural dependency parser. The parser is based on a simple neural network with just one hidden layer and without any recurrent connections, using locally-normalized scores.

The parser offers several transition systems – a projective arc-standard system (Nivre, 2008), partially non-projective link2 system (Gómez-Rodríguez et al., 2014) and a fully non-projective swap system (Nivre, 2009). Several transition oracles are implemented – static oracles, dynamic oracle for the arc-standard system (Goldberg et al., 2014) and a search-based oracle (Straka et al., 2015). Detailed description of the parser architecture and transition systems and oracles can be found in Straka et al. (2016) and Straka et al. (2015).

The parser makes use of FORM, UPOS, FEATS and DEPREL embeddings. The form embeddings are precomputed with `word2vec` using the training data, the other embeddings are initialized randomly, and all embeddings are updated during training.

We again precompute as much network operations as possible for the input embeddings. However, to keep memory requirements and loading times reasonable, we do so only for 1000 most frequent embeddings of every type.

Because the *CoNLL 2017 UD Shared Task* did not allow sentences with multiple roots, we modified all the transition systems in UDPipe 1.1 to generate only one root node and to use the `root` dependency relation only for this node.

3.4 Hyperparameter Search Support

All three described components employ several hyperparameters which can improve performance if tuned correctly. To ease up the process, UDPipe offers random hyperparameter search for all the components – the `run=number` option during training generates pseudorandom but deterministic values for predefined hyperparameters. The hyperparameters are supposed to be tuned for every component individually, and then merged.

3.5 Training the UDPipe 1.1 Baseline System

When developing the *UDPipe 1.1 Baseline System* in the training phase of *CoNLL 2017 UD Shared Task*, the testing data were not yet available for the participants. Therefore a new data split was created from the available training and development data: the performance of the models was evaluated on the development data, and part of the training data was put aside and used to tune the hyperparameters. This *baselinemodel-split* of the UD 2.0 data is provided together with the baseline modes from Straka (2017).

The following subsections describe the details of training the *UDPipe 1.1 Baseline System*.

Tokenizer

The segmenter and tokenizer network employs character embeddings and GRU cells of dimension 24. The network was trained using dropout both before and after the recurrent units, using the Adam optimization algorithm (Kingma and Ba, 2014). Suitable batch size, dropout probability, learning rate and number of training epochs was tuned on the *tune* set.

Tagger

The tagger and the lemmatizer do not use any hyperparameters which require tuning. The guesser hyperparameter were tuned on the tune set.

Parser

The parser network employs form embeddings of dimension 50, and UPOS, FEATS and DEPREL embeddings of dimension 20. The hidden layer has dimension 200, batch consists of 10 words and the network was trained for 10 iterations. The suitable transition system, oracle, learning rate and L2 regularization was chosen to maximize the accuracy on the tune set.

3.6 Evaluation of the UDPipe 1.1 Baseline System

There are three testing collections in *CoNLL 2017 UD Shared Task*: UD 2.0 test data, new parallel treebank (PUD) sets, and four surprise languages.

The *UDPipe 1.1 Baseline System* models were completely trained, released and "frozen" on the UD 2.0 training and development data with a new split (see the previous Section 3.5) already in the training phase of the *CoNLL 2017 UD Shared Task* on the UD 2.0 training data, unlike the participant systems, which could use the full training data for training and development data for tuning.

We used the *UDPipe 1.1 Baseline System* models for evaluation of the completely new parallel treebank (PUD) set and completely new surprise languages in the following way:

For the new parallel treebank sets we utilized the "main" treebank for each language (e.g., for Finish `fi` instead of `fi_ftb`). This arbitrary decision was a lucky one – after the shared task evaluation, the performance on the parallel treebanks was shown to be significantly worse if different treebanks than the "main" were used (even if they were larger or provided higher LAS on their own test set). The reason seem to be the inconsistencies among the treebanks of the same language – the Universal Dependencies are yet not so universal as everyone would like.

To parse the surprise languages, we employed a baseline model which resulted in highest LAS F1-score on the surprise language sample data – resulting in Finnish FTB, Polish, Finnish FTB and Slovak models for the surprise languages Buryat, Kurmanji, North Sámi and Upper Sorbian, respectively. Naturally, most words of a surprise language are not recognized by a baseline model for a different language. Conveniently, the UPOS tags and FEATS are shared across languages, allowing the baseline model to operate similarly to a delexicalized parser.

4 UDPipe 1.2 Participant System

We further updated the *UDPipe 1.1 Baseline System* to participate in *CoNLL 2017 UD Shared Task* with an improved *UDPipe 1.2 Participant System*.

As participants of the shared task, we trained the system using the whole training data and searched for hyperparameters using the development data (instead of using the *baselinemodelsplit* described in Section 3.5). Although the data size increase is not exactly a change in the system itself, it improves performance, especially for smaller treebanks.

4.1 Hyperparameter Changes

While tokenization and segmentation is straightforward in some languages, it is quite complex in others (notably in Japanese and Chinese, which do not use spaces for word separation, or in Vietnamese, in which many tokens contain spaces). In order to improve the performance on these languages we increased the embedding dimension and GRU cell dimension in the tokenizer from 24 to 64.

We increased form embedding dimension in the parser from 50 to 64 (larger dimensions showed no more improvements on the development set) and also trained the parser for 20 iterations over the training data instead of 10.

Furthermore, instead of using beam of size 5 during parsing as in *UDPipe 1.1 Baseline System*, we tuned the beam size individually for each treebank, choosing 5, 10, 15 or 20 according to resulting LAS on a development set.

4.2 Merging Treebanks of the Same Language

For several languages, there are multiple treebanks available in the UD 2.0 collection. Ideally, one would merge all training data of all treebanks of a given language. However, according to our preliminary experiments, the annotation is not perfectly consistent even across treebanks of the same language. Still, additional training data, albeit imperfect, could benefit small treebanks.

We therefore attempt to exploit these multiplex treebanks by enriching each treebank's training data with training data from other treebanks of the same language. Given a treebank for which another treebanks of the same language exist, we evaluate performance of several such expansions

Treebank	Maximum sentence length	Changed sentence boundary log-probability	Every sentence log-probability
Gothic	20	-0.5	-0.9
Latin-PROIEL	25	-0.4	-0.7
Slovenian-SST	15	-0.7	-0.9

Table 1: Hyperparameters for joint segmentation and parsing.

and choose the best according to LAS score on the development data of the treebank in question. We extend the original training data by adding random sentences from the additional treebanks of the same language – we consider subsets containing $\frac{1}{4}$, $\frac{1}{2}$, 1 and 2 times the size of the original treebank.

4.3 Joint Sentence Segmentation and Parsing

Some treebanks are very difficult to segment into sentences due to missing punctuation, which harms the parser performance. We segment three smallest treebanks of this kind (namely Gothic, Latin-PROIEL and Slovenian-SST) jointly with the parser, by choosing such sentence segmentation which maximizes likelihood of their parse trees.

In order to determine the segmentation with maximum parsing likelihood, we evaluate every possible segmentation with sentences up to a given maximum length L. Because likelihoods of parse trees are independent, we can utilize dynamic programming and find the best segmentation in polynomial time by parsing sentences of lengths 1 to L at every location in the original text. Therefore, the procedure has the same complexity as parsing text which is circa $L^2/2$ times longer than the original one.

Additionally, we incorporate the segmentation suggested by the tokenizer in the likelihood of the parse trees – we multiply the tree likelihood by a fixed probability for each sentence boundary different than the one returned by the tokenizer.

However, if a transition-based parser is used, the optimum solution for the algorithm described so far would probably be to segment the text into one-token sentences, due to the fact that for a single word there is only one possible sequence of transitions (to make the word a root node), which has therefore probability one. Consequently, we introduce a third hyperparameter, which is an additional "cost" for every sentence.

We tuned the three described hyperparameters for every treebank independently to maximize LAS score on development set. The chosen hyperparameter values are shown in Table 1.

We expect graphical parsing models to benefit even more from this kind of joint segmentation – for every word, one can compute the probability distribution of attaching it as a dependent to all words within a distance of L (including the word itself, which represents the word being a root node). Then, the likelihood of a single-word sentence would not be one, but would take into account the possibility of attaching the word as a dependent to every near word.

5 Experiments and Results

The official *CoNLL 2017 UD Shared Task* evaluation was performed using a TIRA platform (Potthast et al., 2014), which provided virtual machines for every participants' systems. During test data evaluation, the machines were disconnected from the internet, and reset after the evaluation finished – this way, the entire test sets were kept private even during the evaluation.

In addition to official results, we also report results of supplementary experiments. These were evaluated after the shared task, using the released test data (Nivre et al., 2017b). All results are produced using the official evaluation script.

Because only plain text (and not gold tokenization) is used as input, all results are in fact F1-scores and always take tokenization performance into account.

The complete *UDPipe 1.2 Participant System* scores are shown in Table 2. We also include LAS F1-score of the *UDPipe 1.1 Baseline System* for reference. Note that due to time constraints, some *UDPipe 1.2 Participant System* submitted models did not generate any XPOS and lemmas. In these cases, we show XPOS and lemmatization results using post-competition models and typeset them in italic.

| Treebank | UDPipe 1.2 Participant System | | | | | | | | | | | Baseline |
	Tokens	Words	Sents	Words	UPOS	XPOS	Feats	AllTags	Lemmas	UAS	LAS	LAS
Ancient Greek	99.96	99.96	98.73	99.96	85.55	*43.69*	73.30	*43.67*	82.89	65.37	**57.39**	56.04
Ancient Greek-PROIEL	100.00	100.00	47.09	100.00	95.60	*93.34*	87.66	*84.85*	92.73	71.72	**66.51**	65.22
Arabic	99.98	93.71	81.77	93.71	88.26	83.27	83.40	82.08	87.34	71.69	**66.06**	65.30
Basque	99.96	99.96	99.50	99.96	92.33	99.96	87.25	84.66	93.49	75.59	**70.45**	69.15
Bulgarian	99.92	99.92	92.85	99.92	97.72	94.57	95.55	94.01	94.60	88.82	**84.92**	83.64
Catalan	99.97	99.97	99.03	99.97	98.00	98.00	97.20	96.56	97.87	88.69	**85.53**	85.39
Chinese	89.55	89.55	98.20	89.55	83.47	83.38	88.28	82.13	89.54	61.81	**57.89**	57.40
Croatian	99.90	99.90	95.56	99.90	95.88	99.90	84.34	83.43	94.33	83.73	**77.73**	77.18
Czech	99.93	99.93	92.30	99.93	98.23	92.71	91.97	91.60	97.82	86.73	**83.19**	82.87
Czech-CAC	99.97	99.96	100.00	99.96	98.34	*91.92*	90.53	*90.36*	*97.31*	88.21	**84.40**	82.46
Czech-CLTT	99.34	99.34	94.19	99.34	95.49	*88.07*	86.14	*85.04*	96.79	80.52	**76.69**	71.64
Danish	99.60	99.60	78.97	99.60	95.28	99.60	94.37	93.25	94.51	78.91	**75.28**	73.38
Dutch	99.80	99.80	76.95	99.80	91.33	88.05	89.23	86.94	89.77	76.50	**70.52**	68.90
Dutch-LassySmall	99.99	99.99	81.83	99.99	97.43	99.99	97.17	96.39	97.99	82.76	**80.15**	78.15
English	99.03	99.03	75.33	99.03	93.50	92.88	94.44	91.48	96.10	80.34	**77.25**	75.84
English-LinES	99.92	99.92	87.40	99.92	94.87	*92.01*	99.39	*98.34*	79.06		**74.92**	72.94
English-ParTUT	99.57	99.55	98.40	99.55	93.41	*91.92*	91.45	*89.83*	96.39	81.13	**76.89**	73.64
Estonian	99.89	99.89	93.66	99.89	87.60	89.98	81.14	78.99	80.96	68.65	**60.01**	58.79
Finnish	99.69	99.69	86.75	99.69	94.49	95.68	91.42	90.35	86.49	80.74	**77.26**	73.75
Finnish-FTB	99.97	99.96	85.54	99.96	92.28	91.05	92.53	89.41	88.68	79.69	**75.31**	74.03
French	99.76	98.88	94.58	98.88	95.49	98.88	95.42	94.26	96.59	84.09	**80.50**	80.75
French-ParTUT	99.85	98.97	97.76	98.97	95.38	*85.35*	91.23	*82.06*	94.87	84.03	**80.17**	77.38
French-Sequoia	99.76	99.06	84.60	99.06	95.63	99.06	94.74	93.59	96.82	84.06	**81.35**	79.98
Galician	99.93	99.93	96.18	99.93	96.93	96.44	99.70	96.08	96.93	81.95	**77.73**	77.31
Galician-TreeGal	99.62	98.66	85.35	98.66	91.08	87.70	89.84	86.90	92.56	71.59	**66.31**	65.82
German	99.67	99.67	79.35	99.67	90.72	94.65	80.46	76.26	95.38	74.15	**68.61**	69.11
Gothic	100.00	100.00	24.12	100.00	94.32	94.87	87.06	85.03	92.45	69.26	**62.80**	59.81
Greek	99.87	99.87	90.00	99.87	95.35	95.35	89.89	88.62	94.44	84.31	**80.67**	79.26
Hebrew	99.98	85.16	100.00	85.16	80.87	80.87	77.57	76.78	79.58	62.06	**57.86**	57.23
Hindi	100.00	100.00	99.20	100.00	95.75	94.82	90.12	87.57	98.00	91.45	**87.28**	86.77
Hungarian	99.81	99.81	95.54	99.81	90.80	99.81	70.59	69.57	88.40	72.36	**66.54**	64.30
Indonesian	100.00	100.00	91.73	100.00	93.43	100.00	99.52	93.42	100.00	81.67	**75.47**	74.61
Irish	99.40	99.40	94.78	99.40	88.86	87.90	76.27	73.53	85.45	73.10	**62.87**	61.52
Italian	99.91	99.83	97.11	99.83	97.31	*97.06*	97.20	96.26	*97.34*	88.62	**86.11**	85.28
Japanese	90.97	90.97	95.01	90.97	88.19	90.97	90.95	88.19	90.19	75.81	**74.49**	72.21
Kazakh	96.07	95.63	81.23	95.63	50.69	50.56	46.06	39.57	59.46	41.77	**25.43**	24.51
Korean	99.69	99.69	92.41	99.69	94.22	89.13	99.34	89.13	99.32	66.64	**60.30**	59.09
Latin	99.99	99.99	98.56	99.99	83.66	68.03	72.75	68.02	51.85	57.57	**47.02**	43.77
Latin-ITTB	99.89	99.89	82.58	99.89	96.83	*91.58*	93.50	*89.71*	*97.61*	79.74	75.84	**76.98**
Latin-PROIEL	100.00	100.00	19.56	100.00	95.00	95.08	87.94	86.89	94.91	66.45	**61.55**	57.54
Latvian	98.94	98.94	98.32	98.94	88.40	75.00	82.02	74.45	86.76	68.38	**61.80**	59.95
Norwegian-Bokmaal	99.79	99.79	96.38	99.79	96.83	99.79	95.25	94.38	96.66	86.62	**83.89**	83.27
Norwegian-Nynorsk	99.93	99.93	92.08	99.93	96.54	99.93	95.02	94.15	96.48	85.86	**82.74**	81.56
Old Church Slavonic	99.99	99.99	40.94	99.99	93.55	93.60	86.72	85.43	90.69	72.60	**66.29**	62.76
Persian	100.00	99.65	97.76	99.65	96.02	95.94	96.09	95.36	93.58	84.18	**80.33**	79.24
Polish	99.98	99.87	99.18	99.87	95.43	83.36	83.46	81.35	93.34	86.31	**80.21**	78.78
Portuguese	99.66	99.54	89.24	99.54	96.30	72.63	93.36	71.59	96.70	86.30	**82.72**	82.11
Portuguese-BR	99.96	99.86	96.71	99.86	97.07	97.07	99.72	97.05	98.75	88.18	**85.97**	85.36
Romanian	99.67	99.67	93.72	99.67	96.62	95.87	96.05	95.71	96.54	85.74	**80.32**	79.88
Russian	99.90	99.90	96.59	99.90	94.69	94.38	84.17	82.61	74.91	80.94	**76.15**	74.03
Russian-SynTagRus	99.58	99.58	97.97	99.58	98.91	99.58	93.45	93.11	95.43	89.35	**86.80**	86.76
Slovak	100.00	100.00	84.26	100.00	92.85	77.32	79.61	76.93	86.17	80.78	**75.63**	72.75
Slovenian	99.96	99.96	98.86	99.96	96.11	88.01	88.33	87.50	95.27	85.37	**81.84**	81.15
Slovenian-SST	99.87	99.87	13.13	99.87	91.78	*86.40*	85.32	*82.33*	93.79	59.26	**53.94**	46.45
Spanish	99.91	99.74	95.26	99.74	95.54	99.74	96.10	93.70	95.89	85.32	**81.95**	81.47
Spanish-AnCora	99.97	99.95	98.26	99.95	98.14	98.14	97.57	96.89	98.09	87.91	**84.95**	83.78
Swedish	99.86	99.86	95.57	99.86	95.66	93.92	94.43	92.85	95.48	81.67	**77.58**	76.73
Swedish-LinES	99.97	99.97	86.43	99.97	94.26	*91.27*	99.60	*90.04*	98.53	80.14	**75.57**	74.29
Turkish	99.85	97.92	96.89	97.92	91.51	90.58	86.70	84.60	89.60	60.78	**53.78**	53.19
Ukrainian	99.66	99.66	94.84	99.66	87.33	70.77	71.00	69.74	86.64	69.28	**61.09**	60.76
Urdu	100.00	100.00	98.32	100.00	92.13	89.93	80.31	76.03	93.04	83.86	**77.09**	76.69
Uyghur	99.94	99.94	65.31	99.94	76.09	79.04	99.94	75.57	99.94	53.49	33.21	**34.18**
Vietnamese	84.26	84.26	92.87	84.26	75.29	73.30	83.93	73.26	83.54	44.99	**39.97**	37.47
Arabic-PUD	80.85	90.81	98.95	90.81	70.39	0.00	22.73	0.00	0.00	54.57	**44.34**	43.14
Czech-PUD	99.28	99.28	95.40	99.28	96.57	89.92	88.33	87.69	95.37	84.50	79.67	**79.80**
German-PUD	97.90	97.94	90.75	97.94	84.46	20.40	31.77	1.55	3.10	73.75	66.05	**66.53**
English-PUD	99.74	99.74	95.57	99.74	94.11	92.99	94.19	90.13	95.47	82.80	**79.21**	78.95
Spanish-PUD	99.48	99.43	94.14	99.43	88.17	1.76	54.21	0.00	3.43	84.96	**77.99**	77.65
Finnish-PUD	99.63	99.63	92.20	99.63	95.84	0.00	93.75	0.00	86.50	83.89	**80.86**	78.65
French-PUD	99.81	98.86	93.33	98.86	88.00	2.39	58.65	0.00	4.79	79.64	**74.19**	73.63
Hindi-PUD	98.78	98.78	93.26	98.78	84.69	33.09	18.11	4.80	0.00	65.56	**52.53**	50.85
Italian-PUD	99.64	99.22	94.11	99.22	93.10	*2.47*	57.26	*2.47*	95.52	87.39	**84.03**	83.70
Japanese-PUD	92.41	92.41	95.04	92.41	90.02	7.65	53.75	7.07	91.39	79.26	**78.36**	76.28
Portuguese-PUD	99.27	99.39	95.94	99.39	88.45	0.00	59.22	0.00	12.57	80.32	**74.43**	73.96
Russian-PUD	97.25	97.25	98.51	97.25	85.86	78.82	38.20	34.28	0.00	76.69	**69.37**	68.31
Swedish-PUD	98.35	98.35	94.44	98.35	91.16	88.07	74.58	73.09	84.55	75.43	**70.88**	70.62
Turkish-PUD	99.13	96.93	90.87	96.93	71.38	0.00	23.67	0.00	0.09	53.58	34.12	**34.53**
Buryat (surprise)	99.35	99.35	91.81	99.35	84.12	99.35	81.65	78.08	81.40	41.64	21.58	**31.50**
Kurmanji (surprise)	99.01	98.85	97.02	98.85	90.04	89.84	81.61	80.62	89.76	46.33	**32.89**	32.35
North Sámi (surprise)	99.88	99.88	98.79	99.88	86.81	88.98	81.93	77.76	81.86	45.53	**33.62**	30.60
Upper Sorbian (surprise)	99.84	99.84	90.69	99.84	90.30	99.84	74.20	72.43	87.70	63.34	**55.76**	53.83
Average Score	98.89	98.63	88.68	98.63	91.22	*79.48*	82.50	*73.47*	82.64	75.39	**69.52**	68.35

Table 2: Full results of *UDPipe 1.2 Participant System* and LAS F1-score of *UDPipe 1.1 Baseline System* for reference. The results in italic are not part of the official results and were generated using post-competition models due to time constraints.

Treebank	Enlarged training data using other treebanks							Original training data only						
	UPOS	XPOS	Feats	AllTags	Lemmas	UAS	LAS	UPOS	XPOS	Feats	AllTags	Lemmas	UAS	LAS
Ancient Greek	**85.55**	*43.69*	73.30	*43.67*	*82.89*	**65.37**	57.39	82.37	**72.33**	**85.82**	**72.32**	82.63	64.05	**57.44**
Ancient Greek-PROIEL	95.60	*93.34*	87.66	*84.85*	*92.73*	**71.72**	**66.51**	**95.74**	**95.94**	**88.49**	**87.04**	92.66	71.29	66.49
Czech-CAC	**98.34**	*91.92*	**90.53**	*90.36*	*97.31*	**88.21**	**84.40**	98.17	90.64	89.43	88.51	97.04	86.17	81.88
Czech-CLTT	95.49	*88.07*	86.14	*85.04*	*96.79*	**80.52**	**76.69**	**96.28**	86.86	**87.02**	86.75	95.56	78.66	74.67
English-LinES	94.87	*92.01*	99.39	*90.41*	98.34	79.06	74.92	**94.94**	**92.56**	**99.92**	**90.87**	**99.92**	**79.30**	**75.20**
English-ParTUT	**93.41**	*91.92*	91.45	*89.83*	96.39	**81.13**	**76.89**	93.08	**92.85**	**92.23**	**90.84**	**96.50**	79.86	75.31
French-ParTUT	**95.38**	*85.35*	91.23	*82.06*	*94.87*	**84.03**	**80.17**	94.48	**94.23**	**91.89**	**90.75**	94.29	83.24	79.07
Italian	**97.31**	*97.06*	**97.20**	*96.26*	*97.34*	**88.62**	**86.11**	97.22	97.04	97.00	96.14	97.28	88.53	85.72
Latin-ITTB	96.83	*91.58*	93.50	*89.71*	*97.61*	79.74	75.84	**97.15**	**92.64**	**93.51**	**91.24**	**97.73**	**80.03**	**76.26**
Slovenian-SST	**91.78**	*86.40*	**85.32**	*82.33*	*93.79*	**59.26**	**53.94**	88.90	81.59	81.77	79.12	91.39	53.60	47.50
Swedish-LinES	94.26	*91.27*	99.60	*90.04*	98.53	80.14	**75.57**	**94.33**	**91.76**	**99.97**	**90.56**	**99.97**	**80.25**	75.45
Italian-PUD	93.10	*2.47*	**57.26**	*2.47*	95.52	**87.39**	**84.03**	**93.18**	2.47	57.19	2.47	**95.57**	86.87	83.61

Table 3: The effect of additional training data from other treebanks of the same language in *UDPipe 1.2 Participant System*.

Treebank	GRU-based segmentation followed by parsing			Joint segmentation and parsing		
	Sents	UAS	LAS	Sents	UAS	LAS
Gothic	**32.46**	69.04	62.23	24.12	**69.26**	**62.80**
Latin-PROIEL	**30.37**	66.11	60.63	19.56	**66.45**	**61.55**
Slovenian-SST	**17.76**	57.93	51.95	13.13	**59.26**	**53.94**

Table 5: Joint segmentation and parsing in *UDPipe 1.2 Participant System*, optimized to maximize parsing likelihood, in comparison with sequential segmentation and parsing.

Beam size	UAS	LAS
1	74.36	68.46
5	75.33	69.45
10	75.39	69.51
15	75.41	69.53
20	**75.42**	**69.54**
Best on development data for each treebank	75.39	69.52

Table 7: *UDPipe 1.2 Participant System* parsing scores with various beam sizes.

In order to make the extensive results more visual, we show relative difference of baseline LAS score using the grey bars (on a scale that ignores 3 outliers). We use this visualization also in later tables, always showing relative difference to the first occurrence of the metric in question.

The effect of enlarging training data using other treebanks of the same language (Section 4.2) is evaluated in Table 3. We include only those treebanks in which the enlarged training data result in better LAS score and compare the performance to cases in which only the original training data is used.

The impact of tokenizer dimension 64 compared to dimension 24 can be found in Table 4. We also include the effect of not using the suffix rules for multi-word token splitting, and not using multi-word token splitting at all. As expected, for many languages the dimension 64 does not change the results, but yields superior performance for languages with either difficult tokenization or sentence segmentation.

The improvement resulting from joint sentence segmentation and parsing is evaluated in Table 5. While the LAS and UAS F1-scores of the joint approach improves, the sentence segmentation F1-score deteriorates significantly.

The overall effect of search-based oracle with various transition systems on parsing accuracy is summarized in Table 6. The search-based oracle improves results in all cases, but the increase is only slight if a dynamic oracle is also used. Note however that dynamic oracles for non-projective systems are usually either very inefficient (for link2, only $\mathcal{O}(n^8)$ dynamic oracle is proposed in Gómez-Rodríguez et al. (2014)) or not known (as is the case for the swap system).

Furthermore, if only a static oracle is used, partially or fully non-projective systems yield better overall performance than a projective one. Yet, a dynamic oracle improves performance of the projective system to the extent it yield better results (which is further improved by utilizing also a search-based oracle).

The influence of beam size on UAS and LAS scores is analyzed in Table 7. According to the results, tuning beam size for every treebank independently is worse than using large beam size all the time.

Finally, model size and runtime performance of individual UDPipe components are outlined in Table 8. The median of complete model size is circa 13MB and the speed of full processing (tokenization, tagging and parsing with beam size 5) is approximately 1700 words per second on a single core of an Intel Xeon E5-2630 2.4GHz processor.

Treebank	UDPipe 1.2 Participant System				Tokenizer dim 24			No suffix rules		No token splitting	
	Tokens	Words	Sents	LAS	Words	Sents	LAS	Words	LAS	Words	LAS
Ancient Greek	99.96	**99.96**	98.73	57.39	**99.96**	**98.85**	**57.42**	**99.96**	57.39	**99.96**	57.39
Ancient Greek-PROIEL	100.00	**100.00**	47.09	66.51	**100.00**	45.14	65.79	**100.00**	**66.51**	**100.00**	**66.51**
Arabic	99.98	93.71	81.77	66.06	**93.71**	80.89	**66.08**	92.89	65.13	78.39	45.84
Basque	99.96	**99.96**	99.50	70.45	**99.96**	99.08	70.39	**99.96**	**70.45**	**99.96**	**70.45**
Bulgarian	99.92	**99.92**	92.85	84.92	99.91	92.54	84.87	**99.92**	**84.92**	**99.92**	**84.92**
Catalan	99.97	**99.97**	99.03	85.53	99.96	**99.03**	85.52	99.77	85.17	99.67	84.93
Chinese	89.55	**89.55**	98.20	57.89	89.25	**98.50**	57.63	**89.55**	**57.89**	**89.55**	**57.89**
Croatian	99.90	99.90	95.56	77.73	**99.92**	**96.98**	**77.83**	99.90	77.73	99.90	77.73
Czech	99.93	**99.93**	92.30	83.19	99.92	91.82	83.16	**99.93**	**83.19**	99.80	82.96
Czech-CAC	99.97	**99.96**	100.00	84.40	**99.96**	99.76	**84.40**	**99.96**	**84.40**	99.72	84.03
Czech-CLTT	99.34	99.34	94.19	76.69	**99.52**	**96.49**	**77.30**	99.34	76.69	99.31	76.65
Danish	99.60	**99.60**	78.97	75.28	99.58	**80.07**	**75.43**	**99.60**	75.28	**99.60**	75.28
Dutch	99.80	99.80	76.95	70.52	**99.84**	**77.62**	70.09	99.80	**70.52**	99.80	**70.52**
Dutch-LassySmall	99.99	**99.99**	81.83	80.15	**99.99**	74.84	79.18	**99.99**	**80.15**	**99.99**	**80.15**
English	99.03	**99.03**	75.33	77.25	98.97	75.67	77.24	**99.03**	**77.25**	**99.03**	**77.25**
English-LinES	99.92	**99.92**	87.40	74.92	99.90	86.59	**74.96**	**99.92**	74.92	**99.92**	74.92
English-ParTUT	99.57	99.55	98.40	76.89	**99.61**	97.19	**77.04**	99.54	76.86	99.45	76.75
Estonian	99.89	**99.89**	93.66	60.01	99.88	**93.75**	59.99	**99.89**	**60.01**	**99.89**	**60.01**
Finnish	99.69	**99.69**	86.75	77.26	**99.69**	84.70	77.11	**99.69**	**77.26**	**99.69**	**77.26**
Finnish-FTB	99.97	**99.96**	85.54	75.31	99.94	84.72	75.03	99.95	75.28	99.74	75.08
French	99.76	98.88	94.58	80.50	98.89	94.09	80.41	98.88	80.50	**95.54**	74.98
French-ParTUT	99.85	**98.97**	97.76	80.17	**98.97**	97.38	80.06	**98.97**	**80.17**	95.00	74.43
French-Sequoia	99.76	99.06	84.60	81.35	99.04	84.00	81.34	99.06	**81.35**	95.07	74.74
Galician	99.93	**99.93**	96.18	77.73	**99.94**	95.98	**77.81**	**99.93**	77.73	**99.93**	77.73
Galician-TreeGal	99.62	98.66	85.35	66.31	98.70	**86.69**	**66.32**	98.09	65.48	87.58	48.87
German	99.67	99.66	79.35	68.61	**99.68**	79.34	68.41	99.67	**68.61**	97.17	64.81
Gothic	100.00	**100.00**	24.12	62.80	**100.00**	20.75	62.08	**100.00**	**62.80**	**100.00**	**62.80**
Greek	99.87	**99.87**	90.00	80.67	**99.87**	**90.44**	80.54	**99.87**	**80.67**	**99.87**	**80.67**
Hebrew	99.98	**85.16**	100.00	57.86	85.12	99.59	57.83	81.73	54.60	57.12	26.11
Hindi	100.00	**100.00**	99.20	87.28	**100.00**	99.20	87.28	**100.00**	**87.28**	**100.00**	**87.28**
Hungarian	99.81	**99.81**	95.54	66.54	**99.81**	95.58	**66.63**	**99.81**	66.54	**99.81**	66.54
Indonesian	100.00	**100.00**	91.73	75.47	**100.00**	90.71	**75.48**	**100.00**	75.47	**100.00**	75.47
Irish	99.40	99.40	94.78	62.87	**99.56**	94.14	**63.00**	99.40	62.87	99.40	62.87
Italian	99.91	**99.83**	97.11	86.11	99.78	96.91	85.97	99.58	85.53	88.92	68.98
Japanese	90.97	**90.97**	95.01	74.49	90.02	**95.01**	73.19	**90.97**	**74.49**	**90.97**	**74.49**
Kazakh	96.07	95.63	81.23	25.43	92.74	**81.56**	24.39	95.36	**25.95**	95.36	**25.95**
Korean	99.69	**99.69**	92.41	60.30	99.67	92.04	60.08	**99.69**	**60.30**	**99.69**	**60.30**
Latin	99.99	**99.99**	98.56	47.02	100.00	98.35	46.96	**99.99**	**47.02**	**99.99**	**47.02**
Latin-ITTB	99.89	99.89	82.58	75.84	**99.94**	82.49	**75.91**	99.89	75.84	99.89	75.84
Latin-PROIEL	100.00	**100.00**	19.56	61.55	**100.00**	18.43	**61.55**	**100.00**	**61.55**	**100.00**	**61.55**
Latvian	98.94	**98.94**	98.32	61.80	98.89	98.37	**61.81**	**98.94**	61.80	**98.94**	61.80
Norwegian-Bokmaal	99.79	**99.79**	96.38	83.89	99.78	95.79	83.86	**99.79**	**83.89**	**99.79**	**83.89**
Norwegian-Nynorsk	99.93	**99.93**	92.08	82.74	**99.93**	92.03	82.68	**99.93**	**82.74**	**99.93**	**82.74**
Old Church Slavonic	99.99	99.99	40.94	66.29	**100.00**	39.14	66.15	99.99	**66.29**	99.99	**66.29**
Persian	100.00	**99.65**	97.76	80.33	**99.65**	**98.74**	80.30	99.48	80.06	99.08	79.42
Polish	99.98	99.87	**99.18**	80.21	**99.88**	99.00	80.20	99.09	77.98	98.60	76.67
Portuguese	99.66	99.54	**89.24**	82.72	99.55	88.75	82.63	99.29	82.11	88.36	64.71
Portuguese-BR	99.96	**99.86**	96.71	85.97	99.85	**96.80**	**85.98**	**99.86**	85.97	89.41	67.97
Romanian	99.67	**99.67**	93.72	80.32	99.62	**93.85**	80.29	**99.67**	**80.32**	**99.67**	**80.32**
Russian	99.90	99.90	**96.59**	76.15	**99.91**	96.48	76.11	99.90	**76.15**	99.90	**76.15**
Russian-SynTagRus	99.58	**99.58**	**97.97**	86.80	99.50	97.72	86.70	**99.58**	**86.80**	**99.58**	**86.80**
Slovak	100.00	**100.00**	84.26	75.63	99.99	83.14	75.43	**100.00**	**75.63**	**100.00**	**75.63**
Slovenian	99.96	**99.96**	98.86	81.84	99.93	98.85	81.74	**99.96**	**81.84**	**99.96**	**81.84**
Slovenian-SST	99.87	99.87	13.13	53.94	**99.97**	15.38	53.86	99.87	**53.94**	99.87	**53.94**
Spanish	99.91	**99.74**	95.26	81.95	99.70	94.89	81.92	99.41	81.32	96.55	77.75
Spanish-AnCora	99.97	**99.95**	98.26	84.95	**99.95**	98.15	**84.95**	99.73	84.51	99.45	83.74
Swedish	99.86	**99.86**	95.57	77.58	99.78	93.17	77.30	**99.86**	**77.58**	**99.86**	**77.58**
Swedish-LinES	99.97	**99.97**	86.43	75.57	99.96	85.73	75.44	**99.97**	**75.57**	**99.97**	**75.57**
Turkish	99.85	**97.92**	96.89	53.78	**97.92**	**97.09**	53.73	97.28	52.58	96.04	50.88
Ukrainian	99.66	99.66	94.84	61.09	**99.77**	**94.89**	**61.21**	99.66	61.09	99.66	61.09
Urdu	100.00	**100.00**	98.32	77.09	**100.00**	**98.60**	**77.11**	**100.00**	77.09	**100.00**	77.09
Uyghur	99.94	**99.94**	65.31	33.21	99.85	**67.23**	33.18	**99.94**	**33.21**	**99.94**	**33.21**
Vietnamese	84.26	**84.26**	92.87	39.97	82.57	92.26	38.45	**84.26**	**39.97**	**84.26**	**39.97**
Arabic-PUD	80.85	90.81	98.95	44.34	**90.87**	**99.10**	**44.37**	89.91	43.92	80.85	36.61
Czech-PUD	99.28	99.28	95.40	79.67	**99.29**	**96.29**	**79.74**	99.28	79.67	99.13	79.46
German-PUD	97.90	**97.94**	90.75	66.05	97.83	86.58	65.43	**97.94**	**66.05**	95.58	62.62
English-PUD	99.74	**99.74**	95.57	79.21	99.66	**97.22**	**79.34**	**99.74**	79.21	**99.74**	79.21
Spanish-PUD	99.48	99.43	94.14	77.99	**99.50**	94.36	**78.03**	99.30	77.78	96.46	74.94
Finnish-PUD	99.63	**99.63**	**92.20**	80.86	99.60	91.87	**80.92**	**99.63**	80.86	**99.63**	80.86
French-PUD	99.81	98.86	93.33	74.19	**98.88**	**96.38**	**74.31**	98.86	74.19	96.15	69.79
Hindi-PUD	98.78	98.78	**93.26**	52.53	**98.84**	90.92	**52.54**	98.78	52.53	98.78	52.53
Italian-PUD	99.64	99.22	94.11	**84.03**	**99.25**	**94.40**	83.95	99.05	83.72	89.56	68.04
Japanese-PUD	92.41	**92.41**	95.04	78.36	90.95	**95.04**	76.00	**92.41**	**78.36**	**92.41**	**78.36**
Portuguese-PUD	99.27	99.39	**95.94**	74.43	**99.44**	95.21	74.37	99.24	74.18	89.49	60.18
Russian-PUD	97.25	97.25	98.51	69.37	**97.38**	**99.10**	**69.57**	97.25	69.37	97.25	69.37
Swedish-PUD	98.35	98.35	94.44	70.88	**98.41**	**94.47**	**70.88**	98.35	**70.88**	98.35	**70.88**
Turkish-PUD	99.13	**96.94**	90.87	34.12	96.31	**92.20**	34.02	96.02	32.56	95.99	32.15

Table 4: Impact of tokenizer dimension 64 versus 24, no suffix rules for multi-word token splitting, and no multi-word token splitting at all in the *UDPipe 1.2 Participant System*.

Transition system and oracle	No search-based oracle		Search-based oracle	
	UAS	LAS	UAS	LAS
Arc standard system with static oracle	74.29	68.27	74.80	68.87
Arc standard system with dynamic oracle	75.31	69.36	**75.40**	69.51
Swap system with static lazy oracle	74.73	68.76	75.16	69.27
Link2 system with static oracle	74.79	68.76	75.21	69.29
Any system, static oracle	74.72	68.71	75.21	69.31
Any system, any oracle	75.27	69.31	75.38	**69.52**

Table 6: The overall effect of search-based oracle on various transition systems.

Model configuration	Model size [MB]	Model speed [kwords/s]
Tokenizer dim 24	0.04 (0.03–0.15)	27.7 (20–37)
Tokenizer dim 64	0.20 (0.19–0.31)	6.0 (4.9–8.6)
Tagger&lemmatizer	9.4 (2.3–24.8)	6.5 (2.1–14)
Parser beam size 1	3.2 (1.9–6.9)	14.9 (12–19)
Parser beam size 5		2.7 (2.2–3.6)
Complete model	13.2 (4.4–31.9)	1.7 (1.2–2.3)

Table 8: *UDPipe 1.2 Participant System* model size and runtime performance, displayed as a median for all the treebanks, together with the 5th and 95th percentile. The complete model consists of a tokenizer with character embedding and GRU cell dimension 64, a tagger, a lemmatizer and a parser with beam size 5.

6 Conclusions and Future Work

We described our contributions to *CoNLL 2017 UD Shared Task*: *UDPipe 1.1 Baseline System* and *UDPipe 1.2 Participant System*. Both these systems and the pretrained models are available at `http://ufal.mff.cuni.cz/udpipe` under open-source Mozilla Public Licence (MPL). Binary tools as well as bindings for C++, Python, Perl, Java and C# are provided.

As our future work, we consider using deeper models in UDPipe for tokenizers, POS taggers and especially for the parser.

Acknowledgments

This work has been partially supported and has been using language resources and tools developed, stored and distributed by the LIN-DAT/CLARIN project of the Ministry of Education, Youth and Sports of the Czech Republic (project LM2015071). This research was also partially supported by OP VVV projects CZ.02.1.01/0.0/0.0/16_013/0001781 and CZ.02.2.69/0.0/0.0/16_018/0002373, and by SVV project number 260 453.

References

Daniel Andor, Chris Alberti, David Weiss, Aliaksei Severyn, Alessandro Presta, Kuzman Ganchev, Slav Petrov, and Michael Collins. 2016. Globaly normalized transition-based neural networks. In *Association for Computational Linguistic*. http://arxiv.org/abs/1603.06042.

Steven Bird, Ewan Klein, and Edward Loper. 2009. *Natural Language Processing with Python*. O'Reilly Media, Inc., 1st edition.

Danqi Chen and Christopher Manning. 2014. A fast and accurate dependency parser using neural networks. In *Proceedings of the 2014 Conference on Empirical Methods in Natural Language Processing (EMNLP)*. Association for Computational Linguistics, Doha, Qatar, pages 740–750. http://www.aclweb.org/anthology/D14-1082.

KyungHyun Cho, Bart van Merrienboer, Dzmitry Bahdanau, and Yoshua Bengio. 2014. On the properties of neural machine translation: Encoder-decoder approaches. *CoRR* abs/1409.1259. http://arxiv.org/abs/1409.1259.

Ronan Collobert, Jason Weston, Léon Bottou, Michael Karlen, Koray Kavukcuoglu, and Pavel Kuksa. 2011. Natural language processing (almost) from scratch. *The Journal of Machine Learning Research* 12:2493–2537.

Jacob Devlin, Rabih Zbib, Zhongqiang Huang, Thomas Lamar, Richard M. Schwartz, and John Makhoul. 2014. Fast and robust neural network joint models for statistical machine translation. In *Proceedings of the 52nd Annual Meeting of the Association for Computational Linguistics, ACL 2014, June 22-27, 2014, Baltimore, MD, USA, Volume 1: Long Papers*. pages 1370–1380. http://aclweb.org/anthology/P/P14/P14-1129.pdf.

Timothy Dozat and Christopher D. Manning. 2016. Deep biaffine attention for neural dependency parsing. *CoRR* abs/1611.01734. http://arxiv.org/abs/1611.01734.

Chris Dyer, Miguel Ballesteros, Wang Ling, Austin Matthews, and Noah A. Smith. 2015. Transition-based dependency parsing with stack long short-term memory. In *Proceedings of the 53rd Annual Meeting of the Association for Computational Linguistics and the 7th International Joint*

Conference on Natural Language Processing (Volume 1: Long Papers). Association for Computational Linguistics, Beijing, China, pages 334–343. http://www.aclweb.org/anthology/P15-1033.

Yoav Goldberg, Francesco Sartorio, and Giorgio Satta. 2014. A tabular method for dynamic oracles in transition-based parsing. *TACL* 2:119–130. http://www.aclweb.org/anthology/Q14-1010.

Carlos Gómez-Rodríguez, Francesco Sartorio, and Giorgio Satta. 2014. A polynomial-time dynamic oracle for non-projective dependency parsing. In *Proceedings of the 2014 Conference on Empirical Methods in Natural Language Processing (EMNLP)*. Association for Computational Linguistics, Doha, Qatar, pages 917–927. http://www.aclweb.org/anthology/D14-1099.

Sepp Hochreiter and Jürgen Schmidhuber. 1997. Long short-term memory. *Neural Comput.* 9(8):1735–1780. https://doi.org/10.1162/neco.1997.9.8.1735.

Diederik P. Kingma and Jimmy Ba. 2014. Adam: A method for stochastic optimization. *CoRR* abs/1412.6980. http://arxiv.org/abs/1412.6980.

Adhiguna Kuncoro, Miguel Ballesteros, Lingpeng Kong, Chris Dyer, Graham Neubig, and Noah A. Smith. 2016. What do recurrent neural network grammars learn about syntax? *CoRR* abs/1611.05774. http://arxiv.org/abs/1611.05774.

Wang Ling, Tiago Luís, Luís Marujo, Ramón Fernandez Astudillo, Silvio Amir, Chris Dyer, Alan W. Black, and Isabel Trancoso. 2015. Finding function in form: Compositional character models for open vocabulary word representation. *CoRR* abs/1508.02096. http://arxiv.org/abs/1508.02096.

Tomas Mikolov, Ilya Sutskever, Kai Chen, Gregory S. Corrado, and Jeffrey Dean. 2013. Distributed representations of words and phrases and their compositionality. In *Advances in Neural Information Processing Systems 26: 27th Annual Conference on Neural Information Processing Systems 2013. Proceedings of a meeting held December 5-8, 2013, Lake Tahoe, Nevada, United States.*. pages 3111–3119. http://papers.nips.cc/paper/5021-distributed-representations-of-words-and-phrases-and-their-compositionality.

Joakim Nivre. 2008. Algorithms for deterministic incremental dependency parsing. *Comput. Linguist.* 34(4):513–553. https://doi.org/10.1162/coli.07-056-R1-07-027.

Joakim Nivre. 2009. Non-projective dependency parsing in expected linear time. In *Proceedings of the Joint Conference of the 47th Annual Meeting of the ACL and the 4th International Joint Conference on Natural Language Processing of the AFNLP: Volume 1 - Volume 1*. Association for Computational Linguistics, Stroudsburg, PA, USA, ACL '09, pages 351–359. http://dl.acm.org/citation.cfm?id=1687878.1687929.

Joakim Nivre, Željko Agić, Lars Ahrenberg, et al. 2017a. Universal Dependencies 2.0. LINDAT/CLARIN digital library at the Institute of Formal and Applied Linguistics, Charles University, Prague. http://hdl.handle.net/11234/1-1983.

Joakim Nivre, Željko Agić, Lars Ahrenberg, et al. 2017b. Universal dependencies 2.0 – CoNLL 2017 shared task development and test data. LINDAT/CLARIN digital library at the Institute of Formal and Applied Linguistics, Charles University. http://hdl.handle.net/11234/1-2184.

Joakim Nivre, Marie-Catherine de Marneffe, Filip Ginter, Yoav Goldberg, Jan Hajič, Christopher Manning, Ryan McDonald, Slav Petrov, Sampo Pyysalo, Natalia Silveira, Reut Tsarfaty, and Daniel Zeman. 2016. Universal Dependencies v1: A multilingual treebank collection. In *Proceedings of the 10th International Conference on Language Resources and Evaluation (LREC 2016)*. European Language Resources Association, Portorož, Slovenia, pages 1659–1666.

Martin Potthast, Tim Gollub, Francisco Rangel, Paolo Rosso, Efstathios Stamatatos, and Benno Stein. 2014. Improving the reproducibility of PAN's shared tasks: Plagiarism detection, author identification, and author profiling. In Evangelos Kanoulas, Mihai Lupu, Paul Clough, Mark Sanderson, Mark Hall, Allan Hanbury, and Elaine Toms, editors, *Information Access Evaluation meets Multilinguality, Multimodality, and Visualization. 5th International Conference of the CLEF Initiative (CLEF 14)*. Springer, Berlin Heidelberg New York, pages 268–299. https://doi.org/10.1007/978-3-319-11382-1_22.

Milan Straka. 2017. CoNLL 2017 shared task - UDPipe baseline models and supplementary materials. LINDAT/CLARIN digital library at the Institute of Formal and Applied Linguistics, Charles University. http://hdl.handle.net/11234/1-1990.

Milan Straka, Jan Hajič, and Jana Straková. 2016. UDPipe: trainable pipeline for processing CoNLL-U files performing tokenization, morphological analysis, POS tagging and parsing. In *Proceedings of the 10th International Conference on Language Resources and Evaluation (LREC 2016)*. European Language Resources Association, Portorož, Slovenia.

Milan Straka, Jan Hajič, Jana Straková, and Jan Hajič jr. 2015. Parsing universal dependency treebanks using neural networks and search-based oracle. In *Proceedings of Fourteenth International Workshop on Treebanks and Linguistic Theories (TLT 14)*.

Jana Straková, Milan Straka, and Jan Hajič. 2014. Open-source tools for morphology, lemmatization, pos tagging and named entity recognition. In *Proceedings of 52nd Annual Meeting of the*

Association for Computational Linguistics: System Demonstrations. Association for Computational Linguistics, Baltimore, Maryland, pages 13–18. http://www.aclweb.org/anthology/P14-5003.

Ashish Vaswani, Noam Shazeer, Niki Parmar, Jakob Uszkoreit, Llion Jones, Aidan N. Gomez, Lukasz Kaiser, and Illia Polosukhin. 2017. Attention is all you need. *CoRR* abs/1706.03762. http://arxiv.org/abs/1706.03762.

Zhilin Yang, Ruslan Salakhutdinov, and William W. Cohen. 2016. Multi-task cross-lingual sequence tagging from scratch. *CoRR* abs/1603.06270. http://arxiv.org/abs/1603.06270.

Daniel Zeman, Martin Popel, Milan Straka, Jan Hajič, Joakim Nivre, Filip Ginter, Juhani Luotolahti, Sampo Pyysalo, Slav Petrov, Martin Potthast, Francis Tyers, Elena Badmaeva, Memduh Gökırmak, Anna Nedoluzhko, Silvie Cinková, Jan Hajič jr., Jaroslava Hlaváčová, Václava Kettnerová, Zdeňka Urešová, Jenna Kanerva, Stina Ojala, Anna Missilä, Christopher Manning, Sebastian Schuster, Siva Reddy, Dima Taji, Nizar Habash, Herman Leung, Marie-Catherine de Marneffe, Manuela Sanguinetti, Maria Simi, Hiroshi Kanayama, Valeria de Paiva, Kira Droganova, Hĕctor Martínez Alonso, Hans Uszkoreit, Vivien Macketanz, Aljoscha Burchardt, Kim Harris, Katrin Marheinecke, Georg Rehm, Tolga Kayadelen, Mohammed Attia, Ali Elkahky, Zhuoran Yu, Emily Pitler, Saran Lertpradit, Michael Mandl, Jesse Kirchner, Hector Fernandez Alcalde, Jana Strnadova, Esha Banerjee, Ruli Manurung, Antonio Stella, Atsuko Shimada, Sookyoung Kwak, Gustavo Mendonça, Tatiana Lando, Rattima Nitisaroj, and Josie Li. 2017. CoNLL 2017 Shared Task: Multilingual Parsing from Raw Text to Universal Dependencies. In *Proceedings of the CoNLL 2017 Shared Task: Multilingual Parsing from Raw Text to Universal Dependencies*. Association for Computational Linguistics.

UParse: the Edinburgh system for the CoNLL 2017 UD shared task

Clara Vania, Xingxing Zhang, and **Adam Lopez**
Institute for Language, Cognition and Computation
School of Informatics
University of Edinburgh
`{c.vania, x.zhang}@ed.ac.uk, alopez@inf.ed.ac.uk`

Abstract

This paper presents our submissions for the CoNLL 2017 UD Shared Task. Our parser, called UParse, is based on a neural network graph-based dependency parser. The parser uses features from a bidirectional LSTM to produce a distribution over possible heads for each word in the sentence. To allow transfer learning for low-resource treebanks and surprise languages, we train several multilingual models for related languages, grouped by their genus and language families. Out of 33 participants, our system achieves rank 9th in the main results, with 75.49 UAS and 68.87 LAS F-1 scores (average across 81 treebanks).

1 Introduction

Dependency parsing aims to automatically extract dependencies between words in a sentence, in the form of tree structure. These dependencies define the grammatical structure of the sentence, which makes it beneficial for many natural language applications, such as question answering (Cui et al., 2005), machine translation (Carreras and Collins, 2009), and information extraction (Angeli et al., 2015). The most common approaches for dependency parsing are transition-based (Nivre et al., 2006) or graph-based (McDonald et al., 2005). Recent works also apply neural network approaches for dependency parsing (Chen and Manning, 2014; Dyer et al., 2015; Kiperwasser and Goldberg, 2016; Zhang et al., 2017), particularly for learning rich feature representations that improve parser accuracy.

To train a high-quality parser, one typically needs a large treebank, annotated with some linguistic information, such as part of speech (POS) tags, lemmas, and morphological features. However, human annotations are expensive. As a result, most of the work has been focused on few languages, such as English, Czech, or Chinese.

The Universal Dependencies (UD; Nivre et al. (2016)) is an initiative to develop consistent treebank annotations across many languages. It provides an opportunity to perform model transfer – using model trained on high-resource languages to parse low-resource languages, allowing the development of treebanks for many more languages. Several works (McDonald et al., 2011; Zhang and Barzilay, 2015; Duong et al., 2015a,b; Guo et al., 2015, 2016) have shown that this technique can help improve accuracy for low-resource languages, and in fact recent work of Ammar et al. (2016) demonstrated that it is possible to train a single multilingual model that works well both in low-resource and high-resource settings.

The CoNLL 2017 UD Shared Task (Zeman et al., 2017) uses Universal Dependencies version 2.0 (Nivre et al., 2017), with training data consists of 64 treebanks from 45 languages. Some of the challenges are the truly low-resource treebanks (e.g., Kazakh and Uyghur with only 30 and 100 training sentences, respectively), small treebanks without development data (e.g., Irish, French-ParTUT, Galician-TreeGal, Ukrainian), and the surprise languages and treebanks needed to be parse during test phase.

To address these challenges, we designed our system for the shared task to use both monolingual and multilingual models. In particular:

- We train one monolingual model per high-resource treebank in the training set.

- For low-resource treebanks, we train several multilingual models, each for related languages grouped by their genus and language families.

Proceedings of the CoNLL 2017 Shared Task: Multilingual Parsing from Raw Text to Universal Dependencies, pages 100–110,
Vancouver, Canada, August 3-4, 2017. © 2017 Association for Computational Linguistics

- For surprise languages, we train several delexalized parsers using treebanks that are closest to the surprise languages in terms of language family.

Our parsing model uses pretrained word vectors, gold universal POS tags (UPOS), and gold morphological analysis (XFEATS, if available). For the multilingual models, we also use language ID and replace pre-trained word vectors with multilingual word vectors. For the delexicalized models, we remove the word vectors from our feature set because we want to use the model for other languages which use different vocabularies.

We submitted three systems, which are described in Section 5. The final ranking of the shared task brings our parser to the ninth place, with average UAS and LAS, 75.49 and 68.87, respectively. On the surprise languages, our system reaches the 6th rank, with 39.17 LAS.

2   System Description

Our system, called UParse, is a combination of monolingual, multilingual, and delexicalized models. In this section, we describe our parsing model which extends DENSE, the neural network graph-based parser of Zhang et al. (2017).

2.1   DENSE Parser

DENSE (**D**ependency **N**eural **Se**lection) is a neural graph-based parser which generates dependency tree by predicting the heads of each word in a sentence. Given an input sentence of length N^1, the parser first produces N ⟨head, dependent⟩ dependency arcs by greedily selecting the most likely head word. If the predicted dependency arcs do not result a (projective) tree structure, a maximum spanning tree algorithm will be used to adjust the output to a (projective) tree. In the following, we will describe the DENSE parser in details.

Token Representations. In the first step, the parser computes the representation of each word in the sentence. The objective is to encode both local (lexical meaning and POS tag) and global information (word position and context). To do this, the parser uses a bidirectional LSTM (bi-LSTMs), which have shown to be effective in capturing long-term dependencies. More formally, let

$S = (w_0, w_1, \ldots, w_N)$ be the input sentence of length N, where w_0 denotes the artificial ROOT token. Each input token w_i is represented by $\mathbf{x}_i$, which is a concatenation of its word and POS tag embeddings, $\mathbf{e}(w_i)$ and $\mathbf{e}(t_i)$, respectively.

$$\mathbf{x}_i = [\mathbf{e}(w_i); \mathbf{e}(t_i)] \tag{1}$$

These representations are the input to a bi-LSTM, which produces a sentence-specific representation of token w_i computed by concatenating the hidden states of a forward and a backward LSTM:

$$\mathbf{a}_i = [\mathbf{h}_i^f; \mathbf{h}_i^b] \tag{2}$$

where $\mathbf{h}_i^f$ and $\mathbf{h}_i^b$ denotes the hidden states of the forward and backward LSTMs.

Head Predictions. For each token w_i, the parser computes the probability of w_j being the head as:

$$P_{head}(w_j|w_i, S) = \frac{\exp(g(\mathbf{a}_j, \mathbf{a}_i))}{\Sigma_{k=0}^N \exp(g(\mathbf{a}_k, \mathbf{a}_i))} \tag{3}$$

where $\mathbf{a}_i$ and $\mathbf{a}_j$ are the word representations of w_i and w_j, respectively. Function g is a neural network with a single layer which computes the associative score between the two words:

$$g(\mathbf{a}_j, \mathbf{a}_i) = \mathbf{v}_a^T \cdot \tanh(\mathbf{U}_a \cdot \mathbf{a}_j + \mathbf{W}_a \cdot \mathbf{a}_i) \tag{4}$$

Note that, this step is similar to the neural attention mechanism in the sequence-to-sequence models (Bahdanau et al., 2015). The model is trained to minimize the negative log likelihood of the gold standard ⟨head, dependent⟩ arcs of all the training sentences. At test time, the parser greedily choose the most probable head for each word in the sentence.

Adjusting Tree Outputs. In many cases, the individual predictions form a tree. However, if this is not the case, a maximum spanning tree (MST) algorithm is used to constrain the set of predictions to form a tree. DENSE can use two algorithms: Chu-Liu-Edmonds (Chu and Liu, 1965; Edmonds, 1967) algorithm to generating non-projective trees; and the Eisner algorithm (Eisner, 1996) to generate projective trees. The decision of the MST algorithms depends on the language's treebank. For the shared task, we assume that each language can produce non-projective trees.

---

[1] As the convention in dependency parsing, we add a dummy ROOT token to the sentence. Therefore, the resulting length of the sentence will be $N + 1$.

Model	Word	Multi-Word	UPOS	XFEATS	LID
MONO	✓		✓	✓	
MULTI		✓	✓	✓	✓
DELEX			✓	✓	

Table 1: Feature set used for each type of model in UParse. Multi-Word denotes the multilingual word embeddings. XFEATS feature is only used if the annotation is available in the training data.

Label Predictions. After obtaining the unlabeled dependency trees, the parser needs to predict labels. To do this, a two-layer rectifier network (Glorot et al., 2011) is used. More formally, to predict the arc label between w_i and w_j, the classifier takes as input the concatenation of the local (Eq. 1) and global (Eq. 2) vector representations of both words, $[\mathbf{a}_i; \mathbf{a}_j; \mathbf{x}_i; \mathbf{x}_j]$ and predicts a valid dependency label.

Zhang et al. (2017) presents more detailed account of the parsing model.

2.2 UParse

Next, we describe UParse, the extended version of DENSE which we use for the UD shared task. As mentioned in Section 1, UParse is a combination of monolingual, multilingual, UDPipe baseline, and delexicalized models. In general, the key difference between DENSE and UParse is in the type of features used for training. UParse uses richer linguistic features, namely word embeddings, universal POS tag (UPOS), morphological analysis (XFEATS), and language ID (LID). This design is mostly inspired by the work of Ammar et al. (2016) and Straka et al. (2016) for monolingual and multilingual parsing models. Each feature is represented by its vector representations and we concatenate them together to represent each input token which will be fed into the bi-LSTMs. Specifically, we modify Eq. 1 to

$$\mathbf{x}_i = [\mathbf{e}(w_i); \mathbf{e}(t_i); \mathbf{e}(m_i); \mathbf{e}(lid_i)] \qquad (5)$$

where $\mathbf{e}(m_i)$ and $\mathbf{e}(lid_i)$ denotes the embeddings of XFEATS and language ID, respectively.[2] During training our system uses gold annotations (tokenization, UPOS, and XFEATS) provided in the data. At test time, it uses predicted annotations produced by UDPipe (Straka et al., 2016).

Table 1 shows different feature set used in each type of model in the UParse. We employ

the original DENSE architecture for the monolingual models in UParse, with an additional feature (XFEATS, if available). For the multilingual models, we replace the standard word embeddings with multilingual word embeddings (Section 2.3). This is important since we need to project word vectors of different languages to the same vector space. We also use language ID as a feature, to inform the parser about the language of the sentence it is currently parsing. This allows the model to learn not only transferable dependency features across languages, but also the language-specific features.

2.3 Multilingual Word Embeddings

Following Ammar et al. (2016), we adapt the robust projection approach of Guo et al. (2016) to build our multilingual word embeddings. The idea is to train word embeddings of a source language and project them to obtain word embeddings for the target languages. For the shared task, we use English pre-trained word vectors trained on the Wikipedia data (Bojanowski et al., 2016) as our source embeddings. Next, we use OPUS data (Tiedemann, 2012, 2009) to build alignment dictionaries for languages that have parallel text with English. Specifically, we use parallel corpora of Europarl, Global Voices, Wikipedia, and hrWaC (for Croatian).

To build the alignment dictionaries, we use `fast_align` toolkit (Dyer et al., 2013). We then compute vector for each target word using the weighted average of its aligned English word embeddings, weighted by the alignment probabilities. A limitation of this approach is that it creates embeddings for target words that appear in the parallel data. Thus, the final step of this approach also compute embeddings for other target words not aligned with the source words by averaging the embeddings of all aligned target words within an edit distance of 1. The token level embeddings are shared across languages.

3 Preliminary Experiments

Prior to our participation in the shared task, we ran a number of preliminary experiments that informed the design of the final system. Our shared task submission is based on these results.

In our preliminary experiments, our main goal is to evaluate the multilingual model of UParse. These experiments are mainly inspired by the

---

[2] We treat XFEATS as an atomic symbol.

Type	Model	Languages							Average
		de	en	es	fr	it	pt	sv	
MONO	UDPipe	82.9	87.5	87.1	84.5	90.2	87.2	86.2	86.5
	UParse	**86.8**	**88.7**	**89.2**	87.1	91.4	88.0	88.2	**88.5**
MULTI	UParse	85.9	87.4	88.3	**87.6**	**91.8**	**89.0**	**88.8**	88.4

Table 2: UAS results for monolingual and multilingual model of UParse on the Universal Dependencies version 1.2.

Type	Model	Languages							Average
		de	en	es	fr	it	pt	sv	
MONO	UDPipe	78.6	85.0	84.5	81.0	88.1	84.7	83.2	83.6
	UParse	**80.4**	**85.5**	**85.5**	**83.1**	88.9	84.2	82.7	84.3
MULTI	MALOPA	78.9	85.4	84.3	82.4	**89.1**	86.2	**84.5**	**84.4**
	UParse	77.9	85.1	84.3	81.9	89.0	**86.5**	81.1	83.7

Table 3: LAS results for monolingual and multilingual model of UParse on the Universal Dependencies version 1.2. MALOPA is the multilingual parser of Ammar et al. (2016).

work of Ammar et al. (2016). To compare our results, we use the same datasets from Universal Dependencies version 1.2 (Nivre et al., 2015), for seven languages: English, French, German, Italian, Spanish, Swedish, and Portuguese. The training data for the first five languages consists of more than 10K training sentences, while for Portuguese and Swedish, there are 8.8K and 4.3K training sentences, respectively. For simplicity, we also follow their experimental setup for training optimization (more detail is reported in Section 4). In addition, we also compare our parser performance for the monolingual models with UDPipe parser.

Table 2 and 3 present the performance of our parser compared to UDPipe (monolingual) and MALOPA (multilingual) parsers. In terms of UAS, our multilingual model achieves the best scores, except for English, German, and French. The results for LAS are slightly different. We found that for languages where we have more than 10K training sentences, our monolingual model outperforms the other models, with an exception on Italian. For the smaller treebanks, although we see UAS improvements for Portuguese and Swedish when we use multilingual model, we only obtain LAS improvement on Portuguese. We believe that these mixed results are due to poor accuracy of our label classifier, since the UAS results demonstrate that the parser itself is quite effective in predicting the dependency arcs.

4 Experiments

This section describes the experimental design, training, and also our submissions to the shared task. After looking at the results of our preliminary experiments, we decided to train both monolingual and multilingual parsers, evaluate them on the shared task development data and choose the best settings for our submissions.

4.1 Language Groups

To build the multilingual models, we first group the treebanks such that treebanks of related languages will be trained in a single model. We use genus and language family information taken from the World Atlas of Language Structures(WALS; Dryer and Haspelmath (2013)) to group the languages. For each treebank in which the language is not related to any other treebanks, it will be in a singleton group, hence the same as a monolingual model. For classic languages like Ancient Greek, Latin, Gothic, and Old Church Slavonic, we group them to the same group, instead of using the WALS information. Table 4 shows the language groups used in UParse.

4.2 Training

In the preprocessing step, following the common setup in parsing, we remove multiword tokens and language specific dependency relations. For the multilingual training, we also combine treebanks of the same language in the same training data. We also use two additional datasets: pre-trained

Group	Languages
Classic	Ancient Greek, Latin, Gothic
	Old Church Slavonic
Finnic	Finnish
Germanic	Danish, Dutch, English, German
	Norwegian, Swedish
Indic	Hindi, Urdu
Romance	Catalan, French, Italian
	Portuguese, Spanish
Slavic	Bulgarian, Croatian, Czech
	Polish, Russian, Slovak
	Slovenian, Ukrainian
Semitic	Arabic, Hebrew
Turkic	Kazakh, Turkish, Uyghur

Table 4: Language groups used for building UParse multilingual models. Finish language has two treebanks, we group them together in the same group.

word embeddings from Bojanowski et al. (2016) and OPUS parallel data (Tiedemann, 2012, 2009).

Unless we explicitly mention in the description, we follow the same training configurations as described in Zhang et al. (2017). We use two-layer bi-LSTMs with 150 hidden units, and set embedding size for {words, UPOS, XFEATS, LID} to {300, 30, 40, 10}, respectively. The word embedding size matches that of the pre-trained embeddings. We did not use the Czech-CLLT or any ParTUT treebanks for training since they contain many long sentences (the longest sentence in the Czech-CLLT treebank consists of 534 words). At test time, we parse these treebanks using the models trained on the same language. We trained our models on an Nvidia GPU card; training a monolingual model takes 1-2 hours, while training a multilingual model takes 4-5 hours.

Word embeddings. For monolingual training, we initialize the embeddings with the pre-trained ones and keep them fixed during training. For the multilingual models, we first create multilingual word embeddings as described in Section 2.3, using OPUS parallel data and English as the source language. Unlike Ammar et al. (2016) and Guo et al. (2016), we also share representations for words which are used by more than one language. For example, if *system* appears in the English and German data, we only use a single vector to represent it. Of course, this means we allow parameter sharing across words with the same forms,

but different meanings. But on the other hand, it also enables named entities and loanwords to have the same representation across languages. We initialize the embeddings with the multilingual word embeddings and update them during training.[3] For all models, embeddings for words with no pretrained representation are initialized uniformly at random in the range [-0.1, 0.1].

Optimization for multilingual training. For multilingual training, we follow Ammar et al. (2016) when updating the parameters. Specifically, we use mini-batch updates in which we uniformly sampled (without replacement) the same number of sentences for each treebank, until all sentences in the smallest treebank are used. In other words, each epoch will use $N \times L$ sentences, where N is the number of sentences in the smallest treebank and L is the number of languages.

4.3 Truly Low-Resource Treebanks

There are some challenges when training the truly low-resource treebanks, i.e., treebanks with less than 2K sentences, with no other treebanks from the same language available. For example, Vietnamese treebank only has 1400 sentences with no related languages in terms of genus and language family. Ideally, we want to apply multilingual learning for these treebanks since we do not have enough examples to train them using monolingual models. Moreover, languages like Kazakh and Uyghur have 100 training sentences or fewer and no development data, which makes it difficult to do multilingual training as described above. Our initial experiments show that multilingual learning helps improve accuracy of the truly low-resource treebanks (with less than 1K training sentences), but degrades accuracy of the high-resource treebanks. This is because using our training set up, each epoch will only consists of small number of sentences per language. Irish is particularly challenging, with only 566 training sentences, no development data, and no related languages. Our training strategy for these particular cases are as follows:

Estonian and Hungarian. These languages are belong to the Uralic language family. Since Finnish has two treebanks with large training data, we train two more multilingual models for each, using additional Finnish treebanks.

---

[3]We did not fix the embeddings since in our preliminary experiments, it gave us lower accuracy.

We do not use a single model to train both Estonian and Hungarian since Estonian has more training sentences than Hungarian.

Greek. We train a multilingual model for Greek, using training data from Ancient Greek and Greek treebanks.[4]

Irish. Since this language does not have any related languages, we use delexicalized model of Czech. We chose Czech since the language has the largest treebank.

Kazakh and Uyghur. For the two languages, since the training data are very small, we use a single delexicalized model of Turkish. We only use Turkish data during training, but include both Kazakh and Uyghur training data in the development set.

4.4 Surprise Languages and Treebanks

For the surprise languages, since we do not have any training data, we train delexicalized models on related languages. In particular, we use delexicalized Russian for Buryat, Persian for Kurmanji, Finnic for North Sami, and Czech for Upper Sorbian. Note that the delexicalized models of Russian, Finnic, and Czech use all the treebanks of the language, thus allowing transfer learning between different treebanks of the same language. For example, to train a delexicalized model of Russian, we use both UD_Russian and UD_Russian-SynTagRus treebanks.

For the surprise treebanks from known languages, we simply use a parser trained on other treebanks in that language.

5 Results and Analysis

5.1 Initial Results on Development Data

During the training phase, we evaluated the performance of our monolingual and multilingual systems using the official development data. Since we use gold annotations (tokenization, UPOS, and XFEATS) as our features, we compare our performance with UDPipe baseline which also use gold annotations. Table 5 shows the average UAS and LAS of the monolingual and multilingual systems. Similar to our preliminary results, we see improvements on UAS for the multilingual model, but with

Model	Avg. UAS	Avg. LAS
Baseline	83.29	**79.53**
MONO	79.53	78.44
MULTI	**85.76**	77.55

Table 5: Average UAS and LAS of the monolingual versus multilingual models. The baseline is UDPipe with gold annotations.

LAS lower than the monolingual or even the UDPipe system. When we look at the results for individual treebanks, we found that our models are especially achieved lower LAS than the baseline system on the smaller treebanks.

5.2 Submission

The UD shared task employs TIRA (Potthast et al., 2014) to evaluate all systems. When we deployed our system on the TIRA virtual machine, we encountered two problems which break the evaluation script. First, our system sometimes produces multiple roots in the prediction, which the script rejects. To address this, we post-processed the predicted tree by taking the first prediction as the root, and connect other roots to the first root with a clausal component label, ccomp.[5] The second problem occurs when the test data has sentence longer than the maximum sentence length in the training data.[6] Because we had limited time to address this, we used the following algorithm: Let n be the maximum length of sentence allowed by the parsing model. For each sentences with length k, where $k > n$:

1. Parse the first n words in the sentence.

2. For the rest $k - n$ words, connect each word with the previous word, and label the arc between them using a heuristic label (DIST), or a random label (RAND). We simply take the most frequent label between the head POS and the dependent POS in the training data for DIST.

We decided to use the combination of monolingual, multilingual, UDPipe (only for the primary system, UP-1), and delexicalized models for our primary system. For each treebank, we pick the

---

[4]This specific model is slightly different, one might assume that Ancient Greek and Modern Greek are highly related.

[5]We choose this label based from our observation on the multiple roots prediction. Most of the time, our parser predicts multiple roots if the sentences are too long and contain multiple clauses.

[6]In the current training setup, the maximum sentence length is fixed.

Model	Avg. LAS
UP-1	**73.66**
UP-2	73.30
UP-3	73.29

Table 6: Macro-averaged LAS F1 score on development data.

Treebank name	Model
Estonian*	Finnic-Estonian
Gothic	Classic
Hungarian*	Finnic-Hungarian
Irish*	DEL-Czech
Kazakh*	DEL-Turkic
Old Church Slavonic*	Classic
Slovak*	Slavic
Swedish	Germanic
Swedish-LinES	Germanic
Uyghur*	DEL-Turkic
Buryat	DEL-Russian
Kurmanji	DEL-Persian
North_Sami	DEL-Finnic
Upper_Sorbian	DEL-Czech

Table 7: List of treebanks which use multilingual or delexicalized models in UParse. (*) denotes treebanks which use UDPipe models in UP-1. The bottom part of the table shows the models used to parse surprise languages.

best model based on its performance on the development data. We use UDPipe models for 24 treebanks in which we achieved lower performance than the baseline on the development data (denoted by (*) in Table 9). UP-2 and UP-3 do not use any UDPipe models. Table 7 lists all treebanks which use multilingual or delexicalized models for parsing. Our final submission consists of three different systems:

1. UP-1: UParse + DIST + UDPipe

2. UP-2: UParse + DIST

3. UP-3: UParse + RAND

Table 6 shows the macro-averaged LAS F1 scores for all the systems.

5.3 Results on Test Data

Table 8 shows the results of our primary system of LAS, UAS, and CLAS (Nivre and Fang, 2017). The more detailed results for each treebank and system is given in Table 9. Similar to the results

Metric	Score
LAS	68.87
UAS	75.49
CLAS	63.55

Table 8: LAS, UAS, and CLAS results of our primary system, UP-1.

on development data (Table 6), UP-1 achieves the best macro-average F1 score out of the three systems. The results of UP-2 and UP-3 are quite similar, which is not surprising since there are only a few long sentences in the test data.

We further observe the performance of the UDPipe baseline model versus UParse models, by comparing the performance of UP-1 and UP-2 on the 24 treebanks (treebanks with (*) in Table 9). Based on the results, our system achieves lower LAS-F1 scores on 16 treebanks, which are either treebanks with small training data or treebanks with long sentences, for which we did not train any model. For the other six treebanks, our system achieves higher LAS-F1 scores than the UDPipe baseline system, with 4 treebanks predicted using the multilingual models.

Our system is deployed on the TIRA virtual machine, which is a quad-core CPU with 16GB RAM. It took 2 hours and 43 minutes for our primary system to parse the official test data.

6 Conclusion and Future Work

We described UParse, our system for the CoNLL UD Shared Task 2017. Our observation from the overall results suggested that our parsing model outperforms the UDPipe baseline model, except in cases when there is little training data available. Our approach to perform multilingual learning by transferring models from high-resource to low-resource treebank seems to be quite effective in predicting the dependency arcs, but less for the label predictions. However, we observed some improvements for a number of treebanks when we use a multilingual model trained using treebanks from related languages.

In the light of these results, some possible directions for the future work include improving the label predictions of the parsing model and exploring the possibilities to use character-level models, as they have shown to be effective for parsing morphologically rich languages (Ballesteros et al., 2015). Another interesting direction is to combine

Treebank Code	LAS F-1 score		
	UP-1	UP-2	UP-3
ar_pud	45.3	45.3	45.3
ar	66.35	66.35	66.3
bg*	**83.64**	83.46	83.46
bxr	21.63	21.63	21.63
ca	86.8	86.8	86.8
cs_cac	85.57	85.57	85.57
cs_cltt*	**71.64**	66.74	66.37
cs_pud	81.06	81.06	81.06
cs	85.24	85.24	85.24
cu*	62.76	**64.24**	64.24
da	73.46	73.46	73.46
de_pud	67.36	67.36	67.36
de	70.09	70.09	70.09
el*	**79.26**	76.93	76.93
en_lines	73.28	73.28	73.28
en_partut*	**73.64**	69.63	69.63
en_pud	79.54	79.54	79.54
en	76.42	76.42	76.41
es_ancora	86.01	86.01	86.01
es_pud	79.2	79.2	79.2
es	83.02	83.02	83.02
et*	**58.78**	56.26	56.26
eu	69.85	69.85	69.85
fa	79.97	79.97	79.97
fi_ftb*	**74.04**	73.77	73.77
fi_pud	79.66	79.66	79.66
fi	75.35	75.35	75.35
fr_partut*	**77.38**	76.05	76.05
fr_pud	74.44	74.44	74.44
fr_sequoia	78.57	78.57	78.57
fr	81.58	81.58	81.58
ga*	**61.52**	36.31	36.2
gl_treegal	64.18	64.18	64.18
gl	78.08	78.08	78.08
got	60.71	60.71	60.71
grc_proiel	64.48	64.48	64.45
grc	57.22	57.22	57.22
he	57.6	57.6	57.6
hi_pud	51.89	51.89	51.89
hi	87.2	87.2	87.2
hr*	**77.18**	76.28	76.28

Treebank Code	LAS F-1 score		
	UP-1	UP-2	UP-3
hsb	59.24	59.24	59.24
hu*	**64.3**	57.37	57.37
id	75.01	75.01	75.01
it_pud	85.13	85.13	85.13
it	86.62	86.62	86.62
ja_pud	74.64	74.64	74.64
ja*	**72.21**	70.51	70.51
kk	21.96	21.96	21.96
kmr	39.76	39.76	39.76
ko*	**59.09**	58.74	58.74
la_ittb	79.35	79.35	79.35
la_proiel	56.93	56.93	56.91
la*	43.77	**46.07**	46.07
lv*	**59.95**	57.09	57.09
nl_lassysmall	79.56	79.56	79.56
nl	69.9	69.9	69.9
no_bokmaal	83.81	83.81	83.81
no_nynorsk	81.91	81.91	81.91
pl*	78.78	**79.69**	79.69
pt_br	86.38	86.38	86.38
pt_pud	74.76	74.76	74.76
pt	83.12	83.12	83.12
ro	80.45	80.45	80.45
ru_pud	68.64	68.64	68.64
ru_syntagrus	89.18	89.18	89.18
ru*	74.03	**74.86**	74.76
sk*	72.75	**74.77**	74.77
sl_sst	46.97	46.97	46.97
sl*	**81.15**	81.09	81.09
sme	36.04	36.04	36.04
sv_lines	74.04	74.04	74.04
sv_pud	70.44	70.44	70.44
sv	75.29	75.29	75.29
tr_pud	32.63	32.63	32.63
tr*	**53.22**	51.69	51.69
ug*	**34.18**	20.8	20.8
uk*	60.76	**60.78**	60.78
ur	76.35	76.35	76.35
vi*	**37.47**	37.14	37.14
zh*	**57.4**	56.14	56.14
Average LAS	**68.87**	68.09	68.09

Table 9: LAS F-1 scores for each treebank in the test data. (*) denotes treebanks which are predicted using UDPipe baseline models in the UP-1 system and the best accuracies are shown in **bold**.

both morphological analysis and also sub-word unit representation (characters, character n-grams, or morphemes) and investigate whether these features are transferable across languages with similar typology.

Acknowledgments

We would like to thank Sameer Bansal, Jianpeng Cheng, Jonathan Mallinson, and the anonymous reviewers for the helpful feedbacks. Clara Vania is supported by the Indonesian Endowment Fund for Education (LPDP), the Centre for Doctoral Training in Data Science, funded by the UK EPSRC (grant EP/L016427/1), and the University of Edinburgh.

References

Waleed Ammar, George Mulcaire, Miguel Ballesteros, Chris Dyer, and Noah Smith. 2016. Many languages, one parser. *Transactions of the Association for Computational Linguistics* 4:431–444. https://www.transacl.org/ojs/index.php/tacl/article/view/892.

Gabor Angeli, Melvin Jose Johnson Premkumar, and Christopher D. Manning. 2015. Leveraging linguistic structure for open domain information extraction. In *Proceedings of the 53rd Annual Meeting of the Association for Computational Linguistics and the 7th International Joint Conference on Natural Language Processing (Volume 1: Long Papers)*. Association for Computational Linguistics, Beijing, China, pages 344–354. http://www.aclweb.org/anthology/P15-1034.

Dzmitry Bahdanau, Kyunghyun Cho, and Yoshua Bengio. 2015. Neural machine translation by jointly learning to align and translate. *Proceedings of the 3rd International Conference on Learning Representations* .

Miguel Ballesteros, Chris Dyer, and Noah A. Smith. 2015. Improved transition-based parsing by modeling characters instead of words with lstms. In *Proceedings of the 2015 Conference on Empirical Methods in Natural Language Processing*. Association for Computational Linguistics, Lisbon, Portugal, pages 349–359. http://aclweb.org/anthology/D15-1041.

Piotr Bojanowski, Edouard Grave, Armand Joulin, and Tomas Mikolov. 2016. Enriching word vectors with subword information. *arXiv preprint arXiv:1607.04606* .

Xavier Carreras and Michael Collins. 2009. Nonprojective parsing for statistical machine translation. In *Proceedings of the 2009 Conference on Empirical Methods in Natural Language Processing: Volume 1 - Volume 1*. Association for Computational Linguistics, Stroudsburg, PA, USA, EMNLP '09, pages 200–209. http://dl.acm.org/citation.cfm?id=1699510.1699537.

Danqi Chen and Christopher Manning. 2014. A fast and accurate dependency parser using neural networks. In *Proceedings of the 2014 Conference on Empirical Methods in Natural Language Processing (EMNLP)*. Association for Computational Linguistics, Doha, Qatar, pages 740–750. http://www.aclweb.org/anthology/D14-1082.

Y. J. Chu and T. H. Liu. 1965. On the shortest arborescence of a directed graph. *Science Sinica* 14.

Hang Cui, Renxu Sun, Keya Li, Min-Yen Kan, and Tat-Seng Chua. 2005. Question answering passage retrieval using dependency relations. In *Proceedings of the 28th Annual International ACM SIGIR Conference on Research and Development in Information Retrieval*. ACM, New York, NY, USA, SIGIR '05, pages 400–407. https://doi.org/10.1145/1076034.1076103.

Matthew S. Dryer and Martin Haspelmath, editors. 2013. *WALS Online*. Max Planck Institute for Evolutionary Anthropology, Leipzig. http://wals.info/.

Long Duong, Trevor Cohn, Steven Bird, and Paul Cook. 2015a. Low resource dependency parsing: Cross-lingual parameter sharing in a neural network parser. In *Proceedings of the 53rd Annual Meeting of the Association for Computational Linguistics and the 7th International Joint Conference on Natural Language Processing (Volume 2: Short Papers)*. Association for Computational Linguistics, Beijing, China, pages 845–850. http://www.aclweb.org/anthology/P15-2139.

Long Duong, Trevor Cohn, Steven Bird, and Paul Cook. 2015b. A neural network model for low-resource universal dependency parsing. In *Proceedings of the 2015 Conference on Empirical Methods in Natural Language Processing*. Association for Computational Linguistics, Lisbon, Portugal, pages 339–348. http://aclweb.org/anthology/D15-1040.

Chris Dyer, Miguel Ballesteros, Wang Ling, Austin Matthews, and Noah A. Smith. 2015. Transition-based dependency parsing with stack long short-term memory. In *Proceedings of the 53rd Annual Meeting of the Association for Computational Linguistics and the 7th International Joint Conference on Natural Language Processing (Volume 1: Long Papers)*. Association for Computational Linguistics, Beijing, China, pages 334–343. http://www.aclweb.org/anthology/P15-1033.

Chris Dyer, Victor Chahuneau, and Noah A. Smith. 2013. A simple, fast, and effective reparameterization of ibm model 2. In *Proceedings of the 2013 Conference of the North American Chapter of the Association for Computational Linguistics: Human

Language Technologies. Association for Computational Linguistics, Atlanta, Georgia, pages 644–648. http://www.aclweb.org/anthology/N13-1073.

Jack Edmonds. 1967. Optimum branchings. *Journal of Research of the National Bureau of Standards B* 71(4):233–240.

Jason Eisner. 1996. Efficient normal-form parsing for combinatory categorial grammar. In *Proceedings of the 34th Annual Meeting of the Association for Computational Linguistics*. Association for Computational Linguistics, Santa Cruz, California, USA, pages 79–86. https://doi.org/10.3115/981863.981874.

Xavier Glorot, Antoine Bordes, and Yoshua Bengio. 2011. Deep sparse rectifier neural networks. In *International Conference on Artificial Intelligence and Statistics*. Cadiz, Spain, pages 315–323.

Jiang Guo, Wanxiang Che, David Yarowsky, Haifeng Wang, and Ting Liu. 2015. Cross-lingual dependency parsing based on distributed representations. In *Proceedings of the 53rd Annual Meeting of the Association for Computational Linguistics and the 7th International Joint Conference on Natural Language Processing (Volume 1: Long Papers)*. Association for Computational Linguistics, Beijing, China, pages 1234–1244. http://www.aclweb.org/anthology/P15-1119.

Jiang Guo, Wanxiang Che, David Yarowsky, Haifeng Wang, and Ting Liu. 2016. A representation learning framework for multi-source transfer parsing. https://www.aaai.org/ocs/index.php/AAAI/AAAI16/paper/view/12236.

Eliyahu Kiperwasser and Yoav Goldberg. 2016. Simple and accurate dependency parsing using bidirectional lstm feature representations. *Transactions of the Association for Computational Linguistics* 4:313–327. https://transacl.org/ojs/index.php/tacl/article/view/885.

Ryan McDonald, Koby Crammer, and Fernando Pereira. 2005. Online large-margin training of dependency parsers. In *Proceedings of the 43rd Annual Meeting of the Association for Computational Linguistics (ACL'05)*. Association for Computational Linguistics, Ann Arbor, Michigan, pages 91–98. https://doi.org/10.3115/1219840.1219852.

Ryan McDonald, Slav Petrov, and Keith Hall. 2011. Multi-source transfer of delexicalized dependency parsers. In *Proceedings of the 2011 Conference on Empirical Methods in Natural Language Processing*. Association for Computational Linguistics, Edinburgh, Scotland, UK., pages 62–72. http://www.aclweb.org/anthology/D11-1006.

Joakim Nivre, Željko Agić, Maria Jesus Aranzabe, Masayuki Asahara, Aitziber Atutxa, Miguel Ballesteros, John Bauer, Kepa Bengoetxea, Riyaz Ahmad Bhat, Cristina Bosco, Sam Bowman, Giuseppe G. A. Celano, Miriam Connor, Marie-Catherine de Marneffe, Arantza Diaz de Ilarraza, Kaja Dobrovoljc, Timothy Dozat, Tomaž Erjavec, Richárd Farkas, Jennifer Foster, Daniel Galbraith, Filip Ginter, Iakes Goenaga, Koldo Gojenola, Yoav Goldberg, Berta Gonzales, Bruno Guillaume, Jan Hajič, Dag Haug, Radu Ion, Elena Irimia, Anders Johannsen, Hiroshi Kanayama, Jenna Kanerva, Simon Krek, Veronika Laippala, Alessandro Lenci, Nikola Ljubešić, Teresa Lynn, Christopher Manning, Ctlina Mrnduc, David Mareček, Héctor Martínez Alonso, Jan Mašek, Yuji Matsumoto, Ryan McDonald, Anna Missilä, Verginica Mititelu, Yusuke Miyao, Simonetta Montemagni, Shunsuke Mori, Hanna Nurmi, Petya Osenova, Lilja Øvrelid, Elena Pascual, Marco Passarotti, Cenel-Augusto Perez, Slav Petrov, Jussi Piitulainen, Barbara Plank, Martin Popel, Prokopis Prokopidis, Sampo Pyysalo, Loganathan Ramasamy, Rudolf Rosa, Shadi Saleh, Sebastian Schuster, Wolfgang Seeker, Mojgan Seraji, Natalia Silveira, Maria Simi, Radu Simionescu, Katalin Simkó, Kiril Simov, Aaron Smith, Jan Štěpánek, Alane Suhr, Zsolt Szántó, Takaaki Tanaka, Reut Tsarfaty, Sumire Uematsu, Larraitz Uria, Viktor Varga, Veronika Vincze, Zdeněk Žabokrtský, Daniel Zeman, and Hanzhi Zhu. 2015. Universal dependencies 1.2 LINDAT/CLARIN digital library at Institute of Formal and Applied Linguistics, Charles University in Prague. http://hdl.handle.net/11234/1-1548.

Joakim Nivre, Marie-Catherine de Marneffe, Filip Ginter, Yoav Goldberg, Jan Hajič, Christopher Manning, Ryan McDonald, Slav Petrov, Sampo Pyysalo, Natalia Silveira, Reut Tsarfaty, and Daniel Zeman. 2016. Universal Dependencies v1: A multilingual treebank collection. In *Proceedings of the 10th International Conference on Language Resources and Evaluation (LREC 2016)*. European Language Resources Association, Portoro, Slovenia, pages 1659–1666.

Joakim Nivre and Chiao-Ting Fang. 2017. Universal dependency evaluation. In *Proceedings of the NoDaLiDa 2017 Workshop on Universal Dependencies (UDW 2017)*. pages 86–95.

Joakim Nivre, Johan Hall, Jens Nilsson, Gülşen Eryiğit, and Svetoslav Marinov. 2006. Labeled pseudo-projective dependency parsing with support vector machines. In *Proceedings of the Tenth Conference on Computational Natural Language Learning (CoNLL-X)*. Association for Computational Linguistics, New York City, pages 221–225. http://www.aclweb.org/anthology/W/W06/W06-2933.

Joakim Nivre et al. 2017. Universal Dependencies 2.0. LINDAT/CLARIN digital library at the Institute of Formal and Applied Linguistics, Charles University, Prague, http://hdl.handle.net/11234/1-1983. http://hdl.handle.net/11234/1-1983.

Martin Potthast, Tim Gollub, Francisco Rangel, Paolo Rosso, Efstathios Stamatatos, and Benno Stein. 2014. Improving the reproducibility of PAN's shared tasks: Plagiarism detection, author identification, and author profiling. In Evangelos Kanoulas, Mihai Lupu, Paul Clough, Mark Sanderson, Mark Hall, Allan Hanbury, and Elaine Toms, editors, *Information Access Evaluation meets Multilinguality, Multimodality, and Visualization. 5th International Conference of the CLEF Initiative (CLEF 14)*. Springer, Berlin Heidelberg New York, pages 268–299. https://doi.org/10.1007/978-3-319-11382-1_22.

Milan Straka, Jan Hajič, and Jana Straková. 2016. UDPipe: trainable pipeline for processing CoNLL-U files performing tokenization, morphological analysis, POS tagging and parsing. In *Proceedings of the 10th International Conference on Language Resources and Evaluation (LREC 2016)*. European Language Resources Association, Portoro, Slovenia.

Jörg Tiedemann. 2009. News from OPUS - A collection of multilingual parallel corpora with tools and interfaces. In N. Nicolov, K. Bontcheva, G. Angelova, and R. Mitkov, editors, *Recent Advances in Natural Language Processing*, John Benjamins, Amsterdam/Philadelphia, Borovets, Bulgaria, volume V, pages 237–248.

Jörg Tiedemann. 2012. Parallel data, tools and interfaces in opus. In Nicoletta Calzolari (Conference Chair), Khalid Choukri, Thierry Declerck, Mehmet Ugur Dogan, Bente Maegaard, Joseph Mariani, Jan Odijk, and Stelios Piperidis, editors, *Proceedings of the Eight International Conference on Language Resources and Evaluation (LREC'12)*. European Language Resources Association (ELRA), Istanbul, Turkey.

Daniel Zeman, Martin Popel, Milan Straka, Jan Hajič, Joakim Nivre, Filip Ginter, Juhani Luotolahti, Sampo Pyysalo, Slav Petrov, Martin Potthast, Francis Tyers, Elena Badmaeva, Memduh Gökırmak, Anna Nedoluzhko, Silvie Cinková, Jan Hajič jr., Jaroslava Hlaváčová, Václava Kettnerová, Zdeňka Urešová, Jenna Kanerva, Stina Ojala, Anna Missilä, Christopher Manning, Sebastian Schuster, Siva Reddy, Dima Taji, Nizar Habash, Herman Leung, Marie-Catherine de Marneffe, Manuela Sanguinetti, Maria Simi, Hiroshi Kanayama, Valeria de Paiva, Kira Droganova, Hĕctor Martínez Alonso, Hans Uszkoreit, Vivien Macketanz, Aljoscha Burchardt, Kim Harris, Katrin Marheinecke, Georg Rehm, Tolga Kayadelen, Mohammed Attia, Ali Elkahky, Zhuoran Yu, Emily Pitler, Saran Lertpradit, Michael Mandl, Jesse Kirchner, Hector Fernandez Alcalde, Jana Strnadova, Esha Banerjee, Ruli Manurung, Antonio Stella, Atsuko Shimada, Sookyoung Kwak, Gustavo Mendonça, Tatiana Lando, Rattima Nitisaroj, and Josie Li. 2017. CoNLL 2017 Shared Task: Multilingual Parsing from Raw Text to Universal Dependencies. In *Proceedings of the CoNLL 2017 Shared Task: Multilingual Parsing from Raw Text to Universal Dependencies*. Association for Computational Linguistics.

Xingxing Zhang, Jianpeng Cheng, and Mirella Lapata. 2017. Dependency parsing as head selection. In *Proceedings of the 15th Conference of the European Chapter of the Association for Computational Linguistics: Volume 1, Long Papers*. Association for Computational Linguistics, Valencia, Spain, pages 665–676. http://www.aclweb.org/anthology/E17-1063.

Yuan Zhang and Regina Barzilay. 2015. Hierarchical low-rank tensors for multilingual transfer parsing. In *Proceedings of the 2015 Conference on Empirical Methods in Natural Language Processing*. Association for Computational Linguistics, Lisbon, Portugal, pages 1857–1867. http://aclweb.org/anthology/D15-1213.

Multi-Model and Crosslingual Dependency Analysis

Johannes Heinecke, Munshi Asadullah
Orange Labs
2 avenue Pierre Marzin
F - 22300 Lannion, France
`{johannes.heinecke,munshi.asadullah}@orange.com`

Abstract

This paper describes the system of the team Orange-Deskiñ, used for the *CoNLL 2017 UD Shared Task*. We based our approach on an existing open source tool (BistParser), which we modified in order to produce the required output. Additionally we added a kind of pseudo-projectivisation. This was needed since some of the task's languages have a high percentage of non-projective dependency trees. In most cases we also employed word embeddings. For the 4 surprise languages, the data provided seemed too little to train on. Thus we decided to use the training data of typologically close languages instead. Our system achieved a macro-averaged LAS of 68.61% (10th in the overall ranking) which improved to 69.38% after bug fixes.

1 Introduction

For our work in our lab (Orange-Deskiñ) we needed a robust dependency analysis for written French with the highest Labeled Attachment Score (LAS)[1] possible, using a wide range of dependency relations. Having worked in the past on rule based dependency analysis, it became obvious that we need to adopt a more modern approach to dependency analysis. Thus during the last year we tried several freely available open source tools available (e.g. MaltParser[2], Google's SyntaxNet[3], Standford Dependency Tools[4], Bist-

Parser[5] and HTParser[6]), trained on different Treebanks (notably French Sequoia (Candito et al., 2014) and Universal Dependencies (McDonald et al., 2013)). All combinations of tools and treebanks had some advantages and some inconveniences. For instance, the underlying linguistic models of the treebanks are not the same or some tools would not accept CONLLU input but only raw text and apply their own segmentation and POS tagging.

In a next step we enriched the French treebanks with additional information like lemmas, morphological features and more fine-graded XPOS in addition to the about 20 UPOS categories of the treebanks (UD-French v1.2 does not contain neither lemmas nor morphological features) and conducted a new training/test/evaluation cycle. Since the initial results for French were encouraging we tried the same approaches with other languages, such as the languages proposed for *CoNLL 2017 UD Shared Task* (Zeman et al., 2017). However, for participation at the shared task, we relied exclusively on the data provided by Universal Dependencies (Nivre et al., 2016, 2017b), also for French in spite of our previous work.

For the shared task we have trained models separately for each language. So strictly speaking, this is not a multilingual but a monolingual multi-model approach.

2 System Description

2.1 Software

For the shared task, we used an (older) version of BistParser for all treebanks (ud-treebanks-conll2017). BistParser (Kiperwasser and Goldberg, 2016) is a transition based parser (Nivre (2008), and which uses the arc-hybrid transition

---

[1]Since we are interested in semantic relations a good CLAS score (Nivre and Fang, 2017) is even more relevant.

[2]`http://www.maltparser.org/`

[3]`https://www.tensorflow.org/versions/r0.11/tutorials/syntaxnet/`

[4]`https://nlp.stanford.edu/software/stanford-dependencies.shtml`

[5]`https://github.com/elikip/bist-parser`

[6]`https://github.com/elikip/htparser`

Proceedings of the CoNLL 2017 Shared Task: Multilingual Parsing from Raw Text to Universal Dependencies, pages 111–118,
Vancouver, Canada, August 3-4, 2017. © 2017 Association for Computational Linguistics

system (Kuhlmann et al., 2011)) with the three "basic" transitions LEFT ARC, RIGHT ARC and SHIFT. Since the shared task requires that output dependency trees have exactly one root, we modified BistParser accordingly by deleting the additional ROOT node added to each sentence in the original version of this parser. BistParser uses a bidirectional LSTM neural network. Currently BistParser uses forms and XPOS for both learning and predicting. We have started implementing the use of feature column as well, but this has not been used for the *CoNLL 2017 UD Shared Task*.

Some of the languages in the shared task have a large percentage of non-projective sentences. We thus decided to implement a pseudo-projectivisation (Kübler et al., 2009, p. 37) of the input sentences before training or predicting. The output sentences are than de-projectivised. Sometimes of course, the de-projectivisation can fail, especially if there are other dependency relation errors. Our tests showed, however, that the overall result for most languages is still better than without any pseudo-projectivisation.

Finally we implemented filters which ignore the special CONLLU lines for multi-word tokens (`2-3 ...`) and elliptic insertions (`4.1 ...`) and reinsert those lines after predicting.

In order to reduce memory usage during training and prediction, we modified BistParser and the underlying CNN library[7] to load word embeddings only for the words present in the training or test data. For the same reason we modified BistParser to read sentences one by one, to predict, and to output the result, instead of reading the entire test file at once[8].

2.2 Training Data

We trained our models using all treebanks provided by the *CoNLL 2017 UD Shared Task*. Since for some of the languages there were no development treebanks available, we split the training treebank in order to get a small development corpus (10% of the training corpus is split to test during development). This posed a certain problem for treebanks like Kazakh and Uyghur, which are hopelessly small (31 and 100 sentences respectively). Eventhough both languages are geneti-

cally and typologically very close to Turkish (3685 sentences), we finally trained on those small treebanks for time constraints (with more time available we would have experimented with various other parameters and a cross-lingual approach).

In most cases, adding word embeddings improved the LAS considerably. We downloaded the language specific corpora provided[9] by the task organisers and calculated our own word embeddings with Mikolov's `word2vec` (Mikolov et al., 2013)[10], which gave better results than the 100-dimensional word embeddings provided. In order to get the best results, we cleaned the text corpora (e.g. deleting letter-digit combinations and separating punctuation symbols such as commas, question marks etc. by a white space from the preceding token). For those languages which use an alphabet which has case distinction (Latin, Cyrillic and Greek) we put everything in lowercase. Finally we trained word embeddings with 300 and 500 dimensional vectors respectively. For all other parameters of `word2vec` we used the default setting, apart from the lower frequency limit, which we increased to 15 words.

The word embeddings were calculated on a server with a 32 core CPU running Ubuntu 14.04[11]. For the biggest text corpora like English (9 billion words), German (5,9 billion words), Indonesian (5 billion words) French (4,8 billion words) training for 500 dimensional word vectors took up to 6 hours (English).

A similar approach to `word2vec` is fastText The fundamental difference is the adoption of the "subword model" described in Bojanowski et al. (2016). A subword model is described as a open model allowing each word to be represented not only by the word itself but also the subword components of the word in combination. Subword components can be n-grams with varying values for n, stems, root words, prefixes, and suffixes or any other possible formalism. As a matter of fact, `word2vec` can been seen as the minimum configuration of fastText where only the words are considered. FastText has been demonstrated (Joulin et al., 2016) to perform rather well in two different tasks i.e. sentiment analysis and tag prediction. For the *CoNLL 2017 UD Shared Task* we finally

---

[7]`https://github.com/clab/cnn-v1`, CNN has meanwhile evolved to Dynet (`https://github.com/clab/dynet`)

[8]The code is available at `https://github.com/CoNLL-UD-2017/Orange-Deskin`

[9]`https://lindat.mff.cuni.cz/repository/xmlui/handle/11234/1-1989`

[10]`https://code.google.com/archive/p/word2vec/`

[11]Intel Xeon CPU E5-2640 v3 at 2.60GHz.

used `word2vec`, since the results were similar, but fastText was taking significantly more time to train.

3 Training and development

We trained all treebanks without any word embeddings, with 300 and with 500 dimensional word embeddings. For BistParser, the only other parameter we changed was the size of the first hidden layer (default 100) which we set to 50 (or lower, especially for languages whose treebanks are very small). Every sentence of the training treebanks was pseudo-projectivised before training. Using the weighted LAS, we then chose the best combination of parameters for each language. Since the python version of CNN (used by our adaptation of BistParser) does not support GPU, training was slow[12]. Thus we stopped training usually after 15 epochs unless the intermediary results were promising enough to continue. Figure 1 shows the system architecture. The upper part represents the data flow for the training, the lower part represents the predicting phase.

We did all training on two Ubuntu 16.04 servers[13] with 64 GB RAM. As said above, the version of the CNN library we used, does not run on GPU, so all training was single threaded. The training processes used up to 15 GB RAM, and took between 1 minute (Kazakh) and 53 hours (Czech). depending on the size of the treebank. This corresponds to 0.5 to 3 seconds per sentence during training. Training for the surprise languages (using treebanks of typologically close languages, cf. section, 4), took significantly longer (up to 90 hours for Czech).

Training was on the gold values (form, lemma, XPOS, UPOS, deprel, head) of the training treebanks[14], however, both, the development set (on the Tira-platform) and the final test set use the UDPipe output e.g. lemma, XPOS or UPOS (Straka et al., 2016) which may be erroneous. So we expected a certain drop of LAS for the tests. In order to be prepared, we tried to add erroneous lemmas and UPOS in the training data. This, however, did not produce better results, so we abandoned the

---

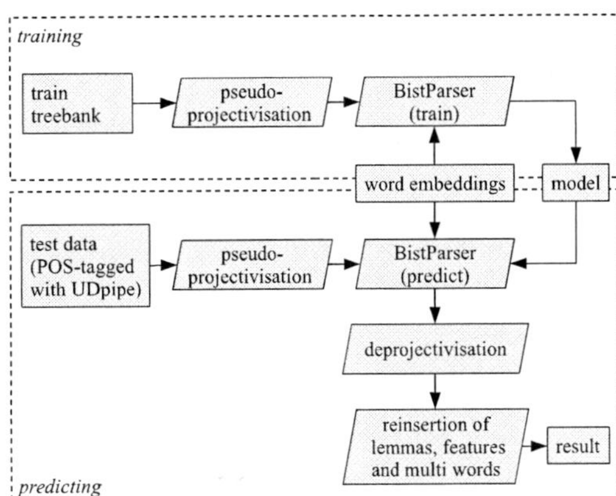

Figure 1: Schema of the system architecture

idea. Knowing that training takes a certain time we did not POS-tag the training treebanks with UDpipe to have similar "noise" than the test treebanks. The final results obtained with the development corpora (or split from train corpora when there were no development corpora) are shown in table 1. We did not (yet) use the morphological features (column 6). First tests on French showed that a slight increase in LAS is possible, so we will work on this in the future.

With 16GB RAM on the virtual machine provided by Tira (Potthast et al., 2014)[15] the 56 development corpora (on the Tira platform) were processed in about 130 minutes.

4 Surprise languages

The biggest challenge were the 4 surprise languages. Having only between 20 and 109 sentences to train on (even less if we wanted to split it into a train and development corpus) did not help (see table 2 for some details). Since the word embedding files where also rather small we chose not to train on the languages themselves, but to keep all of the provided sentences for the development corpus. So we first tried three similar approaches in order to be able to predict dependency relations for these languages:

1. lumping together 2000 sentences of 11 typologically different languages (German, Irish, Russian, Spanish, Turkisch, Arabic, Persian, Indonesian, Basque, Finnish and Estonian)

2. lumping together 5000 sentences of 11 typologically different languages (as above)

---

[12]The successor of CNN, Dynet, supports GPU, but since BistParser learns on a phrase by phrase base, no gain in time can be observed.

[13]Intel Xeon CPU E5-1620 v4 at 3.50GHz and Intel Core i7-6900K CPU at 3.20GHz respectively.

[14]Apart from numerous punctuation symbols with wrong heads, we found several bad annotations for words as well in different languages.

[15]The tests are run on the Tira platform (`http://www.tira.io`), we used Ubuntu 16.04 as operating system

treebank	number of dimensions of word embeddings	size of hidden layer	weighted LAS	treebank	number of dimensions of word embeddings	size of hidden layer	weighted LAS
ar	300	50	76.75	hu	300	40	64.72
bg	300	100	83.62	id	300	50	71.82
ca	300	50	85.67	it	500	100	86.34
cs	300	50	87.08	it-ParTUT	300	100	79.54
cs-CAC	300	100	85.93	ja	500	100	91.04
cs-CLTT	500	100	78.95	kk	300	100	31.53
cu	500	40	75.18	ko	300	50	73.76
da	500	40	72.46	la	300	50	54.40
de	300	50	78.03	la-ITTB	300	50	72.32
el	300	100	80.59	la-PROIEL	300	50	70.49
en	300	50	84.60	lv	300	50	69.47
en-LinES	500	40	77.83	nl	500	100	78.70
en-ParTUT	300	50	79.93	nl-LassySmall	500	100	73.99
es	300	50	80.29	no-Bokmaal	300	50	82.19
es-AnCora	500	100	85.60	no-Nynorsk	300	50	80.25
et	300	50	67.68	pl	500	40	86.78
eu	300	50	65.65	pt	300	50	91.21
fa	500	40	84.23	pt-BR	500	100	87.22
fi	300	100	77.84	ro	300	50	80.10
fi-FTP	300	50	82.70	ru	300	50	80.22
fr	500	100	83.64	ru-SynTagRus	300	50	82.06
fr-ParTut	500	100	83.03	sk	500	40	82.67
fr-Sequoia	300	50	80.42	sl	300	50	86.62
ga	500	100	64.84	sl-sst	300	100	60.24
gl	300	50	78.46	sv	500	100	80.01
gl-TreeGal	500	100	70.04	sv-LinES	300	50	79.73
got	none	100	68.53	tr	300	50	56.60
grc	500	40	58.21	ug	500	40	42.35
grc-PROIEL	300	50	66.81	uk	300	50	75.77
he	300	50	78.87	ur	500	100	80.89
hi	500	40	89.70	vi	500	100	71.06
hr	300	100	72.56	zh	500	100	78.28

Table 1: Development results (without surprise languages)

3. lumping together 2000 sentences of 23 typologically different languages (as above and Chinese, Japanese, Korean, Vietnamese, Romanian, Latin, Greek, Ancient Greek, Hebrew, Urdu and Hungarian)

	hsb	sme	kmr	bxr
sentences	109	20	65	20
words	460	147	242	153
has XPOS	no	yes	yes	no
has features	yes	yes	yes	yes

Table 2: Statistics on the data of the surprise languages

In all three cases we replaced the forms of all closed word classes (i.e. all but nouns, adjectives and verbs) with the corresponding UPOS in the training and in the test corpus (for the *CoNLL 2017 UD Shared Task* we inserted the original forms again after predicting the dependency relations. The "mix" is then trained with a hidden layer size of either 100 or 50, but without word embeddings. We initially tested these models using the test corpus for the Tamil treebank (UD v2.0). Using the "mix" with 23 languages (3) resulted in the best weighted LAS, 35.2% (35.3% if using a hidden layer size of 50). The weighted LAS for the surprise languages is shown in table 3.

language	hidden layer size	
	50	100
Upper Sorbian (hsb)	59.5%	63.2%
Northern Sami (sme)	49.2%	47.5%
Kurmanji (kmr)	28.9%	29.2%
Buryat (bxr)	25.3%	26.3%

Table 3: Weighted LAS of the surprise languages using a model trained on 23 languages

By replacing words of the closed word classes by their UPOS we tried to get similar corpora for training (on languages other than the surprise language) and predicting (surprise languages), assuming that the syntactical structures are similar enough, especially if we use only typologically close languages (see below). This technique avoids also the problem of different alphabets for typologically close languages, since we use UPOS and not character chains.

Eventhough these results were encouraging, we hoped an increase of the weighted LAS should still be feasible. Especially since some of the surprise languages are typologically (very) close to languages within the Universal Dependency corpus: Upper Sorbian is a slavonic language very close to Czech (and slightly less close to Polish). Northern Sami shares quite a lot of typological features with the Finnic branch of the Fenno-Ugric languages (here Finnish and Estonian), and Kurmanji shares at least some typolological feature with Persian (both are from the Iranian subgroup of the Indo-European language family. However Buryat, a Mongolian language, is not typologically close to any of the shared task's languages. Even though Turkish seems close enough, to our surprise Hindi was finally the best guess. With Urdu, which is very similar to Hindi apart from the fact that it uses the Arabic alphabet instead of Devanagari, the LAS was less good.

As for the language mix, we replaced the forms of the closed word classes in the training corpora by the corresponding UPOS (except nouns, verbs and adjectives) and trained the modified treebanks (cf. tables 4 and 5, best configuration in bold).

Upper Sorbian		Northern Sami	
cs (100)	**69.5%**	**fi (100)**	**52.9%**
cs (50)	67.5%	fiu[16](100)	51.7%
pl (50)	56.9%	fiu (50)	49.7%
pl (100)	51.9%	fi (50)	50.8%

Table 4: Weighted LAS using typologically close languages (with hidden layer size)

Kurmanji		Buryat	
fa (100)	**36.7%**	**hi (50)**	**32.0%**
fa (50)	35.8%	hi (100)	28.1%
hi (50)	22.2%	ur (50)	28.0%
hi (100)	22.0%	tr (100)	27.6%
ur (100)	20.6%	fi (100)	21.8%
ur (50)	20.6%	tr (50)	19.4%
		ja (50)	18.0%

Table 5: Weighted LAS using typologically close languages (with hidden layer size)

The reason for not replacing nouns, adjectives, and verbs is simple: Leaving the original words of the training corpus language and the test corpus language, means while the parser predicts, it comes across a word which it has never seen during training. But since it has the UPOS, it has

---

[16]*fiu* represents the Fenno-Ugric languages, in our case a mix of Finnish, Estonian and Hungaric

treebank	development results	final test results	difference
ar	76.75	67.26	-9.49
ar-pud (*unavailable for dev.*)		44.77	
bg	83.62	85.06	1.44
bxr (*surprise lg*)	32.00	25.25	-6.75
ca	85.67	86.24	0.57
cs	87.08	84.33	-2.75
cs-CAC	85.93	83.98	-1.95
cs-CLTT	78.95	72.99	-5.96
cs-pud (*unavailable for dev.*)		79.49	
cu	75.18	64.26	-10.92
da	72.46	73.54	1.08
de	78.03	73.38	-4.65
de-pud (*unavailable for dev.*)		69.75	
el	80.59	80.69	0.10
en	84.60	77.51	-7.09
en-LinES	77.83	73.36	-4.47
en-ParTUT	79.93	75.78	-4.15
en-pud (*unavailable for dev.*)		79.67	
es	80.29	83.03	2.74
es-AnCora	85.60	85.57	-0.03
es-pud (*unavailable for dev.*)		78.78	
et	67.68	58.98	-8.70
eu	65.65	65.29	-0.36
fa	84.23	80.87	-3.36
fi	77.84	73.97	-3.87
fi-FTP	82.70	78.64	-4.06
fi-pud (*unavailable for dev.*)		77.52	
fr	83.64	80.58	-3.06
fr-ParTut (*)	83.03	77.26	(tested with fr)
fr-pud (*unavailable for dev.*)		74.63	
fr-Sequoia	80.42	81.54	1.12
ga	64.84	63.10	-1.74
gl	78.46	79.66	1.20
gl-TreeGal (*)	70.04	22.46	(tested with gl)
got	68.53	57.97	-10.56
grc	58.21	54.10	-4.11
grc-PROIEL	66.81	65.50	-1.31
he	78.87	58.07	-20.8
hi	89.70	87.09	-2.61
hi-pud (*unavailable for dev.*)		51.02	
hr	72.56	77.11	4.55

treebank	development results	final test results	difference
hsb (*surprise lg*)	69.50	58.25	-11.25
hu	64.72	64.59	-0.13
id	71.82	73.64	1.82
it	86.34	86.65	0.31
it-ParTuT	79.54	(*withdrawn*)	
it-pud (*unavailable for dev.*)		84.89	
ja	91.04	73.37	-17.67
ja-pud (*unavailable for dev.*)		76.74	
kk	31.53	21.31	-10.22
kmr (*surprise lg*)	36.70	38.31	1.61
ko	73.76	67.76	-6.00
la	54.40	43.16	-11.27
la-ITTB	72.32	76.42	4.10
la-PROIEL	70.49	60.44	-10.05
lv	69.47	61.52	-7.95
nl	78.70	70.33	-8.37
nl-LassySmall	73.99	77.58	3.59
no-Bokmaal	82.19	83.79	1.60
no-Nynorsk	80.25	81.69	1.44
pl	86.78	81.71	-5.07
pt	91.21	76.40	-14.81
pt-BR	87.22	87.07	-0.15
pt-pud (*unavailable for dev.*)		69.00	
ro	80.10	81.34	1.24
ru	80.22	76.28	-3.94
ru-pud (*unavailable for dev.*)		69.58	
ru-SynTagRus	82.06	87.10	5.04
sk	82.67	75.97	-6.7
sl	86.62	82.38	-4.24
sl-sst (*)	60.24	40.25	(tested with sl)
sme (*surprise lg*)	52.90	33.08	-19.82
sv	80.01	78.85	-1.16
sv-LinES	79.73	74.28	-5.45
sv-pud (*unavailable for dev.*)		70.82	
tr	56.60	55.21	-1.39
tr-pud (*unavailable for dev.*)		34.36	
ug	42.35	34.24	-8.11
uk	75.77	62.30	-13.47
ur	80.89	77.93	-2.96
vi	71.06	39.12	-31.94
zh	78.28	59.33	-18.95
average	74.40	68.61	

Table 6: comparison of training results (on development corpora) and final results. Due to an error, the models for the treebanks marked (*) were unfortunately not used for the tests.

an idea what to do. If we took UPOS for verbs, nouns, and adjectives, this meant that the whole training (and test) corpus would only contain one single verb (namely VERB), noun (NOUN) and adjective (ADJ). Tests showed, that the parser got confused, since it encountered the same verb, noun or adjective in very different syntactic contexts. Of course, this applies also to prepositions or adverbs but keeping the open word classes gave the best development results.

As expected, Upper Sorbian and Norther Sami give quite acceptable results using models trained on Czech and Finnish respectively. Due to the fact that the provided treebanks for Kazakh and Uyghur are both very small we tried to apply the same approach of using the training corpus of a typologically close language (here Turkish). However, the results were disappointing. Thus, we continue to use the models trained on very small corpora for these two languages in the shared task. Possibly the fact that the raw text corpus used to calculate word embeddings for Kazakh and Uyghur are much bigger than those of the surprise languages allowed to produce usable word embeddings. If so, this would mean that word embeddings play a very prominent role in data driven dependency parsing.

5   Results of the Shared Task

Our final macro-averaged LAS F1 score on the *CoNLL 2017 UD Shared Task* test data (Nivre et al., 2017a) was 68.61%, (10th out of 33)[17]. The details show that our approach worked well for the bigger treebanks and the surprise languages (where we ended up as 8th). In general, the results per language are slightly lower than those we had during training on the development corpora (cf. table 1). This is due to the fact we did our training on forms, lemmas, UPOS and XPOS of the training corpus, which are gold. In the test data, lemmas, UPOS and XPOS (if present), however, are predicted by UDpipe, and do contain some errors with respect to the gold standard.

After the end of the test phase, we discovered a bug in our chain, which concerned languages, which have only UPOS data. In this case the UPOS information was totally discarded by error. Thus all training and testing are done only on the forms[18].

Further we made en error uploading the models for the `gl_TreeGal`, `fr_parTut` and `sl_sst` treebanks. During the tests the models trained on the basic `gl`, `fr` and `sl` treebanks were used instead. After the test phase we corrected these errors. Fortunately, their impact was not that hard. Apart from the result for `gl_TreeGal` and `sl_sst`, which went up to 66.13% (from 22.46%) and to 47.68 (from 40.25) respectively once the correct model was used, the results for the other corpora changed only slightly, the global results could have been 69.38%. All results are shown in table 6. The column on the right shows the difference between the results of the development corpora and test data. For some languages, the test results are unexpectedly lower than the results on the development corpora. For `gl_TreeGal`, `fr_parTut` and `sl_sst`, this is due to errors when installing our system on the Tira-platform. The lower performance on languages like Chinese, Ukrainian, Vietnamese or Latin (both ITTB and PROIEL) seems to be caused by the nature of the test corpora themselves. Systems of other participants seem to drop in performance as well; for all these languages our system is still around the 10th position of the global ranking. Perhaps a cause may be the fact that the XPOS we use (predicted by UDpipe) contain more errors than average for the Chinese, Ukrainian or Vietnamese treebanks than for languages where our test score is closer to the development score.

Acknowledgments

We would like to thank the developpers of Bist-Parser, Eliyahu Kiperwasser and Yoav Goldberg, and the developper of the CNN library (Chris Dyer) for making them available as open source on GitHub. Finally we would like to thank our colleague Ghislain Putois for help on all aspects on neural networks.

References

Piotr Bojanowski, Edouard Grave, Armand Joulin, and Tomas Mikolov. 2016. Enriching word vectors with subword information. *CoRR* abs/1607.04606. http://arxiv.org/abs/1607.04606.

---

[18]This concerns the treebanks da, en-LinES, es, eu, fr, fr-Sequoia, hr, hu, id, ja, nl-LassySmall, no-Bokmaal, no-Nynorsk, ru-SynTagRus and sv-LinEs.

Marie Candito, Guy Perrier, Bruno Guillaume, Corentin Ribeyre, Karën Fort, Djamé Seddah, and Éric de la Clergerie. 2014. Deep syntax annotation of the sequoia french treebank. In *Proc. of LREC 2014*. Reykjavík, Iceland.

Armand Joulin, Edouard Grave, Piotr Bojanowski, and Tomas Mikolov. 2016. Bag of tricks for efficient text classification. *CoRR* abs/1607.01759. http://arxiv.org/abs/1607.01759.

Eliyahu Kiperwasser and Yoav Goldberg. 2016. Easy-first dependency parsing with hierarchical tree lstms. *TACL* 4:445–461. https://transacl.org/ojs/index.php/tacl/article/view/798.

Sandra Kübler, Ryan McDonald, and Joakim Nivre. 2009. *Dependency Parsing*. Morgan and Claypool Publishers.

Marco Kuhlmann, Carlos Gómez-Rodríguez, and Giorgio Satta. 2011. Dynamic programming algorithms for transition-based dependency parsers. In *Proceedings of the 49th Annual Meeting of the Association for Computational Linguistics: Human Language Technologies - Volume 1*. Association for Computational Linguistics, Stroudsburg, PA, USA, HLT '11, pages 673–682. http://dl.acm.org/citation.cfm?id=2002472.2002558.

Ryan McDonald, Joakim Nivre, Yvonne Quirmbach-Brundage, Yoav Goldberg, Dipanjan Das, Kuzman Ganchev, Keith Hall, Slav Petrov, Hao Zhang, Oscar Täckström, Claudia Bedini, Núria Bertomeu, and Castelló Jungmee Lee. 2013. Universal dependency annotation for multilingual parsing. In *Proc. of ACL 2013*.

Tomas Mikolov, Kai Chen, Greg Corrado, and Jeffrey Dean. 2013. Efficient estimation of word representations in vector space. *CoRR* abs/1301.3781. http://arxiv.org/abs/1301.3781.

Joakim Nivre. 2008. Algoritms for deterministic incremental dependency parsing. *Computational Linguistics* 34(4):513–553.

Joakim Nivre, Željko Agić, Lars Ahrenberg, et al. 2017a. Universal dependencies 2.0 CoNLL 2017 shared task development and test data. LINDAT/CLARIN digital library at the Institute of Formal and Applied Linguistics, Charles University. http://hdl.handle.net/11234/1-2184.

Joakim Nivre, Marie-Catherine de Marneffe, Filip Ginter, Yoav Goldberg, Jan Hajič, Christopher Manning, Ryan McDonald, Slav Petrov, Sampo Pyysalo, Natalia Silveira, Reut Tsarfaty, and Daniel Zeman. 2016. Universal Dependencies v1: A multilingual treebank collection. In *Proceedings of the 10th International Conference on Language Resources and Evaluation (LREC 2016)*. European Language Resources Association, Portorož, Slovenia, pages 1659–1666.

Joakim Nivre and Chiao-Ting Fang. 2017. Universal dependency evaluation. In *Proceedings of the NoDaLiDa 2017 Workshop on Universal Dependencies (UDW 2017)*. Association for Computational Linguistics, Gothenburg, Sweden, pages 86–95. http://www.aclweb.org/anthology/W17-0411.

Joakim Nivre et al. 2017b. Universal Dependencies 2.0. LINDAT/CLARIN digital library at the Institute of Formal and Applied Linguistics, Charles University, Prague. http://hdl.handle.net/11234/1-1983.

Martin Potthast, Tim Gollub, Francisco Rangel, Paolo Rosso, Efstathios Stamatatos, and Benno Stein. 2014. Improving the reproducibility of PAN's shared tasks: Plagiarism detection, author identification, and author profiling. In Evangelos Kanoulas, Mihai Lupu, Paul Clough, Mark Sanderson, Mark Hall, Allan Hanbury, and Elaine Toms, editors, *Information Access Evaluation meets Multilinguality, Multimodality, and Visualization. 5th International Conference of the CLEF Initiative (CLEF 14)*. Springer, Berlin Heidelberg New York, pages 268–299. https://doi.org/10.1007/978-3-319-11382-1_22.

Milan Straka, Jan Hajič, and Jana Straková. 2016. UD-Pipe: trainable pipeline for processing CoNLL-U files performing tokenization, morphological analysis, POS tagging and parsing. In *Proceedings of the 10th International Conference on Language Resources and Evaluation (LREC 2016)*. European Language Resources Association, Portorož, Slovenia.

Daniel Zeman, Martin Popel, Milan Straka, Jan Hajič, Joakim Nivre, Filip Ginter, Juhani Luotolahti, Sampo Pyysalo, Slav Petrov, Martin Potthast, Francis Tyers, Elena Badmaeva, Memduh Gökırmak, Anna Nedoluzhko, Silvie Cinková, Jan Hajič jr., Jaroslava Hlaváčová, Václava Kettnerová, Zdeňka Urešová, Jenna Kanerva, Stina Ojala, Anna Missilä, Christopher Manning, Sebastian Schuster, Siva Reddy, Dima Taji, Nizar Habash, Herman Leung, Marie-Catherine de Marneffe, Manuela Sanguinetti, Maria Simi, Hiroshi Kanayama, Valeria de Paiva, Kira Droganova, Héctor Martínez Alonso, Hans Uszkoreit, Vivien Macketanz, Aljoscha Burchardt, Kim Harris, Katrin Marheinecke, Georg Rehm, Tolga Kayadelen, Mohammed Attia, Ali Elkahky, Zhuoran Yu, Emily Pitler, Saran Lertpradit, Michael Mandl, Jesse Kirchner, Hector Fernandez Alcalde, Jana Strnadova, Esha Banerjee, Ruli Manurung, Antonio Stella, Atsuko Shimada, Sookyoung Kwak, Gustavo Mendonça, Tatiana Lando, Rattima Nitisaroj, and Josie Li. 2017. CoNLL 2017 Shared Task: Multilingual Parsing from Raw Text to Universal Dependencies. In *Proceedings of the CoNLL 2017 Shared Task: Multilingual Parsing from Raw Text to Universal Dependencies*. Association for Computational Linguistics.

TurkuNLP: Delexicalized Pre-training of Word Embeddings for Dependency Parsing

Jenna Kanerva[1,2], Juhani Luotolahti[1,2], and Filip Ginter[1]
[1]Turku NLP Group
[2]University of Turku Graduate School (UTUGS)
University of Turku, Finland
`jmnybl@utu.fi, mjluot@utu.fi, figint@utu.fi`

Abstract

We present the TurkuNLP entry in the *CoNLL 2017 Shared Task on Multilingual Parsing from Raw Text to Universal Dependencies*. The system is based on the UDPipe parser with our focus being in exploring various techniques to pre-train the word embeddings used by the parser in order to improve its performance especially on languages with small training sets. The system ranked 11th among the 33 participants overall, being 8th on the small treebanks, 10th on the large treebanks, 12th on the parallel test sets, and 26th on the surprise languages.

1 Introduction

In this paper we describe the TurkuNLP entry in the *CoNLL 2017 Shared Task on Multilingual Parsing from Raw Text to Universal Dependencies* (Zeman et al., 2017). The Universal Dependencies (UD) treebank collection (Nivre et al., 2017b) has 70 treebanks for 50 languages with cross-linguistically consistent annotation. Of these, the 63 treebanks which have at least 10,000 tokens in their test section are used for training and testing the systems. Further, a parallel corpus consisting of 1,000 sentences in 14 languages was developed as an additional test set, and finally, the shared task included test sets for four "surprise" languages not known until a week prior to the test phase of the shared task (Nivre et al., 2017a). No training data was provided for these languages — only a handful of sentences was given as an example. As an additional novelty, participation in the shared task involved developing an end-to-end parsing system, from raw text to dependency trees, for all of the languages and treebanks. The participants were provided with automatically predicted word and sentence segmentation as well as morphological tags for the test sets, which they could choose to use as an alternative to developing own segmentation and tagging. These baseline segmentations and morphological analyses were provided by UDPipe v1.1 (Straka et al., 2016).

In addition to the manually annotated treebanks, the shared task organizers also distributed a large collection of web-crawled text for all but one of the languages in the shared task, totaling over 90 billion tokens of fully dependency parsed data. Once again, these analyses were produced by the UDPipe system. This automatically processed large dataset was intended by the organizers to complement the manually annotated data and, for instance, support the induction of word embeddings.

As an overall strategy for the shared task, we chose to build on an existing parser and focus on exploring various methods of pre-training the parser and especially its embeddings, using the large, automatically analyzed corpus provided by the organizers. We expected this strategy to be particularly helpful for languages with only a little training data. On the other hand we put only a minimal effort into the surprise languages. We also chose to use the word and sentence segmentation of the test datasets, as provided by the organizers. As we will demonstrate, the results of our system correlate with the focus of our efforts. Initially, we focused on the latest ParseySaurus parser (Alberti et al., 2017), but due to the magnitude of the task and restrictions on time, we finally used the UDPipe parsing pipeline of Straka et al. (2016) as the basis of our efforts.

2 Word Embeddings

The most important component of our system is the novel techniques we used to pre-train the

Proceedings of the CoNLL 2017 Shared Task: Multilingual Parsing from Raw Text to Universal Dependencies, pages 119–125,
Vancouver, Canada, August 3-4, 2017. © 2017 Association for Computational Linguistics

word embeddings. Our word embeddings combine three important aspects: 1) delexicalized syntactic contexts for inducing word embeddings, 2) word embeddings built from character n-grams, and 3) post-training injection and modification of embeddings for unseen words.

2.1 Delexicalized Syntactic Contexts

Word embeddings induced from large text corpora have been a key resource in many NLP task in recent years. In many common tools for learning word embeddings, such as word2vec (Mikolov et al., 2013), the context for a focus word is a sliding window of words surrounding the focus word in linear order. Levy and Goldberg (2014) extend the context with dependency trees, where the context is defined as the words nearby in the dependency tree with additionally the dependency relation attached to the context words, for example *interresting/amod*.

In Kanerva et al. (2017), we show that word embeddings trained in a strongly syntactic fashion outperform standard word2vec embeddings in dependency parsing. In particular, the context is fully delexicalized — instead of using words in the word2vec output layer, only part-of-speech tags, morphological features and syntactic functions are predicted. This delexicalized syntactic context is shown to lead to higher performance as well as generalize better across languages.

In our shared task submission we build on top of the previous work and optimize the embeddings even closer to the parsing task: We extend the original delexicalized context to also predict parsing actions of a transition-based parser. From the existing parse trees in the raw data collection, we create the transition sequence used to produce the tree and for each word collect features describing the actions taken when the word is on top-2 positions of the stack, e.g. if the focus word is first on stack, what is the next action. Our word–context pairs are illustrated in Table 1. In this way, we strive to build embeddings which relate together words which appear in similar configurations of the parser.

2.2 Word embeddings from character n-grams

It is known that the initial embeddings affect the performance of neural dependency parsers and pre-training the embedding matrix prior to training has an important effect on the performance of

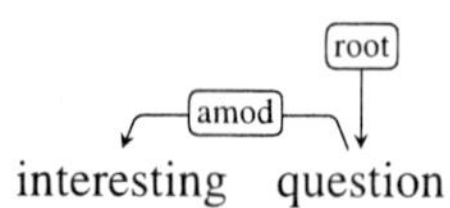

input	context
interesting	ADJ
interesting	Degree=Pos
interesting	amod
question	NOUN
question	Number=Sing
question	root
question	Dep_amod
interesting	stack1_shift
interesting	stack2_left-arc
interesting	stack2_left_amod
question	stack1_left-arc
question	stack1_left_amod
question	stack1_root

character four-grams
interesting, char_$int, char_inte, char_nter, char_tere, char_eres, char_rest, char_esti, char_stin, char_ting, char_ing$
question, char_$que, char_ques, char_uest char_esti, char_stio, char_tion, char_ion$

Table 1: Delexicalized contexts and character n-grams for word embeddings

neural systems (Chen and Manning, 2014; Andor et al., 2016).

Since the scope of languages in the task is large, the embeddings used for this dependency parsing task need to be able to be representative of languages with both large and small available resources, and also they need to be able to capture morphological information for languages with complex morphologies as well as those with less morphological variation.

To address better the needs of small languages with very little of data available as well as morphologically rich languages, we build our word embedding models with methods used in the popular fastText[1] representation of Bojanowski et al. (2016). They suggest, instead of tokens, to use character n-grams as the basic units in building embeddings for words. First, words are turned into character n-grams and embeddings are learned separately for each of these character n-grams. Secondly, word vectors are assembled from these

---

[1] https://github.com/facebookresearch/fastText

trained character embeddings by averaging all character n-grams present in a word. To make the embeddings more informative, the n-grams include special markers for the beginning and the end of the token, allowing the model for example to learn special embeddings for word suffixes which are often used as inflectional markers. In addition to the n-grams, a vector for the full word is also trained, and when final word vectors are produced, the full word vector is treated similarly as other n-grams and is averaged as part of the final product along with the rest. This allows for the potential benefits of token level embeddings to be materialized in our model.

Table 1 demonstrates the splitting of a word into character four-grams with special start and end markers. When learning embeddings for these character n-grams, context for each n-gram is replicated from the original word context, i.e. each character n-gram created from the word *interesting* gets the delexicalized context assigned for that word, namely *ADJ, Degree=Pos, amod, stack1_shift, stack2_left-arc, stack2_left_amod* in the example Table 1.

This procedure offers multiple advantages. One of them is the ability to construct embeddings for previously unseen words, a common occurrence especially with languages with small training corpora. With these character n-gram embeddings we are basically able to build an embedding for any word, except very few cases where we do not find any of the character n-grams from our trained model. Another advantage of this embedding scheme is its better ability to address the morphological variation compared to plain token based embeddings.

2.3 Data and Parameters

For the training of word embeddings for each language we took training data from the treebank training section and the automatically analyzed raw corpus (Ginter et al., 2017). Using also the treebank training section is important for very small languages where there is very little of raw data, especially for Old Church Slavonic where the raw data has only 29,000 tokens compared to 37,500 tokens in the treebank training set, while for big languages it barely makes any difference as the treebank data gets buried under the mass of raw data. For each language we build character n-gram

embedding models using word2vecf software[2] by Levy and Goldberg (2014) with negative sampling, skip-gram architecture, embeddings dimensionality of 100, delexicalized syntactic contexts explained in Section 2.1 and character n-grams of length 3-6. The maximum size of raw data used is limited to 50 million unique sentences in order to keep the training times bearable, and sentences longer that 30 tokens are discarded. Languages with only very limited resources we run 10 training iterations, but for rest only one iteration is used. These character n-gram models explained in detail in Section 2.2 can then be used to build word embeddings for arbitrary words, only requiring that at least one of the extracted character n-grams is present in our embedding model.

For parsing we also used the parameters optimized for UDPipe baseline system and changed only parts related to pre-trained embeddings. As we do not perform further parameter optimization, we trained our models always using the full training set, also in cases where different development sets were not provided. For small treebanks without development data, we did not test our models in advance but trusted methods tested on other treebanks to generalize also for these. For each language we include 100-dim word embeddings trained using our methods described in Sections 2.1 and 2.2. Additionally, pre-trained feature embeddings are trained for upos+feat combinations included in the xpostag column. These embeddings are trained using the transition actions as delixicalized context, and vectors for full feature combinations are constructed from individual features using the same character n-gram method as in the word embeddings (one feature is now the same as one character n-gram).

3 Parsing Pipeline

Our submission builds on top of the UDPipe parsing pipeline by Straka et al. (2016). We use data segmented by the UDPipe baseline systems as our system input, and then morphological analysis and syntactic parses are produced with our own UDPipe models. The UDPipe morphological tagger (MorphoDiTa (Straková et al., 2014)) is run as-is with parameters optimized for the baseline system (released together with the baseline models). The only exception is that we replaced the language-specific postag (*xpostag*) column with a combined

---

universal postag (*upostag*) and morphological features (*feats*), and trained the tagger to produce this instead of the language-specific postags. We did not expect this to affect the tagging accuracy, but instead it was used to provide pre-trained feature embeddings for the parser.

We further modified the UDPipe parser to allow including new embedding matrices after the model has been trained. This gives us an easy way to add embeddings for arbitrary words without a need of training a new parsing model. As we are able to create word embeddings for almost any word using our character n-gram embeddings described in Section 2.2, we are able to collect vocabulary from the data we are parsing, create vectors for previously unseen words and inject these vectors into the parsing model. This method essentially eliminates all out of vocabulary words.

3.1 Post-training modifications of word embeddings

The UDPipe parser uses the common technique of adjusting the word embeddings during training. The magnitude of the change imposed by the parser depends on the frequency of the word in the training data and, naturally, only words seen in the training set are subject to this training-phase adjustment. Therefore, we implemented a step whereby we transfer the parser adjustments onto the words not seen in the training data. For every such unseen word, we calculate its translation in the vector space by summing the parser-induced changes of known words in its neighborhood. These are weighted by their cosine similarity with the unknown word, using a linear function mapping similarities in the $[0.5, 1.0]$ interval into weights in the $[0.0, 1.0]$ range. I.e. known words with similarity below 0.5 do not contribute, and thereafter the weighting is linear. The overall effect of this modification observed in our development runs was marginal.

3.2 Parallel test sets (PUD)

Parallel test sets are parsed with a model trained on the default treebank of a language (the one without any treebank-specific suffix). For many languages only one treebank exists and no choice is needed, but for some there are two or even more choices. We chose to use these treebanks without treebank suffixes as the very first treebank included for a language will receive just the language code without the treebank suffix while newer treebanks will get a distinguishable treebank suffix. It then means that the default treebanks without suffixes have been part of the UD collection longer, many of these originating from the Google's Universal Treebank collection (McDonald et al., 2013). We hypothesized these treebanks to be more harmonized to the UD guidelines and apply better to the new test sets.

3.3 Surprise languages

In this work we did not concentrate on parsing the four surprise languages, and only used a very naive approach to complete the submission of all required test sets. For each surprise language we simply picked one existing model among all models trained for regular treebanks. We parsed the small sample of example sentences (about 20 sentences for each language) with all existing models, and picked the one which maximized the LAS score (Kazakh for Buryat, Galician-TreeGal for Kurmanji, Portuguese for North Sami and Slovenian for Upper Sorbian) without doing any treebank size, language family or related language evaluation. The only change in the parsing model is that during parsing, we mask all word embeddings, this way preventing the parser to use the vector for unknown word too often. This makes our parsing model delexicalized as all word embeddings are zeroed after training and not used in parsing, with the exception that parsing model is trained using information from word embeddings.

4 Results

The participating systems are tested using TIRA platform (Potthast et al., 2014), where the system must be deployed on a virtual machine and the test sets are processed without direct access to the data. Overall rank of our system in the official evaluation is 11th out of 33 participating teams with a macro-averaged labeled attachment score (LAS) of 68.59%.[3] On macro-LAS score across all treebanks, we are clearly behind the winning system (Stanford, 76.30%), but our pre-trained word embeddings are able to improve over the baseline UDPipe by 0.24% points on average. When looking only at treebanks with very little of training data we gain on average 2.38% over the baseline system. The same number for the big treebanks

---

[3]Full list of the official results can be found at `http://universaldependencies.org/conll17/results.html`.

only is +1.15%, +0.23% for parallel test sets and -16.55% for surprise languages. Based on these numbers we can clearly see that we managed to get a substantial improvement over the baseline system on very small languages where we also assumed our word embeddings to be most helpful. Instead, our very naive approach for handling surprise languages is clearly not sufficient, and a better approach should have been implemented. Detailed results of our system are shown in Table 2.

On official evaluation our system ranked sixth on universal part-of-speech tagging and second on morphological features. We see modest improvement of +0.22% (*upos*) and +0.27% (*feats*) over the baseline models. As word embeddings are not used in tagging and we use the same parameters as the baseline system, the only modification we did in tagging is that instead of using language-specific postags (*xpostag*), we concatenated universal postag and morphological features into xpostag column and trained the tagger to produce this concatenation.

5 Conclusions

We have presented our entry in the *CoNLL 2017 Shared Task on Multilingual Parsing from Raw Text to Universal Dependencies*, with the 11th rank of 33 participants. During the development, we have focused on exploring various ways of pre-training the embeddings used by the parser, as well as providing embeddings also for the unknown words in the data to be parsed. In particular, we have proposed a method of pre-training the embeddings using an entirely delexicalized output layer of the word2vec skip-gram model. This mode of pre-training the embeddings is shown to be superior to the usual approach of pre-training with the standard word2vec skip-gram with negative sampling. We have also explored, here with only a minimal improvement to the score, the possibility of post-hoc application of the adjustments effected by the parser on the word embeddings during the training phase. All our components used in this paper are freely available at `https://github.com/TurkuNLP/conll17-system`.

Acknowledgments

This work was supported by the Finnish Academy and the Kone Foundation. Computational resources were provided by CSC – IT Center for Science, Finland.

References

Chris Alberti, Daniel Andor, Ivan Bogatyy, Michael Collins, Dan Gillick, Lingpeng Kong, Terry Koo, Ji Ma, Mark Omernick, Slav Petrov, et al. 2017. Syntaxnet models for the conll 2017 shared task. *arXiv preprint arXiv:1703.04929* .

Daniel Andor, Chris Alberti, David Weiss, Aliaksei Severyn, Alessandro Presta, Kuzman Ganchev, Slav Petrov, and Michael Collins. 2016. Globally normalized transition-based neural networks. *arXiv preprint arXiv:1603.06042* .

Piotr Bojanowski, Edouard Grave, Armand Joulin, and Tomas Mikolov. 2016. Enriching word vectors with subword information. *arXiv preprint arXiv:1607.04606* .

Danqi Chen and Christopher D Manning. 2014. A fast and accurate dependency parser using neural networks. In *EMNLP*. pages 740–750.

Filip Ginter, Jan Hajič, Juhani Luotolahti, Milan Straka, and Daniel Zeman. 2017. CoNLL 2017 shared task - automatically annotated raw texts and word embeddings. LINDAT/CLARIN digital library at the Institute of Formal and Applied Linguistics, Charles University. http://hdl.handle.net/11234/1-1989.

Jenna Kanerva, Sampo Pyysalo, and Filip Ginter. 2017. Delexicalized contexts for pure dependency-based word embeddings. In *Proceedings of the International Conference on Dependency Linguistics (Depling'17)*. Under review.

Omer Levy and Yoav Goldberg. 2014. Dependency-based word embeddings. In *Proceedings of ACL*.

Ryan T McDonald, Joakim Nivre, Yvonne Quirmbach-Brundage, Yoav Goldberg, Dipanjan Das, Kuzman Ganchev, Keith B Hall, Slav Petrov, Hao Zhang, Oscar Täckström, et al. 2013. Universal dependency annotation for multilingual parsing. In *ACL (2)*. pages 92–97.

Tomas Mikolov, Kai Chen, Greg Corrado, and Jeffrey Dean. 2013. Efficient estimation of word representations in vector space. In *Proceedings of ICLR*.

Joakim Nivre, Željko Agić, Lars Ahrenberg, et al. 2017a. Universal dependencies 2.0 CoNLL 2017 shared task development and test data. LINDAT/CLARIN digital library at the Institute of Formal and Applied Linguistics, Charles University. http://hdl.handle.net/11234/1-2184.

Joakim Nivre et al. 2017b. Universal Dependencies 2.0. LINDAT/CLARIN digital library at the Institute of Formal and Applied Linguistics, Charles University, Prague, http://hdl.handle.net/11234/1-1983. http://hdl.handle.net/11234/1-1983.

Big Treebanks					
Treebank	Rank	LAS F1	Treebank	Rank	LAS F1
ar	17	65.74	hr	9	78.57
bg	11	84.85	hu	10	65.61
ca	11	85.64	id	12	74.87
cs	13	83.48	it	15	85.66
cs_cac	8	84.28	ja	15	72.81
cs_cltt	11	73.83	ko	11	66.93
cu	11	65.43	la_ittb	9	78.99
da	12	74.61	la_proiel	11	59.86
de	17	69.32	lv	8	62.13
el	13	79.93	nl	14	69.59
en	11	76.68	nl_lassysmall	14	79.06
en_lines	8	74.77	no_bokmaal	13	83.60
en_partut	13	74.48	no_nynorsk	10	82.35
es	15	81.79	pl	12	80.11
es_ancora	15	84.15	pt	10	82.91
et	10	59.79	pt_br	12	86.36
eu	13	70.22	ro	10	80.71
fa	20	76.54	ru	17	74.69
fi	9	75.82	ru_syntagrus	13	86.79
fi_ftb	9	75.59	sk	12	74.72
fr	12	80.61	sl	8	82.77
fr_sequoia	10	81.12	sv	12	77.35
gl	17	77.66	sv_lines	13	74.46
got	9	61.52	tr	13	54.69
grc	8	59.83	ur	14	77.06
grc_proiel	7	68.04	vi	14	38.07
he	16	57.50	zh	12	58.71
hi	7	87.75			
			All	10	74.19

Parellel Test Sets			Surprise Test Sets		
Treebank	Rank	LAS F1	Treebank	Rank	LAS F1
ar_pud	27	42.34	bxr	26	14.22
cs_pud	11	80.02	hsb	25	34.67
de_pud	17	66.78	kmr	23	22.19
en_pud	9	79.61	sme	27	10.99
es_pud	12	78.02	**All**	26	20.52
fi_pud	8	79.61			
fr_pud	14	74.17	Small Treebanks		
hi_pud	8	51.87	Treebank	Rank	LAS F1
it_pud	12	84.18	fr_partut	12	78.83
ja_pud	19	76.09	ga	7	64.25
pt_pud	12	74.09	gl_treegal	9	66.47
ru_pud	8	69.11	kk	2	28.31
sv_pud	16	69.90	la	9	47.91
tr_pud	15	34.09	la_ittb	9	78.99
All	12	68.56	la_proiel	11	59.86
			sl_sst	11	47.50
All treebanks			ug	6	36.51
Treebank	Rank	LAS F1	uk	7	63.70
All	11	68.59	**All**	8	54.18

Table 2: Rank and labeled attachment score for our system in the official evaluation.

Martin Potthast, Tim Gollub, Francisco Rangel, Paolo Rosso, Efstathios Stamatatos, and Benno Stein. 2014. Improving the reproducibility of PAN's shared tasks: Plagiarism detection, author identification, and author profiling. In Evangelos Kanoulas, Mihai Lupu, Paul Clough, Mark Sanderson, Mark Hall, Allan Hanbury, and Elaine Toms, editors, *Information Access Evaluation meets Multilinguality, Multimodality, and Visualization. 5th International Conference of the CLEF Initiative (CLEF 14)*. Springer, Berlin Heidelberg New York, pages 268–299. https://doi.org/10.1007/978-3-319-11382-1_22.

Milan Straka, Jan Hajič, and Jana Straková. 2016. UD-Pipe: trainable pipeline for processing CoNLL-U files performing tokenization, morphological analysis, POS tagging and parsing. In *Proceedings of the 10th International Conference on Language Resources and Evaluation (LREC 2016)*. European Language Resources Association, Portoro, Slovenia.

Jana Straková, Milan Straka, and Jan Hajič. 2014. Open-Source Tools for Morphology, Lemmatization, POS Tagging and Named Entity Recognition. In *Proceedings of 52nd Annual Meeting of the Association for Computational Linguistics: System Demonstrations*. Association for Computational Linguistics, Baltimore, Maryland, pages 13–18. http://www.aclweb.org/anthology/P/P14/P14-5003.pdf.

Daniel Zeman, Martin Popel, Milan Straka, Jan Hajič, Joakim Nivre, Filip Ginter, Juhani Luotolahti, Sampo Pyysalo, Slav Petrov, Martin Potthast, Francis Tyers, Elena Badmaeva, Memduh Gökırmak, Anna Nedoluzhko, Silvie Cinková, Jan Hajič jr., Jaroslava Hlaváčová, Václava Kettnerová, Zdeňka Urešová, Jenna Kanerva, Stina Ojala, Anna Missilä, Christopher Manning, Sebastian Schuster, Siva Reddy, Dima Taji, Nizar Habash, Herman Leung, Marie-Catherine de Marneffe, Manuela Sanguinetti, Maria Simi, Hiroshi Kanayama, Valeria de Paiva, Kira Droganova, Hĕctor Martínez Alonso, Hans Uszkoreit, Vivien Macketanz, Aljoscha Burchardt, Kim Harris, Katrin Marheinecke, Georg Rehm, Tolga Kayadelen, Mohammed Attia, Ali Elkahky, Zhuoran Yu, Emily Pitler, Saran Lertpradit, Michael Mandl, Jesse Kirchner, Hector Fernandez Alcalde, Jana Strnadova, Esha Banerjee, Ruli Manurung, Antonio Stella, Atsuko Shimada, Sookyoung Kwak, Gustavo Mendonça, Tatiana Lando, Rattima Nitisaroj, and Josie Li. 2017. CoNLL 2017 Shared Task: Multilingual Parsing from Raw Text to Universal Dependencies. In *Proceedings of the CoNLL 2017 Shared Task: Multilingual Parsing from Raw Text to Universal Dependencies*. Association for Computational Linguistics.

The parse is darc and full of errors: Universal dependency parsing with transition-based and graph-based algorithms

Kuan Yu **Pavel Sofroniev** **Erik Schill** **Erhard Hinrichs**

Department of Linguistics, University of Tübingen

{kuan.yu,pavel.sofroniev,erik.schill}@student.uni-tuebingen.de
erhard.hinrichs@uni-tuebingen.de

Abstract

We developed two simple systems for dependency parsing: *darc*, a transition-based parser, and *mstnn*, a graph-based parser. We tested our systems in the *CoNLL 2017 UD Shared Task*, with darc being the official system. Darc ranked 12th among 33 systems, just above the baseline. Mstnn had no official ranking, but its main score was above the 27th. In this paper, we describe our two systems, examine their strengths and weaknesses, and discuss the lessons we learned.

1 Introduction

Universal Dependencies (UD) (Nivre et al., 2016) is a cross-linguistically consistent annotation scheme for dependency-based treebanks. UD version 2.0 (UD2) (Nivre et al., 2017b,a) provided the datasets for the *CoNLL 2017 Shared Task: Multilingual Parsing from Raw Text to Universal Dependencies* (Zeman et al., 2017). In the shared task participating systems were evaluated through the *TIRA* platform (Potthast et al., 2014). The main evaluation metric was the labeled attachment F_1-score (LAS). 33 systems completed the official evaluation, including the baseline *UDPipe* (Straka et al., 2016).

We submitted a primary system *darc* and a secondary system *mstnn*, with the primary system partaking in the official evaluation. Both are open sourced under the *MIT* license.[1] The two systems differ only in the parsing algorithm. Darc is equipped with a *transition-based non-projective/projective* parser. Mstnn is equipped with a *graph-based non-projective unlabeled* parser and a standalone labeler. Both sys-

tems utilize a *neural network classifier* with similar input features.

In this paper, we start with a description of our treatments for different datasets in the shared task, and then the separate descriptions of our two parsers, followed by an analysis of the results.

2 Treatments for datasets

We were tasked with producing parsed outputs for 81 test-sets, either from raw texts or from segmented and tagged inputs produced by the baseline system.

The outputs were required to conform to the *CoNLL-U* format.[2] In this format, each node in a dependency-graph has ten fields named *ID, FORM, LEMMA, UPOSTAG, XPOSTAG, FEATS, HEAD, DEPREL, DEPS*, and *MISC*, where ID, HEAD, and DEPREL defines an edge. Segmentation establishes the graph/sentence boundaries while filling in ID, FORM, and MISC. Tagging fills in LEMMA, UPOSTAG, XPOSTAG, and FEATS.

63 test-sets have corresponding treebanks in UD2. These treebanks were the only training resources we used.

2.1 Big treebanks

The majority of the treebanks in UD2 (55/63) consist of train-sets and dev-sets. These are the big treebanks.

For segmentation and tagging, we trained UD-Pipe models on the train-sets and used the dev-sets for parameter tuning.[3] The only hyperparameter tuned by the dev-sets was the number of training iterations. All the other hyperparameters were

---

[1] https://github.com/CoNLL-UD-2017/darc

[2] http://universaldependencies.org/format.html

[3] Danish, Finnish-FTB, and Slovenian-SST treebanks are missing the SpaceAfter=No information in MISC. For training the tokenizers, this information was added.

Proceedings of the CoNLL 2017 Shared Task: Multilingual Parsing from Raw Text to Universal Dependencies, pages 126–133,
Vancouver, Canada, August 3-4, 2017. © 2017 Association for Computational Linguistics

simply taken from the baseline models (Straka, 2017), because of our limited computing power.

The gold-standard train-sets were re-tagged by our UDPipe models to produce training data for our parsers.

2.2 Small treebanks

The remainder of the treebanks (8/63) consist only of train-sets. These are the small treebanks.

Here we consulted the approach of the baseline system, which split the train-sets into three parts: train, tune, and dev. For our UDPipe models, both the train-sets and tune-sets were used for training, and the dev-sets for tuning. For our parser models, the entirety of treebanks was used for training, and all hyperparameters took the default values.

2.3 Parallel test-sets

The 14 parallel test-sets have no corresponding treebanks, but the corresponding languages exist. For these we used the preprocessed inputs from the baseline system, and picked our parser models according to the languages. If multiple treebanks exist for the same language, we took the model trained on the first one.

2.4 Surprise languages

4 test-sets have no corresponding languages, though small samples of gold-standard data were released as part of the shared task. Again, we used the preprocessed inputs from the baseline system.

For each sample we applied our existing parser models to pick the best treebank for training a delexicalized model. These delexicalized models rely mostly on UPOSTAG, but may utilize FEATS as well. This setting, along with the other hyperparameters, were tuned by the sample data.[4]

3 Primary system: darc

Our primary system employs a transition-based parser.

We adapted our parser from Chen and Manning (2014), who used a neural network classifier in a transition-based parsing algorithm known as the *arc-standard* system (Nivre, 2008).

The neural network classifier requires little feature engineering, and therefore is easily adaptable for different languages, making it ideal for UD parsing. However, the arc-standard system is only applicable to projective parsing, while over half of the treebanks in UD2 have more than 10% non-projective sentences in the train-sets. For this reason, we adopted a non-projective variant by adding a *swap* action to the transition system (Nivre, 2009; Nivre et al., 2009). We chose either the projective or the non-projective algorithm based on how they performed for each treebank. In the end, we used the non-projective one for all but three treebanks.[5]

3.1 The transition algorithm

The algorithm produces a directed acyclic graph from a sequence of nodes $[w_0, w_1, \ldots, w_n]$, which are the syntactic tokens of a sentence, where w_0 is a pseudo root node. The transition system consists of several transition actions defined over *configurations*. Each configuration is a triple consisting of a stack σ, a buffer β, and a set of edges A. From the initial configuration $c_0 \colon (\sigma \colon [w_0], \beta \colon [w_1, w_2, \ldots, w_n], A \colon \{\})$, a series of transition actions are taken to produce a terminal configuration $c_m \colon (\sigma \colon [w_0], \beta \colon [\,], A)$.

Possible transition actions are listed below. A different action is defined for each l in the set of dependency labels.

shift
$$(\sigma, [w_i | \beta], A) \mapsto ([w_i | \sigma], \beta, A)$$

left_arc$_l$
$$([w_j, w_i | \sigma], \beta, A) \mapsto ([w_j | \sigma], \beta, A \cup \{(w_j, l, w_i)\})$$

right_arc$_l$
$$([w_j, w_i | \sigma], \beta, A) \mapsto ([w_i | \sigma], \beta, A \cup \{(w_i, l, w_j)\})$$
$$\text{where } 0 \neq i$$

swap
$$([w_j, w_i | \sigma], \beta, A) \mapsto ([w_j | \sigma], [w_i | \beta], A)$$
$$\text{where } 0 < i < j$$

3.2 Input features

As input features, we use the set of 18 graph nodes from Chen and Manning (2014):

- The top three words on the stack & buffer

- The first & second leftmost & rightmost children of the top two words on the stack

---

[4] In the end, we used the Polish treebank for Buryat and Kurmanji, Finnish for North Sami, and Slovenian for Upper Sorbian. The FEATS field was used in the models for Buryat and North Sami.

[5] Persian, Spanish, and Vietnamese.

- The leftmost-of-leftmost & rightmost-of-rightmost children of the top two words on the stack

For each node we take its FORM, LEMMA, UPOSTAG, FEATS, and DEPREL fields. Each field is represented through an embedding into the real vector space. However, some treebanks have no informative LEMMA. For these treebanks we omit the LEMMA embedding, and double the dimension of the FORM embedding.[6]

All embeddings are trainable, except for the FEATS embedding. Each FEATS is represented by a vector of binary values, indicating the presence or absence of any attribute-value pairs in the morphological vocabulary of its affiliated treebank.

In any transition configuration, some nodes may be missing, for which special dummy members are in all embeddings. Special members are also appointed for the root node. For FORM and LEMMA, all hapaxes are replaced with a single arbitrary symbol.

Table 1 lists the number of rows (min, max & avg) and columns (dim) in the embedding matrices.

field	min	max	avg	dim
FORM	70	58562	9070	32
LEMMA	89	29972	6321	32
UPOSTAG	13	19	18	12
DEPREL	21	55	37	16

Table 1: Shapes of embedding matrices

The amount of parameters in the embedding matrices for FORM and LEMMA are substantial. Initializing these parameters with pretrained embeddings has been shown to be beneficial (Chen and Manning, 2014). To produce embeddings which are more suitable for capturing syntactic information, we used the tool developed by Ling et al. (2015).[7]

The embeddings for UPOSTAG and DEPREL are randomly initialized from the $uniform(-0.5, 0.5)$ distribution.

---

[6]Korean, Portuguese-BR, English-LinES, Indonesian, Swedish-LinES, and Uyghur.

[7]`https://github.com/wlin12/wang2vec/` with options `{-type 3 -hs 0 -min-count 2 -window 7 -sample 0.1 -negative 7 -iter 20}`; Though in fact `[-min-count 2]` had no effect, as we had all hapaxes replaced by an obscure symbol.

3.3 Feedforward neural network

Our neural network classifier is implemented in *Keras* (Chollet et al., 2015) with the *TensorFlow* backend (Abadi et al., 2015).

The inputs are first transformed by a hidden layer with 256 rectified linear units (*ReLU*), then by a second, similar hidden layer, and finally by a *softmax* layer with as many units as the number of transition actions. The softmax output assigns a probability prediction for each action.

The weights for all layers are initialized in a random uniform distribution following He et al. (2015). The ReLU layers have their biases initialized to ones, in order to alleviate the dying ReLU problem. The network is trained through backpropagation by the *AdaMax* (Kingma and Ba, 2014) algorithm.

In our experiments, we found it helpful to apply *dropout* (Srivastava et al., 2014) to both the trainable embedding layers and the hidden layers. For our network, 25% dropout rate seems to be the optimal. The 50% dropout rate suggested by Srivastava et al. (2014) requires extending the sizes of these layers, which would result in a polynomial amount of increase in the number of parameters. Even though we did find a slight improvement in accuracy with a larger network and a higher dropout rate, we rejected extending the network because of our limited computing power.

For regularization, we apply the *unit-norm* constraint to the trainable embeddings, which ensures that each column of the embedding matrices is a unit vector. We found this helpful for stabilizing the accuracy in later iterations and achieving higher scores. We also experimented with the *max-norm* constraint, which only forces the norms of the column vectors to be no greater than the max-norm; We found that it can be better than the unit-norm constraint, but only for certain optimal max-norm values, which were different for every dataset.

3.4 Training and parsing

These hyperparameters are tuned during training, with their default values marked bold:

- Algorithm: projective, **non-projective**

- Batch-size: 16, **32**, 64

- Iterations: maximally **16**

Our parser is greedy during parsing. From any configuration, only the action with the highest probability prediction is taken to advance into the next configuration. In case the action suggested by the classifier is illegal, the next best action is taken.

The transition algorithm does not prevent multiple nodes from being attached to the pseudo root node. However, this is not allowed in the UD treebanks. When this occurs, we keep the first attachment, and attach the other nodes to that node with the *parataxis* label.

Apart from the regular syntactic nodes, the CoNLL-U format allows for *empty-words* and *multi-words*. We completely ignore the empty-words. We keep track of the multi-words, but ignore them during parsing.

The evaluation is only concerned with the UD labels, and not the language-specific subtypes. For example, *acl:relcl* is considered to be the same as *acl*. We experimented with removing the language specific information before parsing, and we found it to be helpful in some cases, but harmful in others. Either way, the differences are negligible.

3.5 A comparison with Parsito

Our parser is very similar to the *Parsito* parser (Straka et al., 2015) incorporated in UDPipe, which is also a transition-based parser with a feedforward neural network classifier.

The primary difference is in the training. Our parser uses only a *static oracle*, while Parsito supports a *dynamic oracle*, and may additionally utilize a *search-based oracle*.

The static oracle produces transition sequences which must lead to the gold-standard parse trees. A classifier trained only on the gold-standard transition sequences is not robust against its own errors. When an error is made, the parser arrives in a configuration which it has never seen before. To help the classifier make the best decision possible in any configuration, the dynamic oracle (Goldberg and Nivre, 2012) explores erroneous transitions suggested by the classifier itself. Parsito's search-based oracle applies the *SEARN* algorithm (Daumé et al., 2009) to mitigate this problem.

Moreover, in addition to the projective and non-projective transition systems, Parsito supports *link2* (Attardi, 2006), a partially non-projective transition algorithm, which was used for more than one-third of the baseline models.

Despite the limitations of our parser in comparison with UDPipe's Parsito, it achieved comparable results in the shared task.

4 Secondary system: mstnn

In our secondary system, a graph-based non-projective unlabeled parser and a labeler are used.

4.1 Unlabeled parsing

We adapted the *MSTParser* (McDonald et al., 2005) with a neural network classifier. Starting with a fully connected directed graph, the classifier scores the edges between every two nodes, and then the *Chu-Liu-Edmonds' algorithm* (Chu and Liu, 1965; Edmonds, 1967) is applied to find the *maximum spanning arborescence*. The algorithm was implemented using *NetworkX* (Hagberg et al., 2008).

The neural network classifier accepts the following inputs:

- The distance between the two nodes (the arithmetic difference of their ID)

- FORM & LEMMA of the two nodes

- UPOSTAG of the two nodes and their left & right & left-of-left & right-of-right neighbors

- FEATS of the two nodes and their left & right neighbors

All features are constructed the same as in the primary system, except for the added distance feature.[8] The structure of the neural network is also the same, except that the output layer consists of a single *sigmoid* unit. The probability prediction of the sigmoid unit is taken as the score associated with the dependency arc in consideration.

4.2 Labeling

For labeling the edges, we implemented a linear *support-vector classifier* (Cortes and Vapnik, 1995) using *LIBLINEAR* (Fan et al., 2008) through *scikit-learn* (Pedregosa et al., 2011).[9]

Input features to the classifier are the FORM, LEMMA, UPOSTAG, and FEATS fields of the two nodes, plus the UPOSTAG of their left & right neighbors. The FEATS field is represented in the

---

[8] Also as in the primary system, some features were omitted for certain treebanks.

[9] All hyperparameters used the default values.

	ranking	darc	baseline	ÚFAL	best score	best system
all treebanks	12	68.41	68.35	69.52	76.30	Stanford (Stanford)
big treebanks	15	73.31	73.04	74.38	81.77	Stanford (Stanford)
small treebanks	12	52.46	51.80	53.75	61.49	C2L2 (Ithaca)
parallel test-sets	16	67.96	68.33	69.00	73.73	Stanford (Stanford)
surprise languages	18	34.47	37.07	35.96	47.54	C2L2 (Ithaca)
Old Church Slavonic	7	66.37	62.76	62.76	76.84	IMS (Stuttgart)
Gothic	8	61.92	59.81	62.80	71.36	IMS (Stuttgart)
Hindi	8	87.50	86.77	87.28	91.59	Stanford (Stanford)
German PUD	25	65.09	66.53	66.05	74.86	Stanford (Stanford)
Buryat	25	15.61	31.50	21.58	32.24	IMS (Stuttgart)
Korean	25	58.30	59.09	60.30	82.49	Stanford (Stanford)

Table 2: Official results (LAS)

	UAS				LAS			
	mstnn	darc	baseline	ÚFAL	mstnn	darc	baseline	ÚFAL
all treebanks	71.03	74.22	74.41	**75.39**	61.13	68.41	68.35	**69.52**
Ancient Greek	**66.29**	64.92	62.74	65.37	54.78	**58.20**	56.04	57.39
Irish	**73.61**	72.81	72.08	73.10	57.55	**62.97**	61.52	62.87
Turkish	**61.45**	61.33	60.48	60.78	52.44	**54.70**	53.19	53.78
Uyghur	52.05	**53.79**	53.58	53.49	**34.32**	34.28	34.18	33.21

Table 3: Secondary results

same way as described above, while the other features are constructed through *one-hot* encoding.

5 Results

The official test-run took 1 hour 47 minutes on a single-core *Intel Xeon* CPU, which included segmentation, tagging, and parsing. The secondary system took 3 hours and 14 minutes.

In Table 2, we report our official LAS (labeled attached F_1-score) and our rankings among the 33 systems.[10] We compare our system against the baseline (UDPipe 1.1), ÚFAL (UDPipe 1.2), and the best systems. Included are the macro-averaged scores for all and some subsets of the treebanks, plus three of our best-ranking & worst-ranking per-treebank scores.

Our official system was far from the best, but it was comparable to the two UDPipe systems, despite having a much simpler parser. Parsing aside, it had the highest all-tags F_1-score with 73.92%, thanks to the *MorphoDiTa* (Straková et al., 2014) tool incorporated in UDPipe. However, the base-

line was very close with 73.74%.

In general, our primary system (darc) outperformed our secondary system (mstnn), both in LAS and UAS (unlabeled attached F_1-score). However, mstnn occasionally achieved better UAS or LAS, as shown in Table 3.

6 Discussions

In Section 3.5 we made a comparison between our darc parser and UDPipe's Parsito parser. Specifically, Parsito supports better oracles and an additional transition algorithm. We attribute the comparable performance of our much simpler parser to the following factors:

- We used more training data.

  The baseline models were trained on subsets of the train-sets, while using the rest for parameter tuning, leaving the dev-sets untouched. Our models were trained on the entire train-sets, and tuned on the dev-sets.

  We believe this was the reason that we ranked above the baseline but below ÚFAL.

- We used LEMMA when possible.

---

[10] http://universaldependencies.org/conll17/
results.html

In our experiments, we fixed the dimensionality of the lexical space, namely the target real vector space where we embed the lexical representation (FORM and/or LEMMA) of the vocabulary. We found that splitting the dimensions between FORM and LEMMA, as opposed to dedicating exclusively to either one, consistently produced the best results.

Further evidence of this is that for four out of the six treebanks where LEMMA was not used, darc performed worse than the baseline.

Splitting the lexical space between FORM and LEMMA actually decreases the number of parameters in the embedding matrices, comparing with using FORM alone, because LEMMA has fewer types.

- We had a better representation for FEATS.

Simply treating FEATS as atomic symbols is subject to data sparsity as shown in Table 4.

FEATS	max	avg
type count	2487	430
hapax type count	561	92
entry type count	112	44

Table 4: Statistics for FEATS

Different types of FEATS are merely different combinations of morphological entries, aka the attribute-value pairs. They are compound symbols with a visible structure, which should be preserved.

Our representation is explained in Section 3.2. We experimented with normalizing the FEATS vectors into unit vectors by their L^2-norm, or into probability distributions by their L^1-norm as in Alberti et al. (2015). But simple binary indicators seemed to work the best.

Despite the generally similar performance of the original MSTParser in comparison with transition-based parsers with similar learning algorithms, our own mstnn did not meet the expectation, when compared against darc.

The graph-based approach and the transition-based approach are faced with different challenges, and produces different types of errors (McDonald and Nivre, 2007). The former suffers less from the errors of local decisions, but the latter usually benefits from richer features. In our case, the neural network classifier in mstnn used much less information from neighboring nodes than the classifier in darc.

The separate labeler in mstnn was also suboptimal. From UAS to LAS, the absolute drop was 4% higher for mstnn than it was for darc, which actually means a 15.6% higher increase in error rate. This exemplified a general problem with the pipeline approach: Errors made in each step of the pipeline stack up quickly, which is made even worse by the snowball effect, where errors made in one step bring about more errors in the following steps. Another problem is that in a pipeline, the information necessary for making the correct decisions in one step may not be available until later. We experimented with unlabeled parsing using darc, and despite facing a much simpler task than labeled parsing, it yielded lower UAS.

The pipeline approach is a common weakness of our both systems. We believe that for tasks such as this one, an integrated end-to-end system is more desirable.

Acknowledgments

We thank Dr. Çağrı Çöltekin for his encouragement and expert support, which made this work possible. We also thank Dr. Daniël de Kok for his counseling and the anonymous reviewers for their advice.

References

Martín Abadi, Ashish Agarwal, Paul Barham, Eugene Brevdo, Zhifeng Chen, Craig Citro, Greg S. Corrado, Andy Davis, Jeffrey Dean, Matthieu Devin, Sanjay Ghemawat, Ian Goodfellow, Andrew Harp, Geoffrey Irving, Michael Isard, Yangqing Jia, Rafal Jozefowicz, Lukasz Kaiser, Manjunath Kudlur, Josh Levenberg, Dan Mané, Rajat Monga, Sherry Moore, Derek Murray, Chris Olah, Mike Schuster, Jonathon Shlens, Benoit Steiner, Ilya Sutskever, Kunal Talwar, Paul Tucker, Vincent Vanhoucke, Vijay Vasudevan, Fernanda Viégas, Oriol Vinyals, Pete Warden, Martin Wattenberg, Martin Wicke, Yuan Yu, and Xiaoqiang Zheng. 2015. TensorFlow: Large-scale machine learning on heterogeneous systems. Software available from tensorflow.org. http://tensorflow.org/.

Chris Alberti, David Weiss, and Slav Petrov. 2015. Improved transition-based parsing and tagging with neural networks .

Giuseppe Attardi. 2006. Experiments with a multilanguage non-projective dependency parser. In *Proceedings of the Tenth Conference on Computational Natural Language Learning*. Association for Computational Linguistics, pages 166–170.

Danqi Chen and Christopher D Manning. 2014. A fast and accurate dependency parser using neural networks. In *EMNLP*. pages 740–750.

François Chollet et al. 2015. Keras. `https://github.com/fchollet/keras`.

Yoeng-Jin Chu and Tseng-Hong Liu. 1965. On shortest arborescence of a directed graph. *Scientia Sinica* 14(10):1396.

Corinna Cortes and Vladimir Vapnik. 1995. Support-vector networks. *Machine learning* 20(3):273–297.

Hal Daumé, John Langford, and Daniel Marcu. 2009. Search-based structured prediction. *Machine learning* 75(3):297–325.

Jack Edmonds. 1967. Optimum branchings. *Journal of Research of the National Bureau of Standards B* 71(4):233–240.

Rong-En Fan, Kai-Wei Chang, Cho-Jui Hsieh, Xiang-Rui Wang, and Chih-Jen Lin. 2008. Liblinear: A library for large linear classification. *Journal of machine learning research* 9(Aug):1871–1874.

Yoav Goldberg and Joakim Nivre. 2012. A dynamic oracle for arc-eager dependency parsing. In *COLING*. pages 959–976.

Aric A. Hagberg, Daniel A. Schult, and Pieter J. Swart. 2008. Exploring network structure, dynamics, and function using NetworkX. In *Proceedings of the 7th Python in Science Conference (SciPy2008)*. Pasadena, CA USA, pages 11–15.

Kaiming He, Xiangyu Zhang, Shaoqing Ren, and Jian Sun. 2015. Delving deep into rectifiers: Surpassing human-level performance on imagenet classification. In *Proceedings of the IEEE international conference on computer vision*. pages 1026–1034.

Diederik Kingma and Jimmy Ba. 2014. Adam: A method for stochastic optimization. *arXiv preprint arXiv:1412.6980* .

Wang Ling, Chris Dyer, Alan Black, and Isabel Trancoso. 2015. Two/too simple adaptations of word2vec for syntax problems. In *Proceedings of the 2015 Conference of the North American Chapter of the Association for Computational Linguistics: Human Language Technologies*. Association for Computational Linguistics.

Ryan McDonald, Fernando Pereira, Kiril Ribarov, and Jan Hajič. 2005. Non-projective dependency parsing using spanning tree algorithms. In *Proceedings of the conference on Human Language Technology and Empirical Methods in Natural Language Processing*. Association for Computational Linguistics, pages 523–530.

Ryan T McDonald and Joakim Nivre. 2007. Characterizing the errors of data-driven dependency parsing models. In *EMNLP-CoNLL*. pages 122–131.

Joakim Nivre. 2008. Algorithms for deterministic incremental dependency parsing. *Computational Linguistics* 34(4):513–553.

Joakim Nivre. 2009. Non-projective dependency parsing in expected linear time. In *Proceedings of the Joint Conference of the 47th Annual Meeting of the ACL and the 4th International Joint Conference on Natural Language Processing of the AFNLP: Volume 1-Volume 1*. Association for Computational Linguistics, pages 351–359.

Joakim Nivre, Željko Agić, Lars Ahrenberg, et al. 2017a. Universal dependencies 2.0 CoNLL 2017 shared task development and test data. LINDAT/CLARIN digital library at the Institute of Formal and Applied Linguistics, Charles University. http://hdl.handle.net/11234/1-2184.

Joakim Nivre, Marie-Catherine de Marneffe, Filip Ginter, Yoav Goldberg, Jan Hajič, Christopher Manning, Ryan McDonald, Slav Petrov, Sampo Pyysalo, Natalia Silveira, Reut Tsarfaty, and Daniel Zeman. 2016. Universal Dependencies v1: A multilingual treebank collection. In *Proceedings of the 10th International Conference on Language Resources and Evaluation (LREC 2016)*. European Language Resources Association, Portoro, Slovenia, pages 1659–1666.

Joakim Nivre, Marco Kuhlmann, and Johan Hall. 2009. An improved oracle for dependency parsing with online reordering. In *Proceedings of the 11th international conference on parsing technologies*. Association for Computational Linguistics, pages 73–76.

Joakim Nivre et al. 2017b. Universal Dependencies 2.0. LINDAT/CLARIN digital library at the Institute of Formal and Applied Linguistics, Charles University, Prague, `http://hdl.handle.net/11234/1-1983`. http://hdl.handle.net/11234/1-1983.

F. Pedregosa, G. Varoquaux, A. Gramfort, V. Michel, B. Thirion, O. Grisel, M. Blondel, P. Prettenhofer, R. Weiss, V. Dubourg, J. Vanderplas, A. Passos, D. Cournapeau, M. Brucher, M. Perrot, and E. Duchesnay. 2011. Scikit-learn: Machine learning in Python. *Journal of Machine Learning Research* 12:2825–2830.

Martin Potthast, Tim Gollub, Francisco Rangel, Paolo Rosso, Efstathios Stamatatos, and Benno Stein. 2014. Improving the reproducibility of PAN's shared tasks: Plagiarism detection, author identification, and author profiling. In Evangelos Kanoulas, Mihai Lupu, Paul Clough, Mark Sanderson, Mark Hall, Allan Hanbury, and Elaine Toms, editors, *Information Access Evaluation meets Multilinguality, Multimodality, and Visualization. 5th International Conference of the CLEF Initiative*

(CLEF 14). Springer, Berlin Heidelberg New York, pages 268–299. https://doi.org/10.1007/978-3-319-11382-1_22.

Nitish Srivastava, Geoffrey E Hinton, Alex Krizhevsky, Ilya Sutskever, and Ruslan Salakhutdinov. 2014. Dropout: a simple way to prevent neural networks from overfitting. *Journal of Machine Learning Research* 15(1):1929–1958.

Milan Straka. 2017. CoNLL 2017 shared task - UDPipe baseline models and supplementary materials. LINDAT/CLARIN digital library at the Institute of Formal and Applied Linguistics, Charles University. http://hdl.handle.net/11234/1-1990.

Milan Straka, Jan Hajič, and Jana Straková. 2016. UDPipe: trainable pipeline for processing CoNLL-U files performing tokenization, morphological analysis, POS tagging and parsing. In *Proceedings of the 10th International Conference on Language Resources and Evaluation (LREC 2016)*. European Language Resources Association, Portoro, Slovenia.

Milan Straka, Jan Hajič, Jana Straková, and Jan Hajič jr. 2015. Parsing universal dependency treebanks using neural networks and search-based oracle. In *Proceedings of Fourteenth International Workshop on Treebanks and Linguistic Theories (TLT 14)*.

Jana Straková, Milan Straka, and Jan Hajic. 2014. Open-source tools for morphology, lemmatization, pos tagging and named entity recognition. In *ACL (System Demonstrations)*. pages 13–18.

Daniel Zeman, Martin Popel, Milan Straka, Jan Hajič, Joakim Nivre, Filip Ginter, Juhani Luotolahti, Sampo Pyysalo, Slav Petrov, Martin Potthast, Francis Tyers, Elena Badmaeva, Memduh Gökırmak, Anna Nedoluzhko, Silvie Cinková, Jan Hajič jr., Jaroslava Hlaváčová, Václava Kettnerová, Zdeňka Urešová, Jenna Kanerva, Stina Ojala, Anna Missilä, Christopher Manning, Sebastian Schuster, Siva Reddy, Dima Taji, Nizar Habash, Herman Leung, Marie-Catherine de Marneffe, Manuela Sanguinetti, Maria Simi, Hiroshi Kanayama, Valeria de Paiva, Kira Droganova, Hěctor Martínez Alonso, Hans Uszkoreit, Vivien Macketanz, Aljoscha Burchardt, Kim Harris, Katrin Marheinecke, Georg Rehm, Tolga Kayadelen, Mohammed Attia, Ali Elkahky, Zhuoran Yu, Emily Pitler, Saran Lertpradit, Michael Mandl, Jesse Kirchner, Hector Fernandez Alcalde, Jana Strnadova, Esha Banerjee, Ruli Manurung, Antonio Stella, Atsuko Shimada, Sookyoung Kwak, Gustavo Mendonça, Tatiana Lando, Rattima Nitisaroj, and Josie Li. 2017. CoNLL 2017 Shared Task: Multilingual Parsing from Raw Text to Universal Dependencies. In *Proceedings of the CoNLL 2017 Shared Task: Multilingual Parsing from Raw Text to Universal Dependencies*. Association for Computational Linguistics.

A Novel Neural Network Model for Joint POS Tagging and Graph-based Dependency Parsing

Dat Quoc Nguyen, Mark Dras and **Mark Johnson**
Department of Computing
Macquarie University, Australia
`dat.nguyen@students.mq.edu.au`
`{mark.dras, mark.johnson}@mq.edu.au`

Abstract

We present a novel neural network model that learns POS tagging and graph-based dependency parsing jointly. Our model uses bidirectional LSTMs to learn feature representations shared for both POS tagging and dependency parsing tasks, thus handling the feature-engineering problem. Our extensive experiments, on 19 languages from the Universal Dependencies project, show that our model outperforms the state-of-the-art neural network-based Stack-propagation model for joint POS tagging and transition-based dependency parsing, resulting in a new state of the art. Our code is open-source and available together with pre-trained models at: `https://github.com/datquocnguyen/jPTDP`.

Keywords: Neural network, POS tagging, Dependency parsing, Bidirectional LSTM, Universal Dependencies, Multilingual parsing.

1 Introduction

Dependency parsing has become a key research topic in NLP in the last decade, boosted by the success of the CoNLL 2006, 2007 and 2017 shared tasks on multilingual dependency parsing (Buchholz and Marsi, 2006; Nivre et al., 2007a; Zeman et al., 2017). McDonald and Nivre (2011) identify two types of data-driven methodologies for dependency parsing: graph-based approaches (Eisner, 1996; McDonald et al., 2005; Koo and Collins, 2010) and transition-based approaches (Yamada

and Matsumoto, 2003; Nivre, 2003). Most traditional graph- or transition-based parsing approaches manually define a set of core and combined features associated with one-hot representations (McDonald and Pereira, 2006; Nivre et al., 2007b; Bohnet, 2010; Zhang and Nivre, 2011; Martins et al., 2013; Choi and McCallum, 2013). Recent work shows that using deep learning in dependency parsing has obtained state-of-the-art performances. Several authors represent the core features with dense vector embeddings and then feed them as inputs to neural network-based classifiers (Chen and Manning, 2014; Weiss et al., 2015; Pei et al., 2015; Andor et al., 2016). In addition, others propose novel neural architectures for parsing to handle feature-engineering (Dyer et al., 2015; Cheng et al., 2016; Zhang et al., 2016; Wang and Chang, 2016; Kiperwasser and Goldberg, 2016a,b; Dozat and Manning, 2017; Ma and Hovy, 2017; Peng et al., 2017).

Part-of-speech (POS) tags are essential features used in most dependency parsers. In real-world parsing, those dependency parsers rely heavily on the use of automatically predicted POS tags, thus encountering error propagation problems. Li et al. (2011), Straka et al. (2016) and Nguyen et al. (2016) show that parsing accuracies drop by 5+% when utilizing automatic POS tags instead of gold ones. Some attempts have been made to avoid using POS tags during dependency parsing (Dyer et al., 2015; Ballesteros et al., 2015), however, these approaches still additionally use the automatic POS tags to achieve the best accuracy. Alternatively, joint learning both POS tagging and dependency parsing has gained more attention because: i) more accurate POS tags could lead to improved parsing performance and ii) the the syntactic context of a parse tree could help resolve POS

Proceedings of the CoNLL 2017 Shared Task: Multilingual Parsing from Raw Text to Universal Dependencies, pages 134–142,
Vancouver, Canada, August 3-4, 2017. © 2017 Association for Computational Linguistics

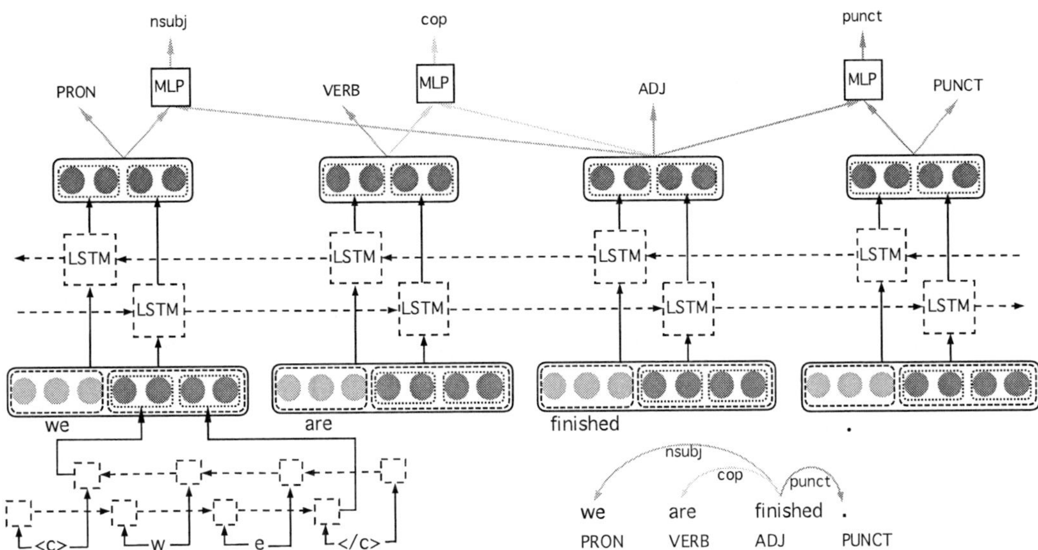

Figure 1: Illustration of our jPTDP for joint POS tagging and graph-based dependency parsing.

ambiguities (Li et al., 2011; Hatori et al., 2011; Lee et al., 2011; Bohnet and Nivre, 2012; Qian and Liu, 2012; Wang and Xue, 2014; Zhang et al., 2015; Alberti et al., 2015; Johannsen et al., 2016; Zhang and Weiss, 2016).

In this paper, we propose a novel neural architecture for joint POS tagging and graph-based dependency parsing. Our model learns latent feature representations shared for both POS tagging and dependency parsing tasks by using BiLSTM— the bidirectional LSTM (Schuster and Paliwal, 1997; Hochreiter and Schmidhuber, 1997). Not using any external resources such as pre-trained word embeddings, experimental results on 19 languages from the Universal Dependencies project show that: our joint model performs better than strong baselines and especially outperforms the neural network-based Stack-propagation model for joint POS tagging and transition-based dependency parsing (Zhang and Weiss, 2016), achieving a new state of the art.

2 Our joint model

In this section, we describe our new model for joint **POS t**agging and **d**ependency **p**arsing, which we call **jPTDP**. Figure 1 illustrates the architecture of our new model. We learn shared latent feature vectors representing word tokens in an input sentence by using BiLSTMs. Then these shared feature vectors are further used to make the predic-

tion of POS tags as well as fed into a multi-layer perceptron with one hidden layer (MLP) to decode dependency arcs and another MLP to predict relation types for labeling the predicted arcs.

BiLSTM-based latent feature representations: Given an input sentence s consisting of n word tokens $w_1, w_2, ..., w_n$, we represent each word w_i in s by an embedding $\mathbf{e}_{w_i}^{(\bullet)}$. Plank et al. (2016) and Ballesteros et al. (2015) show that character-based representations of words help improve POS tagging and dependency parsing performances. So, we also use a sequence BiLSTM (BiLSTM$_{\text{seq}}$) to compute a character-based vector representation for each word w_i in s. For a word type w consisting of k characters $w = c_1 c_2 ... c_k$, the input to the sequence BiLSTM consists of k character embeddings $\mathbf{c}_{1:k}$ in which each embedding vector $\mathbf{c}_j$ represents the jth character c_j in w; and the output is the character-based embedding $\mathbf{e}_w^{(*)}$ of the word type w, computed as:

$$\mathbf{e}_w^{(*)} = \text{BiLSTM}_{\text{seq}}(\mathbf{c}_{1:k})$$

For the ith word w_i in the input sentence s, we create an input vector $\mathbf{e}_i$ which is a concatenation ($\circ$) of the corresponding word embedding and character-based embedding vectors:

$$\mathbf{e}_i = \mathbf{e}_{w_i}^{(\bullet)} \circ \mathbf{e}_{w_i}^{(*)}$$

Then, we feed the sequence of input vectors $\mathbf{e}_{1:n}$ with an additional index i corresponding to a context position into another BiLSTM (BiLSTM$_{\text{ctx}}$), resulting in shared feature vectors $\boldsymbol{v}_i$ representing the ith words w_i in the sentence s:

$$\boldsymbol{v}_i = \text{BiLSTM}_{\text{ctx}}(\mathbf{e}_{1:n}, i)$$

POS tagging: Using shared BiLSTM-based latent feature vector representations, then we follow a common approach to compute the cross-entropy objective loss $\mathcal{L}_{\text{POS}}(\hat{\mathbf{t}}, \mathbf{t})$, in which $\hat{\mathbf{t}}$ and $\mathbf{t}$ are the sequence of predicted POS tags and sequence of gold POS tags of words in the input sentence s, respectively (Goldberg, 2016; Plank et al., 2016).

Arc-factored graph-based parsing: Dependency trees can be formalized as directed graphs. An arc-factored parsing approach learns the scores of the arcs in a graph (Kübler et al., 2009). Then, using an efficient decoding algorithm (in particular, we use the Eisner (1996)'s algorithm), we can find a maximum spanning tree—the highest scoring parse tree—of the graph from those arc scores:

$$\text{score}(s) = \underset{\hat{y} \in \mathcal{Y}(s)}{\text{argmax}} \sum_{(h,m) \in \hat{y}} \text{score}_{\text{arc}}(h, m)$$

where $\mathcal{Y}(s)$ is the set of all possible dependency trees for the input sentence s while $\text{score}_{\text{arc}}(h, m)$ measures the score of the arc between the head h^{th} word and the modifier m^{th} word in s. Following Kiperwasser and Goldberg (2016b), we score an arc by using a MLP with one-node output layer (MLP$_{\text{arc}}$) on top of the BiLSTM$_{\text{ctx}}$:

$$\text{score}_{\text{arc}}(h, m) = \text{MLP}_{\text{arc}}(\boldsymbol{v}_h \circ \boldsymbol{v}_m)$$

where $\boldsymbol{v}_h$ and $\boldsymbol{v}_m$ are the shared BiLSTM-based feature vectors representing the hth and m^{th} words in s, respectively. We then compute a margin-based hinge loss $\mathcal{L}_{\text{arc}}$ with loss-augmented inference to maximize the margin between the gold unlabeled parse tree and the highest scoring incorrect tree (Kiperwasser and Goldberg, 2016b).

Dependency relation types are predicted in a similar manner. We use another MLP on top of the BiLSTM$_{\text{ctx}}$ for predicting relation type of an head-modifier arc. Here, the number of the nodes in the output layer of this MLP (MLP$_{\text{rel}}$) is the number of relation types. Given an arc (h, m), we compute a corresponding output vector as:

$$\mathbf{v}_{(h,m)} = \text{MLP}_{\text{rel}}(\boldsymbol{v}_h \circ \boldsymbol{v}_m)$$

Then, based on MLP output vectors $\mathbf{v}_{(h,m)}$, we also compute another margin-based hinge loss $\mathcal{L}_{\text{rel}}$ for relation type prediction, using only the gold labeled parse tree.

Joint model training: The final training objective function of our joint model is the sum of the POS tagging loss $\mathcal{L}_{\text{POS}}$, the structure loss $\mathcal{L}_{\text{arc}}$ and the relation labeling loss $\mathcal{L}_{\text{rel}}$. The model parameters, including word embeddings, character embeddings, two BiLSTMs and two MLPs, are learned to minimize the sum of the losses.

Discussion: Prior neural network-based joint models for POS tagging and dependency parsing are feed-forward network- and transition-based approaches (Alberti et al., 2015; Zhang and Weiss, 2016), while our model is a BiLSTM- and graph-based method. Our model can be considered as a two-component mixture of a tagging component and a parsing component. Here, the tagging component can be viewed as a simplified version without the additional auxiliary loss for rare words of the BiLSTM-based POS tagging model proposed by Plank et al. (2016). The parsing component can be viewed as an extension of the graph-based dependency model proposed by Kiperwasser and Goldberg (2016b), where we replace the input POS tag embeddings by the character-based representations of words.

3 Experiments

3.1 Experimental setup

Following Zhang and Weiss (2016) and Plank et al. (2016), we conduct multilingual experiments on 19 languages from the Universal Dependencies (UD) treebanks[1] v1.2 (Nivre et al., 2015), using the universal POS tagset (Petrov et al., 2012) instead of the language specific POS tagset.[2] For dependency parsing, the evaluation metric is the labeled attachment score (LAS). LAS is the percentage of words which are correctly assigned both dependency arc and relation type.

---

[1] `http://universaldependencies.org/`

[2] Zhang and Weiss (2016) and Plank et al. (2016) experimented on 19 and 22 languages, respectively. For consistency, we use 19 languages as in Zhang and Weiss (2016).

Method	ar	bg	da	de•	en	es	eu•	fa	fi•	fr	hi	id	it	iw	nl	no	pl•	pt	sl•	AVG
	10.3	12.3	15.6	11.9	9.1	7.3	17.8	8.2	24.4	5.7	4.6	13.8	5.7	10.9	18.8	11.2	23.1	10.0	19.9	12.7
PART-OF-SPEECH TAGGING																				
UDPipe	98.7	97.8	95.8	90.7	94.5	95.0	93.1	96.9	**94.9**	95.9	95.8	**93.6**	97.2	94.8	89.2	97.2	96.0	97.4	95.6	95.3
TnT [⊕]	97.8	96.8	94.3	92.6	92.7	94.6	93.4	96.0	93.6	94.5	94.5	93.2	96.2	93.7	88.5	96.3	95.6	96.3	94.9	94.5
CRF [⊕]	97.6	96.4	93.8	91.4	93.4	94.2	91.6	95.7	90.3	95.1	96.0	93.0	96.4	93.6	90.0	96.2	94.0	96.3	94.8	94.2
BiLSTM-aux	**98.9**	**98.0**	**96.2**	92.6	94.5	95.1	**94.7**	**97.2**	94.9	95.8	96.2	93.1	**97.6**	**95.8**	**93.3**	97.6	**96.4**	**97.5**	**97.6**	**95.9**
Stack-prop	-	-	-	-	-	-	-	-	-	-	-	-	-	-	-	-	-	-	-	95.4
Our **jPTDP**	98.8	97.4	95.8	**92.7**	**94.7**	**95.9**	93.7	96.8	94.6	**96.0**	**96.4**	93.1	97.5	95.5	91.4	97.4	96.3	**97.5**	97.1	95.7
▽-Chars	3.1	2.4	3.9	2.3	1.6	0.8	4.3	0.8	5.4	1.1	0.3	3.7	1.4	1.6	6.6	2.7	4.7	3.1	5.7	2.9
DEPENDENCY PARSING																				
UDPipe	76.0	**84.7**	74.8	71.8	80.2	79.7	69.7	79.7	**76.3**	77.8	87.5	73.9	85.7	77.1	71.3	84.5	79.4	**81.3**	80.2	78.5
B'15 [*]	75.6	83.1	69.6	72.4	77.9	78.5	67.5	74.7	73.2	77.4	85.9	72.3	84.1	73.1	69.5	82.4	78.0	79.9	80.1	76.6
PipelineP$_{tag}$[*]	73.7	83.6	72.0	73.0	79.3	79.5	63.0	78.0	66.9	78.5	87.8	73.5	84.2	75.4	70.3	83.6	73.4	79.5	79.4	76.6
RBGParser [*]	75.8	83.6	73.9	73.5	79.9	79.6	68.0	78.5	65.4	78.9	87.7	74.2	84.7	77.6	72.4	83.9	75.4	**81.3**	80.7	77.6
Stack-prop	77.0	84.3	73.8	74.2	80.7	80.7	70.1	78.5	74.5	**80.0**	88.9	74.1	85.8	77.5	**73.6**	84.7	79.2	80.4	**81.8**	78.9
Our **jPTDP**	**79.0**	83.9	**75.8**	75.8	82.0	82.4	73.2	81.5	75.0	**80.0**	87.3	**75.7**	**86.4**	**79.2**	66.8	**84.9**	82.5	79.3	81.7	**79.6**
▽-Chars	3.8	4.1	4.5	3.6	1.4	2.3	12.0	1.1	11.1	0.2	0.3	4.1	1.9	1.9	5.4	2.3	10.6	3.4	9.2	4.4

Table 1: Universal POS tagging accuracies and LAS scores computed on all tokens (including punctuation) on test sets for 19 languages in UD v1.2. The language codes with • refer to morphologically rich languages. Numbers (in the second top row) right below language codes are out-of-vocabulary rates. **UDPipe** is the trainable pipeline for processing CoNLL-U files (Straka et al., 2016). **TnT** denotes the second order HMM-based TnT tagger (Brants, 2000). **CRF** denotes the Conditional random fields-based tagger, presented in Plank et al. (2014). **BiLSTM-aux** refers to the state-of-the-art (SOTA) BiLSTM-based POS tagging model with an additional auxiliary loss for rare words (Plank et al., 2016). Note that the (old) language code for Hebrew "**iw**" is referred to as "**he**" as in Plank et al. (2016). [⊕]: Results are reported in Plank et al. (2016). **Stack-prop** refers to the SOTA Stack-propagation model for joint POS tagging and transition-based dependency parsing (Zhang and Weiss, 2016). ▽-**Chars** denotes the absolute accuracy decrease of our jPTDP, when the character-based representations of words are not taken into account. **B'15** denotes the character-based stack LSTM model for transition-based dependency parsing (Ballesteros et al., 2015). **Pipeline**P$_{tag}$ refers to a greedy version of the approach proposed by Alberti et al. (2015). **RBGParser** refers to the graph-based dependency parser with tensor decomposition, presented in Lei et al. (2014). [*]: Results are reported in Zhang and Weiss (2016).

3.2 Implementation details

Our jPTDP is implemented using DYNET v2.0 (Neubig et al., 2017).[3] We optimize the objective function using Adam (Kingma and Ba, 2014) with default DYNET parameter settings and no mini-batches. We use a fixed random seed, and we do not utilize pre-trained embeddings in any experiment. Following Kiperwasser and Goldberg (2016b) and Plank et al. (2016), we apply a word dropout rate of 0.25 and Gaussian noise with $\sigma = 0.2$. For training, we run for 30 epochs, and evaluate the *mixed accuracy* of correctly assigning POS tag together with dependency arc and relation type on the development set after each training epoch. We perform a minimal grid search of hyper-parameters on English. We find that the highest mixed accuracy on the English develop-ment set is when using 64-dimensional character embeddings, 128-dimensional word embeddings, 128-dimensional BiLSTM states, 2 BiLSTM layers and 100 hidden nodes in MLPs with one hidden layer.[4] We then apply those hyper-parameters to all 18 remaining languages.

3.3 Main results

Table 1 compares the POS tagging and dependency parsing results of our model jPTDP with results reported in prior work, using the same experimental setup.

Regarding POS tagging, our joint model jPTDP generally obtains similar POS tagging accuracies to the BiLSTM-aux model (Plank et al.,

---

[3] https://github.com/clab/dynet

[4] On English, carried out on a computer with 2.2 GHz Core i7 processor, jPTDP took 6 hours for training with these hyper-parameters, and then obtained a joint tagging and parsing speed of 700 words/second.

2016). Our model also achieves higher averaged POS tagging accuracy than the joint model Stack-propagation (Zhang and Weiss, 2016). There are slightly higher tagging results obtained by BiLSTM-aux when utilizing pre-trained word embeddings for initialization, as presented in Plank et al. (2016). However, for a fair comparison to both Stack-propagation and our jPTDP, we only compare to the results reported without using the pre-trained word embeddings.

In terms of dependency parsing, in most cases, our model jPTDP outperforms Stack-propagation. It is somewhat unexpected that our model produces about 7% absolute lower LAS score than Stack-propagation on Dutch (**nl**). A possible reason is that the hyper-parameters we selected on English are not optimal for Dutch. Another reason is due to a large number of non-projective trees in Dutch test set ($106/386 \approx 27.5\%$), while we use the Eisner's decoding algorithm, producing only projective trees (Eisner, 1996). Without taking "nl" into account, our averaged LAS score over all remaining languages is 1.1% absolute higher than Stack-propagation's.

One reason for our better LAS is probably because jPTDP uses character-based representations of words, while Stack-propagation uses feature representations for suffixes and prefixes which might not be as useful as character-based representations for capturing unknown words. The last row in Table 1 shows an absolute LAS improvement of 4.4% on average when comparing our jPTDP with its simplified version of not using character-based representations: specifically, morphologically rich languages get an averaged improvement of 9.3 %, vice versa 2.6% for others.[5] So, our jPDTP is particularly good for morphologically rich languages, with 1.7% higher averaged LAS than Stack-propagation over these languages.

4   MQuni at the CoNLL 2017 shared task

Our team MQuni participated with jPTDP in the CoNLL 2017 shared task on multilingual parsing from raw text to universal dependencies (Zeman et al., 2017). Training data are 60+ universal dependency treebanks for 40+ languages from UD v2.0 (Nivre et al., 2017a). We do not use any external resource, and we use a fixed random seed and a fixed set of hyper-parameters as presented in Section 3.2 for all treebanks.[6] For each treebank, we train a joint model for *universal* POS tagging and dependency parsing. We evaluate the mixed accuracy on the development set after each training epoch, and select the model with the highest mixed accuracy. Note that for each "surprise" language where there are only few sample sentences with gold-standard annotation or a "small" treebank whose development set is not available, we simply split its sample or training set into two parts with a ratio 4:1, and then use the larger part for training and the smaller part for development.

For parsing from raw text to universal dependencies, we utilize CoNLL-U test files pre-processed by the baseline UDPipe 1.1 (Straka et al., 2016). These pre-processed CoNLL-U test files are available to all participants who do not want to train their own models for any steps preceding the dependency analysis, including: tokenization, word segmentation, sentence segmentation, POS tagging and morphological analysis. Note that we only employ the tokenization, word and sentence segmentation, and we do not care about the POS tagging and morphological analysis pre-processed by UDPipe 1.1. Recall that we perform universal POS tagging and dependency parsing jointly. In addition, when we encounter an additional parallel test set in a language where multiple training treebanks exist, i.e. a parallel test set marked with language code suffix "_pud" such as "ar_pud", "cs_pud" and "de_pud", we simply use the model trained for its corresponding language code prefix, e.g., "ar", "cs" and "de".

Table 2 presents our official parsing results from the CoNLL 2017 shared task on UD parsing (Zeman et al., 2017). We obtain 1% absolute higher averaged scores than the baseline UDPipe 1.1 (Straka et al., 2016) in both categories: big treebank test sets (denoted as **Big** in Table 2) and parallel test sets (denoted as **PUD** in Table 2). Specifically, we obtain a highest rank at 8th place for the **PUD** category, showing that our parsing model jPTDP is particularly good when it is applied to a real practical application in out-of-domain data. Unlike the baseline UDPipe 1.1 and others, for each surprise language, we simply

---

[5]To determine a morphologically rich language, we take as a proxy for morphological richness the number of noun cases $>=$ 4, with this value obtained from WALS (http://wals.info/) where available or Wikipedia otherwise.

[6]Except for the biggest treebank UD_Czech (cs) consisting of 68K training sentences, due to a limited computation resource, we used 64-dimensional word embeddings and 32-dimensional character embeddings. Then it took 30 hours to complete training process for UD_Czech.

System	All (81)	Big (55)	PUD (14)	Sma. (8)	Sur. (4)	R_{-S}
UDPipe 1.2	69.52_8	74.38_9	69.00_9	53.75_9	35.96_{14}	8
UDPipe 1.1	68.35_{13}	73.04_{17}	68.33_{13}	51.80_{15}	37.07_{11}	15
MQuni	68.05_{14}	74.03_{12}	69.28_8	51.58_{17}	14.48_{28}	10

Table 2: Official macro-averaged LAS F1 scores of MQuni and baselines from the CoNLL 2017 shared task on UD parsing (Zeman et al., 2017): `http://universaldependencies.org/conll17/results-las.html`. "**All**" refers to the averaged score over all 81 test sets, which is used as the main metric for ranking participating systems. **Big**: the averaged score over 55/81 test sets whose training treebanks are big and have development data available. **PUD**: the averaged score over 14/81 test sets that are additional parallel ones, produced separately and their domain may be different from their training data. **Sma.**: the averaged score over 8/81 test sets whose training treebanks are small, i.e., they lack development data and some of them have very little training data. **Sur.**: the averaged score over 4/81 remaining test sets for surprise languages. Here the *subscript* denotes the official rank out of 33 participating systems. R_{-S} is the system rank where the 4 surprise language test sets are not taken into account.

train a joint model just on the sample data of few sentences with gold-standard annotation provided before the test phase, i.e., we utilize neither external resources nor a cross-lingual technique nor a delexicalized parser. So, it is not surprising that we obtain a very low averaged score over the 4 surprise language test sets. When the 4 surprise language test sets are not taken into account, we obtain a rank in top-10 participating systems.

In fact, it is hard to make a clear comparison between our jPTDP and the parsing models used in other top participating systems. This is because other systems use various external resources and/or better pre-processing modules and/or construct ensemble models for dependency parsing.[7] For example, UDPipe 1.2 only extends the word and sentence segmenters of the baseline UDPipe 1.1. Consequently, UDPipe 1.2 obtains 0.1% absolute higher in the macro-averaged word segmentation score[8] and 0.2% higher in the macro-

averaged sentence segmentation score[9] than the baseline UDPipe 1.1, resulting in 1+% better in the macro-averaged LAS F1 score though they use exactly the same parsing model. See Zeman et al. (2017) for an overview of the methods, algorithms, resources and software used for all other participating systems.[10]

It is worth noting that for universal POS tagging, we obtain a highest rank at **4**[th] place for the **Big** category (i.e., 4th on average over 55 big treebank test sets).[11] In this **Big** category, we also obtain better rank than both UDPipe 1.2 and 1.1.

5 Conclusion

In this paper, we describe our novel model for joint POS tagging and graph-based dependency parsing, using bidirectional LSTM-based feature representations. Experiments on 19 languages from the Universal Dependencies (UD) v1.2 show that our model obtains state-of-the-art results in both POS tagging and dependency parsing.

With our joint model, we participated in the CoNLL 2017 shared task on UD parsing (Zeman et al., 2017). Given that we followed a strict closed setting while other top participating systems did not, we still obtained very competitive results. So, we believe our joint model can serve as a new strong baseline for further models in both POS tagging and dependency parsing tasks.

For future comparison, we provide in Table 3 the POS tagging, UAS and LAS accuracies with respect to gold-standard segmentation on the UD v2.0—CoNLL 2017 shared task test sets (Nivre et al., 2017b). Our code is open-source and available at: `https://github.com/datquocnguyen/jPTDP`.

Acknowledgments

This research was supported by a Google award through the Natural Language Understanding Focused Program, and under the Australian Research Council's *Discovery Projects* funding scheme (project number DP160102156). This research

---

[7]Combining multiple treebanks available for a language or similar languages to obtain larger training data is also considered as a manner of exploiting external data.

[8]Word segmentation results are available at: `http://universaldependencies.org/conll17/results-words.html`

[9]Sentence segmentation results are available at: `http://universaldependencies.org/conll17/results-sentences.html`

[10]Outlined at: `http://universaldependencies.org/conll17/systems-in-a-nutshell.html`

[11]Universal POS tagging results are available at: `http://universaldependencies.org/conll17/results-upos.html`

ltcode	UPOS	UAS	LAS	ltcode	UPOS	UAS	LAS	ltcode	UPOS	UAS	LAS
ar_pud	79.34	68.78	56.81	fr_partut	95.34	84.75	80.68	lv	90.27	69.28	61.50
ar	95.18	84.16	77.82	fr_pud	89.85	83.50	78.14	nl_lassysmall	95.82	79.74	75.29
bg	97.49	88.53	84.20	fr_sequoia	97.27	86.00	83.25	nl	91.15	78.47	71.39
bxr	43.21	28.79	14.04	fr	96.70	87.69	84.51	no_bokmaal	97.43	88.25	85.33
ca	98.10	88.62	85.59	ga	88.35	73.43	62.24	no_nynorsk	97.07	86.30	83.12
cs_cac	98.53	87.52	83.47	gl_treegal	92.83	75.45	68.46	pl	96.18	88.60	82.70
cs_cltt	97.20	79.61	74.84	gl	96.86	83.77	80.40	pt_br	97.64	90.40	88.32
cs_pud	95.96	85.26	79.83	got	94.27	77.78	70.27	pt_pud	88.41	81.49	75.15
cs	98.41	88.03	84.35	grc_proiel	94.73	73.25	67.34	pt	96.58	87.88	84.54
cu	92.81	81.96	73.22	grc	86.97	54.87	47.57	ro	96.72	87.04	81.37
da	95.80	80.87	76.89	he	95.53	86.65	80.91	ru_pud	86.26	78.88	70.15
de_pud	85.62	78.34	71.34	hi_pud	85.19	64.54	51.97	ru_syntagrus	98.11	89.73	87.08
de	92.83	80.16	75.66	hi	96.41	90.68	86.71	ru	95.31	82.14	77.12
el	96.18	85.07	81.55	hr	96.19	85.46	79.32	sk	94.48	81.26	75.51
en_lines	94.67	79.21	74.60	hsb	51.13	29.88	17.06	sl_sst	88.84	63.25	55.01
en_partut	94.17	81.25	76.56	hu	91.81	74.05	66.82	sl	96.87	84.75	81.25
en_pud	94.74	85.49	81.64	id	93.10	83.41	76.84	sme	33.12	22.80	8.23
en	94.82	85.29	81.64	it_pud	93.51	89.30	85.58	sv_lines	94.73	81.52	76.19
es_ancora	98.28	88.48	85.50	it	97.62	90.28	87.26	sv_pud	91.60	77.73	72.05
es_pud	88.59	87.55	80.28	ja_pud	97.08	94.40	93.26	sv	96.05	83.35	78.85
es	96.32	87.66	84.05	ja	96.56	94.07	92.41	tr_pud	72.60	57.14	35.50
et	87.62	69.44	59.15	kk	51.11	44.25	22.91	tr	93.42	67.39	59.14
eu	93.15	77.86	72.56	kmr	47.72	31.59	18.79	ug	72.49	57.79	39.48
fa	96.38	85.98	81.91	ko	93.47	79.89	74.75	uk	88.09	71.03	61.03
fi_ftb	92.63	82.48	76.54	la_ittb	97.44	78.81	74.65	ur	92.96	86.05	79.27
fi_pud	96.15	83.15	79.31	la_proiel	94.23	71.75	64.78	vi	86.78	64.88	55.63
fi	94.95	81.89	77.50	la	83.26	57.79	44.60	zh	92.36	78.57	72.99

Table 3: Universal POS tagging accuracies (labeled as UPOS), UAS and LAS scores of our jPTDP model with respect to gold-standard segmentation on the UD v2.0—CoNLL 2017 shared task test sets (Nivre et al., 2017b). UAS refers to the unlabeled attachment score. **ltcode** denotes the language treebank code. The 4 surprise language tests are *bxr*, *hsb*, *kmr* and *sme*. The 8 small treebank tests are *fr_partut*, *ga*, *gl_treegal*, *kk*, *la*, *sl_sst*, *ug* and *uk*. The 14 parallel test sets are marked with the language code suffix "_pud". The 55 remaining test sets are for big treebanks.

was also supported by NICTA, funded by the Australian Government through the Department of Communications and the Australian Research Council through the ICT Centre of Excellence Program. The first author was supported by an International Postgraduate Research Scholarship—which is an Australian Government Research Training Program Scholarship—and a NICTA NRPA Top-Up Scholarship.

References

Chris Alberti, David Weiss, Greg Coppola, and Slav Petrov. 2015. Improved Transition-Based Parsing and Tagging with Neural Networks. In *Proceedings of EMNLP*. pages 1354–1359.

Daniel Andor, Chris Alberti, David Weiss, Aliaksei Severyn, Alessandro Presta, Kuzman Ganchev, Slav Petrov, and Michael Collins. 2016. Globally Normalized Transition-Based Neural Networks. In *Proceedings of ACL*. pages 2442–2452.

Miguel Ballesteros, Chris Dyer, and Noah A. Smith. 2015. Improved Transition-based Parsing by Modeling Characters instead of Words with LSTMs. In *Proceedings of EMNLP*. pages 349–359.

Bernd Bohnet. 2010. Very high accuracy and fast dependency parsing is not a contradiction. In *Proceedings of COLING*. pages 89–97.

Bernd Bohnet and Joakim Nivre. 2012. A Transition-Based System for Joint Part-of-Speech Tagging and Labeled Non-Projective Dependency Parsing. In *Proceedings of EMNLP-CoNLL*. pages 1455–1465.

Thorsten Brants. 2000. TnT: A Statistical Part-of-Speech Tagger. In *Proceedings of ANLP*. pages 224–231.

Sabine Buchholz and Erwin Marsi. 2006. CoNLL-X shared task on multilingual dependency parsing. In *Proceedings of CoNLL*. pages 149–164.

Danqi Chen and Christopher Manning. 2014. A fast and accurate dependency parser using neural networks. In *Proceedings of EMNLP*. pages 740–750.

Hao Cheng, Hao Fang, Xiaodong He, Jianfeng Gao, and Li Deng. 2016. Bi-directional Attention with Agreement for Dependency Parsing. In *Proceedings of EMNLP*. pages 2204–2214.

Jinho D. Choi and Andrew McCallum. 2013. Transition-based dependency parsing with selectional branching. In *Proceedings of ACL*. pages 1052–1062.

Timothy Dozat and Christopher D. Manning. 2017. Deep Biaffine Attention for Neural Dependency Parsing. In *Proceedings of ICLR*.

Chris Dyer, Miguel Ballesteros, Wang Ling, Austin Matthews, and Noah A. Smith. 2015. Transition-Based Dependency Parsing with Stack Long Short-Term Memory. In *Proceedings of ACL-IJCNLP*. pages 334–343.

Jason M. Eisner. 1996. Three New Probabilistic Models for Dependency Parsing: An Exploration. In *Proceedings of COLING*. pages 340–345.

Yoav Goldberg. 2016. A Primer on Neural Network Models for Natural Language Processing. *Journal of Artificial Intelligence Research* 57:345–420.

Jun Hatori, Takuya Matsuzaki, Yusuke Miyao, and Jun'ichi Tsujii. 2011. Incremental Joint POS Tagging and Dependency Parsing in Chinese. In *Proceedings of IJCNLP*. pages 1216–1224.

Sepp Hochreiter and Jürgen Schmidhuber. 1997. Long short-term memory. *Neural Computation* 9(8):1735–1780.

Anders Johannsen, Željko Agić, and Anders Søgaard. 2016. Joint part-of-speech and dependency projection from multiple sources. In *Proceedings of ACL (Volume 2: Short Papers)*. pages 561–566.

Diederik P. Kingma and Jimmy Ba. 2014. Adam: A Method for Stochastic Optimization. *CoRR* abs/1412.6980.

Eliyahu Kiperwasser and Yoav Goldberg. 2016a. Easy-First Dependency Parsing with Hierarchical Tree LSTMs. *Transactions of ACL* 4:445–461.

Eliyahu Kiperwasser and Yoav Goldberg. 2016b. Simple and Accurate Dependency Parsing Using Bidirectional LSTM Feature Representations. *Transactions of ACL* 4:313–327.

Terry Koo and Michael Collins. 2010. Efficient Third-Order Dependency Parsers. In *Proceedings of ACL*. pages 1–11.

Sandra Kübler, Ryan McDonald, and Joakim Nivre. 2009. *Dependency Parsing*. Synthesis Lectures on Human Language Technologies, Morgan & cLaypool publishers.

John Lee, Jason Naradowsky, and David A. Smith. 2011. A discriminative model for joint morphological disambiguation and dependency parsing. In *Proceedings of ACL-HLT (Volume 1)*. pages 885–894.

Tao Lei, Yu Xin, Yuan Zhang, Regina Barzilay, and Tommi Jaakkola. 2014. Low-Rank Tensors for Scoring Dependency Structures. In *Proceedings of ACL (Volume 1: Long Papers)*. pages 1381–1391.

Zhenghua Li, Min Zhang, Wanxiang Che, Ting Liu, Wenliang Chen, and Haizhou Li. 2011. Joint Models for Chinese POS Tagging and Dependency Parsing. In *Proceedings of EMNLP*. pages 1180–1191.

Xuezhe Ma and Eduard H. Hovy. 2017. Neural Probabilistic Model for Non-projective MST Parsing. *CoRR* abs/1701.00874.

Andre Martins, Miguel Almeida, and Noah A. Smith. 2013. Turning on the Turbo: Fast Third-Order Non-Projective Turbo Parsers. In *Proceedings of ACL (Volume 2: Short Papers)*. pages 617–622.

Ryan McDonald, Koby Crammer, and Fernando Pereira. 2005. Online large-margin training of dependency parsers. In *Proceedings of ACL*. pages 91–98.

Ryan McDonald and Joakim Nivre. 2011. Analyzing and integrating dependency parsers. *Computational Linguistics* 37(1):197–230.

Ryan McDonald and Fernando Pereira. 2006. Online Learning of Approximate Dependency Parsing Algorithms. In *Proceedings of EACL*. pages 81–88.

Graham Neubig, Chris Dyer, Yoav Goldberg, Austin Matthews, Waleed Ammar, Antonios Anastasopoulos, Miguel Ballesteros, David Chiang, Daniel Clothiaux, Trevor Cohn, Kevin Duh, Manaal Faruqui, Cynthia Gan, Dan Garrette, Yangfeng Ji, Lingpeng Kong, Adhiguna Kuncoro, Gaurav Kumar, Chaitanya Malaviya, Paul Michel, Yusuke Oda, Matthew Richardson, Naomi Saphra, Swabha Swayamdipta, and Pengcheng Yin. 2017. DyNet: The Dynamic Neural Network Toolkit. *arXiv preprint arXiv:1701.03980* .

Dat Quoc Nguyen, Mark Dras, and Mark Johnson. 2016. An empirical study for Vietnamese dependency parsing. In *Proceedings of ALTA*. pages 143–149.

Joakim Nivre. 2003. An efficient algorithm for projective dependency parsing. In *Proceedings of IWPT*.

Joakim Nivre, Željko Agić, Lars Ahrenberg, et al. 2017a. Universal Dependencies 2.0. http://hdl.handle.net/11234/1-1983.

Joakim Nivre, Željko Agić, Lars Ahrenberg, et al. 2017b. Universal dependencies 2.0 - CoNLL 2017 shared task development and test data. http://hdl.handle.net/11234/1-2184.

Joakim Nivre, Željko Agić, Maria Jesus Aranzabe, et al. 2015. Universal Dependencies 1.2. http://hdl.handle.net/11234/1-1548.

Joakim Nivre, Johan Hall, Sandra Kübler, Ryan McDonald, Jens Nilsson, Sebastian Riedel, and Deniz Yuret. 2007a. The CoNLL 2007 Shared Task on Dependency Parsing. In *Proceedings of the CoNLL Shared Task Session of EMNLP-CoNLL 2007*.

Joakim Nivre, Johan Hall, Jens Nilsson, Atanas Chanev, Gülsen Eryigit, Sandra Kübler, Svetoslav Marinov, and Erwin Marsi. 2007b. MaltParser: A language-independent system for data-driven dependency parsing. *Natural Language Engineering* 13(2):95–135.

Wenzhe Pei, Tao Ge, and Baobao Chang. 2015. An effective neural network model for graph-based dependency parsing. In *Proceedings of ACL-IJCNLP*. pages 313–322.

Hao Peng, Sam Thomson, and Noah A. Smith. 2017. Deep Multitask Learning for Semantic Dependency Parsing. In *Proceedings of ACL*.

Slav Petrov, Dipanjan Das, and Ryan T. McDonald. 2012. A Universal Part-of-Speech Tagset. In *Proceedings of LREC*. pages 2089–2096.

Barbara Plank, Dirk Hovy, Ryan McDonald, and Anders Søgaard. 2014. Adapting taggers to Twitter with not-so-distant supervision. In *Proceedings of COLING: Technical Papers*. pages 1783–1792.

Barbara Plank, Anders Søgaard, and Yoav Goldberg. 2016. Multilingual Part-of-Speech Tagging with Bidirectional Long Short-Term Memory Models and Auxiliary Loss. In *Proceedings of ACL (Volume 2: Short Papers)*. pages 412–418.

Xian Qian and Yang Liu. 2012. Joint Chinese Word Segmentation, POS Tagging and Parsing. In *Proceedings of EMNLP-CoNLL*. pages 501–511.

M. Schuster and K.K. Paliwal. 1997. Bidirectional recurrent neural networks. *IEEE Transactions on Signal Processing* 45(11):2673–2681.

Milan Straka, Jan Hajic, and Jana Strakov. 2016. UD-Pipe: Trainable Pipeline for Processing CoNLL-U Files Performing Tokenization, Morphological Analysis, POS Tagging and Parsing. In *Proceedings of LREC*.

Wenhui Wang and Baobao Chang. 2016. Graph-based Dependency Parsing with Bidirectional LSTM. In *Proceedings of ACL (Volume 1: Long Papers)*. pages 2306–2315.

Zhiguo Wang and Nianwen Xue. 2014. Joint POS Tagging and Transition-based Constituent Parsing in Chinese with Non-local Features. In *Proceedings of ACL (Volume 1: Long Papers)*. pages 733–742.

David Weiss, Chris Alberti, Michael Collins, and Slav Petrov. 2015. Structured training for neural network transition-based parsing. In *Proceedings of ACL-IJCNLP*. pages 323–333.

Hiroyasu Yamada and Yuji Matsumoto. 2003. Statistical dependency analysis with support vector machines. In *Proceedings IWPT*.

Daniel Zeman, Martin Popel, Milan Straka, Jan Hajič, Joakim Nivre, Filip Ginter, Juhani Luotolahti, Sampo Pyysalo, Slav Petrov, Martin Potthast, Francis Tyers, Elena Badmaeva, Memduh Gökırmak, Anna Nedoluzhko, Silvie Cinková, Jan Hajič jr., Jaroslava Hlaváčová, Václava Kettnerová, Zdeňka Urešová, Jenna Kanerva, Stina Ojala, Anna Missilä, Christopher Manning, Sebastian Schuster, Siva Reddy, Dima Taji, Nizar Habash, Herman Leung, Marie-Catherine de Marneffe, Manuela Sanguinetti, Maria Simi, Hiroshi Kanayama, Valeria de Paiva, Kira Droganova, Héctor Martínez Alonso, Hans Uszkoreit, Vivien Macketanz, Aljoscha Burchardt, Kim Harris, Katrin Marheinecke, Georg Rehm, Tolga Kayadelen, Mohammed Attia, Ali Elkahky, Zhuoran Yu, Emily Pitler, Saran Lertpradit, Michael Mandl, Jesse Kirchner, Hector Fernandez Alcalde, Jana Strnadova, Esha Banerjee, Ruli Manurung, Antonio Stella, Atsuko Shimada, Sookyoung Kwak, Gustavo Mendonça, Tatiana Lando, Rattima Nitisaroj, and Josie Li. 2017. CoNLL 2017 Shared Task: Multilingual Parsing from Raw Text to Universal Dependencies. In *Proceedings of the CoNLL 2017 Shared Task: Multilingual Parsing from Raw Text to Universal Dependencies*.

Yuan Zhang, Chengtao Li, Regina Barzilay, and Kareem Darwish. 2015. Randomized greedy inference for joint segmentation, pos tagging and dependency parsing. In *Proceedings of NAACL-HLT*.

Yuan Zhang and David Weiss. 2016. Stack-propagation: Improved Representation Learning for Syntax. In *Proceedings of ACL (Volume 1: Long Papers)*. pages 1557–1566.

Yue Zhang and Joakim Nivre. 2011. Transition-based dependency parsing with rich non-local features. In *Proceedings ACL-HLT*. pages 188–193.

Zhisong Zhang, Hai Zhao, and Lianhui Qin. 2016. Probabilistic Graph-based Dependency Parsing with Convolutional Neural Network. In *Proceedings of ACL (Volume 1: Long Papers)*. pages 1382–1392.

A non-DNN Feature Engineering Approach to Dependency Parsing – FBAML at CoNLL 2017 Shared Task

Xian Qian
xianqian@fb.com

Yang Liu
yangli@fb.com

Facebook Applied Machine Learning / 1 Facebook Way

Abstract

For this year's multilingual dependency parsing shared task, we developed a pipeline system, which uses a variety of features for each of its components. Unlike the recent popular deep learning approaches that learn low dimensional dense features using non-linear classifier, our system uses structured linear classifiers to learn millions of sparse features. Specifically, we trained a linear classifier for sentence boundary prediction, linear chain conditional random fields (CRFs) for tokenization, part-of-speech tagging and morph analysis. A second order graph based parser learns the tree structure (without relations), and a linear tree CRF then assigns relations to the dependencies in the tree. Our system achieves reasonable performance – 67.87% official averaged macro F1 score.

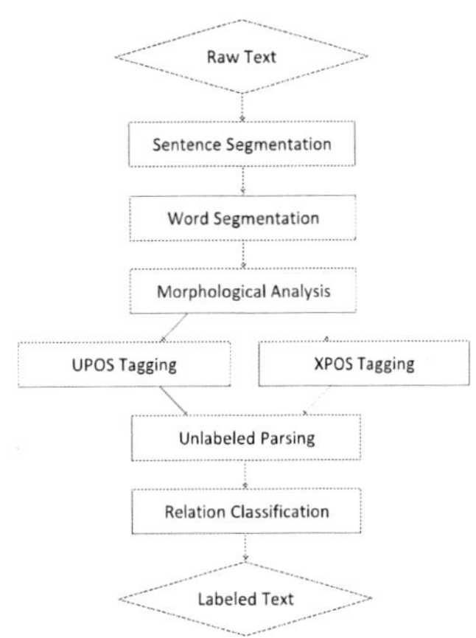

Figure 1: System architecture: pipeline components for universal dependency parsing.

1 Introduction

Our system for the universal dependency parsing shared task in CoNLL 2017 (Zeman et al., 2017) follows a typical pipeline framework.

The system architecture is shown in Figure 1, which consists of the following components : (1) sentence segmentor, which segments raw text into sentences, (2) tokenizer that tokenizes sentences into words, or performs word segmentation for Asian languages, (3) morphologic analyzer generates morphologic features, (4) part-of-speech (POS) tagger generates universal POS tags and language specific POS tags, (5) parser predicts tree structures without relations, (6) a relation predictor assigns relations to the dependencies in the tree.

For each component, we take a non deep learning based approach, that is the typical structured linear classifier that learns sparse features, but requires heavy feature engineering.

Sentence segmentation, tokenization, POS tagger and morphologic analyzer are based on linear chain CRFs (Lafferty et al., 2001), and the relation predictor is based on linear tree CRFs. We train the pipeline for each language independently using the training portion of the treebank and the official word embeddings for 45 languages provided by the organizers. Our system components are implemented in C++ with no third party toolkits. Due to the time limit, we did not optimize our system for speed or memory.

Proceedings of the CoNLL 2017 Shared Task: Multilingual Parsing from Raw Text to Universal Dependencies, pages 143–151,
Vancouver, Canada, August 3-4, 2017. © 2017 Association for Computational Linguistics

2 System Components

2.1 Sentence Segmentation

2.1.1 Task setup

We cast sentence segmentation as a classification problem at the character level, determining whether a character is the end of the sentence character (EOS). To obtain the gold labels, we aligned the raw text file with the conllu file with annotations.

Since most characters are not sentence boundaries, using all the characters will make the data very imbalanced. To address this problem, we only consider a character as a candidate trigger if it is labeled as EOS at least once in the training data. Intuitively this would prune many characters as EOS characters should be punctuation marks. However, we noticed that for English (possibly other languages too) many sentences in the data end without punctuation, and thus the last character of the sentence will be added into the EOS character trigger set. To reduce the size of the triggers, we use a three label scheme for the characters.

- Label N for the character following the end of a sentence, and before the beginning of the next sentence. A typical example for this is the space between two sentences. Even for cases when punctuation marks are omitted, this applies to the space separating the two sentences.

- Label E represents a character is the end of a sentence, and its next character is the beginning of the next sentence. This category is introduced for sentences that are not split by space. For example, *past few years,...Great to have you on board!*, 'G' is the beginning of the second sentence, '.' before 'G' has a label of 'E'.

- Label O is used for all other cases. Note that a punctuation mark that ends a sentence will have a label of 'O' if there is a space following the sentence. In this case, EOS information is obtained by the 'N' label for the space.

Using this scheme, during testing, an EOS character is found if it is labeled as E or its next character is labeled as N. For training, we collect the characters labeled as E or N in the training set as candidates. Table 1 shows the number of candidates for each language. This significantly reduces

languages	#trigger characters
cs_cltt, et, it, lv, pt, pt_br	3
en_lines, sl	4
no_nynorsk	5
no_bokmaal	6
ru_syntagrus	7
en	8
cs	14
zh	20
ja	23
others	2

Table 1: Number of trigger characters for EOS detection.

the number of trigger candidates compared to considering all the characters.

2.1.2 Features

We use a linear classifier for EOS detection. We tune the feature templates on the English development data, and apply to all the other languages. Detailed feature templates are described in Table 2. Features include the surrounding characters and their lower cases. For character types, we use digit and letters, and keep the other symbols. Take *12:00pm* as an example, it is represented as: *00:00aa*, where we replace all digits by '0' and all lower cased letters by 'a'. For languages that have spaces between words, we also use the surrounding 'words' split by spaces and the current character. For example, for the following example: *comes this story: President Bush* for character 'y', we have word features: $word_{-2}=this$, $word_{-1}=stor$, $word_1=:$, $word_2=President$.

2.2 Tokenization

2.2.1 Methodology

We use a sequence labeling model for tokenization. Each character will be labeled as one of the following tags:

- B: beginning of a multi-character token,

- I: inside a multi-character token,

- E: end of a multi-character token,

- S: single character token,

- O: other.

The labels are generated by aligning the raw text with the gold sentence segmentation with the word form column of the conllu table.

$char_i, -3 \leq i \leq +3$
$char_i char_{i+1}, -3 \leq i \leq +2$
$lowchar_i, -3 \leq i \leq +3$
$lowchar_i lowchar_{i+1}, -3 \leq i \leq +2$
$chartype_i, -3 \leq i \leq +3$
$chartype_i chartype_{i+1}, -3 \leq i \leq +2$
$word_i, i = -2, -1, 1, 2$
$wordtype_i, i = -2, -1, 1, 2$

Table 2: Feature templates for sentence segmentation. $char_i$ is the ith character to the right of current character, $char_{-i}$ is the ith character to the left of the current character. $lowchar$ is the lower cased character, $chartype$ is the character type, it can be digit, upper cased letter, lower cased letter or other. $word_i$ is surrounding 'words' splitted by spaces and the current character. $wordtype$ is the concatenation of character types

$chartype_0, chartype_{-1} chartype_0$
$word_{-1}, word_1$
$word_{-1} chartype_0, word_1 chartype_0$
$chartype_{-1} chartype_0, chartype_0 chartype_1$
transition feature

Table 3: Tokenization feature templates for languages with space between words (except Chinese and Japanese).

2.2.2 Features

Linear chain CRF is used to learn the model with character and word n-gram features. We used two sets of feature templates, one for languages having spaces between words including English, Arabric etc., the other for languages without spaces including Chinese and Japanese, as shown in Table 3 and 4. The first feature template set is tuned on English development set, the second one is tuned on Chinese development set.

2.3 POS Tagging and Morph Analysis

2.3.1 Methodology

For morphological analysis and POS tagging, we use the same model setup and features, therefore we group them together in this section. We used linear chain CRFs for these tasks (a sequence labeling task for each word in the sequence). As the morph features consist of several fields separated by a special symbol, we treat the prediction of each field as an independent task, and then combine the predictions from different models. For

$char_i char_{i+1}, -2 \leq i \leq 1$
$word_{-1}, word_1$
$char_0 word_{\text{left to current character}}$
$char_0 word_{\text{right to current character}}$
$word_{\text{left to current character}}$
$word_{\text{right to current character}}$
$word_{\text{left to left character}}$
$word_{\text{right to left character}}$
$word_{\text{left to right character}}$
$word_{\text{right to right character}}$
transition feature
transition feature + current character

Table 4: Tokenization feature templates for Chinese and Japanese. Words in these languages are obtained by maximum forward/backward matching.

POS tagging (both universal (UPOS) and language specific POS (XPOS) tagging), we use the same set of features as used for morph analysis, and the automatically predicted morph features. For languages that have multiple labels in XPOS tag, we use a similar strategy as for morph analysis, i.e., learning multiple taggers and combine the results.

2.3.2 Features

The list of feature templates are shown in Table 5. Note for POS tagging, as mentioned above, one additional feature is the morph feature, which comes from the automatic morph models.

The basic features includes word and lower cased word n-grams, prefixes and suffixes. With these features, the baseline UPOS tagger achieves 94.78% accuracy on the English development set. Since we do not use deep learning based approaches, incorporating pretrained word embeddings is not straightforward for linear classifiers. In our system, we clustered the word vectors using k-means, where $k = 2048$ and 10000, and then used the cluster n-grams as features.

2.4 Unlabeled Dependency Parsing

2.4.1 Methodology

Our dependency parser consists of two components, one is the unlabeled parser which only predicts the tree structures, the other is relation type prediction that assigns dependency relations to the dependencies. Originally, we trained a third order parser with word/POS/morph n-gram features, but it is too slow to extract features, especially

$word_i, -2 \leq i \leq 2$
$word_i char_{i+1}, -2 \leq i \leq 1$
$cluster_0, cluster_i cluster_{i+1}, i = -1, 0$
$lowerCasedWord_0$
$prefix_{i,j}, i = -1, 0, 1, 1 \leq j \leq 6$
$suffix_{i,j}, i = -1, 0, 1, 1 \leq j \leq 6$
$word_0 prefix_{i,j}, i = -1, 1, 1 \leq j \leq 6$
$word_0 suffix_{i,j}, i = -1, 1, 1 \leq j \leq 6$
$morph$ (invalid for morph analysis)
transition features

Table 5: Feature templates for morph analysis and POS tagging, where $prefix_{i,j}$ is the length = j prefix of the ith word to the right of current word, $cluster_i$ is the cluster id of $word_i$

the third order features. So we chose to build a second order parser to balance speed and performance. We developed two versions of dependency parsers, one is pseudo-projective parser that handles treebanks that are nearly projective (projective dependencies % > 95%), the other is the 1-endpoint-crossing parser (Pitler et al., 2013; Pitler, 2014) that processes treebanks with more non-projective dependencies (projective dependencies % < 95%), such as Dutch-LassySmall, Ancient_Greek, Ancient_Greek-PROIEL, Basque, Latin-PROIEL and Latin. We modified the original third order 1-endpoint-crossing parsing algorithm to guarantee the unique derivation of any parse tree, because we need the top k parse trees for training.

2.4.2 Features

Our original third order parser includes 1000+ feature templates, and generated more than 100 million features on English data. As the features consume too much memory, making the parser rather slow, we kept only 260 templates, and use second order parser instead, which generated 15 million features. Most of the feature templates come from the previous works (Koo and Collins, 2010; McDonald et al., 2005), including word, POS ngrams and their combinations. We also add some morphology and word cluster n-grams. Detailed feature templates are described in Table 6.

2.5 Relation Classification

2.5.1 Methodology

Once the tree structure of a parse tree is obtained, we train a linear tree CRF to assign the relation

type to each arc in the tree. Given a tree represented as a collection of arcs: $\mathcal{T} = \{e\}$, the tree CRF represents the potential function of $\mathcal{T}$ as the sum of the potential functions of arcs and arc pair chains:

$$\phi(\mathcal{T}) = \sum_e \phi(e) + \sum_{e \to e'} \phi(e \to e') \qquad (1)$$

where $\phi(e)$ is the linear combination of node features in the CRF and $\phi(e \to e')$ is the linear combination of transition features in the CRF.

2.5.2 Features

For each arc $p \to c$, we use the same feature templates as in Table 6 to generate node features. For transition features, we simply use the relation type bigrams, i.e., relation(g $\to$ p)relation(p $\to$ c).

3 CoNLL Shared Task Results

3.1 Implementation details

All the classifiers, including linear chain CRF, tree CRF and second order dependency parser, are trained using 10-best MIRA (McDonald et al., 2005). Parameters are averaged to avoid overfitting. We found that k best MIRA consistently outperforms averaged perceptron about $0.1 - 0.2\%$ for all tasks.

For CRFs and the parser, we used the lazy decoding algorithm (Huang and Chiang, 2005) for fast k-best candidate generation, the complexity is nearly the same as 1-best decoding. Specifically, the time complexity for CRFs is $O(nL^2 + nk \log(k))$, and $O(n^4 + nk \log(k))$ for the parser. where n is the length of sentence.

Both CRFs are optimized for fast tagging: strings like words, POS tags are mapped to bit strings for efficient concatenation to generate feature strings, while the parser is not optimized. The actual running time for 1-endpoint-crossing parser is about 1.8 times of projective parser, though theoretically it should be 50x times slower. The main reason is that feature generating is much more slower than decoding, which is actully the same for both parsers. For fast training, we use hogwild strategy to update the parameters using 30 threads. Empirical results on English development data showed that compared with standard MIRA that only used single thread, the hogwild strategy get 5x speedup, the parser can be trained within 2.5 hours. While the performance is very competitive, only lost 0.1% UAS.

$p_i.word,$	$c_i.word,$	$-2 \leq i \leq 2$
$p_i.word\ p_{i+1}.word,$	$c_i.word\ c_{i+1}.word,$	$-2 \leq i \leq 1$
$p_i.word\ c_j.word,$ $c_i.word\ s_j.word,$	$g_i.word\ c_j.word,$	$-1 \leq i,j \leq 1$
$g_i.word\ p_j.word\ c_k.word,$ $p_i.word\ c_j.word\ s_k.word,$		$-1 \leq i,j,k \leq 1$
$p_i.word\ c_j.word\ c_{j+1}.word,$	$-1 \leq i \leq 1,$	$-1 \leq j \leq 0$
$p_i.word\ p_{i+1}.word\ c_j.word,$	$-1 \leq i \leq 0,$	$-1 \leq j \leq 1$
$g_0.word\ p_i.word\ c_j.word\ c_{j+1}.word,$	$-1 \leq i \leq 1,$	$-1 \leq j \leq 0$
$g_0.word\ p_i.word\ p_{i+1}.word\ c_j.word,$	$-1 \leq i \leq 0,$	$-1 \leq j \leq 1$
$p_i.word\ c_j.word\ c_{j+1}.word\ s_0.word,$	$-1 \leq i \leq 1,$	$-1 \leq j \leq 0$
$p_i.word\ p_{i+1}.word\ c_j.word\ s_0.word,$	$-1 \leq i \leq 0,$	$-1 \leq j \leq 1$
replace $word$ above by $upos, xpos, lowCasedWord, wordCluster, morph$		
combine the templates above with distance and direction of arcs		

Table 6: Feature templates for unlabeled dependency parsing, where p_i, c_i, g_i, s_i are the ith token right to the parent, child, grand parent, sibling. (to the left, if $i < 0$)

To cluster word vectors, we implemented fast k means using triangle inequality. We let k means run 20 iterations using 45 threads to quickly generate clusters. For languages without pretrained word vectors, such as *en_lines*, we use word vectors from *en* instead.

For surprised languages, we trained POS tagger, morphological analyzer and parser using the example data. The word cluster features are derived by running word2vec on the unlabeled dataset, and k-means clustering. For sentence segmentation and tokenization, we just used the models trained on English data, since the example dataset is quite limited.

3.2 Results on development data

The feature sets are tuned on English development data, except some languages specific tasks such as Chinese word segmentation. Table 7 shows the results on development dataset. We have the following observation regarding feature effect.

- Character type features are useful for sentence segmentation, which made 13% absolute F1 score improvement.

- Morphological features help the parser, resulting in an UAS 0.5% absolute F1 score improvement.

- For tokenization, word features i.e., $word_{-1}$ and $word_1$ in Table 3 are useful, which made 1% absolute F1 score improvement.

- Lemma features do not have a big effect on parsing. We compared using the gold lemma features vs. the automatically generated ones,

with about 0.3% improvement from the former, and only 0.1% using the latter. Because of this our system did not do lemmartization for all the languages.

- Word cluster features have limited gains. We tried two different ways to convert the pretrained word vectors to binary features:

(1) find the k nearest neighbors ($k = 3$ in experiments) in the embedding space, and use these neighors as features;

(2) cluster the words into k clusters, ($k = 8, 16, \ldots, 2048, 10000, 100000$), and used the cluster features.

The results on the English development set showed that the two approaches performed quite the same, both achieving 94.92% UPOS accuracy, 0.15% improvement over the baseline. In addition, we noticed that the word cluster features did not help when k is small. In our system submission, we used $k = 2048, 10000$ to generate the clusters.

It is worth pointing out that such improvement from using the cluster features is quite limited compared to using embeddings in deep learning based methods. For example, using stacked word and character bi-LSTM-CRFs (Lample et al., 2016) achieved 95.75% POS tagging accuracy, and 96.00% using word+prefix/suffix embedding. We suspect that the converting real valued features to binary features (cluster features) loses too much information.

Language	Sentence	Words	UPOS	XPOS	Feats	UAS	LAS
ar	87.89%	92.15%	87.51%	81.08%	78.83%	70.33%	65.03%
bg	91.32%	99.77%	97.36%	75.72%	89.78%	87.75%	83.30%
ca	99.30%	99.73%	97.89%	97.92%	95.63%	88.69%	85.41%
cs	96.09%	99.96%	98.71%	92.11%	88.65%	89.46%	86.11%
cs_cac	99.50%	100.00%	99.00%	88.60%	83.94%	87.47%	84.26%
cs_cltt	74.36%	99.33%	89.20%	70.17%	65.97%	71.70%	68.37%
da	87.39%	100.00%	95.65%	0.00%	89.51%	79.36%	75.40%
de	93.68%	99.91%	93.39%	95.74%	79.83%	84.16%	79.76%
el	94.37%	99.78%	94.76%	94.80%	84.85%	81.99%	78.60%
en	81.43%	98.92%	93.89%	92.22%	92.23%	81.63%	78.11%
en_partut	95.73%	99.37%	94.37%	93.76%	88.81%	80.60%	76.35%
es	98.75%	99.70%	96.24%	0.00%	95.00%	86.95%	83.71%
es_ancora	96.66%	99.74%	97.93%	97.77%	95.64%	87.73%	84.74%
et	93.21%	99.07%	89.27%	91.13%	74.46%	71.24%	59.57%
eu	100.00%	99.99%	94.95%	0.00%	83.97%	76.87%	70.12%
fa	98.74%	99.48%	95.75%	95.52%	94.33%	83.27%	78.84%
fi	89.33%	99.77%	94.93%	96.07%	88.01%	78.73%	74.26%
fi_ftb	85.02%	100.00%	92.96%	0.00%	88.60%	78.78%	73.34%
fr	97.73%	99.16%	96.27%	0.00%	94.87%	87.67%	85.03%
fr_sequoia	90.58%	98.83%	96.05%	0.00%	92.82%	83.03%	80.43%
gl	96.68%	99.96%	96.83%	95.32%	99.79%	83.17%	79.89%
got	26.87%	100.00%	94.29%	95.23%	80.63%	70.46%	62.89%
grc	99.34%	100.00%	88.35%	77.68%	84.01%	68.13%	60.82%
grc_proiel	42.42%	100.00%	96.20%	96.54%	86.50%	74.26%	68.52%
he	99.49%	84.12%	80.55%	80.66%	75.41%	62.52%	57.81%
hi	98.55%	100.00%	96.33%	95.11%	87.43%	92.20%	88.09%
hr	97.48%	99.89%	96.64%	0.00%	81.14%	82.20%	76.22%
hu	98.19%	99.95%	93.40%	0.00%	59.68%	73.99%	64.48%
it	97.02%	99.44%	96.92%	96.28%	95.44%	87.65%	85.36%
it_partut	96.62%	99.16%	95.16%	94.89%	92.60%	82.55%	79.02%
ko	90.61%	97.91%	91.54%	86.50%	97.57%	62.80%	55.05%
la_ittb	77.03%	99.87%	96.75%	0.00%	88.37%	75.85%	70.70%
la_proiel	22.81%	100.00%	95.62%	95.37%	84.94%	68.66%	62.19%
lv	94.30%	99.66%	91.76%	26.01%	69.57%	72.57%	64.15%
nl	93.25%	99.66%	94.49%	0.00%	89.96%	82.82%	77.86%
nl_lassysmall	81.01%	99.81%	96.32%	0.00%	93.48%	79.35%	74.41%
no_bokmaal	96.08%	99.88%	97.28%	0.00%	91.16%	86.64%	83.22%
no_nynorsk	93.90%	99.94%	96.54%	0.00%	91.27%	84.78%	81.28%
pl	99.56%	99.17%	95.54%	0.00%	77.10%	84.51%	79.17%
pt	90.71%	99.53%	96.70%	0.00%	92.86%	87.45%	84.66%
pt_br	96.71%	99.82%	97.65%	97.57%	99.70%	89.23%	87.01%
ro	97.47%	99.63%	96.58%	9.64%	89.17%	86.94%	81.59%
ru	93.09%	99.79%	95.48%	94.35%	79.82%	82.12%	77.38%
ru_syntagrus	97.29%	99.72%	98.10%	0.00%	90.25%	88.91%	86.14%
sk	76.09%	99.93%	94.94%	0.87%	69.04%	82.74%	77.20%
sl	99.59%	99.94%	97.38%	14.87%	81.19%	87.41%	84.31%
sv	96.17%	99.88%	95.66%	0.00%	89.63%	80.57%	76.05%
sv_lines	87.19%	99.97%	94.89%	66.27%	99.97%	80.30%	75.22%
tr	96.98%	96.61%	89.31%	88.25%	77.59%	60.47%	52.49%
ur	99.10%	99.99%	93.46%	91.47%	77.62%	84.81%	78.02%
vi	97.40%	85.98%	78.32%	75.69%	85.84%	49.67%	44.20%
zh	98.50%	93.81%	87.21%	87.39%	92.25%	67.97%	62.75%

Table 7: Performance of our system on development dataset. XPOS accuracy for some languages are quite low due to the format issue.

Language	Sentence	Word	UPOS	XPOS	Feats	UAS	LAS
ar	85.69%	91.45%	86.59%	80.83%	78.27%	70.16%	64.89%
bg	91.5%	99.82%	97.67%	76.65%	90.18%	87.96%	83.89%
ca	99.35%	99.77%	97.68%	97.68%	95.35%	88.48%	85.02%
cs_cac	99.76%	99.94%	98.43%	87.99%	83.95%	87.54%	83.27%
cs_cltt	91.99%	99.59%	96.65%	83.34%	78.42%	80.26%	76.08%
cs	95.1%	99.99%	98.53%	91.45%	87.96%	88.14%	84.43%
cu	37.46%	100%	94.8%	95.02%	80.78%	73.68%	66.91%
da	81.41%	100%	95.84%	0%	90.55%	79.48%	75.59%
de	78.78%	99.61%	92.42%	96.74%	78.28%	79.17%	74.26%
el	28.28%	100%	95.75%	95.9%	84.99%	67.8%	61.53%
en_lines	86.95%	99.96%	95.4%	63.43%	99.96%	79.27%	74.67%
en_partut	98.1%	99.31%	94.2%	93.43%	88.49%	80.83%	76.68%
en	78.01%	98.98%	94.09%	93.46%	92.9%	80.8%	77.57%
es_ancora	98.67%	99.72%	97.87%	97.87%	95.66%	87.13%	83.81%
es	87.08%	99.98%	94.88%	62.88%	99.98%	80.33%	74.89%
et	92.63%	99.28%	89.9%	92.01%	75.16%	69.98%	58.48%
eu	99.75%	99.99%	94.59%	0%	83.32%	77.28%	70.76%
fa	99.25%	99.44%	95.86%	95.74%	94.4%	82.11%	77.74%
fi_ftb	86.46%	99.98%	93.11%	0%	89.1%	78.16%	72.08%
fi	89.48%	99.6%	95.15%	96.15%	88.07%	78.87%	74.51%
fr_sequoia	82.97%	99.19%	96.4%	0%	93.33%	82.91%	80.3%
fr	92.49%	98.84%	95.68%	0%	94.27%	83.83%	80.38%
gl	96.14%	99.98%	96.98%	95.82%	99.78%	83%	79.79%
got	28.35%	100%	94.85%	95.7%	81.73%	70.13%	62.64%
grc	98.96%	100%	87.25%	75.43%	81.13%	66.23%	58.42%
he	99.49%	80.93%	77.34%	77.34%	71.84%	58.54%	54.25%
hi	99.11%	99.99%	96.4%	95.8%	87.71%	92.31%	88.15%
hr	95.92%	99.88%	96.13%	0%	78.71%	82.95%	76.63%
hu	94.1%	99.75%	92.63%	0%	59.13%	74.22%	64.37%
id	92.14%	99.96%	93.41%	0%	99.46%	82.27%	75.74%
it	98.76%	99.56%	97.29%	97.17%	96.02%	88.42%	86.01%
ja	94.64%	93.32%	91.04%	0%	93.3%	80.71%	79.25%
ko	90.99%	98.24%	92.51%	88.35%	97.9%	68.14%	61.14%
la_ittb	92.91%	99.97%	97.49%	0%	91.59%	82.08%	77.62%
la_proiel	28.28%	100%	95.75%	95.9%	84.99%	67.8%	61.53%
lv	98.8%	99.45%	90.09%	26.52%	68.6%	69.15%	60.94%
nl_lassysmall	82.8%	99.93%	97.74%	0%	95.74%	84.92%	81.81%
nl	76.83%	99.79%	92.04%	0%	87.45%	77.93%	72%
no_bokmaal	96.26%	99.85%	96.64%	0%	90.78%	85.8%	82.6%
no_nynorsk	80.51%	96.99%	28.19%	0%	25.88%	23.91%	6.57%
pl	98.73%	98.99%	95.66%	0%	77.12%	84.05%	78.61%
pt_br	96.63%	99.83%	97.42%	97.42%	99.7%	87.57%	85.41%
pt	91.67%	99.34%	96.51%	0%	92.24%	85.15%	82.03%
ro	94.79%	99.64%	96.71%	9.43%	89.06%	86.68%	81.19%
ru_syntagrus	97.97%	99.69%	98.2%	0%	90.38%	89.36%	86.83%
ru	95.75%	99.81%	95.49%	95.24%	80.24%	81.58%	76.53%
sk	82.04%	99.98%	94.22%	0.9%	68.49%	81.58%	76.23%
sl	99.24%	99.93%	96.92%	14.55%	81.73%	85.74%	82.19%
sv_lines	87.08%	99.98%	94.88%	62.88%	99.98%	80.33%	74.89%
sv	94.92%	99.84%	96.05%	0%	89.81%	82.31%	77.7%
tr	96.32%	97.13%	91.3%	90.45%	78.62%	61.69%	53.08%
ur	97.67%	100%	93.17%	91.23%	78.21%	85.22%	78.61%
vi	92.44%	83.8%	75.84%	72.94%	83.56%	46.16%	40.89%
zh	98.5%	94.57%	88.36%	88.4%	92.9%	70.35%	65.15

Table 8: Official performance of our system on big treebanks. For language no_nynorsk, we used the model trained on another language, thus got very poor result.

Language	Sentence	Word	UPOS	XPOS	Feats	UAS	LAS
fr_partut	98.5%	98.88%	95.26%	95.04%	90.07%	84.2%	80.06%
ga	94.75%	99.64%	90.79%	89.9%	71.95%	76.51%	66.49%
gl_treegal	86.74%	97.91%	91.89%	86.48%	83.83%	73.44%	67.97%
kk	71.84%	94.45%	56.76%	57.13%	36.46%	44.67%	23.99%
la	98.14%	99.99%	88.57%	68.96%	67.45%	59.83%	48.33%
sl_sst	17.58%	100%	91.78%	13.97%	75.6%	56.73%	49.53%
ug	67.13%	96.94%	74.76%	76.87%	96.94%	54.54%	34.57%%
uk	92.49%	99.82%	90.08%	8.95%	62.26%	73.52%	65.17%
ar_pud	99.4%	89.08%	69.85%	0%	21.16%	53.74%	44.31%
cs_pud	96.13%	98.48%	96.32%	87.99%	83.56%	85.12%	79.76%
de_pud	88.4%	96.28%	83.82%	20.29%	30.75%	75.61%	69.19%
en_pud	98.06%	99.59%	94.46%	93.43%	91.38%	83.56%	79.88%
es_pud	94.88%	99.24%	88.01%	0%	54.03%	84.27%	77.09%
fr_pud	96.55%	96.63%	87.56%	0%	57.52%	78.74%	73.67%
hi_pud	1.17%	92.38%	79.04%	34.5%	13.38%	54.7%	43.46%
it_pud	93.97%	99.08%	93.19%	2.48%	57.18%	87.72%	84.41%
ja_pud	96.6%	93.57%	91.7%	0%	54.72%	82.04%	81.25%
pt_pud	97.32%	98.51%	88%	0%	58.8%	78.75%	72.85%
ru_pud	97.23%	97.15%	85.67%	79.23%	37.33%	77.5%	69.46%
sv_pud	94.11%	98.39%	92.54%	0%	69.4%	75.94%	70.76%
tr_pud	93%	94.94%	68.8%	0%	22.41%	52.75%	31.53%
bxr	90.62%	97.46%	49.11%	0%	39.9%	36.42%	17.08%
hsb	72.93%	94.32%	63.89%	0%	35.05%	37.58%	24.58%
kmr	92.91%	91.45%	58.03%	56.45%	31.56%	33.98%	25.85%
sme	98.09%	96.52%	53.98%	57.7%	30.7%	31.22%	17.1%

Table 9: Official performance of our system on small treebanks, PUD treebanks and suprise languages.

3.3 Official Results and Analysis

Detailed numbers for official runs on the test set (Nivre et al., 2017) are listed in Table 8 and Table 9.

Our system ranked the 15th among the 33 submissions. Unfortunately, we found that for one language (no_nynorsk), we used the model trained on another language, therefore the performance is poor. Changing to the correct model would change our results from 67.87% averaged macro F1 score to 68.78%. For two languages *la* and *grc_proiel*, we trained the 1-endpoint-crossing parser, but used the projective parser for testing due to memory issue. On the development dataset, we found that such strategy lost about 0.5% LAS due to the inconsistent decoding algorithms between training and testing. For PUD treebanks that have no corresponding training portion, we used the model trained on the non-PUD dataset, e.g., used the model trained on *en* to parse *en_pud*.

Regarding speed, our parser is not optimized for running time nor memory. It spent 67 hours to parse all the languages using 10 threads. The peak memory usage is about 89GB when parsing *grc_proiel*. The most time consuming part in our system is feature generation that has a complexity of $O(n^3T)$, where $T = 260$ is the number of templates.

4 Conclusion and Future Work

We described our system for the universal dependency parsing task that relies heavily on feature engineering for each component in the pipeline. Our system achieves reasonable performance. An important observation we have is regarding the pretrained word embeddings. Unlike neural net based parsers that can effectively use large unlabeled data by pretrained word embedding, pictures of semi-supervised learning approaches for feature engineering based systems are unclear. Though we tried different ways in our work, the improvement is quite limited. In our future work, we plan to combine our system with neural net based approaches and explore some other semi-superivsed learning techniques.

References

Liang Huang and David Chiang. 2005. Better k-best parsing. In *Proceedings of the Ninth International Workshop on Parsing Technology*. Association for Computational Linguistics, Stroudsburg, PA, USA, Parsing '05, pages 53–64. http://dl.acm.org/citation.cfm?id=1654494.1654500.

Terry Koo and Michael Collins. 2010. Efficient third-order dependency parsers. In *Proceedings of the 48th Annual Meeting of the Association for Computational Linguistics*. Association for Computa-

tional Linguistics, Uppsala, Sweden, pages 1–11.
http://www.aclweb.org/anthology/P10-1001.

John D. Lafferty, Andrew McCallum, and Fernando
C. N. Pereira. 2001. Conditional random fields:
Probabilistic models for segmenting and labeling sequence data. In *Proceedings of the Eighteenth International Conference on Machine Learning*. Morgan Kaufmann Publishers Inc., San Francisco, CA, USA, ICML '01, pages 282–289.
http://dl.acm.org/citation.cfm?id=645530.655813.

Guillaume Lample, Miguel Ballesteros, Sandeep
Subramanian, Kazuya Kawakami, and Chris
Dyer. 2016. Neural architectures for named
entity recognition. *CoRR* abs/1603.01360.
http://arxiv.org/abs/1603.01360.

Ryan McDonald, Koby Crammer, and Fernando
Pereira. 2005. Online large-margin training of dependency parsers. In *Proceedings of the 43rd
Annual Meeting of the Association for Computational Linguistics (ACL'05)*. Association for Computational Linguistics, Ann Arbor, Michigan, pages
91–98. https://doi.org/10.3115/1219840.1219852.

Joakim Nivre et al. 2017. Universal Dependencies
2.0 CoNLL 2017 shared task development and test
data. LINDAT/CLARIN digital library at the Institute of Formal and Applied Linguistics, Charles University, Prague, `http://hdl.handle.net/
11234/1-2184`. http://hdl.handle.net/11234/1-
2184.

Emily Pitler. 2014. A crossing-sensitive
third-order factorization for dependency
parsing. *Transactions of the Association for Computational Linguistics* 2:41–54.
https://www.transacl.org/ojs/index.php/tacl/article/view/193.

Emily Pitler, Sampath Kannan, and Mitchell
Marcus. 2013. Finding optimal 1-endpoint-
crossing trees. *Transactions of the Association for Computational Linguistics* 1:13–24.
https://www.transacl.org/ojs/index.php/tacl/article/view/23.

Daniel Zeman, Filip Ginter, Jan Hajič, Joakim Nivre,
Martin Popel, Milan Straka, and et al. 2017. CoNLL
2017 Shared Task: Multilingual Parsing from Raw
Text to Universal Dependencies. In *Proceedings of
the CoNLL 2017 Shared Task: Multilingual Parsing
from Raw Text to Universal Dependencies*. Association for Computational Linguistics, pages 1–20.

A non-projective greedy dependency parser with bidirectional LSTMs

David Vilares
Universidade da Coruña
LyS Group
Departamento de Computación
Campus de Elviña s/n, 15071
A Coruña, Spain
david.vilares@udc.es

Carlos Gómez-Rodríguez
Universidade da Coruña
FASTPARSE Lab, LyS Group
Departamento de Computación
Campus de A Elviña s/n, 15071
A Coruña, Spain
carlos.gomez@udc.es

Abstract

The LyS-FASTPARSE team presents BIST-COVINGTON, a neural implementation of the Covington (2001) algorithm for non-projective dependency parsing. The bidirectional LSTM approach by Kiperwasser and Goldberg (2016) is used to train a greedy parser with a dynamic oracle to mitigate error propagation. The model participated in the *CoNLL 2017 UD Shared Task*. In spite of not using any ensemble methods and using the baseline segmentation and PoS tagging, the parser obtained good results on both macro-average LAS and UAS in the *big treebanks* category (55 languages), ranking 7th out of 33 teams. In the *all treebanks* category (LAS and UAS) we ranked 16th and 12th. The gap between the *all* and *big* categories is mainly due to the poor performance on four parallel PUD treebanks, suggesting that some 'suffixed' treebanks (e.g. Spanish-AnCora) perform poorly on cross-treebank settings, which does not occur with the corresponding 'unsuffixed' treebank (e.g. Spanish). By changing that, we obtain the 11th best LAS among all runs (official and unofficial). The code is made available at https://github.com/CoNLL-UD-2017/LyS-FASTPARSE

1 Introduction

Dependency parsing is one of the core structured prediction tasks researched by computational linguists, due to the potential advantages that obtaining the syntactic structure of a text has in many natural language processing applications, such as machine translation (Miceli-Barone and Attardi, 2015; Xiao et al., 2016), sentiment analysis (Socher et al., 2013; Vilares et al., 2017) or information extraction (Yu et al., 2015).

The goal of a dependency parser is to analyze the syntactic structure of sentences in one or several human languages by obtaining their analyses in the form of dependency trees. Let $w = [w_1, w_2, ..., w_{|w|}]$ be an input sentence, a *dependency tree* for w is an edge-labeled directed tree $T = (V, E)$ where $V = \{0, 1, 2, \ldots, |w|\}$ is the set of nodes and $E = V \times D \times V$ is the set of labeled arcs. Each arc, of the form (i, d, j), corresponds to a syntactic *dependency* between the words w_i and w_j; where i is the index of the *head* word, j is the index of the *child* word and d is the *dependency type* representing the kind of syntactic relation between them.[1] We will write $i \xrightarrow{d} j$ as shorthand for $(i, d, j) \in E$ and we will omit the dependency types when they are not relevant.

A dependency tree is said to be non-projective if it contains two arcs $i \rightarrow j$ and $k \rightarrow l$ where $min(i, j) < min(k, l) < max(i, j) < max(k, l)$, i.e., if there is any pair of arcs that cross when they are drawn over the sentence, as shown in Figure 1. Unrestricted non-projective parsing allows more accurate syntactic representations than projective parsing, but it comes at a higher computational cost, as there is more flexibility in how the tree can be arranged so that more operations are usually needed to explore the much larger search space.

Non-projective transition-based parsing has been actively explored in the last decade (Nivre and Nilsson, 2005; Attardi, 2006; Nivre, 2008, 2009; Gómez-Rodríguez and Nivre, 2010; Gómez-Rodríguez et al., 2014). The success of neural networks and word embeddings for pro-

---

[1] Following common practice, we are using node 0 as a dummy root node that acts as the head of the syntactic root(s) of the sentence.

Proceedings of the CoNLL 2017 Shared Task: Multilingual Parsing from Raw Text to Universal Dependencies, pages 152–162,
Vancouver, Canada, August 3-4, 2017. © 2017 Association for Computational Linguistics

Figure 1: A non-projective dependency tree

jective dependency parsing (Chen and Manning, 2014) also encouraged research on neural non-projective models (Straka et al., 2016). However, to the best of our knowledge, no neural implementation is available of unrestricted non-projective transition-based parsing with a dynamic oracle. Here, we present such an implementation for the Covington (2001) algorithm using bidirectional long short-term memory networks (LSTM) (Hochreiter and Schmidhuber, 1997), which is the main contribution of this paper.

The system is evaluated at the *CoNLL 2017 UD Shared Task*: *end-to-end multilingual parsing using Universal Dependencies* (Zeman et al., 2017). The goal is to obtain a Universal Dependencies v2.0 representation (Nivre et al., 2016) of a collection of raw texts in different languages.

2   End-to-end multilingual parsing

Given a raw text, we: (1) segment and tokenize sentences and words, (2) apply part-of-speech (PoS) tagging over them and (3) obtain the dependency structure for each sentence.

2.1   Segmentation and PoS tagging

For these two steps we relied on the output provided by UDpipe v1.1 (Straka et al., 2016), which was provided as a baseline model for the shared task.

2.2   The BIST-COVINGTON parser

BIST-COVINGTON is built on the top of three core ideas: a non-projective transition-based parsing algorithm (Covington, 2001; Nivre, 2008), a neural scoring model with bidirectional long short-term memory networks as feature extractors that feed a multilayer perceptron (Kiperwasser and Goldberg, 2016), and a dynamic oracle to mitigate error propagation (Gómez-Rodríguez and Fernández-González, 2015).

2.2.1   The Covington (2001) algorithm

The idea of Covington's algorithm is quite intuitive: any pair of words w_i, w_j in w have a chance to be connected, so we need to consider all such pairs to determine the type of relation that exists between them (i.e. $i \xrightarrow{d} j$, $j \xrightarrow{d} i$ or none). One pair (i, j) is compared at a time. We will be referring to the indexes i and j as the *focus words*. It is straightforward to conclude that the theoretical complexity of the algorithm is $\mathcal{O}(|w|^2)$.

Covington's algorithm can be easily implemented as a transition system (Nivre, 2008). The set of transitions used in BIST-COVINGTON and their preconditions is specified in Table 1. Each transition corresponds to a parsing configuration represented as a 4-tuple $c = (\lambda_1, \lambda_2, \beta, A)$, such that:

- λ_1, λ_2 are two lists storing the words that have been already processed in previous steps. λ_1 contains the already processed words for which the parser still has not decided, in the current state, the type of relation with respect to the focus word j, located at the top of β. λ_2 contains the already processed words for which the parser has already determined the type of relation with respect to j in the current step.

- β contains the words to be processed.

- A contains the set of arcs already created.

Given a sentence w the parser starts at an initial configuration $c_s = ([0], [], [1, ..., |w|], \{\})$ and will apply valid transitions until reaching a final configuration c_f such that $c_f = (\lambda_1, \lambda_2, [], A)$. Figure 2 illustrates an intermediate parsing configuration for our introductory example.

<table>
<tr><td colspan="4" align="center">λ₁</td><td align="center">λ₂</td><td colspan="2" align="center">β</td></tr>
<tr><td>He</td><td>gave</td><td>a</td><td>talk</td><td>yesterday</td><td>about</td><td>parsing</td></tr>
<tr><td>1</td><td>2</td><td>3</td><td>4</td><td>5</td><td>6</td><td>7</td></tr>
</table>

A = [(0,2), (2,1), (4,3), (2,5), (2,4)]

Figure 2:   A parsing configuration for our introductory example just before creating a non-projective RIGHT ARC *talk → about*.

2.2.2   A dynamic oracle for Covington's algorithm (Gómez-Rodríguez and Fernández-González, 2015)

Given a gold dependency tree, τ_g, and a parser configuration c, we can define a loss function

153

Transitions

LEFT ARC	$(\lambda_1\|i, \lambda_2, j\|\beta, A)$	$(\lambda_1, i\|\lambda_2, j\|\beta, A \cup \{(j, d, i)\})$
RIGHT ARC	$(\lambda_1\|i, \lambda_2, j\|\beta, A)$	$(\lambda_1, i\|\lambda_2, j\|\beta, A \cup \{(i, d, j)\})$
SHIFT	$(\lambda_1, \lambda_2, i\|\beta, A)$	$(\lambda_1 \cdot \lambda_2\|i, [], \beta, A)$
NO-ARC	$(\lambda_1\|i, \lambda_2, \beta, A)$	$(\lambda_1 \cdot i\|\lambda_2, \beta, A)$

Preconditions

LEFT ARC	$i > 0$ *and* $\not\exists(k \to i) \in A$ *and* $\not\exists(i \to ... \to j)$
RIGHT ARC	$\not\exists(k \to j) \in A$ *and* $\not\exists(j \to ... \to i)$
NO-ARC	$i > 0$

Table 1: Set of transitions for BIST-COVINGTON as described in Nivre (2008). $a \to ... \to b$ indicates there is a path in the dependency tree that allows to reach b from a

$\mathcal{L}(c, \tau_g)$ that determines the minimum number of missed arcs of τ_g across the possible outputs (A) of final configurations that can be reached from c, i.e., the least possible number of errors with respect to τ_g that we can obtain from c. A static (traditional) oracle is only defined on canonical transition sequences that lead to the gold tree, so that $\mathcal{L}(c, \tau_g) = 0$ at every step during the training phase. However, during the test phase such training strategy might end up in serious error propagation, as it is difficult for the parser to recover from wrong configurations that it has never seen, resulting from suboptimal transitions that increase loss. A dynamic oracle (Goldberg and Nivre, 2012) explores such wrong configurations during the training phase to overcome this issue. Instead of always picking the optimal transition during training, the parser moves with probability x to an erroneous (loss-increasing) configuration, namely the one with the highest score among those that increase loss.

To compute $\mathcal{L}$ for non-projective trees we used the approach proposed by Gómez-Rodríguez and Fernández-González (2015, Algorithm 1). This dynamic oracle can be computed in $\mathcal{O}(|w|)$ although the current implementation in BIST-COVINGTON is $\mathcal{O}(|w|^3)$. To choose the dependency type corresponding to the selected transition (in case it is a LEFT or RIGHT ARC), we look at the gold treebank.

2.2.3 The BIST-parsers (Kiperwasser and Goldberg, 2016)

The original set of BIST-parsers is composed of a projective transition-based model using the arc-hybrid algorithm (Kuhlmann et al., 2011) and a graph-based model inspired in Eisner (1996). They both rely on bidirectional LSTM's (BILSTM's). We kept the main architecture of the arc-hybrid BIST-parser and changed the parsing algorithm to that described in §2.2.1 and §2.2.2. We encourage the reader to consult Kiperwasser and Goldberg (2016) for a detailed explanation of their architecture, but we now try to give a quick overview of its use as the core part of BIST-COVINGTON.[2]

In contrast to traditional parsers (Nivre et al., 2006; Martins et al., 2010; Rasooli and Tetreault, 2015), BIST-parsers rely on embeddings as inputs instead of on discrete events (co-occurrences of words, tags, features, etc.). Embeddings are low-dimensional vectors that provide a continuous representation of a linguistic unit (word, PoS tag, etc.) based on its context (Mikolov et al., 2013).

Let $\mathbf{w}=[\mathbf{w}_1, ..., \mathbf{w}_{|w|}]$ be a list of word embeddings for a sentence, let $\mathbf{u}=[\mathbf{u}_1, ..., \mathbf{u}_{|w|}]$ be the corresponding list of universal PoS tag embeddings, $\mathbf{t}=[\mathbf{t}_1, ..., \mathbf{t}_{|w|}]$ the list of specific PoS tag embeddings, $\mathbf{f}=[\mathbf{f}_1, ..., \mathbf{f}_{|w|}]$ the list of morphological features ("feats" column in the Universal Dependencies data format) and $\mathbf{e}=[\mathbf{e}_1, ..., \mathbf{e}_{|w|}]$ a list of external word embeddings; an input $\mathbf{x}_i$ for a word w_i to BIST-COVINGTON is defined as:[3]

$$\mathbf{x}_i = \mathbf{w}_i \circ \mathbf{u}_i \circ \mathbf{t}_i \circ \mathbf{f}_i \circ \mathbf{e}_i$$

where $\circ$ is the concatenation operator.

Let $\text{LSTM}(\mathbf{x})$ be an abstraction of a standard long short-term memory network that processes the sequence $\mathbf{x} = [\mathbf{x}_1, ..., \mathbf{x}_{|\mathbf{x}|}]$, then a BILSTM encoding of its ith element, $\text{BILSTM}(\mathbf{x}, i)$ can be

---

[2] Including some additional capabilities that we included especially for BIST-COVINGTON.

[3] It might turn out that for some treebank/language some of this information is not available, in which case the unavailable elements are considered as empty lists.

defined as:

$$\text{BILSTM}(\mathbf{x}, i) = \text{LSTM}(\mathbf{x}_{1:i}) \circ \text{LSTM}(\mathbf{x}_{|\mathbf{x}|:i})$$

In the case of multilayer BILSTM'S (BIST-parsers allow it), given n layers, the output of the BILSTM$_m$ is fed as input to BILSTM$_{m+1}$. From the BILSTM network we take a hidden vector $\mathbf{h}$, which can contain the output hidden vectors for: the x leftmost words in β, the rightmost y of λ_1, and the z leftmost and v rightmost words in λ_2.

The hidden vector $\mathbf{h}$ is used to feed a multilayer perceptron with one hidden layer and four output neurons that predicts which transition to take. The output is computed as $W_2 \cdot tanh(W \cdot \mathbf{h} + b) + b_2$, where W, W_2, b and b_2 correspond to the weight matrices and bias vectors of the hidden and output layer of the perceptron. Similarly, BIST-parsers (including BIST-COVINGTON) use a second perceptron with one hidden layer to predict the dependency type. In this case the output layer corresponds to the number of dependency types in the training set.

2.3 Postprocessing

BIST-COVINGTON as it is allows parses with multiple roots, i.e., with several nodes assigned as children of the dummy root. This was not allowed however by the task organizers, as it is enforced by Universal Dependencies that only one word per sentence must depend on the dummy root. To overcome this, the output is postprocessed according to Algorithm 1. Basically, we look for the first verb rooted at 0, or for the first word whose head is 0 if there is no verb, and reassign all other words to the selected term:

3 Experiments

We here describe the official treebanks used in the shared task (§3.1), the general setup used to train the models (§3.2) and some exceptions to said general setup that were applied to special cases (§3.3). We also discuss the experimental results obtained by our system in the shared task (§3.4).

3.1 CoNLL 2017 treebanks

3.1.1 Training/development splits

60 treebanks from 45 languages were released to train the models, based on Universal Dependencies 2.0 (Nivre et al., 2017a). Most of them already contained official training and development splits. A few others lacked a development set. For these, we applied a training/dev random split

---

Algorithm 1 Multiple to single node root

```
1:  procedure TO_SINGLE(V, E)
        ▷ Get the nodes rooted at zero (those whose head has to
        be reassigned)
2:      RO ← []
3:      for i in V do
4:          if head(i) = 0 then
5:              append(RO, i)
        ▷ We select the first verb linked to the dummy root to
        remove multiple roots
6:      if len(RO) > 1 then
7:          closest_head ← RO[0]
8:          for r0 in RO do
9:              if utag(r0) = VERB then
10:                 closest_head ← r0
11:                 break
        ▷ Reassign the head of the invalid nodes (rooted to the
        dummy root) to closest_head
12:         for r0 in RO do
13:             if r0 ≠ closest_head then
14:                 head(r0) ← closest_head
```

(80/20) over the original training set. All development sets were only used to evaluate and tune the trained models. *No development set* was used to train any of the runs, as specified in the task guidelines.

Additionally, four *surprise languages* (truly low resource languages), were considered by the organization for evaluation: Buryat, Kurmanji, North Sami and Upper Sorbian. For these, the organizers only released a tiny sample set consisting of very few sentences annotated according to the UD guidelines.

3.1.2 Test splits

The organizers provided a test split for each of the treebanks released in the training phase, including the surprise languages. Additionally, they provided test sets corresponding to 14 parallel treebanks in different languages translated from a unique source. All of these test sets (Nivre et al., 2017b) were hidden from the participating teams until the shared task had ended. Using the TIRA environment (Potthast et al., 2014) provided for the shared task, participants could execute runs on them, but not see the outputs or the results.

3.2 General setup

We used the gold training treebanks to train the parsing models. We trained one model per treebank. No predicted training treebank (predicted universal and/or specific tags and morphological features) was used for training, except for the case of Portuguese (see §3.3.1).

Embeddings: Word embeddings are set to size 100 and universal tag embeddings to 25. Language-specific tag and morphological feature embeddings are used and set to size 25, if they are available for the treebank at hand. Using external word embeddings seems to be beneficial to improve parsing performance (Kiperwasser and Goldberg, 2016), but it also makes models take more time and especially much more memory to train. The external word embeddings used in this work (the ones pretrained by the *CoNLL 2017 UD Shared Task* organizers[4]) are of size 100. Due to lack of enough computational resources, we only had time to train 38 models (mainly corresponding to the smallest treebanks) including this information. Models trained with external word embeddings are marked in Table 3 with ⋆.

Parameters: Adam is used as optimizer (Kingma and Ba, 2014). Models were trained for up to 30 epochs, except for the two smallest training sets (Kazakh and Uyghur), where models were trained for up to 100 epochs. The size of the output of the stacked BILSTM was set to 512. For very large treebanks (e.g. Czech or Russian-SyntagRus) or treebanks where sentences are very long (e.g. Arabic), we set it to 256, also to counteract the lack of physical resources to finish the task on time. These models are marked in Table 3 with •. The number of BILSTM layers is set to 2. To choose a transition, BIST-COVINGTON looks at the embeddings of: the first word in β, the rightmost three words in λ_1, and the leftmost and rightmost word in λ_2 (i.e., following the notation in Section 2.2.3, we set $x = 1$, $y = 3$, $z = 1$ and $v = 1$).

Other relevant features of the setup: Aggressive exploration is applied to the dynamic oracle, as in the original arc-hybrid BIST-PARSER.

3.3 Special cases

For some treebanks, we followed a different strategy due to various issues. We enumerate the changes below:

3.3.1 The Portuguese model

Surprisingly, the model trained on the Portuguese treebank suffered a significant loss with respect to the UDpipe baseline when parsing the full predicted (segmentation and tagging) development file. We first hypothesized this was due to a low accuracy on predicting the "feats" column in comparison to other languages, as they are pretty sparse. To try to overcome this, we trained a model without considering them, but it did not solve the problem. Our second option was to train a Portuguese model on its predicted training treebank.[5] Additionally, despite being a relative large treebank, we included external word embeddings to boost performance. This helped us to obtain a performance similar to that reported by UDpipe.

3.3.2 Surprise languages

As training an accurate parser with so little data might be a hard task , especially in the case of *data-hungry* deep learning models, we used other training treebanks for this purpose. We built a set of parsers inspired on the approach presented by Vilares et al. (2016), who find that training a multilingual model on merged harmonized treebanks might actually have a positive impact on parsing the corresponding monolingual treebank. In this particular case, we are assuming that a trained model over multilingual treebanks might be able to capture similar treebank structures for unseen languages.

In particular, we: (1) ran every trained monolingual model on the sample sets, (2) for each surprise language, we chose the top three languages where the corresponding models obtained the best performance and (3) trained a parser taking the first 2 000 sentences of the training sets corresponding to such languages and merging them.

Thus, we did not use the provided sample data for training, but only as a development set to choose suitable source languages for our crosslingual approach.

3.3.3 Parallel (PUD) treebanks

The only information our models knew about the parallel treebanks during the testing phase was the language in which they were written. To parse these languages we follow a simplistic approach, using the models we had already trained on the provided training corpora: (1) if there is only one model trained on the same language we take that model, (2) else if there is more than one model trained on that language, we take the one trained over the largest treebank (in number of sentences),

---

[4]`http://hdl.handle.net/11234/1-1989`

[5]We used the predicted tokenization and tagging provided by UDpipe.

otherwise (3) we parse the PUD treebank using the English model.[6]

3.4 Results

Official and unofficial results for our model and for the rest of participants on the test set can be found at the task website: `http://universaldependencies.org/conll17/results.html`, but in this section we detail the results obtained by BIST-COVINGTON.

3.4.1 Results on *small* and *big* treebanks categories

Table 2 shows the performance on the test sets for the treebanks where an official training set was released.

In Table 3 we summarize our results on the development sets for those treebanks that provided an official one. Although not shown for brevity and clarity reasons, it is easy to check for the reader that BIST-COVINGTON outperformed the baseline UDpipe[7] for all these treebanks on the gold configuration (gold segmentation, gold tags). The same is true, except for Chinese (-0.69 decrease in LAS) and Portuguese (-0.09), in the fully predicted configuration (end-to-end parsing). It is easy to conclude from the table that including external word embeddings has a positive effect in most of the treebanks we had time to try. This is especially true when performing end-to-end parsing, where only for three languages (English-LinES, Gothic and Old Church Slavonic) a negative effect was observed.[8]

Table 4 shows the top three selected languages for each surprise treebank, the performance of the monolingual and multilingual (merged) models on them on the sample set (used as dev set), and also shows the performance of the multilingual models in the official test sets.

Table 5 shows our performance on the PUD treebanks (test sets). There are 4 PUD treebanks for which we obtained a poor performance: Spanish, Finnish, Portuguese and Russian. Average LAS loss with respect to the top system in the cor-

---

[6]This latter case should and did never happen, as the task organizers specified in advance that the parallel treebanks would correspond to languages with existing treebanks, but we included it as a fallback mechanism.

[7]`http://universaldependencies.org/conll17/baseline.html`

[8]Due to not so rich embeddings and/or the model finishing earlier than expected during training. See §5.

Treebank	LAS
Ancient_Greek -PROIEL	67.85_8
Ancient_Greek	59.83_6
Arabic	66.54_{10}
Basque	73.27_5
Bulgarian	85.76_6
Catalan	85.37_{18}
Chinese	56.76_2
Croatian	77.91_{11}
Czech-CAC	82.71_{16}
Czech-CLTT	68.92_{23}
Czech	83.77_{11}
Danish	75.27_{11}
Dutch-LassySmall	82.49_6
Dutch	71.89_7
English-LinES	73.47_{13}
English-ParTUT	74.50_{12}
English	76.00_{14}
Estonian	61.79_7
Finnish-FTB	76.80_7
Finnish	76.11_8
French-ParTUT	72.09_{25}
French-Sequoia	77.77_{23}
French	79.86_{20}
Galician-TreeGal	65.42_{17}
Galician	79.24_{12}
German	68.35_{22}
Gothic	62.07_7
Greek	81.43_6
Hebrew	59.28_9
Hindi	86.88_{15}
Hungarian	66.00_9
Indonesian	72.94_{23}
Irish	58.05_{22}
Italian	85.60_{16}
Japanese	72.68_{17}
Kazakh	16.20_{26}
Korean	63.85_{14}
Latin-ITTB	79.58_7
Latin-PROIEL	61.45_7
Latin	48.92_7
Latvian	63.05_7
Norwegian-Bokmaal	84.49_8
Norwegian-Nynorsk	83.10_7
Old_Church_Slavonic	67.21_4
Persian	77.68_{17}
Polish	82.09_7
Portuguese-BR	86.74_9
Portuguese	80.91_{19}
Romanian	80.58_{11}
Russian-SynTagRus	87.55_9
Russian	76.98_8
Slovak	76.47_6
Slovenian-SST	43.80_{21}
Slovenian	82.92_7
Spanish-AnCora	86.83_7
Spanish	83.24_8
Swedish-LinES	75.04_{10}
Swedish	77.33_{13}
Turkish	57.22_5
Ukrainian	61.21_{15}
Urdu	78.31_9
Uyghur	27.92_{23}
Vietnamese	38.33_{12}

Table 2: BIST-COVINGTON results on the test sets, for those treebanks from which a training set was provided (*small* and *big* treebanks categories)

Treebank	Gold treebank LAS no E	E	Predicted treebank LAS no E	E
Ancient_Greek -PROIEL	81.44	N/A	70.5	N/A
Ancient_Greek*	71.01	**71.31**	60.41	**61.25**
Arabic*•	79.12	**79.71**	64.37	**65.62**
Basque*	81.53	**82.06**	72.00	**73.42**
Bulgarian*	89.88	**90.46**	84.33	**85.30**
Catalan•	90.63	N/A	87.21	N/A
Chinese	80.34	N/A	55.31	N/A
Croatian*	**83.86**	83.64	78.04	**78.74**
Czech-CAC•	88.64	N/A	84.93	N/A
Czech-CLTT•	82.28	N/A	68.03	N/A
Czech•	90.70	N/A	85.47	N/A
Danish*	83.85	**85.78**	74.92	**76.94**
Dutch-LassySmall*	86.59	**86.65**	76.78	**77.50**
Dutch	86.82	N/A	76.47	N/A
English-LinES*	**83.74**	83.05	**76.48**	76.44
English-ParTUT*	84.15	**84.60**	76.24	**77.07**
English	**88.02**	N/A	76.7	N/A
Estonian*	79.26	**80.21**	61.09	**62.80**
Finnish-FTB	**89.00**	N/A	76.43	N/A
Finnish	86.51	N/A	76.96	N/A
French-Sequoia	89.14	N/A	81.79	N/A
French•	89.86	N/A	85.8	N/A
Galician*•	84.22	82.58	80.17	79.03
German	87.63	N/A	73.61	N/A
Gothic*	80.82	**81.17**	**60.84**	60.82
Greek*	86.03	**86.37**	79.74	**80.05**
Hebrew*•	**85.26**	85.13	62.18	**62.39**
Hindi	93.42	N/A	87.41	N/A
Hungarian*	80.84	**81.30**	69.16	**70.43**
Indonesian	80.39	N/A	74.91	N/A
Italian-ParTUT*	86.20	**86.83**	78.90	**79.56**
Italian	90.30	N/A	86.05	N/A
Japanese*	**96.48**	96.46	73.99	**74.20**
Korean	68.66	N/A	60.18	N/A
Latin-ITTB	84.21	N/A	72.22	N/A
Latin-PROIEL	79.37	N/A	61.98	N/A
Latvian*	**77.25**	76.55	63.12	**63.62**
Norwegian-Bokmaal	91.45	N/A	85.13	N/A
Norwegian-Nynorsk	91.06	N/A	83.38	N/A
Old_Church_Slavonic*	**84.59**	84.52	**66.93**	66.66
Persian*•	86.85	N/A	80.44	81.45
Polish*	91.04	**91.25**	81.43	**82.18**
Portuguese-BR•	90.91	N/A	86.41	N/A
Portuguese*•	**94.94**	93.09	79.3	**84.00**
Romanian*	**85.08**	84.44	80.97	**81.01**
Russian-SynTagRus•	91.91	N/A	88.29	N/A
Russian*	85.12	**86.07**	78.02	**79.09**
Slovak*	87.61	**88.39**	75.59	**77.35**
Slovenian*	92.28	**93.14**	82.48	**84.15**
Spanish-AnCora•	90.50	N/A	86.21	N/A
Spanish•	87.90	N/A	84.25	N/A
Swedish-LinES*	84.23	**84.44**	76.39	**76.86**
Swedish*	84.88	**85.03**	76.41	**76.64**
Turkish*	61.66	**64.46**	55.05	**57.60**
Urdu*	**87.63**	87.50	77.43	**77.49**
Vietnamese*	72.21	**72.58**	42.27	**42.94**

Table 3: BIST-COVINGTON results on the dev set, for those treebanks that have an official dev set (all treebanks except French-ParTUT, Irish, Galician-TreeGal, Kazakh, Slovenian-SST, Kazakh, Uyghur and Ukrainian). ⋆ indicates the model was also trained with external word embeddings (E). • indicates the BILSTM output dimension was 256. The performance of some models is likely to be improved, as its training finished earlier than expected due to lack of time to finish it or memory issues (see also §5)

responding treebank was 32.47, which implied a LAS loss up to 1.60 points in the official global ranking. We hypothesized that taking the model

Surprise language	Top 3 treebanks	Sample set Monolingual	Sample set Multilingual	Test set Multi
Buryat	Hindi	36.60		
	German	32.68	43.14	28.65$_5$
	Korean	27.45		
Kurmanji	Romanian	38.84		
	Czech	37.19	39.26	32.08$_{16}$
	Slovenian	31.40		
North Sami	Estonian	45.38		
	Finnish	40.82	57.14	32.58$_{14}$
	Finnish-FTB	40.14		
Upper Sorbian	Slovenian	65.22		
	Slovak	64.78	70.65	52.50$_{15}$
	Bulgarian	61.09		

Table 4: LAS on the surprise languages sample sets for: (1) top 3 best performing monolingual models for which there is an official training treebank and (2) a multilingual model trained on the first 2 000 sentences of each of such treebanks. For the multilingual models, the last column shows its performance on the test sets (subscripts indicate our ranking in that language)

trained on the largest treebank of the same language was the safest option to parse PUD texts, but in retrospective this clearly was not the optimal choice. Those four PUD treebanks were parsed with models trained on Universal Dependencies (UD) treebanks whose official name has a *suffix* (i.e. Spanish-Ancora, Finnish-FTB, Portuguese-BR and Russian-SyntagRus), which were larger than the unsuffixed UD treebank. However, we think such a poor performance surpasses what can be reasonably expected from an universal treebank written in the same language. From Table 5 it is reasonable to conclude that such suffixed treebanks parse more than poorly on cross-treebank settings, in comparison to the model trained on the unsuffixed treebank (rightmost column). We wonder if this can be an indicator of those treebanks sharing universal dependency types, but diverging in terms of syntactic structures, which caused the low LAS scores in those cases.

A possible contributing factor to this could be that the annotators of the parallel treebanks used guidelines from the unsuffixed treebanks, or automatic output trained on them, as a starting point from the annotation process. At the point of writing we cannot confirm whether this is the case, as documentation for the PUD treebanks is not yet publicly available.

PUD treebank	Trained on largest treebank (official)	LAS	Trained on uns. treebank (unofficial)	LAS
Arabic	Arabic	45.12_{11}	=	
Czech	Czech	80.13_{10}	=	
German	German	66.29_{19}	=	
English	English	78.79_{16}	=	
Spanish	Spanish-Ancora	$53.73_{30}\downarrow$	Spanish	78.90
Finnish	Finnish-FTB	$40.66_{28}\downarrow$	Finnish	80.70
French	French	73.15_{23}	=	
Hindi	Hindi	51.15_{13}	=	
Italian	Italian	83.84_{15}	=	
Japanese	Japanese	76.09_{18}	=	
Portuguese	Portuguese-BR	$54.75_{27}\downarrow$	Portuguese	72.84
Russian	Russian-SyntagRus	$44.69_{31}\downarrow$	Russian	70.00
Swedish	Swedish	69.60_{17}	=	
Turkish	Turkish	34.96_{4}	=	

Table 5: LAS/UAS performance on the PUD treebanks (test sets). The $\downarrow$ symbol indicates a drastic gap in performance with respect the average performance of BIST-COVINGTON. We show how parsing the PUD treebank with a model trained on the corresponding unsuffixed treebank clearly improves the LAS accuracy.

4 Discussion

BIST-COVINGTON worked very well on languages where official training/development sets were available, what the organizers named *big treebanks* (55 treebanks), category where we ranked 7th out of 33 systems, both for LAS and UAS metrics, in spite of not using any ensemble method and not performing custom tokenization, segmentation or tagging.

More in detail, we ranked in the top ten LAS for 35 languages, where 32 belong to the category of *big treebanks*: Arabic (10th), Bulgarian (6th), Buryat (5th), Czech-PUD (10th), Old Church Slavonic (4th), Greek (6th), Spanish (8th), Spanish-Ancora (7th), Estonian (7th), Basque (5th), Finnish (8th), Finnish-ftb (7th), Gothic (7th), Ancient_Greek (6th), Ancient_Greek-PROIEL (8th), Hebrew (9th), Hungarian (9th), Latin (7th), Latin-ITB (7th), Latin-PROIEL (7th), Latvian (7th), Dutch (7th), Dutch-lassysmall (6th), Norwegian-Bokmaal (8th), Norwegian-Nynorsk (7th), Polish (7th), Portuguese-BR (9th), Russian (8th), Russian-Syntagrus(9th), Slovak (6th), Slovenian (7th), Swedish-LinES (10th), Turkish (5th), Turkish-PUD (4th) and Ukrainian (9th).

We failed on a subset of the PUD treebanks. As previously explained, the main gap came from the Spanish, Russian, Portuguese and Finnish PUD treebanks. We analyzed those treebanks based on existing UD CoNLL treebanks. We parsed them

with the model trained on the largest treebank that shared the language. It turned out that those PUD treebanks that were parsed with suffixed treebanks (e.g. Spanish-Ancora or Russian-SynTagRus) obtained a very low performance, something that did not happen when parsing them with the model trained on the corresponding unsuffixed treebank (e.g. Spanish or Russian). In cases where there was only one UD treebank sharing the language, our approach worked reasonably well, in spite of the simplistic strategy followed (e.g. Turkish-PUD or Czech-PUD).

We did not perform too well either on the set of *small treebanks* (French-ParTUT, Irish, Galician-TreeGal, Kazakh, Slovenian-SST, Uyghur and Ukrainian). This was somewhat expected for two reasons: (1) neural models that are fed with continuous vector representations are usually data-hungry and (2) the submitted model was only trained on our training split; we did not include the *ad-hoc* dev sets for those languages as a part of the final training data.

We believe that the cases where the parser did not work well were due to external causes (e.g. the chosen cross-treebank strategy), as shown in the case of the PUD treebanks. Unofficial results such as the ones in Table 5 show that this can be easily addressed to push BIST-COVINGTON to obtain competitive results in those treebanks too.

5 Hardware requirements and issues

Our models required DyNet (Neubig et al., 2017), which allocates memory when it is launched. We ran them on CPU. To train the models we used two servers with 128GB of RAM memory each. Estimating the required memory to allocate to train each model was a hard task for us. Dynet does not currently have a garbage collector,[9] so many models ran out of memory even before finishing their training, probably due to wrong memory estimations to complete this phase, and our lack of resources to allocate memory for many treebanks at a time. We observed that models such as Arabic with external word embeddings could take up to 64GB during the training phase.

The performance on the dev set of our trained models was close, but not equal, in our training machine and in TIRA. This might be caused by a serialization versioning issue: `https://`

---

[9]`https://github.com/clab/dynet/issues/418`

To safely run a large trained model with external embeddings we recommend at least 32GB of RAM memory. We think a safe estimate to run any model without external embeddings would be something between 15 and 20GB.

The current version of BIST-COVINGTON is not very fast. Average speed (tokens/second) over all test treebanks was 18.27. The fastest models were Kazakh (66.36), Uyghur (54.11) and Czech-PUD (45.79) and the slowest ones Czech-CLTT (5.37), Latin-PROIEL (7.69) and Galician-TreeGal (8.19). To complete the testing phase of the shared task, BIST-COVINGTON took around 28 hours. These times correspond to those of the official evaluation on the TIRA virtual machine. Several factors influence these speeds. Firstly, RNN approaches tend to be slower than feedforward approaches (e.g., reported speeds for the original transition-based BIST-parser by Kiperwasser and Goldberg (2016) are an order of magnitude behind those of Chen and Manning (2014), although the latter is also much less accurate). Secondly, parsing UD data for different languages accurately requires using more linguistic information (e.g. feature embeddings), increasing the model size with respect to models evaluated on simpler settings like the English Penn Treebank. Finally, we are aware that Covington's algorithm may become slower when sentences are too long due to its quadratic worst-case complexity, an issue that is likely to happen due to the predicted segmentation (the organizers actually informed that some treebanks contained sentences of about 300 words).

6 Conclusion

This paper presented BIST-COVINGTON, a bidirectional LSTM implementation of the Covington (2001) algorithm for non-projective transition-based dependency parsing. Our model was evaluated on the end-to-end multilingual parsing with universal dependencies shared task proposed at CoNLL 2017. For segmentation and part-of-speech tagging our model relied on the official UDpipe baseline. The official results located us 7th out of 33 teams in the *big treebanks* category, in spite of not using any ensemble method.

As future work, there is room for improvement. Due to lack of resources to train the models and complete the task on time, we could not train all models using external word embeddings, which has been shown to produce a significant overall improvement. Jackniffing (Agić and Schluter, 2017) might be a simple way to improve the LAS scores. Finally, it would be interesting to implement the non-monotonic version of the Covington transition system, together with approximate dynamic oracles (Fernández-González and Gómez-Rodríguez, 2017), shown to improve accuracy over the regular Covington parser.

Acknowledgments

David Vilares is funded by an FPU Grant 13/01180. Carlos Gómez-Rodríguez has received funding from the European Research Council (ERC), under the European Union's Horizon 2020 research and innovation programme (FASTPARSE, grant agreement No 714150). Both authors have received funding from the TELEPARES-UDC project from MINECO.

References

Željko Agić and Natalie Schluter. 2017. How (not) to train a dependency parser: The curious case of jackknifing part-of-speech taggers. In *The 54th Annual Meeting of the Association for Computational Linguistics (ACL 2017)*.

Giuseppe Attardi. 2006. Experiments with a multilanguage non-projective dependency parser. In *Proceedings of the Tenth Conference on Computational Natural Language Learning*. Association for Computational Linguistics, pages 166–170. http://dl.acm.org/citation.cfm?id=1596276.1596307.

Danqi Chen and Christopher Manning. 2014. A fast and accurate dependency parser using neural networks. In *Proceedings of the 2014 Conference on Empirical Methods in Natural Language Processing (EMNLP)*. Doha, Qatar, pages 740–750. http://www.aclweb.org/anthology/D14-1082.

Michael A Covington. 2001. A fundamental algorithm for dependency parsing. In *Proceedings of the 39th annual ACM southeast conference*. Citeseer, pages 95–102.

Jason M Eisner. 1996. Three new probabilistic models for dependency parsing: An exploration. In *Proceedings of the 16th conference on Computational linguistics-Volume 1*. Association for Computational Linguistics, pages 340–345. https://arxiv.org/pdf/cmp-lg/9706003.pdf.

Daniel Fernández-González and Carlos Gómez-Rodríguez. 2017. A full non-monotonic transition system for unrestricted non-projective parsing. In *Proceedings of the 55th Annual Meeting of the Association for Computational Linguistics (in press)*. Association for Computational Linguistics.

Yoav Goldberg and Joakim Nivre. 2012. A dynamic oracle for arc-eager dependency parsing. In *COLING*. pages 959–976. http://www.aclweb.org/anthology/C12-1059.

Carlos Gómez-Rodríguez and Daniel Fernández-González. 2015. An efficient dynamic oracle for unrestricted non-projective parsing. *Volume 2: Short Papers* page 256. http://aclweb.org/anthology/P/P15/P15-2042.pdf.

Carlos Gómez-Rodríguez and Joakim Nivre. 2010. A transition-based parser for 2-planar dependency structures. In *Proceedings of the 48th Annual Meeting of the Association for Computational Linguistics*. Association for Computational Linguistics, pages 1492–1501. http://aclweb.org/anthology/P/P10/P10-1151.pdf.

Carlos Gómez-Rodríguez, Francesco Sartorio, and Giorgio Satta. 2014. A polynomial-time dynamic oracle for non-projective dependency parsing. In *Proceedings of the 2014 Conference on Empirical Methods in Natural Language Processing (EMNLP)*. pages 917–927. http://aclweb.org/anthology/D/D14/D14-1099.pdf.

Sepp Hochreiter and Jürgen Schmidhuber. 1997. Long short-term memory. *Neural computation* 9(8):1735–1780.

Diederik Kingma and Jimmy Ba. 2014. Adam: A method for stochastic optimization. *arXiv preprint arXiv:1412.6980* https://arxiv.org/pdf/1412.6980.pdf.

Eliyahu Kiperwasser and Yoav Goldberg. 2016. Simple and accurate dependency parsing using bidirectional lstm feature representations. *Transactions of the Association for Computational Linguistics* 4:313–327. http://transacl.org/ojs/index.php/tacl/article/view/885.

Marco Kuhlmann, Carlos Gómez-Rodríguez, and Giorgio Satta. 2011. Dynamic programming algorithms for transition-based dependency parsers. In *Proceedings of the 49th Annual Meeting of the Association for Computational Linguistics: Human Language Technologies-Volume 1*. Association for Computational Linguistics, pages 673–682. http://aclweb.org/anthology/P/P11/P11-1068.pdf.

André FT Martins, Noah A Smith, Eric P Xing, Pedro MQ Aguiar, and Mário AT Figueiredo. 2010. Turbo parsers: Dependency parsing by approximate variational inference. In *Proceedings of the 2010 Conference on Empirical Methods in Natural Language Processing*. Association for Computational Linguistics, pages 34–44. http://aclweb.org/anthology/D/D10/D10-1004.pdf.

Antonio Valerio Miceli-Barone and Giuseppe Attardi. 2015. Non-projective dependency-based pre-reordering with recurrent neural network for machine translation. In *The 53rd Annual Meeting of the Association for Computational Linguistics and The 7th International Joint Conference of the Asian Federation of Natural Language Processing*.

Tomas Mikolov, Ilya Sutskever, Kai Chen, Greg S Corrado, and Jeff Dean. 2013. Distributed representations of words and phrases and their compositionality. In *Advances in neural information processing systems*. pages 3111–3119. https://papers.nips.cc/paper/5021-distributed-representations-of-words-and-phrases-and-their-compositionality.pdf.

Graham Neubig, Chris Dyer, Yoav Goldberg, Austin Matthews, Waleed Ammar, Antonios Anastasopoulos, Miguel Ballesteros, David Chiang, Daniel Clothiaux, Trevor Cohn, Kevin Duh, Manaal Faruqui, Cynthia Gan, Dan Garrette, Yangfeng Ji, Lingpeng Kong, Adhiguna Kuncoro, Gaurav Kumar, Chaitanya Malaviya, Paul Michel, Yusuke Oda, Matthew Richardson, Naomi Saphra, Swabha Swayamdipta, and Pengcheng Yin. 2017. Dynet: The dynamic neural network toolkit. *arXiv preprint arXiv:1701.03980* https://arxiv.org/abs/1701.03980.

Joakim Nivre. 2008. Algorithms for deterministic incremental dependency parsing. *Computational Linguistics* 34(4):513–553. http://dl.acm.org/citation.cfm?id=1479205.

Joakim Nivre. 2009. Non-projective dependency parsing in expected linear time. In *Proceedings of the Joint Conference of the 47th Annual Meeting of the ACL and the 4th International Joint Conference on Natural Language Processing of the AFNLP: Volume 1-Volume 1*. Association for Computational Linguistics, pages 351–359. http://aclweb.org/anthology/P/P09/P09-1040.pdf.

Joakim Nivre, Željko Agić, Lars Ahrenberg, et al. 2017a. Universal Dependencies 2.0. LINDAT/CLARIN digital library at the Institute of Formal and Applied Linguistics, Charles University, Prague, http://hdl.handle.net/11234/1-1983. http://hdl.handle.net/11234/1-1983.

Joakim Nivre, Željko Agić, Lars Ahrenberg, et al. 2017b. Universal dependencies 2.0 CoNLL 2017 shared task development and test data. LINDAT/CLARIN digital library at the Institute of Formal and Applied Linguistics, Charles University. http://hdl.handle.net/11234/1-2184.

Joakim Nivre, Marie-Catherine de Marneffe, Filip Ginter, Yoav Goldberg, Jan Hajič, Christopher Manning, Ryan McDonald, Slav Petrov, Sampo Pyysalo, Natalia Silveira, Reut Tsarfaty, and Daniel Zeman. 2016. Universal Dependencies v1: A multilingual treebank collection. In *Proceedings of the 10th International Conference on Language Resources and Evaluation (LREC 2016)*. European Language Resources Association, Portoro, Slovenia, pages 1659–1666. http://www.lrec-conf.org/proceedings/lrec2016/pdf/348_Paper.pdf.

Joakim Nivre, Johan Hall, and Jens Nilsson. 2006. Maltparser: A data-driven parser-generator for dependency parsing. In *Proceedings of LREC*. volume 6, pages 2216–2219. http://www.lrecconf.org/proceedings/lrec2006/pdf/162_pdf.pdf.

Joakim Nivre and Jens Nilsson. 2005. Pseudo-projective dependency parsing. In *Proceedings of the 43rd Annual Meeting on Association for Computational Linguistics*. Association for Computational Linguistics, pages 99–106. http://aclweb.org/anthology/P/P05/P05-1013.pdf.

Martin Potthast, Tim Gollub, Francisco Rangel, Paolo Rosso, Efstathios Stamatatos, and Benno Stein. 2014. Improving the reproducibility of PAN's shared tasks: Plagiarism detection, author identification, and author profiling. In Evangelos Kanoulas, Mihai Lupu, Paul Clough, Mark Sanderson, Mark Hall, Allan Hanbury, and Elaine Toms, editors, *Information Access Evaluation meets Multilinguality, Multimodality, and Visualization. 5th International Conference of the CLEF Initiative (CLEF 14)*. Springer, Berlin Heidelberg New York, pages 268–299. https://doi.org/10.1007/978-3-319-11382-1_22.

Mohammad Sadegh Rasooli and Joel Tetreault. 2015. Yara parser: A fast and accurate dependency parser. *arXiv preprint arXiv:1503.06733* https://arxiv.org/pdf/1503.06733.pdf.

Richard Socher, Alex Perelygin, Jean Y Wu, Jason Chuang, Christopher D Manning, Andrew Y Ng, Christopher Potts, et al. 2013. Recursive deep models for semantic compositionality over a sentiment treebank. In *Proceedings of the conference on empirical methods in natural language processing (EMNLP)*. volume 1631, page 1642.

Milan Straka, Jan Hajic, and Jana Straková. 2016. Udpipe: Trainable pipeline for processing conll-u files performing tokenization, morphological analysis, pos tagging and parsing. In *Proceedings of the Tenth International Conference on Language Resources and Evaluation (LREC 2016)*. http://www.lrecconf.org/proceedings/lrec2016/pdf/873_Paper.pdf.

David Vilares, Carlos Gómez-Rodríguez, and Miguel A. Alonso. 2016. One model, two languages: training bilingual parsers with harmonized treebanks. In *The 54th Annual Meeting of the Association for Computational Linguistics*. pages 425–431. http://aclweb.org/anthology/P/P16/P16-2069.pdf.

David Vilares, Carlos Gómez-Rodríguez, and Miguel A Alonso. 2017. Universal, unsupervised (rule-based), uncovered sentiment analysis. *Knowledge-Based Systems* 118:45–55.

Tong Xiao, Jingbo Zhu, Chunliang Zhang, and Tongran Liu. 2016. Syntactic skeleton-based translation. In *Proceedings of the Thirtieth AAAI Conference on Artificial Intelligence, February 12-17, 2016, Phoenix, Arizona, USA.*. pages 2856–2862. http://www.aaai.org/ocs/index.php/AAAI/AAAI16/paper/view/11933

Mo Yu, Matthew R Gormley, and Mark Dredze. 2015. Combining word embeddings and feature embeddings for fine-grained relation extraction. In *HLT-NAACL*. pages 1374–1379.

Daniel Zeman, Martin Popel, Milan Straka, Jan Hajič, Joakim Nivre, Filip Ginter, Juhani Luotolahti, Sampo Pyysalo, Slav Petrov, Martin Potthast, Francis Tyers, Elena Badmaeva, Memduh Gökırmak, Anna Nedoluzhko, Silvie Cinková, Jan Hajič jr., Jaroslava Hlaváčová, Václava Kettnerová, Zdeňka Urešová, Jenna Kanerva, Stina Ojala, Anna Missilä, Christopher Manning, Sebastian Schuster, Siva Reddy, Dima Taji, Nizar Habash, Herman Leung, Marie-Catherine de Marneffe, Manuela Sanguinetti, Maria Simi, Hiroshi Kanayama, Valeria de Paiva, Kira Droganova, Héctor Martínez Alonso, Hans Uszkoreit, Vivien Macketanz, Aljoscha Burchardt, Kim Harris, Katrin Marheinecke, Georg Rehm, Tolga Kayadelen, Mohammed Attia, Ali Elkahky, Zhuoran Yu, Emily Pitler, Saran Lertpradit, Michael Mandl, Jesse Kirchner, Hector Fernandez Alcalde, Jana Strnadova, Esha Banerjee, Ruli Manurung, Antonio Stella, Atsuko Shimada, Sookyoung Kwak, Gustavo Mendonça, Tatiana Lando, Rattima Nitisaroj, and Josie Li. 2017. CoNLL 2017 Shared Task: Multilingual Parsing from Raw Text to Universal Dependencies. In *Proceedings of the CoNLL 2017 Shared Task: Multilingual Parsing from Raw Text to Universal Dependencies*. Association for Computational Linguistics.

LIMSI@CoNLL'17: UD Shared Task

Lauriane Aufrant[1,2]   **Guillaume Wisniewski**[1]

[1]LIMSI, CNRS, Univ. Paris-Sud, Université Paris-Saclay, 91 405 Orsay, France
[2]DGA, 60 boulevard du Général Martial Valin, 75 509 Paris, France
{lauriane.aufrant,guillaume.wisniewski}@limsi.fr

Abstract

This paper describes LIMSI's submission to the *CoNLL 2017 UD Shared Task*, which is focused on small treebanks, and how to improve low-resourced parsing only by *ad hoc* combination of multiple views and resources. We present our approach for low-resourced parsing, together with a detailed analysis of the results for each test treebank. We also report extensive analysis experiments on model selection for the PUD treebanks, and on annotation consistency among UD treebanks.

1 Introduction

This paper describes LIMSI's submission to the *CoNLL 2017 UD Shared Task* (Zeman et al., 2017), dedicated to parsing Universal Dependencies (Nivre et al., 2016) on a wide array of languages. Our team's work is focused on small treebanks, under 1,000 training sentences. To improve low-resourced parsing, we propose to leverage base parsers, either monolingual or cross-lingual, by combining them with a cascading method: each parser in turn annotates some of the tokens, and has access to previous predictions on other tokens to help current prediction; in the end each token is annotated by exactly one parser. Compared to the official baseline, this combination method yields significant improvements on several small treebanks, as well as a few larger ones.

Overall, according to the official results, our system achieves 67.72 LAS and is ranked 17th out of 33 participants, while the baseline (UD-Pipe 1.1) achieves 68.35 LAS and is ranked 13th. This is mostly due to huge drops from the baseline on a few languages, for which we submitted one of the official baseline models. Analyzing these drops (see §4.5) unveils that strong annota-

tion divergences remain among UD treebanks of the same language. If for these treebanks we had submitted the exact same models as the baseline submission, our system would have been ranked 9th, achieving 68.90 LAS. In the unofficial, post-evaluation ranking, it is ranked 12th.

In §2, we present the design of our system, the base parsers we use and how we combine them. Official results are reported in §3; the strategy adopted for each group of treebanks is presented in §4, along with per-treebank detailed analyses.

2 System overview

Our system consists of several strategies, summarized in Figure 1: depending on the treebank size, we build and compare several parsers with various designs, and finally submit the parser or parsers combination performing best on development data. For a few languages, we also improve preprocessing by correcting errors in the tokenization predicted by UDPipe (Straka et al., 2016).

Most of the parsers we consider are based on the literature or our previous works, but for some languages, we also experiment with a new method for combining base parsers. This method is designed to better leverage each available resource in a low-resource context. Indeed, state-of-the-art methods for low-resourced parsing generally focus on exploiting one type of resource (e.g. parallel data) to build a model, neglecting the others. On the contrary, our approach aims at using all available resources together, since when data is scarce, we can hardly afford ignoring a given information source.

The main idea of our approach is that various kinds of parsing algorithms and training data (monolingual, cross-lingual, delexicalized, parallel data) provide different, complementary views on the dependency structure of the language at hand. We intend to leverage this complementar-

163

Proceedings of the CoNLL 2017 Shared Task: Multilingual Parsing from Raw Text to Universal Dependencies, pages 163–173,
Vancouver, Canada, August 3-4, 2017. © 2017 Association for Computational Linguistics

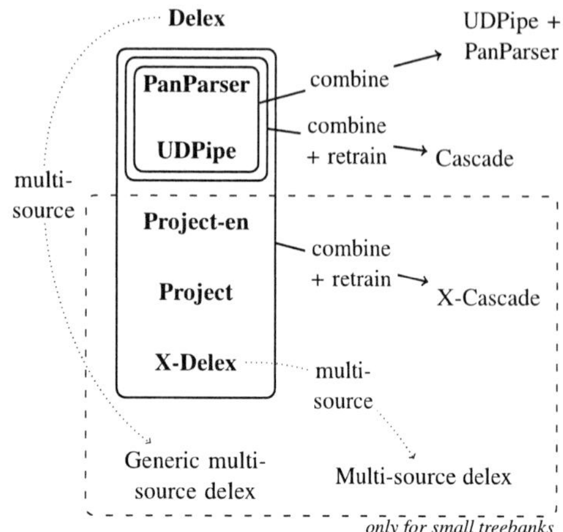

Figure 1: The various strategies contained in our system. The strategies written in bold consist of a single model, the others are combinations of models. For each language, the best strategy is selected on development data.

ity with a selective combination of several base parsers.

For instance, a cross-lingual delexicalized parser intuitively provides insights on the main syntactic structures, presumably shared because of linguistic similarities (typically assessed using linguistic knowledge), while a monolingual parser can learn target-specific structures in target data. On one hand, if monolingual data is too small, it does not contain enough information on the main syntactic structures, and the cross-lingual parser will be more accurate; it should be preferred for this kind of dependencies. On the other hand, knowing the main structure of the sentence can help in identifying fine-grained, target-specific structures; when it is not available in monolingual data, we want the cross-lingual parser to provide this information to the monolingual parser (e.g. as additional features).

Hence, we propose that some part of the syntax is preassigned to each base parser, which is retrained to specialize on that part, and to make use of the syntactic insights provided by other, more generic parsers. We achieve this with a cascading method (Alpaydin and Kaynak, 1998) and preestimated competence regions (Kuncheva, 2004, Chapter 6): each component of the cascade is assigned a competence region, i.e. a subset of the tokens on which it is assumed *a priori* to perform well, it annotates only these tokens and the

subsequent parsers are only allowed to complete this partial tree. In the cascade, each component parser trains and annotates the input based on its predecessors; this requires (a) parsers with partial trees as output, (b) to predict parses that include a given set of dependency constraints, and (c) to train parsers to use such constraints. Figure 2 summarizes the method.

The base parsers that we compare and combine are introduced in §2.1, and §2.2 describes how the cascades are implemented and the competence regions are chosen. §2.3 and §2.4 address other technical aspects of our submission: model selection among our multiple strategies, and input preprocessing.

2.1 Base parsers

2.1.1 Training data

In our system, we do not distinguish languages with or without development data, nor surprise languages. For all languages, we use train/tune/dev splits of the UD data (Nivre et al., 2017a), following the splits provided with the official baseline (Straka, 2017).[1] We perform a similar split for the surprise languages, retaining the 10 first sentences for the trainset and the 4 last sentences for the devset.

We always use gold tokenization and segmentation during training, but to improve robustness to noisy tags, all models are trained on treebanks with predicted tags, provided by the task organizers.[2]

We use the word embeddings provided by the organizers, computed on monolingual data preprocessed by UDPipe.[3]

Parallel data from the OPUS platform (Tiedemann, 2012) is preprocessed as follows: for each pair, all corpora are concatenated, tokenized and annotated by UDPipe, and word aligned with fast align (Dyer et al., 2013).

2.1.2 Monolingual

We consider four monolingual parsers:

---

[1]However, in the case of Uyghur and Kazakh, whose tunesets are particularly small and can hinder our method, we reallocate sentences from trainsets to tunesets, to reach 15 tuning sentences. Still, to prevent train-tune overlaps, the initial tuneset is used when evaluating the official UDPipe model.

[2]Except for the sample treebanks of the surprise languages, for which only gold tags are released.

[3]We also compute such embeddings for the surprise languages, using the same process.

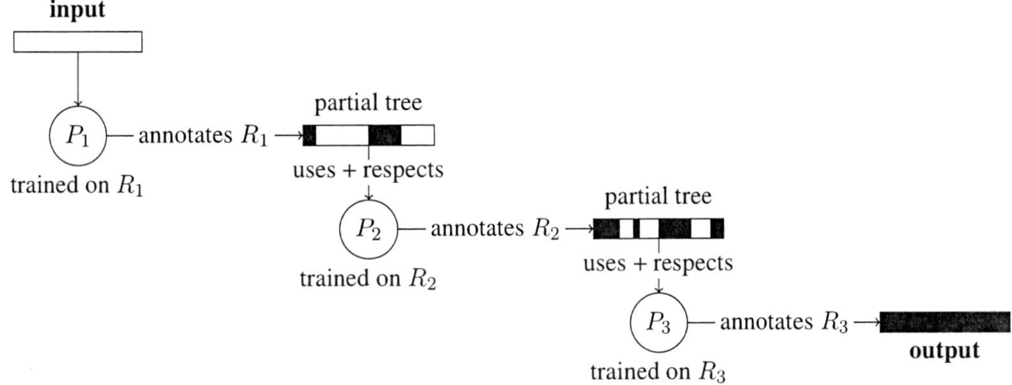

Figure 2: Processing of an input sentence by a 3-component cascade. The cascade contains parsers P_1, P_2 and P_3, which have been respectively assigned the competence regions R_1, R_2 and R_3; each token belongs to exactly one region. On the input sentence, the white areas represent tokens whose head is unknown, while the black areas represent tokens whose head has already been predicted.

UDPipe We apply the official UDPipe 1.1 base-line models (Straka, 2017). For the surprise languages, we train our own model.[4]

PanParser This is an in-house implementation (Aufrant and Wisniewski, 2016) of a transition-based parser, using the ArcEager system and an averaged perceptron. Hyperparameters to tune are the number of epochs, the use of the universal morphological features, the use of word embeddings concatenated to the feature vectors, and the size of the beam (either 8 or 1, i.e. greedy). In any case the parser trains with dynamic oracles, with the restart strategy of Aufrant et al. (2017). Relation labels are predicted in a second step, which enables to use features of the whole parse tree for this prediction.

Delex This is the same as the PanParser models, except that all lexicalized features are removed, including word embeddings.

UDPipe+PanParser As relation labels are sometimes better predicted by PanParser than UDPipe, we also consider combining their outputs at prediction time: we first annotate the input with UDPipe, discard the predicted labels and replace them with labels predicted by PanParser on UDPipe trees.

2.1.3 Cross-lingual

For each treebank under 1,000 training sentences, we apply cross-treebank techniques to build additional parsers.

First, for each target treebank, we transform every source treebank by delexicalizing it and applying the WALS rewrite rules of Aufrant et al. (2016). We then compute, for each such treebank, its similarity to the target treebank, using the KL_{cpos^3} divergence metric (Rosa and Zabokrtsky, 2015).

We select the source among treebanks over 2,000 sentences, by retaining the languages requiring the smallest number of rewrite rules (i.e. the smallest number of divergent WALS features), and then choosing the (transformed) treebank minimizing the KL_{cpos^3} divergence.

When the selected source is of the same language, we use domain adaptation techniques, otherwise we turn to cross-lingual methods. However, domain adaptation was not used in the final submission as it did not bring significant improvements on the corresponding treebanks (French-ParTUT, Galician-TreeGal and Czech-CLTT), and is not detailed here.

We consider five cross-lingual parsers:

Project-en Based on parallel data with English, we use the partial projection technique of Lacroix et al. (2016). Similarly to Lacroix et al. (2016), alignment links are filtered by PoS agreement and non-projective parses are filtered out; for some pairs there are not many trees with high coverage,

---

[4]We use the same hyperparameters as the smallest UD treebank (Kazakh), including word embeddings pretrained on their trainsets.

so we adopt the following heuristic: we select all trees with coverage over 20% if there are less than 5,000, trees with coverage over 80% if there are more than 5,000 (up to 10,000), or the 5,000 trees with highest coverage otherwise. Training on partial trees is enabled by PanParser; PanParser hyperparameters are tuned on the target tuning data.

Project This model is the same as Project-en, but using parallel data between the selected source and the target. Depending on the language, the language pair may be similar enough to compensate for the reduced amount of parallel data.

X-Delex We train a delexicalized PanParser model on the selected source treebank, transformed by the WALS rules. In order to increase train-test similarity, especially for Uyghur and Kazakh whose tagging accuracy is particularly low (under 70%), we also experimented with artificial noise added to the source tags (either random or designed to match the error types of the target tagger) but it was not conclusive. Hyperparameters are tuned on the target tuning data.

Generic multi-source delex This language-independent model first parses the input with all Delex models, then computes the output tree as a maximum spanning tree over all (unweighted) candidate parses; relation labels result from a vote of all Delex models, for each dependent token.

Multi-source delex This is a language-dependent variant of the previous model, where delexicalized models (excluding the target) are trained on the transformed treebanks, and their contributions to tree combination and vote on labels are weighted by $\left(1/KL_{cpos^3}\right)^4$, following Rosa and Zabokrtsky (2015). We experiment with three heuristics to reduce the source set: retaining only treebanks over 2,000 sentences, treebanks that minimize the number of rewrite rules, and the top 5 treebanks according to the KL_{cpos^3} metric; the best heuristic depends on the language and is tuned on target data.

Most base parsers are trained in a few hours on CPU, using a single thread (excluding hyperparameter tuning); exceptions are for instance Czech and Russian-SynTagRus, whose treebanks are notably large, and parser projection to Hungarian, due to parallel data much larger than other pairs.

2.2 Cascade combination

Implementing a cascade parser relies on three features of PanParser:

- Training parsers for partial output: training data annotations are filtered according to the competence region, and during training, the model is penalized when it attaches unannotated tokens.
- Predicting parses under constraints: the search space is reduced at prediction time, according to a partial tree.
- Training parsers under constraints: the search space is reduced at training time, by preannotating the training data with all previous components of the cascade.

Hence, each component parser is retrained[5] both to specialize on its competence region, and to take into account the knowledge provided by the previous components. To ensure that the final output is complete, the last component trains on full parses and annotates any remaining token.

As these features do not exist in UDPipe, we do not retrain the UDPipe models, but still include them in the cascade by predicting without constraints, filtering the output according to competence regions, and restoring the constraint trees as a postprocessing step. This way, they annotate more tokens than needed, and do not use the knowledge from previous components, but they can still provide useful knowledge to later components.

Confidence filtering Sometimes the output contains a few noisy dependencies on top of the dependencies belonging to the competence region. To help distinguishing those, we add confidence filtering with ensembling: for each component, 5 parsers are trained, and only the dependencies predicted by at least 3 parsers are retained (using maximum spanning tree techniques for combination).

Relation labels As in base PanParser models, relation labels are predicted in a second step, using features from the whole predicted parse tree. Since each label is predicted independently, the competence regions are computed only *after* training, without retraining: at test time we simply use the label predicted by the competent classifier.

---

[5] For each retrained component, hyperparameter values are reused from the corresponding base parser.

For each component separately, label prediction is trained on full data, preannotated with parse trees resulting from the whole cascade, and competence regions are computed for these label classifiers.

Competence regions To compute the regions, we group the dependencies into classes according to the PoS of the child and parent (e.g. DETs depending on NOUNs, or NOUNs depending on VERBs), evaluate each base parser on tuning data, and assign each 'PoS-PoS' class to the model that annotates it best. We do not assign classes that are too small (less than 5 occurrences) or have low accuracy (under 0.2). By design, any unassigned class defaults to the last component of the cascade, which in our experiments is always the monolingual PanParser model.

Choice of components We apply the cascade combination method both in monolingual and in cross-lingual configurations. In each case, we try out several subsets of components, training cascades for each subset, and tune this choice separately for the heads and the labels.[6]

In monolingual configurations (denoted Cascade), when the scores of UDPipe and PanParser on tuning data are close enough, we hypothesize that their views may complement one another, and train cascades with the following component candidates: either UDPipe followed by PanParser, or UDPipe alone, or PanParser alone. Hence, we compare 3 cascades on the head prediction task, and 3 computations of competence regions on the label prediction task.

In cross-lingual configurations (denoted X-Cascade), the cascades are trained with the best projected parser (either Project or Project-en, when they exist), followed by X-Delex, the target UDPipe and the target PanParser. We try removing one or both of X-Delex and UDPipe, thus comparing 4 cascades.

2.3 Model selection

For each treebank, we compare all base and cascade parsers, and retain the parser yielding the best LAS on the provided development set (using gold tokenization). However, in some languages this dataset was particularly small and consequently biased, which often led to selecting the wrong model, as will be seen in §4.

For the PUD treebanks, i.e. extra test sets of a UD language but which do not correspond to a given UD treebank, when there are several UD treebanks for the same language, we choose the model whose LAS on own development data is the highest. This corresponds in practice to choosing the largest treebank (in number of sentences), except for Swedish-LinES. This choice is analyzed in detail in §4.5.

2.4 Preprocessing

For most languages, we rely solely on the UDPipe preprocessing as provided by the organizers. Tokenization is customized only for the 3 languages with lowest tokenization accuracy on development data: Vietnamese, Chinese and Japanese.

Vietnamese In the UD 2.0 guidelines, spaces are allowed inside words. While in most treebanks such words are rare, in Vietnamese whitespaces denote syllable boundaries as well as word boundaries, and words containing spaces are consequently much more frequent. The low tokenization accuracy (F_1=83.99) of the baseline UDPipe is mostly due to errors on such words.

UDPipe's tokenization is postprocessed to improve the recognition of words containing spaces. To achieve this, we use a PMI criterion, assuming that pairs of tokens which mostly appear together are very likely a single word. When two consecutive (orthographic) tokens have a very high (resp. low) PMI, they are joined into a single word (resp. split, if UDPipe had joined them). We do not allow words with more than 2 orthographic tokens; in case of conflict the pair with highest PMI is joined.

PMI values are computed using the unigram and bigram counts of orthographic tokens in the crawled monolingual data (after UDPipe tokenization, to segment punctuation); in case of OOV the pair remains unchanged. We set the PMI lower- and upperbounds to $\log 5$ and $\log 400$.

Chinese and Japanese We rely on UDPipe for sentence segmentation, and then use KyTea (Neubig et al., 2011) to tokenize each sentence. KyTea models are trained on UD Chinese and Japanese training treebanks.

For all three languages, the newly tokenized input is then morphologically annotated by UDPipe.

---

[6]Depending on the data sizes, the cascades train in a few hours to two days on CPU, using 5 threads.

3 Overall results

As part of the *CoNLL 2017 UD Shared Task*, we evaluated our system on the TIRA platform (Potthast et al., 2014). Evaluation runs on the virtual machine took 10.5 hours on a single thread, using up to 6GB RAM.

Table 1 presents our overall results as published by the organizers, compared to the UDPipe 1.1 baseline.

Results rank our model first in tokenization and second in morphological tagging, although these improvements are due to our tokenization improvements on only 3 languages.

Regarding LAS, and according to the various strategies that were adopted, our system presents various behaviors depending on the treebank group, and sometimes even among treebanks of the same group, e.g. surprise languages (see §4.4).

However, the publication of the results, and careful comparison with the baseline UDPipe submission, revealed huge unexpected drops on the PUD treebanks, associated to differences in model selection. Consequently, we also submitted an additional, unofficial run, using the same heuristic as the baseline submission: always retain the model trained on the main treebank of the language. The corresponding scores are reported in Table 1 as 'unoff.'. The score differences are mostly explained by biases in PUD treebanks, towards one of the UD treebanks of the given language (see §4.5).

Consequently, our system is ranked below the baseline in the official run, but above the baseline when taking the PUD bias into account.

4 Analysis

In this section, we present the strategy that was adopted for each treebank, along with detailed analysis on the results. The analysis is conducted separately for the treebanks with custom tokenization, the large (over 10,000 training sentences), medium and small (under 1,000 sentences) UD treebanks, and for PUD treebanks.

Throughout the section, we report both official results from the TIRA platform, and our own measures using the official evaluation script on the released test files (Nivre et al., 2017b). The latter are displayed in italics.

	UDPipe [off.]		LIMSI [off.]		LIMSI [unoff.]	
	F1/LAS	Rank	F1/LAS	Rank	F1/LAS	Rank
Tokenization	98.77	8	98.95*	1	98.95*	
All tags	73.74	4	73.86*	2	73.86*	
All treebanks	68.35	13	67.72	17	68.90*	12
Big (55)	73.04	17	73.64*	13	73.64*	
PUD (14)	68.33	13	62.24	26	69.07*	
Small (8)	51.80*	15	51.71	16	51.71	
Surprise (4)	37.07	11	37.57*	9	37.57*	

Table 1: Overall results of the shared task, as published by the organizers. '*' denotes the best scores among the three systems. For each group of treebanks, the number of treebanks it contains is indicated in parentheses. The last column corresponds to the unofficial ranking, which also takes into account later improvements achieved by other teams. The missing ranks are unknown.

4.1 Custom tokenization

For the languages with custom tokenization (Japanese, Chinese and Vietnamese), we use the UDPipe model for parsing. Table 2 displays our improvements on tokenization and the resulting improvements on LAS. It also reports the LAS of the UDPipe models using gold tokenization and sentence segmentation, which singles out the LAS drop due to tokenization issues.

It appears that for all four treebanks, tokenization is an important cause of errors, and that our tokenization improvements (+2 to +4 on F1) result in large LAS improvements (+2 to +8 on F1).

	ja	ja_pud	zh	vi
Trainset size	6,805		3,797	1,330
UDPipe tokenization	89.68	91.06	88.91	82.47
LIMSI tokenization	93.82	94.93	91.35	87.30
UDPipe (gold seg.)	*90.99*	*92.12*	*70.04*	*53.28*
UDPipe LAS	72.21	76.28	57.40	37.47
LIMSI LAS	80.01	82.99	59.98	42.02

Table 2: Tokenization and LAS results on the treebanks with custom tokenization.

4.2 Treebanks over 10,000 sentences

Table 3 reports the scores obtained on the largest treebanks, and the corresponding baselines. It includes evaluation of both UDPipe and PanParser based on gold segmentation, for a better comparison of parsers (as they were trained, tuned and selected using gold segmentation), and an assessment of the LAS drop due to segmentation errors.

	cs	ru_syntagrus	cs_cac	la_ittb	no_bokmaal	fi_ftb	grc_proiel	fr	es_ancora	la_proiel
Trainset size	65,070	46,373	22,304	15,017	14,911	14,231	14,103	13,825	13,589	13,482
UDPipe (GOLD SEG.)	*83.76*	*87.55*	*82.47*	*77.74*	*83.94*	*76.07*	*70.69*	*82.15*	*83.97*	*67.22*
PanParser	*78.65*	*82.41*	*79.80*	*74.78*	*83.38*	*75.49*	*69.03*	*81.33*	*83.50*	*65.36*
UDPipe (F1) (TIRA)	82.87	86.76	82.46	76.98	83.27	74.03	65.22	80.75	83.78	**57.54**
LIMSI (F1)	82.87	86.76	82.46	76.98	83.27	**74.04**	65.22	80.75	83.78	57.51

	es	no_nynorsk	de	hi	ca	it	en	nl	fi	grc
Trainset size	13,477	13,465	13,412	12,638	12,466	12,196	11,915	11,713	11,606	10,902
UDPipe (GOLD SEG.)	*81.97*	*82.71*	*71.33*	*86.84*	*85.46*	*85.90*	*80.72*	*71.10*	*75.41*	*56.16*
PanParser	*80.58*	*81.04*	*72.98*	*85.88*	*84.55*	*85.25*	*79.64*	*70.10*	*73.87*	*52.45*
UDPipe (F1) (TIRA)	81.47	81.56	69.11	86.77	85.39	85.27	75.84	**68.90**	73.75	56.04
LIMSI (F1)	81.47	81.56	**70.89**	**86.82**	85.39	**85.28**	75.84	68.31	73.75	56.04

Table 3: LAS results on the large treebanks. The models selected on development data are underlined. For 3 languages, we selected other models: UDPipe+PanParser for `la_proiel`, a monolingual Cascade (using UDPipe and PanParser) for `hi` and `it`.

	pt_br	bg	sk	pt	ro	hr	sl	pl	ar	nl_lassysmall	eu	he	fa	id	ko	da
Trainset size	9,180	8,461	8,058	7,914	7,640	7,304	6,154	5,795	5,771	5,738	5,126	4,978	4,558	4,253	4,180	4,163
UDPipe (GOLD SEG.)	*85.79*	*84.55*	*74.23*	*83.10*	*80.57*	*77.51*	*81.20*	*79.31*	*73.85*	*81.34*	*69.23*	*78.31*	*79.82*	*75.02*	*60.04*	*74.98*
PanParser	*84.38*	*84.13*	*75.90*	*81.72*	*80.55*	*78.21*	*81.64*	*80.42*	*74.20*	*81.54*	*67.45*	*77.83*	*79.33*	*74.34*	*62.19*	*75.24*
Cascade		*84.09*	*75.19*			*77.28*	*81.24*	*79.88*		*80.48*	*69.31*	*77.60*	*79.30*	*75.18*	*59.60*	*74.92*
UDPipe (F1) (TIRA)	85.36	**83.64**	72.75	82.11	79.88	77.18	81.15	78.78	65.30	78.15	69.15	57.23	79.24	74.61	59.09	73.38
LIMSI (F1)	85.36	83.22	**74.45**	**82.19**	**80.11**	**78.02**	**81.37**	**79.95**	**65.86**	78.15	**69.21**	57.23	79.24	**74.78**	59.09	**73.85**

	sv	cu	ur	ru	tr	got	sv_lines	en_lines	lv	gl	et	fr_sequoia	sl_sst	el	la	en_partut
Trainset size	4,087	3,916	3,840	3,657	3,500	3,217	2,601	2,601	2,197	2,162	2,149	2,119	1,816	1,578	1,133	1,035
UDPipe (GOLD SEG.)	*77.28*	*72.56*	*76.74*	*74.45*	*55.93*	*68.98*	*74.94*	*73.64*	*61.15*	*77.46*	*59.87*	*82.10*	*55.22*	*79.92*	*43.81*	*74.08*
PanParser	*77.14*	*74.58*	*76.26*	*76.07*	*57.41*	*69.50*	*74.68*	*73.87*	*60.99*	*76.74*	*60.96*	*81.76*	*56.62*	*79.58*	*44.17*	*73.89*
Cascade	*76.99*	*72.67*	*75.69*	*75.17*	*57.59*	*69.69*	*73.98*	*72.91*	*59.85*		*59.37*	*82.62*	*55.49*	*80.05*	*43.67*	*72.80*
UDPipe (F1) (TIRA)	76.73	62.76	**76.69**	74.03	53.19	59.81	74.29	72.94	**59.95**	77.31	58.79	79.98	46.45	79.26	**43.77**	**73.64**
LIMSI (F1)	76.73	**65.64**	76.65	**75.65**	**55.23**	**60.94**	74.29	72.94	59.81	77.31	**59.80**	**80.55**	**46.71**	**79.38**	43.55	73.60

Table 4: LAS results on the medium treebanks. The models selected on development data are underlined. For `pt`, `ro`, `sl`, `id`, `ur`, `sl_sst` and `en_partut`, we rather selected UDPipe+PanParser.

In most cases, our submission is simply the baseline UDPipe, as we did not focus on improving the system for large treebanks. Thus, no improvement is reported on these treebanks.

Model selection proves successful on all treebanks except Latin-PROIEL and Dutch. In particular, it detects that the German PanParser is significantly better than UDPipe; considering the PanParser LAS on the other large treebanks, this is unexpected and remains to be investigated.

4.3 Treebanks from 1,000 to 10,000 sentences

The results for the medium treebanks are reported in Table 4. Compared to Table 3, it also includes gold segmentation evaluation of the monolingual Cascades, when they were considered.

As treebank size reduces, PanParser is more and more often the best parser; but with smaller development sets, the number of failures to select the best model increases (12 out of 32 treebanks).

The Cascade model provides significant gains on several treebanks, outperforming both UDPipe and PanParser; it is indeed able to extract knowledge from the lowest parser and use it to improve upon the best parser (see Basque, Indonesian, Turkish, Gothic, French-Sequoia and Greek). However, these gains are not consistent, and despite confidence and tuning mechanisms, the method still requires empirical validation.

4.4 Treebanks under 1,000 sentences

Table 5 presents the last group of UD treebanks, the smallest ones, including surprise languages.

For each treebank, we report several scores, now including Delex, which is a promising candidate to parse the smallest treebanks. When cross-lingual methods are used, we indicate the source treebank and the scores of the projected base parsers (except for the surprise languages lacking parallel data), X-Delex and their combination X-Cascade.

For this group, since the development sets are very small, model selection is not reliable and misses the best model in 5 out of 12 cases. Additionally, the even smaller tuning sets lead for the cascades to poor estimation of competence regions. But the main challenge faced by cascades is noisy tags. Indeed, while preliminary experiments on X-Cascade with gold tags were very promising, turning to predicted tags makes the X-Delex models very unreliable (as their only features are unreliable), and they cannot provide useful insights to the cascade anymore, in which case cascades lack interest.

Regarding Uyghur, Kazakh and the surprise languages, for lack of data we decided to reduce the training set in favor of the tuning set, in the hope that better estimated cascades would compensate for worse base parsers. This proves to be a bad strategy in half the cases, and we end up underperforming the baseline by a large margin in Kazakh and Buryat.

However, X-Cascades still achieve significant improvements over their base parsers in Uyghur, North Sámi and Buryat. This suggests that cascading can indeed prove useful in cross-lingual contexts; with the appropriate amount of data and additional effort on estimation of competence regions and on robustness to noisy tags, it may convey much larger gains.

4.5 Model selection for PUD treebanks

The PUD treebanks are the additional test sets provided for 14 of the languages covered by the UD treebanks. They have been annotated separately and do not correspond to a given UD treebank. As such, processing them with systems trained on UD treebanks is prone to domain adaptation issues: the PUD treebanks contain sentences extracted from newswire and Wikipedia, while UD treebanks also cover several other domains. For some of the PUD languages, several UD treebanks are available, which raises the additional question of choosing training data: either one of the UD treebanks, or all of them.

For the PUD treebanks, we submitted baseline UDPipe models in Czech, English, French, Spanish, Finnish, Portuguese, Russian and Swedish, yet on 5 of these treebanks we suffered huge drops (-9 to -34 LAS) from the official baseline submission. For these, the only difference with the base-

line is that we selected different treebanks. In order to understand these drops, we performed a systematic evaluation of various preprocessing and parser choices, comparing the same system with different training data.

Table 6 reports, for each PUD treebank, the results when applying each UDPipe pipeline on gold segmentation, and when combining each UDPipe preprocesser (segmentation and tagging) with each UDPipe parser. Experiments with PanParser yield consistent results.

In some cases, important drops seem due to incompatible preprocessing between treebanks of the same language: in English, Portuguese and Swedish, the 'main' scores are much lower and 'variant 1' scores much higher when replacing 'main' preprocessing by 'variant 1'. As the preprocessing provided by the organizers was systematically produced by the 'main' UDPipe model, this certainly affected our submission, which used the provided preprocessing even when not using the 'main' parser.

However, comparing results where treebank choices are consistent, it appears that the 'main' treebank always outperforms the variants by a large margin. This is not only due to differences in tokenization, as this occurs also with gold segmentation.

Additionally, in Table 6, the 'All data' results are those obtained with a UDPipe model trained on the concatenation of all treebanks of the language. In most cases they underperform the 'main' model, which confirms that the variant treebanks add mostly noise to the model, from the PUD perspective.

While there may be various explanations to these accuracy differences, what is surprising here is that the best treebank does not seem consistent with common factors of high accuracy (treebank size, domain similarity, treebank consistency). For instance, Russian contains Wikipedia articles and Russian-SynTagRus news (and Russian-PUD consists of both Wikipedia articles and news), but Russian-SynTagRus is much larger than Russian; as such, parsers trained on Russian-SynTagRus should be more accurate on Russian-PUD than Russian, which they are not. Besides, Russian-SynTagRus performs better than Russian on their own test sets, indicating that the treebank does not have strong self-consistency issues. For these reasons, and the additional cue of incompatible pre-

	hu	uk	fr_partut	gl_treegal	ga	cs_cltt	ug	kk	hsb	kmr	sme	bxr
Trainset size	864	733	527	510	481	441	75	12	10	10	10	10
GOLD												
UDPipe	64.67	60.92	78.77	68.50	62.25	72.77	36.66	27.10	32.91*	27.93*	20.72*	12.88*
PanParser	65.60	61.97	79.78	68.36	63.38	74.94	36.21*	23.48*	47.27*	39.38*	31.99*	28.59*
Delex	61.97	59.79	74.14	66.01	59.44	66.42	36.54*	22.75*	46.44*	38.27*	32.84*	29.73*
Cascade	65.46	61.64	79.13	68.75	62.55	73.51	35.83*	23.99*	46.55*	37.80*	31.35*	25.91*
Source	fi_ftb	sk	fr_sequoia	gl	id	cs_cac	tr	tr	sl	fa	et	et
SEG												
Project-en	44.01	52.59			42.48		16.65	13.87	37.77			
Project	36.61	55.52			38.46		23.27	23.08	43.27			
X-Delex	41.42	54.75			38.80		22.89	25.63	62.20	43.32	37.58	26.16
X-Cascade		57.43			60.09		37.35*	22.35*	54.61*	40.26*	37.79*	30.13*
Multi-source									68.78		41.52	
TIRA												
UDPipe (F1)	64.30	60.76	77.38	65.82	61.52	71.64	34.18	**24.51**	53.83	32.35	30.60	**31.50**
LIMSI (F1)	**65.18**	**61.68**	**78.30**	**65.85**	**61.94**	**73.49**	**34.70**	20.94	**57.79**	**35.59**	**31.03**	25.86

Table 5: LAS results on the small treebanks. For the last 4 columns (surprise languages), 'gold seg.' results use gold segmentation *and* gold tagging. '*' denotes parsers whose monolingual training data is smaller than the data used by the UDPipe baseline, hence important score differences. The models selected on development data are underlined. The Multi-source line reports the scores of two models: 'Generic multi-source delex' for sme, and 'Multi-source delex' for hsb, with the heuristic retaining only treebanks over 2,000 sentences.

		cs_pud	en_pud	fr_pud	es_pud	fi_pud	it_pud	pt_pud	ru_pud	sv_pud	ar_pud	de_pud	hi_pud	ja_pud	tr_pud
GOLD SEG.	UDPipe Main	81.10+	79.58*+	75.54+	78.40	78.84+	84.43+	74.32	70.36	73.05+	52.78+	68.03+	52.49+	92.12+	37.37+
	UDPipe Variant 1	75.14	64.67*	68.20	74.38+	48.70*	76.62	72.22+	61.81+	66.58*					
	UDPipe Variant 2	44.67*	65.65	63.57											
SEG MAIN	UDPipe All data	79.32	79.05	74.00	77.58	76.49	83.57	74.27	64.49	69.97					
	UDPipe Main	79.80	78.95	73.63	77.65	78.65	83.70	73.96	68.31	70.62	43.14	66.53	50.85	76.28	34.53
	UDPipe Variant 1	76.58	47.30	68.31	68.40	44.99	80.35	59.50	52.36	49.41					
	UDPipe Variant 2	54.65	66.42	68.18											
+TAGV ARI	UDPipe Main	75.36	63.42	69.04	70.75	52.80	78.43	62.83	68.18	51.63					
	UDPipe Variant 1	73.03	64.28	66.08	71.30	47.27	75.75	69.82	59.87	65.11					
	UDPipe Variant 2	53.32	55.68	64.39											
AGV ARI 2	UDPipe Main	47.31	68.53	63.18											
	UDPipe Variant 1	46.10	45.28	59.20											
	UDPipe Variant 2	41.66	64.82	61.10											
TIRA	UDPipe	79.80	78.95	73.63	**77.65**	**78.65**	**83.70**	**73.96**	**68.31**	**70.62**	43.14	66.53	50.85	76.28	**34.53**
	LIMSI	79.80	78.95	73.63	68.40	44.99	83.69	59.50	52.36	49.41	**43.91**	**68.62**	**50.91**	**82.99**	34.15

Table 6: LAS results on the PUD treebanks. For lang_pud, 'main' denotes the lang treebank. Variants 1 are cs_cac, en_lines, fr_sequoia, es_ancora, fi_ftb, it_partut, pt_br, ru_syntagrus and sv_lines. Variants 2 are cs_cltt, en_partut and fr_partut.

For each language, the largest treebank is annotated with '+' (considering numbers of tokens: fi_ftb contains more sentences than fi, but they are shorter), and '*' indicates treebanks with important domain adaptation issues (i.e. that contain neither Wikipedia nor news data).

Underlined results denote the training treebanks that we used to annotate the PUD treebanks (not necessarily with a UDPipe model). The baseline UDPipe submission corresponds to 'main'+'main'.

For instance, in the cs_pud column, the 3rd row ('gold'+'variant 2') corresponds to gold tokenization and segmentation, tagging with the cs_cltt UDPipe model, and parsing with the cs_cltt UDPipe model. The 8th row ('var1'+'main') corresponds to tokenizing and tagging with the cs_cac UDPipe model, and parsing with the cs UDPipe model.

processings, we speculate that the PUD treebanks are indeed biased towards the main treebank of each language, because of annotation scheme discrepancies between treebanks. Such inconsistencies may be due either to one treebank not following the guidelines, or to underspecified aspects of the guidelines that have been interpreted differently by different teams.

Notably, Arabic and Hindi also present huge drops from their scores on UD test sets, even though they trained only on news; it is possible that here as well, the drops are due only to annotation inconsistencies.

Concluding on this hypothesis would require, however, further analysis of the treebank domains: the scores may still be partially explained by actual domain adaptation issues, e.g. the relative size of each domain in multi-domain treebanks, or details of the domains (style, author, date...) that do not appear in the coarse domain categories (news, Wikipedia, fiction...).

Full examination of the annotation inconsistencies is an ongoing work of the UD project, and is out of the scope of this paper, but during our manual analysis we already noticed that plain text (both in the training data, and the raw input of the test data) is in fact already partially preprocessed, for some UD treebanks. For some, multitoken words are already detected and annotated with '_' instead of spaces: this concerns at least Russian-SynTagRus (phrasal conjunctions and numbers), Finnish-FTB (numbers) and Greek (dates). For others (Danish, Finnish-FTB), plain text is already fully tokenized (except for multiword tokens).

This is not an issue in general, because the UD treebanks are self-consistent on this convention, but it affects the ability of the trained models to process actual raw input. This partially explains the PUD bias, since Russian and Finnish main treebanks have actual raw text, as the PUD ones.

5   Conclusion

Our submission to the *CoNLL 2017 UD Shared Task* focuses on low-resourced dependency parsing. Our system is built upon base parsers, and combines them using a cascading algorithm, in order to leverage small and incomplete data.

This shared task was an opportunity to experiment with this new cascading method in realistic conditions; this is particularly interesting, since this method addresses precisely realistic scenar-

ios where available data does not consist in either large monolingual data or large parallel data, but in various amounts of each resource type.

The method has proved useful in many cases, with sometimes large improvements, but the gains are not consistent enough to be reliable and still require further work. The shared task conditions have indeed uncovered several challenges faced by the method: it lacks confidence mechanisms, delexicalized models are too unreliable, and the lack of development data hinders accurate estimation of competence regions for the components of the cascade.

The improvements we achieve are strongly diminished by huge unexpected drops on a few languages; while this affects our ranking in great proportions, it also enables detailed analysis of the new PUD treebanks, and on how and why they are biased towards the main UD treebanks.

Acknowledgments

This work has been partly funded by the French *Direction générale de l'armement* and by the *Agence Nationale de la Recherche* (ParSiTi project, ANR-16-CE33-0021). We thank Joseph Le Roux for fruitful discussions and comments.

References

Ethem Alpaydin and Cenk Kaynak. 1998. Cascading classifiers. *Kybernetika* pages 369–374.

Lauriane Aufrant and Guillaume Wisniewski. 2016. PanParser: a Modular Implementation for Efficient Transition-Based Dependency Parsing. Technical report, LIMSI-CNRS.

Lauriane Aufrant, Guillaume Wisniewski, and François Yvon. 2016. Zero-resource Dependency Parsing: Boosting Delexicalized Cross-lingual Transfer with Linguistic Knowledge. In *Proceedings of COLING 2016, the 26th International Conference on Computational Linguistics: Technical Papers*. The COLING 2016 Organizing Committee, Osaka, Japan, pages 119–130. http://aclweb.org/anthology/C16-1012.

Lauriane Aufrant, Guillaume Wisniewski, and François Yvon. 2017. Don't Stop Me Now! Using Global Dynamic Oracles to Correct Training Biases of Transition-Based Dependency Parsers. In *Proceedings of the 15th Conference of the European Chapter of the Association for Computational Linguistics: Volume 2, Short Papers*. Association for Computational Linguistics, Valencia, Spain, pages 318–323. http://www.aclweb.org/anthology/E17-2051.

Chris Dyer, Victor Chahuneau, and Noah A. Smith. 2013. A Simple, Fast, and Effective Reparameterization of IBM Model 2. In *Proceedings of the 2013 Conference of the North American Chapter of the Association for Computational Linguistics: Human Language Technologies*. Association for Computational Linguistics, Atlanta, Georgia, pages 644–648. http://www.aclweb.org/anthology/N13-1073.

Ludmila I Kuncheva. 2004. *Combining pattern classifiers: methods and algorithms*.

Ophélie Lacroix, Lauriane Aufrant, Guillaume Wisniewski, and François Yvon. 2016. Frustratingly Easy Cross-Lingual Transfer for Transition-Based Dependency Parsing. In *Proceedings of the 2016 Conference of the North American Chapter of the Association for Computational Linguistics: Human Language Technologies*. Association for Computational Linguistics, San Diego, California, pages 1058–1063. http://www.aclweb.org/anthology/N16-1121.

Graham Neubig, Yosuke Nakata, and Shinsuke Mori. 2011. Pointwise Prediction for Robust, Adaptable Japanese Morphological Analysis. In *Proceedings of the 49th Annual Meeting of the Association for Computational Linguistics: Human Language Technologies*. Association for Computational Linguistics, Portland, Oregon, USA, pages 529–533. http://www.aclweb.org/anthology/P11-2093.

Joakim Nivre, Željko Agić, Lars Ahrenberg, et al. 2017a. Universal Dependencies 2.0. LINDAT/CLARIN digital library at the Institute of Formal and Applied Linguistics, Charles University, Prague. http://hdl.handle.net/11234/1-1983.

Joakim Nivre, Željko Agić, Lars Ahrenberg, et al. 2017b. Universal dependencies 2.0 CoNLL 2017 shared task development and test data. LINDAT/CLARIN digital library at the Institute of Formal and Applied Linguistics, Charles University. http://hdl.handle.net/11234/1-2184.

Joakim Nivre, Marie-Catherine de Marneffe, Filip Ginter, Yoav Goldberg, Jan Hajič, Christopher Manning, Ryan McDonald, Slav Petrov, Sampo Pyysalo, Natalia Silveira, Reut Tsarfaty, and Daniel Zeman. 2016. Universal Dependencies v1: A multilingual treebank collection. In *Proceedings of the 10th International Conference on Language Resources and Evaluation (LREC 2016)*. European Language Resources Association, Portoro, Slovenia, pages 1659–1666.

Martin Potthast, Tim Gollub, Francisco Rangel, Paolo Rosso, Efstathios Stamatatos, and Benno Stein. 2014. Improving the reproducibility of PAN's shared tasks: Plagiarism detection, author identification, and author profiling. In Evangelos Kanoulas, Mihai Lupu, Paul Clough, Mark Sanderson, Mark Hall, Allan Hanbury, and Elaine Toms, editors, *Information Access Evaluation meets Multilinguality, Multimodality, and Visualization. 5th International Conference of the CLEF Initiative (CLEF 14)*. Springer, Berlin Heidelberg New York, pages 268–299. https://doi.org/10.1007/978-3-319-11382-1_22.

Rudolf Rosa and Zdenek Zabokrtsky. 2015. KLcpos3 - a Language Similarity Measure for Delexicalized Parser Transfer. In *Proceedings of the 53rd Annual Meeting of the Association for Computational Linguistics and the 7th International Joint Conference on Natural Language Processing (Volume 2: Short Papers)*. pages 243–249.

Milan Straka. 2017. CoNLL 2017 Shared Task - UDPipe Baseline Models and Supplementary Materials. LINDAT/CLARIN digital library at the Institute of Formal and Applied Linguistics, Charles University. http://hdl.handle.net/11234/1-1990.

Milan Straka, Jan Hajič, and Jana Straková. 2016. UDPipe: trainable pipeline for processing CoNLL-U files performing tokenization, morphological analysis, POS tagging and parsing. In *Proceedings of the 10th International Conference on Language Resources and Evaluation (LREC 2016)*. European Language Resources Association, Portoro, Slovenia.

Jörg Tiedemann. 2012. Parallel Data, Tools and Interfaces in OPUS. In Nicoletta Calzolari (Conference Chair), Khalid Choukri, Thierry Declerck, Mehmet Ugur Dogan, Bente Maegaard, Joseph Mariani, Jan Odijk, and Stelios Piperidis, editors, *Proceedings of the Eight International Conference on Language Resources and Evaluation (LREC'12)*. European Language Resources Association (ELRA), Istanbul, Turkey.

Daniel Zeman, Martin Popel, Milan Straka, Jan Hajič, Joakim Nivre, Filip Ginter, Juhani Luotolahti, Sampo Pyysalo, Slav Petrov, Martin Potthast, Francis Tyers, Elena Badmaeva, Memduh Gökırmak, Anna Nedoluzhko, Silvie Cinková, Jan Hajič jr., Jaroslava Hlaváčová, Václava Kettnerová, Zdeňka Urešová, Jenna Kanerva, Stina Ojala, Anna Missilä, Christopher Manning, Sebastian Schuster, Siva Reddy, Dima Taji, Nizar Habash, Herman Leung, Marie-Catherine de Marneffe, Manuela Sanguinetti, Maria Simi, Hiroshi Kanayama, Valeria de Paiva, Kira Droganova, Héctor Martínez Alonso, Hans Uszkoreit, Vivien Macketanz, Aljoscha Burchardt, Kim Harris, Katrin Marheinecke, Georg Rehm, Tolga Kayadelen, Mohammed Attia, Ali Elkahky, Zhuoran Yu, Emily Pitler, Saran Lertpradit, Michael Mandl, Jesse Kirchner, Hector Fernandez Alcalde, Jana Strnadova, Esha Banerjee, Ruli Manurung, Antonio Stella, Atsuko Shimada, Sookyoung Kwak, Gustavo Mendonça, Tatiana Lando, Rattima Nitisaroj, and Josie Li. 2017. CoNLL 2017 Shared Task: Multilingual Parsing from Raw Text to Universal Dependencies. In *Proceedings of the CoNLL 2017 Shared Task: Multilingual Parsing from Raw Text to Universal Dependencies*. Association for Computational Linguistics.

RACAI's Natural Language Processing pipeline for Universal Dependencies

Stefan Daniel Dumitrescu, Tiberiu Boros and Dan Tufis
Research Institute for Artificial
Intelligence, Romanian Academy
Bucharest, Romania
sdumitrescu@racai.ro, tibi@racai.ro, tufis@racai.ro

Abstract

This paper presents RACAI's approach, experiments and results at *CoNLL 2017 Shared Task: Multilingual Parsing from Raw Text to Universal Dependencies*. We handle raw text and we cover tokenization, sentence splitting, word segmentation, tagging, lemmatization and parsing. All results are reported under strict training, development and testing conditions, in which the corpora provided for the shared tasks is used "as is", without any modifications to the composition of the train and development sets.

1 Introduction

This paper describes RACAI's entry for the CONLL Shared Task on Universal Dependencies parsing. We represent the Research Institute for Artificial Intelligence, in Bucharest, Romania. The shared task refers to processing raw text with the goal of automatically inferring word dependencies. While some approaches require only segmented (tokenized) text, parsing methods that depend on rich feature sets (which is our case), implicitly require that the text is tokenized, POS tagged and lemmatized. The Universal Dependencies (UD) corpus (Nivre et al., 2016, 2017a) uses 3 distinct layers of analysis: (a) a Universal Part-of-Speech layer (UPOS) (Petrov et al., 2011); (b) a language specific part-of-speech layer (XPOS) and (c) a list of language-dependent morphological attributes Zeman (2008). Also, in the current version of UD, tokenization and word-segmentation require different handling strategies (see section 3.2 for details). In what follows we will provide an overview of our system's architecture (section 2) and a detailed description of each module (section 3) used in our process-

ing pipeline, followed by its evaluation (section 4) (Nivre et al., 2017b) on the TIRA platform (Potthast et al., 2014). Though Syntaxnet (Weiss et al., 2015) models were also available, some discrepancies in the token and word-segmentation methodology made the comparison impossible (mainly because the Syntaxnet's output was incompatible with the evaluation script). This work is focused on presenting our system's technical details and individual results. The full comparison between competing systems, as well as the baseline values obtained by UDPipe v1.1 (Straka et al., 2016) are available in Zeman et al. (2017).

2 System Architecture

Figure 1 presents a bird's eye view on the individual modules of the system and how they interconnect.

At runtime, the input of the system is a raw text file. As the file is not sentence split, all new line characters are removed and passed as a single long string to the first module: the **Tokenization and Sentence Splitting (Tok/SS)** (section 3.1). Depending on language, some files are already tokenized, for which we perform only sentence splitting; however, for most languages, we perform both tokenization and sentence-splitting in a single pass. At this point, we obtain a file in the conllu format, passed to the **Compound Word** module (section 3.2). This module looks for words that can (and should) be split in two or more tokens. For example, in German "im" becomes "in dem", or in Polish: "kupiłbym" becomes "kupił by m". Compound words are added as new lines in the conllu file. Next, language independent part of speech (UPOS) tags are added by the **Tag.UPOS** module (section 3.3). Based on the available information so far, the following modules all run in parallel: The **Lemma** (section 3.4), **Tag.XPOS**

Proceedings of the CoNLL 2017 Shared Task: Multilingual Parsing from Raw Text to Universal Dependencies, pages 174–181,
Vancouver, Canada, August 3-4, 2017. © 2017 Association for Computational Linguistics

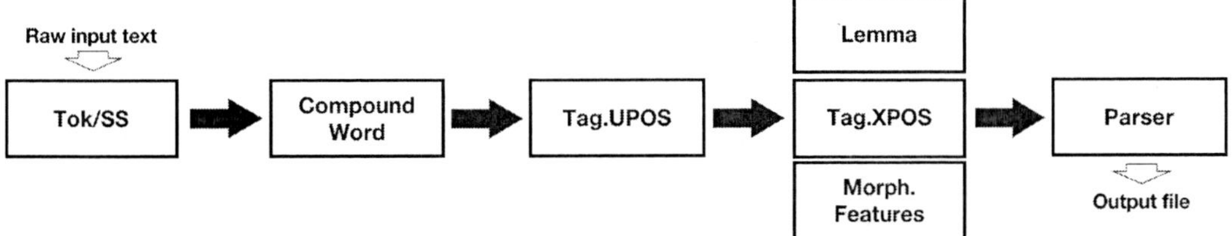

Figure 1: System architecture

and **Morphological Features** modules add lemmas, XPOSes and Morphological Features. The XPOS and Morphological Features modules are language dependent and are described together in section 3.5. Finally, the **Parser** module (section 3.6) adds the final dependencies in the output conllu file.

For the training process we used the available training data in the conllu format. The conllu files provided by the organizers contained "detokenization" information (a SpaceAfter=No flag added to every token that in the original text had no space) and morphological analysis layers: word, lemmas, part-of-speech, language-dependent part-of-speech, morphological attributes and word dependencies (index of the head of each word, as well as the relationship type).

Further details about each information layer will be provided later in the paper, when we introduce the individual processing modules and describe our feature extraction and labeling strategies. During training we use a separate script responsible for preparing the custom training and development sets. Depending on the memory and CPU requirements we trained either the models sequentially (e.g. the parser is memory expensive and the linear classifier for part-of-speech tagging is multi-threaded) or multiple models in parallel (the morphological analysis require far less memory and CPU time - practically the decision trees for all languages in the competition were built and pruned in parallel).

3 System Description

Before we proceed with the description of the modules we must note that some of our methods rely on decision trees (DT) that are built using a custom designed algorithm that relies on the constituency matrix to speed-up computation for the Information Gain (IG) (Equation 1). Also, after the initial trees are built, we use the available development sets to prune them to reduce possible train-data overfitting, leading to improved performance.

$$IG_i(S) = H(S) - \sum_{t \in T} (P(t) \cdot H(t)) \quad (1)$$

where i represents an input feature, $H(S)$ (Equation 2) is the entropy of the initial set S, $H(t)$ the entropy of subset t, and $P(t)$ is the fraction of elements in t over the entire $|S|$. We note $|S|$ as the number of instances in S.

$$H(S) = -\sum_{x=1}^{N} P_x \cdot \log_2 P_x \quad (2)$$

We note this because the above mentioned methodology was not presented elsewhere and we feel the it is an important aspect of our approach (see section 4 for details regarding the model sizes and section 5 for comments).

3.1 Tokenization and Sentence Splitting

The first module in the pipeline is the Tokenizer and Sentence Splitter. Depending on the training data, we actually have 4 distinct tokenizers/sentence splitters merged into our module: the standard Tok/SS for corpora that had both punctuation and was not already tokenized (this is the case for most languages), the character level Tok/SS for Japanese and Chinese, and two versions of the sentence splitter for training data with pre-tokenized sentences that had (e.g. Danish, Finish FTB and Slovene SST), and had not punctuation (e.g. Gothic, Latin Proiel, Ancient Greek Proiel and Old Church Slavonic).

The main tokenizer and sentence splitter is based on DTs. Tokenization and sentence splitting are independent models, and are run in parallel. Based on a number of features (described below), the DT tokenizer model chooses between 4 classes: SPLIT_LEFT, SPLIT_RIGHT,

SPLIT_LEFTRIGHT and NONE, meaning it should split to the left of the current character, right, to put two spaces around the character or not make a split. The DT sentence splitter has only 2 classes: SPLIT and NONE. Training is done in the following manner: (1) initially, we look for specific characters where we might have a word split, marked in the conllu train file by "SpaceAfter=No"; we then normalize the frequency of these characters; iterating again on the training data, we choose only the character that is most probable to initiate a split, based on the normalized frequency; for sentence splitting we perform the same process, the only difference being we pre-seed the character list with a number of punctuation characters like: .-!? etc., because we had cases where *?* for example was not frequent enough to remain in the split list, though it was a valid sentence splitter; (2) we extracted the following features for each split character: current letter, 3 characters before and after (4 for sentence splitting), and for the previous and next words a marker whether or not the word is punctuation only, if it ends with punctuation, if it contains punctuation, if it is uppercase, if it is capitalized and the number of periods in the word; (3) we trained the DT model and pruned the tree based on the dev set. Another small optimization worth mentioning is that we replaced all digits with zeroes to reduce variability in the training data.

The symbol based tokenizer is targeted for Japanese and Chinese where we have to look after each symbol and decide whether to split. The features are simply the current symbol and one symbol to the left and right, with two possible classes: SPLIT (split after the current symbol) and NONE.

The last two Tok/SS address languages that are already tokenized, performing only sentence splitting. For the languages that had no punctuation (e.g. Gothic), the features are 5 characters to the left and 3 to the right (including the current character). For the languages that had punctuation (e.g. Danish) the features are token based: the current token plus 2 tokens before and after; for each token we mark all the features the main tokenizer has for words (if the token is punctuation only, etc.)

Overall, we compared our results on the dev sets against UDPipe's, obtaining good results. However, for a few languages it seems that the decision tree approach is not optimal, yielding low per-

formances. For English, Bulgarian, Korean, Portuguese and other 14 smaller languages, at runtime we directly used the UDPipe tokenization and sentence split conllu files, bypassing this module. This is the only place in the system where we use data that was not generated by us.

3.2 Compound Words

The compound words module has the task of word expansion. For example, in German *"im"* is the contraction of *"in dem"*; in Turkish, *"muhabbetliydi"* is for *"muhabbet li ydi"*. While word expansion could be relatively well solved by using a dictionary (search for the key and replace with expansion tokens), it would fail for unseen words as well as ignoring split-no split decisions depending on POS tags. Our intuition was that we need to represent generated word expansions as parts of the original string (longest common substring or LCS) plus new terminations, either before and/or after the LCS. For example, currency tokens like *"7000€"* should always expand as the first variable part plus the last symbol separately if that last symbol is "€", while the opposite example *"€7000"* should be represented as a static first symbol followed by a variable string (here the numeric amount).

Needless to say, the process of token decomposition into words carries a great weight over the accuracy of the system, because all other modules depend on it: tagging, morphological analysis and parsing. Obviously preserving the head or tail of the original token and concatenating strings at the beginning or end requires different labeling strategies, because any of the words in the decomposition can be written either by keeping the head of the original token and concatenating a suffix or by a prefix and concatenating the tail of the original token. More often than not, one strategy will likely yield a larger number of unique output labels in the training data than the other. As such, the actual difficulty is determining which labeling strategy would be more accurate. We attempted to determine the labeling strategy as follows:

- First, take the training data and generate output labels using all (desired) tagging strategies, generating multiple label sets;

- Then, measure the system entropy for each of the previously generated label sets;

- Finally, use the tagging strategy which generated the lowest-entropy system for training the classifier.

In our approach the labeling scheme was in the form of "n+<*string*>" where n is a number and <*string*> is a string to keep. Consider the following example, where a is the word that will be expanded in two words b c. There are four different output encodings we can choose from: FS_KS, FS_KE, FE_KS and FE_KE. FS means "from start" and denotes that the number n is an **absolute index**, which measures the character span from the beginning of the word, FE is "from end" and denotes that n is a **relative index** and it will express a character span relative to the size of the original token. The meaning of KS is "keep start" and means that the head of the token should be preserved, while KE stands for "keep end" and means that the tail of the original token will be used in building the decomposed token. Now, suppose we write word a as letters $a_1 a_2 a_3 a_4 a_5$ and its first expansion b as $b_1 b_2 b_3 b_4$, and a_{1-2} is equal to b_{1-2} and a_5 is equal to b_4. To obtain the first encoding FS_KS we find the longest common substring *from start* of a and b which is b_{1-2}, of length 2, keeping the rest of b; so, the FS_KS label encoding is $2+ < b_{3-4} >$. Encoding FS_KE means finding the longest common substring from start, while keeping the end: $3 + b_{4-n-3}$.

Our algorithm has to choose between FS and FE labeling schemes, the decision between KS and KE subordinated depending only on the LCS criterion (for each word in the decomposition, we chose to keep the head or tail of the original token depending on which would provide a higher character overlapping).

After determining the best labeling strategy we generated a decision tree using the following features: first four letters, last four letters, wordform (if occurrence frequency was higher than 10 in the training data).

To show how important choosing the appropriate labeling strategy is, on the Hebrew development set we obtained 93% F-score using the FE notation (automatically selected by the system), versus 88% when we forced the system to use FS.

3.3 POS Tagging

The part-of-speech inventory used in this step refers to UPOS tags, an inventory which contains only 17 unique labels. Our tagging methodology is fairly standard: we use a Conditional Random Field to estimate the probability of the i-th tag (t_i), based on the previous tag and a rich set of features (f_i) (Equation 3). During runtime, we use Viterbi to obtain the optimal sequence of labels.

$$P(t_i|t_{i-1}, f_i) \qquad (3)$$

The set of features is composed of (a) the lower-cased wordform, (b) a large number of letter n-grams, with n ranging from 2 to 5 and (c) a feature which we refer to as "writing style". All the features are extracted from a window of 3 words (centered on the current word). The "writing style" feature takes 4 values:

- ALL-CAPS - the word is written in CAPS;

- ALL-LOWER - the word contains only lower-cased symbols;

- F-UPPER - the word starts with a capital letter and all other symbols are lower-cased;

- F-UPPER-START - similar with F-UPPER, only this time the word is also the first token of the sentence.

We use a large number of character combinations (90), which includes **cross-word letter n-grams** and was manually obtained using a trial-and-error process.

To prevent overfitting and obtain a robust model for out-of-vocabulary (OOV) words, we only include a wordform as a feature, if that word's occurrence frequency is higher than a threshold (k) in the training data[1].

3.4 Lemmatizer

Lemmatization is done in two steps. First, the surface wordform and its UPOS (language independent part of speech) is searched in a dictionary created at train time. If the surface form & UPOS match, the corresponding lemma is used (if there is more than one lemma for the surface&UPOS pair, we prefer the most frequent). If not found, we attempt to create the new lemma using a DT. Given a word, we extract the UPOS, the first 4 letters and the last 4 as features. The first and last letters may overlap if the word is smaller than 8 letters, or can be null (encoded as "_") if the word is smaller than 4 letters. The output classes are

---

[1] In our experiments we observed that $k = 10$ is a good choice for many of the languages we used for tunning

Model	Type	Count	Min	Max	Average	St. Dev.
Tokenization	DT	57	0.66 KB	394 KB	18.09 KB	71.09 KB
Sentence Split	DT	64	0.91 KB	345 KB	23.90 KB	54.07 KB
Compound Words	DT	22	0.34 KB	484 KB	50.53 KB	126.68 KB
Lemmatization	DT	56	2.79 KB	370.53 KB	56.36 KB	68.23 KB
Tag.UPOS	CRF	64	2.97 MB	612 MB	121.26 MB	100.09 MB
Morph. Feats.	DT	64	10.46 KB	1.34 MB	170.21 KB	219.05 KB
Tag.XPOS	DT	64	10.64 KB	1.08 MB	111.73 KB	200.39 KB
Parsing	RBG	64	43.41 MB	3.16 GB	1.01 GB	755.5 MB

Table 1: Model types and sizes

strings looking like "*n+<string>*". The *n* represents how many letters to cut from the surface form of the word, and *<string>* means the string to append to the word. For example, given the word *forgotten*, which is a *Verb*, with features *f o r g* and *t t e n*, its output class would be *5+et*, meaning that we need to cut the last 5 letters (to obtain the largest common prefix) and add *et* to obtain the lemma *forget*.

We note that the number of output classes varies between a few hundreds to several thousands depending on the language, but, even for this large number, the results of the DT seem accurate.

3.5 Language Specific Morphological Analysis

Language-specific morphological analysis is a two-fold process that refers to the resolution of (a) the language-dependent part-of-speech (XPOS) tag and (b) a structured set of morphological attributes (in the form of key-value pairs), which are used to encode important information such as gender, number, case etc.

As a rule-of-thumb, the XPOS tag used in morphologically rich languages is a compact representation of the morphological attributes. For instance, the Romanian corpus from the UD data uses a standardized compact representation, which is composed of morphosyntactic descriptors (MSDs) (Erjavec, 2004). Given the similarities between language-specific tags and UD morphological-attributes, in our approach we used the same feature sets for both tasks. The features are composed of: (a) the UPOS tag, (b) the first four characters of the word; (c) the last four characters of the word and (d) the previously mentioned "writing-style" feature. To capture local-dependencies between words we used a context window of 5 centered on the current word.

In this case, we preferred to use decision trees, mainly because of reduced computational requirements and the small-footprint of the output models.

3.6 Parsing

Once the morphological analysis is completed, our processing pipeline relies on RBGParser[2] which is a greedy hill-climbing parser, well described in Zhang et al. (2014a,b); Lei et al. (2014). In our approach, we used branch 1.1.2 of RBG, which we modified in order to be compliant with the current UD version.

The main incompatibility was generated by the presence of multiword tokens. During training we modified the data adapter of the RBGParser to skip multiword tokens and, for the runtime version, we filtered the input for RBG to exclude multiword tokens and we re-aligned the output of RBG with the unparsed dataset, to restore multiword tokens and provide an output compatible with the current UD standard.

The RBG models were built using the default parameters for the "standardModel" predefined configuration, on which we added automatically extracted word embeddings (Mikolov et al., 2013), obtained using word2vec[3]. The word embeddings were computed by applying the Continuous Bag of Words (CBOW) model on the permitted raw-text resources.

Depending on the language, for the computation of word vectors we compiled monolithic corpora composed of Wikipedia Dumps (whenever available) and raw text from UD training.

---

[2]https://github.com/taolei87/RBGParser - accessed 2017-05-24

[3]https://github.com/dav/word2vec - accessed 2017-05-24

Language	Tok	SS	Words	Lemma	UPOS	XPOS	Morpho	UAS	LAS
ar	99.98	60.50	95.50	85.51	90.01	81.96	80.76	76.35	69.32
ar_pud	80.81	98.80	93.34	0	73.54	0	0	59.80	48.73
bg	99.91	92.83	99.91	92.14	97.20	91.45	90.00	87.66	82.47
bxr	99.35	91.81	99.35	81.40	84.12	99.35	78.08	38.46	21.66
ca	99.96	98.95	99.95	84.26	97.60	97.60	95.46	87.98	83.94
cs	99.96	82.83	99.96	95.03	98.07	88.31	85.15	85.97	81.14
cs_cac	100.00	100.00	99.97	96.27	98.38	85.22	81.94	87.18	81.95
cs_cltt	99.82	80.14	99.820	94.56	95.78	83.24	83.00	76.17	68.36
cs_pud	97.98	93.23	97.97	92.00	95.40	83.93	80.01	84.13	77.71
cu	99.96	36.05	99.96	86.38	94.06	94.28	80.76	74.04	67.12
da	100.00	76.85	100.00	94.14	94.62	100.00	90.46	77.15	72.29
de	99.44	76.80	99.45	90.82	91.02	91.27	71.30	76.21	69.14
de_pud	96.72	89.87	96.47	2.71	83.12	19.45	1.36	74.65	65.24
el	99.83	87.56	99.83	91.78	95.78	95.78	84.98	84.03	79.08
en	98.67	73.22	98.67	93.43	92.76	91.67	89.75	78.34	74.44
en_lines	99.92	82.11	99.92	88.36	93.86	90.90	88.98	76.84	70.97
en_partut	99.51	97.51	99.49	94.81	92.93	92.60	90.22	78.11	72.69
en_pud	99.66	97.13	99.66	95.00	93.65	91.81	88.36	82.59	77.79
es	99.94	94.17	99.77	94.17	95.21	99.75	92.04	84.43	79.97
es_ancora	99.95	98.06	99.93	78.56	97.60	97.60	95.56	86.12	82.07
es_pud	99.53	95.27	99.36	3.32	87.55	1.70	0	84.60	76.64
et	99.85	92.53	99.85	79.28	87.53	89.48	77.32	68.69	58.74
eu	99.98	99.83	99.98	88.89	92.44	99.98	80.72	77.31	70.40
fa	99.99	98.01	99.34	96.58	94.92	94.50	93.75	82.69	77.45
fi	99.46	86.05	99.46	81.87	92.56	93.77	85.05	78.23	72.59
fi_ftb	99.90	83.83	99.87	85.58	89.77	85.74	82.94	78.21	72.09
fi_pud	99.39	91.91	99.39	81.06	93.74	0.01	0.01	80.85	75.44
fr	99.72	92.12	98.85	95.41	94.95	98.85	92.18	82.64	78.38
fr_partut	99.75	99.12	98.89	92.86	94.30	90.15	84.69	81.42	76.75
fr_pud	97.43	91.71	96.62	4.82	87.23	2.41	0	77.50	72.18
fr_sequoia	99.77	83.75	99.14	95.66	95.41	99.14	91.94	81.52	77.64
ga	99.73	96.69	99.73	83.33	88.95	83.25	65.64	76.27	65.65
gl	99.92	95.92	99.92	96.94	96.11	95.15	94.88	82.43	78.34
gl_treegal	98.91	84.80	97.97	90.94	90.51	85.60	83.99	71.74	65.22
got	100.00	27.85	100.00	88.80	93.39	93.13	80.18	70.18	62.30
grc	99.98	98.70	99.98	72.35	86.48	72.68	71.44	68.53	60.48
grc_proiel	100.00	43.11	100.00	90.17	95.70	96.03	83.01	74.89	69.47
he	99.98	100.00	88.55	75.64	83.24	83.24	78.17	66.23	60.72
hi	100.00	99.20	100.00	87.09	95.94	95.05	84.93	89.90	85.33
hi_pud	92.27	94.45	92.27	0	78.12	33.23	4.67	57.33	45.57
hr	99.84	95.91	99.84	93.36	95.80	99.84	79.17	84.13	77.03
hsb	99.84	90.69	99.84	87.70	90.30	99.84	72.43	54.24	43.74
hu	99.70	89.75	99.70	80.02	90.52	99.70	67.59	72.34	64.76
id	99.99	88.41	99.99	85.47	92.71	99.99	92.67	80.89	73.86
it	99.92	98.45	99.82	89.40	96.56	95.74	94.19	87.98	84.45
it_pud	99.60	94.56	99.16	88.22	92.50	2.47	2.47	86.73	82.48
ja	87.57	93.18	86.57	86.00	84.82	87.57	84.82	69.14	67.64
ja_pud	89.87	96.21	89.87	88.55	87.78	6.17	5.69	74.92	74.06
kk	94.52	81.50	93.89	51.48	56.49	54.94	35.81	43.01	29.22
kmr	99.01	97.02	98.85	89.76	90.04	89.84	80.62	32.05	14.73
ko	99.73	93.05	99.73	53.80	91.21	81.02	81.02	69.45	62.79
la	99.97	99.20	99.97	31.42	84.58	63.18	62.79	59.15	46.77
la_ittb	99.91	83.10	99.91	94.32	96.68	88.49	84.56	79.61	74.45
la_proiel	100.00	25.80	100.00	88.08	93.73	93.91	80.29	67.68	60.80
lv	99.30	93.30	99.30	84.86	88.62	71.51	69.55	68.54	60.08
nl	99.85	74.52	99.85	77.02	91.19	85.67	83.82	77.32	68.23
nl_lassy	99.93	78.62	99.93	97.13	96.88	99.93	93.82	84.05	79.54
no_bokmaal	99.88	93.11	99.88	95.55	96.04	99.88	90.91	83.84	79.84
no_nynorsk	99.85	91.23	99.85	93.30	95.51	99.85	90.47	82.33	77.83
pl	99.97	99.59	99.89	92.23	95.45	77.72	75.94	85.56	78.29
pt	99.64	89.79	99.49	94.05	96.01	73.24	71.81	85.81	81.92
pt_br	99.95	95.51	99.84	81.13	96.81	96.81	96.80	86.92	83.54
pt_pud	99.29	95.65	99.40	11.87	88.12	0	0	79.85	73.27
ro	99.54	92.60	99.54	95.90	96.02	94.11	93.88	85.75	79.44
ru	99.94	95.30	99.94	74.14	95.15	94.38	77.71	81.06	75.54
ru_pud	97.22	96.93	97.21	0	85.33	78.49	33.85	77.32	68.96
ru_syntag	99.51	98.01	99.51	93.55	97.70	99.51	89.04	89.41	85.41
sk	100.00	83.53	100.00	86.18	94.11	71.55	68.68	80.77	74.26
sl	99.96	99.24	99.96	93.95	96.24	83.08	80.99	84.67	79.61

Language	Tok	SS	Words	Lemma	UPOS	XPOS	Morpho	UAS	LAS
sl_sst	99.82	16.72	99.82	90.64	89.42	77.15	72.58	55.84	48.13
sme	99.88	98.79	99.82	81.86	86.81	88.98	77.76	47.51	35.47
sv	99.59	89.87	99.59	91.62	94.63	87.70	86.42	79.36	73.56
sv_lines	99.90	84.96	99.90	83.82	93.48	89.42	88.02	76.95	70.72
sv_pud	98.39	94.46	98.39	81.73	90.87	83.63	68.71	74.81	68.40
tr	99.76	95.77	97.52	84.83	89.30	87.31	76.01	64.09	55.74
tr_pud	97.61	91.79	95.10	0	68.66	0	0	53.78	33.20
ug	98.57	68.17	98.57	36.73	72.79	74.73	72.41	57.61	38.76
uk	99.65	94.25	99.65	85.16	88.58	65.35	61.26	72.45	63.54
ur	100.00	96.83	100.00	69.78	92.12	89.64	75.35	82.72	75.17
vi	82.47	92.59	82.47	78.18	71.23	50.35	50.25	39.98	34.19
zh	88.91	98.19	88.91	88.38	82.81	82.50	81.14	62.56	57.75

Table 2: Results per language

4 Evaluation

Table 1 presents the types of the individual models and their sizes. We use decision trees for most of the tasks, a CRF model for UPOS tagging and the models RBG Parser creates for the last task of parsing. We can directly see that the DT models are very small, even if they are written in text mode, with the largest average for morphological features of 170 KB. We also note that while there are 64 models for the 64 languages we had training data for, we only created 22 models for the languages that actually had compound words and 56 for lemmatization. The 57 tokenization models do not include the symbol tokenization models for Japanese and Chinese, which are even smaller; also, there were other languages that were pre-tokenized, so no models were created for them (details in section 3.1). The CRF models used for UPOS tagging are significantly larger, with the average of 121MB. Still, with a standard deviation of 100MB, we can say that most models are smaller than 250MB. The largest models are created by RBG, with the model for Czech reaching an impressive 3.16GB. On average, RBG creates models of around 1GB.

Moving on to the system results, we evaluate each task incrementally, starting from tokenization. We obtained a macro-averaged F1 score of 98.58, with a 0.37 difference to the first place. The decision tree approach used, while simple, brought interesting results, like first place for Czech (CLTT), Italian, Irish or Russian.

For sentence splitting, also based on DT, we obtained an average F1 score of 87.52 versus the top score of 89.10. We obtained first place on a number of languages like Hebrew, Basque or Latin. However on Latvian we obtained last place with an F1 of 93.30 versus 98.90. We note that no language-dependent tuning was performed, neither for tokenization nor for sentence splitting. The same features were chosen for all languages. While we did perform tree pruning based on the dev sets, we did not vary and choose the best feature set for each language (e.g. tokenization on some languages was better with a context of 2,2, while for others with context 4,1; we used 3,3 for every language that had punctuation and was not pre-tokenized).

In word segmentation we obtained a score of 98.39 vs 98.81, a difference of only 0.42 percent. Using the DT classifier brought us top places in several languages like Czech (CLTT), Danish, Norwegian (Bokmaal) or Russian.

Lemmatization, also based on decision trees, unfortunately worked really well on only a small number of languages. For example on Farsi we were the first with a 1.5 point difference over second place. Overall, we obtained an F1 score of 77.45 versus the top performer that obtained 83.74.

The morphological features average F1 score of 70.8 brings us relatively close to the top score of 73.92. Again, while not a best performer, the decision tree algorithm we used has shown very good performance compared to more complex algorithms in the competition.

On the language independent parts of speech (UPOSes) we obtained 90.71 vs 93.09. On language dependent parts of speech (XPOSes) we have an average F1 of 78.20 vs the top performer 82.27, a larger difference that for UPOSes.

Finally, on parsing we obtained an UAS of 74.67 vs 81.30 (11th place), and on LAS an F1 score of 67.71 vs 76.3, placing us on the 18th place.

5 Conclusions

The *CoNLL 2017 UD Shared Task* has been a learning experience for us. Considering that so far we only worked mostly on Romanian and English, and only up to the level of POS tagging, we managed to draw a number of conclusions, a few outlined below:

- while the DT algorithm has, on average, below state-of-the-art performance, it is very close to top performers. It sometimes achieves first place on tasks like tokenization or word expansion which follow a simpler and more predictable set of rules. We used a decision tree model because it is a predictable and understandable model, that, for this initial set of experiments allowed us to obtain significant insight on how we should create features and output labels, something that using a neural network would not allow.

- sticking with a method and trying out variations can lead to noticeable improvements. For example, pruning the character list on which to attempt a word split for tokenization based on normalized frequency yielded a more balanced training set. This has led to better results than simply asking whether to split on each character in the unpruned list (an unbalanced training set with most examples being "no split").

- sometimes intuition does not work. Initially, we hypothesized that for the morphological feature prediction task it was natural to attempted to predict each feature individually: we would predict, for every word irrespective of its part of speech, all available features separately. Each feature had an extra class of NONE meaning that it was not appropriate for that particular word, so it would not show up to the final composition of features. The results were actually significantly worse that trying to predict all features at once, as a single class output label, even if the number of such labels was much higher as it contained all combinations seen in the training data for morphological features.

As we viewed the *CoNLL 2017 UD Shared Task* as a learning experience, we attempted all tasks sequentially, even though the main goal of the challenge was the last task: parsing. The only place we used baseline UDPipe files was in the tokenization and sentence splitting where our decision tree approach with no tuning produced results significantly below the baseline. However, we kept our Tok/SS module even for languages where we were 5 points below the base-line, to see what would be the results on the test data. That basically meant that any error in the initial task would be partially propagated in the next one in our processing chain, as each module relies on information from any number of the preceding modules, marginally explaining some of the lower scores in later tasks.

Regarding the system itself we already created a fully functioning on-line version available at our NLP Tools Website[4]. During the last weeks after the shared task ended, we have replaced the decision tree algorithm with our own implementation of a linear classifier, and have obtained superior results. However there the footprint of the model obtained using the linear classifier is, in some cases, 1000 times larger than that of the decision tree classifier (i.e. the Ancient Greek XPOS linear model size is 4.5GB, whereas the DT model is only 4MB). Experiments using a deep neural network (DNN) architecture, trained to predict attributes and XPOS based on character-level features were also performed. Though this approach provided state-of-the art results for some languages, we found it difficult to tune hyper-parameters for all languages. However, for the DNN approach, the model footprint and performance figures (accuracy and computational time) were very appealing.

While one might consider that training independent models for each morphological attribute would provide better results, decision trees, Linear Classifier and DNN performed significantly better, when trained to output all the morphological features at once (softmax one-of-n encoded, not multi-task learning). Additionally, we experimented with multi-task learning (i.e.: using a common network structure, followed by multiple softmax layers) (Collobert and Weston, 2008) and observed that it did not improve the learning process, at least on the corpora and feature sets we used. Further tuning will be done and performance figures evaluated by the UD evaluation script will be reported on the above mentioned website.

Acknowledgments

This work was supported by UEFISCDI, under grant PN-II-PT-PCCA-2013-4-0789, project "Assistive Natural-language, Voice-controlled System for Intelligent Buildings" (2013-2017).

References

Ronan Collobert and Jason Weston. 2008. A unified architecture for natural language processing: Deep neural networks with multitask learning. In *Proceedings of the 25th international conference on Machine learning*. ACM, pages 160–167.

Tomaz Erjavec. 2004. Multext-east version 3: Multilingual morphosyntactic specifications, lexicons and corpora. In *Proceedings of the 4th International Conference on Language Resources and Evaluation (LREC 2004)*.

Tao Lei, Yuan Zhang, Regina Barzilay, and Tommi Jaakkola. 2014. Low-rank tensors for scoring dependency structures. Association for Computational Linguistics.

Tomas Mikolov, Ilya Sutskever, Kai Chen, Greg S Corrado, and Jeff Dean. 2013. Distributed representations of words and phrases and their compositionality. In *Advances in neural information processing systems*. pages 3111–3119.

Joakim Nivre, Marie-Catherine de Marneffe, Filip Ginter, Yoav Goldberg, Jan Hajič, Christopher Manning, Ryan McDonald, Slav Petrov, Sampo Pyysalo, Natalia Silveira, Reut Tsarfaty, and Daniel Zeman. 2016. Universal Dependencies v1: A multilingual treebank collection. In *Proceedings of the 10th International Conference on Language Resources and Evaluation (LREC 2016)*. European Language Resources Association, Portoroz, Slovenia, pages 1659–1666.

Joakim Nivre et al. 2017a. Universal Dependencies 2.0. LINDAT/CLARIN digital library at the Institute of Formal and Applied Linguistics, Charles University, Prague, http://hdl.handle.net/11234/1-1983. http://hdl.handle.net/11234/1-1983.

Joakim Nivre et al. 2017b. Universal Dependencies 2.0 – CoNLL 2017 shared task development and test data. LINDAT/CLARIN digital library at the Institute of Formal and Applied Linguistics, Charles University, Prague, http://hdl.handle.net/11234/1-2184. http://hdl.handle.net/11234/1-2184.

Slav Petrov, Dipanjan Das, and Ryan McDonald. 2011. A universal part-of-speech tagset. *arXiv preprint arXiv:1104.2086* .

Martin Potthast, Tim Gollub, Francisco Rangel, Paolo Rosso, Efstathios Stamatatos, and Benno Stein. 2014. Improving the reproducibility of PAN's shared tasks: Plagiarism detection, author identification, and author profiling. In Evangelos Kanoulas, Mihai Lupu, Paul Clough, Mark Sanderson, Mark Hall, Allan Hanbury, and Elaine Toms, editors, *Information Access Evaluation meets Multilinguality, Multimodality, and Visualization. 5th International Conference of the CLEF Initiative (CLEF 14)*. Springer, Berlin Heidelberg New York, pages 268–299. https://doi.org/10.1007/978-3-319-11382-1_22.

Milan Straka, Jan Hajič, and Jana Straková. 2016. UDPipe: trainable pipeline for processing CoNLL-U files performing tokenization, morphological analysis, POS tagging and parsing. In *Proceedings of the 10th International Conference on Language Resources and Evaluation (LREC 2016)*. European Language Resources Association, Portoroz, Slovenia.

David Weiss, Chris Alberti, Michael Collins, and Slav Petrov. 2015. Structured training for neural network transition-based parsing. *CoRR* abs/1506.06158. http://arxiv.org/abs/1506.06158.

Daniel Zeman. 2008. Reusable tagset conversion using tagset drivers. In *Proceedings of the 6th International Conference on Language Resources and Evaluation (LREC 2008)*.

Daniel Zeman, Filip Ginter, Jan Hajič, Joakim Nivre, Martin Popel, Milan Straka, and et al. 2017. CoNLL 2017 Shared Task: Multilingual Parsing from Raw Text to Universal Dependencies. In *Proceedings of the CoNLL 2017 Shared Task: Multilingual Parsing from Raw Text to Universal Dependencies*. Association for Computational Linguistics, pages 1–20.

Yuan Zhang, Tao Lei, Regina Barzilay, and Tommi Jaakkola. 2014a. Greed is good if randomized: New inference for dependency parsing .

Yuan Zhang, Tao Lei, Regina Barzilay, Tommi Jaakkola, and Amir Globerson. 2014b. Steps to excellence: Simple inference with refined scoring of dependency trees. Association for Computational Linguistics.

---

[4]http://slp.racai.ro/index.php/mlpla-new/

Delexicalized transfer parsing for low-resource languages using transformed and combined treebanks

Ayan Das, Mohammad Affan Zafar, Sudeshna Sarkar
Department of Computer Science and Engineering
Indian Institute of Technology, Kharagpur, WB, India
ayan.das@cse.iitkgp.ernet.in
affanzafar07@gmail.com
sudeshna@cse.iitkgp.ernet.in

Abstract

This paper describes the IIT Kharagpur dependency parsing system in CoNLL-2017 shared task on Multilingual Parsing from Raw Text to Universal Dependencies. We primarily focus on the low-resource languages (surprise languages). We have developed a framework to combine multiple treebanks to train parsers for low resource languages by a delexicalization method. We have applied transformation on the source language treebanks based on syntactic features of the low-resource language to improve performance of the parser. In the official evaluation, our system achieves macro-averaged LAS scores of 67.61 and 37.16 on the entire blind test data and the surprise language test data respectively.

1 Introduction

A dependency parser analyzes the relations among the words in a sentence to determine the syntactic dependencies among them where the dependency relations are drawn from a fixed set of grammatical relations. Dependency parsing is a very important NLP task and has wide usage in different tasks such as question answering, semantic parsing, information extraction and machine translation.

There has been a lot of focus recently on development of dependency parsers for low-resource languages i.e., the languages for which little or no treebanks are available by cross-lingual transfer parsing methods using knowledge derived from treebanks of other languages and the resources available for the low-resource languages (McDonald et al., 2011; Tiedemann, 2015; McDonald et al., 2011; Zeman and Resnik, 2008; Rasooli and Collins, 2015).

The Universal Dependencies (http://universaldependencies.org/) (Nivre et al., 2016) project has enabled the development of consistent treebanks for several languages using an uniform PoS, morphological features and dependency relation tagging scheme. This has immensely helped research in multi-lingual parsing, cross-lingual transfer parsing and the comparison of language structures over several languages.

The CONLL 2017 shared task focusses on learning syntactic parsers starting from raw text that can work over several typologically different languages and even surprise languages for which no training data is available using the common annotation scheme (UD v2). The details of the task are available in the overview paper (Zeman et al., 2017).

For parsing the surprise languages we trained delexicalized parser models. In order to improve performance on the surprise languages we applied syntactic transformation on some source language treebanks based on the information obtained from the "The World Atlas of Language Structures" (WALS) (Haspelmath, 2005) and sample data and used the transformed treebanks to train the parsers for the surprise languages. The details of the treebanks are discussed in Section 3.1.

The rest of the paper is organized as follows. In Section 2 we describe the corpora and resources used to build our system. In Section 3 we describe in details the methods used to train the parser models. In Section 4 we describe the experiments and report the results, and, we conclude in Section 5.

2 Corpus and resources

We used the treebanks (UD v2.0) (Nivre et al., 2017b) which were officially released for the shared task to train our parser models. The dataset

Proceedings of the CoNLL 2017 Shared Task: Multilingual Parsing from Raw Text to Universal Dependencies, pages 182–190,
Vancouver, Canada, August 3-4, 2017. © 2017 Association for Computational Linguistics

consists of 70 treebanks on 50 different languages. There are multiple treebanks for some languages such as Arabic, English, French, Russian etc. For the shared task, only the training and development data was released. The small sample treebanks (approximately 20 sentences per language) for the surprise languages were made available separately one week before the test phase.

We have used the pre-trained word vectors of 50 dimensions provided by the organizers to train the parser models. For tokenization and tagging we used the baseline models provided by the organizers. Our parser models were trained using the Parsito parser (Straka et al., 2015) implemented in UDPipe (Straka et al., 2016) text-processing pipeline system.

3   System description

Our parser worked on parsed the tokenized and tagged files (`*-udpipe.conllu`) provided by the organizers rather than the raw text files. We first discuss the steps for training the models for surprise languages in Section 3.1 followed by methods used to train the models for the new parallel treebanks in Section 3.2 and known treebanks in Section 3.3.

3.1   Surprise language

The surprise languages are Buryat (bxr), Kurmanji (Kurdish) (kmr), North Sámi (sme) and Upper Sorbian (hsb) for which sample data of approximately 20 annotated sentences per language was made available. No training or test data is available for the surprise languages.

We have used cross-lingual parser transfer to develop parsers for the surprise languages using the treebanks of resource-rich languages (McDonald et al., 2011). Annotation projection (Hwa et al., 2005) and delexicalized transfer (Zeman and Resnik, 2008) are the two major methods of cross-lingual parser transfer.

However, annotation projection requires parallel data which is not available for the surprise languages. Hence, we used the delexicalized parser transfer method to train parser models for the surprise languages. Training delexicalized parser involves supervised training of a parser model on a source language (SL) treebank without using any lexical features and then applying the model directly to parse sentences in the target language (TL). Zeman and Resnik (2008) and Søgaard

(2011) have shown that cross-lingual transfer by delexicalization works best for syntactically related language pairs.

The first step was to identify the languages which are syntactically related to the surprise languages and whose treebanks are in Universal Dependency corpus. We observed that Upper Sorbian being a slavonic language is typologically related to Czech, Polish and to some extent Slovak. North Sámi is spoken in the northern parts of Norway, Sweden and Finland. It belongs to the family of Finno-Ugric languages and hence has typological similarities with Estonian, Finnish and Hungarian. Kurmanji has typological similarities with Persian and Turkish. Buryat is spoken in Monglia. Although none of the languages whose treebanks are available in Universal Dependencies corpus belong to the family of Buryat yet we guessed that Kazakh, Tamil, Hindi and Urdu might have some similarities with Buryat based on the syntactic features and phrasal structures of the languages.

In order to verify our guesses, we tested the delexicalized models trained on individual treebanks on the sample data for the surprise languages and ranked them based on LAS. We observed that our guesses were quite close to the actual results except a few cases. Table 3.1 lists the top-5 languages for each of the surprise language based on LAS score. Encouraged by the above results that support our guesses we explored a transformation-based method to further reduce the syntactic differences between the surprise languages and the corresponding source languages. Besides attempting to reduce the syntactic differences between the languages we also experimented with combining the treebanks for which the individual LAS scores were highest to further boost the LAS on the surprise languages.

3.1.1   Syntactic feature based transformation

Aufrant et al. (2016) have shown that local reordering of words of the source sentence using PoS language model and linguistic knowledge derived from WALS improve performance of the delexicalized transfer parser even for syntactically different SL-TL pairs. The reordering features they use are relative orderings of the adjectives, adpositions, articles (definite and indefinite) and demonstratives with respect to the corresponding modified nouns in the TL.

However, for language pairs that differ in the arrangement of verb arguments, local rearrange-

Buryat	Kazakh	Latvian	Hindi	Tamil	Finnish-ftb
	(43.14)	(37.25)	(37.25)	(35.95)	(35.29)
Kurmanji (Kurdish)	Polish	Persian	Bulgarian	Romanian	Czech
	(45.04)	(42.15)	(41.74)	(40.91)	(40.5)
North Sámi	Finnish	Swedish	Estonian	Norwegian	Lithuanian
	(54.42)	(51.02)	(48.98)	(46.26)	(45.58)
Upper Sorbian	Slovak	Slovenian	Bulgarian	Polish	Czech
	(71.5)	(65.9)	(63.91)	(63.48)	(62.83)

Table 1: Top 5 languages whose delex models gave the highest LAS on the surprise language sample data

	81A	84A	87A	85A	37A	38A	88A	86A	aux	cop	ccomp	xcomp	acl	advcl	90A
bxr	SOV	-	pre	post	×	×	pre	pre	post	post	post	-	pre	pre	×
kmr	SOV	-	post	pre	pre	pre	pre	post	pre	post	pre	pre	post	pre	×
sme	SVO	-	pre	post	×	×	×	pre	pre	post	-	pre	post	pre	post
hsb	SVO	-	pre	pre	pre	pre	pre	post	-	-	post	post	post	post	×

Table 2: Ordering of the head-modifier pairs in the target language as derived from the universal dependency treebank statistics. "pre" indicates that the modifier precedes the head, "post" indicates that the modifier succeeds the head and "-" indicates that the ordering cannot be decided. "×" shows that the dependency does apply to the language. Some of the feature identifiers are derived from WALS: 81A - order of subject, object and verb in a sentence, 84A - order of object, oblique and verb, 87A - ordering of ADJ and NOUN, 85A - ordering of ADP and NOUN, 37A/38A - ordering of Definite/Indefinite articles and NOUN, 88A - ordering of Demonstrative and NOUN, 86A - ordering of genitive and NOUN, 90A - ordering of relative clause and VERB

	Our system		Best scores		Our rank
	UAS	LAS	UAS	LAS	
All test data	73.68	67.61	81.30 (Stan.)	76.30 (Stan.)	19
Surprise treebanks	49.98	37.16	58.40 (C2L2)	47.54 (C2L2)	10
Big treebanks	77.32	72.68	85.16 (Stan.)	81.77 (Stan.)	18
New parallel treebanks	74.45	67.42	80.17 (Stan.)	73.73 (Stan.)	17
Small treebanks	59.14	48.33	70.59 (C2L2)	61.49 (C2L2)	22

Table 3: UAS and LAS on blind test as obtained by primary system run and their comparison with the best runs. Stan. and C2L2 refer to the systems submitted by Stanford University and C2L2 (Ithaca) respectively

ments based on PoS tags may not be enough to address the difference between the two languages. Hence, we hypothesize that a reordering of SL sentences based on more generic features such as dependency relations (subject, object, indirect object, clausal complement) might result in improvement in accuracy of the parser.

An example of syntactic transformation In order to illustrate the syntactic difference between two languages we put forth an example for English-Kurmanji (Kurdish) language pair.

The example in figure 1 shows the syntactic difference between the two languages - English and Kurmanji (Kurdish) - and how the transformation of the English sentence makes it syntactically

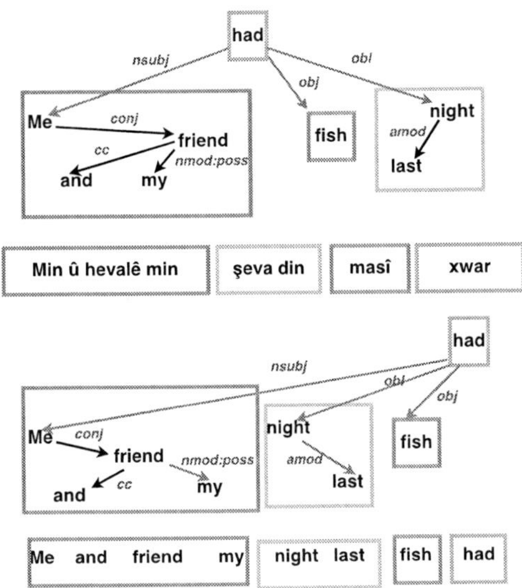

Figure 1: Transformation of English sentence to match the syntax of Kurdish sentence based on the syntactic features of Hindi

closer to Kurmanji (Kurdish). English language sentences have a SVO sentence structure while Kurmanji (Kurdish) has a SOV sentence structure. Moreover, in English the oblique arguments tend to appear after the object in the sentence while in Kurmanji (Kurdish) the oblique arguments tend to appear before the object.

The English sentence "Me and my friend had fish last night" may be translated to Kurmanji (Kurdish) as " *Min û hevalê min şeva din masî xwar (Me and friend my night last fish had)*". In this sentence pair *Me and my friend (Min û hevalê min)* and *fish (masî)* are the subject and the object of the main verb *had (xwar)* and *last night (şeva din)* is the non-core (oblique) argument indicating the time of occurrence of the verb. Also, in Kurmanji (Kurdish), the adjectival modifiers and genitives occur after the modified noun e.g., *hevalê min (friend my)* and *şeva din (night last)*, while in English these modifiers occur before the modified noun e.g. *my friend* and *last night*.

3.1.2 Transformation features

Apart from the features proposed by Aufrant et al. (2016) we obtained the order of subject-object-verb (SOV), order of object-oblique-verb, and the relative order of relative clause, auxiliaries, copula verbs, clausal complements, clausal modifier (adjectival and adverbial) with respect to the modified

verb from WALS and the statistics of sample data. The relative ordering of head-modifier pairs based on the features derived from treebanks was determined using the following heuristic. If a particular order appears in at least 90% cases out of the total number of occurrences of the feature (dependency tag) then we use that ordering corresponding to the feature. Else we do not do any transformation based on that feature. We relied on the WALS features and the statistics of the sample data to derive the syntactic features and ignored the features that did not appear in these two sources. For example, although Buryat, Upper Sorbian and Kurmanji have relative clauses we neither did we find mention of the feature in WALS for the language nor did we find that relation in sample data for these languages. Hence, we did not use that relation during transfer. In Table 3.1 we summarize the transformation features and the corresponding orderings used for each surprise language.

We categorized the dependency relations into six classes.

- **Clausal complements :** ccomp, xcomp

- **Subject :** nsubj, nsubj:pass, csubj, csubj:pass

- **Object :** obj, iobj

- **Modifiers :** acl, advcl, amod, aux, case, cop, det (Pronominal type = Article or Demonstrative, and, Definiteness = Definite, Indefinite)

- **Other dependencies :** Dependency labels that do not belong to the above five classes (cc, conj, punct, mwe, foreign etc.).

Among the determiners we only considered the articles and demonstratives. We further divide the members of class *modifiers* into *pre-modifiers* and *post-modifiers* depending upon the position they take in the sentences with respect to the parent word in TL.

3.1.3 Tree-traversal based transformation algorithm

Given a source language sentence $S = \{w_1, \cdots, w_m\}$, where m is the length of S, let T_S be the parse tree of S. The transformation is carried out in two steps.

- **Step 1:** Remove the words corresponding to the dependency relations that do not hold in the TL from the SL parse tree e.g., remove

Demonstratives when North Sámi is the target language.

- **Step 2:** Rewrite the sentence by a tree-traversal method depending upon the ordering of the head-modifier pairs based on the transformation features.

Corresponding to each target language we have separate transformation procedures. The Procedure BuildTree is common for all the target languages. In this procedure we construct the tree data structure where each node in the tree corresponds to a word in the sentence. Each node consists subject, object, clausal complement, *premodifier*, *postmodifier* and *other-modifier* lists. The lists of a node are filled up only by the dependents of the corresponding word in the dependency tree. The subjects, objects and the clausal complements of the word are added to the corresponding lists. While constructing the pre-modifier, post-modifier and other modifier lists the module refers to a look-up table to obtain the order of the modifiers in the TL and place the modifiers in the corresponding lists. All the lists are not necessarily filled up e.g., if none of the dependents hold a subject relation (nsubj or nsubj:pass) with the word then the subject list of the corresponding node remains empty.

We have separate procedures for transforming the SL trees for each TL. The sentences are transformed by traversing the trees according to the ordering of the dependencies in the TL e.g., the subtrees corresponding to the modifiers in the *pre-modifier* list and the modifiers in the *other-modifier* list that appear before the current word in the SL sentence are traversed first, then the word of the current node is added to the transformed word list, followed by traversal of the subtrees corresponding to the modifiers in the *post-modifier* list and the words in *other-modifiers* list that appear after the current word in the SL sentence. Also, if the TL has SVO sentence structure, first the subtree corresponding to the subject is traversed, the verb is added to the transformed list and finally the subtree corresponding to the object is traversed. Procedure TraverseAnd-TransformTree illustrates the steps used for transforming the SL tree when the the target language follows SOV ordering of verb arguments and the clausal complements occur before the verb.

Lang-uage	Treebanks	Transfo-rmation	Number of tokens
bxr	Kazakh (kk)	-	547
kmr	Polish (pl)	-	175600
	Slovenian (sl)	37A, 38A, 86A, 87A	
sme	Finnish (fi)	-	187920
	Estonian (et)	88A	
	Lithuanian (lt)	85A, 88A, cop, xcomp, acl, advcl	
hsb	Slovak (sk)	-	273680
	Slovak (sk)	81A, 37A, 38A, 86A, ccomp, advcl	
	Slovenian (sl)	37A, 38A, 86A	

Table 4: The treebanks combined to train the parser models for surprise languages in the primary system. The 'Transformation' column lists the syntactic features on which the source treebanks were transformed. '-' implies untransformed treebank

3.1.4 Steps for training the parser for surprise languages

For each language we used the following steps to train the delexicalized parser:

1. We obtained the syntactic features proposed by Aufrant et al. (2016) from WALS and the sample data.

2. Besides the features obtained in step 1, we also derived some more syntactic features from WALS and sample data statistics such as ordering of subject (S)-object (O)-verb (V)

Procedure BuildTree

  input : Source language parse tree T_S
  output: Tree data structure T
1 T = node n_{root}, containing the root word
   (w_{root}), POS ($pos_{w_{root}}$), empty children list
   (cl_{root}), parent link (p_{root}) = $null$
2 **for** *each word w_i in S except the root word* **do**
3   Form a node n_i containing, w_i, pos_{w_i}, cl_i,
       p_i, dependency relation with $p_i = d_i$
4   Add n_i to the children list of p_i
5   Add n_i to the $pre - modifier$,
       $post - modifier$ or $other - modifier$
       list based on TL features
6 return T

---

in a sentence, relative ordering of auxiliaries, copula verbs, clausal complements, adjectival and adverbial clausal modifiers.

3. We transformed all the available treebanks based on the syntactic features described in step 1 and the combination of the features stated in step 1 and 2 using the appropriate transformation procedures.

4. We trained separate delexicalized models for untransformed treebanks and both types of transformations such that corresponding to each source language there are three models - one trained on untransformed treebank and two on transformed treebanks. Universal Dependencies v2.0 corpus consists of 70 treebanks. Hence, after transformation we have $70 \times 3 = 210$ treebanks.

5. We ranked the 210 models based on their LAS on the sample data provided for the surprise language and broke ties based on UAS and chose the top 20 treebanks for our next step.

6. We trained 20 models by combining the treebanks in the top-*k* ordering (top-1, top-2,$\cdots$, top-20) and selected the model that gave the highest LAS on the sample data. The treebanks were combined by concatenating the treebank files to form a single treebank e.g. for the top-2 model, we concatenated the two treebanks which ranked first and second with respect to the LAS on the sample data and used the concatenated treebank to train the top-2 model. In Table 3.1.4 we summarize

---

Procedure TraverseAndTransformTree

  input : Source language parse tree data
         structure T
  output: Transformed source language parse
         tree T_S^R
1 T_S^R = `RearrangeNodes` (T)
2 return T_S^R
3 **Procedure** `RearrangeNodes` (*Root node*
   n_{root} *of tree datastructure* T)
4   Rearranged word sequence (S_R) =
       `TraverseTree` (n_{root})
5      $T_S^R = null$
6   **for** i *in* S_R **do**
7   i_p^R = index of parent of i in S^R
8   Add (i, i_p^R, d_j) to T_S^R
9   return T_S^R
10 **Procedure** `TraverseTree` (*node t*)
11     $S_R = null$
12   **if** *t has empty children list* **then**
13   Add word (w_t) of t to S_R
14   **else**
15   **for** *Child c_t in cl_t with clausal*
          complements ($ccomp, xcomp$)
          dependency relation **do**
16   TraverseTree(c_t)
17   **for** *Child c_t in cl_t with subject*
          ($nsubj$) dependency relation **do**
18   TraverseTree(c_t)
19   **for** *Child c_t in cl_t with $dobj, iobj$*
          dependency relation **do**
20   TraverseTree(c_t)
21   **for** *Child c_t in cl_t that are*
          `pre-modifiers` *of t or in* `other`
          `dependencies` *appearing* **before** *t*
          in S **do**
22   TraverseTree(c_t)
23   Add word (w_t) of t to S_R
24   **for** *Child c_t in cl_t that are*
          `post-modifiers` *of t or in*
          `other dependencies` *appearing*
          after *t in S* **do**
25   TraverseTree(c_t)
26   return S_R

---

the LAS of our combined treebanks on the sample data. We report only those top-k combinations that have been used in the submitted systems.

3.2 Known language, new parallel treebank

New parallel treebanks were provided for 14 languages in the test data. Out of these 14 languages, we trained the models for German, Hindi, Japanese and Turkish on the single UD treebanks available for each of these languages. Multiple treebanks are available for each of the remaining 10 languages, viz, Arabic, Czech, English, Finnish, French, Italian, Portuguese, Russian and Swedish.

For each language with multiple treebanks we followed the following steps:

1. We combined all the treebanks in that language and trained a parser model on the combined treebank.

2. We tested the combined model and the models trained on the individual treebanks on the development sets of all individual treebanks.

3. We used the combined model for the parallel treebank if it gives uniform UAS and LAS scores across all the development sets and gave significant improvement over the models trained on individual treebanks. Else we used the model trained on the treebank that gave best result across all the treebanks.

We used the combined models for Swedish, English, Finnish, French, Italian, Portuguese, Russian. For Arabic and Czech we used the models trained on the main treebanks (lcode: 'ar' and 'cs', tcode: '0') of the respective languages.

3.3 Known language, known treebank

We trained separate models for each of the 70 Universal Dependecies v2.0 treebanks. We used word, PoS and dependency relation embeddings of 50 dimensions. Apart from these parameters we used the default parameter settings of the UDPipe parser to train our models. The 'small' treebanks for which for which no development data was available, we used the training data itself as development data.

4 Experiments and results

Our system comprises of 88 models. 70 models were trained on the individual treebanks available

from `http://universaldependencies.org/`, 14 models were trained for the new parallel treebanks and 4 models for the surprise language. Given the language code (lcode) and treebank code (tcode), our system identifies the parser model corresponding to the input test treebank and parses the sentences in the treebank file.

The systems were ranked based on macro-averaged LAS. The final evaluation of the parser is on blind test data sets (Nivre et al., 2017a) through TIRA platform set up by Potthast et al. (2014). We submitted 9 systems (software$k$, where $k \in \{2, \cdots, 10\}$). The systems differ in the models trained for the surprise languages. The models corresponding to the known language treebanks and the new parallel treebanks were same in all the systems. Since the test set was blind, the first four systems (software 2 to 5) consisted of a combination of models for the surprise languages that were expected to perform best based on the performance on the sample treebanks. The remaining 5 consisted of models corresponding to combinations of top-k (k= 1, 5, 10, 15, 20) models for each of the surprise languages. Table 3.1.3 lists the treebanks combined to train the models for our primary system. We summarize the macro-averaged LAS scores for the surprise languages for the 8 models in Table 3.3. The highest scoring system for the surprise languages (software2) consists of top-2 model for Buryat, top-10 model for Kurmanji (Kurdish) and top-6 models for North Sámi and Upper Sorbian. The results using the primary system is summarized in Table 3.1 and the macro-average over all submitted softwares are listed in Table 3.3.

5 Conclusion

In this work, we have implemented a system for parsing sentences in several typologically different languages with a special focus on surprise languages for the CoNLL 2017 Shared Task. We have developed a system for combining treebanks to train parsers for surprise languages and applied syntactic transformation of source languages based on the syntactic features of the target languages to improve performance on the target languages. We derived the syntactic features from the WALS and sample data provided. On the surprise languages, the macro-averaged LAS F1-score of our primary system is 37.16 while that of the best performing system (Stanford) is 47.54. However,

Combin- ation	bxr		kmr		hsb		sme	
	UAS	LAS	UAS	LAS	UAS	LAS	UAS	LAS
Top-1	63.1	**43.14**	51.2	45.04	76.52	71.52	63.95	54.52
Top-2	62.18	41.81	52.07	**45.87**	78.26	73.7	70.75	57.82
Top-3	58.17	39.22	45.04	40.91	78.26	74.13	70.75	**59.86**
Top-5	54.25	35.95	47.93	41.74	76.52	71.52	62.59	48.98
Top-6	53.59	32.03	48.6	42.43	77.61	74.13	72.11	59.18
Top-10	59.5	40.52	49.6	43.39	76.96	73.7	72.11	55.1
Top-15	58.17	41.18	40.5	35.54	77.83	**74.57**	70.75	59.18
Top-20	53.59	38.56	45.87	42.15	78.04	73.7	67.35	54.42

Table 5: UAS and LAS scores of models trained on treebank combinations on the surprise language sample data

	bxr	kmr	sme	hsb	Macro-averaged LAS F1 score	Overall macro-averaged LAS F1 score
Primary system (software3)	26.60	32.03	35.25	54.78	37.16	67.61
software2	29.98	32.38	33.27	**55.4**	**37.75**	**67.75**
software4	26.60	32.03	**35.25**	53.37	36.81	67.60
software5	29.98	32.38	32.05	53.37	36.94	67.60
Top-1 (software6)	26.60	32.18	32.83	52.92	36.13	67.56
Top-5 (software7)	29.08	**32.97**	32.88	54.85	37.44	67.63
Top-10 (software8)	28.91	32.38	33.03	53.54	36.96	67.62
Top-15 (software9)	**31.65**	32.27	32.05	53.37	37.33	67.62
Top-20 (software10)	30.44	32.51	32.95	53.23	37.28	67.62

Table 6: Comparison of LAS F1 scores of the submitted systems and their macro-averages on the surprise language test data. The system with highest macro-averaged LAS F1 score (software2) is composed of top-2, top-10, top-6, top-6 models for bxr, kmr, sme and hsb respectively. The *software4* is composed of top-1, top-2, top-3, top-15 models for bxr, kmr, sme and hsb respectively and the *software5* is composed of top-2, top-10, top-15, top-15 models for bxr, kmr, sme and hsb respectively. For the remaining systems (software6-10) we combined the top-5, top-10, top-15 and top-20 treebanks respectively.

the macro-averaged LAS F1-score of our best performing system is 37.75. Our rank with respect to the surprise languages is 10.

The overall macro-averaged LAS F1-score of our primary system is 67.61 as compared the best performing system that has an macro-averaged LAS F1 score of 76.30. The overall macro-averaged LAS F1-score of our best-performing system is 67.75. Our overall rank is 19.

References

Lauriane Aufrant, Guillaume Wisniewski, and Franois Yvon. 2016. Zero-resource dependency parsing: Boosting delexicalized cross-lingual transfer with linguistic knowledge. In *Proceedings of COLING 2016, the 26th International Conference on Computational Linguistics: Technical Papers*. The COLING 2016 Organizing Committee, Osaka, Japan, pages 119–130. http://aclweb.org/anthology/C16-1012.

Martin Haspelmath. 2005. *The world atlas of language structures / edited by Martin Haspelmath ... [et al.]*. Oxford University Press Oxford.

Rebecca Hwa, Philip Resnik, Amy Weinberg, Clara Cabezas, and Okan Kolak. 2005. Bootstrapping parsers via syntactic projection across parallel texts. *Natural Language Engineering* 11:11–311.

Ryan McDonald, Slav Petrov, and Keith Hall. 2011. Multi-source transfer of delexicalized dependency parsers. In *Proceedings of the Conference on EMNLP*. Association for Computational Linguistics, Stroudsburg, PA, USA, EMNLP '11, pages 62–72. http://dl.acm.org/citation.cfm?id=2145432.2145440.

Joakim Nivre, Željko Agić, Lars Ahrenberg, et al. 2017a. Universal dependencies 2.0 CoNLL 2017 shared task development and test data. LINDAT/CLARIN digital library at the Institute of Formal and Applied Linguistics, Charles University. http://hdl.handle.net/11234/1-2184.

Joakim Nivre, Marie-Catherine de Marneffe, Filip Ginter, Yoav Goldberg, Jan Hajič, Christopher Manning, Ryan McDonald, Slav Petrov, Sampo Pyysalo, Natalia Silveira, Reut Tsarfaty, and Daniel Zeman. 2016. Universal Dependencies v1: A multilingual treebank collection. In *Proceedings of the 10th International Conference on Language Resources and Evaluation (LREC 2016)*. European Language Resources Association, Portoro, Slovenia, pages 1659–1666.

Joakim Nivre et al. 2017b. Universal Dependencies 2.0. LINDAT/CLARIN digital library at the Institute of Formal and Applied Linguistics, Charles University, Prague, `http://hdl.handle.net/11234/1-1983`. http://hdl.handle.net/11234/1-1983.

Martin Potthast, Tim Gollub, Francisco Rangel, Paolo Rosso, Efstathios Stamatatos, and Benno Stein. 2014. Improving the reproducibility of PAN's shared tasks: Plagiarism detection, author identification, and author profiling. In Evangelos Kanoulas, Mihai Lupu, Paul Clough, Mark Sanderson, Mark Hall, Allan Hanbury, and Elaine Toms, editors, *Information Access Evaluation meets Multilinguality, Multimodality, and Visualization. 5th International Conference of the CLEF Initiative (CLEF 14)*. Springer, Berlin Heidelberg New York, pages 268–299. https://doi.org/10.1007/978-3-319-11382-1_22.

Mohammad Sadegh Rasooli and Michael Collins. 2015. Density-driven cross-lingual transfer of dependency parsers. In *Proceedings of the 2015 Conference on EMNLP*. Association for Computational Linguistics, Lisbon, Portugal, pages 328–338. http://aclweb.org/anthology/D15-1039.

Anders Søgaard. 2011. Data point selection for cross-language adaptation of dependency parsers.

Milan Straka, Jan Hajič, and Jana Straková. 2016. UDPipe: trainable pipeline for processing CoNLL-U files performing tokenization, morphological analysis, POS tagging and parsing. In *Proceedings of the 10th International Conference on Language Resources and Evaluation (LREC 2016)*. European Language Resources Association, Portoro, Slovenia.

Milan Straka, Jan Hajič, Jana Straková, and Jan Hajič jr. 2015. Parsing universal dependency treebanks using neural networks and search-based oracle. In *Proceedings of Fourteenth International Workshop on Treebanks and Linguistic Theories (TLT 14)*.

Jörg Tiedemann. 2015. Improving the cross-lingual projection of syntactic dependencies. In *Proceedings of the 20th Nordic Conference of Computational Linguistics (NODALIDA 2015)*. Linköping University Electronic Press, Sweden, Vilnius, Lithuania, pages 191–199. http://www.aclweb.org/anthology/W15-1824.

D. Zeman and Philip Resnik. 2008. Cross-language parser adaptation between related languages. *NLP for Less Privileged Languages* pages 35 – 35.

Daniel Zeman, Martin Popel, Milan Straka, Jan Hajič, Joakim Nivre, Filip Ginter, Juhani Luotolahti, Sampo Pyysalo, Slav Petrov, Martin Potthast, Francis Tyers, Elena Badmaeva, Memduh Gökırmak, Anna Nedoluzhko, Silvie Cinková, Jan Hajič jr., Jaroslava Hlaváčová, Václava Kettnerová, Zdeňka Urešová, Jenna Kanerva, Stina Ojala, Anna Missilä, Christopher Manning, Sebastian Schuster, Siva Reddy, Dima Taji, Nizar Habash, Herman Leung, Marie-Catherine de Marneffe, Manuela Sanguinetti, Maria Simi, Hiroshi Kanayama, Valeria de Paiva, Kira Droganova, Héctor Martínez Alonso, Hans Uszkoreit, Vivien Macketanz, Aljoscha Burchardt, Kim Harris, Katrin Marheinecke, Georg Rehm, Tolga Kayadelen, Mohammed Attia, Ali Elkahky, Zhuoran Yu, Emily Pitler, Saran Lertpradit, Michael Mandl, Jesse Kirchner, Hector Fernandez Alcalde, Jana Strnadova, Esha Banerjee, Ruli Manurung, Antonio Stella, Atsuko Shimada, Sookyoung Kwak, Gustavo Mendonça, Tatiana Lando, Rattima Nitisaroj, and Josie Li. 2017. CoNLL 2017 Shared Task: Multilingual Parsing from Raw Text to Universal Dependencies. In *Proceedings of the CoNLL 2017 Shared Task: Multilingual Parsing from Raw Text to Universal Dependencies*. Association for Computational Linguistics.

A Transition-based System for Universal Dependency Parsing

Hao Wang[1,2]**, Hai Zhao**[1,2,*]**, Zhisong Zhang**[1,2]
[1]Department of Computer Science and Engineering, Shanghai Jiao Tong University
[2]Key Laboratory of Shanghai Education Commission for Intelligent Interaction
and Cognitive Engineering, Shanghai Jiao Tong University, Shanghai, 200240, China
{wanghao.ftd, zzs2011}@sjtu.edu.cn, zhaohai@cs.sjtu.edu.cn,

Abstract

This paper describes the system for our participation of team *Wanghao-ftd-SJTU* in the *CoNLL 2017 Shared Task: Multilingual Parsing from Raw Text to Universal Dependencies*. In this work, we design a system based on UDPipe[1] for universal dependency parsing, where transition-based models are trained for different treebanks. Our system directly takes raw texts as input, performing several intermediate steps like tokenizing and tagging, and finally generates the corresponding dependency trees. For the special surprise languages for this task, we adopt a delexicalized strategy and predict based on transfer learning from other related languages. In the final evaluation of the shared task, our system achieves a result of 66.53% in macro-averaged LAS F1-score.

1 Introduction

Universal Dependencies (UD) (Nivre et al., 2016, 2017b) and universal dependency parsing take efforts to build cross-linguistically treebank annotation and develop cross-lingual learning to parse many languages even low-resource languages. Universal Dependencies release 2.0[2] (Nivre et al., 2017b) includes rich languages and treebanks resources and the parsing task in CoNLL 2017 is

based on this dataset. In fact, dependency parsing has been adopted as topic of the shared task in CoNLL-X and CoNLL-2007 (Buchholz and Marsi, 2006; Nivre et al., 2007), which have been the milestones for the researching field of parsing. This time, the task is taking a universal annotation version and trying to exploit cross-linguistic similarities between various languages.

In this paper, we describe the system of team *Wanghao-ftd-SJTU* for the *CoNLL 2017 Shared Task: Multilingual Parsing from Raw Text to Universal Dependencies* (Zeman et al., 2017). For this task, we only use provided treebanks to train models without any other resources including pretrained embeddings.

For dependency parsing, there have been two major parsing methods: graph-based and transition-based. The former searches for the final tree through graph algorithms by decomposing trees into factors, utilizing ingenious dynamic programming algorithms (Eisner, 1996; McDonald et al., 2005; McDonald and Pereira, 2006); while the latter parses sentences by making a series of shift-reduce decisions (Yamada and Matsumoto, 2003; Nivre, 2003). In our system, we will utilize the transition-based system for its simplicity and relatively lower computation cost.

Transition-based dependency parsing takes linear time complexity and utilizes rich features to make structural prediction (Zhang and Clark, 2008; Zhang and Nivre, 2011). Specifically, a buffer for input words, a stack for partially built structure and shift-reduce actions are basic elements in a transition-based dependency parsing. For the transition systems of dependency parsing, there have been two major ones: *arc-standard* and *arc-eager* (Nivre, 2008). Our system adopts the former, whose basic algorithm can be described as

*Correspondence author. This paper was partially supported by Cai Yuanpei Program (CSC No. 201304490199 and No. 201304490171), National Natural Science Foundation of China (No. 61170114, No. 61672343 and No. 61272248), National Basic Research Program of China (No. 2013CB329401), Major Basic Research Program of Shanghai Science and Technology Committee (No. 15JC1400103), Art and Science Interdisciplinary Funds of Shanghai Jiao Tong University (No. 14JCRZ04), Key Project of National Society Science Foundation of China (No. 15-ZDA041).

[1]http://ufal.mff.cuni.cz/udpipe

[2]http://universaldependencies.org/

Proceedings of the CoNLL 2017 Shared Task: Multilingual Parsing from Raw Text to Universal Dependencies, pages 191–197,
Vancouver, Canada, August 3-4, 2017. © 2017 Association for Computational Linguistics

following:

$$\text{Start} : \sigma = [ROOT], \beta = w_1, ..., w_n, A = \emptyset$$

1. Shift :

$$\sigma, w_i \mid \beta, A \rightarrow \sigma \mid w_i, \beta, A$$

2. Left-Arc$_r$:

$$\sigma \mid w_i \mid w_j, \beta, A \rightarrow \sigma \mid w_j, \beta, A \cup r(w_j, w_i)$$

3. Right-Arc$_r$:

$$\sigma \mid w_i \mid w_j, \beta, A \rightarrow \sigma \mid w_i, \beta, A \cup r(w_i, w_j)$$

$$\text{Finish} : \sigma = [w], \beta = \emptyset$$

where σ, β, A represent the stack, queue and the actions respectively.

One major difference for parsing between the situation of current and that of ten years ago is that recently we have seen a rising of neural network based methods in the field of Natural Language Processing and parsing has also been greatly changed by the neural methods. With distributed representation for words and sentences and the powerful non-linear calculation ability of the neural networks, we could explore deeper syntactic and maybe semantic meaning in text analysis, and both graph-based (Pei et al., 2015; Wang and Chang, 2016) and transition-based (Chen and Manning, 2014; Weiss et al., 2015; Dyer et al., 2015; Andor et al., 2016) parsing have benefited a lot from neural representation learnings. In our system, the model, which is trained by *UDPipe*, for the transition action predictor is also based on neural network, which is similar to the one of Chen and Manning (2014).

For this shared task, our system is built based on UDpipe (Straka et al., 2016), which provides a pipeline from raw text to dependency structures, including a tokenizer, taggers and the dependency predictor. We trained and tuned the models on different treebanks, and in the final evaluation, a score of 66.53% in macro-averaged LAS F1-score measurement is achieved. In the task, there are several surprise languages which lack of annotated resources, which means it is hard to train specified models for those languages. To tackle this problem, we exploit the universal part-of-speech (POS) tags, which could be represented as cross-lingual knowledge to avoid language-specific information, and adopting a delexicalized and cross-lingual method, which relies solely on universal POS tags and annotated data in close-related languages.

The rest of the paper is organized as follows:

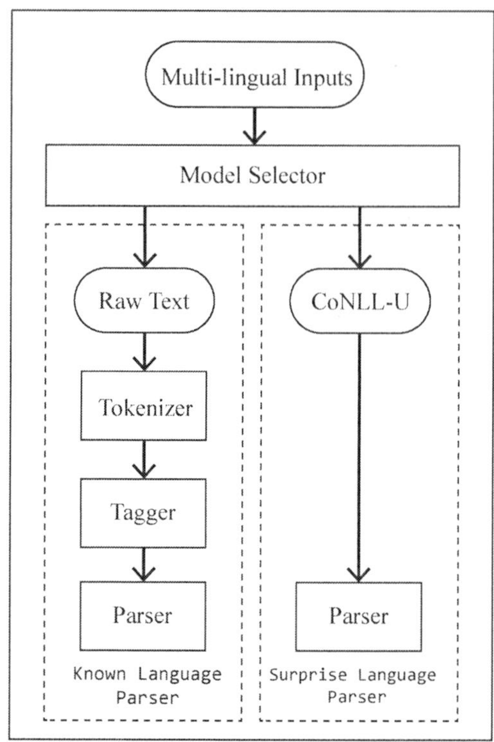

Figure 1: System overview.

Section 2 describes our system overview, Section 3 elaborates the components of the system, Section 4 shows the experiments and results for our participation in the shared task, and Section 5 concludes this paper.

2 System Overview

The overall architecture of our universal dependency parser is shown in Figure 1. The whole system can be divided into two parts: *Known Language Parser* and *Surprise Language Parser*. The former deals with known languages, including rich resource treebanks and low resource treebanks, whose annotations as the training data are accessible, while the latter disposes of the ones without dependency annotations. When the text to be processed by the system is inputed, it is first discriminated as rich-resource or low-resource and then dispatched to the corresponding sub-systems, which will be described as follows.

For the **Known Language Parser**, the related pipeline contains three steps as follow.

(1) **Tokenizer** The raw texts are split into basic units for the latter processing of dependency anal-

ysis, which is the main task of the tokenizer. For all rich resource languages, we train tokenziers using provided training data, including the languages which can be easily tokenized by specific delimiters.

(2) **Tagger** The tokenized texts are labeled by taggers, which provides them with the tags which will be utilized in the later dependency analysis, such as POS and morphological features. Like the previous step, we train taggers for all the rich resource languages.

(3) **Dependency Parser** Tokens and linguistic features generated by taggers are put into the dependency parser to generate the final dependency structures.

For **Surprise Language Parser**, only *Dependency Parser* is needed. We directly take the provided CoNLL-U files which already include the tokens and features as inputs and predicts the results. Without annotated training data, we could not train the tokenizers and taggers for these languages; Meanwhile for the parsing, we adopt a delexicalized and cross-lingual strategy, which will be described later in Section 3.3.

3 System Components

3.1 Model Selector

In the final testing phase of the shared task, there are mainly three types of test data (Nivre et al., 2017a), *Ordinary Provided Resource Test Set* which have corresponding training datasets , *Parallel Test Set* which concerns selected known languages but may have different domain from their training data and *Surprise Languages* whose training annotations are not available in the provided dataset. The model selector aims to discriminate these different input types, and dispatch the inputs to different sub-systems. Specifically, for the first two types which we refer to as Known Language, they will be dealt by the *Known Language Parser*, while the *Surprise Language Parser* will dispose with the surprise languages.

As for *Parallel Test Set*, we use its corresponding treebank without specific domain in treebank name.[3]

---

[3]It may be better if we use the whole treebanks of corresponding language

Parameter Name	Value
tokenize_url	1
allow_spaces	1
iterations	20
batch_size	50
learning_rate	0.005
dropout	0.1

Table 1: Parameters for the training of tokenizers.

Parameter Name	Value
guesser_suffix_rules	8
guesser_prefixes_max	4
guesser_prefix_min_count	10
guesser_enrich_dictionary	0
iterations	20
dimension of upostag	20
dimension of feats	20
dimension of xpostag	20
dimension of form	50
dimension of deprel	20

Table 2: Parameters for the training of taggers.

3.2 Known Language Parser

3.2.1 Tokenizer

In the *Known Language Parser*, the first step is to tokenize the input raw text, generating the basic units for later processing. We train tokenizers for all the languages using *UDPipe*, including those ones which are quite easy to separate using simple rules, like identifying the blank spaces in English. Considering there are some languages that could not be simply tokenized by blank spaces, we adopt this unified treatment for this step. The tokenizers are trained mainly using the *SpaceAfter* features provided in the CoNLL-U files and the parameters of *UDPipe Tokenizer* are shown in Table 1.

3.2.2 Tagger

In the pipeline of dealing known languages, the second step is to provide several light-weighted syntactical and morphological features for the tokenized texts, which will be utilized as the input features in the final parsing step. In our system, we adopt the tagger in *UDPipe*, whose tagging method is based on *MorphoDita* (Straková et al., 2014) and the training method is the classical Averaged Perceptron (Collins, 2002), and the training parameters of *UDPipe Tagger* are provided in Table 2. In this step, the tagger will provide the following outputs:

1. *Lemma*: Lemma or stem of word forms.

2. *UPOS*: Universal POS tags.

3. *XPOS*: Language-specific POS tags.

4. *FEATS*: Morphological features from the universal feature inventory or from a defined language-specific extension.

These features will be used as inputs in the final parsing step for Rich Resource Languages.

3.2.3 Dependency Parser

For the final step, we generate the final dependency outputs with the tokens and features generated by the pre-trained POS taggers. The parser uses *Parsito* (Straka et al., 2015b). *Parsito*[4] is a transition-based parser with neural network classifier, which is similar to the one of (Chen and Manning, 2014). The inputs to the model represent the current configuration of the stack and buffer, including features of the top three nodes on both of them and child nodes of the nodes on the stack. After we projected features to embeddings and concatenated the generated embeddings to representations of features, the vector representations of the input are fed to a hidden layer activated with *tanh*, and the output layer is softmax indicating the probabilities of each possible transition actions.

The parser supports projective and non-projective dependency parsing, which is configured by the option *transition_system*. In Universal Dependencies release 2.0, only UD_Japanese and UD_Galician have no non-projective dependency trees; while UD_Chinese, UD_Polish and UD_Hebrew have a few non-projective trees, around 1% in the treebanks. According to the projective tree quantities of the whole treebanks[5], we train non-projective parsing for most treebanks except UD_Japanese and UD_Galician. In projective parsing, we use dynamic oracle which usually performs better but more slowly. In non-projective parsing, we use static_lazy and search-based oracle (Straka et al., 2015a).

Except *transition_system* option, other configurations of *Parsito* are the same in all the training of different treebanks. For the structured_interval option, we kept the default value 8. To make sure that there is a only single root when parsing, *single_root* option is set to 1. Transition-based

<hr>

[4]http://ufal.mff.cuni.cz/parsito

[5]Projective tree extraction script is from https://github.com/ftyers/ud-scripts

Parameter Name	Value
iteration	20
hidden_layer	200
batch_size	10
learning_rate	0.1
dimension of upostag	20
dimension of feats	20
dimension of xpostag	20
dimension of form	50
dimension of deprel	20

Table 3: Parameters for the training of parsers.

Surprise Language	Source Language
Buryat	Turkish
Kurmanji	Persian
North Sami	Finnish
Upper Sorbian	Czech

Table 4: Surprise languages and corresponding source languages.

method could employ rich features effectively. In our system, we use the linguistic features generated by previous taggers, including lemma, POS tags and morphological features as described in Section 3.2.2. The parameters for the parser training are shown in Table 3.

3.3 Surprise Language Parser

This sub-system deals with the surprise languages without enough training data. We use a simple delexicalized and cross-lingual method, that is, parsing these low resource languages based on the models learned from other languages. This follows the method of (Zeman and Resnik, 2008), which shows that transfer learning for another language based on delexicalized parser can perform well. Although different languages may have different word forms, the underlying syntactic information could overlap and the universal POS tags could be utilized to explore the correlations. To achieve this, we train a dependency parser in a close-relation language (source language) for a surprise language, and then feed the delexicalized POS tag sequence of the surprise language to the source language parser. We consider language family and close area to find the source language for surprise language. Table 4 shows surprise languages and their corresponding source languages we found.

We use delexicalized source language parser to

Treebank's Type	LAS
Big treebanks	71.20.
PUD treebanks	65.55
Small treebanks	52.13
Surprise languages	34.49

Table 5: Results of main types of treebanks.

Surprise Language	LAS	UAS
Buryat	28.11	49.67
Kurmanji	19.85	30.49
North Sami	33.39	45.60
Upper Sorbian	56.60	64.33
Macro-average	34.49	47.52

Table 6: Final LAS scores for the surprise languages.

predict the surprise language's dependency structures. The input is CoNLL-U file in which we filter other linguistic features except Universal POS tags. Blind test results of surprise language are showed in Section 4.

Results	Our System	Best
LAS	66.53	76.30
UAS	72.69	81.30
CLAS	60.85	72.57
UPOS	90.63	93.09
XPOS	79.64	82.27
Morphological Features	82.27	82.58
Morphological Tags	73.81	73.92
Lemmas	81.63	83.74
Sentence segmentation	88.40	89.10
Word Segmentation	98.55	98.81
Tokenization	98.81	98.95

Table 7: Final results for the task.

4 Results

Evaluation process of this shared task is deployed in TIRA [6] (Potthast et al., 2014). LAS is the main scoring metric and we show performances of our system in several types of treebanks in Table 5 using the same groups as the official results. What's more, LAS of our system in Surprise Languages are shown in Table 6. We show several official evaluation results such as LAS, UAS and other results and compared with best results in Table 7.

___
[6]http://www.tira.io/tasks/conll

5 Conclusion

In this paper, we describe the universal dependency parser for our participation in the CoNLL 2017 shared task. The official evaluation shows that our system achieves 66.53% in macro-averaged LAS F1-score measurement on the official blind test. Further improvements could be obtained by more carefully fine-tuning models and adopting more sophisticated neural models.

References

Daniel Andor, Chris Alberti, David Weiss, Aliaksei Severyn, Alessandro Presta, Kuzman Ganchev, Slav Petrov, and Michael Collins. 2016. Globally normalized transition-based neural networks. In *Proceedings of the 54th Annual Meeting of the Association for Computational Linguistics (Volume 1: Long Papers)*. Berlin, Germany, pages 2442–2452.

Sabine Buchholz and Erwin Marsi. 2006. Conll-x shared task on multilingual dependency parsing. In *Proceedings of the Tenth Conference on Computational Natural Language Learning (CoNLL-X)*. Association for Computational Linguistics, New York City, pages 149–164.

Danqi Chen and Christopher Manning. 2014. A fast and accurate dependency parser using neural networks. In *Proceedings of the 2014 Conference on Empirical Methods in Natural Language Processing (EMNLP)*. Doha, Qatar, pages 740–750.

Michael Collins. 2002. Discriminative training methods for hidden markov models: Theory and experiments with perceptron algorithms. In *Proceedings of the 2002 Conference on Empirical Methods in Natural Language Processing*. pages 1–8.

Chris Dyer, Miguel Ballesteros, Wang Ling, Austin Matthews, and Noah A. Smith. 2015. Transition-based dependency parsing with stack long short-term memory. In *Proceedings of the 53rd Annual Meeting of the Association for Computational Linguistics and the 7th International Joint Conference on Natural Language Processing (Volume 1: Long Papers)*. Beijing, China, pages 334–343.

Jason M. Eisner. 1996. Three new probabilistic models for dependency parsing: An exploration. In *Proceedings of the 16th International Conference on Computational Linguistics*. Copenhagen, pages 340–345.

Ryan McDonald, Koby Crammer, and Fernando Pereira. 2005. Online large-margin training of dependency parsers. In *Proceedings of the 43rd Annual Meeting of the Association for Computational Linguistics (ACL'05)*. Ann Arbor, Michigan, pages 91–98.

Ryan McDonald and Fernando Pereira. 2006. Online learning of approximate dependency parsing algorithms. In *Proceedings of the 11th Conference of the European Chapter of the ACL (EACL 2006)*. pages 81–88.

Joakim Nivre. 2003. An efficient algorithm for projective dependency parsing. In *Proceedings of the 8th International Workshop on Parsing Technologies (IWPT)*. pages 149–160.

Joakim Nivre. 2008. Algorithms for deterministic incremental dependency parsing. *Computational Linguistics* 34(4):513–553.

Joakim Nivre, Željko Agić, Lars Ahrenberg, et al. 2017a. Universal dependencies 2.0 CoNLL 2017 shared task development and test data. LINDAT/CLARIN digital library at the Institute of Formal and Applied Linguistics, Charles University. http://hdl.handle.net/11234/1-2184.

Joakim Nivre, Marie-Catherine de Marneffe, Filip Ginter, Yoav Goldberg, Jan Hajič, Christopher Manning, Ryan McDonald, Slav Petrov, Sampo Pyysalo, Natalia Silveira, Reut Tsarfaty, and Daniel Zeman. 2016. Universal Dependencies v1: A multilingual treebank collection. In *Proceedings of the 10th International Conference on Language Resources and Evaluation (LREC 2016)*. Portoro, Slovenia, pages 1659–1666.

Joakim Nivre, Johan Hall, Sandra Kübler, Ryan McDonald, Jens Nilsson, Sebastian Riedel, and Deniz Yuret. 2007. The CoNLL 2007 shared task on dependency parsing. In *Proceedings of the CoNLL Shared Task Session of EMNLP-CoNLL 2007*. Association for Computational Linguistics, Prague, Czech Republic, pages 915–932.

Joakim Nivre et al. 2017b. Universal Dependencies 2.0. LINDAT/CLARIN digital library at the Institute of Formal and Applied Linguistics, Charles University, Prague. http://hdl.handle.net/11234/1-1983.

Wenzhe Pei, Tao Ge, and Baobao Chang. 2015. An effective neural network model for graph-based dependency parsing. In *Proceedings of the 53rd Annual Meeting of the Association for Computational Linguistics and the 7th International Joint Conference on Natural Language Processing (Volume 1: Long Papers)*. Beijing, China, pages 313–322.

Martin Potthast, Tim Gollub, Francisco Rangel, Paolo Rosso, Efstathios Stamatatos, and Benno Stein. 2014. Improving the reproducibility of PAN's shared tasks: Plagiarism detection, author identification, and author profiling. In Evangelos Kanoulas, Mihai Lupu, Paul Clough, Mark Sanderson, Mark Hall, Allan Hanbury, and Elaine Toms, editors, *Information Access Evaluation meets Multilinguality, Multimodality, and Visualization. 5th International Conference of the CLEF Initiative (CLEF 14)*. Berlin Heidelberg New York, pages 268–299.

Milan Straka, Jan Hajic, Jana Straková, and Jan Hajic jr. 2015a. Parsing universal dependency treebanks using neural networks and search-based oracle. In *International Workshop on Treebanks and Linguistic Theories (TLT14)*. page 208.

Milan Straka, Jan Hajič, and Jana Straková. 2016. UDPipe: trainable pipeline for processing CoNLL-U files performing tokenization, morphological analysis, pos tagging and parsing. In *Proceedings of the Tenth International Conference on Language Resources and Evaluation (LREC'16)*. Paris, France.

Milan Straka, Jan Hajič, Jana Straková, and Jan Hajič jr. 2015b. Parsing universal dependency treebanks using neural networks and search-based oracle. In *Proceedings of Fourteenth International Workshop on Treebanks and Linguistic Theories (TLT 14)*.

Jana Straková, Milan Straka, and Jan Hajič. 2014. Open-Source Tools for Morphology, Lemmatization, POS Tagging and Named Entity Recognition. In *Proceedings of 52nd Annual Meeting of the Association for Computational Linguistics: System Demonstrations*. Baltimore, Maryland, pages 13–18.

Wenhui Wang and Baobao Chang. 2016. Graph-based dependency parsing with bidirectional lstm. In *Proceedings of the 54th Annual Meeting of the Association for Computational Linguistics (Volume 1: Long Papers)*. Berlin, Germany, pages 2306–2315.

David Weiss, Chris Alberti, Michael Collins, and Slav Petrov. 2015. Structured training for neural network transition-based parsing. In *Proceedings of the 53rd Annual Meeting of the Association for Computational Linguistics and the 7th International Joint Conference on Natural Language Processing (Volume 1: Long Papers)*. Beijing, China, pages 323–333.

Hiroyasu Yamada and Yuji Matsumoto. 2003. Statistical dependency analysis with support vector machines. In *Proceedings of the 8th International Workshop on Parsing Technologies (IWPT)*. pages 195–206.

Daniel Zeman, Martin Popel, Milan Straka, Jan Hajič, Joakim Nivre, Filip Ginter, Juhani Luotolahti, Sampo Pyysalo, Slav Petrov, Martin Potthast, Francis Tyers, Elena Badmaeva, Memduh Gökırmak, Anna Nedoluzhko, Silvie Cinková, Jan Hajič jr., Jaroslava Hlaváčová, Václava Kettnerová, Zdeňka Urešová, Jenna Kanerva, Stina Ojala, Anna Missilä, Christopher Manning, Sebastian Schuster, Siva Reddy, Dima Taji, Nizar Habash, Herman Leung, Marie-Catherine de Marneffe, Manuela Sanguinetti, Maria Simi, Hiroshi Kanayama, Valeria de Paiva, Kira Droganova, Hĕctor Martínez Alonso, Hans Uszkoreit, Vivien Macketanz, Aljoscha Burchardt, Kim Harris, Katrin Marheinecke, Georg Rehm, Tolga Kayadelen, Mohammed Attia, Ali Elkahky, Zhuoran Yu, Emily Pitler, Saran Lertpradit, Michael

Mandl, Jesse Kirchner, Hector Fernandez Alcalde, Jana Strnadova, Esha Banerjee, Ruli Manurung, Antonio Stella, Atsuko Shimada, Sookyoung Kwak, Gustavo Mendonça, Tatiana Lando, Rattima Nitisaroj, and Josie Li. 2017. CoNLL 2017 Shared Task: Multilingual Parsing from Raw Text to Universal Dependencies. In *Proceedings of the CoNLL 2017 Shared Task: Multilingual Parsing from Raw Text to Universal Dependencies*. Association for Computational Linguistics.

Daniel Zeman and Philip Resnik. 2008. Cross-language parser adaptation between related languages. In *IJCNLP*. pages 35–42.

Yue Zhang and Stephen Clark. 2008. A tale of two parsers: Investigating and combining graph-based and transition-based dependency parsing. In *Proceedings of the 2008 Conference on Empirical Methods in Natural Language Processing*. Honolulu, Hawaii, pages 562–571.

Yue Zhang and Joakim Nivre. 2011. Transition-based dependency parsing with rich non-local features. In *Proceedings of the 49th Annual Meeting of the Association for Computational Linguistics: Human Language Technologies*. Portland, Oregon, USA, pages 188–193.

Corpus Selection Approaches for Multilingual Parsing from Raw Text to Universal Dependencies

Ryan Hornby[1] and **Clark Taylor**[2] and **Jungyeul Park**[3]
[1]BASIS Oro Valley, Oro Valley, AZ
`ryanhornby1999@gmail.com`
[2]Department of Computer Science, University of Arizona
`cgtboy1988@email.arizona.edu`
[3]Department of Linguistics, University of Arizona
`jungyeul@email.arizona.edu`

Abstract

This paper describes UALing's approach to the *CoNLL 2017 UD Shared Task* using corpus selection techniques to reduce training data size. The methodology is simple: We use similarity measures to select a corpus from available training data (even from multiple corpora for surprise languages) and use the resulting corpus to complete the parsing task. The training and parsing is done with the baseline UDPipe system (Straka et al., 2016). While our approach reduces the size of training data significantly, it retains performance within 0.5% of the baseline system. Due to the reduction in training data size, our system performs faster than the naïve, complete corpus method. Specifically, our system runs in less than 10 minutes, ranking it among the fastest entries for this task. Our system is available at `https://github.com/CoNLL-UD-2017/UALING`.

1 Introduction

Universal Dependencies (UDs) (Nivre et al., 2016) includes corpora from different languages annotated with identical types of labels. This allows for the examination of different theoretical (Schuster and Manning, 2016) and practical applications such as the *CoNLL 2017 UD Shared Task* (Zeman et al., 2017).[1] The specific practical task presented here involves using these corpora in a supervised learning approach in order to achieve the task's goal: Training with the multilingual UD data in order to find dependency relationships not just for

these known languages, but also for unknown or little-known language.[2]

1.1 Theoretical Concepts

Supervised learning occurs when humans encode their judgment into a set of data, which is in turn used to train statistical models with the ultimate goal of using these models to make accurate predictions for previously unseen datasets—which are often too large (and costly) or otherwise unavailable for humans to judge manually. Building these models of human judgment is necessary in cases where explicit rules are too complex to encode, ambiguous, or where such rules are not known; rather than explicitly and programatically encoding rules, supervised learning models "learn" or at least "contain" the rules through models generated from human-judged data. Ideally, the models are used to apply those same rules to the unseen datasets.

The rules contained in human-judged training data are, necessarily, constrained to the domain from which the data derives.[3] Unknown domains—such as unknown languages—are difficult to handle, because the rules from another known domain do not necessarily apply and the rules for the target domain are thus not readily known. Creating new corpora for specific domains (which occurs often for biomedical-domain data, for instance) drastically improves accuracy for the given corpus domain (Clegg and Shepherd, 2005). The UD corpora extend training data across

---

[1]`http://universaldependencies.org/conll17`

[2]"Little-known" here implies that the language has little to no human-annotated data—also known as under-resourced languages.

[3]What constitutes a "domain" may vary across different contexts. Here, the term is used generally to denote sources of data for which there exist significant similarity in grammatical rules, such as entire languages or much smaller topics. In the context of the task, "domain" generally refers to a single language, as our target data is of unknown topics but of a single language.

Proceedings of the CoNLL 2017 Shared Task: Multilingual Parsing from Raw Text to Universal Dependencies, pages 198–206,
Vancouver, Canada, August 3-4, 2017. © 2017 Association for Computational Linguistics

numerous different language-domains. However, adapting currently known data to new domains (including new languages) is a difficult problem, particularly when human judgment is not available to aid in the adaption.

Similarly, in many cases training data contains rules not relevant or even contradictory to those in unseen data. This occurs both interdomain—where the training data contains data from a domain which is not relevant to the unseen data—and intradomain—where training data from a domain is not relevant to other data in the same domain.[4] This data may not be necessary to building supervised learning models because it does not contain relevant rules; in some circumstances, training data may even introduce rules to the model which contradict rules in the unseen data.[5] Still other training data contains rules of marginal significance to the model, where such rules apply only to an extremely small segment of unseen data.

Without using supervised learning methods which actively adapt the rules of these data types to incoming unseen data, it is possible to (1) improve algorithmic and model performance by removing contradictory-rule training data, (2) improve algorithmic performance without model performance loss by removing irrelevant-rule training data, and (3) improve algorithmic performance without significant performance loss by removing marginal-significance rule data.

1.2 Resulting Methodology

For this paper, we introduce several methods of automated corpus refinement in order to improve and at best optimize supervised learning by accomplishing the goals enumerated above. Specifically, we propose and evaluate the use of similarity measures to refine the training data set; these similarity metrics "select" training data of the same domain and data which is closest in linguistic rules to the target, unseen data from available corpora.

Using only this similar training data ought to remove data containing contradictory or irrelevant rules. Furthermore, similarity metrics provide an opportunity to scale the included data by including only the **most** similar data above a threshold, which also has the potential to remove marginal-significance training data. This method allows us to drastically reduce corpus size while retaining only the most similar—and, ideally, best—training data. The overall effect on supervised learning performance depends on how well the employed similarity metric matches underlying rule similarity.

To accomplish this, we create a corpus processing pipeline in Java which calculates similarity and selects data. In this implementation, the development data set for monolingual parsing is considered a feature vector (§3), and similarity (§2) is calculated between this vector and each sentence in the single monolingual training data of the language. We try to find a *fixed* selection threshold (where sentences above the threshold are kept in the new training dataset) for all languages for monolingual parsing that provides the greatest performance, though performance-per-compression metrics are also valuable in some contexts. The sample data set for surprise languages also constitutes a feature vector (§4), and the program calculates the similarity between this vector and each sentence in the training data of all other languages. We evaluate *various* selection thresholds to adapt the under-resourced situation for each surprise language. We use UDPipe 1.1 (Straka et al., 2016) as the baseline system and the UD version 2.0 datasets (Nivre et al., 2017). We are able to reduce the size of training data down to 76.25% of the original in average using the proposed method while retaining UD parsing results are comparable to the baseline system. We can actually increase result accuracies for certain languages by using the resulting compressed training datasets.

2 Similarity

In our methodology, we employ cosine similarity as our similarity metric. The cosine similarity measure is applied to two latent vectors in two datasets. Let $\cos(d_1, d_2)$ be the cosine similarity, which is calculated as follows:

$$\cos(d_1, d_2) = \frac{V_{d_1} \cdot V_{d_2}}{\|V_{d_1}\|\|V_{d_2}\|} \quad (1)$$

where two feature vectors of V_{d_1} and V_{d_2} are

---

[4]Both interdomain and intradomain data are considered and dealt with by the method proposed here, though the task focuses on interdomain problems when considering different language domains. Pure corpus compression, as also discussed herein, tends to focus on the intradomain problem.

[5]To illustrate, when considering supervised learning approaches to parts-of-speech annotating, in the domain of formal scientific literature the word "as" might more often be used as a conjunction (as a synonym of "because") while in journalism it might be more often used as an adverb. Models trained on these different domains would likely result in different outcomes when labeling parts-of-speech due to these differences.

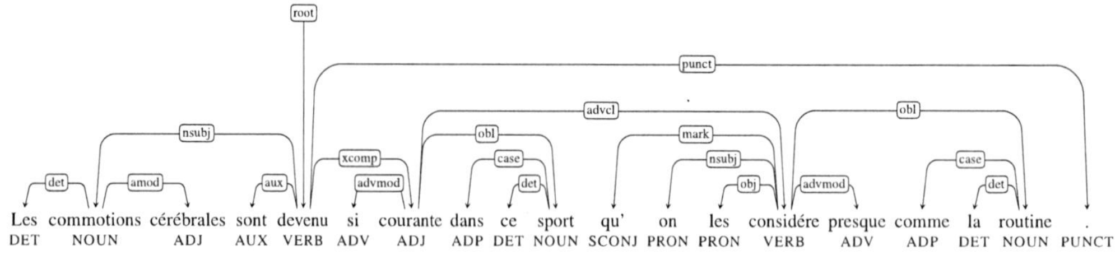

Figure 1: Treebank example: tri-gram POS sequences and dependency relationship between POS labels are extracted for features of the similarity measure.

from training and development datasets. Among the 64 languages with training data, 56 provide development data as well. Therefore, we focus on 56 languages for the proposed corpus selection approaches. The entire development data set makes one vector, and then the similarity is calculated between this vector and every sentence in the training data.

Various feature vectors are described in §3 and §4 for the monolingual and cross-lingual corpus selection approaches. For monolingual parsing, we use training and development corpora of the single language set for similarity measurement, extracting the most pertinent training data from the single corpus in order to compress and/or refine it. For cross-lingual parsing when we deal with surprise languages, we use training corpora from all languages, comparing the target language data to all known UD language corpora. This extracts the most similar data from other languages, with the hope that it is also similar in language grammar and structure—and, hence, similar in annotation.

3 Monolingual Corpus Selection Approaches

We use the following features for monolingual parsing:

1. tri-gram POS sequences

2. dependency relationships between two POS labels

Tri-gram POS sequences represent the tri-gram universal POS labels (Petrov et al., 2012). Dependency relationships represents the part of speech labels of a dependent and a dependee, and their dependency relationships.

3.1 Feature extraction

Tri-gram POS sequences are extracted from Universal POS labels of the sentence such as DET NOUN ADJ, NOUN ADJ AUX, etc. (See Figure 1). Uni-gram and bi-gram POS sequences are excluded because we found them to not be distinctive between the languages with Universal POS labels that we examined. We also extract dependency relationships between POS labels for the similarity measure such as NOUN nsubj VERB for *commotions ... devenu* where *commotions*/NOUN is dependent on *devenu*/VERB with nsubj dependency relation.[6] Figure 2 shows two results by using the different thresholds for tri-gram POS sequences and POS-dep-POS. Using similarity measures to select the subset of the original training data, the proposed method slightly outperforms the results obtained by the original training data set with the similarity threshold $\theta = 0.1$. Actually, it improves the parsing result by 0.01% and 0.15% only using 94% and 77% of the original training datasets for German and Dutch, respectively.

Table 1 shows our entire results of the corpus selection method for monolingual parsing on the dev datasets using label attachment score (LAS) per treebank. We train the full training datasets, and trimmed datasets using similarity of tri-gram POS sequences (pos) and POS-dep-POS (dep). We also train the monolingual parsing models by using results the intersection of two similarity measures (intersection). All results are tested on the dev datasets without 8 languages which do not provide dev datasets.[7] Table 1 also shows results from the

---

[6]While current feature selection is based on Universal POS labels, using language-specific POS labels for feature selection is one possible way to extend our approach for the *monolingual* corpus selection.

[7] We also exclude results of ru_syntagrus from the table because of internal formatting errors that our corpus selection method produced.

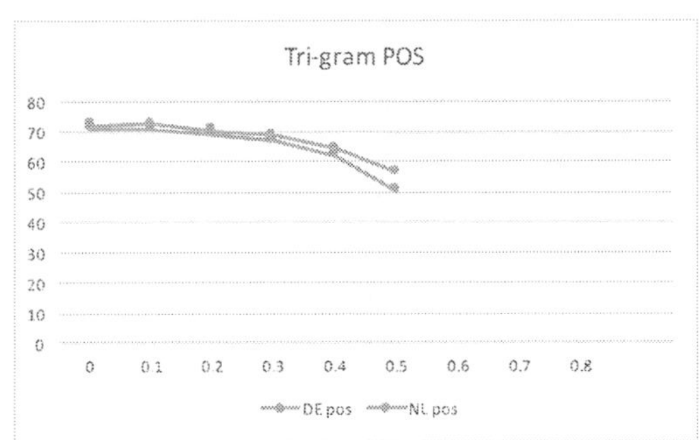
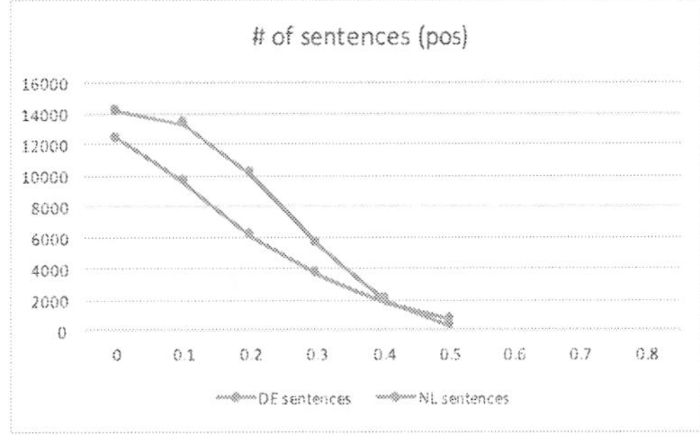

(a) Tri-gram POS sequences

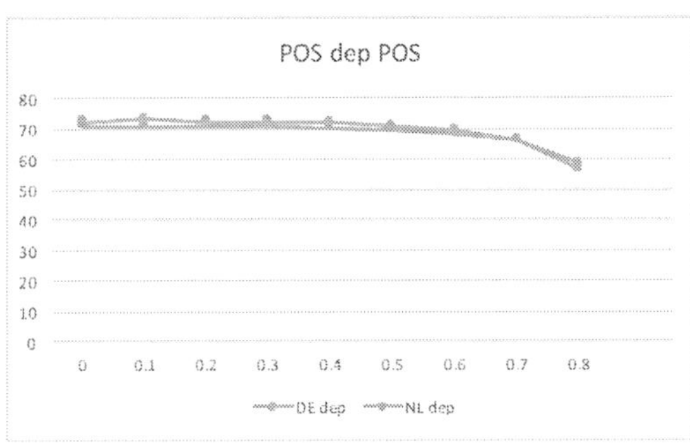
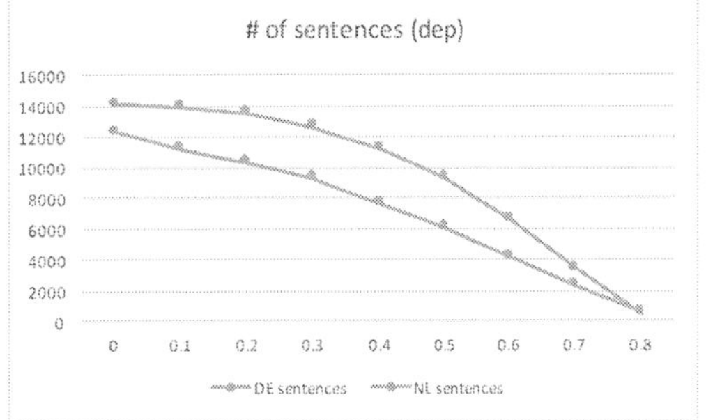

(b) POS dep POS

Figure 2: Threshold estimation using Dutch (NL) and German (DE): Similarity thresholds for tri-gram POS sequences and POS-dep-POS. Y-axis shows LAS (left) and the number of sentences (right).

method of length-based corpus selection (length). Since the sentence lengths decay after the peak (of the distribution of the numbers of sentences), our length-based approach to reduce the data set by length is to count the number of sentences before the peak and keep up to that many sentences after the peak.[8] In Table 1, we also indicate ratios of training datasets. This compression amount uses the scale indicated by the entire (*full*) and its compressed rates. For example, while grc uses 54.76% (▇▇▭) of the full training data set for *length*, its results decreases only by 2.54%. Actually, grc uses only 83.54% (▇▇▇▭) for *intersection*, it outperforms by 0.41%. We improve parsing results for 33 languages on dev data using the proposed corpus selection method by measuring similarity.

[8]This method resulted in some languages having up to 80% of the sentences removed because the peak sentence length was a small number of words. In order to make sure that only the outliers in length are removed we change the algorithm so that the peak value was between ten and twenty words long. This fixes the problem where languages with a low peak length having a large amount of sentences removed.

3.2 Discussion

Besides features that we presented, we also investigate a length-based approach to select the training data. Instead of using the peak of the distribution of the numbers of sentences as in Table 1, we calculate the simple average numbers of words of the sentences in the dev data set. Then, we obtain the training data set using thresholds with $average \pm scale$ for the number of words, where $scale$ is the number of $\max(|avg - max|, |avg - min|)$ words of the sentence in the dev data set. max and min are the maximum and the minimum numbers of words of the sentences. Figure 3 shows results and the number of sentences in the trimmed training datasets using length thresholds. We vary scale multipliers from 1 to 5. Filtering based on sentence length can potentially remove unnecessary size from the training data and possibly remove some inaccuracy, assuming that longer sentences increase entropy and become inherently less predictable. However, as Figure 3 indicated this *simple* length-based approach cannot keep up with the baseline results. While corpus compression levels compare to the similarity-

	full	length	pos	dep	intersection
grc	49.79	47.24	48.67	49.49	50.20
grc_proiel	65.87	57.95	65.66	66.40	66.69
ar	66.99	51.59	65.56	65.87	67.14
eu	67.48	52.35	66.94	67.86	67.32
bg	83.55	82.30	82.86	83.19	82.98
ca	81.80	75.23	81.26	81.05	81.59
zh	66.20	51.45	66.30	66.45	66.35
hr	73.87	72.64	73.41	74.23	74.33
cs_cac	79.89	73.24	79.81	79.48	79.74
cs_cltt	67.93	55.10	68.00	68.27	68.00
cs	79.42	76.48	79.42	79.03	79.42
da	72.68	59.66	73.29	73.78	73.83
nl_lassysmall	73.05	58.06	73.57	74.12	72.88
nl	72.31	60.26	72.46	73.00	71.56
en	77.67	76.50	77.72	77.78	77.16
en_lines	73.77	55.38	73.39	74.35	73.68
en_partut	75.66	56.99	74.30	74.97	74.30
et	60.11	44.93	59.87	60.46	59.75
fi	74.99	73.30	73.90	74.76	73.81
fi_ftb	75.17	75.17	73.49	74.04	73.18
fr	83.29	80.75	83.54	83.57	83.15
fr_sequoia	81.73	80.41	81.74	81.82	81.74
gl	74.95	42.68	74.31	74.95	74.31
de	70.80	66.15	70.81	70.98	70.33
got	66.84	60.09	66.65	67.90	66.76
el	75.41	65.71	75.08	75.08	75.08
he	75.46	73.90	75.18	74.35	75.49
hi	85.85	77.60	85.62	85.49	85.49
hu	67.23	60.76	66.54	66.37	66.54
id	71.88	70.05	71.67	71.65	71.14
it	83.21	79.19	81.48	83.08	82.57
it_partut	77.32	65.10	77.24	78.22	77.24
ja	92.42	82.50	92.12	91.99	92.06
ko	51.05	51.05	51.26	51.78	50.53
la_ittb	69.43	58.16	69.48	68.71	68.54
la_proiel	65.58	65.58	65.14	65.51	64.58
lv	63.02	48.34	61.97	62.78	62.87
no_bokmaal	82.34	79.81	81.06	81.59	81.40
no_nynorsk	80.20	79.93	79.95	80.07	79.72
cu	71.26	64.04	71.14	71.90	70.63
fa	75.93	50.92	75.73	75.88	75.29
pl	78.81	71.11	78.71	78.96	77.77
pt_br	83.44	80.95	83.28	82.87	83.61
pt	81.87	80.74	81.87	80.74	81.87
ro	77.70	69.25	77.14	77.74	76.72
ru	54.21	50.80	54.63	53.77	53.94
sk	75.10	65.66	73.61	75.06	73.69
sl	79.72	69.10	79.19	79.73	79.20
es_ancora	80.35	79.65	80.54	80.57	81.02
es	81.57	79.64	80.72	81.29	81.51
sv_lines	73.43	69.37	73.92	73.40	73.19
sv	72.88	68.01	71.97	72.92	72.47
tr	53.91	45.92	51.95	54.19	51.99
ur	75.23	66.55	74.60	75.36	74.20
vi	54.16	44.44	53.82	53.38	54.10
average	72.6545	64.9818	72.2545	71.3636	71.0727

Table 1: Monolingual corpus selection results on dev datasets. The numerical entries are LAS, and the bar indicates corpus compression amount. Length-based is trimmed based on the length of sentences in training data. Tri-gram POS sequences and POS-relation-POS are trimmed based on similarities between full training and dev data. *intersection* applies two feature extraction together (POS sequences and POS-relation-POS trimming). Threshold is fixed for all languages (0.1). We also indicate ratios of trimming of training datasets alongside parsing results.

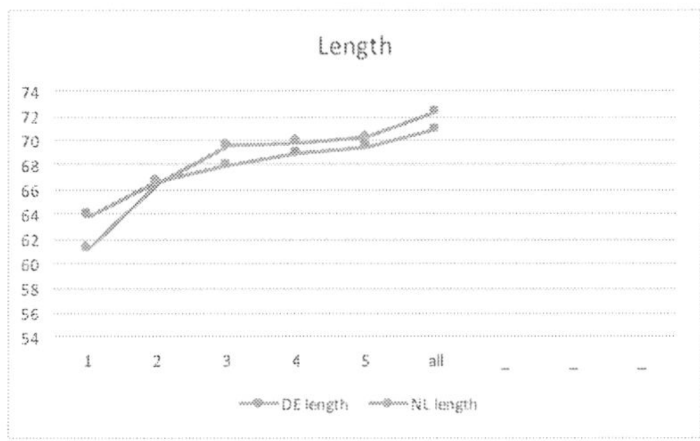
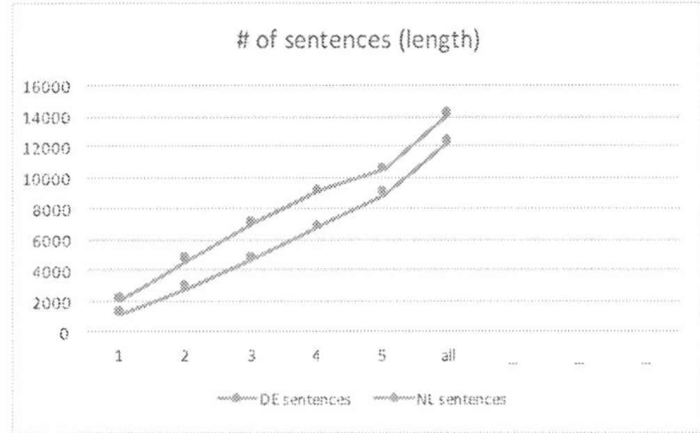

Figure 3: Threshold estimation for Dutch (nl) and German (de): Length scale thresholds based on the average number of words in the dev data set. Y-axis shows LAS (left) and the number of sentences (right).

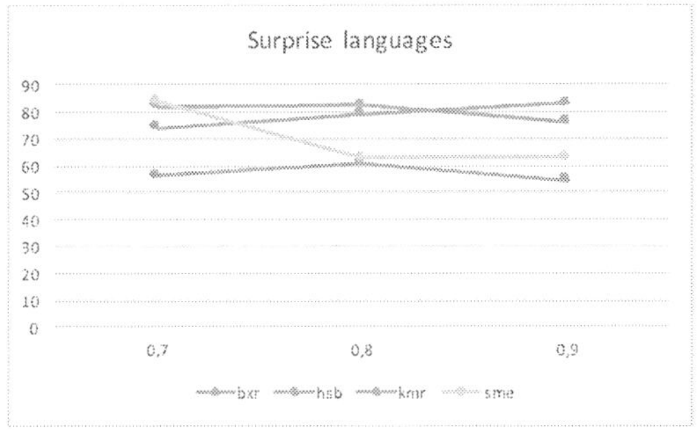

Figure 4: Threshold estimation for surprise languages: we fix 0.3 for tri-gram POS sequences and we vary between 0.7 and 0.9 for POS-dep-POS. Y-axis shows LAS.

based approaches, parsing results drop significantly. The empirical reasons that naive length-based approaches do not work well may be worth further consideration, but as a general matter the length metric is overly simplistic and may omit significant amounts of pertinent training data; similarity metrics, by contrast, attempt to retain the most pertinent data.

4 Cross-lingual Similarities for Surprise Language Parsing

We use the same similarity measures to identify the training data of the surprise language. Since surprise languages are provided without training data, we select the training datasets from training datasets of *all* languages by calculating similarities with sample datasets of surprise languages. Figure 4 shows threshold estimation for surprise languages. We fix the similarity threshold at 0.3 for tri-gram POS sequences because larger thresholds provide too little training data, and the smaller thresholds do not compress adequately. Thus, we

tune based on resulting corpus size.

We vary similarity threshold between 0.7 and 0.9 for POS-dep-POS. 0.3 for tri-gram POS sequences and 0.7 for POS-dep-POS both result in a size of about 25% of the training data set for monolingual corpus selection.

5 Results

For the submitted official results through TIRA (Potthast et al., 2014), we use the *intersection* model for all languages. Since we focus on the corpus selection, we do not perform additional preprocessing and we use the provided training datasets as they are. We fix 0.1 both for tri-gram POS sequences and POS-dep-POS because it gives the best results for dev datasets for monolingual training. We fix 0.3 for tri-gram POS sequences and we use the thresholds described in Table 2 for POS-dep-POS to select training datasets from all languages for surprise language parsing. We provide the basic parsing model for PUD treebanks, for example, we use cs parsing model for

bxr	hsb	kmr	sme
0.8	0.9	0.8	0.7

Table 2: POS-dep-POS thresholds for surprise languages

lang	BASELINE UDPipe 1.1	UALING
All treebanks	68.35	65.24
Big treebanks only	73.04	69.59
PUD treebanks only	68.33	64.29
Small treebanks only	51.80	**52.27**
Surprise languages only	37.07	34.57

Table 3: Summary of LAS results

cs_pud treebank without any modification. We obtain 65.24% LAS F_1 score for the submitted model where we position 22nd. Table 3 and 4 show the summaries of LAS and results per treebank, respectively.

6 Discussion and Conclusion

In this paper, we introduced the idea of refining the training datasets to UD parsing and cross-lingual parsing to select training datasets from the same language and other languages, respectively. While our approach reduced the size of training data significantly, we retained performance within 0.5% of the baseline system. Additionally, corpus refinement methods can also be of utmost importance in trimming the size of training data for algorithmically intense algorithms or large scale system deployment runtime performance. A total runtime on entire treebanks is only around 10min with a default setting, which is fast enough; additional optimization may improve this. The size of parsing models is smaller than the baseline because we use only the subset of the entire training datasets. Even though we don't use any external data, our final results are competitive to the baseline system even with smaller datasets. The current results presented here show promise, and there exists potential for further refinement by, for instance, using different similarity metrics. Exploring different similarity metrics may further enhance performance for other NLP tasks as well as UD parsing.

References

Andrew B. Clegg and Adrian J. Shepherd. 2005. Evaluating and Integrating Treebank Parsers on a Biomedical Corpus. In *Proceedings of the ACL Workshop on Software*. Association for Computational Linguistics, Ann Arbor, Michigan, pages 14–33. http://www.aclweb.org/anthology/W05-1102.

Joakim Nivre, Željko Agić, Lars Ahrenberg, et al. 2017. Universal dependencies 2.0 CoNLL 2017 shared task development and test data. LINDAT/CLARIN digital library at the Institute of Formal and Applied Linguistics, Charles University. http://hdl.handle.net/11234/1-2184.

Joakim Nivre, Marie-Catherine de Marneffe, Filip Ginter, Yoav Goldberg, Jan Hajic, Christopher D. Manning, Ryan McDonald, Slav Petrov, Sampo Pyysalo, Natalia Silveira, Reut Tsarfaty, and Daniel Zeman. 2016. Universal Dependencies v1: A Multilingual Treebank Collection. In Luis von Ahn, editor, *Proceedings of the Tenth International Conference on Language Resources and Evaluation (LREC 2016)*. European Language Resources Association (ELRA), Portorož, Slovenia.

Slav Petrov, Dipanjan Das, and Ryan McDonald. 2012. A Universal Part-of-Speech Tagset. In *Proceedings of the Eighth International Conference on Language Resources and Evaluation (LREC-2012)*. European Language Resources Association (ELRA), Istanbul, Turkey, pages 2089–2096.

Martin Potthast, Tim Gollub, Francisco Rangel, Paolo Rosso, Efstathios Stamatatos, and Benno Stein. 2014. Improving the Reproducibility of PAN's Shared Tasks:. In Evangelos Kanoulas, Mihai Lupu, Paul Clough, Mark Sanderson, Mark Hall, Allan Hanbury, and Elaine Toms, editors, *Information Access Evaluation. Multilinguality, Multimodality, and Interaction: Proceedings of the 5th International Conference of the CLEF Initiative (CLEF 2014)*, Springer International Publishing, Sheffield, UK, pages 268–299. https://doi.org/10.1007/978-3-319-11382-1_22.

Sebastian Schuster and Christopher D. Manning. 2016. Enhanced English Universal Dependencies: An Improved Representation for Natural Language Understanding Tasks. In *Proceedings of the Tenth International Conference on Language Resources and Evaluation (LREC 2016)*. European Language Resources Association (ELRA), Paris, France.

Milan Straka, Jan Hajic, and Jana Straková. 2016. UD-Pipe: Trainable Pipeline for Processing CoNLL-U Files Performing Tokenization, Morphological Analysis, POS Tagging and Parsing. In *Proceedings of the Tenth International Conference on Language Resources and Evaluation (LREC 2016)*. European Language Resources Association (ELRA), Paris, France.

Daniel Zeman, Martin Popel, Milan Straka, Jan Hajič, Joakim Nivre, Filip Ginter, Juhani Luotolahti, Sampo Pyysalo, Slav Petrov, Martin Potthast, Francis Tyers, Elena Badmaeva, Memduh Gökırmak, Anna Nedoluzhko, Silvie Cinková, Jan Hajič jr., Jaroslava Hlaváčová, Václava Kettnerová, Zdeňka Urešová, Jenna Kanerva, Stina Ojala, Anna Missilä, Christopher Manning, Sebastian Schuster, Siva Reddy, Dima Taji, Nizar Habash, Herman Leung, Marie-Catherine de Marneffe, Manuela Sanguinetti, Maria Simi, Hiroshi Kanayama, Valeria de Paiva, Kira Droganova, Hěctor Martínez Alonso, Hans Uszkoreit, Vivien Macketanz, Aljoscha Burchardt, Kim Harris, Katrin Marheinecke, Georg Rehm, Tolga Kayadelen, Mohammed Attia, Ali Elkahky, Zhuoran Yu, Emily Pitler, Saran Lertpradit, Michael Mandl, Jesse Kirchner, Hector Fernandez Alcalde, Jana Strnadova, Esha Banerjee, Ruli Manurung, Antonio Stella, Atsuko Shimada, Sookyoung Kwak, Gustavo Mendonça, Tatiana Lando, Rattima Nitisaroj, and Josie Li. 2017. CoNLL 2017 Shared Task: Multilingual Parsing from Raw Text to Universal Dependencies. In *Proceedings of the CoNLL 2017 Shared Task: Multilingual Parsing from Raw Text to Universal Dependencies*. Association for Computational Linguistics.

	BASELINE UDPipe 1.1	UALING		BASELINE UDPipe 1.1	UALING
ar	65.30	61.86	hsb	53.83	46.78
ar_pud	43.14	42.57	hu	64.30	64.18
bg	83.64	82.43	id	74.61	72.59
bxr	31.50	19.15	it	85.28	84.01
ca	85.39	81.93	it_pud	83.70	82.31
cs	82.87	78.04	ja	72.21	71.75
cs_cac	82.46	79.59	ja_pud	76.28	75.61
cs_cltt	71.64	**71.86**	kk	24.51	**24.75**
cs_pud	79.80	76.75	kmr	32.35	**40.57**
cu	62.76	61.35	ko	59.09	52.61
da	73.38	72.61	la	43.77	**44.62**
de	69.11	66.00	la_ittb	76.98	73.29
de_pud	66.53	63.65	la_proiel	57.54	54.53
el	79.26	78.43	lv	59.95	59.73
en	75.84	72.84	nl	68.90	66.14
en_lines	72.94	72.55	nl_lassysmall	78.15	72.99
en_partut	73.64	73.59	no_bokmaal	83.27	80.56
en_pud	78.95	76.42	no_nynorsk	81.56	79.16
es	81.47	78.73	pl	78.78	78.24
es_ancora	83.78	80.90	pt	82.11	36.40
es_pud	77.65	76.31	pt_br	85.36	82.58
et	58.79	**58.85**	pt_pud	73.96	35.76
eu	69.15	66.77	ro	79.88	76.68
fa	79.24	76.23	ru	74.03	73.56
fi	73.75	73.06	ru_pud	68.31	67.64
fi_ftb	74.03	72.60	ru_syntagrus	86.76	52.22
fi_pud	78.65	77.22	sk	72.75	**72.95**
fr	80.75	77.30	sl	81.15	79.29
fr_partut	77.38	**78.29**	sl_sst	46.45	46.09
fr_pud	73.63	72.03	sme	30.60	**31.77**
fr_sequoia	79.98	79.12	sv	76.73	75.32
ga	61.52	**62.20**	sv_lines	74.29	72.63
gl	77.31	74.02	sv_pud	70.62	69.43
gl_treegal	65.82	**66.12**	tr	53.19	50.69
got	59.81	57.62	tr_pud	34.53	33.55
grc	56.04	52.56	ug	34.18	**34.97**
grc_proiel	65.22	62.07	uk	60.76	**61.12**
he	57.23	55.79	ur	76.69	74.92
hi	86.77	85.56	vi	37.47	35.98
hi_pud	50.85	50.83	zh	57.40	55.85
hr	77.18	74.59			
			avg	68.35	65.24

Table 4: LAS results per treebank. We highlight the score where we can improve the results compared to the baseline system.

From Raw Text to Universal Dependencies – Look, No Tags!

Miryam de Lhoneux[*] **Yan Shao**[*] **Ali Basirat**[*] **Eliyahu Kiperwasser**[†]
Sara Stymne[*] **Yoav Goldberg**[†] **Joakim Nivre**[*]

[*]Department of Linguistics and Philology
Uppsala University
Uppsala, Sweden

[†]Computer Science Department
Bar-Ilan University
Ramat-Gan, Israel

Abstract

We present the Uppsala submission to the CoNLL 2017 shared task on parsing from raw text to universal dependencies. Our system is a simple pipeline consisting of two components. The first performs joint word and sentence segmentation on raw text; the second predicts dependency trees from raw words. The parser bypasses the need for part-of-speech tagging, but uses word embeddings based on universal tag distributions. We achieved a macro-averaged LAS F1 of 65.11 in the official test run and obtained the 2nd best result for sentence segmentation with a score of 89.03. After fixing two bugs, we obtained an unofficial LAS F1 of 70.49.

1 Introduction

The CoNLL 2017 shared task differs from most previous multilingual dependency parsing tasks not only by using cross-linguistically consistent syntactic representations from the UD project (Nivre et al., 2016), but also by requiring systems to start from raw text, as opposed to pre-segmented and (often) pre-annotated words and sentences. Since systems are only evaluated on their output dependency trees (and indirectly on the word and sentence segmentation implicit in these trees), developers are free to choose what additional linguistic features (if any) to predict as part of the parsing process.

The Uppsala team has adopted a minimalistic stance in this respect and developed a system that does not predict any linguistic structure over and above a segmentation into sentences and words and a dependency structure over the words of each sentence. In particular, the system makes no use of part-of-speech tags, morphological features, or lemmas, despite the fact that these annotations are available in the training and development data.

In this way, we go against a strong tradition in dependency parsing, which has generally favored pipeline systems with part-of-speech tagging as a crucial component, a tendency that has probably been reinforced by the widespread use of data sets with gold tags from the early CoNLL tasks (Buchholz and Marsi, 2006; Nivre et al., 2007). Even models that perform joint inference, like those of Hatori et al. (2012) and Bohnet et al. (2013), depend heavily on part-of-speech tags, so we were unlikely to reach top scores in the shared task without them. However, from a scientific perspective, we thought it would be interesting to explore how far we can get with a bare-bones system that does not predict redundant linguistic categories. In addition, we take inspiration from recent work showing that character-based representations can at least partly obviate the need for part-of-speech tags (Ballesteros et al., 2015).

The Uppsala system is a very simple pipeline consisting of two main components. The first is a model for joint sentence and word segmentation, which uses the BiRNN-CRF framework of Shao et al. (2017) to predict sentence and word boundaries in the raw input and simultaneously marks multiword tokens that need non-segmental analysis. The latter are handled by a simple dictionary lookup or by an encoder-decoder network. We use a single universal model regardless of writing system, but train separate models for each language. The segmentation component is described in more detail in Section 2.

The second main component of our system is a greedy transition-based parser that predicts the dependency tree given the raw words of a sentence. The starting point for this model is the transition-based parser described in Kiperwasser and Goldberg (2016b), which relies on a BiLSTM to learn

207

Proceedings of the CoNLL 2017 Shared Task: Multilingual Parsing from Raw Text to Universal Dependencies, pages 207–217,
Vancouver, Canada, August 3-4, 2017. © 2017 Association for Computational Linguistics

informative features of words in context and a feed-forward network for predicting the next parsing transition. The parser uses the arc-hybrid transition system (Kuhlmann et al., 2011) with greedy inference and a dynamic oracle for exploration during training (Goldberg and Nivre, 2013). For the shared task, the parser has been modified to use character-based representations instead of part-of-speech tags and to use pseudo-projective parsing to capture non-projective dependencies (Nivre and Nilsson, 2005). The parsing component is further described in Section 3.

Our original plans included training a single universal model on data from all languages, with cross-lingual word embeddings, but in the limited time available we could only start exploring two simple enhancements. First, we constructed word embeddings based on the RSV model (Basirat and Nivre, 2017), using universal part-of-speech tags as contexts (Section 4). Secondly, we used multilingual training data for languages with little or no training data (Section 5).

Our system was trained only on the training sets provided by the organizers (Nivre et al., 2017a). We did not make any use of large unlabeled data sets, parallel data sets, or word embeddings derived from such data. After evaluation on the official test sets (Nivre et al., 2017b), run on the TIRA server (Potthast et al., 2014), the Uppsala system ranked 23 of 33 systems with respect to the main evaluation metric, with a macro-average LAS F1 of 65.11. We obtained the 2nd highest score for sentence segmentation overall (89.03), and top scores for word segmentation on several languages (but with relatively high variance).

However, after the test phase was concluded, we discovered two bugs that had affected the results negatively. For comparison, we therefore also include post-evaluation results obtained after eliminating the bugs but without changing anything else, resulting in a macro-average LAS F1 of 70.49. Because of the nature of one of the bugs, the corrected results were obtained by running our system on a local server instead of the official TIRA server (see Section 6). We discuss our results in Section 6 and refer to the shared task overview paper (Zeman et al., 2017) for a thorough description of the task and an overview of the results.

2   Sentence and Word Segmentation

We model joint sentence and word segmentation as a character-level sequence labeling problem in a Bi-RNN-CRF model (Huang et al., 2015; Ma and Hovy, 2016). We simultaneously predict sentence boundaries and word boundaries and identify multi-word tokens that require further transduction.

In the BiRNN-CRF architecture, characters – regardless of writing system – are represented as dense vectors and fed into the bidirectional recurrent layers. We employ the gated recurrent unit (GRU) (Cho et al., 2014) as the basic recurrent cell. Dropout (Srivastava et al., 2014) is applied to the output of the recurrent layers, which are concatenated and passed further to the first order chain CRF layer. The CRF layer models conditional scores over all possible boundary tags given the features extracted by the BiRNN from the vector representations of the input characters. Incorporating the transition scores between the successive labels, the optimal sequence of labels that indicate different types of boundaries can be obtained efficiently via the Viterbi algorithm.

As illustrated in Figure 1, following Shao et al. (2017), we employ the boundary tags B, I, E, and S to indicate a character positioned at the beginning (B), inside (I), or at the end (E) of a word, or occurring as a single-character word (S). To this standard tag set, we add four corresponding tags (K, Z, J, D) to label corresponding positions in multi-word tokens, and a special tag X to mark characters, mostly spaces, that do not belong to words/tokens. Finally, we mark a character that occurs at the end of a sentence. T is employed if the character is a single-character word and U is used otherwise.

Multi-word tokens are transcribed without considering contextual information. For most languages, the number of unique multi-word tokens is rather limited and can be covered by dictionaries built from the training data. However, if there are more than 200 unique multi-word tokens contained in the training data, we employ an attention-based encoder-decoder (Bahdanau et al., 2014) equipped with shared long-short term memory (LSTM) (Hochreiter and Schmidhuber, 1997) as the basic recurrent cell. At test time, multi-word tokens are first queried in the dictionary. If not found, the segmented words are generated via the encoder-decoder as a sequence-to-sequence trans-

```
Characters:  ... La sede del condado es Ottawa. En ...
Tags:        ... BEXBIIEXKZJXBIIIIIEXBEXBIIIIETXBE ...
```

Figure 1: Tags employed for sentence and word segmentation. Note that the token `del` is a multiword token that should be transcribed to `de` and `el` and should therefore be tagged `KZJ` instead of `BIE`.

Character embedding size	50
GRU/LSTM state size	200
Optimizer	Adagrad
Initial learning rate (main)	0.1
Decay rate	0.05
Gradient Clipping	5.0
Initial learning rate (encoder-decoder)	0.3
Dropout rate	0.5
Batch size	10

Table 1: Hyper-parameters for segmentation.

duction.

Table 1 shows the hyper-parameters adopted for the main network as well as the encoder-decoder, which is trained separately from the main network. We use one set of parameters for all treebanks. The weights of the neural networks, including the embeddings, are initialized using the scheme introduced in Glorot and Bengio (2010). The network is trained using back-propagation, and all embeddings are fine-tuned during training by back-propagating gradients. Adagrad (Duchi et al., 2011) with mini-batches is employed for optimization. The initial learning rate η_0 is updated with a decay rate ρ as $\eta_t = \frac{\eta_0}{\rho(t-1)+1}$ when training the main network, where t is the index of the current epoch. We use early stopping (Yao et al., 2007) with respect to the performance of the model on the validation sets. For the encoder-decoder, 5% of the training data is randomly subtracted for validation. The score is calculated via how many outputs exactly match the references. For the main network, the F1-score is employed to measure the performance of the model after each epoch during training on the development set.

The general segmentation model is applied to all languages with small variations for Chinese and Vietnamese. For Chinese, the concatenated trigram model introduced in Shao et al. (2017) is employed. For Vietnamese, we first separate punctuation marks and then use space-delimited units as the basic elements for boundary prediction.

Bug in test results: After the official evaluation, we discovered a bug in the segmenter, which affected words and punctuation marks immediately before sentence boundaries. After fixing the bugs, both word segmentation and sentence segmentation results improved, as seen from our post-evaluation results included in Section 6.

3 Dependency Parsing

The transition-based parser from Kiperwasser and Goldberg (2016b) uses a configuration containing a buffer B, a stack Σ, and a set of arcs A. In the initial configuration, all words from the sentence plus a root node are in the buffer and the arc set is empty. A terminal configuration has a buffer with just the root and an empty stack, and the arc set then forms a tree spanning the input sentence. Parsing consists in performing a sequence of transitions from the initial configuration to the terminal one, using the arc-hybrid transition system, which allows three types of transitions, SHIFT, LEFT-ARC$_d$ and RIGHT-ARC$_d$, defined as in Figure 2.

The LEFT-ARC$_d$ transition removes the first item on top of the stack (i) and attaches it as a modifier to the first item of the buffer j with label d, adding the arc (j, d, i). The RIGHT-ARC$_d$ transition removes the first item on top of the stack (j) and attaches it as a modifier to the next item on the stack (i), adding the arc (i, d, j). The SHIFT transition moves the first item of the buffer i to the stack. To conform to the constraints of UD representations, we have added a new precondition to the LEFT-ARC$_d$ transition to ensure that the special root node has exactly one dependent. Thus, if the potential head i is the root node, LEFT-ARC$_d$ is only permissible if the stack contains exactly one element (in which case the transition will lead to a terminal configuration). This precondition is applied only at parsing time and not during training.

A configuration c is represented by a feature function $\phi(\cdot)$ over a subset of its elements and for each configuration, transitions are scored by a classifier. In this case, the classifier is a multi-layer perceptron (MLP) and $\phi(\cdot)$ is a concatenation of BiLSTM vectors on top of the stack and the be-

$$c_0(x = (w_1, \ldots, w_n)) = ([\,], [1, \ldots, n, 0], \emptyset)$$

Initialization: $c_0(x = (w_1, \ldots, w_n)) = ([\,], [1, \ldots, n, 0], \emptyset)$

Termination: $C_t = \{c \in C \mid c = ([\,], [0], A)\}$

Transition		**Condition**
LEFT-ARC$_d$	$(\sigma\|i, j\|\beta, A) \Rightarrow (\sigma, j\|\beta, A \cup \{(j, d, i)\})$	$j \neq 0 \lor \sigma = [\,]$
RIGHT-ARC$_d$	$(\sigma\|i\|j, \beta, A) \Rightarrow (\sigma\|i, \beta, A \cup \{(i, d, j)\})$	
SHIFT	$(\sigma, i\|\beta, A) \Rightarrow (\sigma\|i, \beta, A)$	$i \neq 0$

Figure 2: Transitions for the arc-hybrid transition system with an artificial root node (0) at the end of the sentence. The stack Σ is represented as a list with its head to the right (and tail σ) and the buffer B as a list with its head to the left (and tail β).

ginning of the buffer. The MLP scores transitions together with the arc labels for transitions that involve adding an arc (LEFT-ARC$_d$ and RIGHT-ARC$_d$). For more details, see Kiperwasser and Goldberg (2016b).

The main modification of the parser for the shared task concerns the construction of the BiLSTM vectors, where we remove the reliance on part-of-speech tags and instead add character-based representations. For an input sentence of length n with words $w_1, \ldots, w_n$, we create a sequence of vectors $x_{1:n}$, where the vector x_i representing w_i is the concatenation of a word embedding, a pretrained embedding, and a character vector. We construct a character vector $ch_e(w_i)$ for each w_i by running a BiLSTM over the characters ch_j ($1 \leq j \leq m$) of w_i:

$$ch_e(w_i) = \text{BiLSTM}(ch_{1:m})$$

As in the original parser, we also concatenate these vectors with pretrained word embeddings $pe(w_i)$. The input vectors x_i are therefore:

$$x_i = e(w_i) \circ pe(w_i) \circ ch_e(w_i)$$

Our pretrained word embeddings are further described in Section 4. A variant of word dropout is applied to the word embeddings, as described in Kiperwasser and Goldberg (2016a), and we apply dropout also to the character vectors.

Finally, each input element is represented by a BiLSTM vector, v_i:

$$v_i = \text{BiLSTM}(x_{1:n}, i)$$

For each configuration c, the feature extractor concatenates the BiLSTM representations of core elements from the stack and buffer. Both the embeddings and the BiLSTMs are trained together with the model. The model is represented in Figure 3.

Internal word embedding dimension	100
Pre-trained word embedding dimension	50
Character embedding dimension	12
Character BI-LSTM Dimensions	100
Hidden units in MLP	100
BI-LSTM Layers	2
BI-LSTM Dimensions (hidden/output)	200 / 200
α (for word dropout)	0.25
Character dropout	0.33
p_{agg} (for exploration training)	0.1

Table 2: Hyper-parameter values for parsing.

With the aim of training a multilingual parser, we additionally created a variant of the parser which adds a language embedding to input vectors in a spirit similar to what is done in Ammar et al. (2016). In this setting, the vector for each word x_i is the concatenation of a word embedding, a pretrained word embedding, a character vector, and a language embedding l_i with the language corresponding to the word. As was mentioned in the introduction, our experiments with this model was limited to the languages with little data. Those experiments are described in Section 5.

$$x_i = e(w_i) \circ pe(w_i) \circ ch_e(w_i) \circ e(l_i)$$

The final change we made to the parser was to use pseudo-projective parsing to deal with non-projective dependencies. Pseudo-projective parsing, as described in Nivre and Nilsson (2005), consists in a pre-processing and a post-processing step. The pre-processing step consists in projectivising the training data by reattaching some of the dependents and the post-processing step attempts to deprojectivise trees in output parsed data. In order for information about non-projectivity to be recoverable after parsing, when

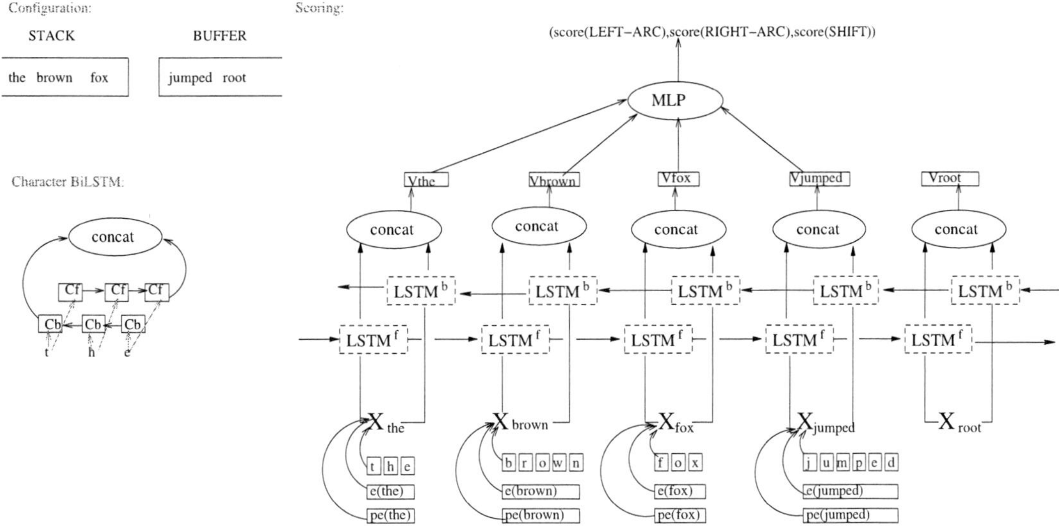

Figure 3: Illustration of the neural model scheme of the transition-based parser when calculating the scores of the possible transitions in a given configuration. The configuration (stack and buffer) is depicted in the top left corner. Each transition is scored using an MLP that is fed the vectors of the first word in the buffer and the three words at the top of the stack, and a transition is picked greedily. Each vector is a BiLSTM encoding of the word. Each x_i is a concatenation of a word vector, a character vector, and an additional external embedding vector for the word. Character vectors are obtained using a BiLSTM over the characters of the word. An example is given at the bottom left of the figure. The figure depicts a single-layer BiLSTM, while in practice we use two layers. When parsing a sentence, we iteratively compute scores for all possible transitions and apply the best scoring action until the final configuration is reached.

projectivising, arcs are renamed to encode information about the original parent of dependents which get re-attached. We used MaltParser (Nivre et al., 2006) for this. More specifically, we used the *head* schema, as described in Nivre and Nilsson (2005). This method increases the size of the dependency label set. In order to keep training efficient, we cap the number of dependency relations to the 200 most frequently occurring ones in the training set.

We did no hyper-parameter tuning for the parser component but instead mostly used the values that had been found to work well in Kiperwasser and Goldberg (2016b), except for the BiLSTM hidden layer which we increased as we had increased the dimensions of the output layer by using pseudo-projective parsing. The hyper-parameter values we used are in Table 2. We used the dynamic oracle as well as the extended feature set (the top 3 items on the stack together with their rightmost and leftmost modifiers as well as the first item on the buffer and its leftmost modifier). We trained the parsers for 30 epochs and picked the model that gave the best LAS score on the development sets for languages for which we had a development set, the last epoch otherwise.

The code is available at https://github.com/UppsalaNLP/uuparser.

Bug in test results: Our official test run suffered from a bug in the way serialization is handled in dynet. As reported in https://github.com/clab/dynet/issues/84, results may differ if the machine on which a model is used does not have the exact same version of boost as the machine on which the model was trained. Our post-evaluations results were obtained by using exactly the same models but parsing the test data on the machine on which they were trained.

4 Pre-Trained Word Embeddings

Our word embedding method is based on the RSV method introduced by Basirat and Nivre (2017). RSV extracts a set of word vectors in three main steps. First it builds a co-occurrence matrix for words that appear in certain contexts. Then, it normalizes the data distribution in the co-occurrence matrix by a power transformation. Finally, it builds a set of word vectors from the singular vectors of the transformed co-occurrence matrix.

We propose to restrict the contexts used in RSV to a set of universal features provided by the UD corpora. The universal features can be any combination of universal POS tags, dependency relations, and other universal tags associated with words. Given the set of universal features, each word is associated with a high-dimensional vector whose dimensions correspond to the universal features. The space formed by these vectors can be seen as a multi-lingual syntactic space which captures the universal syntactic properties provided by the UD corpora.

We define the set of universal features as $\{t_w, t_h, (t_w, d, t_h)\}$, where t_w and t_h are the universal POS tags of the word of interest and its parent in a dependency tree, and d is the dependency relation between them. It results in a set of *universal word vectors* with fairly large dimensions, $13\,794$. The values of the vector elements are set with the probability of seeing each universal feature given the word. These vectors are then centered around their mean and the final word vectors are built from the top k right singular vectors of the matrix formed by the high-dimensional universal word vectors:

$$\Upsilon = \lambda\sqrt{v}\mathbf{V}_{vk} \qquad (1)$$

where v is the size of vocabulary, $\mathbf{V}$ is the matrix of right singular vectors, λ is the scaling factor that controls the variance of the data.

The word vectors are extracted from the training part of the UD corpora for all words whose frequencies exceed 5, resulting in $204,024$ unique words. The number of dimensions, k, is set to 50 and the scaling parameter λ is set to 0.1 as suggested by Basirat and Nivre (2017). Adding these pre-trained word embeddings improved results on development sets by 0.44 points on average.

5 Multilingual Models

The shared task contained four surprise languages, Buryat, Kurmanji, North Sami, and Upper Sorbian, for which there was no data available until the last week, when we had a few sample sentences for each language. Two of the ordinary languages, Kazakh and Uyghur, had a similar situation, since they had less than 50 sentences in their training data. We therefore decided to treat those two languages like the surprise languages.

For segmentation, we utilized the small amount of available annotated data as development sets. We applied all the segmentation models trained on larger treebanks and adopted the one that achieved the highest F1-score as the segmentation model for the surprise language. We thus selected Bulgarian for Buryat, Slovenian for North Sami, Czech for Upper Sorbian, Turkish for Kurmanji, Russian for Kazakh as well as Persian for Uyghur.

For parsing, we trained our parser on a small set of languages. For each surprise language, we used the little data we had for that language, and in addition a set of other languages, which we will call support languages. In this setting we took advantage of the language embedding implemented in the parser. Since the treebanks for the support languages have very different sizes, we limited the number of sentences from each treebank used per epoch to 2263 for North Sami and 2500 for the other languages, in order ot use a more balanced sample. For each epoch we randomly picked a new sample of sentences for each treebank larger than this ceiling. We chose the support languages for each surprise language based on four criteria:

- Language relatedness, by including the languages that were most closely related to each surprise language.

- Script, by choosing at least one language sharing the same script as each surprise language, which might help our character embeddings.

- Geographical closeness to the surprise language, since geographically close languages often influence each other and can share many traits and have loan words.

- Performance of single models, by evaluating individual models for all other languages on each surprise language, and choosing support languages from the set of best performing languages.

We used a single multi-lingual model for Kazakh and Uyghur, since they are related. Table 3 shows the support languages used for each surprise language. Since we used all available surprise language data in the training, we could not use it also as development data, to pick the best epoch. We instead used the average LAS score on the development data for all support languages that had available development data. We did not use the pseudo-projective method for the surprise languages, and we did not use pre-trained word embeddings.

Surprise	Support languages
Buryat	Russian-SynTagRus[gps], Russian[gs], Japanese[pr], Kazakh[ps], Bulgarian[s]
Kurmanji	Turkish[gs], Persian[r], Finnish-FTB[ps], German[ps], Slovenian-SST[ps]
North Sami	Finnish[rs], Finnish-FTB[prs], Estonian[rs], Hungarian[prs], Norwegian-Nynorsk[gps]
Upper Sorbian	Czech[prs], Slovak[prs], Slovenian[prs], Polish[prs], German[gs]
Kazakh+Uyghur	Russian-SynTagRus[gps], Hungarian[p], Turkish[pr], Persian[s], Arabic[s]

Table 3: Support languages, and treebanks, used for each surprise language. Superscripts show reason for inclusion: r(elated), s(cript), g(eography), p(erformance).

6   Results and Discussion

Table 4 summarizes the results for the Uppsala system with respect to dependency accuracy (LAS F1) as well as sentence and word segmentation. For each metric, we report our official test score (Test), the corrected score after eliminating the two bugs described in Section 2 and Section 3 (Corr),[1] and the difference between the corrected score and the official UDPipe baseline (Straka et al., 2016) (positive if we beat the baseline and negative otherwise). To make the table somewhat more readable, we have also added a simple color coding. Post-evaluation scores that are significantly higher/lower than the baseline are marked with two shades of green/red, with brighter colors for larger differences. Thresholds have been set to 1 and 3 points for LAS, 0.5 and 1 points for Sentences, and 0.1 and 0.5 points for Words.

Looking first at the LAS scores, we see that our system improves over the baseline in most cases and by a comfortable margin. In addition, we think we can distinguish three clear patterns:

- Our post-evaluation results are substantially worse than the baseline (only) on the six low-resource languages. This indicates that our cross-lingual models perform poorly without the help of part-of-speech tags when there is little training data. It should, however, also be kept in mind that the baseline had a special advantage here as it was allowed to train segmenters and taggers using jack-knifing on the test sets.

- Our post-evaluation results are substantially better than the baseline on languages with writing systems that differ (more or less) from European style alphabetic scripts, including Arabic, Chinese, Hebrew, Japanese, Korean, and Vietnamese. For all languages except Korean, this can be partly (but not wholly) explained by more accurate word segmentation results.

- Our post-evaluation results are substantially better than the baseline for a number of morphologically rich languages, including Ancient Greek, Arabic, Basque, Czech, Finnish, German, Latin, Polish, Russian, and Slovenian. This shows that character-based representations are effective in capturing morphological regularities and compensate for the lack of explicit morphological features.

To further investigate the efficiency of our cross-lingual models, we ran them for two of the support languages with medium size training data that were not affected by the capping of data. Table 5 shows the results of this investigation. For Estonian the North Sami cross-lingual model that includes the closely related Finnish, was better than the monolingual model. For Hungarian, on the other hand, the monolingual model was better than both cross-lingual models. The model for North Sami, with related languages did perform better than the model for Kazakh+Uyghur with only unrelated languages, however. These results indicate that cross-lingual training without part-of-speech tags can help for a language with a medium sized treebank, but it seems that closely related support languages are needed, which was not the case for any of the surprise languages.

For word segmentation, we have already noted that our universal model works well on some of the most challenging languages, such as Chinese, Japanese and Vietnamese, and also on the Semitic languages Arabic and Hebrew. This is not surprising, given that the model was first developed for Chinese word segmentation, but it is interesting to

---

[1]Note that the overview paper mentions the second of these bugs (i.e. the dynet bug) and reports our results with only that bug fixed. Note also that, for practical reasons, all our post-evaluation results were obtained on the system where models had been trained, as mentioned in the introduction.

Language	LAS F1			Sentences			Words		
	Test	Corr	Diff	Test	Corr	Diff	Test	Corr	Diff
ar	65.96	68.68	3.38	77.32	78.21	-6.36	94.81	94.99	1.30
ar_pud	47.34	50.70	7.56	97.18	98.66	-1.34	94.32	95.30	4.48
bg	81.25	85.38	1.74	93.36	95.23	2.40	99.70	99.91	0.00
bxr	17.14	18.01	-13.49	86.93	87.37	-4.44	97.77	97.71	-1.64
ca	85.42	87.08	1.69	99.43	99.59	0.64	99.78	99.79	-0.18
cs	85.88	86.83	3.96	93.97	92.79	0.76	99.96	99.98	0.08
cs_cac	83.66	85.75	3.29	99.76	99.68	-0.32	99.97	99.99	0.00
cs_cltt	59.84	75.67	4.03	92.99	96.95	1.89	99.54	99.78	0.43
cs_pud	80.21	82.27	2.47	94.18	95.55	-0.88	98.42	99.25	-0.04
cu	57.88	67.04	4.28	39.71	43.72	7.67	99.73	99.94	-0.02
da	70.63	77.70	4.32	81.12	83.41	4.05	99.93	100.00	0.31
de	72.61	75.27	6.16	80.47	81.47	2.36	99.44	99.67	0.02
de_pud	68.04	70.90	4.37	87.16	86.83	0.34	96.42	96.43	-1.57
el	72.77	80.46	1.20	90.38	91.09	0.30	99.83	99.80	-0.08
en	75.88	79.62	3.78	76.91	80.26	7.04	98.38	99.05	0.38
en_lines	67.52	75.80	2.86	86.84	87.17	1.33	99.82	99.96	0.02
en_partut	63.55	76.11	2.47	98.20	98.10	0.59	99.55	99.54	0.05
en_pud	75.61	80.49	1.54	95.28	96.15	-0.98	99.45	99.59	-0.07
es	82.17	84.26	2.79	95.37	94.16	0.01	99.81	99.84	0.15
es_ancora	84.60	86.79	3.01	98.06	98.46	1.41	99.89	99.92	-0.03
es_pud	78.16	79.01	1.36	93.41	93.39	-0.03	99.39	99.34	-0.13
et	49.01	58.67	-0.12	92.74	93.23	8.03	99.69	99.90	0.13
eu	69.84	73.82	4.67	99.67	100.00	0.42	99.97	100.00	0.04
fa	76.13	81.89	2.65	98.75	99.50	1.50	99.32	99.61	-0.03
fi	74.59	78.41	4.66	90.88	91.48	6.92	99.62	99.71	0.08
fi_ftb	71.85	76.25	2.22	86.98	87.16	3.33	99.91	99.99	0.11
fi_pud	76.22	80.05	1.40	92.02	91.64	-2.03	99.39	99.59	-0.02
fr	80.36	83.66	2.91	93.85	94.32	0.73	99.50	99.53	0.66
fr_partut	69.17	80.84	3.46	99.13	99.50	1.50	99.01	99.50	0.55
fr_pud	73.51	75.25	1.62	93.52	91.33	-0.99	97.38	97.34	-0.83
fr_sequoia	74.96	82.85	2.87	81.89	84.95	1.20	99.31	99.48	0.42
ga	52.81	63.35	1.83	95.70	95.35	-0.46	99.62	99.78	0.49
gl	74.09	79.01	1.70	96.36	96.83	0.68	99.91	99.96	0.04
gl_treegal	56.79	65.85	0.03	82.71	83.79	2.16	98.42	98.23	-0.39
got	56.69	62.62	2.81	29.65	35.01	7.16	100.00	100.00	0.00
grc	50.94	58.83	2.79	98.70	98.93	0.50	96.78	99.98	0.03
grc_proiel	63.86	69.04	3.82	49.31	48.86	5.75	99.99	99.98	-0.02
he	63.72	67.75	10.52	99.29	99.69	0.30	91.18	91.19	6.37
hi	74.34	89.13	2.36	99.29	99.11	-0.09	92.74	99.99	-0.01
hi_pud	45.15	53.31	2.46	94.85	95.00	4.17	92.27	98.65	0.84
hr	75.43	79.51	2.33	97.75	97.25	0.33	99.90	99.91	-0.02
hsb	45.63	47.92	-5.91	91.65	89.88	-0.81	99.28	98.76	-1.08
hu	54.55	65.90	1.60	96.56	97.65	3.80	99.85	99.89	0.07
id	72.11	76.13	1.52	92.66	93.55	2.40	100.00	100.00	0.01
it	84.84	87.33	2.05	99.07	99.38	2.28	99.85	99.86	0.13
it_pud	83.28	85.59	1.89	93.39	93.90	-2.68	99.27	99.28	0.11
ja	65.71	81.54	9.33	94.92	94.92	0.00	84.26	93.59	3.91
ja_pud	71.80	83.26	6.98	97.31	97.31	2.42	86.34	94.30	3.24
kk	18.24	17.14	-7.37	87.52	86.26	4.88	96.56	96.46	1.55
kmr	19.37	20.39	-11.96	94.49	94.08	-2.94	97.15	97.06	-1.79
ko	69.87	74.72	15.63	92.39	93.01	-0.04	99.63	99.99	0.26
la	38.93	46.26	2.49	98.04	97.41	-0.68	100.00	100.00	0.01
la_ittb	80.04	82.34	5.36	94.34	92.93	-0.31	99.97	99.99	0.00
la_proiel	58.74	63.17	5.63	30.24	34.66	8.86	99.99	100.00	0.00
lv	52.36	59.75	-0.20	93.45	93.65	-4.94	99.20	99.13	0.22
nl	69.83	74.41	5.51	75.15	76.16	-0.98	99.73	99.85	-0.03
nl_lassysmall	77.56	83.58	5.43	85.33	87.00	8.38	99.85	99.97	0.04
no_bokmaal	83.22	86.04	2.77	96.44	96.20	0.44	99.84	99.87	0.12
no_nynorsk	81.12	84.41	2.85	94.56	93.67	2.44	99.93	99.92	0.07
pl	77.39	82.33	3.55	98.91	99.46	0.55	99.90	99.93	0.05
pt	80.97	83.25	1.14	90.33	90.43	0.64	99.37	99.45	-0.07
pt_br	86.15	88.19	2.83	96.51	97.04	0.20	99.80	99.87	0.03
pt_pud	72.43	74.48	0.52	93.58	94.50	-1.15	98.39	98.48	-0.94
ro	79.40	81.68	1.80	96.57	96.02	2.60	99.77	99.75	0.11
ru	71.65	77.99	3.96	97.16	96.91	0.49	99.83	99.90	-0.01
ru_pud	65.22	70.78	2.47	98.66	98.80	-0.15	97.31	97.34	0.16
ru_syntagrus	88.04	89.61	2.85	98.64	98.78	0.97	99.51	99.63	0.06
sk	69.35	75.98	3.23	85.32	87.17	3.64	99.97	99.96	-0.04
sl	80.14	84.16	3.01	98.67	98.11	-1.13	99.96	99.97	0.01
sl_sst	36.97	46.76	0.31	19.03	19.52	2.80	97.75	100.00	0.18
sme	11.70	11.72	-18.88	98.27	97.59	-1.20	98.44	96.75	-3.13
sv	73.45	79.86	3.13	97.26	95.96	-0.41	99.86	99.77	-0.07
sv_lines	69.42	76.37	2.08	87.89	88.12	1.68	99.86	99.99	0.01
sv_pud	62.40	69.52	-1.10	84.63	81.14	-9.06	98.56	98.47	0.21
tr	48.29	52.84	-0.35	96.29	96.44	-0.19	96.57	97.51	-0.38
tr_pud	29.79	32.84	-1.69	92.08	90.75	-3.16	96.82	96.93	0.31
ug	28.35	30.98	-3.20	68.76	69.36	5.81	97.82	98.74	0.22
uk	47.00	59.33	-1.43	90.04	92.18	-0.41	99.41	99.52	-0.29
ur	64.96	79.31	2.62	98.60	98.60	0.28	94.55	100.00	0.00
vi	37.99	42.68	5.21	87.30	89.49	-3.10	86.63	86.70	4.23
zh	60.47	65.25	7.85	98.20	98.80	0.61	93.81	93.43	4.52
Average	65.11	70.49	2.14	89.03	89.48	0.99	98.20	98.79	0.30

Table 4: Results for LAS F1, sentence and word segmentation. Test = official test score; Corr = corrected
score; Diff = difference Corr − Baseline.

Language	Models		
	sme	kk-ug	mono
Hungarian	62.67	61.64	65.91
Estonian	59.59	–	58.46

Table 5: LAS F1 scores comparing cross-lingual and monolingual models.

see that it generalizes well and gives competitive results also on European style alphabetic scripts, where it is mostly above or very close to the baseline. After fixing the bug mentioned in Section 2, our word segmentation results are only 0.02 below the best official result.

The sentence segmentation results are generally harder to interpret, with much greater variance and really low scores especially for some of the classical languages that lack modern punctuation. Nevertheless, we can conclude that performing sentence segmentation jointly with word segmentation is a viable approach, as our system achieved the second highest score of all systems on sentence segmentation in the official test results. After bug fixing, it is better than any of the official results.

All in all, we are pleased to see that a bare-bones model, which does not make use of part-of-speech tags, morphological features or lemmas, can give reasonable performance on a wide range of languages.

7 Conclusion

We have described the Uppsala submission to the CoNLL 2017 shared task on parsing from raw text to universal dependencies. The system consists of a segmenter, which extracts words and sentences from a raw text, and a parser, which builds a dependency tree over the words of each sentence, without relying on part-of-speech tags or any other explicit morphological analysis. Our post-evaluation results (after correcting two bugs) are on average 2.14 points above the baseline, despite very poor performance on surprise languages, and the system has competitive results especially on languages with rich morphology and/or non-European writing systems. Given the simplicity of our system, we find the results very encouraging.

There are many different lines of future research that we want to pursue. First of all, we want to explore the use of multilingual models with language embeddings, trained on much larger data sets than was practically possible for the shared task. In this context, we also want to investigate the effectiveness of our multilingual word embeddings based on universal part-of-speech tags, deriving them from large parsed corpora instead of the small training sets that were used for the shared task. Finally, we want to extend the parser so that it can jointly predict part-of-speech tags and (selected) morphological features. This will allow us to systematically study the effect of using explicit linguistic categories, as opposed to just relying on inference from raw words and characters. For segmentation, we want to investigate how our model deals with multiword tokens across languages.

Acknowledgments

We are grateful to the shared task organizers and to Dan Zeman in particular, and we acknowledge the computational resources provided by CSC in Helsinki and Sigma2 in Oslo through NeIC-NLPL (www.nlpl.eu). Our parser will be made available in the NLPL dependency parsing laboratory.

References

Waleed Ammar, George Mulcaire, Miguel Ballesteros, Chris Dyer, and Noah Smith. 2016. Many languages, one parser. *Transactions of the Association for Computational Linguistics* 4:431–444.

Dzmitry Bahdanau, Kyunghyun Cho, and Yoshua Bengio. 2014. Neural machine translation by jointly learning to align and translate. *arXiv preprint arXiv:1409.0473* .

Miguel Ballesteros, Chris Dyer, and Noah A. Smith. 2015. Improved transition-based parsing by modeling characters instead of words with LSTMs. In *Proceedings of the Conference on Empirical Methods in Natural Language Processing (EMNLP)*. pages 349–359.

Ali Basirat and Joakim Nivre. 2017. Real-valued syntactic word vectors (RSV) for greedy neural dependency parsing. In *Proceedings of the 21st Nordic Conference on Computational Linguistics (NoDaLiDa)*. pages 21–28.

Bernd Bohnet, Joakim Nivre, Igor Boguslavsky, Richárd Farkas, Filip Ginter, and Jan Hajič. 2013. Joint morphological and syntactic analysis for richly inflected languages. *Transactions of the Association for Computational Linguistics* 1:415–428.

Sabine Buchholz and Erwin Marsi. 2006. CoNLL-X shared task on multilingual dependency parsing. In *Proceedings of the 10th Conference on Computational Natural Language Learning (CoNLL)*. pages 149–164.

Kyunghyun Cho, Bart Van Merriënboer, Dzmitry Bahdanau, and Yoshua Bengio. 2014. On the properties of neural machine translation: Encoder-decoder approaches. *arXiv preprint arXiv:1409.1259* .

John Duchi, Elad Hazan, and Yoram Singer. 2011. Adaptive subgradient methods for online learning and stochastic optimization. *Journal of Machine Learning Research* 12(Jul):2121–2159.

Xavier Glorot and Yoshua Bengio. 2010. Understanding the difficulty of training deep feedforward neural networks. In *Aistats*. pages 249–256.

Yoav Goldberg and Joakim Nivre. 2013. Training deterministic parsers with non-deterministic oracles. *Transactions of the Association for Computational Linguistics* 1:403–414.

Jun Hatori, Takuya Matsuzaki, Yusuke Miyao, and Jun'ichi Tsujii. 2012. Incremental joint approach to word segmentation, POS tagging, and dependency parsing in Chinese. In *Proceedings of the 50th Annual Meeting of the Association for Computational Linguistics (ACL)*. pages 1045–1053.

Sepp Hochreiter and Jürgen Schmidhuber. 1997. Long short-term memory. *Neural computation* 9(8):1735–1780.

Zhiheng Huang, Wei Xu, and Kai Yu. 2015. Bidirectional lstm-crf models for sequence tagging. *arXiv preprint arXiv:1508.01991* .

Eliyahu Kiperwasser and Yoav Goldberg. 2016a. Easy-first dependency parsing with hierarchical tree LSTMs. *Transactions of the Association for Computational Linguistics* 4:445–461.

Eliyahu Kiperwasser and Yoav Goldberg. 2016b. Simple and accurate dependency parsing using bidirectional LSTM feature representations. *Transactions of the Association for Computational Linguistics* 4:313–327.

Marco Kuhlmann, Carlos Gómez-Rodríguez, and Giorgio Satta. 2011. Dynamic programming algorithms for transition-based dependency parsers. In *Proceedings of the 49th Annual Meeting of the Association for Computational Linguistics (ACL)*. pages 673–682.

Xuezhe Ma and Eduard Hovy. 2016. End-to-end sequence labeling via bi-directional LSTM-CNNs-CRF. In *Proceedings of the 54th Annual Meeting of the Association for Computational Linguistics*. pages 1064–1074.

Joakim Nivre, Željko Agić, Lars Ahrenberg, et al. 2017a. Universal Dependencies 2.0. LINDAT/CLARIN digital library at the Institute of Formal and Applied Linguistics, Charles University, Prague. http://hdl.handle.net/11234/1-1983.

Joakim Nivre, Željko Agić, Lars Ahrenberg, et al. 2017b. Universal dependencies 2.0 CoNLL 2017 shared task development and test data. LINDAT/CLARIN digital library at the Institute of Formal and Applied Linguistics, Charles University. http://hdl.handle.net/11234/1-2184.

Joakim Nivre, Marie-Catherine de Marneffe, Filip Ginter, Yoav Goldberg, Jan Hajič, Christopher Manning, Ryan McDonald, Slav Petrov, Sampo Pyysalo, Natalia Silveira, Reut Tsarfaty, and Daniel Zeman. 2016. Universal Dependencies v1: A multilingual treebank collection. In *Proceedings of the 10th International Conference on Language Resources and Evaluation (LREC 2016)*. European Language Resources Association, Portorož, Slovenia, pages 1659–1666.

Joakim Nivre, Johan Hall, Sandra Kübler, Ryan McDonald, Jens Nilsson, Sebastian Riedel, and Deniz Yuret. 2007. The CoNLL 2007 shared task on dependency parsing. In *Proceedings of the CoNLL Shared Task of EMNLP-CoNLL 2007*. pages 915–932.

Joakim Nivre, Johan Hall, and Jens Nilsson. 2006. Maltparser: A data-driven parser-generator for dependency parsing. In *Proceedings of the 5th International Conference on Language Resources and Evaluation (LREC)*. pages 2216–2219.

Joakim Nivre and Jens Nilsson. 2005. Pseudo-projective dependency parsing. In *Proceedings of the 43rd Annual Meeting of the Association for Computational Linguistics (ACL)*. pages 99–106.

Martin Potthast, Tim Gollub, Francisco Rangel, Paolo Rosso, Efstathios Stamatatos, and Benno Stein. 2014. Improving the reproducibility of PAN's shared tasks: Plagiarism detection, author identification, and author profiling. In Evangelos Kanoulas, Mihai Lupu, Paul Clough, Mark Sanderson, Mark Hall, Allan Hanbury, and Elaine Toms, editors, *Information Access Evaluation meets Multilinguality, Multimodality, and Visualization. 5th International Conference of the CLEF Initiative (CLEF 14)*. Springer, Berlin Heidelberg New York, pages 268–299.

Yan Shao, Christian Hardmeier, Jörg Tiedemann, and Joakim Nivre. 2017. Character-based joint segmentation and POS tagging for Chinese using bidirectional RNN-CRF. ArXiv e-prints: 1704.01314 (cs.CL).

Nitish Srivastava, Geoffrey E Hinton, Alex Krizhevsky, Ilya Sutskever, and Ruslan Salakhutdinov. 2014. Dropout: a simple way to prevent neural networks from overfitting. *Journal of Machine Learning Research* 15(1):1929–1958.

Milan Straka, Jan Hajič, and Jana Straková. 2016. UDPipe: trainable pipeline for processing CoNLL-U files performing tokenization, morphological analysis, POS tagging and parsing. In *Proceedings of the 10th International Conference on Language Resources and Evaluation (LREC 2016)*. European Language Resources Association, Portorož, Slovenia.

Yuan Yao, Lorenzo Rosasco, and Andrea Caponnetto. 2007. On early stopping in gradient descent learning. *Constructive Approximation* 26(2):289–315.

Daniel Zeman, Martin Popel, Milan Straka, Jan Hajič, Joakim Nivre, Filip Ginter, Juhani Luotolahti, Sampo Pyysalo, Slav Petrov, Martin Potthast, Francis Tyers, Elena Badmaeva, Memduh Gökırmak, Anna Nedoluzhko, Silvie Cinková, Jan Hajič jr., Jaroslava Hlaváčová, Václava Kettnerová, Zdeňka Urešová, Jenna Kanerva, Stina Ojala, Anna Missilä, Christopher Manning, Sebastian Schuster, Siva Reddy, Dima Taji, Nizar Habash, Herman Leung, Marie-Catherine de Marneffe, Manuela Sanguinetti, Maria Simi, Hiroshi Kanayama, Valeria de Paiva, Kira Droganova, Hěctor Martínez Alonso, Hans Uszkoreit, Vivien Macketanz, Aljoscha Burchardt, Kim Harris, Katrin Marheinecke, Georg Rehm, Tolga Kayadelen, Mohammed Attia, Ali Elkahky, Zhuoran Yu, Emily Pitler, Saran Lertpradit, Michael Mandl, Jesse Kirchner, Hector Fernandez Alcalde, Jana Strnadova, Esha Banerjee, Ruli Manurung, Antonio Stella, Atsuko Shimada, Sookyoung Kwak, Gustavo Mendonça, Tatiana Lando, Rattima Nitisaroj, and Josie Li. 2017. CoNLL 2017 Shared Task: Multilingual Parsing from Raw Text to Universal Dependencies. In *Proceedings of the CoNLL 2017 Shared Task: Multilingual Parsing from Raw Text to Universal Dependencies*. Association for Computational Linguistics.

Initial Explorations of CCG Supertagging for Universal Dependency Parsing

Burak Kerim Akkus, Heval Azizoglu and Ruket Cakici

Computer Engineering Department

Middle East Technical University

Ankara, Turkey

{burakkerim,heval.azizoglu,ruken}@ceng.metu.edu.tr

Abstract

In this paper we describe the system by METU team for universal dependency parsing of multilingual text. We use a neural network-based dependency parser that has a greedy transition approach to dependency parsing. CCG supertags contain rich structural information that proves useful in certain NLP tasks. We experiment with CCG supertags as additional features in our experiments. The neural network parser is trained together with dependencies and simplified CCG tags as well as other features provided.

1 Introduction

Combinatory Categorial Grammar (Steedman, 2000) (CCG) is widely used for natural language processing for its desirable properties of generative expressiveness and its transparent interface of syntax and underlying semantic interpretation. CCG has been used for creating fast and accurate parsers (Hockenmaier and Steedman, 2002), (Clark and Curran, 2007), (Auli and Lopez, 2011), (Lewis and Steedman, 2014). In addition to this, the structural information in the CCG categories, which is a lexicalised grammar, has been shown to improve performance of various other systems when used indirectly. Examples are multilingual dependency parsing and machine translation (Ambati et al., 2013a; Çakıcı, 2008; Birch et al., 2007).

In this paper, we describe a system we created for CoNLL Shared Task of 2017 (Zeman et al., 2017) Multilingual Parsing from Raw Text to Universal Dependencies (Nivre et al., 2016, 2017b) [1]. We use CCG categories induced from the CCGBank (Hockenmaier and Steedman, 2007) to

supertag different languages with these structural information-packed tags. We aim to show that CCG categories for English may be used to improve parsing results for other languages, especially similar ones.

In the next section, we give a brief background on the dependency parsing problem and CCG categories that have been shown to improve performance on various tasks either directly or indirectly. Section 3 gives the implementation details for the METU system and in Section 4 results are discussed.

2 Background

Combinatory Categorial Grammar is a lexicalised grammar formalism that has a transparent syntax-semantics interface which means one can create rich semantic interpretations in parallel with parsing (Steedman, 2000). Several fast and highly accurate CCG parsers have been introduced in the literature. These parsers make use of the CCG-Bank (Hockenmaier and Steedman, 2002) that is created by inducing a CCG Grammar from the Penn Treebank (Marcus et al., 1993). The CCG categories of each word are extracted and referred to as supertags or CCG tags throughout the paper.

Different types of supertags such as the ones encoding predicate argument structure or morphosyntactic information have been shown to increase parsing performance in several studies starting with Bangalore and Joshi (1999). The importance of supertagging in parsing accuracy has been shown in various studies such as Falenska et al. (2015), Ouchi et al. (2014) and Foth et al. (2006) for different types of supertags such as combinations of dependency labels and dependent positions, and by Clark and Curran (2004) for CCG categories as supertags. The use of induced CCG grammar was also evaluated as an extrinsic

---

[1] Results are announced at `http://universaldependencies.org/conll17/results.html`

218

Proceedings of the CoNLL 2017 Shared Task: Multilingual Parsing from Raw Text to Universal Dependencies, pages 218–227,
Vancouver, Canada, August 3-4, 2017. © 2017 Association for Computational Linguistics

model in Bisk et al. (2016). They show that although using full CCG derivation trees is superior, CCG lexicon-based grammars also increase performance in a semantics task.

CCG categories have been successfully used in parsing studies as external features and were shown to increase the performance. Note that this use of CCG categories does not allow us to fully access the power of CCG formalism but rather provides a way to use the rich structural information as a means of supertags. Çakıcı (2008) first uses automatically-induced CCG categories from the Turkish treebank as extended (fine) tags (Buchholz and Marsi, 2006) in Mac-Donald's parser (McDonald et al., 2005). Then they were used for Hindi dependency parsing by Ambati et al. (2013a). Birch et al. (2007) and Nadejde et al. (2017) showed that statistical machine translation benefits from using structurally rich CCG categories (supertags/tags) in the source or target language.

Chen and Manning (2014) proposed a neural network classifier for use in a greedy, transition-based dependency parser. They created a three layer network in which the input layer is fed with word, POS tag and label embeddings, and after the feed forward step, the error is back-propagated to the input layer in order to tune embeddings. They randomly initialized the POS tag and label embeddings, however, as pre-trained word vectors, they used a combination of the embeddings in Collobert et al. (2011) and their trained 50 dimensional word2vec vectors. As this parser only learns and uses dense features with word representations, its parsing speed is at least two times faster than its closest opponent while also improving the accuracy by 2% for English and Chinese. Andor et al. (2016) also created a transition-based dependency parser based on neural networks and word embeddings after the Chen and Manning (2014) work. They proposed to use global instead of local model normalizations to overcome label bias problem with feed forward neural networks. Their parser achieved higher accuracies than former studies in English, Chinese and some other languages as stated in their results.

Dozat and Manning (2016) created a neural network oriented graph based dependency parser. They used bi-affine classifiers to predict arcs and labels. They achieved state-of-the-art or competent accuracies on graph-based parsing for six languages. They improved LAS and UAS score by 1% from previous most accurate graph based parser.

Transition-based dependency parser created by (Kuncoro et al., 2016) is performing as current state-of-the-art with using recurrent neural network grammars. They also outperform most performing graph based parser with increasing attachment scores by almost 2% for English.

3 Method

Gold-standard CCG categories do not exist for languages except a few ones. In order to explore the effects of CCG supertagging on multilingual universal dependencies we assign simplified CCG-based supertags to the multilingual data by using dependency relations from English CCGbank (Hockenmaier and Steedman, 2007). We label training and development data sets for different languages using a tagger trained on English supertagged data and then we use the supertagged training and development data sets for each language in training CCG-based supertaggers and dependency parsers for test data sets in UD treebanks.

Figure 1 shows the overall system that we use for the multilingual universal dependency parsing task (Zeman et al., 2017). We train separate models for dependency parsing for each language.

Section 3.1 explains how we transfer CCG-based supertags to UD training and development data sets, Section 3.2 explains how we train a sequence tagger for assigning supertags to test data and finally Section 3.3 explains how the dependency parser is trained using these supertags.

3.1 Assigning CCG Categories Using Dependency Relations

Dependency relations and predicate-argument structures encoded in CCG categories are parallel most of the time, even though the parent-child directions are different in many cases. Figure 2 shows a sentence from PTB (and CCGbank) with dependency relations above the sentence and predicate-argument relations below the sentence. Many of the edges are symmetric in dependency relations and predicate-argument structure derived from the lexical categories. Figure 3 shows an enlarged view of a part of the sentence in Figure 2 in order to make the labels clearer.

In order to supertag the data, first, the CCGbank

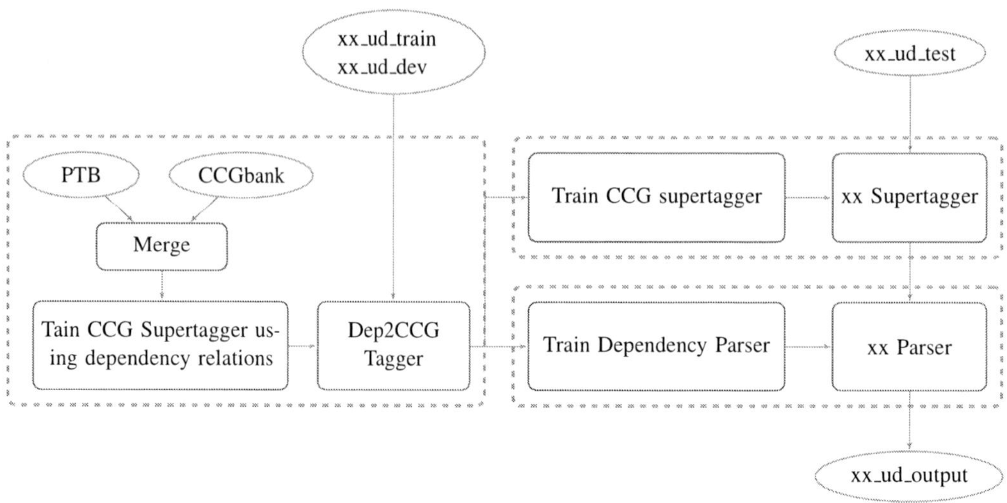

Figure 1: System overview

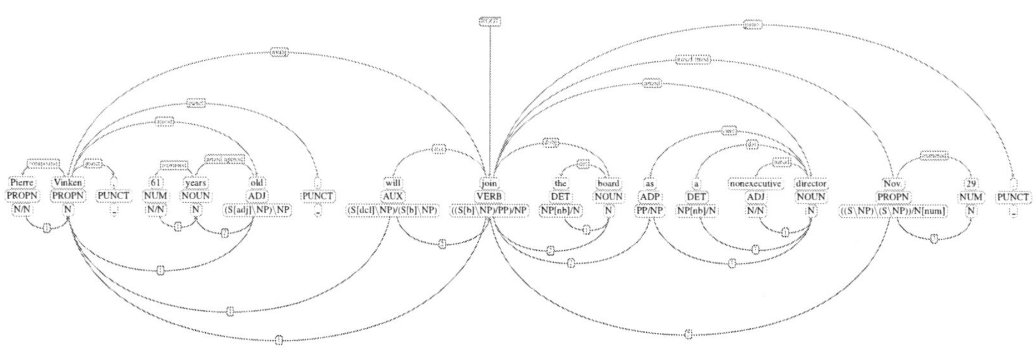

Figure 2: Example: wsj_0001.1

(Hockenmaier and Steedman, 2007) and the Penn Treebank (Marcus et al., 1993) are merged by converting PTB to CONLLU format using Stanford CoreNLP tool (Manning et al., 2014). We then aligned the tokens in both data sets so that CCG categories from CCGbank can be transfered to the MISC field in the CONLLU data.

CCG category	$(S[dcl]\backslash NP)/(S[b]\backslash NP)$
Without subcategories	$(S\backslash NP)/(S\backslash NP)$
Without directions	(S-NP)-(S-NP)

Table 1: Category simplification for supertags

A logistic regression classifier is trained to label the tokens in training and development sets using Scikit-Learn (Pedregosa et al., 2011). The classifier only uses universal part-of-speech tags and de-

	CCG category	Simplified category
en	$(S\backslash NP)\backslash(S\backslash NP)$	(S-NP)-(S-NP)
tr	$(S\backslash NP[nom])/(S\backslash NP[nom])$	(S-NP)-(S-NP)

Table 2: Two adverb categories that take a verb as their arguments in Turkish and English

pendency relations as its features since other features are not common among languages. We use an overly simplified version of CCG categories by removing directional information and features from the CCG supertags. This over-generalization results in decreasing the supertagging accuracy, however, it is necessary so that the English dependency directional information is not imposed on other languages with different word orders. Table 1 shows the simplification of a CCG category

220

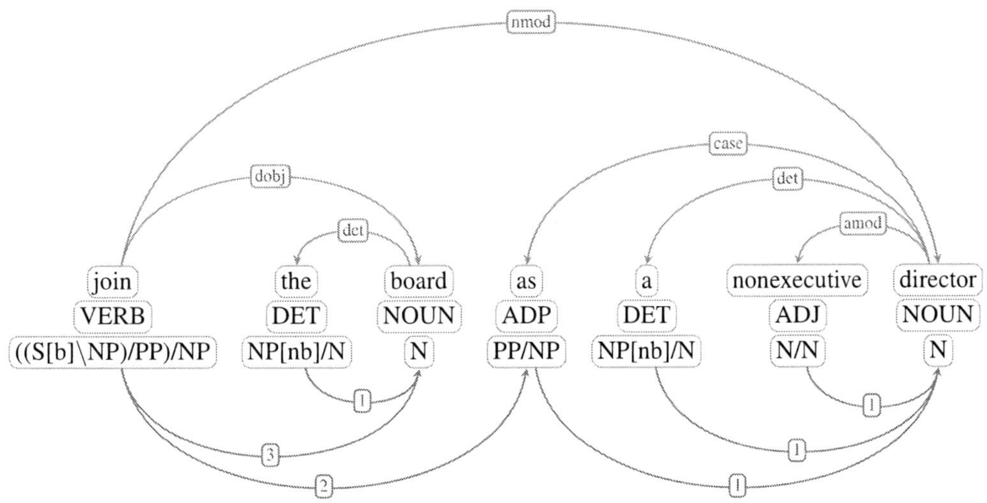

Figure 3: Example: A part of wsj_0001.1

to create a supertag. In Table 2, two adverbs are shown with different CCG categories in two languages. Note that the directions of the slashes in the original forms are different due to different word-order in these languages..

We use dependency relation labels between the word, its head, the head of the head, its dependents and the dependents of its head as features in the tagger. We also use universal part of speech tags for each one of the mentioned words. In English, the only language for which we have the gold standard CCG tags and dependency relations aligned, the re-tagging accuracy is 91.78%. If we additionally use extended part-of-speech tags and CCG argument positions as labels relative to (before or after) the current word, the accuracy increases to 93.55% on English for CCG categories with directional information. However, these are not universal in all languages, so we drop these features. Table 3 shows the features that are extracted for a sample word.

We run this tagger, trained on English CCG data, on every language to generate training and development files with CCG-based supertags for training supetaggers and dependency parsers that will work on test data.

3.2 CCG Sequence Tagging for Training

A supertagger for each language is built using CCG-based supertags transferred with dependency relations. This tagger is a CRF model (Lafferty et al., 2001) built using CRFSuite (Okazaki, 2007). The features are word, part-of-speech tags, key-value pairs in FEATS columns, prefixes and suffixes up to 5 characters, previous and following words and POS tags in a 2-token window. The CRF supertagger on CCGbank with these features (trained only on sections 02-05, tested on section 00) has an accuracy of 93.74%. Lewis and Steedman (2014) give 91.3%, Curran et al. (2007) give 92.6% accuracy with their maximum entropy tagger.

Table 4 show features extracted for the word "çalışacak" in sentence "İnşaatta çalışacak vasıfsız işçilerin ..."

KEY	VALUE	KEY	VALUE
idx	16	pos	NOUN
head_pos	VERB	head_rel	dobj
h_head_pos	VERB	h_head_rel	dobj-ccomp
dep_count	4	h_dep_count	3
dep_1_pos	DET	dep_1_rel	det
dep_2_pos	ADJ	dep_2_rel	amod
dep_3_pos	NOUN	dep_3_rel	nmod
dep_4_pos	NOUN	dep_4_rel	nmod
h_dep_1_pos	NOUN	h_dep_1_rel	nsubj
h_dep_2_pos	AUX	h_dep_2_rel	aux
h_dep_3_pos	NOUN	h_dep_3_rel	dobj

Table 3: Features used in the tagger

KEY	VALUE	KEY	VALUE
Aspect	Perf	Mood	Ind
Polarity	Pos	Tense	Fut
VerbForm	Part	hyp	False
num	False	pnc	False
upp	False	prefix_1	ç
prefix_2	ça	prefix_3	çal
prefix_4	çalı	prefix_5	çalış
suffix_1	k	suffix_2	ak
suffix_3	cak	suffix_4	acak
w	çalışacak	w+1	vasıfsız
w+2	işçilerin	w-1	İnşaatta
w-2	word-1	p	VERB
p+1	ADJ	p+2	NOUN
p-1	NOUN	p-2	POS-1
x	Verb	x+1	Adj
x+2	Noun	x-1	Noun
x-2	XPOS-1		

Table 4: Features used in the tagger

The tagger tries to recover the supertags that are assigned using the dependency relations. On English, the recovery accuracy is 87.36%. Table 5 shows the accuracy of the supertagger on several languages. Note that these are not based on the correct CCG categories but on the assigned supertags via the tagger explained on Section 3.1. This tagger is used on test data preprocessed by UDpipe (Straka et al., 2016) with POSTAGS and FEATS. Then the tagged test data is passed to the dependency parser.

Language	CCG Accuracy
ar	83.47
el	88.90
en	87.36
es	89.70
de	86.45
fr	91.41
he	86.55
tr	77.97
zh	83.83

Table 5: CCG tagger accuracy on several languages

3.3 Dependency Parsing

Two different dependency parsers are experimented with in this study which are powered by two different techniques. First, CCG-based supertags are integrated into the maximum-spanning tree parser ()MSTParser) (McDonald et al., 2005; McDonald, 2006) which is known as the first high-performing graph-based dependency parser. This parser uses discrete local features as input, and thus, the supertags are directly added to this set of features. This implementation shows us the effect of supertagging in a system where the similarities between the supertag groups are not captured semantically. The following parameters are used in all experiments unless otherwise stated:

$order = 2,$

$loss\ type = no\ punctuation,$

$decode\ type = projective.$

We use the Chen and Manning (2014) neural network-based dependency parser to observe how similarities in our supertags affect the model. This parser has been chosen as a baseline as it is the pioneer in using word embeddings for all the features in parsing process. Furthermore, it was given as the parser in the baseline system in Straka et al. (2016) that we compare our results with. In our parser CCG tags are represented with 100 dimensional vectors instead of discrete features. The supertags are obtained from the CCG-based supertagger described in the previous section. In experiments, the following parameters are used: $embedding\ size = 100$ and $hidden\ layer\ size = 200$. For word embeddings, pre-trained 100 dimensional word embeddings by Ginter et al. (2017) are used. For POS tags and supertags, vectors are initialized randomly and are fed to the neural network during training.

4 Results

First, we present our experiments before the release of the test data, then we present the results on the shared task.

4.1 Pre-evaluation

In MSTParser pre-evaluation experiments, we use the Penn Treebank Wall Street Journal segmentation split as sections 2-21 for training and section 23 as the test set. Extra training parameters are as the following:

$training - k = 5$

$loss - type = nopunc$

$decode - type = proj$

$order = 2$

unless stated otherwise in the results. Detailed

descriptions of these parameters can be found in McDonald et al. (2006). These parameters reproduce similar results as McDonald and Pereira (2006) which we use as a baseline to compare our improvements. The version in which the CCG supertags were added also uses the same configuration. Table 6 shows labelled and unlabelled accuracies in detail in these experiments. Accuracy results are obtained from the evaluator built in MSTParser itself. Training and testing times were similar throughout different experiments explained here.

Parser Configuration	UAS	LAS
MSTParser (1st order)	90.7	87.6
MSTParser (2nd order)	91.4	88.3
- xpos (2nd order)	91.1	88.0
- xpos + CCG tags (2nd order)	94.3	90.5
+ CCG tags (2nd order)	94.5	90.8

Table 6: Accuracy on MSTParser with CCG supertags in English (pre-evaluation)

In the pre-evaluation Chen and Manning (2014)'s parser experiment, we also use the Penn Treebank for English as sections 2-21 for training, section 22 as development and section 23 as the test set. For word embedding file, GloVe 50 dimensional data is used (Pennington et al., 2014). Extra configurational parameters are:

$-maxIter : 20000$
$-trainingThreads : 10$
$-embeddingSize : 50$

where $maxIter$ stands for maximum iteration step in neural network training, $trainingThreads$ for number of threads to use during training and $embeddingSize$ for embedding vector size for words, POS tags and supertags.

Reproduction of the results from the original study and our results with our supertags are given in Table 7. These results are obtained by the evaluation method of the original parser.

Also, in the pre-evaluation phase, we test our Chen and Manning (2014) parser-based system on Turkish, German and French data. Shared task-provided data is used for training and development purposes. Word embeddings are used as 100 dimensional vectors from Ginter et al. (2017). Except this difference, all other configuration param-

Parser Configuration	UAS	LAS
Chen & Manning	91.3	89.8
Chen & Manning + CCG supertags	95.7	94.6

Table 7: Accuracy on (Chen and Manning, 2014) parser with CCG tags in English (pre-evaluation)

eters are the same as in English experiments. Table 8 shows the results. As we see in the results, the tagger predicting the French supertags transferred from English data performs well since the two languages are similar. Also, German tags are inferrable as it is also close to English in grammatical structure. On the other hand, this is not relevant for Turkish, as grammatically, the two languages are quite different. Word order is one of the major differences between these two languages that might have affected the results.

Language	pre-UAS	pre-LAS	post-UAS	post-LAS
Turkish	74.0	61.1	65.8	54.9
German	90.3	80.7	85.4	76.9
French	90.7	75.0	88.1	73.5

Table 8: Accuracy on the Chen and Manning (2014) parser with CCG-based supertags in other languages (pre-evaluation). pre-UAS and pre-LAS stands for accuracies obtained with Chen & Manning, while post-UAS and post-LAS with Chen & Manning + Supertags.

Language	Shared Task Baseline	Our Result
English	82.25	73.40
Spanish	76.76	77.54
Turkish	52.06	48.53
German	71.53	67.97
French	74.57	77.48

Table 9: Our CONLL 2017 Shared task results vs Shared Task baselines (LAS F1 Score)

4.2 Shared Task

In Table 9, we give our shared task results with baselines. Here, we see a drop in accuracy compared to our pre-evaluation phase. The main differences between the systems are pre-trained embedding source and embedding sizes for words, POS tags and labels. In our development experiments, we believe, we are able to capture similarities between POS tags and supertags more efficiently as the embedding size is smaller and the cardinalities of these groups are quite low. This also applies to word embeddings. Other than this, the training iteration count remains the same during experiments. This may be required as we increase the number of features and it needs to be tuned.

For each of the PUD treebanks, we select a model trained on the same language. For some of the languages for which we cannot train a parser, either due to lack of training data or word vectors, and also for the surprise languages, we selected a similar language in the same language family. Table 10 shows the model assignments for the unknown languages.

Language	Selected	Language	Selected
bxr	ru	kmr	fa
sme	fi	hsb	cs
ar_pud	ar	cs_pud	cs
de_pud	de	en_pud	en
es_pud	es	fi_pud	fi
fr_partut	fr	fr_pud	fr
ga	en	gl_treegal	gl
got	de	hi_pud	hi
it_pud	it	ja_pud	ja
kk	tr	la	la_ittb
pt_pud	pt	ru_pud	ru
sl_sst	sl	sv_pud	sv
tr_pud	tr	ug	tr
uk	ru		

Table 10: Selected models for surprise languages and ones without models on training data

Table 11 shows the LAS score of the system on different categories of treebanks as reported in the Shared task paper. All treebanks are shown with the official macro-averaged LAS F1 score. As expected, the system performs better on big treebanks where there are more data instances. PUD treebanks have a big treebank in the same language, therefore the results are close. The difference between our system and the best performing ones is bigger for the small treebanks. The reason for this is that we only train on the language dataset itself and do not use data from other languages for the small treebanks. This causes sparsity issues with the supertagger and the parser. We

try to use model trained on a similar language for the surprise languages, however this does not result in a reasonable accuracy since the lexicons are usually very different even if the languages are from the same family and the supertagging relies mostly on the lexical entries and features extracted from them since we do not have the dependency information while decoding. POS tagging error that propagates through the pipeline also affects the performance.

Language Set	LAS F1 Score
All treebanks	61.98
Big treebanks only	68.77
PUD treebanks only	65.30
Small treebanks only	30.84
Surprise languages only	19.39

Table 11: Test results of different categories

Table 12 shows the results of our system on TIRA (Potthast et al., 2014) evaluations of UD test data for each language (Nivre et al., 2017a).

5 Conclusion and Future Work

We experimented with the effects of introducing CCG-based supertags on multilingual universal dependency parsing by taking a radical approach of transferring CCG categories from English to other languages. We used the similarities in dependency formalism and the universal POS tags in order to create CCG lexicons for each language included in the shared task. Since this is a diverse set of languages from different language families and different structural and orthographic properties this transferring is not ideal for many languages.

The existing CCG lexicons for languages such as Turkish were not used for the task since the universal dependency release of Turkish and the dependency treebank the Turkish CCG lexicon were induced from are not aligned on word/tokenization level. Therefore we could not provide accuracy on that data.

We hypothesise that using CCG lexicons from a different language family, especially one with a different word order, may increase the performance of the supertaggers since English only covers a small subset of syntactic properties in a diverse set of languages.

Language	LAS F1 Score	Language	LAS F1 Score
ar_pud	42.68	ar	63.81
bg	82.07	bxr	18.18
ca	82.43	cs_cac	79.52
cs_cltt	68.71	cs_pud	77.06
cs	79.89	cu	60.33
da	68.09	de_pud	65.94
de	67.97	el	76.71
en_lines	70.36	en_partut	72.38
en_pud	75.97	en	73.40
es_ancora	80.89	es_pud	75.26
es	77.54	et	52.08
eu	59.01	fa	75.73
fi_ftb	72.13	fi_pud	69.47
fi	66.46	fr_partut	71.50
fr_pud	71.15	fr_sequoia	75.96
fr	77.48	ga	13.26
gl_treegal	42.91	gl	75.25
got	20.05	grc_proiel	60.08
grc	49.11	he	55.32
hi_pud	49.63	hi	84.54
hr	71.39	hsb	19.59
hu	52.40	id	68.83
it_pud	80.99	it	83.01
ja_pud	74.69	ja	70.62
kk	16.48	kmr	15.86
ko	64.25	la_ittb	70.90
la_proiel	52.23	la	17.21
lv	56.34	nl_lassysmall	71.12
nl	64.73	no_bokmaal	78.51
no_nynorsk	76.19	pl	76.40
pt_br	83.17	pt_pud	68.97
pt	76.48	ro	76.75
ru_pud	65.81	ru_syntagrus	80.88
ru	71.40	sk	70.96
sl_sst	38.00	sl	78.14
sme	23.95	sv_lines	71.93
sv_pud	67.38	sv	74.06
tr_pud	29.24	tr	48.53
ug	15.66	uk	31.68
ur	75.40	vi	36.51
zh	53.84		

Table 12: Test results

After a manual alignment and tagging procedure, the Turkish data can be used in both training and evaluation. We can also group the languages and use similar families of languages to train a common system for them in the future.

One important addition to future work is to induce the CCG supertags in each language including the smaller datasets similar to the approaches used in (Ambati et al., 2013b,a; Çakıcı, 2008) and use these tags in our experiments. We believe adding the specific directional information in CCG categories will help in making more use of the information in the potentially very rich supertags.

Combining two or more CCG lexicons and tagging with the combined model might also be an interesting experiment.

For parsing, we plan to experiment with different word embedding sizes and tune the deep learning parameters. Other than these, we will experiment over neural networks integrated into graph-based dependency parsers. In future, we are planning to use pre-trained POS and CCG tag embeddings in our experiments. If these embeddings can be extracted from corpora on all available tags, this will reduce training time and increase parsing accuracy.

References

Bharat Ram Ambati, Tejaswini Deoskar, and Mark Steedman. 2013a. Using CCG categories to improve hindi dependency parsing. In *Proceedings of the 51st Annual Meeting of the Association for Computational Linguistics, ACL 2013, 4-9 August 2013, Sofia, Bulgaria, Volume 2: Short Papers*. pages 604–609.

Bharat Ram Ambati, Tejaswini Deoskar, and Mark Steedman. 2013b. Using ccg categories to improve hindi dependency parsing. In *ACL (2)*. pages 604–609.

Daniel Andor, Chris Alberti, David Weiss, Aliaksei Severyn, Alessandro Presta, Kuzman Ganchev, Slav Petrov, and Michael Collins. 2016. Globally normalized transition-based neural networks. *arXiv preprint arXiv:1603.06042* .

Michael Auli and Adam Lopez. 2011. Efficient ccg parsing: A* versus adaptive supertagging. In Dekang Lin, Yuji Matsumoto, and Rada Mihalcea, editors, *ACL '11: Proceedings of the 49th Annual Meeting on Association for Computational Linguistics*. The Association for Computer Linguistics, pages 1577–1585.

Srinivas Bangalore and Aravind K Joshi. 1999. Supertagging: An approach to almost parsing. *Computational linguistics* 25(2):237–265.

Alexandra Birch, Miles Osborne, and Philipp Koehn. 2007. Ccg supertags in factored statistical machine translation. In *Proceedings of the Second Workshop on Statistical Machine Translation*. Association for Computational Linguistics, pages 9–16.

Yonatan Bisk, Siva Reddy, John Blitzer, Julia Hockenmaier, and Mark Steedman. 2016. Evaluating induced ccg parsers on grounded semantic parsing. In *EMNLP*.

Sabine Buchholz and Erwin Marsi. 2006. CoNLL-X shared task on multilingual dependency parsing. In *Proceedings of the 10th Conf. on Computational Natural Language Learning (CoNLL-X)*. SIGNLL.

Ruket Çakıcı. 2008. *Wide-Coverage Parsing for Turkish*. Ph.D. thesis, University of Edinburgh.

Danqi Chen and Christopher D Manning. 2014. A fast and accurate dependency parser using neural networks. In *EMNLP*. pages 740–750.

Stephen Clark and James R. Curran. 2004. The importance of supertagging for wide-coverage ccg parsing. In *Proceedings of the 20th International Conference on Computational Linguistics*. Association for Computational Linguistics, Stroudsburg, PA, USA, COLING '04. https://doi.org/10.3115/1220355.1220396.

Stephen Clark and James R. Curran. 2007. Wide-coverage efficient statistical parsing with CCG and log-linear models. *Computational Linguistics* 33(4).

Ronan Collobert, Jason Weston, Léon Bottou, Michael Karlen, Koray Kavukcuoglu, and Pavel Kuksa. 2011. Natural language processing (almost) from scratch. *Journal of Machine Learning Research* 12(Aug):2493–2537.

Timothy Dozat and Christopher D Manning. 2016. Deep biaffine attention for neural dependency parsing. *arXiv preprint arXiv:1611.01734* .

Agnieszka Falenska, Anders Bjorkelund, Ozlem Cetinoglu, and Wolfgang Seeker. 2015. Stacking or supertagging for dependency parsing what's the difference? In *Proceedings of the 14th International Conference on Parsing Technologies*. Association for Computational Linguistics, Bilbao, Spain, pages 118–129. http://www.aclweb.org/anthology/W15-2215.

Kilian Foth, Tomas By, and Wolfgang Menzel. 2006. Guiding a constraint dependency parser with supertags. In *Proceedings of the 21st International Conference on Computational Linguistics and the 44th annual meeting of the Association for Computational Linguistics*. Association for Computational Linguistics, pages 289–296.

Filip Ginter, Jan Hajič, Juhani Luotolahti, Milan Straka, and Daniel Zeman. 2017. CoNLL 2017 shared task - automatically annotated raw texts and word embeddings. LINDAT/CLARIN digital library at the Institute of Formal and Applied Linguistics, Charles University. http://hdl.handle.net/11234/1-1989.

Julia Hockenmaier and Mark Steedman. 2002. Generative models for statistical parsing with combinatory categorial grammar. In *ACL '02: Proceedings of the 40th Annual Meeting on Association for Computational Linguistics*. pages 335–342.

Julia Hockenmaier and Mark Steedman. 2007. Ccgbank: a corpus of ccg derivations and dependency structures extracted from the penn treebank. *Computational Linguistics* 33(3):355–396.

Adhiguna Kuncoro, Miguel Ballesteros, Lingpeng Kong, Chris Dyer, Graham Neubig, and Noah A Smith. 2016. What do recurrent neural network grammars learn about syntax? *arXiv preprint arXiv:1611.05774* .

John Lafferty, Andrew McCallum, Fernando Pereira, et al. 2001. Conditional random fields: Probabilistic models for segmenting and labeling sequence data. In *Proceedings of the eighteenth international conference on machine learning, ICML*. volume 1, pages 282–289.

Mike Lewis and Mark Steedman. 2014. A* CCG parsing with a supertag-factored model. In *Proceedings of the 2014 Conference on Empirical Methods in Natural Language Processing, EMNLP 2014, October 25-29, 2014, Doha, Qatar, A meeting of SIGDAT, a Special Interest Group of the ACL*. pages 990–1000.

Christopher D. Manning, Mihai Surdeanu, John Bauer, Jenny Finkel, Steven J. Bethard, and David McClosky. 2014. The Stanford CoreNLP natural language processing toolkit. In *Association for Computational Linguistics (ACL) System Demonstrations*. pages 55–60. http://www.aclweb.org/anthology/P/P14/P14-5010.

Mitchell P Marcus, Mary Ann Marcinkiewicz, and Beatrice Santorini. 1993. Building a large annotated corpus of english: The penn treebank. *Computational linguistics* 19(2):313–330.

Ryan McDonald. 2006. *Discriminative Learning and Spanning Tree Algorithms for Dependency Parsing*. Ph.D. thesis, University of Pennsylvania.

Ryan McDonald, Koby Crammer, and Fernando Pereira. 2005. Online large-margin training of dependency parsers. In *Proceedings of ACL 2005*. Ann Arbor, MI, USA.

Ryan McDonald et al. 2006. Mstparser readme. http://www.seas.upenn.edu/˜strctlrn/MSTParser/README.

Ryan T McDonald and Fernando CN Pereira. 2006. Online learning of approximate dependency parsing algorithms. In *EACL*. pages 81–88.

Maria Nadejde, Siva Reddy, Rico Sennrich, Tomasz Dwojak, Marcin Junczys-Dowmunt, Philipp Koehn, and Alexandra Birch. 2017. Syntax-aware neural machine translation using ccg. *arXiv preprint arXiv:1702.01147* .

Joakim Nivre, Željko Agić, Lars Ahrenberg, et al. 2017a. Universal dependencies 2.0 CoNLL 2017 shared task development and test data. LINDAT/CLARIN digital library at the Institute of Formal and Applied Linguistics, Charles University. http://hdl.handle.net/11234/1-2184.

Joakim Nivre, Marie-Catherine de Marneffe, Filip Ginter, Yoav Goldberg, Jan Hajič, Christopher Manning, Ryan McDonald, Slav Petrov, Sampo Pyysalo, Natalia Silveira, Reut Tsarfaty, and Daniel Zeman. 2016. Universal Dependencies v1: A multilingual treebank collection. In *Proceedings of the 10th International Conference on Language Resources and Evaluation (LREC 2016)*. European Language Resources Association, Portoro, Slovenia, pages 1659–1666.

Joakim Nivre et al. 2017b. Universal Dependencies 2.0. LINDAT/CLARIN digital library at the Institute of Formal and Applied Linguistics, Charles University, Prague, http://hdl.handle.net/11234/1-1983. http://hdl.handle.net/11234/1-1983.

Naoaki Okazaki. 2007. Crfsuite: a fast implementation of conditional random fields (crfs). http://www.chokkan.org/software/crfsuite/.

Hiroki Ouchi, Kevin Duh, and Yuji Matsumoto. 2014. Improving dependency parsers with supertags. In *EACL*. pages 154–158.

F. Pedregosa, G. Varoquaux, A. Gramfort, V. Michel, B. Thirion, O. Grisel, M. Blondel, P. Prettenhofer, R. Weiss, V. Dubourg, J. Vanderplas, A. Passos, D. Cournapeau, M. Brucher, M. Perrot, and E. Duchesnay. 2011. Scikit-learn: Machine learning in Python. *Journal of Machine Learning Research* 12:2825–2830.

Jeffrey Pennington, Richard Socher, and Christopher D. Manning. 2014. Glove: Global vectors for word representation. In *Empirical Methods in Natural Language Processing (EMNLP)*. pages 1532–1543. http://www.aclweb.org/anthology/D14-1162.

Martin Potthast, Tim Gollub, Francisco Rangel, Paolo Rosso, Efstathios Stamatatos, and Benno Stein. 2014. Improving the reproducibility of PAN's shared tasks: Plagiarism detection, author identification, and author profiling. In Evangelos Kanoulas, Mihai Lupu, Paul Clough, Mark Sanderson, Mark Hall, Allan Hanbury, and Elaine Toms, editors, *Information Access Evaluation meets Multilinguality, Multimodality, and Visualization. 5th International Conference of the CLEF Initiative (CLEF 14)*. Springer, Berlin Heidelberg New York, pages 268–299. https://doi.org/10.1007/978-3-319-11382-1_22.

Mark Steedman. 2000. *The Syntactic Process*. MIT Press, Cambridge, MA.

Milan Straka, Jan Hajič, and Jana Straková. 2016. UDPipe: trainable pipeline for processing CoNLL-U files performing tokenization, morphological analysis, POS tagging and parsing. In *Proceedings of the 10th International Conference on Language Resources and Evaluation (LREC 2016)*. European Language Resources Association, Portoro, Slovenia.

Daniel Zeman, Martin Popel, Milan Straka, Jan Hajič, Joakim Nivre, Filip Ginter, Juhani Luotolahti, Sampo Pyysalo, Slav Petrov, Martin Potthast, Francis Tyers, Elena Badmaeva, Memduh Gökırmak, Anna Nedoluzhko, Silvie Cinková, Jan Hajič jr., Jaroslava Hlaváčová, Václava Kettnerová, Zdeňka Urešová, Jenna Kanerva, Stina Ojala, Anna Missilä, Christopher Manning, Sebastian Schuster, Siva Reddy, Dima Taji, Nizar Habash, Herman Leung, Marie-Catherine de Marneffe, Manuela Sanguinetti, Maria Simi, Hiroshi Kanayama, Valeria de Paiva, Kira Droganova, Hěctor Martínez Alonso, Hans Uszkoreit, Vivien Macketanz, Aljoscha Burchardt, Kim Harris, Katrin Marheinecke, Georg Rehm, Tolga Kayadelen, Mohammed Attia, Ali Elkahky, Zhuoran Yu, Emily Pitler, Saran Lertpradit, Michael Mandl, Jesse Kirchner, Hector Fernandez Alcalde, Jana Strnadova, Esha Banerjee, Ruli Manurung, Antonio Stella, Atsuko Shimada, Sookyoung Kwak, Gustavo Mendonça, Tatiana Lando, Rattima Nitisaroj, and Josie Li. 2017. CoNLL 2017 Shared Task: Multilingual Parsing from Raw Text to Universal Dependencies. In *Proceedings of the CoNLL 2017 Shared Task: Multilingual Parsing from Raw Text to Universal Dependencies*. Association for Computational Linguistics.

CLCL (Geneva) DINN Parser:
a Neural Network Dependency Parser Ten Years Later

Christophe Moor
University of Geneva
`Christophe.Moor@etu.unige.ch`

Paola Merlo
University of Geneva
`Paola.Merlo@unige.ch`

James Henderson
XRCE / University of Geneva
`James.Henderson@unige.ch`

Haozhou Wang
University of Geneva
`Haozhou.Wang@unige.ch`

Abstract

This paper describes the University of Geneva's submission to the CoNLL 2017 shared task Multilingual Parsing from Raw Text to Universal Dependencies (listed as the CLCL (Geneva) entry). Our submitted parsing system is the grandchild of the first transition-based neural network dependency parser, which was the University of Geneva's entry in the CoNLL 2007 multilingual dependency parsing shared task, with some improvements to speed and portability. These results provide a baseline for investigating how far we have come in the past ten years of work on neural network dependency parsing.

1 Introduction

The system described in this paper is the grandchild of the first transition-based neural network dependency parser (Titov and Henderson, 2007b), which was the University of Geneva's entry in the CoNLL 2007 multilingual dependency parsing shared task (Titov and Henderson, 2007a). The system has undergone some developments and modifications, in particular the faster discriminative version introduced by Yazdani and Henderson (2015), but in many respects the design and implementation of this parser is unchanged since 2007. One of our motivations for our submission to this CoNLL 2017 multilingual dependency parsing shared task is to provide a baseline to evaluate to what extent recent advances in neural network models and training do in fact improve performance over "traditional" recurrent neural networks. We are listed in the table of results as the CLCL (Geneva) entry.

As with previous work using the Incremental Neural Network architecture (e.g. Henderson, 2003), the main philosophy of our submission is that we build language universal inductive biases into the model structure of the recurrent neural network, but we do not do any feature engineering. Training the neural network induces language-specific hidden representations automatically. To provide such a baseline, we use UDPipe for all pre-processing (Straka et al., 2016), and Malt Parser for all projectivisation (Nivre et al., 2006). The only exception is our strategy for surprise languages, discussed below.

These goals match well the aim of the 2017 Universal dependencies shared task, described in the introductory overview (Zeman et al., 2017). This task makes true cross-linguistic comparison possible thanks to the universal dependency annotation project, which underlies the data used in this shared task. We train exactly the same parsing model on every language, thereby allowing further comparisons. In addition, the feature induction abilities of the recurrent neural network help minimise any remaining cross-lingual differences due to pre-processing or annotation.

2 Data

We use only the provided treebanks. For large treebanks, we train the model on the UD treebank (Nivre et al., 2017a), with some tuning of meta-parameter using the development set.

For surprise languages, we train on the concatenation of the treebank for the language, no matter how small, and the treebank of an identified source language with a larger treebank. In post-testing experiments, we also apply this same strategy to other small treebanks, resulting in substantial improvements (average 43% better) over the submitted results.

We don't use externally trained word embeddings (we trained our own internally to the parser) or any other data resource.

Proceedings of the CoNLL 2017 Shared Task: Multilingual Parsing from Raw Text to Universal Dependencies, pages 228–236,
Vancouver, Canada, August 3-4, 2017. © 2017 Association for Computational Linguistics

3 Preprocessing

Tokenisation, word and sentence segmentation is provided by UD pipe (Straka et al., 2016). We do not use the morphological transducers from Apertium/Giellatekno that had been made available for the shared task.

Because our parser can only produce projective dependency trees, we apply the projectivisation transformation of the Malt parser package (Nivre et al., 2006) to all treebanks before training.

4 Parser

We apply a single DINN parser to each language. We do not use any ensemble methods. This makes our results more useful for comparison, and allows our model to be used within an ensemble with other parsers.

We use the parser described in Yazdani and Henderson (2015), the Discriminative Incremental Neural Network parser (DINN). Like the previous version of this parser (Titov and Henderson, 2007b), it uses a recurrent neural network (RNN) to predict the actions for a fast shift-reduce dependency parser. Decoding is done with a beam search where pruning occurs after each shift action. The RNN model has an output-dependent structure that matches locality in the parse structure, making it an "incremental" neural network (INN, previously called SSN). This INN computes hidden vectors that encode the preceding partial parse, and estimates the probabilities of the parser actions given this history. Unlike the previous generative INN parser, DINN is a discriminative parser, using lookahead instead of word prediction. In order to combine beam search with a discriminative model, word predictions are replaced by a binary correctness probability which is trained discriminatively.

4.1 Transition-Based Neural Network Parsing

In DINN, the neural network is used to estimate the conditional probabilities of a transition-based statistical parsing model.

4.1.1 The Probabilistic Parsing Model

In shift-reduce dependency parsing, a parser configuration consists of a stack P of words, the queue Q of words and the partial labelled dependency trees constructed by the previous history of parser actions. The parser starts with an empty stack P and all the input words in the queue Q. It stops when it reaches a configuration with an empty queue Q, with any words left on the stack then being attached to ROOT. We use an arc-eager algorithm, which has 4 actions that all manipulate the word s on top of the stack P and the word q on the front of the queue Q: *Left-Arc$_r$* adds a dependency arc from q to s labelled r, then popping s from the stack. *Right-Arc$_r$* adds an arc from s to q labelled r. *Reduce* pops s from the stack. *Shift* shifts q from the queue to the stack. For exact details, see Titov and Henderson (2007b).

To model parse trees, we model the sequences of parser actions which generate them. We take a history based approach to model these sequences of parser actions. So, at each step of the parse sequence, the parser chooses between the set of possible next actions using an estimate of its conditional probability, where T is the parse tree, $D^1 \cdots D^m$ is its equivalent sequence of shift-reduce parser actions and S is the input sentence:

$$
\begin{aligned}
P(T|S) &= P(D^1 \cdots D^m|S) \\
&= \prod_t P(D^t|D^1 \cdots D^{t-1}, S)
\end{aligned}
$$

Unlike in previous dependency parser evaluations, the evaluation script for this shared task requires that exactly one word be attached to the ROOT node of the sentence. We implemented this constraint by modifying the calculation of the set of possible next actions. If an action will lead to a parser configuration where all possible ways of finishing the parse result in more than one word being attached to ROOT, then that action is not a possible action.

4.1.2 Estimating Action Probabilities

To estimate each $P(D^t|D^1 \cdots D^{t-1}, S)$, we need to condition on the unbounded sequences $D^1 \cdots D^{t-1}$ and S. To condition on the words in the queue, we use a bounded lookahead:

$$
P(T|S) \approx \prod_t P(D^t|D^1 \cdots D^{t-1}, w^t_{a_1} \cdots w^t_{a_k})
$$

where $w^t_{a_1} \cdots w^t_{a_k}$ is the first k words on the front of the queue at time t. At every *Shift*, one word is moved from the lookahead onto the stack and a new word from the input is added to the lookahead.

To estimate the probability of a decision at time t conditioned on the history of actions $D^1 \cdots D^{t-1}$,

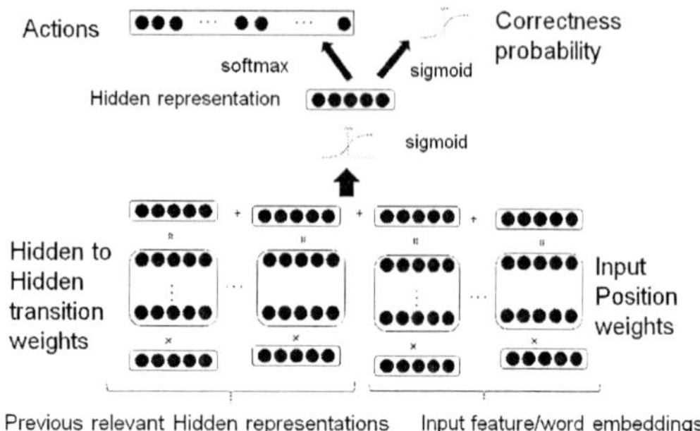

Figure 1: DINN computations for one decision

we use a recurrent neural network to induce hidden representations of the parse history sequence. The relevant information about the parse history at time t is encoded in the hidden representation vector h^t, of size d.

$$\prod_t P(D^t|D^1 \cdots D^{t-1}, w^t_{a_1} \cdots w^t_{a_k}) = \prod_t P(D^t|h^t)$$

This model is depicted in Figure 1. The hidden representation at time t is computed from selected previous hidden representations, plus pre-defined features. The model defines a set of link types $c \in \mathcal{C}$ which select previous states $t_c < t$ and connect them to the current hidden layer h^t via the hidden-hidden weights W^c_{HH}. The model also defines a set of features $f \in \mathcal{F}$ calculated from the previous decision and the current queue and stack, which are connected to the current hidden layer via the input-hidden weights W_{IH}:

$$h^t = \sigma\left(\sum_{c \in \mathcal{C}} h^{t_c} W^c_{HH} + \sum_{f \in \mathcal{F}} W_{IH}(f,:)\right)$$

where σ is the sigmoid function and $W(i,:)$ is row i of matrix W.

The probability of each decision is estimated with a softmax layer (a normalised exponential) with outputs for all decisions that are possible at this step, conditioned on the hidden representation.

$$P(D^t{=}d|h^t) = \frac{e^{h^t W_{HO}(:,d)}}{\sum_{d'} e^{h^t W_{HO}(:,d')}}$$

where W_{HO} is the weight matrix from hidden representations to the outputs.

4.1.3 Hidden and Input Features

$\mathcal{C}$ and $\mathcal{F}$ are the only hand-coded parts of the model. Because $\mathcal{C}$ defines the recurrent connections in the neural network, it is responsible for passing information about the unbounded parse history to the current decision. Because RNNs are biased towards learning correlations which are close together in the connected sequence of hidden layers, we exploit this bias by making the structure of the neural network match the structure of the output parse. This is achieved by including previous states in $\mathcal{C}$ if they had a word on the top of the stack or front of the queue which are also relevant to the current decision. In the version we use in this experiment, we use a minimal set of these link types, specified in section 5.

The input features $\mathcal{F}$ are typical of any statistical model. But in the case of neural networks, it is common to decompose the parametrisation of these features into a matrix for the feature role (e.g. front-of-the-queue) and a vector for the feature value (e.g. a word). This decomposition of features overcomes feature sparsity, because the same value vector can be shared across multiple roles. Word embedding vectors are the most common example of this decomposition.

Unlike in the previous versions of the parser, Yazdani and Henderson (2015) added feature decompositions in the definition of the input-to-hidden weights W_{IH}.

$$W_{IH}(f,:) = W_{emb.}(val(f),:) W^{role(f)}_{HH}$$

Every row in $W_{emb.}$ is an embedding for a feature value, which may be a word, lemma, POS tag, or dependency relation. $val(f)$ is the index of the value for feature role $role(f)$, for example the particular word that is at the front of the queue. The matrix $W^{role(f)}_{HH}$ is the feature role matrix, which maps the feature value embedding to the role-value feature vector for the given feature role $role(f)$. For simplicity, we assume here that the size of the embeddings and the size of the hidden representations of the DINN are the same. In this way, the parameters of the embedding matrix $W_{emb.}$ is shared among various feature input link types $role(f)$, which can improve the model in the case of sparse features f.

We train our own word embeddings within the parsing model, using only the parsed training data. We tried initialising with Facebook embeddings on a sample of languages, but random initialisation worked better.

Unlike Yazdani and Henderson (2015), we did not cache any features, either in testing or in training. Caching can have a big impact on speed, but it has not been shown to improve accuracies.

4.1.4 Discrimination of Correct Partial Parses

Unlike in the previous generative models, the above formulas for computing the probability of a parse make independence assumptions, in that words to the right of $w_{a_k}^t$ are assumed to be independent of D^t. And even for words in the lookahead, it can be difficult to learn correlations with the unstructured lookahead string. If a discriminative model uses normalised estimates for decisions, then once a wrong decision is made there is no way for the estimates to express that this decision has lead to a structure that is incompatible with the current or future lookahead string (see Lafferty et al. (2001) for more discussion). For this reason, there is no obvious way to make effective use of beam search for a normalised discriminative model.

To overcome this problem, DINN estimates a correctness probability after every *Shift* action. This output is trained to discriminate correct from incorrect parse prefixes, using the same hidden representation as used to predict parser actions, as depicted in Figure 1. A beam search is then used to consider multiple possible partial parses so that the correctness probability can be used to select between them. The total score of a parse is the multiplication of the probabilities of all its actions with the correctness probabilities at the shift of each word. For more details on this technique, see Yazdani and Henderson (2015).

5 Experimental Settings

The implementation of DINN uses a parameter file to define the hidden-hidden connections, the input-hidden features, training meta-parameters, and various other parameters of the parser. We use the same settings for all languages. For the official submission, we used the following settings.

- We used a frequency cutoff for words/lemmas of 3.
- We did not normalise the input string to lowercase.
- We always used all the available training and development set.
- Search beam size is 10.
- Hidden layer size is 80.
- The size of the internally calculated embeddings is 50.

- Word embeddings are initialised randomly.
- We do not apply any feature caching.
- Validation occurs at every iteration.
- The configurations of the Input-to-Hidden layer connections are as follows:
    + Look at 4 last elements in the stack and 4 next elements from the input (Except the treebanks fr, ko, it_partut, grc_proiel, cu, where we look at 5 last elements from the stack.)
    + For each element, use all possible features from UDPipe (except UPoS if XPoS exists).
- The configurations of the Hidden-to-Hidden layer connections are as follows:

Closest	Current	H-to-H
Queue	Queue	+
Top	Top	+
Queue	Top	+

In this specification of the hidden-to-hidden connections, Queue refers to the front of the input queue and Top refers to the top of the stack in the parser configuration. This specification uses the same simplified set of connections between hidden states used in Yazdani and Henderson (2015). We assume that the induced hidden features primarily relate to the word on the top of the syntactic stack and the word at the front of the queue, since these are the words used in any action. To decide which previous state's hidden features are most relevant to the current decision, we look at these words in the current parser configuration. For each such word, we look for previous states where the top of the stack or the front of the queue was the same word. If more than one previous state matches, then the hidden vector of the most recent one is used. If no state matches, then no connection is made.

5.1 Training

One aspect of the current implementation which is basically unchanged from ten years ago is the training protocol. Learning rates and weight decay regularisation rates are reduced during training whenever there is a decrease in accuracy on the development set, and early stopping is used to prevent overtraining. Training and development splits are those provided by the shared task. The development set is also used to select which iteration's

Language	abbr.	dev. LAS	test LAS	Rank /33
Ancient Greek	grc	54.98	54.56	15
Ancient Greek-PROIEL	grc_proiel	63.30	62.83	18
Arabic	ar	63.37	64.17	23
Basque	eu	62.73	62.47	26
Bulgarian	bg	82.46	83.50	18
Catalan	ca	82.88	82.83	24
Chinese	zh	52.51	54.89	25
Croatian	hr	72.80	73.78	27
Czech	cs	83.36	82.52	18
Czech-CAC	cs_cac	82.07	81.35	23
Czech-CLTT	cs_cltt	63.98	69.16	22
Danish	da	69.94	69.43	27
Dutch	nl	73.75	67.70	22
Dutch-LassySmall	nl_lassysmall	68.84	73.97	22
English	en	75.69	75.09	22
English-LinES	en_lines	73.03	72.68	21
English-ParTUT	en_partut	71.97	71.78	25
Estonian	et	53.32	52.67	26
Finnish	fi	64.38	63.93	27
Finnish-FTB	fi_ftb	75.69	76.26	8
French	fr	83.74	79.85	21
French-ParTUT	fr_partut		17.85	30
French-Sequoia	fr_sequoia	76.35	76.36	25
Galician	gl	76.04	75.93	23
Galician-TreeGal	gl_treegal		2.76	30
German	de	72.76	69.59	16
Gothic	got	57.47	57.72	21
Greek	el	76.93	77.80	23
Hebrew	he	58.93	55.36	24
Hindi	hi	87.20	86.80	17
Hungarian	hu	53.81	50.95	27
Indonesian	id	68.33	69.45	26
Irish	ga		4.30	30
Italian	it	84.01	85.05	19
Japanese	ja	73.22	71.85	23
Kazakh	kk		1.00	29
Korean	ko	57.39	61.08	18
Latin	la		5.72	31
Latin-ITTB	la_ittb	69.00	75.81	18
Latin-PROIEL	la_proiel	55.28	54.07	22
Latvian	lv	60.06	59.28	22
Norwegian-Bokmaal	no_bokmaal	82.37	82.44	20
Norwegian-Nynorsk	no_nynorsk	80.73	79.34	21
Old Church Slavonic	cu	62.80	62.45	20
Persian	fa	75.74	75.86	23
Polish	pl	80.32	79.83	14
Portuguese	pt	81.83	79.74	22
Portuguese-BR	pt_br	84.75	84.00	21
Romanian	ro	77.27	77.34	23
Russian	ru	73.03	72.03	22
Russian-SynTagRus	ru_syntagrus	83.78	83.89	23
Slovak	sk	73.70	73.30	18
Slovenian	sl	80.31	81.32	14
Slovenian-SST	sl_sst		4.37	30
Spanish	es	81.92	79.96	22
Spanish-AnCora	es_ancora	81.63	81.26	23
Swedish	sv	71.86	76.06	20
Swedish-LinES	sv_lines	73.07	73.82	18
Turkish	tr	48.42	47.91	18
Ukrainian	uk		7.87	30
Urdu	ur	75.37	76.01	20
Uyghur	ug		9.29	27
Vietnamese	vi	39.14	35.77	25
MEAN		71.17	62.83	

Table 1: DINN and Universal Dependencies treebanks - official results.

model to use in testing. Recent advances in optimisation methods for neural networks — such as AdaGrad and mini-batch – are obvious modifications to compare against the reported results.

To deal with small treebanks without development sets, we use a fixed training protocol developed by looking at the training of models with other small training sets. We run for a total of 8 iterations and changed the learning rate and weight decay values every other iteration.

5.2 Dealing with surprise languages and other small datasets

To build a model for the surprise languages, we use simple cross-lingual techniques. For the official test phase, we identified the most similar languages to the surprise language with a string-based technique, concatenated the treebanks, trained and tested on the surprise languages.

The string-based technique constructs a list of words for each language. We used the sample data for the surprise language and the training data for the languages for which we have enough resources. Call these languages with big data sets $\mathcal{B}$. We denote $\mathcal{T}$ as the set of lists of words of $\mathcal{B}$, and t is a word in $\mathcal{T}$. For a given surprise language, we calculate the similarity score S for each t. We treat two words as similar if and only if the first three characters of these two words are identical and the edit distance between these two words is less than or equal to 1. We choose the language that has the best S for training our model for the surprise language. This procedure yields the following similar languages for training. We call them source languages.

Buryat: Russian (rus_syntagrus), Turkish (tr)
Upper Sorbian: Czeck (cs), Norwegian (no_bokmaal)
Kurmanji: Spanish (es), Turkish (tr)
North Sami: Czech (cs), Finnish (fi_ftb)

To train a parser for the surprise language, we concatenate the datasets for the source languages with three copies of the dataset for the target language. Because our frequency threshold is three, this means that all words in the target language dataset are included in the vocabulary. Then we trained a parser on this concatenated dataset, using the surprise language corpus also as a development set.

In addition to the surprise languages, there are other languages whose available data is just enough for a small training set without any development set. For the submitted test run, we did

Language	Abbrev.	LAS	rank
Buryat	bxr	22.59	16
Kurmanji	kmr	22.20	22
North Sami	sme	23.99	21
Upper Sorbian	hsb	48.50	18
Mean on surprise languages		29.32	

Table 2: DINN and Universal Dependencies treebanks - official results on surprise languages.

Language	Abbrev.	LAS	rank
Arabic-PUD	ar_pud	42.61	25
Czech-PUD	cs_pud	79.17	18
English-PUD	en_pud	78.22	18
Finnish-PUD	fi_pud	64.91	24
French-PUD	fr_pud	74.93	9
German-PUD	de_pud	67.76	15
Hindi-PUD	hi_pud	51.31	10
Italian-PUD	it_pud	83.28	21
Japanese-PUD	ja_pud	76.21	16
Portuguese-PUD	pt_pud	73.01	17
Russian-PUD	ru_pud	67.22	16
Spanish-PUD	es_pud	75.90	22
Swedish-PUD	sv_pud	68.92	21
Turkish-PUD	tr_pud	29.01	25
Mean on PUD treebanks		66.60	

Table 3: DINN and Universal Dependencies treebanks - official results on PUD Treebanks.

not do anything special for these datasets (other than the training schedule discussed above), training parsing models on the individual datasets. But in subsequent experiments we tried treating them in the same way as surprise languages, with much improved results, discussed below.

6 Test Phase Results

Evaluation was run on the provided TIRA platform (Potthast et al., 2014) using the data provided by the organisers (Nivre et al., 2017b), but blind to us, as described in the introduction. The results of our submission are shown in the next three tables. Accuracy by LAS is shown in Table 1. Accuracy on surprise languages is shown in Table 2. Accuracy on parallel UD data is shown in Table 3.

6.1 Analysis of results

Our results are 25th over the 33 participants globally, 22nd on the large treebanks only, 19th on the PUD treebanks only, 30th on the small treebanks with only 6% accuracy (see below), 20th on sur-

233

Language	abbr.	Training runtimes			Testing runtimes	
		T/s	NUI	UTH	DPT	W/s
Ancient Greek	grc	0.0714	14	3.18	177	125.056
Ancient Greek-PROIEL	grc_proiel	0.0663	25	6.84	99	137.899
Arabic	ar	0.2698	144	65.56	259	116.753
Basque	eu	0.1001	66	9.90	175	137.686
Bulgarian	bg	0.1360	57	19.17	84	191.536
Catalan	ca	0.1998	23	16.75	404	139.807
Chinese	zh	0.3020	13	4.36	71	178.352
Croatian	hr	0.0990	56	11.84	93	156.269
Czech	cs	0.1256	26	62.14	1130	140.959
Czech-CAC	cs_cac	0.1615	43	45.29	87	125.425
Czech-CLTT	cs_cltt	0.2688	10	0.35	110	94.373
Danish	da	0.0835	58	5.90	69	149.739
Dutch	nl	0.3163	16	17.33	80	143.225
Dutch-LassySmall	nl_lassysmall	0.2697	14	6.33	75	140.667
English	en	0.0829	17	4.91	163	154.282
English-LinES	en_lines	0.0931	12	0.85	127	134.661
English-ParTUT	en_partut	0.1037	105	3.30	79	154.975
Estonian	et	0.1613	129	13.08	73	165.795
Finnish	fi	0.0842	137	39.16	118	155.000
Finnish-FTB	fi_ftb	0.1797	20	14.96	86	182.837
French	fr	0.1297	19	9.95	289	123.758
French-ParTUT	fr_partut	0.1226	8	0.17		
French-Sequoia	fr_sequoia	0.0829	429	22.05	63	158.937
Galician	gl	0.1402	15	1.33	177	168.232
Galician-TreeGal	gl_treegal	0.1183	8	0.16		
German	de	0.0853	124	41.47	80	154.350
Gothic	got	0.0484	32	1.46	60	168.567
Greek	el	0.1107	14	0.72	63	160.937
Hebrew	he	0.1074	132	20.64	68	167.765
Hindi	hi	0.0929	9	3.09	213	165.338
Hungarian	hu	0.1308	168	5.55	69	165.478
Indonesian	id	0.1072	127	16.93		
Irish	ga	0.1166	8	0.15		
Italian	it	0.1049	16	5.99	79	150.734
Italian-ParTUT	it_partut	0.1165	22	0.78	83	166.349
Japanese	ja	0.1336	242	64.33		
Kazakh	kk	0.0968	8	0.01		
Korean	ko	0.1734	35	7.42	58	191.345
Latin	la	0.2819	8	0.84		
Latin-ITTB	la_ittb	0.1741	146	111.61	80	129.138
Latin-PROIEL	la_proiel	0.1206	30	14.27	86	143.756
Latvian	lv	0.2741	18	3.17	60	168.800
Norwegian-Bokmaal	no_bokmaal	0.1099	174	83.38	222	163.824
Norwegian-Nynorsk	no_nynorsk	0.1375	83	44.94	190	164.474
Old Church Slavonic	cu	0.0403	17	0.78	54	187.037
Persian	fa	0.4894	18	11.74	112	141.357
Polish	pl	0.1520	46	11.84	53	193.623
Portuguese	pt	0.6852	10	15.86	83	130.735
Portuguese-BR	pt_br	0.5102	13	17.81	191	168.215
Romanian	ro	0.6079	15	20.37	126	135.508
Russian	ru	0.2192	14	3.28	81	146.630
Russian-SynTagRus	ru_syntagrus	0.1073	19	27.66	804	147.297
Slovak	sk	0.0888	16	3.35	72	172.778
Slovenian	sl	0.1882	13	4.40	86	163.523
Slovenian-SST	sl_sst	0.0917	8	0.44		
Spanish	es	0.2132	15	12.60	271	137.089
Spanish-AnCora	es_ancora	0.2073	99	81.54	367	142.605
Swedish	sv	0.1406	77	12.94	63	155.508
Swedish-LinES	sv_lines	0.2144	15	2.45	120	137.183
Turkish	tr	0.1115	148	16.90	79	126.722
Ukrainian	uk	0.1356	8	0.26		
Urdu	ur	0.3030	7	2.38	101	144.366
Uyghur	ug	0.1000	8	0.02		
Vietnamese	vi	0.1536	317	18.93	67	171.851
MAX			429	111.61	1130.000	193.623
MEAN		0.1727		16.83	152.389	152.576

Table 4: Training and testing runtimes. T/s: Training time per sentence; NUI: Number of useful iterations; UTH: Useful training time (hours); DPT: Development parsing time (seconds); W/s: Words/sec.

Model	Training				Testing		
	Training set	Dev. set	LAS	LAS deproj	LAS	LAS deproj	DINN Official LAS
FrenchParTUT	fr+ fr_partut	fr	85.08	85.09	78.14	78.14	17.85
GalicianTreeGal	gl+gl_treegal	gl	75.88	75.88	60.94	60.94	2.76
Irish	ga+it_partut	it_partut	75.99	75.99	59.44	59.44	4.30
Kazakh	kk+ja	ja	93.10	93.10	18.03	18.03	1.00
Latin	la+grc	grc	55.64	56.86	43.22	43.59	5.72
SlovenianSST	sl+sl_sst	sl	81.09	81.52	47.91	47.99	4.37
Ukrainian	lv+uk	lv	62.84	62.94	59.64	59.64	7.87
Uyghur	ug+bg	bg	83.40	83.49	29.66	29.66	9.29
Mean on small treebanks			76.63	76.86	49.62	49.68	6.64

Table 5: Small treebanks as surprise language, Run 5.1 UD PMor (20/05).

prise languages. They are rather firmly in the bottom third, around 22nd-25th place. They rarely beat the baseline. They are well above the baseline or close to it (above or below) for twelve treebanks (Fi_ftp, 8th, well above; fr_pud, 9th/33, well above; grc, 15th, just under; hi, 17th, just above; hi_pud, 10th, well above; it, 19th; ja_pud, 16th just below; ko, 18th, well above; la_ittb, 18th, same; pl, 14th, above; sk, 18th, above; sl, 14th a little above.)

There are a number of treebanks where the submitted parser does very poorly (fr_partut, 17%; ga, 4%; gl_treegal, 2.75%; kk, 1%; la, 6%; sl_sst, 4%; ug, 9%; uk, 8%). These are all small treebanks with no development set, which we treated in the same way as all other treebanks. As discussed in the post-test results section, treating these treebanks with the same approach that we used for surprise languages yielded instead results on-average 43% LAS better.

6.2 Resources used

Table 4 shows the training and parsing times, calculated on the training and development sets, respectively. Our shared task submission was prepared primarily by one computer science MSc student.

7 Post-Test Results

In the post-test results, we aim to increase the performance on the small treebanks, and correct errors in the submitted system.

7.1 Postprocessing, if any

In the submitted parser, we overlooked the need to deprojectivise the output of the parser. In the post-test results, we run the Malt parser deprojectivisation routine on the output of the DINN parser before doing evaluation. Deprojectivisation makes no or little difference for most languages, but there

is an improvement on some. Improvements range from zero to 1.3% LAS score, with an average improvement of 0.16%. We report some deprojectivisation results on small treebanks in Table 5.

7.2 Dealing with small treebank languages

In the test phase, we train on small treebanks. Given that our results were particularly unsatisfactory on small treebanks, in the post-test phase, we tried a different technique: we treated small treebanks like surprise languages.

For small treebanks, we identified the best source language by exhaustively searching all the possible languages. As with surprise languages, we then concatenated three copies of the small treebank to the larger treebank and trained a parser on this combined dataset. Table 5 shows the treebank configurations and results on the development set and test set. This new method raises the total average score of our parser by 4.20% LAS.

8 Conclusions and Future Work

With this submission, we have shown how a neural network dependency parser whose main architecture is largely unchanged from ten years ago performs with respect to the state of the art. These results can serve as a baseline for future work evaluating to what extent recently proposed methods have a measurable impact on neural network dependency parser accuracy.

Acknowledgements

We would like to thank Corentin Ribeyre for his help in getting the endeavour started and the Language and Communication Network at the university of Geneva for support. We also thank Majid Yazdani for his help understanding the original code base.

References

James Henderson. 2003. Inducing history representations for broad coverage statistical parsing. In *Proceedings of the 2003 Conference of the North American Chapter of the Association for Computational Linguistics on Human Language Technology - Volume 1*. Association for Computational Linguistics, Stroudsburg, PA, USA, NAACL '03, pages 24–31.

John D. Lafferty, Andrew McCallum, and Fernando C. N. Pereira. 2001. Conditional random fields: Probabilistic models for segmenting and labeling sequence data. In *Proceedings of the Eighteenth International Conference on Machine Learning*. Morgan Kaufmann Publishers Inc., San Francisco, CA, USA, ICML '01, pages 282–289. http://dl.acm.org/citation.cfm?id=645530.655813.

Joakim Nivre, Johan Hall, and Jens Nilsson. 2006. Maltparser: A data-driven parser-generator for dependency parsing. In *Proceedings of the Fifth International Conference on Language Resources and Evaluation (LREC-2006)*. pages 2216–2219.

Joakim Nivre et al. 2017a. Universal Dependencies 2.0. LINDAT/CLARIN digital library at the Institute of Formal and Applied Linguistics, Charles University, Prague, http://hdl.handle.net/11234/1-1983. http://hdl.handle.net/11234/1-1983.

Joakim Nivre et al. 2017b. Universal Dependencies 2.0 CoNLL 2017 shared task development and test data. LINDAT/CLARIN digital library at the Institute of Formal and Applied Linguistics, Charles University, Prague, http://hdl.handle.net/11234/1-2184. http://hdl.handle.net/11234/1-2184.

Martin Potthast, Tim Gollub, Francisco Rangel, Paolo Rosso, Efstathios Stamatatos, and Benno Stein. 2014. Improving the reproducibility of PAN's shared tasks: Plagiarism detection, author identification, and author profiling. In Evangelos Kanoulas, Mihai Lupu, Paul Clough, Mark Sanderson, Mark Hall, Allan Hanbury, and Elaine Toms, editors, *Information Access Evaluation meets Multilinguality, Multimodality, and Visualization. 5th International Conference of the CLEF Initiative (CLEF 14)*. Springer, Berlin Heidelberg New York, pages 268–299. https://doi.org/10.1007/978-3-319-11382-1_22.

Milan Straka, Jan Hajič, and Jana Straková. 2016. UDPipe: trainable pipeline for processing CoNLL-U files performing tokenization, morphological analysis, POS tagging and parsing. In *Proceedings of the 10th International Conference on Language Resources and Evaluation (LREC 2016)*. Portorož, Slovenia, publisher = European Language Resources Association, isbn = 978-2-9517408-9-1.

Ivan Titov and James Henderson. 2007a. Fast and robust multilingual dependency parsing with a generative latent variable model. In *Proceedings of the CoNLL Shared Task Session of EMNLP-CoNLL 2007*. Association for Computational Linguistics, Prague, Czech Republic, pages 947–951. http://www.aclweb.org/anthology/D/D07/D07-1099.

Ivan Titov and James Henderson. 2007b. A latent variable model for generative dependency parsing. In *Proceedings of the 10th International Conference on Parsing Technologies*. Association for Computational Linguistics, Stroudsburg, PA, USA, IWPT '07, pages 144–155.

Majid Yazdani and James Henderson. 2015. Incremental recurrent neural network dependency parser with search-based discriminative training. In *Proceedings of the Nineteenth Conference on Computational Natural Language Learning*. Association for Computational Linguistics, Beijing, China, pages 142–152. http://www.aclweb.org/anthology/K15-1015.

Daniel Zeman, Filip Ginter, Jan Hajič, Joakim Nivre, Martin Popel, Milan Straka, and et al. 2017. CoNLL 2017 Shared Task: Multilingual Parsing from Raw Text to Universal Dependencies. In *Proceedings of the CoNLL 2017 Shared Task: Multilingual Parsing from Raw Text to Universal Dependencies*. Association for Computational Linguistics, pages 1–20.

A Fast and Lightweight System for Multilingual Dependency Parsing

Tao Ji, Yuanbin Wu, Man Lan
Department of Computer Science and Technology
East China Normal University
10132130251@stu.ecnu.edu.cn
{ybwu, mlan}@cs.ecnu.edu.cn

Abstract

Following Kiperwasser and Goldberg (2016), we present a multilingual dependency parser with a bidirectional-LSTM (BiLSTM) feature extractor and a multi-layer perceptron (MLP) classifier. We trained our transition-based projective parser in UD version 2.0 datasets without any additional data. The parser is fast, lightweight and effective on big treebanks.

In the *CoNLL 2017 Shared Task: Multilingual Parsing from Raw Text to Universal Dependencies*, the official results show that the macro-averaged LAS F1 score of our system *Mengest* is 61.33%.

1 Introduction

Developing tools that can process multiple languages has always been an important goal in NLP. Ten years ago, CoNLL 2006 (Buchholz and Marsi, 2006) and CoNLL 2007 (Nivre et al., 2007) Shared Task were a major milestone for multilingual dependency parsing. The *CoNLL 2017 UD Shared Task* (Zeman et al., 2017) is an extension of the tasks addressed in previous years. Unlike CoNLL 2006 and CoNLL 2007, the focus of the *CoNLL 2017 UD Shared Task* is learning syntactic dependency parsers on a universal syntactic annotation standard. This shared task requires participants to parse raw texts from different languages, which vary both in typology and training set size.

The *CoNLL 2017 UD Shared Task* provided universal dependencies description from LREC 2016 (Nivre et al., 2016), two datasets, which are UD version 2.0 datasets (Nivre et al., 2017b) and this task test datasets (Nivre et al., 2017a), two baseline models, which are UDPipe (Straka et al., 2016) and SyntaxNet (Weiss et al., 2015), and the evaluation platform TIRA (Potthast et al., 2014).

In this paper, We present our multilingual dependency parsing system *Mengest* for *CoNLL 2017 UD Shared Task*. The system contains a BiLSTM feature extractor for feature representation and a MLP classifier for the transition system. The inputs of our system are word form (lemma or stem, which depending on the particular treebank) and part of speech (POS) tags (coarse-grained and fine-grained) for each token. Based on this input, the system finds a governor for each token, and assigns a universal dependency relation label to each syntactic dependency. Our official submission obtains 61.33% macro-averaged LAS F1 score on all treebanks.

The rest of this paper is organized as follows. Section 2 discusses the transition-based model (Kiperwasser and Goldberg, 2016) and our implementation. Section 3 explains how our system deals with parallel sets and surprise languages. Finally, we present experimental and official results in Section 4.

2 System Description

We implement a transition-based projective parser following Kiperwasser and Goldberg (2016). The system consists of a BiLSTM feature extractor and an MLP classifier. We describe their model and our implementation in the following sections in detail.

2.1 Arc-Hybrid System

In this work, we use the arc-hybrid transition system (Kuhlmann et al., 2011). In the arc-hybrid system, a configuration $c = (\alpha, \beta, A)$ consists of a stack α, a buffer β, and a set of dependency arcs A. Given n words sentence $s = w_1, \cdots, w_n$, the initial configuration $c = (\emptyset, \{1, 2, \cdots, n, root\}, \emptyset)$ with an empty stack, an empty arc set, and a full buffer $\beta = 1, 2, \cdots, n, root$, where $root$ is the special root index. The terminal configuration set

Proceedings of the CoNLL 2017 Shared Task: Multilingual Parsing from Raw Text to Universal Dependencies, pages 237–242,
Vancouver, Canada, August 3-4, 2017. © 2017 Association for Computational Linguistics

contains configurations with an empty stack, an arc set and a buffer containing only *root*.

For each configuration $c = (\sigma|s_1|s_0, b_0|\beta, A)$, the arc-hybrid system has 3 kinds of transitions, $T = \{\text{SHIFT}, \text{LEFT}_l, \text{RIGHT}_l\}$:

$$\text{SHIFT}(c) = (\sigma|s_1|s_0|b_0, \beta, A)$$
$$s.t. \ |\beta| > 0$$
$$\text{LEFT}_l(c) = (\sigma|s_1, b_0|\beta, A \cup \{(b_0, s_0, l)\})$$
$$s.t. \ |\beta| > 0, |\sigma| > 0$$
$$\text{RIGHT}_l(c) = (\sigma|s_1, b_0|\beta, A \cup \{(s_1, s_0, l)\})$$
$$s.t. \ |\sigma| > 0, s_0 \neq root$$

The SHIFT transition moves the first item of the buffer (b_0) to the stack. The LEFT$_l$ transition removes the first item on top of the stack (s_0) and attaches it as a modifier to b_0 with label l, adding the arc (b_0, s_0, l) to arc set A. The RIGHT$_l$ transition removes s_0 from the stack and attaches it as a modifier to the next item on the stack (s_1), adding the arc (s_1, s_0, l) to arc set A.

We apply a classifier to determine the best action for a configuration. Following Chen and Manning (2014), we use a MLP with one hidden layer. The score of the transition $t \in T$ is defined as:

$$MLP_\theta(\phi(c)) = W^2 \cdot tanh(W^1 \cdot \phi(c) + b^1) + b^2$$
$$\text{SCORE}_\theta(\phi(c), t) = MLP_\theta(\phi(c))[t]$$

where $\theta = \{W^1, W^2, b^1, b^2\}$ are the model parameters, $\phi(c)$ is the feature representation of the configuration c. $MLP_\theta(\phi(c))[t]$ denotes an indexing operation taking the output element which is the class of transition t.

2.2 The Feature Representation

We consider two types of feature repersentations $\phi(c)$ of a configuration: *simple* and *extended*.

Simple: For an input sequence $s = w_1, \cdots, w_n$, we associate each word w_i with a vector x_i:

$$x_i = e(w_i) \circ e(p_i) \circ e(q_i)$$

where $e(w_i)$ is the embedding vector of word w_i, $e(p_i)$ is the embedding vector of POS tag p_i, $e(q_i)$ is the embedding vector of coarse-grained POS (CPOS) tag q_i. The embeddings $e(w_i), e(p_i), e(q_i)$ are randomly initialized (without pre-training) and jointly trained with the parsing model. Then, in order to encode context features, we use a 2-layer sentence level BiLSTM on top of $x_{1:n}$:

$$\vec{h}_t = LSTM(\vec{h}_{t-1}, x_i, \vec{\theta})$$
$$\overleftarrow{h}_t = LSTM(\overleftarrow{h}_{t+1}, x_i, \overleftarrow{\theta})$$
$$v_i = \vec{h}_i \circ \overleftarrow{h}_i$$

$\vec{\theta}$ are the model parameters of the forward hidden sequence $\vec{h}$. $\overleftarrow{\theta}$ are the model parameters of the backward hidden sequence $\overleftarrow{h}$. The vector v_i is our final vector representation of ith token in s, which has took into account both the entire history $\vec{h}_i$ and the entire future $\overleftarrow{h}_i$ by concatenating the matching Long Short-Term Memory Network (LSTM).

For $\phi(c)$, our simple feature function is the concatenated BiLSTM vectors of the top 3 items on the stack and the first item on the buffer. A configuration c is represented by:

$$\phi(c) = v_{s_2} \circ v_{s_1} \circ v_{s_0} \circ v_{b_0}$$

Extended: We add the feature vectors corresponding to the right-most and left-most modifiers of s_0, s_1 and s_2, as well as the left-most modifier of b_0, reaching a total of 11 BiLSTM vectors as extended feature representation. As we will see in experimental sections, using the extended set does indeed improves parsing accuracies.

2.3 Training Details

The training objective is to make the score of correct transitions always above the scores of incorrect transitions. We use a margin-based criteria. Assume T_{gold} is the set of gold transitions at the current configuration c. At each time stamp, the objective function tries to maximize the margin between T_{gold} and $T - T_{gold}$. The hinge loss of a configuration c is defined as:

$$Loss_\theta(c) = \big(1 - \max_{t_o \in T_{gold}} \text{SCORE}_\theta(\phi(c), t_o)$$
$$+ \max_{t_p \in (T - T_{gold})} \text{SCORE}_\theta(\phi(c), t_p)\big)_+$$

Our system use the backpropagation algorithm to calculate the gradients of the entire network (including the MLP and the BiLSTM).

Since our parser can only deal with projective dependency trees, we exclude all training examples with non-projective dependencies. This approach undoubtedly downgrades the performance of our system, we plan to use pseudo-projective approach to improve it in the future work.

3 Multilingual Dependency Parsing

There are 81 treebanks in the *CoNLL 2017 UD Shared Task*, including 55 big treebanks, 14 PUD treebanks (additional parallel test sets), 8 small treebanks and 4 surprise language treebanks. For each language treebank of UD version 2.0 training sets, we train a parser only using its monolingual training set (no cross-lingual features). In total, we trained 61 models, 55 on big treebanks and 6 on small treebanks[1]. Our system reads the CoNLL-U files predicted by UDPipe, and uses morphology (lemmas, UPOS, XPOS) predicted by UDPipe.

3.1 Dealing with Parallel Test Sets

There are 14 additional parallel test sets. Our system simply selects one trained model when we encounter a parallel test set where multiple training treebanks exist. For example, although we don't have English-PUD training set but we have English, English-LinES and English-ParTUT training set. So we only use the model trained on English training set to predict English-PUD test set.

3.2 Dealing with Surprise Languages

There are 4 surprise languages in the *CoNLL 2017 UD Shared Task*. Our system simply use the model trained on English to predict 4 surprise languages, without looking at the input words.

4 Results

We trained our system based on a MacBook Air with a Intel Core i5 1.6 GHz CPU and 4G memory. We used the official TIRA (Potthast et al., 2014) to evaluate the system. We used Dynet neural network library to build our system (Neubig et al., 2017).

The hyper-parameters of the final system used for all the reported experiments are detailed in Table 1.

4.1 Token Representation

We compare two constructions of x_i:

- lemma and POS tag ($w_i \circ p_i$).

- lemma, POS tag and CPOS tag ($w_i \circ p_i \circ q_i$).

The performance of different token representations on 4 example languages are given in Table 2. The results show that the CPOS tag improves the LAS measure between 0.5% and 0.72%.

Word embedding dimension	100
POS tag embedding dimension	25
CPOS tag embedding dimension	10
Label embedding dimension	25
Hidden units in MLP	100
BiLSTM layers	2
BiLSTM hidden layer dimensions	125
BiLSTM output layer dimensions	125
α (for word dropout)	0.25
Learning rate	0.1
Optimization algorithm	Adam

Table 1: Hyper-parameter values used in shared task.

Language	$w_i \circ p_i$	$w_i \circ p_i \circ q_i$
Bulgarian(bg)	83.78	84.28
Catalan(ca)	85.67	86.26
German(de)	70.77	71.49
English(en)	75.91	76.42

Table 2: The LAS score of two different token representations on the 4 treebanks: Bulgarian(bg), Catalan(ca), German(de), English(en).

4.2 BiLSTM Feature Representation

Performances of simple feature representation and extended feature representation are given in Table 3. The results show that the extended feature representation slightly increases the performance of our system. while the simple feature representation can significantly speed up the system.

	Simple Feature			Extended Feature		
	LAS	train(sec)	test(sec)	LAS	train(sec)	test(sec)
bg	84.24	205.6	22.4	84.28	287.9	29.1
ca	85.74	663.5	37.2	86.26	878.5	48.8
de	71.15	416.8	29.8	71.49	733.2	37.4
en	76.18	375.6	24.5	76.42	524.8	31.1

Table 3: Comparison of Simple and Extended feature representations, we report LAS score, offline training time, and TIRA testing time.

4.3 Overall Performances

In our final submitted system to the shared task, we used lemmas, POS tags and CPOS tags in token representation and selected extended feature representation.

The macro-average LAS of the 55 big treebanks is 68.37% and the results for each language are

---

[1] In UD version 2.0 datasets, Kazakh and Uyghur only contain development set, no training set.

Language	LAS(max)	Language	LAS(max)	Language	LAS(max)	Language	LAS(max)
ar	65.65(72.90)	bg	84.28(89.81)	ca	86.26(90.70)	cs	83.85(90.17)
cs_cac	83.22(90.43)	cs_cltt	68.42(85.82)	cu	48.95(76.84)	da	72.78(82.97)
de	71.49(80.71)	el	78.72(87.38)	en	76.42(82.23)	en_lines	72.66(82.09)
en_partut	73.74(84.46)	es	75.41(87.29)	es_ancora	78.64(89.99)	et	55.40(71.65)
eu	62.89(81.44)	fa	61.43(86.31)	fi	69.86(85.64)	fi_ftb	75.13(86.81)
fr	80.07(85.51)	fr_sequoia	79.00(87.31)	gl	79.28(83.23)	got	57.02(71.36)
grc	49.30(73.19)	grc_proiel	60.61(75.28)	he	58.10(68.16)	hi	86.76(91.59)
hr	76.59(85.25)	hu	57.85(77.56)	id	74.40(79.19)	it	86.14(90.68)
ja	73.00(91.13)	ko	63.21(82.49)	la_ittb	74.37(87.02)	la_proiel	54.07(71.55)
lv	59.50(74.01)	nl	68.84(80.48)	nl_lassysmall	71.53(87.71)	no_bokmaal	75.96(89.88)
no_nynorsk	70.97(88.81)	pl	67.63(90.32)	pt	62.85(87.65)	pt_br	79.71(91.36)
ro	64.38(85.92)	ru	56.56(83.65)	ru_syntagrus	82.42(92.60)	sk	60.48(86.04)
sl	61.28(91.51)	sv	61.43(85.87)	sv_lines	61.09(82.89)	tr	49.11(62.79)
ur	61.77(82.28)	vi	31.67(47.51)	zh	58.03(68.56)		

Table 4: The LAS F1 score of our system and best system on the 55 big treebanks: ar, bg, ca, cs, cs_cac, cs_cltt, cu, da, de, el, en, en_lines, en_partut, es, es_ancora, et, eu, fa, fi, fi_ftb, fr, fr_sequoia, gl, got, grc, grc_proiel, he, hi, hr, hu, id, it, ja, ko, la_ittb, la_proiel, lv, nl, nl_lassysmall, no_bokmaal, no_nynorsk, pl, pt, pt_br, ro, ru, ru_syntagrus, sk, sl, sv, sv_lines, tr, ur, vi, zh.

Language	LAS(max)	Language	LAS(max)	Language	LAS(max)	Language	LAS(max)
fr_partut	72.40(88.13)	ga	55.07(70.06)	gl_treegal	61.17(74.34)	kk	_(29.22)
la	38.00(63.37)	sl_sst	23.77(59.07)	ug	_(43.51)	uk	20.61(75.33)

Table 5: The LAS F1 score of our system and best system on the 8 small treebanks: fr_partut, ga, gl_treegal, kk, la, sl_sst, ug, uk.

Language	LAS(max)	Language	LAS(max)	Language	LAS(max)	Language	LAS(max)
ar_pud	43.70(49.94)	cs_pud	80.44(84.42)	de_pud	69.13(74.86)	en_pud	79.02(85.51)
es_pud	72.61(81.05)	fi_pud	71.77(88.47)	fr_pud	73.92(78.81)	hi_pud	51.07(54.49)
it_pud	83.79(88.14)	ja_pud	76.66(83.75)	pt_pud	59.32(78.48)	ru_pud	52.73(75.71)
sv_pud	54.83(78.49)	tr_pud	22.52(38.22)				

Table 6: The LAS F1 score of our system and best system on the 14 PUD treebanks (additional parallel test sets): ar_pud, cs_pud, de_pud, en_pud, es_pud, fi_pud, fr_pud, hi_pud, it_pud, ja_pud, pt_pud, ru_pud, sv_pud, tr_pud.

Language	LAS(max)	Language	LAS(max)	Language	LAS(max)	Language	LAS(max)
bxr	12.44(32.24)	hsb	14.19(61.70)	kmr	8.62(47.53)	sme	10.00(48.96)

Table 7: The LAS F1 score of our system and best system on the 4 surprise language treebanks: bxr, hsb, kmr, sme.

shown in Table 4. The macro-average LAS of the 8 small treebanks is 33.88% and the results for each language are shown in Table 5. The macro-average LAS of the 14 PUD treebanks is 63.68% and the results for each language are shown in Table 6. The macro-average LAS of the 4 surprise language treebanks is 11.31% and the results for each language are shown in Table 7. The macro-averaged LAS F1 score of our system on all treebanks is 61.33%.

4.4 Computational Efficiencies

The parser is fast. Offline training time is about 300 words/sec. Prediction time on the official TIRA is about 400 words/sec without asking for more resources.

Memory requirements are lower than 512M for each language.

5 Conclusions

In this paper, we present a fast and lightweight multilingual dependency parsing system for the *CoNLL 2017 UD Shared Task*, which composed of a BiLSTMs feature extractor and a MLP classifier. Our system only uses UD version 2.0 datasets (without any additional data). The parser makes a good ranking at some of the big treebanks. The results suggests that the simple BiLSTM extractor is a reasonable baseline for multilingual dependency parsing. We will continue to improve our system and add cross-lingual techniques in our future work.

Acknowledgments

We would like to thank the *CoNLL 2017 UD Shared Task* organizers (Jan Hajič, Daniel Zeman, Joakim Nivre, Filip Ginter, Slav Petrov, Milan Straka , Martin Popel, Eduard Bejček, Martin Potthast et al.).

This research is supported by NSFC(61402175).

References

Sabine Buchholz and Erwin Marsi. 2006. Conll-x shared task on multilingual dependency parsing. In *Proceedings of the Tenth Conference on Computational Natural Language Learning, CoNLL 2006, New York City, USA, June 8-9, 2006*. pages 149–164. http://aclweb.org/anthology/W/W06/W06-2920.pdf.

Danqi Chen and Christopher D Manning. 2014. A fast and accurate dependency parser using neural networks. In *Empirical Methods in Natural Language Processing (EMNLP)*.

Eliyahu Kiperwasser and Yoav Goldberg. 2016. Simple and accurate dependency parsing using bidirectional LSTM feature representations. *TACL* 4:313–327. https://transacl.org/ojs/index.php/tacl/article/view/885.

Marco Kuhlmann, Carlos Gómez-Rodríguez, and Giorgio Satta. 2011. Dynamic programming algorithms for transition-based dependency parsers. In *The 49th Annual Meeting of the Association for Computational Linguistics: Human Language Technologies, Proceedings of the Conference, 19-24 June, 2011, Portland, Oregon, USA*. pages 673–682. http://www.aclweb.org/anthology/P11-1068.

Graham Neubig, Chris Dyer, Yoav Goldberg, Austin Matthews, Waleed Ammar, Antonios Anastasopoulos, Miguel Ballesteros, David Chiang, Daniel Clothiaux, Trevor Cohn, Kevin Duh, Manaal Faruqui, Cynthia Gan, Dan Garrette, Yangfeng Ji, Lingpeng Kong, Adhiguna Kuncoro, Gaurav Kumar, Chaitanya Malaviya, Paul Michel, Yusuke Oda, Matthew Richardson, Naomi Saphra, Swabha Swayamdipta, and Pengcheng Yin. 2017. Dynet: The dynamic neural network toolkit. *arXiv preprint arXiv:1701.03980* .

Joakim Nivre, Željko Agić, Lars Ahrenberg, et al. 2017a. Universal dependencies 2.0 CoNLL 2017 shared task development and test data. LINDAT/CLARIN digital library at the Institute of Formal and Applied Linguistics, Charles University. http://hdl.handle.net/11234/1-2184.

Joakim Nivre, Marie-Catherine de Marneffe, Filip Ginter, Yoav Goldberg, Jan Hajič, Christopher Manning, Ryan McDonald, Slav Petrov, Sampo Pyysalo, Natalia Silveira, Reut Tsarfaty, and Daniel Zeman. 2016. Universal Dependencies v1: A multilingual treebank collection. In *Proceedings of the 10th International Conference on Language Resources and Evaluation (LREC 2016)*. European Language Resources Association, Portoro, Slovenia, pages 1659–1666.

Joakim Nivre, Johan Hall, Sandra Kübler, Ryan T. McDonald, Jens Nilsson, Sebastian Riedel, and Deniz Yuret. 2007. The conll 2007 shared task on dependency parsing. In *EMNLP-CoNLL 2007, Proceedings of the 2007 Joint Conference on Empirical Methods in Natural Language Processing and Computational Natural Language Learning, June 28-30, 2007, Prague, Czech Republic*. pages 915–932. http://www.aclweb.org/anthology/D07-1096.

Joakim Nivre et al. 2017b. Universal Dependencies 2.0. LINDAT/CLARIN digital library at the Institute of Formal and Applied Linguistics, Charles University, Prague, http://hdl.handle.net/

11234/1-1983.   http://hdl.handle.net/11234/1-1983.

Martin Potthast, Tim Gollub, Francisco Rangel, Paolo Rosso, Efstathios Stamatatos, and Benno Stein. 2014.   Improving the reproducibility of PAN's shared tasks: Plagiarism detection, author identification, and author profiling.   In Evangelos Kanoulas, Mihai Lupu, Paul Clough, Mark Sanderson, Mark Hall, Allan Hanbury, and Elaine Toms, editors, *Information Access Evaluation meets Multilinguality, Multimodality, and Visualization. 5th International Conference of the CLEF Initiative (CLEF 14)*. Springer, Berlin Heidelberg New York, pages 268–299. https://doi.org/10.1007/978-3-319-11382-1_22.

Milan Straka, Jan Hajič, and Jana Straková. 2016. UDPipe: trainable pipeline for processing CoNLL-U files performing tokenization, morphological analysis, POS tagging and parsing.   In *Proceedings of the 10th International Conference on Language Resources and Evaluation (LREC 2016)*. European Language Resources Association, Portoro, Slovenia.

David Weiss, Chris Alberti, Michael Collins, and Slav Petrov. 2015. Structured training for neural network transition-based parsing.   *CoRR* abs/1506.06158. http://arxiv.org/abs/1506.06158.

Daniel Zeman, Martin Popel, Milan Straka, Jan Hajič, Joakim Nivre, Filip Ginter, Juhani Luotolahti, Sampo Pyysalo, Slav Petrov, Martin Potthast, Francis Tyers, Elena Badmaeva, Memduh Gökırmak, Anna Nedoluzhko, Silvie Cinková, Jan Hajič jr., Jaroslava Hlaváčová, Václava Kettnerová, Zdeňka Urešová, Jenna Kanerva, Stina Ojala, Anna Missilä, Christopher Manning, Sebastian Schuster, Siva Reddy, Dima Taji, Nizar Habash, Herman Leung, Marie-Catherine de Marneffe, Manuela Sanguinetti, Maria Simi, Hiroshi Kanayama, Valeria de Paiva, Kira Droganova, Hěctor Martínez Alonso, Hans Uszkoreit, Vivien Macketanz, Aljoscha Burchardt, Kim Harris, Katrin Marheinecke, Georg Rehm, Tolga Kayadelen, Mohammed Attia, Ali Elkahky, Zhuoran Yu, Emily Pitler, Saran Lertpradit, Michael Mandl, Jesse Kirchner, Hector Fernandez Alcalde, Jana Strnadova, Esha Banerjee, Ruli Manurung, Antonio Stella, Atsuko Shimada, Sookyoung Kwak, Gustavo Mendonça, Tatiana Lando, Rattima Nitisaroj, and Josie Li. 2017. CoNLL 2017 Shared Task: Multilingual Parsing from Raw Text to Universal Dependencies. In *Proceedings of the CoNLL 2017 Shared Task: Multilingual Parsing from Raw Text to Universal Dependencies*. Association for Computational Linguistics.

The ParisNLP entry at the ConLL UD Shared Task 2017:
A Tale of a #ParsingTragedy

Éric de La Clergerie[1]   Benoît Sagot[1]   Djamé Seddah[2,1]

(1) Inria   (2) Université Paris Sorbonne

`{firstname.lastname}@inria.fr`

Abstract

We present the ParisNLP entry at the UD CoNLL 2017 parsing shared task. In addition to the UDpipe models provided, we built our own data-driven tokenization models, sentence segmenter and lexicon-based morphological analyzers. All of these were used with a range of different parsing models (neural or not, feature-rich or not, transition or graph-based, etc.) and the best combination for each language was selected. Unfortunately, a glitch in the shared task's Matrix led our model selector to run generic, weakly lexicalized models, tailored for surprise languages, instead of our dataset-specific models. Because of this #ParsingTragedy, we officially ranked 27th, whereas our real models finally unofficially ranked 6th.

1 Introduction

The Universal Dependency parsing shared task (Zeman et al., 2017) was arguably the hardest shared task the field has seen since the CoNLL 2006 shared task (Buchholz and Marsi, 2006) where 13 languages had to be parsed in gold token, gold morphology mode, while its follow up in 2007 introduced an out-of-domain track for a subset of the 2006 languages (Nivre et al., 2007). The SANCL "parsing the web" shared task (Petrov and McDonald, 2012) introduced the parsing of English non-canonical data in gold token, predicted morphology mode and saw a large decrease of performance compared to what was usually reported in English parsing of the Penn Treebank . As far as we know, the SPMRL shared tasks (Seddah et al., 2013, 2014) were first to introduce a non gold tokenization, predicted morphology, scenario for two morphologically rich languages, Arabic

and Hebrew while, for other languages, complex source tokens were left untouched (Korean, German, French...). Here, the Universal Dependency (hereafter "UD") shared task introduced an end-to-end parsing evaluation protocol where none of the usual stratification layers were to be evaluated in *gold* mode: tokenization, sentence segmentation, morphology prediction and of course syntactic structures had to be produced[1] for 46 languages covering 81 datasets. Some of them are low-resource languages, with training sets containing as few as 22 sentences. In addition, an out-of-domain scenario was *de facto* included via a new 14-language parallel test set. Because of the very nature of the UD initiative, some languages are covered by several treebanks (English, French, Russian, Finnish...) built by different teams, who interpreted the annotation guidelines with a certain degree of freedom when it comes to rare, or simply not covered, phenomena.[2] Let us add that our systems had to be deployed on a virtual machine and evaluated in a total blind mode with different metadata between the trial and the test runs.

All those parameters led to a multi-dimension shared task which can loosely be summarized by the following "equation":

$$Lang.Tok.WS.Seg.Morph.DS.OOD.AS.Exp,$$

where $Lang$ stands for Language, Tok for tokenization, WS for word segmentation, Seg for sentence segmentation, $Morph$ for predicted morphology, DS for data scarcity, OOD for out-of-domainness, AS for annotation scheme, Exp for experimental environment.

---

[1] Although baseline prediction for all layers were made available through Straka et al.'s (2016) pre-trained models or pre-annotated development and test files.

[2] See for example, the discrepancy between fr$_{\text{partut}}$ and the other French treebanks regarding the annotation of the not so rare *car* conjunction, 'for/because', and the associated syntactic structures, cf. `https://github.com/UniversalDependencies/docs/issues/432`.

Proceedings of the CoNLL 2017 Shared Task: Multilingual Parsing from Raw Text to Universal Dependencies, pages 243–252,
Vancouver, Canada, August 3-4, 2017. © 2017 Association for Computational Linguistics

In this shared task, we earnestly tried to cover all of these dimensions, ranking #3 in UPOS tagging and #5 in sentence segmentation. But we were ultimately strongly impacted by the Exp parameter (cf. Section 6.3), a parameter we could not control, resulting in a disappointing rank of #27 out of 33. Once this variable was corrected, we reached rank #6.[3]

Our system relies on a strong pre-processing pipeline, which includes lexicon-enhanced statistical taggers as well as data-driven tokenizers and sentence segmenters. The parsing step proper makes use for each dataset of one of 4 parsing models: 2 non-neural ones (transition and graph-based) and extensions of these models with character and word-level neural layers.

2 Architecture and Strategies

In preparation for the shared task, we have developed and adapted a number of different models for tokenization[4] and sentence segmentation, tagging—predicting UPOS and the values for a (manually selected, language-independent) subset of the morphological attributes (hereafter "partial MSTAGs")— and parsing. For each dataset for which training data was available, we combined different pre-processing strategies with different parsing models and selected the best performing ones based on parsing F-scores on the development set in the predicted token scenario. Whenever no development set was available, we achieved this selection based on a 10-fold cross-evaluation on the training set.

Our baseline pre-processing strategy consisted in simply using the data annotated using UDPipe (Straka et al., 2016) provided by the shared task organizers. We also developed new tools of our own, namely a tagger as well as a joint tokenizer and sentence segmenter. We chose whether to use the baseline UDPipe annotations or our own annotations for each of the following steps: sentence segmentation, tokenization, and tagging (UPOS and partial MSTAGs). We used UDPipe-based information in all configurations for XPOS, lemma, and word segmentation, based on an *a posteriori* character-level alignment algorithm.

At the parsing level, we developed and tried five different parsers, both neural and non-neural, which are variants of the shift-reduce (hereafter "SR") and maximum spanning-tree algorithms (hereafter "MST"). The next two sections describe in more detail our different pre-processing and parsing architectures, give insights into their performance, and show how we selected our final architecture for each dataset.

3 Pre-processing

3.1 Tagging

Tagging architecture Taking advantage of the opportunity given by the shared task, we developed a new part-of-speech tagging system inspired by our previous work on MElt (Denis and Sagot, 2012), a left-to-right maximum-entropy tagger relying on features based on both the training corpus and, when available, an external lexicon. The two main advantages of using an external lexicon as a source of additional features are the following: (i) it provides the tagger with information about words unknown to the training corpus; (ii) it allows the tagger to have a better insight into the right context of the current word, for which the tagger has not yet predicted anything.

Whereas MElt uses the `megam` package to learn tagging models, our new system, named alVW-Tagger, relies on Vowpal Wabbit.[5] One of Vowpal Wabbit's major advantages is its training speed, which allowed us to train many tagger variants for each language, in order to assess, for each language, the relative performance of different types of external lexicons and different ways to use them as a source of features. In all our experiments, we used VW in its default multiclass mode, i.e. using a squared loss and the one-against-all strategy. Our feature set is a slight extension of the one used by MElt (cf. Denis and Sagot, 2012).

The first improvement over MElt concerns how information extracted from the external lexicons is used: instead of only using the categories provided by the lexicon, we also use morphological features. We experimented different modes. In the baseline mode, the category provided by the lexicon is the concatenation of a UPOS and a sequence of morphological features, hereafter the "full category". In the F mode ("ms mode" in Table 1), only the UPOS is used (morphological features

---

[3]`http://universaldependencies.org/conll17/results-unofficial.html`

[4]We follow the shared task terminology in differentiating tokenization and word segmentation. A tokenizer only performs token segmentation (i.e. source tokens), and does not predict word segmentation (i.e. wordforms, or tree tokens).

[5]`https://github.com/JohnLangford/vowpal_wabbit/`

are ignored). In the M mode, both the full category and the sequence of morphological features are used separately. Finally, in the FM mode, both the UPOS and the sequence of morphological features are used separately.

The second improvement over MElt is that alVWTagger predicts both a part-of-speech (here, a UPOS) and a set of morphological features. As mentioned earlier, we decided to restrict the set of morphological features we predict, in order to reduce data sparsity.[6] For each word, our tagger first predicts a UPOS. Next, it uses this UPOS as a feature to predict the set of morphological features as a whole, using an auxiliary model.[7]

Extraction of morphological lexicons   As mentioned above, our tagger is able to use an external lexicon as a source of external information. We therefore created a number of morphological lexicons for as many languages as possible, relying only on data and tools that were allowed by the shared task instructions. We compared the UPOS accuracies on the development sets, or on the training sets in an 10-fold setting when no development data was provided, and retained the best performing lexicon for each dataset (see Table 1). Each lexicon was extracted from one of the following sources or several of them, using an *a posteriori* merging algorithm:

- The monolingual lexicons from the Apertium project (lexicon type code "AP" in Table 1);
- Raw monolingual raw corpora provided by the shared task organizers, after application of a basic rule-based tokenizer and the appropriate Apertium or Giellatekno morphological analyzers (codes "APma" or "GTma");
- The corresponding training dataset (code "T") or another training dataset for the same language (code "T*dataset*");
- The UDPipe-annotated corpora provided by the shared task organizers (code "UDP");
- A previously extracted lexicon for another language, which we automatically "translated" using a dedicated algorithm, which we provided, as a seed, with a bilingual lexicon automatically extracted from OPUS sentence-aligned data (code "TR*source_language*").

All lexical information not directly extracted from UDPipe-annotated data or from training data was converted to the UD morphological categories (UPOS and morphological features).

For a few languages only (for lack of time), we also created expanded versions of our lexicons using word embeddings re-computed on the raw data provided by the organizers, assigning to words unknown to the lexicon the morphological information associated with the closest known word (using a simple euclidian distance on the word embedding space).[8] When the best performing lexicon is one of these extended lexicons, it is indicated in Table 1 by the "-e" suffix.

3.2   Tokenization and sentence segmentation

Using the same architecture as our tagger, yet without resorting to external lexicons, we developed a data-driven tokenizer and sentence segmenter, which runs as follows. First, a simple rule-based pre-tokenizer is applied to the raw text of the training corpus, after removing all sentence boundaries.[9,10] This pre-tokenizer outputs a sequence of "pre-tokens," in which, at each pre-token boundary, we keep trace of whether a whitespace was present in the raw text or not at this position. Next, we use the gold train data to label each pre-token boundary with one of the following labels: not a token boundary (NATB), token boundary (TB), sentence boundary (SB).[11] This model can then be applied on raw text, after the pre-tokenizer has been applied. It labels each pre-token boundary, resulting in the following decisions depending on whether it corresponds to a whitespace in the raw text or not: (i) if it predicts NATB at a non-whitespace boundary, the boundary is removed; (ii) if it predicts NATB at a whitespace boundary, it results in a token-with-space; (iii) if it predicts TB (resp. SB) at a non-whitespace boundary, a token (resp. sentence) boundary is created and "SpaceAfter=No" is added to the preceedings token; (iv) if it predicts

---

[6]The list of features we retained is the following: Case, Gender, Number, PronType, VerbForm, Mood, and Voice.

[7]We also experimented with per-feature prediction, but it resulted in slightly lower accuracy results on average, as measured on development sets.

[8]We did not used the embeddings provided by the organizers because we experimentally found that the 10-token window used to train these embeddings resulted in less accurate results than when using smaller windows, especially when the raw corpus available was of a limited size.

[9]Apart from paragraph boundaries whenever available.

[10]On languages such as Japanese and Chinese, each non-latin character is a pre-token on its own.

[11]Our tokenizer and sentence segmenter relies on the almost same features as the tagger, except for two special features, which encode whether the current pre-token is a strong (resp. weak) punctuation, based on two manually crafted lists.

| Dataset | ours (best setting) | | | UDPipe |
	lexicon type	ms mode	overall acc.	overall acc.
ar	AP-e	M	**94.71**	94.57
bg	AP	F	97.61	**97.72**
ca	AP-e	FM	**98.42**	98.15
cs	AP	M	**98.83**	98.48
cs_{cac}	Tcs		**99.24**	98.78
cs_{cltt}	AP+Tcs	F	**94.34**	92.06
cu	T	F	**95.15**	94.07
da	AP		**96.30**	95.19
de	AP	M	**92.70**	91.39
el	AP	F	**95.53**	94.17
en	AP	F	**94.68**	94.43
en_{lines}	AP	FM	**96.08**	94.75
en_{partut}	AP+T	FM	**95.90**	94.39
es	AP		**96.47**	96.24
es_{ancora}	AP	FM	**98.39**	98.16
et	GTms	FM	**89.28**	87.52
eu	AP	F	**94.48**	92.80
fa	*no lexicon*		96.04	**96.17**
fi	GTms	FM	**95.06**	94.52
fi_{ftb}	GTms	F	**92.50**	92.34

| Dataset | ours (best setting) | | | UDPipe |
	lexicon type	ms mode	overall acc.	overall acc.
fr	AP-e		**97.30**	97.08
$fr_{sequoia}$	AP-e	FM	**97.54**	96.60
ga	UDP	M	—	—
gl	AP	FM	**97.45**	96.77
got	T		**94.53**	94.22
grc	$Tgrc_{proiel}$-e		**89.56**	81.54
grc_{proiel}	UDP-e	FM	**96.40**	96.01
he	AP	FM	**96.68**	95.72
hi	AP	F	**96.59**	95.79
hr	TRsl	M	**96.94**	96.15
hu	T		**93.90**	92.31
id	AP	M	92.98	**93.36**
it	AP	F	**97.55**	97.23
it_{partut}	Trit	M	**97.89**	95.16
ja	*no lexicon*		**96.87**	96.72
kk	APms		—	—
ko	*no lexicon*		**93.77**	93.68
la_{ittb}	TRit+T		**97.15**	96.86
la_{proiel}	TRit+T-e	FM	**95.62**	95.43
lv	AP	FM	**93.43**	90.81

| Dataset | ours (best setting) | | | UDPipe |
	lexicon type	ms mode	overall acc.	overall acc.
nl	AP	F	**94.70**	94.07
$nl_{lassysmall}$	AP+Tnl	F	**96.74**	95.65
$no_{bokmaal}$	AP		**97.66**	97.34
$no_{nynorsk}$	AP	M	**97.23**	96.74
pl	AP	M	**97.03**	95.34
pt	AP	FM	**97.21**	97.00
pt_{br}	AP+Tpt	FM	**97.96**	97.40
ro	AP		**97.34**	96.98
ru	AP	M	**96.62**	94.95
$ru_{syntagrus}$	AP	FM	**98.54**	98.20
sk	TRcs	FM	**96.00**	93.14
sl	AP	FM	**97.82**	96.34
sv	AP	FM	**96.32**	95.17
sv_{lines}	AP	F	**96.01**	94.63
tr	APma	FM	**93.65**	92.25
ug	UDP		—	—
uk	AP	M	—	—
ur	AP		**93.01**	92.45
vi	*no lexicon*		88.60	**88.68**
zh	AP+UDP		**91.40**	91.21

Table 1: UPOS accuracies for the UDPipe baseline and for our best alVWTagger setting.

TB (resp. SB) at a whitespace boundary, a token (resp. sentence) boundary is created.

We compared our tokenization and sentence segmentation results with the UDPipe baseline on development sets. Whenever the UDPipe tokenization and sentence segmentation scores were both better, we decided to use them in all configurations. Other datasets, for which tokenization and sentence segmentation performance is shown in Table 2, were split into two sets: those on which our tokenization was better but sentence segmentation was worse—for those, we forced the UDPipe sentence segmentation in all settings—, and those for which both our tokenization and sentence segmentation were better.

3.3 Preprocessing model configurations

As mentioned in Section 2, we used parsing-based evaluation to select our pre-processing strategy for each corpus. More precisely, we selected for each dataset one of the following strategies:

1. UDPIPE: the UDPipe baseline is used and provided as such to the parser.
2. TAG: the UDPipe baseline is used, except for the UPOS and MSTAG information, which is provided by our own tagger.
3. TAG+TOK+SEG and TAG+TOK: we apply our own tokenization and POS-tagger to produce UPOS and MSTAG information; sentence segmentation is performed either by us (TAG+TOK+SEG (available for datasets with "yes" in the last column in Table 2) or by the UDPipe baseline (TAG+TOK, available for datasets with "no" in Table 2).

| Dataset | ours | | UDPIPE | | Use our |
	tok. F-sc.	sent. F-sc.	tokenis. F-sc.	sent. F-sc.	sent. seg.?
ar	99.54	**92.75**	**99.99**	77.99	yes
ca	99.95	**99.01**	**99.97**	98.77	yes
cs_{cac}	**100.00**	99.5	**100.00**	99.09	yes
cu	99.98	**39.44**	**100.00**	37.09	yes
da	**100.00**	84.01	99.68	**84.36**	no
el	99.57	**92.61**	**99.87**	88.67	yes
et	99.69	**90.82**	**99.79**	84.91	yes
eu	99.93	**99.42**	**99.99**	99.00	yes
fa	99.95	**99.42**	**100.00**	97.14	yes
fi	99.54	**87.76**	**99.69**	86.47	yes
fi_{ftb}	**100.00**	**85.94**	99.94	82.52	yes
gl	**99.73**	**96.8**	99.06	92.44	yes
got	99.99	**28.95**	**100.00**	23.51	yes
hu	99.74	**96.83**	**99.91**	94.55	yes
it	99.73	**96.31**	**99.82**	93.20	yes
ja	**92.63**	99.61	89.53	**99.71**	no
la_{ittb}	**99.90**	**78.71**	99.88	77.38	yes
la_{proiel}	**100.00**	**19.92**	99.99	19.76	yes
lv	**99.21**	91.48	98.91	**96.48**	no
$no_{nynorsk}$	99.82	**94.30**	**99.92**	93.05	yes
pt	**99.89**	**90.23**	99.82	89.27	yes
vi	**87.25**	92.23	83.99	**96.28**	no

Table 2: Tokenization and sentence segmentation accuracies for the UDPipe baseline and our tokenizer (restricted to those datasets for which we experimented the use of our own tokenization).

Whenever we used our own tokenization and not that of the UDPipe baseline, we used a character-level alignment algorithm to map this information to our own tokens.

Table 1 shows the configuration retained for each language for which a training set was provided in advance.[12] For surprise language

---

[12]Note that our parsing-performance-based selection strategy did not always result in the same outcome as what we would have been chosen based solely on the comparison of our own tools with UDPipe's baseline. For instance, our new tagger gets better results than UDPipe in UPOS tagging on all development corpora but one, yet we used UDPipe-based UPOS for 24 non-PUD corpora.

datasets, we always used the UDPipe configuration.[13] For PUD corpora, we used the same configuration as for the basic dataset for the same language (for instance, we used for the fr$_{pud}$ dataset the same configuration as that chosen for the fr dataset).[14] Table 1 indicates for each dataset which configuration was retained.

4 Parsing Models

We used 4 base parsers, all implemented on top of the DYALOG system (de La Clergerie, 2005), a logic-programming environment (*à la* Prolog) specially tailored for natural language processing, in particular for tabulation-based dynamic programming algorithms.

Non-neural parsing models The first two parsers are feature-based and use no neural components. The most advanced one is DYALOG-SR, a shift-reduce transition-based parser, using dynamic programming techniques to maintain beams (Villemonte De La Clergerie, 2013). It accepts a large set of transition types, besides the usual `shift` and `reduce` transitions of the arc-standard strategy. In particular, to handle non-projectivity, it can use different instances of `swap` transitions, to swap 2 stack elements between the 3 topmost ones. A `noop` transition may also be used at the end of parsing paths to compensate differences in path lengths. Training is done with a structured averaged perceptron, using early aggressive updates, whenever the oracle falls out of the beam, or when a violation occurs, or when a margin becomes too high, etc.[15]

Feature templates are used to combine elementary standard features:

- Word features related to the 3 topmost stack elements $s_{i=0\cdots2}$, 4 first buffer elements $I_{j=1\cdots4}$, leftmost/rightmost children $[lr]s_i$ /grandchildren of the stack elements $[lr]2s_i$, and governors. These features include the lexical form, lemma, UPOS, XPOS,

morphosyntactic features, Brown-like clusters (derived from word embeddings), and flags indicating capitalization, numbers, etc.

- Binned distances between some of these elements
- Dependency features related to the leftmost/rightmost dependency labels for s_i (and dependent $[lr]s_i$), label set for the dependents of s_i and $[lr]s_i$, and number of dependents
- Last action (+label) leading to the current parsing state.

The second feature-based parser is DYALOG-MST, a parser developed for the shared task and implementing the Maximum Spanning Tree (MST) algorithm (McDonald et al., 2005). By definition, DYALOG-MST may produce non-projective trees. Being recent and much less flexible than DYALOG-SR, it also relies on a much smaller set of first-order features and templates, related to the source and target words of a dependency edge, plus its label and binned distance. It also exploits features related to the number of occurrences of a given POS between the source and target of an edge (inside features) or not covered by the edge but in the neighborhood of the nodes (outside features). Similar features are also implemented for punctuation.

Neural parsing models Both feature-based parsers were then extended with a neural-based component, implemented in C++ with DyNet (Neubig et al., 2017). The key idea is that the neural component can provide the best parser action or, if aksed, a ranking of all possible actions. This information is then used as extra features to finally take a decision. The 2 neural-based variants of DYALOG-SR and DYALOG-MST, straightforwardly dubbed DYALOG-SRNN and DYALOG-MSTNN, implement a similar architecture, the one for DYALOG-SRNN being a bit more advanced and stable. Moreover, DYALOG-MSTNN was only found to be the best choice for a very limited number of treebanks. In addition to these models, we also investigated a basic version of DYALOG-SRNN that only uses, in a feature-poor setting, its character-level component and its joint action prediction, and which provides the best performance on 3 languages. The following discussion will focus on DYALOG-SRNN.

The architecture is inspired by Google's PARSEYSAURUS (Alberti et al., 2017), with a first left-to-right char LSTM covering the whole

---

[13] For surprise languages, the UDPipe baseline was trained on data not available to the shared task participants.

[14] Because of a last-minute bug, we used the TAG configuration for tr$_{pud}$ and pt$_{pud}$ although we used the UDPIPE configuration for tr and pt. We also used the TAG setting for fi$_{pud}$ rather than the TAG+TOK+SEG setting used for fi.

[15] By "violation," we mean for instance adding an edge not present in the gold tree, a first step towards dynamic oracles. We explored this path further for the shared task through dynamic programming exploration of the search space, yet did not observe significant improvements yet.

sentence and (artificial) whitespaces introduced to separate tokens.[16] The output vectors of the char LSTM at the token separations are used as (learned) word embeddings that are concatenated (when present) with both the pre-trained ones provided for the task and the UPOS tags predicted by the external tagger. The concatenated vectors serve as input to a word bi-LSTM that is also used to predict UPOS tags as a joint task (training with the gold tags provided as oracle). For a given word w_i, its final vector representation is the concatenation of the output of the bi-LSTM layers at position i with the LSTM-predicted UPOS tag.

The deployment of the LSTMs is done once for a given sentence. Then, for any parsing state, characterized by the stack, buffer, and dependency components mentioned above, a query is made to the neural layers to suggest an action. The query fetches the final vectors associated with the stack, buffer, and dependent *state* words, and completes it with input vectors for 12 (possibly empty) label dependencies and for the last action. The number of considered state words is a hyper-parameter of the system, which can range between 10 and 19, the best and default value being 10, covering the 3 topmost stack elements and 6 dependent children, but only the first buffer lookahead word[17] and no grandchildren. Through a hidden layer and a softmax layer, the neural component returns the best action `paction` (and `plabel`) but also the ranking and weights of all possible actions. The best action is used as a feature to guide the decision of the parser in combination with the other features, the final weight of an action being a linear weighted combination of the weights returned by both perceptron and neural layers.[18]

A dropout rate of 0.25 was used to introduce some noise. The Dynet AdamTrainer was chosen for gradient updates, with its default parameters. Many hyperparameters are however available as options, such as the number of layers of the char and word LSTMs, the size of input, hidden and output dimensions for the LSTMs and feedforward layers. A partial exploration of these parameters was run on a few languages, but not in a systematic way given the lack of time and the huge

number of possibilities. Clearly, even if we did try 380 distinct parsing configurations through around 16K training runs,[19] we are still far away from language-specific parameter tuning, thus leaving room for improvement.

5   Results

Because of the greater flexibility of transition-based parsers, MST-based models were only used for a few languages. However, our results, provided in the Appendix, show the good performance of these models, for instance on Old Church Slavonic (cu), Gothic (got), Ancient Greek (grc), and Kazakh (kk). Already during development, it was surprising to observe, for most languages, a strong preference for either SR-based models or MST-based ones. For instance, for Ancient Greek, the best score in gold token mode for a MST-based model is 62.43 while the best score for a SR-based one is 60.59. On the other hand, for Arabic (ar), we get 74.87 for the best SR model and 71.44 for the best MST model.

Altogether, our real, yet unofficial scores are encouraging (ranking #6 in LAS) while our official UPOS tagging, sentence segmentation and tokenization results ranked respectively #3, #6 and #5. Let us note that our low LAS official results, #27, was the result of a mismatch between the trial and test experimental environments provided by the organizers (cf. Section 6.3). However, we officially ranked #5 on surprise languages, which were not affected by this mismatch.

6   Discussion

While developing our parsers, training and evaluation were mostly performed using the UDPipe pre-processing baseline with predicted UPOS and MSTAGs but gold tokenization and gold sentence segmentation. For several (bad) reasons, only in the very last days did we train on files tagged with our preprocessing chain. Even later, evaluation (but no training) was finally performed on dev files with predicted segmentation and tokenization, done by either UDPipe or by our pre-processing chains (TAG, TAG+TOK+SEG or TAG+TOK). Based on the results, we selected, for each language and treebank, the best preprocessing configuration and the best parsing model.

---

[16]A better option would be to add whitespace only when present in the original text.

[17]We suppose the information relative to the other lookahead words are encapsulated in the final vector of the first lookahead word.

[18]The best way to combine the weights of the neural and feature components remains a point to further investigate.

[19]We count as a training run the conjunction of a parser configuration, a treebank, and a beam size. Please note that a synthesis may be found at `http://alpage.inria.fr/~clerger/UD17/synthesis.html`

In general, we observed that neural-based models without features often worked worse than pure feature-based parsers (such as `srcat`), but great when combined with features. We believe that, being quite recent, our neural architecture is not yet up-to-date and that we still have to evaluate several possible options. Between using no features (`srnnsimple` and `srnncharsimple` models) and using a rich feature set (`srnnpx` models), where the predicted actions `paction` and `plabel` may be combined with other features, we also tested, for a few languages, a more restricted feature set with no combinations of `paction` and `plabel` with other features (`srnncharjoin` models). These latter combinations are faster to train and reach good scores, as shown in Table 3.

Lang	srcat	srnn charsimple	srnn charjoin	px
sk	76.85	67.85	78.87	80.84
cs$_{cac}$	84.48	77.07	84.80	84.85
lv	63.86	59.57	66.95	68.74
ko	54.43	57.19	70.91	71.45

Table 3: Neural models & feature impact (Dev)

For the treebanks without dev files, we simply did a standard training, using a random 80/20-split of the train files. Given more time, we would have tried transfer from other treebanks when available (as described below).

To summarize, a large majority of 47 selected models were based on DYALOG-SRNN with a rich feature set, 29 of them relying on predicted data coming from our processing chains (TAG or TAG+TOK+SEG), the other ones relying on the tags and segmentation predicted by UDPipe. 10 models were based on DYALOG-MSTNN, with 5 of them relying on our preprocessing chain. Finally, 5 (resp. 2) were simply based on DYALOG-SR (resp. DYALOG-MST), none of them using our preprocessing.

6.1 OOV Handling

Besides the fact that we did not train on files with predicted segmentation, we are also aware of weaknesses in handling unknown words in test files. Indeed, at some point, we made the choice to filter the large word-embedding files by the vocabulary found in the train and dev files of each dataset. We made the same for the clusters we derived from word embeddings. It means that unknown words have no associated word embed-

dings or clusters (besides a default one). The impact of this choice is not yet clear but it should be a relatively significant part of the performance gap between our score of the dev set (with predicted segmentation) and on the final test set.[20]

6.2 Generic Models

We also started exploring the idea of transferring information between close languages, such as Slavic languages. Treebank families were created for some groups of related languages by randomly sampling their respective treebanks as described in Table 4. A fully generic treebank was also created by randomly sampling 41k sentences from almost all languages (1k sentences per primary treebank).

Model	Languages	#sent.
ZZNorthGerman	da, no, sv	8k
ZZRoman	fr, ca, es, it, pt, ro, gl	20k
ZZSouthSlavic	bg, cu, hr, sl	16k
ZZWestSlavic	cs, pl, sk	9k
ZZWestGerman	de, du, nl	12k
ZZGeneric	sampling main 46 lang.	41k

Table 4: Generic models partition

The non-neural parsers were trained on these new treebanks, using much less lexicalized information (no clusters, no word embeddings, no lemmas, and keeping only UPOS tags, but keeping forms and lemmas when present). We tested using the resulting models, whose named are prefixed with "ZZ", as base models for further training on some small language treebanks. However, preliminary evaluations did not show any major improvement and, due to lack of time, we put on hold this line of research, while keeping our generic parsers as backup ones.

Some of these generic parsers were used for the 4 surprise languages, with Upper Sorbian using a ZZSlavic parser[21] (LAS=56.22), North Saami using ZZFinnish (LAS=37.33), and the two other ones using the fully generic parser (Kurmanji LAS=34.8; Buryat LAS=28.55).

6.3 The Tragedy

Ironically, the back-off mechanism we set up for our model selection was also a cause of failure and salvation. Because of the absence of the `name`

---

²⁰An average of 0.4 points between dev and tests. Dev results available at `goo.gl/1yuC8L`.

²¹We had planned to use a ZZWSlavic parser but made a mistake in the configuration file.

field in the test set metadata, which was nevertheless present in the dev run and crucially also in the trial run metadata, the selection of the best model per language was broken and led to the selection of back-off models, either a family one or in most cases the generic one. The Tira blind test configuration prevented us from discovering this experimental discrepancy before the deadline. Once we adapted our wrapper to the test metadata, the appropriate models were selected, resulting in our real run results. It turned out that our non language-specific, generic models performed surprisingly well, with a macro-average F-score of 60% LAS. Of course, except for Ukrainian, our language-specific models reach much better performance, with a macro-average F-score of 70.3%. But our misadventure is an invitation to further investigation.

However, it is unclear at this stage whether or not mixing languages in a large treebank really has advantages over using several small treebanks. In very preliminary experiments on Greek, Arabic, and French, we extracted the 1000 sentences present in the generic treebank for these languages and trained the best generic configuration (`srcat`, beam 6) on each of these small treebanks. As shown in Table 5, the scores on the development sets do not exhibit any improvement coming from mixing languages in a large pool and are largely below the scores obtained on a larger language-specific treebank.

Lang	generic	small	full	size
Greek	76.25	76.29	78.40	1,662
Arabic	57.94	59.84	64.34	6,075
French	78.28	79.59	84.81	14,553

Table 5: Generic pool vs. small treebank vs. full treebank (with `srcat` models (LAS, Dev)

6.4 Impact of the Lexicon

We also investigated the influence of our tagging strategy with respect to the UDPipe baseline. Figure 1 plots the parsing LAS F-scores with respect to training corpus size. It also show the result of logarithmic regressions performed on datasets for which we used the UDPipe baseline for preprocessing versus those for which we used the TAG configuration. As can be seen, using the UDPipe baseline results in a much stronger impact of training corpus size, whereas using our own tagger leads to more stable results. We interpret this

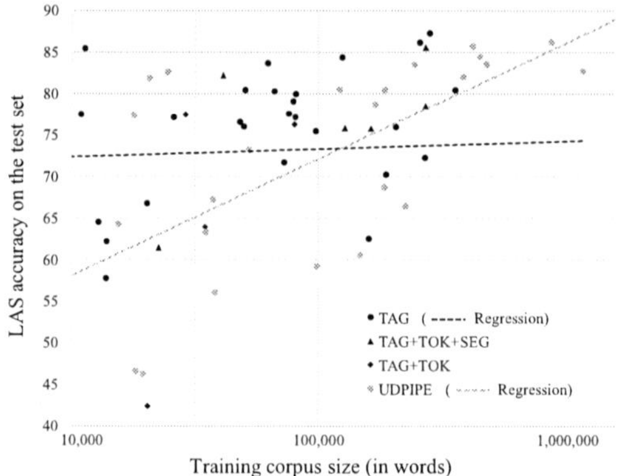

Figure 1: LAS F-score w.r.t. training corpus size

observation as resulting from the influence of external lexicons during tagging, which lowers the negative impact of out-of-training-corpus words on tagging and therefore parsing performance. It illustrates the relevance of using external lexical information, especially for small training corpora.

7 Conclusion

The shared task was a excellent opportunity for us to develop a new generation of NLP components to process a large spectrum of languages, using some of the latest developments in deep learning. However, it was really a challenging task, with an overwhelming number of decisions to take and experiments to run over a short period of time.

We now have many paths for improvement. First, because we have a very flexible but newly developed architecture, we need to stabilize it by carefully selecting the best design choices and parameters. We also plan to explore the potential of a multilingual dataset based on the UD annotation scheme, focusing on cross-language transfer and language-independent models.

Acknowledgments

We thank the organizers and the data providers who made this shared task possible within the core Universal Dependencies framework (Nivre et al., 2016), namely the authors of the UD version 2.0 datasets (Nivre et al., 2017), the baseline UDPipe models (Straka et al., 2016), and of course the team behind the TIRA evaluation platform (Potthast et al., 2014) to whom we owe a lot. This work was funded by the ANR projects ParSiTi (ANR-16-CE33-0021) and SoSweet (ANR-15-CE38-0011-01).

References

Chris Alberti, Daniel Andor, Ivan Bogatyy, Michael Collins, Dan Gillick, Lingpeng Kong, Terry Koo, Ji Ma, Mark Omernick, Slav Petrov, Chayut Thanapirom, Zora Tung, and David Weiss. 2017. SyntaxNet models for the CoNLL 2017 shared task. *CoRR* abs/1703.04929.

Sabine Buchholz and Erwin Marsi. 2006. CoNLL-X shared task on multilingual dependency parsing. In *Proc. of the Tenth Conference on Computational Natural Language Learning*. New York City, USA, pages 149–164.

Éric de La Clergerie. 2005. DyALog: a tabular logic programming based environment for NLP. In *Proceedings of 2nd International Workshop on Constraint Solving and Language Processing (CSLP'05)*. Barcelone, Espagne.

Pascal Denis and Benoît Sagot. 2012. Coupling an annotated corpus and a lexicon for state-of-the-art POS tagging. *Language Resources and Evaluation* 46(4):721–736.

Ryan McDonald, Fernando Pereira, Kiril Ribarov, and Jan Hajič. 2005. Non-projective dependency parsing using spanning tree algorithms. In *Proceedings of the conference on Human Language Technology and Empirical Methods in Natural Language Processing*. pages 523–530.

Graham Neubig, Chris Dyer, Yoav Goldberg, Austin Matthews, Waleed Ammar, Antonios Anastasopoulos, Miguel Ballesteros, David Chiang, Daniel Clothiaux, Trevor Cohn, Kevin Duh, Manaal Faruqui, Cynthia Gan, Dan Garrette, Yangfeng Ji, Lingpeng Kong, Adhiguna Kuncoro, Gaurav Kumar, Chaitanya Malaviya, Paul Michel, Yusuke Oda, Matthew Richardson, Naomi Saphra, Swabha Swayamdipta, and Pengcheng Yin. 2017. Dynet: The dynamic neural network toolkit. *arXiv preprint arXiv:1701.03980* .

Joakim Nivre, Marie-Catherine de Marneffe, Filip Ginter, Yoav Goldberg, Jan Hajič, Christopher Manning, Ryan McDonald, Slav Petrov, Sampo Pyysalo, Natalia Silveira, Reut Tsarfaty, and Daniel Zeman. 2016. Universal Dependencies v1: A multilingual treebank collection. In *Proceedings of the 10th International Conference on Language Resources and Evaluation (LREC 2016)*. Portorož, Slovenia, pages 1659–1666.

Joakim Nivre, Johan Hall, Sandra Kübler, Ryan McDonald, Jens Nilsson, Sebastian Riedel, and Deniz Yuret. 2007. The CoNLL 2007 shared task on dependency parsing. In *Proc. of the CoNLL Shared Task Session of EMNLP-CoNLL 2007*. Prague, Czech Republic, pages 915–932.

Joakim Nivre et al. 2017. Universal Dependencies 2.0. LINDAT/CLARIN digital library at the Institute of Formal and Applied Linguistics, Charles University, Prague, http://hdl.handle.net/11234/1-1983.

Slav Petrov and Ryan McDonald. 2012. Overview of the 2012 shared task on parsing the web. In *Notes of the First Workshop on Syntactic Analysis of Non-Canonical Language (SANCL)*. Montreal, Canada, volume 59.

Martin Potthast, Tim Gollub, Francisco Rangel, Paolo Rosso, Efstathios Stamatatos, and Benno Stein. 2014. Improving the reproducibility of PAN's shared tasks: Plagiarism detection, author identification, and author profiling. In Evangelos Kanoulas, Mihai Lupu, Paul Clough, Mark Sanderson, Mark Hall, Allan Hanbury, and Elaine Toms, editors, *Information Access Evaluation meets Multilinguality, Multimodality, and Visualization. 5th International Conference of the CLEF Initiative (CLEF 14)*. Springer, Berlin Heidelberg New York, pages 268–299.

Djamé Seddah, Sandra Kübler, and Reut Tsarfaty. 2014. Introducing the SPMRL 2014 shared task on parsing morphologically-rich languages. In *Proceedings of the First Joint Workshop on Statistical Parsing of Morphologically Rich Languages and Syntactic Analysis of Non-Canonical Languages*. Dublin, Ireland, pages 103–109.

Djamé Seddah, Reut Tsarfaty, Sandra Kübler, Marie Candito, Jinho Choi, Richárd Farkas, Jennifer Foster, Iakes Goenaga, Koldo Gojenola, Yoav Goldberg, Spence Green, Nizar Habash, Marco Kuhlmann, Wolfgang Maier, Joakim Nivre, Adam Przepiorkowski, Ryan Roth, Wolfgang Seeker, Yannick Versley, Veronika Vincze, Marcin Woliński, Alina Wróblewska, and Eric Villemonte de la Clérgerie. 2013. Overview of the spmrl 2013 shared task: A cross-framework evaluation of parsing morphologically rich languages. In *Proc. of the 4th Workshop on Statistical Parsing of Morphologically Rich Languages: Shared Task*. Seattle, USA.

Milan Straka, Jan Hajič, and Jana Straková. 2016. UDPipe: trainable pipeline for processing CoNLL-U files performing tokenization, morphological analysis, POS tagging and parsing. In *Proceedings of the 10th International Conference on Language Resources and Evaluation (LREC 2016)*. Portorož, Slovenia.

Éric Villemonte De La Clergerie. 2013. Exploring beam-based shift-reduce dependency parsing with DyALog: Results from the SPMRL 2013 shared task. In *4th Workshop on Statistical Parsing of Morphologically Rich Languages (SPMRL'2013)*. Seattle, USA.

Daniel Zeman, Filip Ginter, Jan Hajič, Joakim Nivre, Martin Popel, Milan Straka, and et al. 2017. CoNLL 2017 Shared Task: Multilingual Parsing from Raw Text to Universal Dependencies. In *Proceedings of the CoNLL 2017 Shared Task: Multilingual Parsing from Raw Text to Universal Dependencies*. Vancouver, Canada, pages 1–20.

Appendix: Overall Results

| Dataset | | Preproc. | UPOS tagging | | | Parsing (LAS) | | | |
name	#train wds	mode	acc.	rank	model	real run	real rank	official run	Δ(real−official)
ar	224k	UDPIPE	88.13	8	SR-nn	66.47	11	56.72	9.75
ar$_{pud}$	—	UDPIPE	70.27	8	SR-nn	45.38	10	42.73	2.65
bg	124k	TAG	97.29	25	SR-nn	84.41	13	74.15	10.26
bxr	—	UDPIPE	84.12	1	SR-cat (Generic)	28.55	6	28.55	0
ca	418k	UDPIPE	98.04	3	SR-feats	85.78	11	81.94	3.84
cs	1,173k	UDPIPE	98.13	6	SR-cat	82.72	18	71.30	11.42
cs$_{cac}$	473k	UDPIPE	98.27	8	SR-nn-charjoin	83.56	12	73.62	9.94
cs$_{cltt}$	16k	TAG	97.77	2	SR-nn	76.72	6	58.65	18.07
cs$_{pud}$	—	UDPIPE	96.55	2	SR-cat	79.28	18	72.05	7.23
cu	37k	UDPIPE	93.34	11	MST-nn	67.34	4	63.64	3.70
da	80k	TAG+TOK	96.43	2	SR-nn	76.31	8	73.83	2.48
de	270k	TAG	92.04	6	SR-nn	72.27	12	68.45	3.82
de$_{pud}$	—	TAG	84.58	2	SR-nn	69.79	8	65.16	4.63
el	41k	TAG+TOK+SEG	96.26	3	SR-nn	82.25	5	77.00	5.25
en	205k	TAG	93.52	3	SR-nn	76.00	14	70.20	5.80
en$_{lines}$	50k	TAG	95.99	2	SR-nn	76.01	7	64.77	11.24
en$_{partut}$	26k	TAG	94.78	2	SR-nn	77.21	7	69.29	7.92
en$_{pud}$	—	TAG	94.74	2	SR-nn	80.68	7	75.87	4.81
es	382k	UDPIPE	95.60	5	SR-nn	82.09	13	77.94	4.15
es$_{ancora}$	445k	UDPIPE	98.15	4	SR-feats	84.47	14	76.61	7.86
es$_{pud}$	—	UDPIPE	88.15	5	SR-nn	78.15	11	76.57	1.58
et	23k	TAG+TOK+SEG	89.24	5	SR-nn	61.52	8	56.00	5.52
eu	73k	TAG	94.01	3	SR-nn	71.70	8	50.67	21.03
fa	121k	UDPIPE	96.00	7	SR-nn	80.52	9	61.93	18.59
fi	163k	TAG+TOK+SEG	84.59	4	SR-nn	75.82	9	60.19	15.63
fi$_{ftb}$	128k	TAG+TOK+SEG	93.11	2	MST-nn	75.88	9	40.21	35.67
fi$_{pud}$	—	TAG	95.98	4	SR-nn	79.68	7	62.41	17.27
fr	356k	TAG	95.51	6	SR-nn	80.44	16	76.79	3.65
fr$_{partut}$	18k	UDPIPE	94.46	7	SR-nn	77.40	16	75.15	2.25
fr$_{pud}$	—	TAG	88.54	4	SR-nn	74.82	10	74.70	0.12
fr$_{sequoia}$	51k	TAG	96.78	2	SR-nn	80.48	13	73.55	6.93
ga	14k	TAG	90.00	3	MST-nn	62.23	13	56.35	5.88
gl	79k	TAG	97.42	2	SR-nn	79.06	13	76.81	2.25
gl$_{treegal}$	15k	UDPIPE	90.69	9	SR-nn	64.36	21	65.95	-1.59
got	35k	UDPIPE	93.55	10	MST-nn	63.40	4	58.66	4.74
grc	160k	TAG	88.48	3	MST-nn	62.53	5	47.37	15.16
grc$_{proiel}$	184k	UDPIPE	95.72	7	MST-altcats	68.72	7	49.41	19.31
he	138k	TAG	81.42	4	SR-nn	57.85	15	44.49	13.36
hi	281k	TAG	96.61	3	SR-nn	87.25	10	45.72	41.53
hi$_{pud}$	—	TAG	84.62	4	SR-nn	51.46	10	32.39	19.07
hr	169k	UDPIPE	95.67	12	SR-nn	78.67	9	74.81	3.86
hsb	—	UDPIPE	90.30	1	SR-altcats (SSlavic (!))	56.22	9	56.22	0
hu	20k	TAG	92.19	4	SR-nn	66.82	6	49.82	17
id	98k	TAG	93.59	2	SR-nn	75.47	10	64.84	10.63
it	271k	TAG+TOK+SEG	97.38	3	SR-nn	85.59	17	81.20	4.39
it$_{pud}$	—	TAG+TOK+SEG	93.08	6	SR-nn	84.17	13	81.81	2.36
ja	29k	TAG+TOK	90.00	5	SR-nn	77.52	6	65.15	12.37
ja$_{pud}$	—	TAG+TOK	88.49	25	SR-nn	76.03	20	62.91	13.12
kk	162k	TAG	67.86	1	MST-nn	26.64	4	24.73	1.91
kmr	0.5k	UDPIPE	90.04	1	SR-cat (Generic)	34.80	12	34.80	0
ko	52k	UDPIPE	93.79	7	SR-nn	73.26	6	40.71	32.55
la	18k	UDPIPE	83.39	11	MST-nn	46.59	13	39.91	6.68
la$_{ittb}$	270k	TAG+TOK+SEG	97.39	6	SR-nn	78.51	10	52.38	26.13
la$_{proiel}$	147k	UDPIPE	94.82	8	MST-altcats	60.65	10	42.68	17.97
lv	35k	TAG+TOK	91.10	2	SR-nn	64.03	6	50.52	13.51
nl	186k	TAG	91.57	3	SR-nn	70.28	11	56.11	14.17
nl$_{lassysmall}$	81k	TAG	97.84	2	SR-nn	79.99	10	57.83	22.16
no$_{bokmaal}$	244k	UDPIPE	96.75	6	SR-nn	83.49	14	68.58	14.91
no$_{nynorsk}$	245k	UDPIPE	96.38	7	SR-feats	82.66	10	65.11	17.55
pl	63k	TAG	96.95	2	SR-nn	83.65	6	71.98	11.67
pt	207k	UDPIPE	96.22	6	SR-nn-charjoint	81.87	17	79.21	2.66
pt$_{br}$	256k	TAG	97.54	2	SR-nn	86.17	13	61.30	24.87
pt$_{pud}$	—	TAG	88.88	2	SR-nn-charjoint	74.67	10	75.00	-0.33
ro	185k	UDPIPE	96.40	10	SR-nn	80.47	13	76.69	3.78
ru	76k	TAG	96.60	2	SR-nn	77.61	7	66.83	10.78
ru$_{pud}$	—	TAG	86.66	3	SR-nn	71.55	3	66.17	5.38
ru$_{syntagrus}$	870k	UDPIPE	97.99	4	SR-altcats	86.25	18	54.19	32.06
sk	81k	TAG	95.10	2	SR-nn	77.17	6	67.72	9.45
sl	113k	TAG	97.36	2	SR-nn	85.41	5	80.27	5.14
sl$_{sst}$	19k	UDPIPE	88.82	9	MST-nn	46.27	17	40.15	6.12
sme	—	UDPIPE	86.81	1	SR-cat (Generic)	37.33	5	37.33	0
sv	67k	TAG	96.74	2	SR-nn	80.30	6	76.77	3.53
sv$_{lines}$	48k	TAG	95.83	2	SR-nn	76.61	7	63.50	13.11
sv$_{pud}$	—	TAG	93.43	2	SR-nn	73.65	4	70.83	2.82
tr	38k	UDPIPE	91.22	10	SR-nn	56.03	9	46.38	9.65
tr$_{pud}$	—	TAG	72.65	2	SR-nn	32.74	20	25.78	6.96
ug	2k	TAG	74.06	9	MST-nn	34.82	10	19.65	15.17
uk	13k	TAG	92.10	2	MST-nn	64.58	6	65.52	-0.94
ur	109k	TAG	92.65	6	SR-nn	77.46	12	39.73	37.73
vi	20k	TAG+TOK	77.64	2	SR-nn	42.40	3	33.00	9.40
zh	99k	UDPIPE	82.69	11	SR-nn	59.28	12	45.83	13.45
Overall (macro-average)			91.79	3		70.35	6	60.02	10.33

Universal Joint Morph-Syntactic Processing:
The Open University of Israel's Submission to
The CoNLL 2017 Shared Task

Amir More
Open University of Israel
habeanf@gmail.com

Reut Tsarfaty
Open University of Israel
reutts@openu.ac.il

Abstract

We present the Open University's submission (ID OpenU-NLP-Lab) to the *CoNLL 2017 UD Shared Task* on multilingual parsing from raw text to Universal Dependencies. The core of our system is a joint morphological disambiguator and syntactic parser which accepts morphologically analyzed surface tokens as input and returns morphologically disambiguated dependency trees as output. Our parser requires a lattice as input, so we generate morphological analyses of surface tokens using a data-driven morphological analyzer that derives its lexicon from the UD training corpora, and we rely on UDPipe for sentence segmentation and surface-level tokenization. We report our official macro-average LAS is 56.56. Although our model is not as performant as many others, it does not make use of neural networks, therefore we do not rely on word embeddings or any other data source other than the corpora themselves. In addition, we show the utility of a lexicon-backed morphological analyzer for the MRL Modern Hebrew. We use our results on Modern Hebrew to argue that the UD community should define a UD-compatible standard for access to lexical resources, which we argue is crucial for MRLs and low resource languages in particular.

1 Introduction

The Universal Dependencies (UD) project (Nivre et al., 2016) sets itself apart from previous multilingual parsing initiatives such as the CoNLL (Buchholz and Marsi, 2006; Nivre et al.,

2007) and SPMRL (Seddah et al., 2013, 2014) shared tasks with two key principles: (i) the POS tags, morphological properties, and dependency labels are unified, with enforceable annotation guidelines and (ii) corpora text is provided via a two-level representation of the input stream. With the latter two-level principle in place, corpora can be provided with raw text, syntactic words as the nodes of syntactic trees, and the relationship between them, in a harmonized scheme. This representation is crucial to the participation of Morphologically Rich Languages (MRLs) in end-to-end parsing tasks.

The availability of a wide range of language corpora in this manner provides a unique opportunity for the advancement of (universal) joint morpho-syntactic processing, introduced by Tsarfaty and Goldberg (2008) in a generative setting and advocated for in a variety of settings (Bohnet and Nivre, 2012; Andor et al., 2016; Bohnet et al., 2013; Li et al., 2011; Bohnet and Nivre, 2012; Li et al., 2014; Zhang et al., 2014). To this end, our submission is a joint morpho-syntactic processor in a transition-based framework. We present our submission (OpenU-NLP-Lab), with models trained *only* on the train sets (Nivre et al., 2017b), parsing all 81 test treebanks of UD v2 corpora (Nivre et al., 2017a) participating in the *CoNLL 2017 UD Shared Task* (Zeman et al., 2017).

We use the results of our processor on an MRL to argue that one last piece of the puzzle is missing: a universal scheme for access to lexical resources. We discuss our results for a lexicon-backed approach, compared to a data-driven one. The goal of our submission is to compel the UD community to recognize the need for lexical resources in the context of joint morpho-syntactic processing, and push forward the discussion on a UD annotation-compliant standard for access to

Proceedings of the CoNLL 2017 Shared Task: Multilingual Parsing from Raw Text to Universal Dependencies, pages 253–264,
Vancouver, Canada, August 3-4, 2017. © 2017 Association for Computational Linguistics

lexical resources that could benefit MRLs and low resource languages.

In section 2 we describe our framework and formal settings (2.1), first instantiated individually as a morphological disambiguator (2.2) and dependency parser (2.2), followed by how we unify the two into a joint processor (2.4).

Since the input stream of the processor is a morphological analysis of the tokenized raw text, we describe a universal, data-driven morphological analyzer, and a lexicon-based MA for the MRL Modern Hebrew (2.5).

In section 3, we detail the implementation of our parser (3.1) and specific technical issues we encountered with the official run for the shared task (3.2). We then present our results on all languages in section 4, and present a comparison to processing Modern Hebrew with a lexicon-based morphological analyzer. We discuss directions for future work in section 5, conclude with a summary of our submission in section 6, and urge the UD community to put forth a standard for lexical resource access.

2 Our Framework

We use the transition-based framework of Zhang and Clark (2011), originally designed for syntactic processing using the generalized perceptron and beam search, which we briefly cover in subsection 2.1.

We first describe the standalone transition system and model for morphological disambiguation of (More and Tsarfaty, 2016) (2.2), and Arc Standard transition system together with a rich-linguistic feature model (2.3). We then present our approach to joint morpho-syntactic processing which unifies both transition systems (2.4).

We present our baseline approach to data-driven morphological analysis, followed by our Modern Hebrew lexical resource (2.5).

2.1 Formal Settings

Formally, a transition system is a quadruple (C, T, c_s, C_t) where C is a set of configurations, T a set of transitions between the elements of C, c_s an initialization function, and $C_t \subset C$ a set of terminal configurations. A transition sequence $y = t_n(t_{n-1}(...t_1(c_s(x))))$ for an input x starts with the configuration $c_s(x)$. After n transitions of corresponding configurations $(t_i, c_i) \in T \times C$, the result is a terminal configuration $c_n \in C_t$.

In order to determine *which* transition $t \in T$ to apply given a configuration $c \in C$, we need to define a model that learns to predict the transition that would be chosen by an oracle function $O :$ $C \to T$, which has access to the correct (gold) output.

To define a model, we employ an objective function $F : X \to \mathbb{R}$, which ranks outputs via a scoring of the possible transition sequences $(GEN(x))$ from which outputs are derived, such that the most plausible sequence of transitions is the one that most closely resembles one generated by an oracle:

$$F(x) = argmax_{y \in GEN(x)} Score(y)$$

How we define $Score$ is therefore crucial to the performance of the model, since it must capture the relation of a generated sequence (and its derived output) to that of an oracle's output. To compute $Score(y)$, y is mapped to a global feature vector $\Phi(y) = \{\phi_i(y)\}$ where each feature is a count of occurrences defined by feature functions. Given this vector, $Score(y)$ is calculated as the dot product of $\Phi(y)$ and a weights vector $\vec{\omega}$:

$$Score(y) = \Phi(y) \cdot \vec{\omega} = \sum_{c_j \in y} \sum_i \omega_i \phi_i(c_j)$$

Following Zhang and Clark (2011), we learn the weights vector $\vec{\omega}$ via the *generalized perceptron*, using the *early-update* averaged variant of Collins and Roark (2004).

For decoding, the framework uses the *beam search* algorithm, which helps mitigate otherwise irrecoverable errors in the transition sequence.

2.2 Morphological Disambiguation

The morphological disambiguator (MD) component of our parser is based on More and Tsarfaty (2016), modified only to accommodate UD POS tags and morphological features. We provide a brief exposition of the transition system, and refer the reader to the original paper for an in-depth explanation (More and Tsarfaty, 2016).

The input to the transition-based MD is a lattice L of an input stream of k surface tokens $x = x_1, ..., x_k$, such that $L_i = MA(x_i)$, is generated by a morphological analysis component that analyzes each token separately and returns a lattice for the whole input sentence x. We rely on the UDPipe baseline models (Straka et al., 2016) for sentence segmentation and tokenization.

Each *lattice-arc* in L corresponds to a potential node in the intended dependency tree. A lattice-arc has a *morpho-syntactic representation* (MSR) defined as $m = (b, e, f, t, g)$, with b and e marking the start and end nodes of m in L, f a form, t a universal part-of-speech tag, and g a set of attribute=value universal features.

A configuration $C_{MD} = (L, n, i, M)$ consists of a lattice L, an index n representing a node in L, an index i s.t. $0 \le i < k$ representing a specific token's lattice, and a set of disambiguated morphemes M.

The initial configuration function $c_s(x) = (L, bottom(L), 0, \emptyset)$, where $L = MA(x_1) \circ ... \circ MA(x_k)$, and $n = bottom(L)$, the bottom of the lattice. A configuration is terminal when $n = top(L)$ *and* $i = k$.

To traverse the lattice and disambiguate the input, we define an open set of transitions using the MD_s transition template:

$$MD_s : (L, p, i, M) \rightarrow (L, q, i, M \cup \{m\})$$

Where $p = b$, $q = e$, and s relates the transition to the disambiguated morpheme m using a parameterized delexicalization $s = DLEX_{oc}(m)$:

$$DLEX_{OC}(m) = \begin{cases} (\text{-}, \text{-}, \text{-}, t, g) & \text{if } t \in OC \\ (\text{-}, \text{-}, f, t, g) & \text{otherwise} \end{cases}$$

In words, $DLEX$ projects a morpheme either with or without its form depending on whether or not the POS tag is an open-class with respect to the form. For UD, we redefine:

$$OC = \{ {}^{ADJ,AUX,ADV,PUNCT,NUM,}_{INTJ,NOUN,PROPN,VERB} \}$$

We use the parametric model of More and Tsarfaty (2016) to score the transitions at each step.

Since lattices may have paths of different length and we use beam search for decoding, the problem of variable-length transition sequences arises. We follow More and Tsarfaty (2016), using the $ENDTOKEN$ transition to mitigate the biases induced by variable-length sequences.

2.3 Syntactic Disambiguation

For dependency parsing, we use the Arc Standard configuration, transition system, and oracle function defined in Kübler et al. (2009). A configuration is a triple $C_{DEP} = (\sigma, \beta, A)$ where σ is a stack, β is a buffer, and A a set of labeled arcs.

We present the specific variant of Arc Standard that we use in Figure 2.3. Note that in this variant, arc operations are performed between the top of the stack σ and the head of the buffer β. Additionally, in order to guarantee a single root, for the purposes of the shared task we apply a post processing step in which the first root node encountered (in left-to-right order) is designated as the only root node, and all other root nodes are set as its modifier with the "punct" dependency label.

Of course, this means that our transition system only applies to projective trees — the oracle will indeed fail given a non-projective tree, and our transition system cannot output one. In addition, since we are using the Arc Standard transition system, which has been shown to not be arc-decomposable, we cannot employ a dynamic oracle during training (Goldberg and Nivre, 2012).

The rich-linguistic feature model for our dependency parser, inspired by Zhang and Nivre (2011), applies the rich non-local features to arc standard (where this is possible), such as to accommodate the free word order of MRLs. We provide an appendix with a detailed comparison of the two feature models.

2.4 Joint Morpho-Syntactic Processing

Given standalone morphological and syntactic disambiguation systems in the same framework, we integrate them into a joint morpho-syntactic processor. Our integration is a literal embedding of the two systems, with a deterministic "router" that decides which of the two transition systems should apply a transition to a given configuration — we call this router a *strategy*.

We first must alter the morphological disambiguation transition such that a disambiguated morpheme is enqueued onto β:

$$MD_s : \begin{array}{l} ((L, n, i, M), (\sigma, \beta, A)) \rightarrow \\ ((L, q, j, M \cup \{m\}), (\sigma, [\beta|m], A)) \end{array}$$

We call the set of joint strategies used for the shared task $ArcGreedy_k$, because it will perform a syntactic operation if possible, otherwise it will disambiguate a morpheme. k determines the minimal number of morphemes in the buffer β of the Arc Standard configuration in order to perform a syntactic transition:

$$ArcGreedy_k(c_{md}, (\sigma, \beta, A)) = \begin{array}{ll} T_m & if\ |\beta| \le k \\ T_d & otherwise \end{array}$$

$$\begin{aligned}
\text{Initial} \quad & c_s(x = x_1, ..., x_n) = ([0], [1, ..., n], \emptyset) \\
\text{Terminal} \quad & C_t = \{c \in C \,|\, c = ([0], [], A)\} \\
\text{Transitions} \quad & (\sigma, [i|\beta], A) \rightarrow ([\sigma|i], \beta, A) \hspace{3cm} \text{(SHIFT)} \\
& ([\sigma|i], [j|\beta], A) \rightarrow (\sigma, [j|\beta], A \cup \{(j, l, i)\}) \; \textit{if} \; i \neq 0 \quad \text{(ArcLeft}_l\text{)} \\
& ([\sigma|i], [j|\beta], A) \rightarrow (\sigma, [i|\beta], A \cup \{(i, l, j)\}) \hspace{1.7cm} \text{(ArcRight}_l\text{)}
\end{aligned}$$

Figure 1: The Arc Standard transition system

We set $k = 3$ based on the features we use to predict the syntactic transition.

The *ArcGreedy* approach provides joint processing through the interaction of the two systems through the global score. Together with beam search, this allows a syntactic transition to reverse the ranking of an otherwise higher-scored disambiguation candidate, and vice-versa, although this interaction occurs with a small delay due to the difference between a morphological disambiguation transition and a syntactic transition for the same morpheme.

2.5 Morphological Analysis

The joint parser requires a morphologically analyzed input, in the form of a lattice. However, universal lexical resources are not available for *all* languages participating in the shared task. Therefore, we use the data-driven morphological analyzer from More and Tsarfaty (2016), which derives its lexicon from the training set of a given UD corpora, modified to read/write UDv2-compatible file formats.

As part of our submission, we provide these derived lexica to the community.

In addition, we use the HEBLEX morphological analyzer from More and Tsarfaty (2016), adapted to output lattices conforming to UD annotation standards for universal POS tags and morphological features.

3 Implementation

In this section we describe technical details of implementation 3.1, bugs encountered during the shared task 3.2, and our approach to surprise languages 3.3.

3.1 Technical Details

For sentence segmentation and tokenization, we rely on the UDPipe (Straka et al., 2016) predicted data files. The morphological analysis component and joint morpho-syntactic parser are all implemented in yap[1] (yet another parser), an open-source natural language processor written in Go[2]. Once compiled, the processor is a self-contained binary, without any dependencies on external libraries.

For the shared task the processor was compiled with Go version 1.8.1, and a git tag created for the commit used at the time of the task. During the test phase we wrapped the processor with a python script that invokes two instances concurrently in order to complete processing before the official (final) deadline.

Additionally, in order to train on all treebanks we limited the size of all training sets to the first 50,000 sentences for the parser.

Finally, our training algorithm iterates until convergence, where performance is measured by F_1 for *full morphological disambiguation* when evaluated on languages' respective development sets. We define convergence as two consecutive iterations resulting in a monotonic decrease in F_1 for full MD, and used the best performing model up to that point. For some languages we observed the F_1 never monotonically decreased twice, so after 20 iterations we manually stopped training and used the best performing model.[3]

3.2 Shared Task Bugs

We encountered two serious bugs during training for the shared task, which prevented us from running our joint processor on all treebanks.

First, for some treebanks (cs_cac, cs_cltt, cs_pud, cs, en, fr_sequoia, ru_syntagrus) the serialization code, which relies on Go's built-in encoder package, failed to serialize the in-memory model because it is larger than 2^{30} bytes. Much too our surprise, this is apparently an issue related to the decoder, one the Go maintainers are aware of but have decided not to address.[4] Changing our

---

[1] https://github.com/CoNLL-UD-2017/OpenU-NLP-Lab
[2] https://golang.org
[3] For PUD, we use models of "main" treebanks (no tcode)
[4] https://git.io/nogo

model serialization code was too large a task at the time we found it, so for the aforementioned problematic treebanks we had no choice but to train only the dependency parser, and rely on UDPipe for morphological disambiguation.

Second, close to the time of submitting this paper, we discovered a bug in the morphological disambiguator. The original MD model from More and Tsarfaty (2016) assumed the Hebrew treebank SPMRL annotation (SPMRL citation), in which some clitics are identified by morphological "suffix" features, as opposed to the UD approach which breaks them down as separate syntactic words. As a result, the MD transition system sometimes fails to *distinguish* between lattice-arcs.

As a temporary remedy, we modified the parser such that syntactic words with clitic suffixes have an additional indication as such, to set them apart from syntactic words without clitic suffixes. However, we did not have time to re-run our data-driven morphologically analyzed parses with this fix.

3.3 Surprise Languages

Our strategy for parsing surprise languages was to train a delexicalized (no word-form features) dependency-only parsing model on one treebank per surprise language, which we manually deemed as "close" as follows:

- bxr: ru_syntagrus

- kmr:fa

- sme: fi

- hsb: cs

We relied on the UDPipe predicted data up to and including full morphological disambiguation for all surprise languages.

4 Results and Discussion

In Tables 1 and 2 we present our official results for all languages. For the MRL Modern Hebrew, we train and test parsed using the lexicon-backed morphological analyzer (HEBLEX). When using HEBLEX, we obtained word-segmentation accuracy F_1 score of 87.48, compared to 81.26 in the data-driven MA of the official results, a 33% reduction in error rate.

Although the data-driven results suffer from the aforementioned bug, we do not expect them to change considerably, as we have seen such large differences with similar comparisons for the SPMRL Hebrew treebank. We hope the results from our unofficial run will be more convincing. It is important to note that the best word-segmentation result for Modern Hebrew in the shared task is 91.37.

We argue that although our lexicon-assisted model did not outperform the best model in the shared task, this does not invalidate our position on universal lexical resources. A 91.37 F_1 word-segmentation accuracy on Modern Hebrew is quite low, and in our opinion, still too low for inclusion in practical, real-world applications. We believe it is likely that together with access to lexical resources, more performant models would be able to bridge the gap and reduce this large error rate to a more acceptable level for down-stream tasks.

5 Future Work

In the future, we would like to replace our more traditional linear model with a modern, non-linear neural network-based approach. However, to date there is no solution for *joint* morph-syntactic processing of MRLs, a problem we aim to tackle. In the context of a neural-based solution, we believe that the availability of lexical resources will be crucial for MRLs and low resource languages in particular.

6 Conclusion

We present our submission to the *CoNLL 2017 UD Shared Task*, to the best of our knowledge the first universal, joint morpho-syntactic processor. We report our official result of 56.56. We contrast our results on the MRL Modern Hebrew, as a showcase of the utility of access to a lexicon-backed morphological analyzer.

Our goal is to instigate a discussion in the UD community on the need for a universal scheme for lexical resource access.

Acknowledgements

We would like to thank the CoNLL Shared Task Organizing Committee (COSTOCOM) for their hard word on the task and their timely support. We would also like to thank the TIRA platform team (Potthast et al., 2014) for providing a system that facilitates competition and reproducible research.

	UDPipe		yap				
Treebank	Sentences	Tokens	Words	UPOS	Feats	UAS	LAS
ar	84.57	99.98	92.48	82.73	21.13	53.41	45.01
ar_pud	100	80.89	89.68	65.49	33.49	41.54	31.84
bg	92.83	99.91	99.91	94.47	35.96	80.09	74.23
bxr	91.81	99.35	99.35	84.12	81.65	41.15	26.44
ca	98.95	99.97	99.78	93.55	19.48	80.09	74.53
cs*	92.03	99.9	99.9	98.13	91.01	81.45	76.44
cs_cac*	100	100	99.99	98.27	89.05	84.73	79.43
cs_cltt*	95.06	99.35	99.35	95.41	85.38	76.4	71.68
cs_pud*	96.43	99.29	99.29	96.55	87.34	81.33	75.75
cu	36.05	99.96	99.96	88.52	26.22	65.73	56.19
da	79.36	99.69	99.69	90.02	31.01	70.24	65.28
de	79.11	99.64	99.65	84.32	47.29	55.21	48.05
de_pud	86.49	97.97	97.7	77.61	30.13	52.98	44.05
el	90.79	99.88	99.88	92.29	29.89	77.8	73.41
en*	73.22	98.67	98.67	93.11	93.97	78.09	75.12
en_lines	85.84	99.94	99.94	91.78	99.94	73.5	68.09
en_partut	97.51	99.51	99.48	90.58	37.16	73.47	68.17
en_pud	97.13	99.66	99.66	89.6	32.92	78.27	73.47
es	94.15	99.87	99.42	91.14	42.85	73.51	67.89
es_ancora	97.05	99.97	99.72	93.73	16.99	76.74	71.34
es_pud	93.42	99.52	99.25	84.74	34.59	74.66	67.15
et	85.2	99.77	99.77	78.8	34.19	58.15	45.01
eu	99.58	99.96	99.96	87.06	37.02	66.24	56.37
fa	98	100	99.46	91.5	33.38	69.04	62.89
fi	84.56	99.63	99.63	84.99	29.62	57.65	45.99
fi_ftb	83.83	99.9	99.88	82.41	28.83	63.91	52.73
fi_pud	93.67	99.61	99.61	82.99	28.18	56.51	45.17
fr	93.59	99.75	99.49	92.54	42.33	77.28	71.96
fr_partut	98	99.83	99.44	93.61	34.13	78.84	73.1
fr_pud	92.32	99.1	98.79	84.73	36.8	73.68	67.67
fr_sequoia*	83.75	99.77	99.06	95.4	94.03	81.74	78.92
ga	95.81	99.29	99.29	83.69	28.66	67.69	54.53
gl	96.15	99.92	99.92	95.18	99.69	78.59	74.81
gl_treegal	81.63	99.59	98.02	86.8	22.08	66.68	59.77
got	27.85	100	100	89.19	27.67	59.25	50.06
grc	98.43	99.95	99.95	72.66	35.15	42.39	32.53
grc_proiel	43.11	100	100	89.8	25.26	59.13	51.05
he	99.39	99.94	81.26	73.55	31.71	46.67	41.49
hi	99.2	100	100	92.44	14.94	77.74	69.36
hi_pud	90.83	97.81	97.81	79.93	31.96	55.53	43.06
hr	96.92	99.93	99.93	89.45	19.84	68.49	59.94
hsb	90.69	99.84	99.84	90.3	74.02	64.5	57.14
hu	93.85	99.82	99.82	77.31	26.73	54.56	40.28
id	91.15	99.99	99.99	88.98	96.15	76.13	68.49
it	97.1	99.81	99.5	94.52	38.85	81.98	77.96
it_pud	96.58	99.59	99	88.37	33.98	80.02	75.11
ja	94.92	89.68	89.68	85.2	88.01	70.79	68.68
ja_pud	94.89	91.06	91.06	85.75	54.8	73.09	71.45

Table 1: Official results for the UD Shared Task. We include UDPipe predicted measures for completeness. Our system does not predict lemmas and XPOS, so we do not show them. Treebanks with * were processed by only our dependency parser, relying on UDPipe for morphological disambiguation, due to a technical issue.

	UDPipe		yap				
Treebank	Sentences	Tokens	Words	UPOS	Feats	UAS	LAS
kk	81.38	95.2	94.9	43.87	33.45	36.12	10.49
kmr	97.02	99.01	98.85	90.04	80.72	51.24	38.61
ko	93.05	99.73	99.73	81.9	98.99	60.75	52.37
la	98.09	99.99	99.99	68.32	36.76	37.04	24.3
la_ittb	93.24	99.99	99.99	93.65	31.57	57.99	50.65
la_proiel	25.8	100	100	87.32	26.48	46.46	37.12
lv	98.59	98.91	98.91	80.81	39.93	58.13	47.71
nl	77.14	99.88	99.88	80.07	7.56	50.27	41.9
nl_lassysmall	78.62	99.93	99.93	95.09	47.01	73.8	69.78
no_bokmaal	95.76	99.75	99.75	93.4	40.05	80.68	76.69
no_nynorsk	91.23	99.85	99.85	92.69	40.01	76.51	71.89
pl	98.91	99.99	98.97	86.81	26.09	71.07	63.03
pt	89.79	99.64	99.27	88.48	35.63	59.62	53.67
pt_br	96.84	99.94	99.84	94.44	90.12	83.9	80.65
pt_pud	95.65	99.29	99.2	82.17	37.21	60.51	53.87
ro	93.42	99.64	99.64	93.86	16.29	79.55	72.14
ru	96.42	99.91	99.91	84.32	37.04	64.02	57.09
ru_pud	98.95	97.18	97.18	75.21	35.31	61.06	52.14
ru_syntagrus*	97.81	99.57	99.57	97.99	93.47	84.2	80.1
sk	83.53	100	100	77.99	19.11	57.95	50.25
sl	99.24	99.96	99.96	89.19	23.64	70.95	65.27
sl_sst	16.72	99.82	99.82	83.24	29.7	45.76	37.11
sme	98.79	99.88	99.88	86.81	81.25	45.03	32.57
sv	96.37	99.84	99.84	92.23	34.17	75.96	70.38
sv_lines	86.44	99.98	99.98	91.39	99.98	75.1	69.21
sv_pud	90.2	98.26	98.26	82.66	32.27	68.35	61.42
tr	96.63	99.85	97.17	83.15	35.75	52.72	39.82
tr_pud	93.91	98.86	95.7	61.52	23.36	44.73	23.95
ug	63.55	98.52	98.52	66.15	98.52	20.7	7.35
uk	92.59	99.81	99.81	76.27	30.24	53.24	42.29
ur	98.32	100	100	88.58	14.53	77.95	69.89
vi	92.59	82.47	82.47	71.84	78.23	41.25	36.51
zh	98.19	88.91	88.91	80.08	78.27	58.03	52.93

Table 2: Official results for the UD Shared Task. We include UDPipe predicted measures for completeness. Our system does not predict lemmas and XPOS, so we do not show them. Treebanks with * were processed by only our dependency parser, relying on UDPipe for morphological disambiguation, due to a technical issue.

Appendix

Dependency Features

We use the feature description scheme of Zhang and Nivre (2011) for easy comparison.

Let $c = (S, N, A)$ be a configuration where S is the stack, N is the buffer.

We define an *address* as the location of a node in the partial dependencies trees in S and N of configuration c. An address has a structure name S or N, a subscript integer to access a k-deep node, and characters to access the heads or dependents of the node found at S_k or N_k. For example, the address S_{0h} refers to the head (if such exists) of the partial tree found at the top of the stack. The address N_1 refers to the node that is second in the buffer.

Rich Linguistic Feature Types

In addition to features described in Zhang and Nivre (2011), we define the following attributes:

- f_p - the multi-set of parts of speech of the dependents of a node

- s_f - the multi-set of labels of all dependents of a node

- v_f - the valency (= number) of all dependents of a node

Also, we define C_i as an address generator - it generate a feature for each dependent of the addressed node.

Morphological Augmentation

To allow the inclusion of morphology we add the ability of specifying morphological properties to be added to all features of a feature group. Augmentation of a feature *group* does not cause a replacement of the defined features, it only creates a copy with the addition of morphological properties.

To augment a feature group, all the features to the groups are required to have the same number of addresses. An augmentation specifies a character, either h or x, to specify the host or suffix morphological properties as attributes, respectively. If the group has more than one address, the augmentation must specify an address (a 1-indexed integer offset). Multiple augmentations may be used together.

For example, given the feature group Pairs in table 3, the first few features are $S_w t N_0 w t$, $S_0 w t N_0 w$, $S_w N_0 w t$, etc. All features in the Pairs group have two addresses. An example of a morphological augmentation of the Pairs group is $h1h2$, resulting in the new features $S_0 w t m_h N_0 w t m_h$, $S_0 w t m_h N_0 w m_h$, $S_w m_h N_0 w t m_h$, etc. where m_h is the set of key-value pairs of properties of the respective morphemes at the top of the stack (S_0) and buffer (N_0).

Features

The set of rich non-local features of (Zhang and Nivre, 2011) and the new rich linguistic features defined in this work are shown in table 3. The features are shown side by side to ease the comparison of the two feature sets, along with a column indicating the changes made.

The feature groups are augmented with morphological properties as defined in table 6.

N-L Group	N-L Feature	Ling. Feature	Ling. Group	Change
Single	S_0w	S_0w	Single	
Single	S_0t	S_0t	Single	
Single	S_0wt	S_0wt	Single	
Single	N_0w	N_0w	Single	
Single	N_0t	N_0t	Single	
Single	N_0wt	N_0wt	Single	
Single	N_1w	N_1w	Single	
Single	N_1t	N_1t	Single	
Single	N_1wt	N_1wt	Single	
Single	N_2w	N_2w	Single	
Single	N_2t	N_2t	Single	
Single	N_2wt	N_2wt	Single	
Pairs	S_0wtN_0wt	S_0wtN_0wt	Pairs	
Pairs	S_0wtN_0w	S_0wtN_0w	Pairs	
Pairs	S_0wN_0wt	S_0wN_0wt	Pairs	
Pairs	S_0wtN_0t	S_0wtN_0t	Pairs	
Pairs	S_0tN_0wt	S_0tN_0wt	Pairs	
Pairs	S_0wN_0w	S_0wN_0w	Pairs	
Pairs	S_0tN_0t	S_0tN_0t	Pairs	
Pairs	N_0tN_1t	N_0tN_1t	Pairs	
Three Words	$N_0tN_1tN_2t$	$N_0tN_1tN_2t$	Three Words (A)	
Three Words	$S_0tN_0tN_1t$	$S_0tN_0tN_1t$	Three Words (A)	
Three Words	$S_{0h}tS_0tN_0t$	$S_{0h}tS_0tN_0t$	Three Words (A)	
Three Words	$S_0tN_0tN_{0ld}t$	$S_0tN_0tf_p$	Three Words (B)	$N_{0ld}t \rightarrow N_0f_p$
Three Words	$S_0tS_{0ld}tN_0t$	$S_0tf_pN_0t$	Three Words (B)	$ld/rd \rightarrow f_p$
Three Words	$S_0tS_{0rd}tN_0t$		Three Words (B)	
Distance	S_0wd	S_0wd	Distance	
Distance	S_0td	S_0td	Distance	
Distance	N_0wd	N_0wd	Distance	
Distance	N_0td	N_0td	Distance	
Distance	S_0wN_0wd	S_0wN_0wd	Distance	
Distance	S_0tN_0td	S_0tN_0td	Distance	
Valency	S_0wv_r	S_0wv_f	Valency frames	
Valency	S_0wv_l		Valency frames	
Valency	S_0tv_r	S_0tv_f	Valency frames	$v_r/v_l \rightarrow v_f$
Valency	S_0tv_l		Valency frames	
Valency	N_0wv_l	N_0wv_f	Valency frames	
Valency	N_0tv_l	N_0tv_f	Valency frames	
Unigrams	$S_{0h}w$	$S_{0h}w$	Unigrams (A)	
Unigrams	$S_{0h}t$	$S_{0h}t$	Unigrams (A)	
Unigrams	S_0l	S_0l	Unigrams (A)	
Unigrams	$S_{0ld}w$	$S_0wS_0C_iw$	Unigrams (B)	
Unigrams	$S_{0ld}t$	$S_0wS_0C_it$	Unigrams (B)	
Unigrams	$S_{0ld}l$	$S_0wS_0C_il$	Unigrams (B)	Switch to non-directional bi-lexical dependencies, C_i = for each dependent
Unigrams	$S_{0rd}w$	$S_0tS_0C_iw$	Unigrams (B)	
Unigrams	$S_{0rd}t$	$S_0tS_0C_it$	Unigrams (B)	
Unigrams	$S_{0rd}l$	$S_0tS_0C_il$	Unigrams (B)	
Unigrams	$N_{0ld}w$	$N_0wN_0C_iw$	Unigrams (B)	
Unigrams	$N_{0ld}t$	$N_0wN_0C_it$	Unigrams (B)	
Unigrams	$N_{0ld}l$	$N_0wN_0C_il$	Unigrams (B)	
Unigrams		$N_0tN_0C_iw$	Unigrams	
Unigrams		$N_0tN_0C_it$	Unigrams	New
Unigrams		$N_0tN_0C_il$	Unigrams	
Third Order	$S_{0l2d}w$		Third Order	
Third Order	$S_{0l2d}t$		Third Order	
Third Order	$S_{0l2d}l$		Third Order	
Third Order	$S_{0r2d}w$		Third Order	
Third Order	$S_{0r2d}t$		Third Order	Removed
Third Order	$S_{0r2d}l$		Third Order	
Third Order	$N_{0l2d}w$		Third Order	
Third Order	$N_{0l2d}t$		Third Order	
Third Order	$N_{0l2d}l$		Third Order	
Third Order	$N_0tN_{0ld}tN_{0l2d}t$	N_0tf_p	Third Order	$N_{0l2d}t \rightarrow N_0f_p$
Third Order	$S_{0h2}w$	$S_{0h2}w$	Third Order (A)	
Third Order	$S_{0h2}t$	$S_{0h2}t$	Third Order (A)	
Third Order	$S_{0h}l$	$S_{0h}l$	Third Order (A)	
Third Order	$S_0tS_{0ld}tS_{0l2d}t$	S_0tf_p	Third Order (B)	$ld/rd/l2d/r2d \rightarrow f_p$
Third Order	$S_0tS_{0rd}tS_{0r2d}t$		Third Order (B)	
Third Order	$S_{0h2}tS_{0h}tS_0t$	$S_{0h2}tS_{0h}tS_0t$	Third Order (C)	
LabelSet	S_0wl_p	S_0ws_f	Subcat. frames	
LabelSet	S_0wr_p		Subcat. frames	
LabelSet	S_0tr_p	S_0ws_f	Subcat. frames	$l_p/r_p \rightarrow s_f$
LabelSet	S_0tl_p		Subcat. frames	
LabelSet	N_0wl_p	N_0ws_f	Subcat. frames	
LabelSet	N_0tl_p	N_0ts_f	Subcat. frames	
		S_0wS_0o	Edge Potential	New
		S_0tS_0o	Edge Potential	$o = |\sigma_h| =$ edge potential
		N_0tS_0o	Edge Potential	
		N_0wS_0o	Edge Potential	

Table 3: Rich Non-Local Features vs. Rich Linguistic Features

Feature Group	Morphological Augmentations
Single	h
	x
Pairs	h1h2
	h1x2
	x1h2
Three Words (A)	h1h2
	h1x2
	x1h2
	h1h3
	h1x3
	x1h3
	h2h3
	h2x3
	x2h3
Three Words (B)	h1h3
	h1x3
	x1h3
Valency	h
Unigram (A)	h
	x
Bigram	h1h2
	h1x2
	x1h2
Third Order (A)	h
	x
Third Order (B)	h
	x
Third Order (C)	h1h2
	h1x2
	x1h2
	h1h3
	h1x3
	x1h3
	h2h3
	h2x3
	x2h3

Table 4: Morphological Augmentation of Rich Linguistic Feature Groups

References

Daniel Andor, Chris Alberti, David Weiss, Aliaksei Severyn, Alessandro Presta, Kuzman Ganchev, Slav Petrov, and Michael Collins. 2016. Globally normalized transition-based neural networks. In *Proceedings of the 54th Annual Meeting of the Association for Computational Linguistics, ACL 2016, August 7-12, 2016, Berlin, Germany, Volume 1: Long Papers*. http://aclweb.org/anthology/P/P16/P16-1231.pdf.

Bernd Bohnet and Joakim Nivre. 2012. A transition-based system for joint part-of-speech tagging and labeled non-projective dependency parsing. In *Proceedings of the 2012 Joint Conference on Empirical Methods in Natural Language Processing and Computational Natural Language Learning*. Association for Computational Linguistics, Stroudsburg, PA, USA, EMNLP-CoNLL '12, pages 1455–1465. http://dl.acm.org/citation.cfm?id=2390948.2391114.

Bernd Bohnet, Joakim Nivre, Igor Boguslavsky, Richárd Farkas, Filip Ginter, and Jan Hajic. 2013. Joint morphological and syntactic analysis for richly inflected languages. *TACL* 1:415–428. http://dblp.uni-trier.de/db/journals/tacl/tacl1.html.

Sabine Buchholz and Erwin Marsi. 2006. CoNLL-X shared task on multilingual dependency parsing. In *Proceedings of CoNLL-X*. pages 149–164.

Michael Collins and Brian Roark. 2004. Incremental parsing with the perceptron algorithm. In *Proceedings of the 42Nd Annual Meeting on Association for Computational Linguistics*. Association for Computational Linguistics, Stroudsburg, PA, USA, ACL '04. https://doi.org/10.3115/1218955.1218970.

Yoav Goldberg and Joakim Nivre. 2012. A dynamic oracle for arc-eager dependency parsing. In *COLING 2012, 24th International Conference on Computational Linguistics, Proceedings of the Conference: Technical Papers, 8-15 December 2012, Mumbai, India*. pages 959–976. http://aclweb.org/anthology/C/C12/C12-1059.pdf.

Sandra Kübler, Ryan McDonald, and Joakim Nivre. 2009. *Dependency Parsing*. Number 2 in Synthesis Lectures on Human Language Technologies. Morgan & Claypool Publishers.

Zhenghua Li, Min Zhang, Wanxiang Che, Ting Liu, and Wenliang Chen. 2014. Joint optimization for chinese POS tagging and dependency parsing. *IEEE/ACM Trans. Audio, Speech & Language Processing* 22(1):274–286. https://doi.org/10.1109/TASLP.2013.2288081.

Zhenghua Li, Min Zhang, Wanxiang Che, Ting Liu, Wenliang Chen, and Haizhou Li. 2011. Joint models for chinese pos tagging and dependency parsing. In *Proceedings of the Conference on Empirical Methods in Natural Language Processing*. Association for Computational Linguistics, Stroudsburg, PA, USA, EMNLP '11, pages 1180–1191. http://dl.acm.org/citation.cfm?id=2145432.2145557.

Amir More and Reut Tsarfaty. 2016. Data-driven morphological analysis and disambiguation for morphologically rich languages and universal dependencies. In *Proceedings of COLING 2016, the 26th International Conference on Computational Linguistics: Technical Papers*. The COLING 2016 Organizing Committee, Osaka, Japan, pages 337–348. http://aclweb.org/anthology/C16-1033.

Joakim Nivre, Željko Agić, Lars Ahrenberg, et al. 2017a. Universal dependencies 2.0 CoNLL 2017 shared task development and test data. LINDAT/CLARIN digital library at the Institute of Formal and Applied Linguistics, Charles University. http://hdl.handle.net/11234/1-2184.

Joakim Nivre, Marie-Catherine de Marneffe, Filip Ginter, Yoav Goldberg, Jan Hajič, Christopher Manning, Ryan McDonald, Slav Petrov, Sampo Pyysalo, Natalia Silveira, Reut Tsarfaty, and Daniel Zeman. 2016. Universal Dependencies v1: A multilingual treebank collection. In *Proceedings of the 10th International Conference on Language Resources and Evaluation (LREC 2016)*. European Language Resources Association, Portoro, Slovenia, pages 1659–1666.

Joakim Nivre, Johan Hall, Sandra Kübler, Ryan McDonald, Jens Nilsson, Sebastian Riedel, and Deniz Yuret. 2007. The CoNLL 2007 shared task on dependency parsing. In *Proceedings of the CoNLL Shared Task Session of EMNLP-CoNLL 2007*. pages 915–932.

Joakim Nivre et al. 2017b. Universal Dependencies 2.0. LINDAT/CLARIN digital library at the Institute of Formal and Applied Linguistics, Charles University, Prague, `http://hdl.handle.net/11234/1-1983`. http://hdl.handle.net/11234/1-1983.

Martin Potthast, Tim Gollub, Francisco Rangel, Paolo Rosso, Efstathios Stamatatos, and Benno Stein. 2014. Improving the reproducibility of PAN's shared tasks: Plagiarism detection, author identification, and author profiling. In Evangelos Kanoulas, Mihai Lupu, Paul Clough, Mark Sanderson, Mark Hall, Allan Hanbury, and Elaine Toms, editors, *Information Access Evaluation meets Multilinguality, Multimodality, and Visualization. 5th International Conference of the CLEF Initiative (CLEF 14)*. Springer, Berlin Heidelberg New York, pages 268–299. https://doi.org/10.1007/978-3-319-11382-1_22.

Djamé Seddah, Sandra Kübler, and Reut Tsarfaty. 2014. Introducing the spmrl 2014 shared task on parsing morphologically-rich languages. pages 103–109.

Djame Seddah, Reut Tsarfaty, Sandra Kübler, Marie Candito, D. Jinho Choi, Richárd Farkas, Jennifer Foster, Iakes Goenaga, Koldo Gojenola Galletebeitia, Yoav Goldberg, Spence Green, Nizar Habash, Marco Kuhlmann, Wolfgang Maier, Joakim

Nivre, Adam Przepiórkowski, Ryan Roth, Wolfgang Seeker, Yannick Versley, Veronika Vincze, Marcin Woliński, Alina Wróblewska, and Villemonte Eric de la Clergerie. 2013. Proceedings of the fourth workshop on statistical parsing of morphologically-rich languages. Association for Computational Linguistics, pages 146–182. http://aclweb.org/anthology/W13-4917.

Milan Straka, Jan Hajič, and Jana Straková. 2016. UD-Pipe: trainable pipeline for processing CoNLL-U files performing tokenization, morphological analysis, POS tagging and parsing. In *Proceedings of the 10th International Conference on Language Resources and Evaluation (LREC 2016)*. European Language Resources Association, Portoro, Slovenia.

Reut Tsarfaty and Yoav Goldberg. 2008. Word-based or morpheme-based? annotation strategies for modern Hebrew clitics. In *Proceedings of LREC*.

Daniel Zeman, Martin Popel, Milan Straka, Jan Hajič, Joakim Nivre, Filip Ginter, Juhani Luotolahti, Sampo Pyysalo, Slav Petrov, Martin Potthast, Francis Tyers, Elena Badmaeva, Memduh Gökırmak, Anna Nedoluzhko, Silvie Cinková, Jan Hajič jr., Jaroslava Hlaváčová, Václava Kettnerová, Zdeňka Urešová, Jenna Kanerva, Stina Ojala, Anna Missilä, Christopher Manning, Sebastian Schuster, Siva Reddy, Dima Taji, Nizar Habash, Herman Leung, Marie-Catherine de Marneffe, Manuela Sanguinetti, Maria Simi, Hiroshi Kanayama, Valeria de Paiva, Kira Droganova, Hěctor Martínez Alonso, Hans Uszkoreit, Vivien Macketanz, Aljoscha Burchardt, Kim Harris, Katrin Marheinecke, Georg Rehm, Tolga Kayadelen, Mohammed Attia, Ali Elkahky, Zhuoran Yu, Emily Pitler, Saran Lertpradit, Michael Mandl, Jesse Kirchner, Hector Fernandez Alcalde, Jana Strnadova, Esha Banerjee, Ruli Manurung, Antonio Stella, Atsuko Shimada, Sookyoung Kwak, Gustavo Mendonça, Tatiana Lando, Rattima Nitisaroj, and Josie Li. 2017. CoNLL 2017 Shared Task: Multilingual Parsing from Raw Text to Universal Dependencies. In *Proceedings of the CoNLL 2017 Shared Task: Multilingual Parsing from Raw Text to Universal Dependencies*. Association for Computational Linguistics.

Meishan Zhang, Yue Zhang, Wanxiang Che, and Ting Liu. 2014. Character-level chinese dependency parsing. In *In Proceedings of the ACL*.

Yue Zhang and Stephen Clark. 2011. Syntactic processing using the generalized perceptron and beam search. *Computational Linguistics* 37(1):105–151. https://doi.org/10.1162/coli_a_00037.

Yue Zhang and Joakim Nivre. 2011. Transition-based dependency parsing with rich non-local features. In *Proceedings of the 49th Annual Meeting of the Association for Computational Linguistics: Human Language Technologies: Short Papers - Volume 2*. Association for Computational Linguistics, Stroudsburg, PA, USA, HLT '11, pages 188–193. http://dl.acm.org/citation.cfm?id=2002736.2002777.

A Semi-universal Pipelined Approach to the CoNLL 2017 UD Shared Task

Hiroshi Kanayama   Masayasu Muraoka   Katsumasa Yoshikawa
IBM Research - Tokyo
{hkana,mmuraoka,katsuy}@jp.ibm.com

Abstract

This paper presents the TRL team's system submitted for the CoNLL 2017 Shared Task, "Multilingual Parsing from Raw Text to Universal Dependencies." We ran the system for all languages with our own fully pipelined components without relying on either pre-trained baseline or machine learning techniques. We used only the universal part-of-speech tags and distance between words, and applied deterministic rules to assign labels. The delexicalized models are suitable for cross-lingual transfer or universal approaches. Experimental results show that our model performed well in some metrics and leads discussion on topics such as contribution of each component and on syntactic similarities among languages.

1 Introduction

We tested dependency-based syntactic parsing in 49 languages on Universal Dependencies (Nivre et al., 2015) using 81 corpora from the UD version 2.0 datasets (Nivre et al., 2017). The task is described in the overview paper (Zeman et al., 2017) and the whole system is evaluated on the TIRA platform (Potthast et al., 2014).

Instead of merely pursuing higher scores in the shared task, we adopted several strategies in the design of our parser:

Self-contained system. To keep capabilities to control the input and output of the system, we use only our own components for the whole pipeline including sentence splitter, tokenizer, lemmatizer, PoS tagger, dependency parser and role labeler. We do not rely on any existing preprocessors such as UDPipe

(Straka et al., 2016) and SyntaxNet (Weiss et al., 2015).

One model per language. When there are multiple corpora in a language with different annotation strategies, our system does not optimize models for each corpus, because the real applications do not assume such specific corpora.

No machine learning. We use merely simple statistics with parts of speech of each word and distance between words, and induced deterministic rules. Neither higher order models nor word embeddings are used, thus our system is fully controllable with linguistic knowledge.

Componentized pipeline. Components in the pipeline can be divided and optimized independently so that they are interchangeable with other corresponding components such as the UDPipe tokenizer. Our dependency parser relies only on Universal PoS tags and does not use an extended PoS, lemma nor features annotated by a specific tokenizer.

Our system was composed under these constraints at the sacrifice of overall scores but it performed marginally well, achieving the best participant scores in a number of metrics. The major contributions in this report are as follows:

1. Report of runs without UDPipe with very different results than those obtained from other participants.

2. Experiments in cross-lingual and universal scenarios by using delexicalized statistics of different languages.

3. Simple and reusable techniques to induce rules for PoS tagging and relation labeling.

Proceedings of the CoNLL 2017 Shared Task: Multilingual Parsing from Raw Text to Universal Dependencies, pages 265–273,
Vancouver, Canada, August 3-4, 2017. © 2017 Association for Computational Linguistics

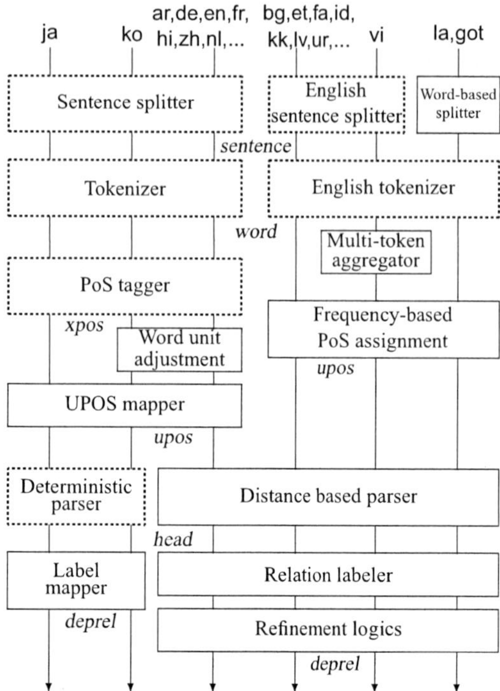

Figure 1: The pipelined architecture for multilingual parsing from raw text. Dotted boxes indicate existing (not UD-compliant) components.

Section 2 describes each components in our pipeline. Section 3 reports our results, including ablation studies and additional experiments in cross-lingual and multilingual settings. Section 4 shows some related prior work related to our approach.

2 Components

Figure 1 illustrates our pipelined architecture for multilingual parsing from raw text. As indicated as dotted boxes in the figure, we exploited in-house engines for sentence splitting, tokenization and PoS tagging for a number of languages and fit them to the UD annotation schemata. For languages which our engine does not cover, we used simple statistics in the training corpus to assign Universal PoS (UPOS). For syntactic parsing, we extracted statistics to predict the head words, taking into account UPOS and distance. To assign relation labels we applied rules induced from the corpus.

The rest of this section describes each component with language specific treatments in the order in the pipeline.

2.1 Sentence splitting

For the sentence splitting we applied existing logics, taking into account language specific punctuations and special cases such as "Mr." in English. For languages that our sentence splitter does not cover, we simply applied the logic for English. For corpora that do not use punctuation at all (*e.g.* got and la_proiel), we identified words that tend to be the first or the last word in a sentence (more than half of appearance *e.g.* "itaque" in Latin as the first word), and used them to split long sentences that had 10 or more words.

2.2 Tokenization

Our in-house engine tokenizer and PoS tagger support 17 languages; ar, cs, da, de, en, es, fr, he, it, ja, ko, nl, pl, pt, tr, ru and zh. For three of them, Japanese (ja), Korean (ko) and Chinese (zh), words are split in very different manner without relying on white spaces [1].

We applied English tokenizer for other languages to simply split words by white spaces and punctuations. For Vietnamese (vi) in which the word units are longer than space-split tokens, we extracted multi-token words from the training corpus and aggregated them in runtime. This raised the word F1 score for vi from 73.7 to 85.1.

There are unignorable mismatches in tokenization strategies between our tokenizer and UD corpora. The major difference is in Korean (ko): while our tokenizer splits particles and suffixes from content words, the UD corpus gives whitespace (*eojeol*) tokenization. Accordingly, we merged those tokens after getting parts of speech of each unit.

We also made adjustments in Turkish (tr) to attach suffixes except for "ki", and in Arabic (ar) to attach the determiner "al". There still remains many differences in other languages but we did not make any other modifications, which resulted in lower word correspondence values (95.5 on average) compared to those of UDPipe (98.6).

2.3 PoS tagging

As well as the tokenization, we applied PoS tags output by our engine for 17 languages to get their own PoS schema; some of them are close to the Penn Treebank style and the others are in different schemes. We adopted those tags as Extended

---

[1]Though the word unit in the Korean corpus in UD2.0 is determined by white space, our tokenizer gives finer tokens by splitting functional words.

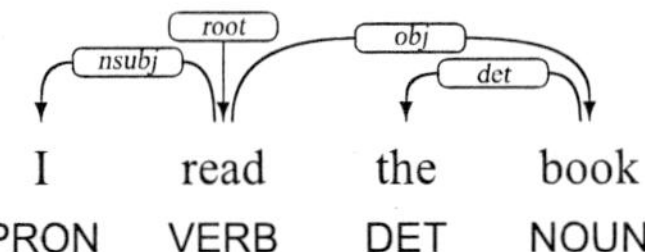

Figure 2: A sample dependency structure of an English sentence.

PoS (XPOS) tags and mapped them to UPOS. The mapper assigns the most frequent UPOS in the training corpus for a combination of XPOS and the lemma of a given word.

By definition, our PoS tagger does not distinguish some of the main verbs (**VERB**) from auxiliary verbs (**AUX**) such as "do" and "have" in English, "avoir" in French and "haber" in Spanish, which causes many parsing errors, and so we added heuristics to change the UPOS using the context.

For other languages the PoS tagger does not cover, we assigned the most frequent UPOS for each surface form in the training corpus. Even with this naïve method we obtained UPOS scores higher than 90 for some languages such as Czech (cs), Persian (fa), Hindi (hi) and Indonesian (id) but it did not work well enough for lower resource languages.

2.4 Dependency parsing

2.4.1 PoS-level models

To keep the simplicity and language universality of the parsing method, we built the first-order delexicalized model for each language[2]. The score of the dependency between two words is determined only by the UPOS of head and dependent words and surface distance between two words.

Figure 2 shows a sample dependency structure for an English sentence and Table 1 shows true (T) and false (F) dependencies found in the sentence in Figure 2. By counting frequencies of these events for all pairs in a sentence, the ratio of correct dependency for a pair of PoS and distance is calculated.

Formally, let h be a head word, d be a dependent, p_w be the UPOS of w, and $\Delta_{d,h}$ be the distance[3] between d and h, so that the score is

---

[2]Not for each corpus, following 'one model par language' policy.

[3]The difference of word IDs of h and d. We cap the maximum distance at 12 (empirically determined), *i.e.* word pairs further than 13 are regarded as $\Delta = 12$.

dependent	head	distance	dependency?
PRON	VERB	1	T
PRON	DET	2	F
PRON	NOUN	3	F
VERB	PRON	-1	F
VERB	DET	1	F
VERB	NOUN	2	F
DET	PRON	-2	F
DET	VERB	-1	F
DET	NOUN	1	T
NOUN	PRON	-3	F
NOUN	VERB	-2	T
NOUN	DET	-1	F

Table 1: True (T) and false (F) dependencies between two words in the sentence in Figure 2. Negative distance means that the head is left to the dependent.

English (en)	
ADJ, NOUN, -1	.238
ADJ, NOUN, 1	.906
ADJ, NOUN, 2	.639
VERB, ADJ, -2	.512
ADP, NOUN, 2	.817
AUX, ADP, 1	.034

French (fr)	
ADJ, NOUN, -1	.959
ADJ, NOUN, 1	.967
ADJ, NOUN, 2	.130
VERB, ADJ, -2	.180
ADP, NOUN, 2	.943
AUX, ADP, 1	.000

Table 2: Examples of dependency scores between two words for English and French. A condition indicates the PoS of dependent and head words, and distance between two words.

$$\frac{\#(\text{T} \mid p_d, p_h, \Delta_{d,h})}{\#(\text{T} \mid p_d, p_h, \Delta_{d,h}) + \#(\text{F} \mid p_d, p_h, \Delta_{d,h})},$$

where $\#(\cdot)$ is the frequency in the training corpus, T denotes that d depends on h and F denotes it does not. The score is set to 0 when the denominator is 0.

Table 2 shows example scores. These statistics reflect universal attributes, for example, smaller distance is preferred, functional words tend not to have dependents, and so on. Also language specific attributes are contained, such as regarding orientation of adjective modification and adpositions.

These scores are used as the weight of the Chu-Liu-Edmonds algorithm (Chu and Liu, 1965; Edmonds, 1967) to obtain the minimum spanning tree to optimize the dependency structures in a sentence. This algorithm can produce a non-projective tree, which frequently appears in languages such as German, Latin and Czech (McDonald et al., 2005).

2.4.2 Language specific cases

Japanese (ja) and Korean (ko) are parsed in a different manner. A common point to both languages is that all content words form right-head structures; consequently, a set of rules selects the syntactically possible head words for a given word by using the syntactic features (Kanayama et al., 2014). Here the dependencies are determined as the nearest baseline among the modification candidates without relying on the statistics of the training corpora.

For 'surprise languages' that do not have training corpora, we use models for languages in the close regions (Russian (ru) for Buryat (bxr), Persian (fa) for Kurmanji (kmr), Finnish (fi) for North Sámi (sme) and Polish (pl) for Upper Sorbian (hsb)) but these selections were not optimal as found in the experiments in Section 3.2.

2.4.3 Exceptional dependencies

The statistic model above is apparently ignorant of the vocabulary and lexical features finer than UPOS level. To capture some phenomena we made two deterministic modifications.

Fixed expressions. Multi-word expressions behave exceptionally in the UPOS-based model. In each language we extracted fixed phrases such as "because of" and "as well as" in English, and in runtime forcibly tagged dependencies for such word sequences with '*fixed*' label. Also, for consecutive appearance of same PoS tags of NOUN, PRON or NUM, a structure with the majority label (one of *flat*, *nmod*, *compound* or *nummod*) is assigned depending on the pairs of language and PoS, *e.g.* give left-head structures with *flat* label for PROPN sequences of Catalan (*ca*).

Consistent words. English UPOS PART is used for possessive "'s" and infinitive "to", which behaves very differently from each other. For such words whose head word is in a consistent direction per dependent word, the score for the other direction is discounted by multiplying 0.1, *e.g.* 0.1 is multiplied for the score

English (en)	
ADP, NOUN, +	*case*
VERB, NOUN,+	*acl*
NOUN, VERB, +	*nsubj*
NOUN, VERB, −	*obj*
ADJ, VERB, −	*xcomp*

Russian (ru)	
ADP, NOUN, +	*case*
VERB, NOUN,+	*amod*
NOUN, VERB, +	*nsubj*
NOUN, VERB, −	*obl*
ADJ, VERB, −	*obl*

Table 3: Examples of label assignment for English and Russian. '+' and '−' indicate the direction of the head word against a dependent; '+' means that the head comes right to a dependent.

of left-head modification of PART: "to" in English.

2.5 Relation label assignment

After getting the tree structures, we assigned dependency labels to each node by referring to the most frequent label between two UPOS tags in the languages. The labels vary by language and orientation of the dependencies as exemplified in Table 3.

In some cases the labels are difficult to deterministically assign merely by using UPOS of two words. In such cases, we applied the following label refinement rules.

Word based constraints. Forcibly change the label for words whose relation labels are mostly consistent ($\geq$ .95), *e.g.* modification by "there" in English should have *expl* label.

Verb arguments. Adjust the label of NOUN, PROPN and PRON when the word is a dependent of VERB with several conditions, *e.g.* set *obl* if the word has a dependent labeled *case* in most of languages.

Pronouns. Change the relation label of PRON as a dependent of VERB to its majority[4] for a surface form. *E.g.* select *obj* for "him" in English.

Conjunctions. When the dependent and head words have the same UPOS and there is CCONJ between the two words, set the label of the dependent as *conj*.

---

[4]Among *nsubj, obj, iobj* and *expl.*

Language	Submitted results (without UDPipe)						UDPipe preprocess					
	Sentence	Words	UPOS	UAS	LAS	WLAS	Sentence	Words	UPOS	UAS	LAS	WLAS
* Average	79.99	95.47	80.45	53.53	43.37	37.33	88.48	98.61	91.02	61.89	52.12	45.75
ar	77.10	92.21	80.05	51.44	39.98	33.40	84.57	93.69	88.13	55.26	46.41	40.53
ar_pud	99.10	**96.05**	73.06	56.59	42.76	35.61	100.00	90.82	70.27	50.05	39.51	33.98
bg	80.71	97.43	88.27	61.26	53.39	46.33	92.83	99.91	97.58	74.43	68.00	63.39
bxr	**93.69**	98.44	47.69	23.40	14.02	4.22	91.81	99.35	84.12	40.35	25.97	19.22
ca	97.25	91.96	85.90	58.31	51.43	40.77	98.95	99.97	98.04	72.85	66.44	56.58
cs	77.90	97.13	93.29	61.32	54.81	51.92	92.03	99.90	98.13	67.24	60.15	57.31
cs_cac	99.76	97.45	92.90	64.88	57.59	53.82	100.00	99.99	98.27	69.40	61.93	57.99
cs_cltt	45.04	88.90	79.91	54.09	48.38	46.30	95.06	99.35	95.41	63.20	56.50	53.48
cs_pud	87.57	97.68	92.67	64.47	58.02	55.20	96.43	99.29	96.55	66.44	59.78	57.34
cu	1.16	99.97	85.52	51.09	35.00	29.90	36.05	99.96	93.34	60.42	45.77	41.04
da	72.76	93.61	79.57	48.62	41.01	34.67	79.36	99.69	95.04	63.15	55.91	50.64
de	69.84	89.86	79.32	49.28	43.23	37.93	79.11	99.65	90.83	62.17	55.87	47.83
de_pud	86.93	93.01	77.55	51.35	43.44	38.46	86.49	98.00	84.38	61.76	53.17	46.38
el	81.03	98.12	86.66	61.06	52.44	41.08	90.79	99.88	95.18	72.34	66.77	59.09
en	64.77	94.31	82.41	56.44	49.56	44.77	73.22	98.67	93.11	62.83	55.98	50.41
en_lines	81.72	98.63	86.90	59.77	52.49	47.25	85.84	99.94	94.53	66.12	57.65	52.00
en_partut	90.61	99.45	88.32	62.48	54.50	46.56	97.51	99.49	93.03	65.19	57.31	49.48
en_pud	94.29	99.04	85.43	60.05	53.94	48.09	97.13	99.66	94.00	66.27	59.82	53.30
es	88.19	96.13	88.82	63.80	57.01	49.03	94.15	99.69	95.60	69.76	63.55	53.34
es_ancora	95.44	98.54	89.35	65.22	55.52	45.81	97.05	99.95	98.15	70.42	60.92	51.31
es_pud	95.40	96.85	84.45	66.68	58.40	50.03	93.42	99.47	88.15	71.92	64.19	54.46
et	80.91	98.73	79.68	49.79	34.05	29.83	85.20	99.77	87.70	58.20	43.25	39.60
eu	91.06	97.52	85.58	53.63	41.80	36.35	99.58	99.96	92.36	59.97	47.51	41.92
fa	96.11	99.07	92.32	56.28	48.40	41.61	98.00	99.64	96.00	60.23	52.12	45.25
fi	80.34	96.10	84.02	45.45	31.51	32.98	84.56	99.63	94.01	51.39	38.23	40.40
fi_ftb	75.42	98.66	78.95	57.45	44.55	34.06	83.83	99.88	91.87	63.80	52.65	42.04
fi_pud	87.50	96.28	85.59	46.67	32.55	35.19	93.67	99.61	95.61	52.92	39.68	43.12
fr	86.99	93.78	85.75	61.71	54.59	50.00	93.59	99.87	95.33	70.25	64.06	57.61
fr_partut	89.99	94.43	86.64	64.75	57.18	51.92	98.00	98.95	94.46	69.93	62.90	54.73
fr_pud	95.85	95.01	81.19	64.04	56.96	51.35	92.32	98.17	87.90	69.42	63.22	56.96
fr_sequoia	67.24	92.70	84.35	59.60	52.75	48.63	83.75	99.06	95.40	70.50	64.35	58.49
ga	95.49	96.44	82.54	61.87	43.80	28.38	95.81	99.29	88.17	65.09	48.30	32.66
gl	90.64	98.39	88.73	64.69	55.70	45.49	96.15	99.92	96.84	68.78	62.96	54.76
gl_treegal	78.79	87.39	71.85	46.75	33.25	27.85	81.63	98.62	90.69	62.92	50.72	41.85
got	3.20	99.90	86.85	51.80	36.92	30.18	27.85	100.00	93.55	58.28	44.97	39.42
grc	41.91	99.96	71.46	41.18	28.63	18.68	98.43	99.95	82.13	47.68	36.16	28.55
grc_proiel	1.42	98.93	87.75	49.97	38.88	26.43	43.11	100.00	95.72	57.61	46.97	36.12
he	98.89	84.45	73.29	47.31	37.10	26.50	99.39	84.82	80.48	51.21	42.52	31.92
hi	90.22	99.06	90.15	66.60	55.15	40.59	99.20	100.00	95.63	71.92	60.45	45.90
hi_pud	94.47	**99.65**	81.48	51.26	36.80	26.09	90.83	97.81	83.75	52.57	39.16	29.68
hr	84.67	98.01	87.71	56.49	45.82	41.33	96.92	99.93	95.67	66.95	57.77	54.60
hsb	68.23	99.51	61.48	30.74	22.15	15.99	90.69	99.84	90.30	51.85	41.96	37.46
hu	88.86	94.42	78.98	46.56	33.75	28.71	93.85	99.82	90.80	61.85	49.66	45.60
id	85.37	99.07	90.54	63.72	54.97	51.56	91.15	99.99	93.32	65.36	57.37	54.87
it	89.05	88.56	77.66	57.96	49.67	46.57	97.10	99.73	97.07	76.45	70.78	61.96
it_pud	**97.81**	89.19	73.72	58.76	50.34	46.67	96.58	99.17	93.07	75.50	70.09	61.20
ja	94.56	**98.59**	**98.45**	**91.14**	**91.13**	**84.45**	94.92	98.49	98.54	61.28	58.54	43.95
* ja_pud	**97.42**	98.89	98.52	88.79	88.71	80.09	94.89	91.06	88.69	64.84	62.31	46.50
kk	**89.35**	95.93	56.39	**45.72**	24.14	18.30	81.38	94.91	50.06	31.53	17.01	13.11
kmr	**98.64**	96.86	35.55	10.59	3.44	3.67	97.02	98.85	90.04	47.66	35.31	28.97
ko	69.87	98.12	76.56	55.54	45.83	42.12	93.05	99.73	93.79	53.11	26.48	20.90
la	62.03	**100.00**	73.24	37.40	23.48	20.35	98.09	99.99	83.39	42.86	29.75	26.54
la_ittb	74.82	99.19	91.33	47.21	37.59	32.05	93.24	99.99	97.21	54.15	44.38	38.52
la_proiel	1.25	99.77	85.27	43.87	27.97	22.30	25.80	100.00	94.82	49.74	34.78	28.95
lv	97.36	98.07	78.66	45.13	34.21	29.09	98.59	98.91	88.37	53.17	43.25	38.83
nl	72.92	92.67	78.53	47.58	39.44	30.28	77.14	99.88	91.00	60.45	50.76	41.36
nl_lassysmall	33.65	93.68	75.54	45.95	35.32	26.90	78.62	99.93	96.86	63.07	52.78	45.58
no_bokmaal	86.72	95.51	87.63	57.07	49.31	42.90	95.76	99.75	96.75	69.57	62.13	55.81
no_nynorsk	80.12	94.88	86.43	54.20	46.83	40.78	91.23	99.75	96.38	66.32	58.91	52.00
pl	97.83	97.19	89.14	68.47	57.83	52.71	98.91	99.88	95.31	76.81	65.44	59.39
pt	77.79	86.46	71.60	52.04	40.46	35.71	89.79	99.52	96.22	72.50	62.11	50.03
pt_br	92.65	88.26	70.12	53.10	43.76	38.87	96.84	99.84	96.97	72.17	64.03	52.71
pt_pud	95.80	88.69	71.70	54.83	44.86	39.42	95.65	99.42	88.45	70.34	60.62	49.06
ro	89.13	96.37	87.64	64.24	53.35	46.51	93.42	99.64	96.40	70.76	62.20	55.63
ru	91.52	93.87	85.62	55.70	45.52	48.67	96.42	99.91	94.47	60.95	51.16	53.69
ru_pud	95.28	**98.29**	80.39	58.58	49.04	52.72	98.95	97.18	85.85	59.33	49.91	54.27
ru_syntagrus	89.75	98.36	89.44	69.49	61.66	51.91	97.81	99.57	97.99	72.58	65.84	56.42
sk	68.30	99.75	81.11	46.60	38.69	31.87	83.53	100.00	92.19	68.28	60.78	57.56
sl	96.49	99.73	86.89	56.55	47.25	39.89	99.24	99.96	96.34	72.11	64.63	60.02
sl_sst	0.52	88.87	77.78	38.65	29.92	24.63	16.72	98.82	88.82	50.20	39.82	35.27
sme	**99.13**	98.28	43.88	27.93	7.47	7.74	98.79	99.88	86.81	46.05	31.46	33.56
sv	89.69	94.51	82.37	54.98	45.17	39.76	96.37	99.84	95.41	67.40	59.48	54.79
sv_lines	79.82	96.59	83.09	57.70	47.13	42.15	86.44	99.98	94.22	68.18	60.47	55.21
sv_pud	**95.52**	95.00	80.36	54.05	42.58	36.82	90.20	98.26	91.16	65.35	56.49	51.29
tr	93.57	88.78	77.25	42.07	30.48	25.91	96.63	97.89	91.22	52.19	39.28	33.70
tr_pud	88.88	88.21	62.02	39.14	21.36	15.17	93.91	96.62	71.05	48.82	25.72	18.36
ug	69.05	98.23	65.27	48.10	23.72	14.37	63.55	98.52	73.63	50.40	31.20	22.55
uk	91.80	98.58	73.97	45.91	33.99	23.45	92.59	99.81	86.72	64.94	52.14	44.82
ur	97.93	97.70	86.31	62.47	50.26	36.55	98.32	100.00	91.71	69.35	56.90	42.73
vi	86.12	85.41	74.53	37.13	31.01	28.50	92.59	82.47	73.82	35.12	29.54	26.32
zh	92.81	83.64	71.31	31.49	25.60	23.24	98.19	88.91	82.69	39.65	33.87	30.99

Table 4: Overall F1 scores over test data (see Section 3.1).

3 Experimental Results

3.1 Overall results

Table 4 shows the results for 81 test corpora in 49 languages including 'surprise languages'.

The left side shows the performance of our system described in Section 2. The scores are the same as those in the official run except for ja_pud data on which we encountered a technical problem in the official run. '∗' denotes that the values were updated from the official score. WLAS denotes "Weighted labeled attachment score", which discounts the functional word attachments by multiplying 0.1 and ignores punctuation.

Numbers in bold letter indicate that our system achieved the best scores among task participants. Our sentence splitting was the best for seven corpora including three surprize languages, and word segmentation was best for five corpora.

Japanese (ja) shows the best score except for sentence splitting[5], but it is exceptional here. As we provided the Japanese UD2.0 data set, we have the consistent tokenization, PoS mapping and label definition with the data set, thus it is straightforward to convert the parsing structure into appropriate UD schema. We intentionally use the naïve method for parsing (nearest baseline), however, we performed the best among the participants due to the high coincidence of the tokenization.

For Kazakh (kk), our approach worked well and achieved the best score in sentence splitting and unlabeled attachment scores (UAS). The absolute score was not high, so this shows the difficulty of the language for machine learning approaches.

Besides the difficult languages in terms of tokenization: Chinese (zh), Vietnamese (vi) and Hebrew (he), some languages show quite low scores for word splitting (*e.g.* pt and tr) due to differences in tokenization policies which our adjustment rules did not cover. Due to the nature of the pipelined architecture, the errors in word splitting directly affect the downstream metrics. Since the UPOS is used for dependency parsing, PoS tagging and PoS mapping errors are critical for parsing scores, both UAS and LAS.

The right side of Table 4 shows the results of our parser using UDPipe for tokenization and PoS tagging. Three columns (Sentence, Words and UPOS) show the scores of UDPipe itself, and the rest of columns show the scores of our parser when

UDPipe was applied for preprocessing. Since UDPipe was trained with the UD corpora the tokenization and PoS tagging performed much better than ours and resulted in scores 8 and 9 points higher than those obtained for UAS and LAS respectively. For Kazakh (kk), Vietnamese (vi) and one of Arabic data (ar_pud), our tokenizer and PoS tagger performed better than UDPipe, resulting in better parsing scores in the left side.

Korean (ko) is another exception. Since our UPOS-based dependency parsing model does not capture the decomposed elements of each token, the parser did not work well after the UDPipe preprocessing. Our deterministic parser can handle the functional words thus it performed better.

3.2 Cross-lingual and universal evaluation

One of the advantages of Universal Dependencies is the capability to test the language independent model and cross-lingual transfer learning. As described in Section 2.4, our dependency parsing models without any lexical information are very general. They therefore can be applied to other languages enabling us to test a universal language model.

Table 5 compares the UAS scores with the cross-lingual and universal settings. The 'Own model' column shows the original score, the 'Best transfer' column shows the score using the model that performed the best among different languages, and the 'Universal' column shows the score obtained with the combined statistics extracted from all of the multilingual corpora. Numbers in **bold** denote that the transfer or universal model outperformed the language specific model. Japanese (ja) and Korean (ko) were not tested here because they did not use compatible models.

The experimental result shows the best models for applying low-resource languages: fi for bxr, cs for kmr, tr for sme and hr for hsb. Also for relatively low-resource languages such as Kazakh (kk) and Ukrainian (uk), the models with larger corpora outperformed their own models. For four French (fr) corpora, the Portuguese (pt) model performed as well as the French model. This suggests the model with three different French corpora generated a noisy model.

It is interesting to consider the 'neighbor' languages in terms of syntax. English and Swedish (sv) selected each other as the closest languages, which suggests that they are selected not only be-

---

[5]Interestingly the sentence splitting score is almost the lowest among participants.

Language	Own model	Best transfer		Universal
Average	53.53			49.06
ar	51.44	ga	47.45	45.47
ar_pud	56.59	ga	55.92	54.53
bg	61.26	cs	60.38	60.19
bxr	23.40	fi	**24.66**	18.10
ca	58.31	es	57.90	57.57
cs	61.32	sl	60.68	59.31
cs_cac	64.88	sl	64.19	62.93
cs_cltt	54.09	sl	52.88	52.34
cs_pud	64.47	sl	64.06	62.43
cu	51.09	got	51.06	47.29
da	48.62	no	48.45	47.56
de	49.28	nl	47.19	47.18
de_pud	51.35	sl	49.92	49.21
el	61.06	de	57.04	58.37
en	56.44	sv	54.84	52.15
en_lines	59.77	sv	58.89	56.05
en_partut	62.48	sv	61.18	58.60
en_pud	60.05	sv	58.55	56.00
es	63.80	pt	63.54	62.51
es_ancora	65.22	ca	64.97	63.96
es_pud	66.68	pt	66.34	65.37
et	49.79	en	48.57	44.14
eu	53.63	hu	47.05	42.78
fa	56.28	la	52.28	51.92
fi	45.45	en	43.98	39.58
fi_ftb	57.45	en	50.92	50.51
fi_pud	46.67	en	45.23	41.83
fr	61.71	pt	61.48	60.18
fr_partut	64.75	it	**64.98**	63.55
fr_pud	64.04	pt	**64.65**	63.56
fr_sequoia	59.60	pt	59.24	57.74
ga	61.87	ro	59.05	57.05
gl	64.69	pt	62.62	60.99
gl_treegal	46.75	pt	**48.64**	**47.67**
got	51.80	grc	50.93	49.22
grc	41.18	no	39.13	39.75
grc_proiel	49.97	got	48.05	46.70
he	47.31	pt	45.35	43.83
hi	66.60	ur	65.48	38.36
hi_pud	51.26	ur	50.83	33.41
hr	56.49	cs	55.36	54.23
hsb	30.74	hr	**32.37**	**32.06**
hu	46.56	fi	46.21	36.04
id	63.72	ro	62.58	61.55
it	57.96	pt	**58.19**	57.09
it_pud	58.76	pt	**59.38**	58.75
ja	91.14	-		-
ja_pud	88.79	-		-
kk	45.72	ur	**47.58**	18.77
kmr	10.59	cs	**12.32**	**12.49**
ko	55.54	-		-
la	37.40	grc	**39.78**	35.83
la_ittb	47.21	cs	45.01	45.19
la_proiel	43.87	got	42.17	41.94
lv	45.13	en	44.80	37.46
nl	47.58	de	45.87	45.65
nl_lassysmall	45.95	la	44.10	43.68
no_bokmaal	57.07	da	55.69	54.70
no_nynorsk	54.20	sv	52.60	51.64
pl	68.47	cs	66.65	66.75
pt	52.04	ca	51.71	50.32
pt_br	53.10	es	53.08	51.56
pt_pud	54.83	es	**54.96**	53.12
ro	64.24	pt	63.60	62.62
ru	55.70	bg	**58.63**	**57.12**
ru_pud	58.58	cs	**64.39**	**62.29**
ru_syntagrus	69.49	fi	58.81	59.63
sk	46.60	cs	**48.82**	**47.45**
sl	56.55	cs	56.21	54.39
sl_sst	38.65	hr	37.35	37.78
sme	27.93	tr	**28.73**	20.31
sv	54.98	en	54.20	51.70
sv_lines	57.70	en	56.93	54.04
sv_pud	54.05	en	53.99	50.47
tr	42.07	ug	37.71	28.81
tr_pud	39.14	ug	36.85	24.12
ug	48.10	ur	45.41	16.20
uk	45.91	sv	**48.14**	**46.15**
ur	62.47	hi	60.35	32.83
vi	37.13	en	33.36	34.15
zh	31.49	tr	27.17	19.58

Table 5: UAS-F1 scores with language specific models, and transfer models (see Section 3.2.

cause of the size of the training corpora. It is also notable that two variants of Norwegian (no) were closest for different languages (Danish (da) and Swedish).

Even the universal model performed well. The drop in UAS scores from the language-specific result was only 4.5 points on average. This shows our method is general enough for multilingual design. Not only for low-resource languages such as Ukrainian and surprise languages, but also for Russian (ru) and Slovak (sk), the universal model outperformed the language specific model.

3.3 Ablation of refinement rules

Table 6 shows the difference in UAS scores when we did not apply one of the sets of rules to change the dependency structures described in Section 2.4 and LAS scores without one of refinements for relation labels described in Section 2.5. The identification of multi word tokens did not work well as expected, and the word level rules made little contribution.

Applying all label refinement rules improved the LAS score by 2.35 points on average. The rules to modify labels for verb arguments were the most important on average. Conjunction rules were very simple but consistently improved for almost all languages. Word-based constraints are good for some languages but may cause side effects. Pronoun rules were good for Gothic (got), which suggests that the Gothic pronouns are relatively consistently used for argument cases *e.g.* "saei" for *nsubj* and "mik" for *obj*.

4 Related Work

Some approaches share the same motivation with ours. Martínez-Alonso et al. (2017) used a small set of UPOS-level attachment rules for parsing and achieved 55 UAS with a universal model with predicted PoS. In this shared task we need to tackle the preprocessing and relation labeling as well which cannot be done in a language agnostic manner. Accordingly, we used minimum statistics for each language and achieved UAS levels similar to those for our own tokenization and PoS prediction, and higher value (by 9 points) when we use the UDPipe preprocessor.

Universal parsing is not our main focus here, but our results in the rightmost column in Table 2 can be used to compare our approach with universal approaches (Ammar et al., 2016).

271

	ΔUAS		ΔLAS				
Language	fixed	const	word	arg	pron	conj	ALL
Average	-0.35	0.06	0.41	1.17	0.18	0.40	2.35
ar	-2.41	0.04	1.51	-0.26	0.00	0.29	1.54
ar_pud	-1.39	0.00	1.44	2.80	-0.01	0.68	4.85
bg	-0.54	0.10	0.88	0.88	0.58	0.73	3.62
bxr	-3.32	0.00	0.00	0.00	0.00	0.00	0.00
ca	1.18	0.05	0.08	0.24	0.49	0.59	1.54
cs	-0.39	0.06	0.24	1.95	0.21	0.50	3.42
cs_cac	-0.13	0.07	0.14	1.93	0.11	1.17	3.72
cs_cltt	0.67	0.06	0.13	0.98	0.02	1.27	2.55
cs_pud	-0.14	0.09	0.08	2.43	0.19	0.60	3.97
cu	0.00	0.16	2.36	2.14	0.49	0.53	6.46
da	0.53	0.04	0.09	1.50	0.01	0.24	2.22
de	-0.01	0.01	0.43	1.56	0.27	0.50	2.94
de_pud	0.00	0.01	0.12	1.77	0.44	0.38	2.91
el	0.04	0.03	1.60	1.55	0.02	0.63	3.77
en	0.04	0.07	0.52	1.57	-0.33	0.40	2.16
en_lines	0.19	0.05	0.59	2.14	-0.35	0.38	2.76
en_partut	0.12	0.03	0.33	1.90	-0.04	0.82	3.00
en_pud	0.02	0.06	0.32	2.12	-0.11	0.48	2.82
es	-0.15	0.05	-0.10	2.14	0.53	0.59	4.27
es_ancora	0.41	0.00	-0.63	0.68	-0.08	0.43	-0.46
es_pud	0.21	0.02	0.20	2.79	0.32	0.54	3.93
et	0.08	0.00	1.14	0.29	0.23	0.05	1.83
eu	-0.16	0.16	1.29	0.37	0.01	0.02	1.62
fa	-4.35	0.19	0.82	1.44	0.00	1.49	3.93
fi	0.13	-0.07	-0.84	0.36	0.14	0.04	-0.29
fi_ftb	0.21	0.12	-0.33	-0.09	0.20	0.07	-0.09
fi_pud	0.09	-0.24	-0.65	0.48	0.10	0.10	0.05
fr	-1.08	0.11	-0.37	2.37	0.40	0.48	4.11
fr_partut	-2.64	0.01	-0.69	2.26	0.24	0.72	3.75
fr_pud	-1.10	0.06	-0.11	2.81	0.40	0.40	4.98
fr_sequoia	0.16	0.05	-0.58	1.75	0.16	0.33	2.95
ga	0.53	0.32	0.46	0.08	0.05	0.44	1.08
gl	-0.45	0.04	0.34	0.99	-0.04	-0.41	0.88
gl_treegal	0.02	0.08	0.28	0.29	0.11	0.80	1.50
got	-0.36	0.15	0.69	1.20	2.18	0.54	4.69
grc	-0.12	0.02	-1.02	1.13	0.12	0.47	0.71
grc_proiel	-0.37	0.01	3.13	1.50	1.07	0.47	6.24
he	0.10	0.09	0.41	0.60	0.02	0.36	1.38
hi	0.03	0.02	0.25	0.95	0.05	-0.01	1.61
hi_pud	0.00	0.03	0.74	0.40	0.27	0.04	1.84
hr	-0.59	0.00	0.75	1.41	0.24	0.81	3.46
hsb	-0.32	0.00	0.29	0.00	0.00	0.66	0.96
hu	-0.07	0.07	0.29	0.26	0.04	0.01	0.64
id	-2.53	0.05	0.05	2.43	-0.03	0.76	3.21
it	0.02	0.06	-0.14	1.99	0.11	0.52	3.13
it_pud	0.16	0.08	-0.01	2.60	0.11	0.43	3.66
kk	0.00	0.00	0.00	0.00	0.00	0.04	0.04
kmr	-9.68	0.00	0.02	0.00	0.00	0.00	0.02
la	-0.06	0.52	0.19	1.58	0.35	0.28	2.36
la_ittb	-0.06	0.02	-0.09	1.48	0.05	0.45	1.89
la_proiel	-0.10	0.02	0.30	2.15	0.65	0.74	3.83
lv	0.20	0.02	0.63	0.21	0.25	0.03	1.12
nl	0.49	0.05	0.59	0.24	0.24	0.63	1.73
nl_lassysmall	0.38	0.05	0.34	0.34	-0.02	0.46	1.15
no_bokmaal	0.04	0.14	0.54	1.73	0.23	0.37	3.03
no_nynorsk	0.13	0.17	0.55	1.42	0.18	0.48	2.83
pl	-0.38	0.02	0.60	0.00	0.49	0.37	2.05
pt	-0.14	0.03	-0.51	0.06	0.00	0.35	-0.09
pt_br	-0.02	0.06	0.58	0.20	0.10	0.39	1.27
pt_pud	0.02	0.10	0.38	0.17	0.03	0.45	1.04
ro	0.91	0.16	1.20	1.68	0.60	0.57	4.15
ru	-0.62	0.16	-0.02	2.85	0.18	0.51	3.84
ru_pud	-0.71	0.00	0.00	3.84	0.36	0.50	5.05
ru_syntagrus	-0.65	0.10	0.04	2.38	0.18	0.55	3.43
sk	-0.75	0.10	0.49	1.12	0.09	0.83	2.67
sl	-0.09	0.00	0.73	2.19	0.26	0.79	4.19
sl_sst	0.11	0.01	1.21	1.30	0.40	0.14	3.62
sme	0.00	0.00	0.00	0.00	0.00	0.04	0.04
sv	1.07	0.11	1.38	2.12	-0.01	0.53	4.17
sv_lines	-0.36	0.18	1.47	2.32	0.22	0.33	4.71
sv_pud	-0.11	0.19	1.55	2.00	0.06	0.40	4.10
tr	0.28	0.00	0.43	0.00	0.26	-0.02	0.74
tr_pud	-0.12	0.00	0.23	0.00	0.07	0.05	0.31
ug	0.00	0.00	0.15	0.00	0.04	0.00	0.19
uk	-0.03	0.03	1.20	0.13	0.10	0.82	2.20
ur	0.03	-0.01	0.44	0.92	0.03	0.06	1.43
vi	-0.53	0.02	0.13	0.57	0.00	0.05	0.75
zh	-0.01	0.05	1.37	0.72	0.00	0.00	2.09

Table 6: Ablation shown by differences in UAS and LAS values.

5 Conclusion

For the CoNLL 2017 Shared Task on multilingual parsing from raw text, we were able to achieve a whole multilingual parser pipeline in a "semi-universal" manner exploiting minimum statistics from the training corpora with deterministic rules for part of speech tagging and label adjustment. Even with a simple and general model we achieved .43 labeled attachment scores on average and showed that the model we propose can be suitably applied to cross-lingual and universal scenarios.

References

Waleed Ammar, George Mulcaire, Miguel Ballesteros, Chris Dyer, and Noah A. Smith. 2016. Many languages, one parser. *TACL* 4:431–444. http://aclweb.org/anthology/Q16-1031.

Y.J. Chu and T.H. Liu. 1965. On the shortest arborescence of a directed graph. *Science Sinica* 14:1396–1400.

J. Edmonds. 1967. Optimum branchings. *Journal of Research of the National Bureau of Standards* 71(B):233–240.

Hiroshi Kanayama, Youngja Park, Yuta Tsuboi, and Dongmook Yi. 2014. Learning from a neighbor: Adapting a Japanese parser for Korean through feature transfer learning. *LT4CloseLang 2014* page 2. http://aclweb.org/anthology/W14-4202.

Héctor Martínez Alonso, Željko Agić, Barbara Plank, and Anders Søgaard. 2017. Parsing universal dependencies without training. In *Proceedings of the 15th Conference of the European Chapter of the Association for Computational Linguistics: Volume 1, Long Papers*. Association for Computational Linguistics, Valencia, Spain, pages 230–240.

Ryan McDonald, Fernando Pereira, Kiril Ribarov, and Jan Hajič. 2005. Non-projective dependency parsing using spanning tree algorithms. In *Proceedings of the conference on Human Language Technology and Empirical Methods in Natural Language Processing*. Association for Computational Linguistics, pages 523–530. www.aclweb.org/anthology/H05-1066.

Joakim Nivre, Željko Agić, Lars Ahrenberg, et al. 2017. Universal dependencies 2.0 — CoNLL 2017 shared task development and test data. LINDAT/CLARIN digital library at the Institute of Formal and Applied Linguistics, Charles University. http://hdl.handle.net/11234/1-2184.

Joakim Nivre, Cristina Bosco, Jinho Choi, Marie-Catherine de Marneffe, Timothy Dozat, Richard

Farkas, Jennifer Foster, Filip Ginter, Yoav Goldberg, Jan Haji, Jenna Kanerva, Veronika Laippala, Alessandro Lenci, Teresa Lynn, Christopher Manning, Ryan McDonald, Anna Missila, Simonetta Montemagni, Slav Petrov, Sampo Pyysalo, Natalia Silveira, Maria Simi, Aaron Smith, Reut Tsarfaty, Veronika Vincze, and Daniel Zeman. 2015. Universal dependencies 1.0.

Martin Potthast, Tim Gollub, Francisco Rangel, Paolo Rosso, Efstathios Stamatatos, and Benno Stein. 2014. Improving the reproducibility of PAN's shared tasks: Plagiarism detection, author identification, and author profiling. In Evangelos Kanoulas, Mihai Lupu, Paul Clough, Mark Sanderson, Mark Hall, Allan Hanbury, and Elaine Toms, editors, *Information Access Evaluation meets Multilinguality, Multimodality, and Visualization. 5th International Conference of the CLEF Initiative (CLEF 14)*. Springer, Berlin Heidelberg New York, pages 268–299. https://doi.org/10.1007/978-3-319-11382-1_22.

Milan Straka, Jan Hajič, and Jana Straková. 2016. UDPipe: trainable pipeline for processing CoNLL-U files performing tokenization, morphological analysis, POS tagging and parsing. In *Proceedings of the 10th International Conference on Language Resources and Evaluation (LREC 2016)*. European Language Resources Association, Portorož, Slovenia.

David Weiss, Chris Alberti, Michael Collins, and Slav Petrov. 2015. Structured training for neural network transition-based parsing. *CoRR* abs/1506.06158. http://arxiv.org/abs/1506.06158.

Daniel Zeman, Martin Popel, Milan Straka, Jan Hajič, Joakim Nivre, Filip Ginter, Juhani Luotolahti, Sampo Pyysalo, Slav Petrov, Martin Potthast, Francis Tyers, Elena Badmaeva, Memduh Gökırmak, Anna Nedoluzhko, Silvie Cinková, Jan Hajič jr., Jaroslava Hlaváčová, Václava Kettnerová, Zdeňka Urešová, Jenna Kanerva, Stina Ojala, Anna Missilä, Christopher Manning, Sebastian Schuster, Siva Reddy, Dima Taji, Nizar Habash, Herman Leung, Marie-Catherine de Marneffe, Manuela Sanguinetti, Maria Simi, Hiroshi Kanayama, Valeria de Paiva, Kira Droganova, Hěctor Martínez Alonso, Hans Uszkoreit, Vivien Macketanz, Aljoscha Burchardt, Kim Harris, Katrin Marheinecke, Georg Rehm, Tolga Kayadelen, Mohammed Attia, Ali Elkahky, Zhuoran Yu, Emily Pitler, Saran Lertpradit, Michael Mandl, Jesse Kirchner, Hector Fernandez Alcalde, Jana Strnadova, Esha Banerjee, Ruli Manurung, Antonio Stella, Atsuko Shimada, Sookyoung Kwak, Gustavo Mendonça, Tatiana Lando, Rattima Nitisaroj, and Josie Li. 2017. CoNLL 2017 Shared Task: Multilingual Parsing from Raw Text to Universal Dependencies. In *Proceedings of the CoNLL 2017 Shared Task: Multilingual Parsing from Raw Text to Universal Dependencies*. Association for Computational Linguistics.

A rule-based system for cross-lingual parsing of Romance languages with Universal Dependencies

Marcos Garcia
LyS Group
Departamento de Letras
Universidade da Coruña
marcos.garcia.gonzalez@udc.gal

Pablo Gamallo
Centro Singular de Investigación en
Tecnoloxías da Información (CiTIUS)
Universidade de Santiago de Compostela
pablo.gamallo@usc.es

Abstract

This article describes *MetaRomance*, a rule-based cross-lingual parser for Romance languages submitted to *CoNLL 2017 Shared Task: Multilingual Parsing from Raw Text to Universal Dependencies*. The system is an almost delexicalized parser which does not need training data to analyze Romance languages. It contains linguistically motivated rules based on PoS-tag patterns. The rules included in *MetaRomance* were developed in about 12 hours by one expert with no prior knowledge in Universal Dependencies, and can be easily extended using a transparent formalism. In this paper we compare the performance of *MetaRomance* with other supervised systems participating in the competition, paying special attention to the parsing of different treebanks of the same language. We also compare our system with a delexicalized parser for Romance languages, and take advantage of the harmonized annotation of Universal Dependencies to propose a language ranking based on the syntactic distance each variety has from Romance languages.

1 Introduction

This article describes the *MetaRomance* parser, which participated at *CoNLL 2017 Shared Task: Multilingual Parsing from Raw Text to Universal Dependencies* (Zeman et al., 2017). *MetaRomance* is a rule-based parser for Romance languages adapted to Universal Dependencies (UD). The system relies on a basic grammar consisting on simple cross-lingual and (almost) delexicalized rules likely to be shared by most Romance lan-

guages. Rules are almost delexicalized because they are mainly applied on Universal PoS-tags, only containing few grammar words (some prepositions and conjunctions) together with a small list of verbs. The grammar was developed by one expert with no prior knowledge in UD in about 12 hours.[1]

As the Universal Dependencies initiative (Nivre et al., 2016) offers linguistic criteria providing a consistent representation across languages, it fits perfectly with our objective of defining cross-lingual rules. In fact, the availability of harmonized treebanks provides an interesting test bench for cross-lingual dependency parsing research (McDonald et al., 2011; Mcdonald et al., 2013; Vilares et al., 2016).

Our participation at this CoNLL 2017 shared task has several experimental objectives. First, we will compare our rule-based approach with the rest of participants, which are likely to be supervised systems, with regard to Romance languages. Namely, we will analyze the performance of several systems on different treebanks of the same language. Then, we will also evaluate the cross-lingual property of our system by comparing it with a supervised delexicalized parser. Last but not least, the analysis of the results in the shared task will allow us to check whether our method might be useful to measure the syntactic distance between Romance and non-Romance languages.

The results of different experiments show that, in spite of its simplicity, *MetaRomance* achieve reasonable results on Romance languages with no training data, and that its performance is relatively uniform across different treebanks of the same language. The delexicalized rules of this system al-

---

[1] The whole system, DepPattern and *MetaRomance*, is freely available at:
https://github.com/CoNLL-UD-2017/
MetaRomance.

Proceedings of the CoNLL 2017 Shared Task: Multilingual Parsing from Raw Text to Universal Dependencies, pages 274–282,
Vancouver, Canada, August 3-4, 2017. © 2017 Association for Computational Linguistics

lowed us to present a classification of all the languages present in the shared task ranked by their syntactic distance from Romance languages.

The remaining of the paper is organized as follows. Section 2 presents some related work on dependency and cross-lingual parsing. Then, we present the architecture of *MetaRomance* in Section 3, and several experiments on Section 4. Finally, we briefly discuss the results and present the conclusions of our work in Sections 5 and 6, respectively.

2   Related Work

In the last 15 years, most work on dependency parsing has been developed within two supervised (data-driven) approaches: deterministic parsing, which is also known as *transition-based parsing* (Yamada and Matsumoto, 2003; Nivre, 2004; Gómez-Rodríguez and Fernández-González, 2012), and non-deterministic strategies, known as *graph-based dependency parsing* (McDonald and Pereira, 2006; Carreras, 2007; Martins et al., 2010).

In opposition to data-driven approaches, many grammar-driven (or rule-based) parsers use finite-state technology, which has attractive properties for syntactic parsing, such as conceptual simplicity, flexibility, and efficiency in terms of space and time. It permits to build robust and deterministic parsers. Most finite-state based parsing strategies use cascades of transducers (Ait-Mokhtar et al., 2002; Oflazer, 2003).

Concerning cross-lingual parsing, there are two main approaches for parsing one language (the target) with resources from one or more source languages: (a) data transfer, and (b) model transfer methods. On the one hand, data transfer approaches obtain annotated treebanks of a target language by projecting the syntactic information from the source data. Some methods use parallel corpora (Hwa et al., 2005; Ganchev et al., 2009; Agić et al., 2016) while others create artificial data taking advantage of machine translation (Tiedemann and Agić, 2016).

On the other hand, the strategies based on model transfer train systems on the source data that can be used to parse a target language (Zeman and Resnik, 2008). The emergence of different initiatives promoting harmonized annotations allowed researchers to explore this approach, using delexicalized models and multi-source strategies (Mc-Donald et al., 2011; Täckström et al., 2012).

More recently, some works addressed multilingual parsing using a single model (trained in a combination of various treebanks) to analyze different languages (Vilares et al., 2016; Ammar et al., 2016).

The growth in cross-lingual parsing research has given rise to a recent shared task at VarDial 2017 (Zampieri et al., 2017), Cross-lingual Dependency Parsing (CLP) (Tiedemann, 2017). CLP is a shared task whose aim is to develop models for parsing selected target languages without annotated training data, but having annotated data in one or two closely related languages (Rosa et al., 2017).

With the emergence of UD as the practical standard for multilingual PoS and syntactic dependency annotation, it is possible to develop universal rule-based strategies requiring no training data, and relying on basic rules exploiting the UD criteria. The Universal Dependency Parser, described in (Martínez Alonso et al., 2017), is a good example of this unsupervised strategy. Our work goes in that direction, but with two differences: the grammar is focused on Romance languages and the parser relies on basic rules implemented as cascades of finite-state transducers.

3   MetaRomance

3.1   The architecture

The core of *MetaRomance*, depicted in Figure 1, consists of the following modules:

- An *adapter* converting CoNLL-U into the format required by the rule-based parser.

- A *MetaRomance grammar* with 150 cross-lingual rules configured to work with tags, labels and linguistic constraints of UD.

- A *grammar compiler* that takes the grammar as input and generates a dependency parser, which is based on finite state transitions.

In order to allow *MetaRomance* to work on raw text, some scripts are provided in addition to the core architecture for converting the tags given by different PoS-taggers (namely, FreeLing (Padró and Stanilovsky, 2012; Garcia and Gamallo, 2010), TreeTagger (Schmid, 1994), and LinguaKit (Garcia and Gamallo, 2015)) into the CoNLL-U format. Thus, *MetaRomance* is able to parse raw text which has been tokenized, lemmatized and PoS-tagged with several systems that provide high-quality analyses for different languages.

3.2 The MetaRomance grammar

The cost of writing the grammar is not high since its size is small and the rules are not language-specific. The strategy we followed to write the *MetaRomance* grammar is based on two methodological principles:

- Start with high-coverage rules.

- Otherwise, develop rules shared by as many Romance languages as possible.

The objective is to find a trade-off between high performance and low effort, i.e. we look for efficiency. Most rules satisfy these two principles, giving rise to a broad-coverage parser. We have not defined non-projective rules since, in general, they have low coverage and are language dependent. Some rules contain information on specific lexical units, but only to identify grammatical words: some prepositions, conjunctions, determiners, and pronouns (and a small and automatically extracted list of verbs). Most phenomena not covered by the grammar are related with some long distance dependencies, including subordinate clauses in non-canonical positions, or complex issues derived from coordination.

Cross-lingual rules were written with DepPattern (Gamallo and González, 2011), a high-level syntactic formalism aimed to write dependency-based grammars. This dependency formalism has been adapted so as to let it interpret Universal Dependencies, more specifically UDv2. All rules were written in about 12 hours by an expert linguist who has skills in the DepPattern formalism, but with no prior knowledge in UD. He took into account the syntactic structure of all Romance languages of the UDv2 treebanks except Romanian. In the following you can see an example of a DepPattern rule:

```
det:   DET [ADJ]? NOUN
Agreement:   gender, number
%
```

The first line contains, divided by the colon, the name of the dependency relation (*det*) together with the PoS context. Here, a determiner will be linked as dependent of a noun (the head), with an optional adjective between them. The second line states that this rule will only be applied if both the dependent and the head agree in gender and number.

As the grammar is not complete, giving rise to partial parses, we implemented a post-editor script linking all tokens without head information to the corresponding sentence root. Moreover, in order to assign a label to each unknown dependency, the script associates dependency names to PoS-tags: e.g., PUNCT is associated with the dependency name "punct", VERB with "xcomp", and so on.

It is worth noting that the rules implemented in *MetaRomance* only make use 25 out of the 37 universal relations defined in the UDv2 guidelines.

3.3 A finite-state transition parser

The parser, automatically generated from the formal grammar, is based on a finite-state transition approach making use of a similar strategy to the shift-reduce algorithm. More precisely, it consists of a set of transducers/rules that *compress* the input sequence of tokens by progressively removing the dependent tokens as soon as dependencies are recognized (Gamallo, 2015). So, at each application of a rule, the system reduces the input and make it easier to find new dependencies in further rule applications. In particular, short dependencies are recognized first and, as a consequence, the input is simplified so as to make lighter the recognition of long distance dependencies. This is inspired by the easy-first strategy.

4 Experiments

This section presents several evaluations of *MetaRomance* using the data provided by the CoNLL 2017 shared task on UD parsing (Nivre et al., 2017). We will show the results of the following experiments:

- Comparison of *MetaRomance* with other supervised approaches on all the testing treebanks of Romance languages.

- Analysis of the performance of several parsers on different treebanks of the same language.

- Comparison of *MetaRomance* with a neural network delexicalized parser for Romance languages.

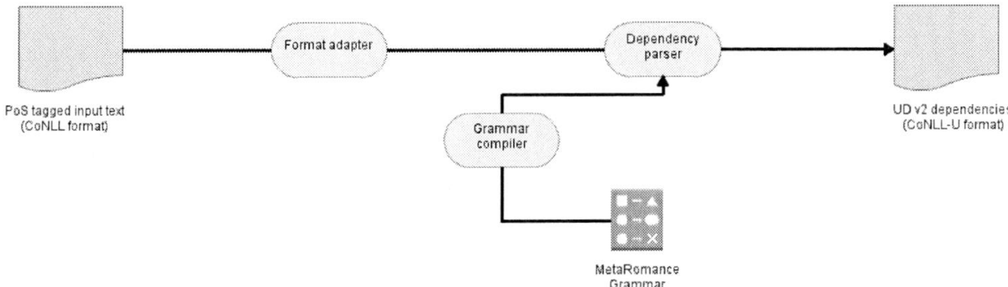

Figure 1: Architecture of *MetaRomance*

- Syntactic distance between Romance and non-Romance languages.

As we had several alignment issues concerning the evaluation of data pre-processed by LinguaKit and FreeLing, all the experiments presented in this paper (as well as the official *MetaRomance* results) used as input the tokenized, lemmatized and PoS-tagged data provided by the UDPipe baseline models.

4.1 Results at CoNLL-2017 shared task

In general, our system obtained low LAS and UAS results in the whole dataset of the shared task (34.05% LAS, 42.55% UAS).[2] The results were mostly expected due to the characteristics of *MetaRomance*: an almost delexicalized parser which does not require training data, with simple rules only based on the syntactic structure of Romance languages.

MetaRomance needed 29 minutes and 155MB of memory to parse all the testing sets on the TIRA virtual machine provided by the shared task (Potthast et al., 2014).

Table 1 shows the official *MetaRomance* results on every treebank of a Romance language evaluated in the shared task. On average, our system achieved F1 results of 58.9 (LAS) and 66.1 (UAS). The worst results were obtained in Romanian; this fact was expected because (a) Romanian is linguistically more distant than the other Romance languages (Gamallo et al., 2017), and (b) we did not implement any dependency rule with this language in mind.

Even if the values in Table 1 are not comparable with most supervised systems in the competition, our simple parser obtained competitive results in some languages, such as *es*, *it*, and *pt*. Interestingly, *MetaRomance* performed better in the *pud* datasets than in the others treebanks of the same languages (with only one exception: UAS results in *pt* and *pt_pud*), while most systems in the shared task decreased their performance in the *pud* datasets in several points. In this respect, *MetaRomance* leaded some supervised approaches in treebanks such as *pt_pud* or *gl_treegal* (this last one with small training data).

Some of the results on different treebanks of the same language have noticeable LAS differences: more than 5 points between *es* and *es_pud*, and about 10% between *pt_br* and the two other treebanks of Portuguese.[3]

In this regard, our next experiment compares the cross-treebank performance of supervised models (i.e., parsing different treebanks of the same language with the same model). To carry out this experiment we trained a UDPipe model (Straka et al., 2016) in each training dataset of Spanish, Galician, and Portuguese. These models were trained using the default parameters of UDPipe 1.1, but removing the lemmas and the morphological features of the treebanks, with a view to building parsers with more robust performance among the different test sets.[4]

---

[2]After correcting a small bug in a script —which produced invalid treebanks for three languages—, we obtained 34.98% LAS and 43.81% UAS. The new results, not present in the official ones, were (LAS/UAS): *bxr*: 19.51/30.22, *cs*: 41.63/47.92, and *tr*: 13.70/23.85.

[3]Concerning Portuguese, it is important to note that (a) Brazilian Portuguese has some syntactic (as well as morphological, orthographic, etc.) differences regarding European Portuguese, and that (b) the *pt_br* treebank does not contain lemmas neither morphological features (and also it has some tokenization issues: e.g., most contractions with the preposition *em* are tokenized as *en*).

[4]Preliminary tests using the baseline models provided by the shared task organization showed that some models trained in one treebank may obtain LAS results with drops of more than 26% when parsing a different treebank of the same lan-

Treebank	LAS	UAS
ca	57.71	65.57
es	59.80	67.20
es_ancora	60.99	69.63
es_pud	65.49	71.68
fr	54.10	62.20
fr_partut	56.17	63.10
fr_sequoia	55.16	60.76
fr_pud	58.67	65.94
gl	54.87	62.59
gl_treegal	57.20	63.87
it	62.96	70.35
it_pud	65.49	71.82
pt	65.50	71.77
pt_br	56.19	65.81
pt_pud	66.35	71.43
ro	45.04	53.90
average	58.86	66.10

Table 1: *MetaRomance* results on the Romance languages test sets (predicted tokens, lemmas, features, and PoS-tags).

Target	*Source*			
Spanish	*es*		*es_ancora*	
	LAS	UAS	LAS	UAS
es	*76.85*	*81.19*	64.25	71.95
es_ancora	67.25	76.43	*79.36*	*83.42*
es_pud	74.88	82.26	67.67	76.77
Galician	*gl*		*gl_treegal*	
	LAS	UAS	LAS	UAS
gl	*73.71*	*77.17*	58.03	68.47
gl_treegal	50.98	63.37	*65.24*	*70.81*
Portuguese	*pt*		*pt_br*	
	LAS	UAS	LAS	UAS
pt	*78.74*	*82.43*	68.00	77.92
pt_br	66.85	76.19	*82.10*	*84.83*
pt_pud	71.59	77.58	67.75	77.87

Table 2: Results of UDPipe models trained in the source treebanks (columns) on the target test sets (rows).

Table 2 includes the LAS and UAS values of each model (in the columns) on the target treebanks (on each row). These numbers clearly show that the results of supervised models are very different when parsing a different treebank to the one used for training, even if both corpus belong to the same language. These differences are much higher than those reported for *MetaRomance*, exceeding 22% in *gl* parsing *gl_treegal*, more than 15% in the analysis of *es* by *es_ancora*, or more than 14 in *pt_br* parsing *pt*. Note, however, than most supervised parsers (except *gl* analyzing *gl_treegal*) achieved better results than those obtained by *MetaRomance*.

These results (both the UDPipe and the *MetaRomance* ones) suggest that careful analyses of the different treebanks are required, aimed at knowing whether these large variations are due to different domains, annotation issues, or linguistic differences.

4.2 Comparison with a cross-lingual delexicalized parser

In the next experiment we compare the performance of *MetaRomance* with a delexicalized parser trained with a combined corpus which includes sentences from every Romance treebank.

This is a competitive supervised baseline in cross-lingual transfer parsing work, which gives us an indication of how our system compares to standard cross-lingual parsers.

We trained 50 UDPipe models by randomly selecting from 1 to 50 sentences of each Romance treebank in the training data. Then, we obtained the average results on all the Romance test treebanks, and plotted them together with the *MetaRomance* performance in Figure 2.

This figure shows that *MetaRomance* obtains similar results ($\approx 59\%$ LAS) to those achieved with about 2,000 tokens of all the Romance treebanks. The learning curve also suggest that it is difficult for cross-lingual models with no lexical features (as *MetaRomance*, which is also delexicalized) to keep increasing their cross-lingual performance on Romance languages. Thus, UDPipe achieves 64% with about 5,000 tokens, but it cannot surpass 65% even with a training corpus of 20,000 tokens.

4.3 Syntactic distance from Romance languages

The last experiment is an attempt to rank all the languages in the shared task with respect to the Romance family, aimed at knowing whether it is possible to use these results as a syntactic distance between Romance and non-Romance languages.

Table 3 includes the UAS values obtained by *MetaRomance* in every language of the dataset.

guage.

Language	UAS	Family	Branch
Italian	71	Ind	Romance
Portuguese	69	Ind	Romance
Spanish	69	Ind	Romance
Catalan	65	Ind	Romance
Galician	63	Ind	Romance
French	63	Ind	Romance
Bulgarian	54	Ind	Slavic
Romanian	53	Ind	Romance
Greek	52	Ind	European
Russian	52	Ind	Slavic
Indonesian	51	Non-Ind	Austronesian
Polish	51	Ind	Germanic
Old Bulgarian	50	Ind	Slavic
Gothic	50	Ind	Germanic
Ukrainian	48	Ind	Slavic
Dutch	48	Ind	Germanic
Croatian	48	Ind	Slavic
Norwegian	48	Ind	Germanic
Danish	46	Ind	Germanic
Hungarian	46	Non-Ind	Uralic
Czech	46	Ind	Slavic
Sorbian	45	Ind	Slavic
English	45	Ind	Germanic
Swedish	44	Ind	Germanic
Slovak	44	Ind	Slavic
German	43	Ind	Germanic
Old Greek	40	Ind	European
Irish	40	Ind	Celtic
Slovene	38	Ind	Slavic
Hebrew	38	Non-Ind	Semitic
Latin	37	Ind	European
Estonian	37	Non-Ind	Uralic
Arabic	37	Non-Ind	Semitic
Latvian	36	Ind	Germanic
Farsi	35	Ind	Indian
Norther Sami	35	Non-Ind	Uralic
Kurdish	35	Ind	Indian
Finnish	34	Non-Ind	Uralic
Russian Buryat	30	Non-Ind	Mongolic
Korean	27	Non-Ind	Koreanic
Turkish	21	Non-Ind	Turkic
Uyghur	18	Non-Ind	Turkic
Vietnamese	18	Non-Ind	Austroasiatic
Kazakh	18	Non-Ind	Turkic
Basque	18	Non-Ind	*isolated*
Hindi	15	Ind	Indian
Chinese	14	Non-Ind	Sino-tibetan
Urdu	13	Ind	Indian
Japanese	8	Non-Ind	Japonic

Table 3: *MetaRomance* results (UAS) on each language of the CoNLL 2017 dataset. Results in languages with more than one treebank are the average values.

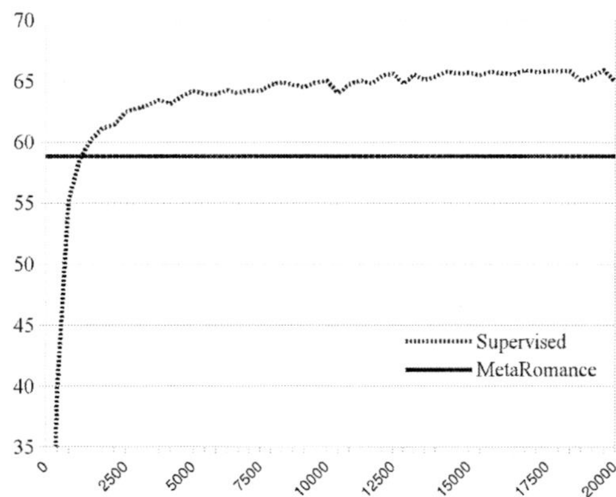

Figure 2: LAS values of *MetaRomance versus* the learning curve (0–20,000 tokens) of a delexicalized UDPipe model trained with random sentences from all the Romance treebanks. Results are average F1 values of all the testing Romance treebanks.

For those languages with more than one treebank we show the average results.[5]

As expected, at the top of the ranking we find Romance languages, on which *MetaRomance* achieves the best results (except on Romanian, slightly surpassed by Bulgarian). With few exceptions, such as the Indian varieties which obtained low values, Indo-european languages have the best results. In general, our system does not reach 40% UAS in Non-Indo-european languages, except in Hungarian and in Indonesian. In this regard, it is worth mentioning that Indonesian (with 51% UAS) has a Subject-Verb-Object word order similar to most European languages (Sneddon, 1996).

5 Discussion

The experiments performed in this paper provided some interesting results that claim for further research in cross-lingual parsing.

On the one hand, there are noticeable differences when parsing different treebanks of the same language, both using a rule-based system and harmonized supervised models. In this respect, it could be interesting to analyze the source of these variations, and *MetaRomance* could be

---

[5]Table 3 follows the language distinction provided by the shared task, even if we are aware that some linguistic varieties may be considered dialects of the same language (e.g., Galician as a variety of Portuguese, Old Bulgarian as a variety of Bulgarian, etc.).

useful for this purpose because it uses linguistically transparent rules based on PoS-tags.

On the other hand, the learning curve of a cross-lingual delexicalized model reinforces the idea that lexical features are required to obtain high-quality parsing results. In this respect, further experiments could compare this learning curve to lexicalized cross-lingual models, which seem to obtain good results in languages from the same linguistic family. Concerning *MetaRomance*, the addition of new rules (both lexicalized and without lexical information) could allow the parser to better analyze different languages.

Finally, and even if this is not a fair comparison, it is worth noting that *MetaRomance* obtained higher results in Romance languages than those achieved by UDP (Martínez Alonso et al., 2017). UDP is a training-free parser based on PageRank and a small set of head attachment rules, being more generic than *MetaRomance* (it can be applied to any language with more homogeneous results than our system). The differences on Romance languages vary between few decimals to more than 6% UAS, but the experiments were performed using different versions of the UD treebanks.[6]

6 Conclusions

This paper presented our submission to the *CoNLL 2017 Shared Task: Multilingual Parsing from Raw Text to Universal Dependencies*. The system, *MetaRomance*, is a fast rule-based parser suited to analyze Romance languages with no training data. It can be used on the top of several PoS-taggers such as LinguaKit, FreeLing, TreeTagger, or in a CoNLL-U file processed by tools such as UDPipe.

This cross-lingual parser contains 150 rules based on PoS-tags patterns, implemented by a linguist in about 12 hours. The *MetaRomance* grammar was written in DepPattern, a formalism that allows experts to easily modify and increase the rules to cover more syntactic phenomena.

Several experiments showed that a simple system such as the proposed in this paper can analyze in a uniform way different treebanks of Romance languages (and also from other linguistic families). Furthermore, a preliminary experiment on cross-lingual delexicalized parsing of Romance languages suggested that lexical features

are needed to increase the parsing performance. Lexical information can be added both to supervised systems and to our rule-based approach.

The grammar provided by *MetaRomance* was also used to present a classification of all the languages of the shared task datasets ranked by their syntactic distance with respect to Romance languages.

Acknowledgments

This work has received financial support from a 2016 BBVA Foundation Grant for Researchers and Cultural Creators, the TelePares project (MINECO, ref:FFI2014-51978-C2-1-R), the Consellería de Cultura, Educación e Ordenación Universitaria (accreditation 2016-2019, ED431G/08), the European Regional Development Fund (ERDF), and from a *Juan de la Cierva-formación* grant (FJCI-2014-22853).

References

Željko Agić, Anders Johannsen, Barbara Plank, Héctor Martínez Alonso, Natalie Schluter, and Anders Søgaard. 2016. Multilingual projection for parsing truly low-resource languages. *Transactions of the Association for Computational Linguistics* 4:301–312.

S. Ait-Mokhtar, J-P Chanod, and C. Roux. 2002. Robustness beyond Shallowness: Incremental Deep Parsing. *Natural Language Engineering* 8(2/3):121–144.

Waleed Ammar, George Mulcaire, Miguel Ballesteros, Cris Dyer, and Noah A. Smith. 2016. Many Languages, One Parser. *Transactions of the Association for Computational Linguistics* 4:431–444.

Xavier Carreras. 2007. Experiments with a higher-order projective dependency parser. In *Proceedings of the CoNLL Shared Task Session of EMNLP-CoNLL 2007*. Association for Computational Linguistics, Prague, pages 957–961.

Pablo Gamallo. 2015. Dependency parsing with compression rules. In *Proceedings of the 14th International Workshop on Parsing Technology (IWPT 2015)*. Association for Computational Linguistics, Bilbao, Spain, pages 107–117.

Pablo Gamallo and Isaac González. 2011. A grammatical formalism based on patterns of part-of-speech tags. *International Journal of Corpus Linguistics* 16(1):45–71.

Pablo Gamallo, José Ramom Pichel, and Iñaki Alegria. 2017. From language identification to language distance. *Physica A* 484:162–172.

---

[6]At this moment it is not possible to perform a better comparison of both systems, because UDP works with UDv1.2 and *MetaRomance* with UDv2.0.

Kuzman Ganchev, Jennifer Gillenwater, and Ben Taskar. 2009. Dependency grammar induction via bitext projection constraints. In *Proceedings of the Joint Conference of the 47th Annual Meeting of the ACL and the 4th International Joint Conference on Natural Language Processing of the AFNLP*. Association for Computational Linguistics, volume 1, pages 369–377.

Marcos Garcia and Pablo Gamallo. 2010. Análise morfossintáctica para português europeu e galego: Problemas, soluçoes e avaliaçao. *Linguamática* 2(2):59–67.

Marcos Garcia and Pablo Gamallo. 2015. Yet another suite of multilingual NLP tools. In *Languages, Applications and Technologies*. Springer, Switzerland, volume 563 of *Communications in Computer and Information Science*, pages 65–75. Revised Selected Papers of the Symposium on Languages, Applications and Technologies (SLATE 2015).

Carlos Gómez-Rodríguez and Daniel Fernández-González. 2012. Dependency parsing with undirected graphs. In *13th Conference of the European Chapter of the Association for Computational Linguistics (EACL)*. Avignon, France, pages 66–76.

Rebecca Hwa, Philip Resnik, Amy Weinberg, Clara Cabezas, and Okan Kolak. 2005. Bootstrapping parsers via syntactic projection across parallel texts. *Natural Language Engineering* 11(03):311–325.

Héctor Martínez Alonso, Zeljko Agic, Barbara Plank, and Anders Søgaard. 2017. Parsing universal dependencies without training. In *15th Conference of the European Chapter of the Association for Computational Linguistics (EACL 2017)*. Valencia, Spain, pages 229–239.

André F. T. Martins, Noah A. Smith, Eric P. Xing, Pedro M. Q. Aguiar, and Mário A. T. Figueiredo. 2010. Turboparsers: Dependency parsing by approximate variational inference. In *Empirical Methods in Natural Language Processing (EMNLP'10)*. Boston, USA.

Ryan Mcdonald, Joakim Nivre, Yvonne Quirmbachbrundage, Yoav Goldberg, Dipanjan Das, Kuzman Ganchev, Keith Hall, Slav Petrov, Hao Zhang, Oscar Täckström, Claudia Bedini, Núria Bertomeu, and Castelló Jungmee Lee. 2013. Universal dependency annotation for multilingual parsing. In *Proceedings of the 51st Annual Meeting of the Association for Computational Linguistics (ACL 2013)*. Association for Computational Linguistics, Sofia, pages 92–97.

Ryan McDonald and Fernando Pereira. 2006. Online Learning of Approximate Dependency Parsing Algorithms. In Association for Computational Linguistics, editor, *Proceedings of the Eleventh Conference of the European Chapter of the Association for Computational Linguistics (EACL 2006)*. Trento, pages 81–88.

Ryan McDonald, Slav Petrov, and Keith Hall. 2011. Multi-source Transfer of Delexicalized Dependency Parsers. In *Proceedings of the Conference on Empirical Methods in Natural Language Processing (EMNLP 2011)*. Association for Computational Linguistics, Edinburgh, United Kingdom, pages 62–72.

Joakim Nivre. 2004. Incrementality in deterministic dependency parsing. In *ACL Workshop on Incremental Parsing: Bringing Engineering and Cognition Together*. Association for Computational Linguistics, Barcelona, pages 50–57.

Joakim Nivre, Željko Agić, Lars Ahrenberg, et al. 2017. Universal dependencies 2.0 – CoNLL 2017 shared task development and test data. LINDAT/CLARIN digital library at the Institute of Formal and Applied Linguistics, Charles University. http://hdl.handle.net/11234/1-2184.

Joakim Nivre, Marie-Catherine de Marneffe, Filip Ginter, Yoav Goldberg, Jan Hajič, Christopher Manning, Ryan McDonald, Sl av Petrov, Sampo Pyysalo, Natalia Silveira, Reut Tsarfaty, and Daniel Zeman. 2016. Universal Dependencies v1: A multilingual treebank collection. In *Proceedings of the 10th International Conference on Language Resources and Evaluation (LREC 2016)*. European Language Resources Association, Portorož, Slovenia, pages 1659–1666.

Kemal Oflazer. 2003. Dependency parsing with an extended finite-state approach. *Computational Linguistics* 29(4):515–544.

Lluís. Padró and Evgeny Stanilovsky. 2012. FreeLing 3.0: Towards Wider Multilinguality. In *Proceedings of the Language Resources and Evaluation Conference (LREC 2012)*. European Language and Resources Association, Istanbul, Turkey, pages 2473–2479.

Martin Potthast, Tim Gollub, Francisco Rangel, Paolo Rosso, Efstathios Stamatatos, and Benno Stein. 2014. Improving the reproducibility of PAN's shared tasks: Plagiarism detection, author identification, and author profiling. In Evangelos Kanoulas, Mihai Lupu, Paul Clough, Mark Sanderson, Mark Hall, Allan Hanbury, and Elaine Toms, editors, *Information Access Evaluation meets Multilinguality, Multimodality, and Visualization. 5th International Conference of the CLEF Initiative (CLEF 14)*. Springer, Berlin Heidelberg New York, pages 268–299.

Rudolf Rosa, Daniel Zeman, David Mareček, and Zdeněk Žabokrtský. 2017. Slavic forest, norwegian wood. In *Proceedings of the Fourth Workshop on NLP for Similar Languages, Varieties and Dialects (VarDial4)*. Association for Computational Linguistics, Stroudsburg, PA, USA, pages 210–219.

Helmut Schmid. 1994. Probabilistic Part-of-Speech Tagging Using Decision Trees. In *International Conference on New Methods in Language Processing*. Manchester, pages 154–163.

James Neil Sneddon. 1996. *Indonesian Reference Grammar*. Allen and Unwin, St. Leonards, Australia.

Milan Straka, Jan Hajič, and Jana Straková. 2016. UD-Pipe: trainable pipeline for processing CoNLL-U files performing tokenization, morphological analysis, POS tagging and parsing. In *Proceedings of the 10th International Conference on Language Resources and Evaluation (LREC 2016)*. European Language Resources Association, Portorož, Slovenia.

Oscar Täckström, Ryan McDonald, and Jakob Uszkoreit. 2012. Cross-lingual word clusters for direct transfer of linguistic structure. In *Proceedings of the 2012 Conference of the North American Chapter of the Association for Computational Linguistics: Human language technologies (NAACL - HLT 2012)*. Association for Computational Linguistics, pages 477–487.

Jörg Tiedemann. 2017. Cross-lingual dependency parsing for closely related languages. In *Proceedings of the Fourth Workshop on NLP for Similar Languages, Varieties and Dialects (VarDial 2017)*. Association for Computational Linguistics, Valencia, pages 131–136.

Jörg Tiedemann and Željko Agić. 2016. Synthetic Treebanking for Cross-Lingual Dependency Parsing. *Journal of Artificial Intelligence Research (JAIR)* 55:209–248.

David Vilares, Miguel A. Alonso, and Carlos Gómez-Rodríguez. 2016. One model, two languages: training bilingual parsers with harmonized treebanks. In *Proceedings of the 54th Annual Meeting of the Association for Computational Linguistics (ACL 2016)*. Berlin, Germany, volume 2, pages 425–431.

Hiroyasu Yamada and Yuji Matsumoto. 2003. Statistically Dependency Analysis with Support Vector Machines. In *Proceedings of 8th International Workshop on Parsing Technologies (IWPT)*. pages 195–206.

Marcos Zampieri, Shervin Malmasi, Nikola Ljubešić, Preslav Nakov, Ahmed Ali, Jörg Tiedemann, Yves Scherrer, and Noëmi Aepli. 2017. Findings of the VarDial Evaluation Campaign 2017. In *Proceedings of the Fourth Workshop on NLP for Similar Languages, Varieties and Dialects (VarDial)*. Valencia.

Daniel Zeman, Martin Popel, Milan Straka, Jan Hajič, Joakim Nivre, Filip Ginter, Juhani Luotolahti, Sampo Pyysalo, Slav Petrov, Martin Potthast, Francis Tyers, Elena Badmaeva, Memduh Gökırmak, Anna Nedoluzhko, Silvie Cinková, Jan Hajič jr., Jaroslava Hlaváčová, Václava Kettnerová, Zdeňka Urešová, Jenna Kanerva, Stina Ojala, Anna Missilä, Christopher Manning, Sebastian Schuster, Siva Reddy, Dima Taji, Nizar Habash, Herman Leung, Marie-Catherine de Marneffe, Manuela Sanguinetti, Maria Simi, Hiroshi Kanayama, Valeria de Paiva, Kira Droganova, Hěctor Martínez Alonso, Hans Uszkoreit, Vivien Macketanz, Aljoscha Burchardt, Kim Harris, Katrin Marheinecke, Georg Rehm, Tolga Kayadelen, Mohammed Attia, Ali Elkahky, Zhuoran Yu, Emily Pitler, Saran Lertpradit, Michael Mandl, Jesse Kirchner, Hector Fernandez Alcalde, Jana Strnadova, Esha Banerjee, Ruli Manurung, Antonio Stella, Atsuko Shimada, Sookyoung Kwak, Gustavo Mendonça, Tatiana Lando, Rattima Nitisaroj, and Josie Li. 2017. CoNLL 2017 Shared Task: Multilingual Parsing from Raw Text to Universal Dependencies. In *Proceedings of the CoNLL 2017 Shared Task: Multilingual Parsing from Raw Text to Universal Dependencies*. Association for Computational Linguistics.

Daniel Zeman and Philip Resnik. 2008. Cross-Language Parser Adaptation between Related Languages. In *Proceedings of the Workshop on NLP for Less Privileged Language at the 3rd International Joint Conference on Natural Language Processing (IJCNLP 2008)*. Asian Federation of Natural Language Processing, Hyderabad, pages 35–42.

Author Index